APPROXIMATE REASONING IN DECISION ANALYSIS

APPROXIMATE REASONING IN DECISION ANALYSIS

Edited by

Madan M. GUPTA
Cybernetics Research Laboratory
University of Saskatchewan
Saskatoon, Canada

and

Elie SANCHEZ
Service Universitaire de Biomathématiques
Faculté de Médecine
Marseille, France

1982

NORTH-HOLLAND PUBLISHING COMPANY – AMSTERDAM • NEW YORK • OXFORD

ISBN: 0 444 86492 x

Publishers:
NORTH-HOLLAND PUBLISHING COMPANY
AMSTERDAM • NEW YORK • OXFORD

Sole distributors for the U.S.A. and Canada:
ELSEVIER SCIENCE PUBLISHING COMPANY, INC.
52 VANDERBILT AVENUE
NEW YORK, N.Y. 10017

Library of Congress Cataloging in Publication Data

Main entry under title:

Approximate reasoning indecision analysis.

Bibliography: p.
1. Statistical decision. 2. Decision-making.
3. Fuzzy sets. I. Gupta, Madan M. II. Sanchez, Elie, 1944- .
QA279.4.A66 1982 519.5'42 82-14308
ISBN 0-444-86492-X (U.S.)

PRINTED IN THE NETHERLANDS

प्रदीपः सर्व्वविद्यानामुपायः सर्व्वकर्म्मणाम् ।
आश्रयः सर्व्वधर्म्माणां शश्वदान्वीक्षिकीमता ॥

(KAUṬILYA.)

" Ānvīkṣikī (Logic) has ever been esteemed as the lamp of all sciences, the resource of all actions and the shelter of all virtues."

न्यायाम्बुधिर्दीधितिकारयुक्तिकल्लोलकोलाहलदुर्विगाहः ।
तस्यापि पातुं न पयः समर्थः किं नाम धीमत्प्रतिमाम्बुवाहः ॥

" Modern Logic is a veritable ocean whose water is saline and which is unapproachable owing to the tumults and uproars of the commentators. Is not then the water of that ocean capable of being drunk? Why not? Intelligent people, like clouds, can easily approach the ocean and drink its water pure and sweet."

Adopted from History of Indian Logic by S.C. Vidyabhusana.

FOREWORD

Since the publication of the two books, "Fuzzy Automata and Decision Processes" (North Holland, 1977) and "Advances in Fuzzy Set Theory and Applications" (North Holland, 1979), there has been a rapid expansion in the theoretical development of fuzzy set theory and its many applications to the hard and soft sciences.

In spite of traditional analysis based upon conventional mathematics, the human thought process has played, and will continue to play, a very important role in knowledge representation and decision analysis. Examples may be found in engineering, medicine, psychology and many other fields where fuzzy information and approximate reasoning are essential to decision making.

These two volumes entitled, "Fuzzy Information and Decision Processes" and "Approximate Reasoning in Decision Analysis" truly reflect the progress made over the last seventeen years since the inception of the fuzzy concepts in 1965. Over 130 world researchers from 21 different countries have reported their research in these two volumes. This international cooperation and exchange of scientific information is a sign of the good and increasing health of this field of Fuzzy Information and Decision Processes.

Peter N. Nikiforuk, Ph.D., D.Sc.
Dean of Engineering
University of Saskatchewan
Saskatoon, Saskatchewan
Canada S7N 0W0

ACKNOWLEDGEMENTS

These two volumes entitled, "Fuzzy Information and Decision Processes" and "Approximate Reasoning in Decision Analysis" represent the work of over one hundred and thirty individuals from twenty one different countries. It is gratifying to acknowledge the devotion of these individuals who have contributed to the exploration of these new theories, to the development of new areas of applications, to the stimulation of the advancement of scientific information, and to the reinforcement of international cooperation in this important field of human decision processes. The Editors record their appreciation to Miss E. Nikiforuk, our research assistant, and Miss Freda Peil, our secretary, who were very helpful during all the editorial phases of these two volumes.

Madan M. Gupta

Elie Sanchez

(Editors)

PREFACE

The subject of information processing and decision analysis, especially using the data arising from human thought and cognition process, has occupied a prominent place in the information processing literature since the inception of Fuzzy Set Theory in 1965. As a result, during the last fifteen years engineering journals as well as those in the social, biological, and medical sciences, have devoted increasing space to articles dealing with the analysis of fuzzy data. Many scientists, mathematicians and social scientists have contributed to this progress but the literature on such a diversified subject is widely scattered. During the decade 1970 - 1980, an important new approach to decision analysis came into prominence. This approach has appeared in the publication of the previous two volumes entitled, "Fuzzy Automata and Decision Processes" (North Holland, 1977) and "Advances in Fuzzy Set Theory and Applications" (North Holland, 1979). Since then, there has been a rapid growth in this theory with many more new applications in different fields. In the present two volumes entitled, "Fuzzy Information and Decision Processes" and "Approximate Reasoning in Decision Analysis" an attempt has been made once again to incorporate the recent advances in both theory and applications.

Initially the project was designed only for one volume, but overwhelming response from the researchers representing over 21 countries forced the editors to enlarge the project to two volumes. The volume entitled, "Fuzzy Information and Decision Processes" contains 45 articles by sixty-three contributors from sixteen different countries.* The second volume entitled "Approximate Reasoning in Decision Analysis" contains 44 articles by seventy-four contributors from seventeen different countries.** Thus the total number of contributors are over 130 from 21 different countries around the world. It is unfortunate that over 50 articles, some of which were of excellent nature, could not be included in these two volumes because of a large constraint on the size.

Initially the proposal was to divide each volume into three parts: introduction, advances in theory, and advances in applications. Some last minute editorial changes were made and each volume was divided according to certain topics. The following is a brief description of each volume with descriptive keywords.

---

* Austria, Belgium, Canada, People's Republic of China, Denmark, France, West Germany, Italy, Japan, Lebanon, The Netherlands, Poland, Romania, Spain, U.K. and U.S.A.

** Austria, Belgium, Brazil, Canada, People's Republic of China, Czechoslovakia, France, West Germany, Hungary, Italy, Japan, Poland, Spain, U.K., U.S.A. and U.S.S.R.

Fuzzy Information and Decision Processes

Part One: Fuzzy Information and Entropy (6 papers)

Keywords: Fuzzy Entropy, fuzzy measures, ordering, subjective entropy, probabilistic set, vagueness, generalized information, lattice evaluation, and separation.

Part Two: Fuzzy Probability, Fuzzy Integrals and Belief Functions (6 papers)

Keywords: Fuzzy measures, probability of fuzzy events, fuzzy numbers, fuzzy Lebesque measure, theory of evidence, subjective probability, degree of belief, and membership function.

Part Three: Fuzzy Mathematical Structures (7 papers)

Keywords: Aggregation, vagueness, relational algebra, L-matrices, category, fuzzy graphs, possibility, lattice theory, fuzzy set structure, ordinal numbers, fuzzy ordering, and fuzzy cardinals.

Part Four: Formalization Of Uncertainty (7 papers)

Keywords: Formalization of vagueness, possibility, plausibility, belief, Dempster's rule, fuzzy reasoning, random sets, possibility distributions, fuzzy set operations, homomorphisms, random vectors, and computer security.

Part Five: Fuzzy Optimization Methods (4 papers)

Keywords: Mathematical programming, fuzzy optimization, topos, and multistage decision making.

Part Six: Aggregation, Multicriteria, Modelling and Fuzzy Ordering (6 papers)

Keywords: Linguistic variables, aggregate planning, multicriteria modelling, social systems, management, fuzzy outranking, scoring methods, interval scale, and preference.

Part Seven: Fuzzy Databases and Question-Answering (4 papers)

Keywords: Database, possibility distribution, fuzzy predicate, question-answering, similarity relations, analogical inference and information retrieval.

Part Eight: Fuzzy Systems and Fuzzy Logic Controllers (5 papers)

Keywords: Fuzzy logics, fuzzy controllers, linguistic controllers, fuzzy systems, multivalued logics, adaptive algorithms, pansystems, and pansymmetry.

Approximate Reasoning in Decision Analysis

Part One: On Membership Functions (3 papers)

Keywords: Membership function, stochastic fuzzy set, relative A-ness, and membership degree.

Part Two: Composite Fuzzy Relations (5 papers)

Keywords: Composite relations, group decision, fuzzy relational equations, L-fuzzy set, LSG operator, fuzzy matrix, eigen fuzzy set, and lattice module-homomorphism.

Part Three: Fuzzy Logic and Inference (5 papers)

Keywords: Fuzzy conditional inference, fuzzy modus ponens, fuzzy modus tollens, syllogism, classification, medical diagnosis, fuzzy switching, and fuzzy functions.

Part Four: Classifications and Similarity Measures (9 papers)

Keywords: Classification algorithms, linguistic variables, fuzzy vectors, feature extraction, fuzzy scale, pseudo-interval, similarity measures, nth level fuzzy sets, vector valued fuzzy sets, texture analysis, linguistic descriptors, speech processing, automatic learning, and neural systems.

Part Five: Expert Systems and Medical Diagnosis (7 papers)

Keywords: Medical diagnosis, expert systems, possibility theory, Dempster and Shafer's theory, damage assessment, computer aided diagnosis, fuzzy heuristics, ECG classification, fuzzy linguistics, fuzzy utilities, and Chinese medicine.

Part Six: Psychological Measurements and Human Behavior (4 papers)

Keywords: Behavior modification, cognitive modelling, linguistic descriptors, psychological measurements, earthquake, and civil evacuation.

Part Seven: Approximate Reasoning and Decision Analysis (7 papers)

Keywords: Linguistic approach, natural language processing, approximate reasoning, linguistic instructions, artificial intelligence, operational research, management, fuzzy decision making, linguistic proposition, dynamic conflict resolution, creative decision, catastrophes, creative decisions rank correlation, and complex planning.

Part Eight: Fuzzy Clustering Algorithms (4 papers)

Keywords: Clustering, possibilistic manipulation, cluster validity, weather forecasting, water pollution control, management practice, and fuzzy hierarchical models.

From the keywords recorded under each heading, it may be noted that the classification is not exclusively devoted to a single topic, but rather there is a considerable amount of overlap. This overlapping of topics constitutes a logical step for such a growing and diversified field. Both of the volumes cover a wide range of theoretical development as well as applications. This diversification of applications indicates that scientists are getting more and more aware of the fact that in real world problems uncertainty arising from human cognition and thought process is a matter of degrees and must be treated rather using a nonconventional approach. In a wide range of problems dealing with hard and soft sciences, it is now getting clear that fuzzy set theory, possibility theory and related notions provide very natural and appropriate tools to model uncertainty.

Readers would note from these two volumes that many new and young researchers are emerging to work in this field. There are many fuzzy working groups that have been formed during the past decade at national and trans-national levels. In the People's Republic of China alone over 250 researchers are engaged working in this field; and a small sample of their work has been reported in these two volumes. Other notable working groups are in India, Japan, North America, U.K., Europe and USSR. And it is gratifying to publish a small amount of their selected work in these two volumes.

Increasingly, the progress of science and technology involves the interaction of ideas from different parts of the world and merging of results from different disciplines. The editors wish to quickly publish these ideas and results which are evolving at an exponential rate. For this reason there are some errors, both in mathematics and english, which could not be corrected.

The editors sincerely hope that these two volumes will complement other works that have appeared and are appearing in scattered scientific journals and other publications.

June 30, 1982

Madan M. Gupta

Elie Sanchez

Editors

LIST OF BOOKS AND JOURNALS ON FUZZY SYSTEMS

1. D. Dubois and H. Prade (1979): "Fuzzy Sets and Systems: Theory and Applications", Academic Press.

2. M.M. Gupta (Editor), G.N. Saridis and B.R. Gaines (Assoc. Editors) (1977): "Fuzzy Automata and Decision Processes", North-Holland.

3. M.M. Gupta (Editor), R.K. Ragade and R.R. Yager (Assoc. Editors) (1979): "Advances in Fuzzy Set Theory and Applications", North-Holland.

4. A. Kaufmann (1972): "Theory of Fuzzy Sets", Merson, Paris.

5. A. Kaufmann (1975): "Theory of Fuzzy Subsets", Academic Press, N.Y.

6. A. Kaufmann (1973): "Introduction a la Theorie des Sous-Ensembles Flous, 1: Elements Theoretiques de Base", Masson et cie, Paris, France.

7. A. Kaufmann (1975A): "Introduction a la Theorie des Sous-Ensembles Flous, 2: Applications a la Linguistique et a la Semantique", Masson et cie, Paris, France.

8. A. Kaufmann (1975B): "Introduction a la Theorie des Sous-Ensembles Flous, 3: Applications a la Classification et la Reconnaissance des Dormes, aux Automates et aux Systems, aux Choix des Critares", Masson et cie, Paris, France.

9. A. Kaufmann (1975): "Introduction to the Theory of Fuzzy Subsets Vol. 1", Academic Press, New York.

10. A. Kaufmann (1976): "Introduction a la Theorie des Sous-Ensembles Flous", Tomes IV, Ed. Masson, Paris.

11. W.J.M. Kickert (1978): "Fuzzy Theories on Decision Making", Nijhoff, Leiden, Boston.

12. C.V. Negoita and D.A. Ralescu (1975): "Applications of Fuzzy Sets to Systems Analysis", Birkhauser Verlag.

13. L.A. Zadeh, K.S. Fu, K. Tanaka and M. Shimura (eds) (1975): "Fuzzy Sets and Their Applications to Cognitive and Decision Processes", Academic Press.

14. International Journal of Fuzzy Sets and Systems, North-Holland.

15. Journal of Fuzzy Mathematics, Huazhong (Central China) University of Science and Technology, Wuhan, Hubei, People's Republic of China.

CONTENTS

FOREWORD vii

ACKNOWLEDGEMENTS viii

PREFACE ix

PART ONE: ON MEMBERSHIP FUNCTIONS

1. On Membership Evaluation in Fuzzy Sets
   B.B. Chaudhuri and D. Dutta Majumder 3

2. Stochastic Fuzziness
   A.M. Norwich and I.B. Turksen 13

3. Membership Degrees Determination From Saaty Matrix Totalities
   V.V. Fedorov, V.B. Kuz'min and A.I. Vereskov 23

PART TWO: COMPOSITE FUZZY RELATIONS

4. Method of Solving the Polynomial Form of Composite Fuzzy Relation Equations and Its Application to a Group Decision Problem
   Ario Ohsato and Takashi Sekiguchi 33

5. An Algorithm to Solve the Max-Min Composite Fuzzy Relational Equations
   Wen-Li Xu, Chiu-feng Wu and Wei-min Cheng 47

6. LSG Powers of An L-Fuzzy Matrix
   Shih-pe Lou and Zhengxiang Tong 51

7. Generalized Inverses of Fuzzy Matrix
   Luo Cheng - Zhong 57

8. The Eigen Fuzzy Sets of a Fuzzy Matrix
   Cao Zhi-qiang 61

PART THREE: FUZZY LOGIC, AND INFERENCE

9. Fuzzy Inference Using Max-$\wedge$ Composition in the Compositional Role of Inference
   Masaharu Mizumoto 67

10. Soft Deduction Rules in Medical Diagnosis Processes
    G. Soula and E. Sanchez 77

11. Imprecise Decision Tables and Their Optimization
    J.M. Francioni, A. Kandel and C.M. Eastman 89

12. New Canonical Forms of Fuzzy Switching Functions
    Masao Mukaidono 97

13. Fuzzy Systems in Civil Engineering
    David Blockley 103

PART FOUR: CLASSIFICATIONS, AND SIMILARITY MEASURES

14. Classification in Fuzzy Environments
V. Kh. Kaipov and A.A. Seliugin 119

15. On The Uncertainty of Fuzzy Classifications
Jiri Šustal 125

16. Character Recognition Using Fuzzy Similarity Relations
B.N. Chatterji 131

17. A Fuzzy Scale Induced by Intransitive Ordering
Yajiro Morita and Yuzo Oka 139

18. Vectorial I-Fuzzy Sets
László T. Kóczy 151

19. Classification of Textures By Vectorial Fuzzy Sets
M. Hajnal and L.T. Kóczy 157

20. The Process of Classification and Learning the Meaning of Linguistic Descriptors of Concepts
J. Aguilar Martin and R. López De Mantaras 165

21. Use of Fuzzy Rules In A Speech Understanding System
Renato De Mori, Piero Laface and Lorenza Saitta 177

22. Toward a Theoretical and Experimental Approach of Fuzzy Learning
A.F. Rocha 191

PART FIVE: EXPERT SYSTEMS, AND MEDICAL DIAGNOSIS

23. A Survey on Medical Diagnosis and Fuzzy Subsets
Klaus-Peter Adlassnig 203

24. CADIAG-2: Computer-Assisted Medical Diagnosis Using Fuzzy Subsets
Klaus-Peter Adlassnig and Gernot Kolarz 219

25. Learning of Fuzzy Production Rules for Medical Diagnosis
Leonardo Lesmo, Lorenza Saitta and Pietro Torasso 249

26. A Rule-Based Inference With Fuzzy Set for Structural Damage Assessment
Mitsuru Ishizuka, K.S. Fu and James T.P. Yao 261

27. SPHINX: An Internactive System for Medical Diagnosis Aids
M. Fieschi, M. Joubert, D. Fieschi, G. Soula and M. Roux 269

28. The Use of Fuzzy Set Theory in Electrocardiological Diagnostics
Etienne E. Kerre 277

29. Fuzzy Set Model for Computerized Diagnosis System In Traditional Chinese Medicine
Guo Rongjian, Xie Min, Ma Binrong and Chen Wuling 283

PART SIX: PSYCHOLOGICAL MEASUREMENTS, AND HUMAN BEHAVIOR

30. Towards Fuzzy Algorithms in Behaviour Modification
V.B. Cervin and Ramesh Jain 291

31. Linguistic Description of Human Judgments in Expert Systems and in the 'Soft' Sciences
Christian Freska 297

32. The Multistage Evaluation Method in Psychological Measurement: An Application of Fuzzy Sets Theory to Psychology
Ma Mou-chao and Cao Zhi-qiang 307

33. Fuzzy Simulation Model of Civil Evacuation from Large-Scale Earthquake-Generated Fires
Fumio Hara 313

PART SEVEN: APPROXIMATE REASONING AND DECISION ANALYSIS

34. A Fuzzy Sets Based Linguistic Approach: Theory and Applications
Piero P. Bonissone 329

35. Recognition of Linguistically Instructed Path to Destination
Haruki Imaoka, Toshiro Terano and Michio Sugeno 341

36. Fuzzy Sets In Few Classical Operational Research Problems
Stefan Chanas 351

37. The Theory of Fuzzy Decisions
Kofi Kissi Dompere 365

38. Dynamic Conflict Resolution Through A Theory of A Displaced Fuzzy Ideal
Yee Leung 381

39. Creative Decision-Making Through Fuzzy Catastrophes
Vladimir Dimitrov 391

40. A Fuzzified Relevance Tree Approach for Solving the Complex Planning
Yasuyoshi Sekita and Masahara Mizumoto 401

PART EIGHT: FUZZY CLUSTERING ALGORITHMS

41. Possibilistic Data Structures for the Representation of Uncertainty
E.H. Ruspini 411

42. Non Metric Fuzzy Clustering Algorithms and Their Cluster Validity
G. Libert and M. Roubens 417

43. Two New Methods in Fuzzy Cluster
Shih-pe Lou, Wha-cheng Cheng and Li-Ming Chao 427

44. A Fuzzy Set Model for the Evaluation of Best Management Practices in Nonpoint Source Water Pollution Policy Formulation
Augustine O. Esogbue 431

PART NINE: BIOGRAPHICAL INFORMATION

45. Biographical Information about the Editors and Contributing Authors 439

TABLE OF CONTENTS OF "FUZZY INFORMATION AND DECISION PROCESSES", EDITED BY M.M. GUPTA AND E. SANCHEZ, NORTH-HOLLAND, 1982 453

PART ONE

ON MEMBERSHIP FUNCTIONS

Approximate Reasoning in Decision Analysis
M.M. Gupta and E. Sanchez (eds.)

ON MEMBERSHIP EVALUATION IN FUZZY SETS

B. B. Chaudhuri and D. Dutta Majumder

Electronics and Communication Sciences Unit,
Indian Statistical Institute,
Calcutta, India

One of the major controversies in using fuzzy set theory for Engineering problems addresses to the unique evaluation of membership function of a fuzzy subset. The problem has been dealt with by various research workers and solutions based on risk function, differential membership, deformation energy, group decision, relative preference system, topological space consideration etc. have been proposed. All the methods have their shortcomings and no general approach is possible as yet. The solution of the problem of finding membership value, especially in pattern recognition context, has been discussed in the present paper. The problem has been subdivided in two major groups according to the availability or non-availability of a mathematical expression for the membership function.

1. INTRODUCTION

Fuzzy set theory, a generalisation of ordinary (or conventional) set theory provides an adequate conceptual framework as well as a mathemetical tool to solve real physical world problems which are usually fuzzy. It can account for inexactness like ambiguity and vagueness, and thus for nonstatistical uncertainty. A list of 1800 references given in [1] speaks about the interest of the investigators exploring the usefulness of the fuzzy set theory in a wide variety of fields ranging from medical diagnosis to industrial control and man-machine communication problems.

It is, however, interesting that the critics [2] speak and the users [3-4] feel about the lack of adequate tools available for evaluating the membership value of a sample in a fuzzy set. Since this evaluation marks the starting point for using the rich theory to a practical problem, many research workers are tempted to choose a membership function heuristically, and thus the choice is not always justified or well-understood. It is easy to find a function that takes values in [0,1] and is monotonic over a range, but the compatibility of a sample to the set may not be reflected by the function and the membership function is not 'good' in the sense of Bellmann et.al. [5]

The sense of 'compatibility' is rather vague. It makes some sense when a set of samples whose membership values, uniformly distributed over [0,1] are known and may be used to test the function in question. This set may be called a 'training set', a terminology borrowed from the discipline of pattern recognition.

However, the basic philosophical problem concerns the construction of a numerical scale for the membership values in such a way that the scale satisfies some conditions imposed on a rational measurement system. The main difficulty lies in constructing a homomorphism from a qualitative preference system to a quantitative preference system and it is here that the ambiguity and idiosyncrasies are likely to be introduced. An approach free from this defect has not yet been found, although modifications have been suggested to reduce it. For example, Kandel and Byatt [6] suggested the use of statistical information whenever available. Fung and Fu [4,7] suggested the problem of eliminating idiosyncrasy as a collective or group decision problem and use a topological space rather than a real interval. Also, when the membership values of simpler action are known, those of complicated actions can be found through hedges [8]. (The famous S and π curves for sets 'large number' and 'young', respectively are examples.) Bremermann [9] and Albin [10] proposed the concept of 'deformation energy' and defined the grade of membership of a given sample dependent on the deformation energy necessary to make the prototype close to the sample in some sense.

It is possible that some or all of the approaches stated above fail for some specific problem. Also, those except in [8] fail to demonstrate an explicit way of finding the membership value of a real data. For example, Bremermann did not define the doformation energy analytically. Recent method by Konchen and Badre [11] is rather a justification of a shape (the S curve) than a quantitative procedure. The relative preferences method due to Saaty [12] is limited by the difficulty of collecting 'consistent' data. The approach in [8], on the other hand, requires membership function of simpler action known and hence has limited applicability. More recently Dishkant [13] found an expression of membership values of a fuzzy variable, which is the sum of many fuzzy variables with known membership functions and satisfying some conditions. The method has similar defect as above.

The present paper is an attempt to solve the problem of finding membership values for practical data. Specially, it aims at answering the problem how to learn about fuzzy membership of samples in a set if some training samples are given. The problem has been subdivided into two major groups depending on the availability or unavailability of a mathematical expression for membership values and are treated in Sec. 2 and Sec. 3 respectively. Each section deals separately with different natures of the prototypes.

2. ESTIMATION OF PARAMETERS OF MEMBERSHIP FUNCTIONS

As pointed out earlier, a mathematical expression for membership function can safely be assumed in certain cases. Apart from the π and S functions of Zadeh, expressions involving similarity and distance measure have been found to be popular. It is assumed that these properties reflect the grade of membership of a sample in a set. Among many others, two simple forms of the membership functions in this class are

$$\mu_A(\underline{x}) = [1 + D(\underline{x},\underline{c})]^{-1} \qquad (1)$$

$$\mu_A(\underline{x}) = \exp[-D(\underline{x},\underline{c})] \qquad (2)$$

where the left side denotes the membership value of a sample with measurement vector $\underline{x}$ in set A while D denotes distance or dissimilarity of $\underline{x}$ with respect to $\underline{c}$, the core point i.e., the point where the membership value is unity.

2.1 Statistical Approach

If D denotes weighted distance in equation (1) or (2), its explicit form may be

$$D(\underline{x},\underline{c}) = (\underline{x} - \underline{c})^t [w] (\underline{x} - \underline{c}) \qquad (3)$$

where $[w]$ denotes an NxN weight matrix, $\underline{x}$ and $\underline{c}$ are N-element column vectors and t denotes transpose. In such cases, it is necessary to estimate $[w]$ and $\underline{c}$ when a set of M prototypes is given.

The estimation process depends on the information about the prototypes. If a statistical information is available with respect to a measurement scale, $\underline{c}$ and $[w]$ can be found as

$$\underline{c} = E(\underline{y})$$
$$w_{ii} = (\sigma_i(\underline{y}))^{-1}, \quad w_{ij} = 0, \ i \neq j \qquad (4)$$

where $E(.)$ and $\sigma_i(.)$ denote the expectation vector and the standard deviation of the i-th feature respectively and $\underline{y}$ is the feature measurement vector of the prototypes.

The above method and some of its variants have been used in membership evaluation of vowel and script recognition problems [14-17]. However, the assumption of expected value as the core point and inverse of standard deviation as weight is quite restrictive. Also, the number of prototypes M may not be large enough to obtain them confidently. In those cases the problem may be solved by the approach given in 2.2.

It should be mentioned that the above method is not the only way of using statistics for membership evaluation. Hersh and Caramazza [18] found membership function based on the assumption that probability of a positive answer to belongingness of a sample $\underline{x}$ to a set A is proportional to its membership value $\mu_A(\underline{x})$. A similar approach in social science problems was used by Nowakowska [19].

2.2 Nonstatistical Approach

Let the measurement vector $\underline{y}_m$ and membership $\mu_A(\underline{y}_m)$ of the m-th prototype be known. Let $\mu_A(\underline{y}_m) = \alpha_m$. Then using equation (1) or (2) we get M equations for $\underline{c}$ and $[w]$. If α_m is not compatible with the expression in the equation (1) or (2), we may arrive at a null solution for $\underline{c}$ and $[w]$. On the other hand we may not know the numerical values of α_m precisely. Thus at best α_m is a good guess. Hence we allow $\mu_A(\underline{y}_m)$ to lie within a range of 2ε about α_m, ie,

$$\alpha_m - \varepsilon \leq \mu_A(\underline{y}_m) \leq \alpha_m + \varepsilon, \quad \varepsilon \geq 0 \qquad (5)$$

such that $\alpha_m - \varepsilon \geq 0$ and $\alpha_m + \varepsilon \leq 1$ (5a) which implies

$$\gamma_m \leq D(\underline{y}_m, \underline{c}) \leq \beta_m \; ; \quad \gamma_m, \beta_m \in R^+ \tag{6}$$

We consider the following 5 cases:

Case 1 $\underline{c}$ is known and [w] is diagonal. Inequality (6) reduces to

$$\gamma_m \leq \sum_{i=1}^{N} w_i (y_{mi} - c_i)^2 \leq \beta_m \tag{6a}$$

There are N unknown w_i to be estimated. Thus at least N samples are needed to get a solution for w_i.

Case 2 $\underline{c}$ is known and [w] is symmetric and not necessarily diagonal. Inequality (6) becomes

$$\gamma_m \leq (\underline{y}_m - \underline{c})^t \, [w] \, (\underline{y}_m - \underline{c}) \leq \beta_m \tag{6b}$$

There are N(N+1)/2 unknown w_{ij}. Hence more samples are needed here.

Case 3 $\underline{c}$ is unknown and [w] is an identity matrix. Here,

$$\gamma_m \leq \sum_{i=1}^{N} (y_{mi} - c_i)^2 \leq \beta_m \tag{6c}$$

There are N parameters to be estimated.

Case 4 $\underline{c}$ is unknown, $w_{ij}=0$ for $i \neq j$ and $w_{ii}=w$ for all i and w is unknown. Then we have

$$\gamma_m \leq \sum_{i=1}^{N} w (y_{mi} - c_i)^2 \leq \beta_m \tag{6d}$$

There are N+1 unknown parameters here.

Case 5 $\underline{c}$ is unknown and [w] is a diagonal matrix. Then inequalities are the same as (6a) with 2N unknowns.

There is, of course, the most general case where [w] is non-diagonal and both $\underline{c}$ and [w] are unknown, the solution of which is quite difficult to obtain. The technique to solve any of the above cases is to start with a large ε such that M inequalities (6) have a common non-empty solution region. Decrease ε in steps so that the solution region shrinks and obtain $\varepsilon=\varepsilon_o$ for which the solution region has sufficiently low hypervolume. Define ε_o as the error of estimation [20].

The solution region (the shaded area) is illustrated in Fig.1 where N=2. To solve for case 1 we need at least two prototypes because there are two unknown w's. In the general case the solution region will have a finite number of corner points. Some kind of average of those corner points is taken as an estimate for the unknown parameters [20].

As for an illustrative example, let us consider a pattern recognition problem

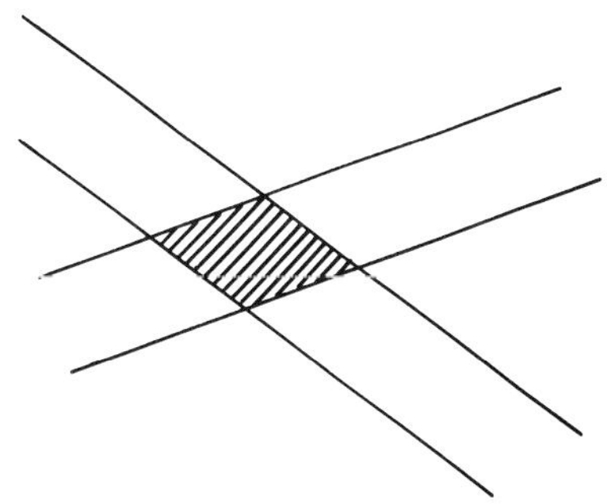

Fig. 1

of English script as shown in Fig.2 where the letter P is considered. The features are defined as the fraction of area covered by the black portion in the concentric rings of equal width. The centre of the rings is the mean position of the black region (X in Fig.2). These features are invariant under translation, rotation and dilation. Four such features (ie, four rings) have been taken in this example. Seven prototypes each of which is a letter P written in different forms have been considered. Approximate membership values of these prototypes to the class 'letter P' have been assumed. The numerical values of the features and membership values are given in Table I. The value of $\underline{c}$ is assumed to be (0.8333, 0.625, 0.241, 0.066). The solution vector obtained for case 1 (N=4, M=7) is also shown in Table I. The solution has been obtained with an error of estimation ε_o=0.0476. The details of the solutions in other cases will be reported elsewhere.

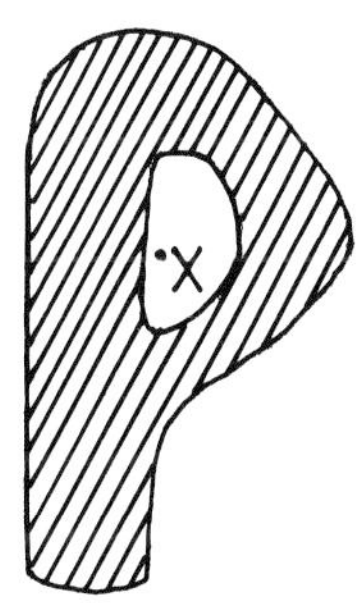

Fig. 2

2.3 Approach for Ordered Prototypes

There is a yet more complex situation

TABLE I

Prototype No.	Feature Vectors				Membership Values
m	y_{m1}	y_{m2}	y_{m3}	y_{m4}	α_m
1	0.833	0.727	0.250	0.064	0.92
2	0.786	0.646	0.221	0.065	0.97
3	0.611	0.735	0.269	0.062	0.80
4	0.294	0.690	0.246	0.061	0.68
5	0.562	0.805	0.303	0.071	0.70
6	0.895	0.589	0.177	0.072	0.70
7	0.381	0.563	0.338	0.066	0.64

Weight Vector Solution $\underline{w}$

w_1	w_2	w_3	w_4
1.1565	3.7521	13.325	5355.3

where even an approximate value of $\mu_A(\underline{y}_m)$ (ie, α_m in the above case) is not known. The prototypes are only rank ordered such that

$$\mu_A(\underline{y}_1) \leq \mu_A(\underline{y}_2) \leq \ \cdots \ \leq \mu_A(\underline{y}_M) \qquad (7)$$

from which $\underline{c}$ and $[w]$ are to be estimated within some range because the exact values are impossible to obtain. Even in that case $\underline{y}_m$ should satisfy some constraints for the solution to exist and remain in a unique range. As an illustrative example let us consider the simple case with two features, $\underline{c}$ known, $[w]$ diagonal and three prototypes such that

$$a_{11}w_1+a_{12}w_2 \geqslant a_{21}w_1+a_{22}w_2 \geqslant a_{31}w_1+a_{32}w_2$$

where $a_{ij}=(y_{ij}-c_j)^2$; $j=1,2$, $i=1,2,3$.

The solution is bounded if

$$\frac{a_{22}-a_{32}}{a_{21}-a_{31}} \geqslant \frac{a_{22}-a_{12}}{a_{11}-a_{21}}$$

which puts some constraints on a_{ij}. Hence it is necessary, in the general case, for the number of prototypes to be large so that the solution is bounded. The constraints under which the solutions are bounded will be discussed elsewhere.

3. MEMBERSHIP EVALUATION WITHOUT A MATHEMATICAL EXPRESSION

The approaches in Section 2 deal with the cases where a mathematical expression for membership function is known. Situations may arise where such an expression is not available and the membership value of a new sample in a set is to be evaluated. The following approaches may be used in those cases.

3.1 Prototype Measurements and Membership Values Known

The simplest case is when the features of the prototypes are measurable and their grades of membership in the set are known. Two ways may be advised to solve the problem: (1) to find a mathematical expression from the known prototypes, (2) to find the membership value of a new sample without the use of an explicit mathematical expression.

The first way may involve expansion through a complete set of orthogonal functions like power series, or seek a simpler expression that fits the prototypes in least square or other sense and use the expression as the membership function. But such an approach, in general, may become intractable, sensitive to prototype number and susceptible to normalisation problem.

Consider the simplest case of linear interpolation. We may find an N-dimensional hyperplane in N+1 dimensional hyperspace with N+1 prototypes about the sample point whose membership is to be found. The membership of ptototypes is represented along N+1 th dimension. The prototypes are chosen such that their degrees of freedom is N, so that the hyperplane can be uniquely defined. The height along N+1 th dimension of the hyperplane at the sample point is the linearly interpolated membership value of the sample if the sample measurement vector is a convex combination of those of the prototypes. Otherwise it is an extrapolated value and may exceed 1. To find a set of prototypes under these restrictions for each new sample is computationally an enormous job. Also, to choose the proper subset one has to start with a set of large cardinality. In that case, the following simple method may be used to reduce the complexity.

Let the prototype vectors $\underline{y}_m$ with known membership values α_m be distributed over a hyperspace $S^N \subset R^N$. A new sample vector $\underline{x} \in S^N$ is to be tested for its membership value. Consider either (a) r prototypes nearest to the new sample, r<M, or (b) the prototypes within a hypercube or hypersphere of size s, and call the prototype vectors $\underline{y}_k$, k=1,2,...r. Find either

$$\alpha_{\underline{x}} = \underset{k}{\operatorname{Min}}\ \mu_A(\underline{y}_k) \tag{8a}$$

or $$\alpha_{\underline{x}} = \frac{1}{r}\sum_{k=1}^{r} \mu_A(\underline{y}_k) \tag{8b}$$

or $$\alpha_{\underline{x}} = \left[\prod_{k=1}^{r} \mu_A(\underline{y}_k)\right]^{1/r} \tag{8c}$$

and $$\mu_A(\underline{x}) \triangleq \alpha_{\underline{x}}$$

It is to be noted that the underlying idea is similar to that in a cluster analysis. This is not surprising since clustering is a powerful learning tool when prior information is meagre. The number r, size s and the alternatives in equation (8) are to be used depending on the problem in hand.

3.2 Prototypes with Unknown Membership Values

Situations may arise when prototypes are measurable but their membership values are unknown. One way to solve the problem is to observe how the data are clustered. Generally, there may be K sets A_k and the M data units are to be optimally partitioned. An objective criterion may be weighted mean squared error among sets, and the partition for which it is minimum is chosen. The weights, properly normalised, imbed fuzzyness in the sets and thus associate a membership value to each prototype in each set.

The clustering procedure described below (called fuzzy ISODATA) has been reported by Dunn [21] and Bezdeck [22] .

Let $\{\mu_k: 1 \le k \le K\}$ be fuzzy subsets of the prototype set $Y = \{\underline{y}_1, \underline{y}_2 \cdots \underline{y}_M\}$. Thus $\mu_k: Y \rightarrow [0,1]$ is the membership function of the k-th fuzzy subset with $\mu_k(\underline{y}_m) = \mu_{km}$ as the grade of membership of $\underline{y}_m$ in fuzzy subset μ_k. Let

$$\sum_{k=1}^{K} \mu_{km} = 1 \quad \text{for } 1 \le m \le M \tag{9}$$

Then the technique is to minimise the objective function

$$J_n(U,\underline{v}) = \sum_{m=1}^{M}\sum_{k=1}^{K} (\mu_{km})^n \,\|\underline{y}_m - \underline{v}_k\|^2 \quad \text{for } n \geqslant 1 \tag{10}$$

where $\underline{v}_k$ is the cluster centre of k th fuzzy set and U is the set of subsets μ_k. The minimisation requires the following conditions to hold

$$\mu_{km} = \left\{\sum_{j=1}^{K}\left[\frac{\|\underline{y}_m - \underline{v}_k\|^2}{\|\underline{y}_m - \underline{v}_j\|^2}\right]^{\frac{1}{n-1}}\right\}^{-1} \quad \text{for all m, k} \tag{11}$$

$$\underline{v}_k = \frac{\sum_{m=1}^{M} (\mu_{km})^n\, \underline{y}_m}{\sum_{m=1}^{M} (\mu_{km})^n} \quad \text{for all k} \tag{12}$$

The procedure to minimise J_n is to start with an initial U and use equations (11) and (12) recursively. The convergence is obtained at I th iteration if

$$|v_k(I+1) - v_k(I)| < \delta v_k(I) \quad \text{for all k} \tag{13}$$

is satisfied for a specified value of δ.

It can be shown that in [23] the method converges to a partition which is locally optimum in the sense of J_n. Each prototype is thus characterised by a membership value in fuzzy set. The method of case 1 above can now be used for the incoming data samples.

TABLE II

Prototype No. m	Membership Values μ_{1m}	μ_{2m}
1	0.089	0.911
2	0.101	0.899
3	0.036	0.964
4	0.070	0.930
5	0.136	0.864
6	0.055	0.945
7	0.023	0.977
8	0.105	0.895
9	0.186	0.814
10	0.079	0.921
11	0.141	0.859
12	0.414	0.586
13	0.663	0.377
14	0.801	0.199
15	0.710	0.290
16	0.944	0.056
17	0.760	0.240
18	0.890	0.110
19	0.984	0.016
20	0.911	0.089
21	0.978	0.022
22	0.874	0.126
23	0.932	0.068
24	0.865	0.135
25	0.932	0.068
	0.944	0.022
x	0.969	0.062
	0.968	0.051

As an illustrative example, consider the 25 prototypes in the sample space shown in Fig.3. The membership value of each of them has been found using fuzzy ISO-DATA for K=2 and is given in Table II. A new sample x in the space is also shown in Fig.3. The membership value of x using equation (8) and considering 3 nearest neighbours is given in Table II for all the three cases in (8).

It may be noted that the membership evaluation can be made adaptive by considering each new x along with the prototypes and using the fuzzy ISODATA over them. Thus the membership values of all samples are shuffled each time a new sample arrives. It increases computation cost, involves storage problem for largo data and has some drawback for on-line use. To reduce computation cost a semi-adaptive system may be considered where n new samples are assigned membership values according to equation (8) and fuzzy ISODATA is used at n+1 th sample, the process being repeated until the data is exhausted.

The family of objective functions J_n in equation (10) is derived from the idea of the Euclidean norm. The use of J_n as well as the assumption that optimised weights satisfying equation (9) are the membership values is questionable. However, when so little information is available to the data set, some assumption must be made to arrive at a workable solution. Different families of J_n like similarity or correlation or potential may be tested in a supervised environment and the family that gives the best result (in the sense of minimum average error or cost) may be accepted in the design.

3.3 Prototype Features Rank-Ordered

As discussed earlier, the features that characterise a fuzzy set are not always measurable. In such cases we can at best expect that the prototypes are rank ordered according to the compatibility of the features in the fuzzy set. Thus for each feature the prototypes may be rank ordered in the set and we want an

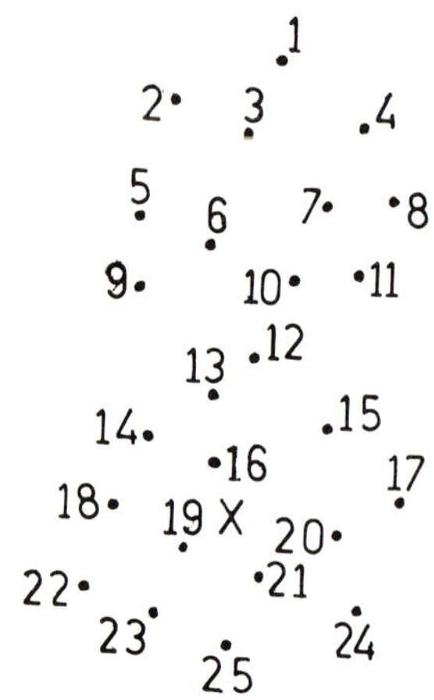

Fig. 3

aggregation of the ordering considering all the features. Let $P_i(k)$ denote the i th prototype to be ordered according to the compatibility of the k th feature in the set such that

$$P_1(k) \geq P_2(k) \geq \dots P_i(k) \geq \dots P_M(k) \quad \text{for all } k \tag{14}$$

It may be noted that ordering (14) is quite different from ordering (7). If the features are independent, (14) can be represented in a K-dimensional space. In order to find the membership values without assuming a functional form it is useful to find a dissimilarity or density or distance measure of the data.

Bartels et al [24] have proposed a distance measure which utilizes only the ordering of data units along each dimension of the space. The basic concept of measuring the distance between two data units is to imagine them as opposite vertices of a hypervolume whose sides are parallel to the axes of the space, The distance is basically the fraction of all data units which fall into this hypervolume and its extentions, as shown in Fig.4. The distance between points 1 and 2 is determined by the number of points in the shaded area, ie, points 3,4,6 and 7. Bartels et al found it necessary to employ a weighting scheme to handle tied values and defined the following:

Interior points (M_i): The number of points in the interior of the hypervolume and its extensions.

Boundary points (M_b): The number of points on the boundary of the hypervolume and its extensions.

Zero points (M_z): The number of points which do not lie either in the interior or on the boundary of the hypervolume but whose value on at least one variable is equal to that of both the points under consideration.

The distance is defined as

$$d_c = 6\,M_i + 3\,M_b + 2\,M_z \tag{15}$$

The choice of weights is intuitive. If the total number of data units is M, the maximum possible value of d_c is 6(M-2) and the normalised distance is

$$d_{nc} = (6\,M_i + 3\,M_b + 2\,M_z)\;/\;6(M-2) \tag{16}$$

This distance fails as a metric in two respects. First, two points need not be identical to be zero distance apart and second, it disobeys the triangular inequality. It is invariant under transformations which preserve the order of the data units along the axes and not invariant under arbitrary orthogonal rotations.

The distance d_{nc} can be used to express membership values if the distance of each point from the seed point is measured. The seed point may be assumed to be the point with the highest rank in the multidimensional space. It is clear that $0 \leq d_{nc} \leq 1$.

To find the membership value of a new sample P_x it is necessary to know its rank in all dimensions. This helps placement of the sample in the multidimensional space. If P_1 and P_2 are its nearest neighbours in ranking such that $d_c(P_1, P_2) = 0$ in the prototype space then either

$$\mu_A(P_1) \geq \mu_A(P_x) \geq \mu_A(P_2)$$
$$\text{or} \quad \mu_A(P_2) \geq \mu_A(P_x) \geq \mu_A(P_1) \tag{17}$$

and define $\mu_A(P_x) = \min\left[\mu_A(P_1),\ \mu_A(P_2)\right]$

There may be problems where it is more convenient to use rank ordering of membership values than getting their numerical values. In those cases the use of equations (15-17) is redundant. However, equations (15-16) give some idea about how to quantify a qualitative preference system and more attention should be paid along this line.

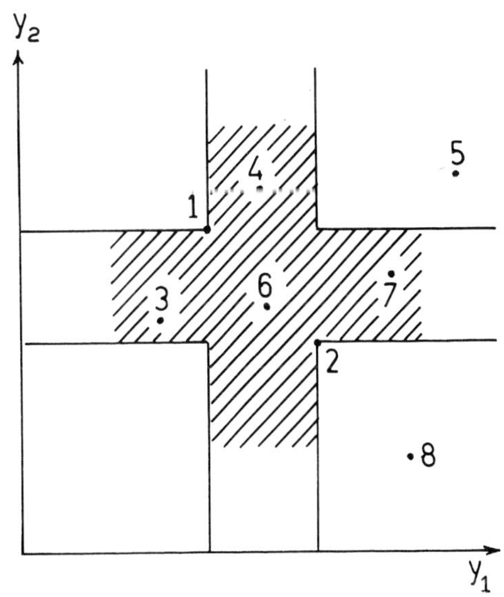

Fig. 4

4. CONCLUSION

The paper has been aimed at discussing the different situations that may arise in evaluating membership values of a fuzzy set in practical problems. The methods described here, however, are not exhaustive. They are discussed mainly from a pattern recognition viewpoint, although applications to other areas are also possible.

In describing the methods, stress has been put to those with computational ease and efficiency. Quite often fuzzy set theory is aimed at solving the problems where samples are not available in a large number. No elaborate description has been made on the methods requiring large number of prototypes, although some of them may be quite effective. Simple illustrative examples have been given whenever possible.

In order to have membership values of prototypes or their rank ordering it is important to become aware of how the human brain processes labels of fuzzy sets. Kochen [25] did some work along this line. Rank ordering of membership values or features may be done in a similar fashion in psychological experiments 26 . Although assignment of numerical values to membership grades even of the prototypes is difficult, they can be guessed approximately and methods in Sections 2.2 or 3.1 may be used. In fact method in Section 2.2 refines the approximation on the aggregate. If guessing is not allowed the approach in Section 3.2 is a possible answer. Also the distance described in Section 3.3 is quite good in quantification of a qualitative preference system.

Finally the methods described here may be refined for use in different practical problems.

Acknowledgement

The authors wish to thank Mr. S. K. Parui for fruitful discussions. The help rendered by Mr. S. Chakraverti and Mr. J. Gupta is also gratefully acknowledged.

REFERENCES

[1] Gupta, M.M., Ragade, R.K. and Yager, R.Y., Eds., Fuzzy set theory and applications (North-Holland, New-York, 1979).

[2] Watanabe, S., A generalised fuzzy set theory, IEEE Trans. Syst. Man Cybernet. Vol.SMC-8, No.10, 756-760 (1978).

[3] Chaudhuri, B.B. and Dutta Majumder, D., Fuzzy sets and possibility theory in reliability studies of man machine systems, in Fuzzy Sets, Wang, P.P. and Cheng, S.K., Eds. (Plenum Press, New York, 1980).

[4] Fung, L.W. and Fu, K.S., Decision-making in a fuzzy environment, Tech. Report No.TR-EE 73-22, School of Engineering Purdue University, Lafayette, Indiana (1973).

[5] Bellmann, R.E., Kalaba, R. and Zadeh, L.A., Abstraction and pattern classification, J. Math. Anal. and Appl., Vol.13, No.1, 1-7 (1966).

[6] Kandel, A. and Byatt, W.J., Fuzzy sets, fuzzy algebra and fuzzy statistics, Proc.IEEE, Vol.66, No.12, 1619-1639 (1978).

[7] Fung, L.W. and Fu, K.S., An axiomatic approach to rational decision-making in a fuzzy environment, in Fuzzy sets and their application to cognitive and decision processes, Zadeh, L.A., Fu, K.S., Tanaka, K. and Shimura, M., Eds. (Academic, New York, 1975).

[8] Zadeh, L.A., Outline of a new approach to the analysis of complex systems and decision processes, IEEE Trans. Syst. Man. Cybernet., Vol. SMC-3, No.1, 28-44 (1973).

[9] Bremermann, H., Pattern recognition by deformable prototypes in structural stability, in The Theory of Catastrophes and Application in Sciences, Springer notes, Vol.25, 15-57 (Springer-Verlag, Berlin, 1976).

[10] Albin, M., Fuzzy sets and their applications to medical diagnosis and pattern recognition, Ph.D Thesis, University of California, Berkeley, 1975.

[11] Kochen, M. and Badre, A.N., On the precision of adjectives which denote fuzzy sets, J.Cybernet. Vol4, No.1, 49-59 (1976).

[12] Saaty, T., Exploring the interface between hierarchies, multiple objectives and fuzzy sets, Int.J.Fuzzy set Syst., Vol.1, No.1, 57-68 (1978).

[13] Dishkant, H., About membership function estimation, Int.J.Fuzzy sets Syst., Vol.5, No.2, 141-147 (1981).

[14] Pal, S.K. and Dutta Majumder, D., Fuzzy sets and decision-making approaches in vowel and speaker recognition, IEEE Trans. Syst. Man Cybernet. Vol.SMC-7, No.8, 625-629 (1977).

[15] Chaudhuri, B.B. and Dutta Majumder, D., Recognition and fuzzy description of sides and symmetries of figures by computer, Int.J.Syst.Sci. Vol.11, No.12, 1435-1445 (1980).

[16] Biswas, P., A fuzzy hybrid model for pattern classification with application to recognition of hand-printed devanagri, Ph.D.Thesis, School of Comp. and Syst.Sci, J.N.University, New Delhi, 1980.

[17] Pal, S.K. and Dutta Majumder, D., A self adaptive fuzzy recognition system for speech sounds, in Fuzzy Sets, Wang, P.P. and Chang, S.K., Eds. (Plenum Press, New York, 1980).

[18] Hersh, H.M. and Caramozza, A., A fuzzy-set approach to modifiers and vaugeness in natural languages, J.Exp.Psychol.Gen., Vol.105, 254-276 (1976).

[19] Nowakowska, M., Fuzzy concepts in the social sciences, Behav. Sci., Vol.22, 107-115 (1977).

[20] Parui, S.K. and Dutta Majumder, D., A procedure to estimate the parameters of a fuzzy membership function, Fuzzy Sets and Systems (Communicated).

[21] Dunn, J.C., A fuzzy relative of the ISODATA process and its use in detecting compact well-separated clusters, J.Cybernet., Vol.3, No.3, 32-57 (1974).

[22] Bezdeck, J.C., Cluster validity with fuzzy sets, J.Cybernet., Vol.3, No.3, 58-73 (1974).

[23] Bezdeck, J.C., A convergence theorem for the fuzzy ISODATA clustering algorithms, IEEE Trans.Pattern Analysis and Machine Intelligence, Vol.PAMI-2, No.1, 1-7 (1980).

[24] Bartels, P.H., Bahr, G.F., Calhoun, D.W. and Wied, G.I., Cell recognition by neighbourhood grouping techniques in TICAS, Acts Cytology, Vol14, No.6, 313-324 (1970).

[25] Kochen, M., Application of fuzzy sets in psychology, in Zadeh, L.A., Fu, K.S., Tanaka, K. and Shimura, M., Eds., Fuzzy sets and their applications to cognitive and decision processes (Academic, New-York, 1975).

[26] Hays, W.L., Quantification in psychology (Prentice-Hall, New-Delhi, 1969).

Approximate Reasoning in Decision Analysis
M.M. Gupta and E. Sanchez (eds.)

STOCHASTIC FUZZINESS

A.M. Norwich and I.B. Turksen

Department of Industrial Engineering
University of Toronto
Toronto, Ontario, M5S 1A4

The stochastic fuzzy set synthesizes the probabilistic and fuzzy models of an ambiguous linguistic term, permitting them to be compared both mathematically and philosophically. Moreover, both the stochastic and the conventional fuzzy set models capture this ambiguity "better" than the probabilistic model, in the sense of a particular quantitative criterion.

KEYWORDS

Semantic uncertainty, membership function, measurement, stochastic fuzzy set, fundamental A-ness, relative A-ness.

1. INTRODUCTION

The theory of fuzzy sets was introduced by L.A. Zadeh in 1965 to model vague or ambiguous adjectives and predicates [1]. The immediate appeal of this theory, due to its philosphical simplicity as well as its mathematical elegance, soon led to its widespread use in diverse applications.

However, two points of controversy sprung up soon after the theory was proposed and have continued unresolved to this day. One originates with critics who see fuzzy sets as totally unnecessary, preferring to represent ambiguous predicates by classical probability theory models. The other originates with fuzzy set adherents themselves, some of whom do in fact use the same model of an ambiguous predicate as the probabilists, but call the resulting probability function a membership function, so that they then may operate on it with fuzzy set calculus rather than probability calculus.

This paper attempts to resolve both these controversies by proposing a new model of fuzziness, called the "stochastic fuzzy set", which enables the comparison to be made, both mathematically and philosophically, between the classical probability model of an ambiguous linguistic term and the traditional model found in fuzzy set literature.

2. OBJECTIVE AND SUBJECTIVE ATTRIBUTES

We will first introduce the terms "objective attribute" and "subjective attribute" of objects in a domain of discourse. An objective attribute A is a linguistic term whose meaning is not open to individual interpretability by any observer. An example is MAN OF AT LEAST 5 FEET IN HEIGHT. Letting Θ denote the empirical domain of discourse (i.e. of objects) and $X(\Theta)$ denote a numerical domain of discourse which can be used to represent Θ, we get: $\Theta = \{\text{different men}\}$, $X(\Theta) = \{\text{numerical heights of men in } \Theta\} = [0,\infty)$ feet, and A = AT LEAST 5 FEET IN HEIGHT. Any objective attribute can be mathematically represented by an ordinary set model--denoted "$\mathfrak{M}_{OS}$"--through a characteristic function $\chi_A(x(\theta))$. For the example just given, A partitions Θ and thus $X(\Theta)$ into two classes I_1 and I_0, corresponding to those objects which do and do not possess the attribute, respectively.

A subjective attribute, A, however, is a linguistic term whose meaning does permit individual interpretability by any observer, so that it may be said to possess "semantic uncertainty" or "fuzziness", whereas an objective attribute possesses none. An example is TALL MAN. A subjective attribute can be represented by the classical "pure probability model", denoted "$\mathfrak{M}_{PP}$", to which we alluded in section 1. This model views semantic uncertainty as being merely statistical uncertainty in the information theoretic sense (i.e. as purely probabilistic) and measures the attribute by the probability function $P_A(x(\theta))$. The value of this function is found by randomly and repeatedly presenting a subject with objects in Θ and receiving either a "yes" or a "no" response to the question "Do you agree that θ is A?" [2,3]. Then

$$P_A(x(\theta)) = \frac{\text{Total number of "yes" responses for } \theta}{\text{Total number of "yes" and "no" responses for } \theta} .$$

The result, for the example of TALL MAN, is shown in Fig. 1. Note that A partitions Θ and thus $X(\Theta)$ into three subsets: the two classes I_1^P and I_0^P, corresponding to those objects which do and do not possess the attribute, respectively, and a "fuzzy region" F^P of those objects which possess it to some intermediate degree (i.e. some

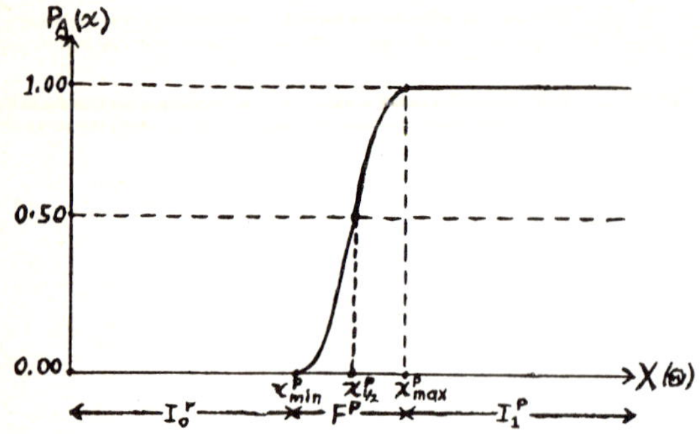

Figure 1.

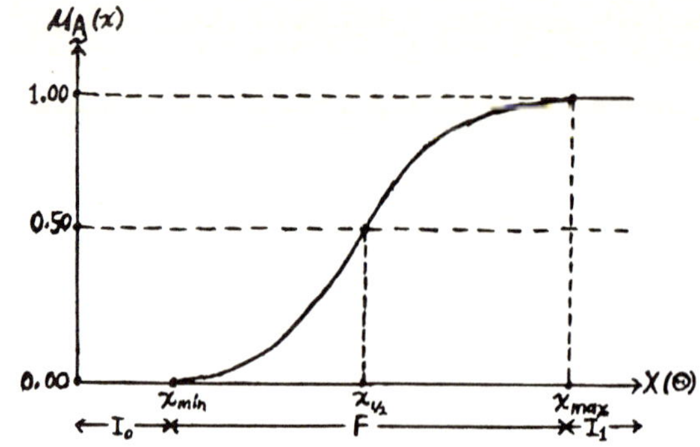

Figure 2.

"yes" and some "no" responses are both obtained for each θ in F^P). $I_0^P \cup I_1^P$ is said to form the "crisp region" of the representation $P_A(x(\theta))$. The superscript "P" denotes that these three subsets come from the pure probability model $\mathcal{M}_{PP}$.

However, fuzzy set theory also proposes a model of subjective attributes. The fuzzy set model of {all objects which are A}, denoted "$\mathcal{M}_{DFS}$" (where the letter "D" signifies the deterministic nature of the model, as described in section 4), is characterized by the membership function $\mu_A(x(\theta))$, which gives the degree of membership in this set. This model, unlike $\mathcal{M}_{PP}$, views semantic uncertainty as different in nature from statistical uncertainty and regards this membership function as not being a probability function at all. That is, $\mathcal{M}_{DFS}$ is seen as generalizing $\mathcal{M}_{OS}$, by extending the characteristic function from the binary lattice range {0,1} to the continuous range [0,1]. The resulting function $\mu_A(x(\theta))$, shown in Fig. 2 for the example of TALL MAN, appears identical in shape to that of the pure probability function $P_A(x(\theta))$: the former also is increasing and reveals a partitioning of X(Θ) into two classes I_1 and I_0, corresponding to those objects which do and do not possess the attribute, respectively, and a fuzzy region F of those objects which possess it to some intermediate degree. $I_0 \cup I_1$ therefore forms the crisp region of the representation $\mu_A(x(\theta))$.

The question immediately arises as to whether $P_A(x(\theta))$ and $\mu_A(x(\theta))$ are identical functions and, if they are not, as to how they differ. As will be demonstrated in section 6, it turns out that the fuzzy region F^P of $P_A(x(\theta))$ is smaller in size than the fuzzy region F of $\mu_A(x(\theta))$, as illustrated in Figs. 1 and 2. Furthermore, empirical evidence indicates that F^P is often very much smaller than F. In order to make such a quantitative comparison as this between $P_A(x(\theta))$ and $\mu_A(x(\theta))$, we must first specify how to measure the membership function, since the method of obtaining the value of $P_A(x(\theta))$ is well established, whereas the method of obtaining the value of $\mu_A(x(\theta))$ is not.

3. MEASURING FUZZINESS

In this paper, only an outline of the measurement of fuzziness will be given, since we have presented a thorough discussion elsewhere [4,5,6,7,8,9] of the issues of representation of the membership function, uniqueness of this representation, and scaling (i.e. actual empirical construction) of the representation.

Since fuzzy set theory concerns itself with subjective attributes and since the measurement of subjective attributes is the province of mathematical psychology, we have investigated the representation and uniqueness of fuzziness through the theory of measurement [10,11,12]. Similarly, we have constructed the membership function by classical psychophysical scaling techniques, in accordance with these models [13,14,15].

Two scaling procedures have been used in our experiments: direct rating and reverse rating. Under direct rating, a subject is randomly and repeatedly given an object θ in the empirical domain Θ (not in the numerical domain X(Θ), since presenting numbers and not objects permits memorization of responses). The subject is asked to express the degree to which s/he feels θ is A by moving a pointer along a continuous, horizontal line segment (representing the range of membership values), where s/he is told that the left-to-right direction represents increasing agreement. (The responses are obtained geometrically rather than numerically by, for example, the subject announcing a degree of agreement from 0 to 1 in graduations of 0.01, because numbers contain inherent biases and also permit memorization of responses.) The membership function value $\mu_A(x(\theta))$ is then obtained by taking the mean value of all responses for each particular object. The result is $\mathcal{M}_{DFS}$.

The reverse rating procedure is essentially a construction of the inverse mapping from the bounded line segment onto the domain of discourse. Here, the subject is randomly and repeatedly presented with a pointer setting representing a degree of agreement that θ is A and asked to choose an object in Θ which corresponds to it (i.e. which has this degree of agreement). The mean value of the responses is again taken to construct the membership function. Both the direct and reverse ratings procedures should yield the same membership function and they have been found to do so for our subjects.

As was mentioned in the last statement in section 2, the method of constructing the psycholinguistic function of the fuzzy set literature has never been clearly established. Thus we are essentially assuming that the function constructed by the standard psychophysical techniques given in this section is that function.

One important consequence of our measurement model is that the membership function appears to be on an interval scale. This means that its lower and upper bounds "0" and "1", as in Fig. 2, are in fact arbitrary in value and should therefore be denoted "B_L" and "B_U", respectively. Thus, $\mu_A(x(\theta))$ is not on the interval [0,1] but on the interval $M \triangleq [B_L, B_U]$.

We now have constructed both the functions $P_A(x(\theta))$ for $\mathfrak{M}_{PP}$ and $\mu_A(x(\theta))$ for $\mathfrak{M}_{DFS}$. In order to compare them mathematically and philosophically, we must introduce the notion of the "stochastic fuzzy set".

4. THE STOCHASTIC FUZZY SET

Each of the direct and reverse rating procedures of section 3 which are used for measuring membership yields a set of responses for any given point which is being rated. Now, however, let us not take the mean response to get the membership function but, rather, let us consider the distribution formed by the responses for each point. So, in direct rating, the set of responses for each point θ in Θ forms a frequency distribution over M, whereas in reverse rating, the set of responses for each point α in M forms a frequency distribution over Θ and therefore over $X(\Theta)$.

Thus, we are now viewing the inconsistency in responses not merely as a noise artifact due to experimental error and as something which should therefore be averaged out. Instead, it is regarded as variability caused by the imprecision (i.e. vagueness or ambiguity) in the definition in the subject's mind of the subjective attribute being scaled and as being, therefore, inherent to fuzziness.

Accordingly, we now view the membership of θ not as a deterministic scalar $\mu_A(x(\theta))$ under direct rating, but as a random variable $\nu_A(x(\theta))$ having a probability density function $p_{\nu_A}(\alpha|x(\theta))$ for $\alpha \varepsilon M$, which is estimated by the frequency distribution of responses. So, $\nu_A = \{\nu_A(x(\theta))\}_{x(\theta)\varepsilon X(\Theta)}$ is a family of such random variables rather than a family of deterministic scalars, $\mu_A = \{\mu_A(x(\theta))\}_{x(\theta)\varepsilon X(\Theta)}$. Letting "$\mathbb{P}$" denote the $[0,\infty)$ range of possible values of the probability density function $p_{\nu_A}(\alpha|x(\theta))$, we may represent the stochastic component of $\nu_A(x(\theta))$ graphically by drawing $\mathbb{P}$ as a third dimension perpendicular to the X x M plane. Thus, the fuzzy set A is no longer represented mathematically by a deterministic (hence the "D" in "$\mathfrak{M}_{DFS}$") curve in the X x M plane (i.e. $A \varepsilon M^X$) but is now a surface in X x M x $\mathbb{P}$ space (i.e. $A \varepsilon \mathbb{P}^{M^X}$). This new model of a subjective attribute, called the "stochastic fuzzy set" is denoted "$\mathfrak{M}_{SFS}$". An example is given in Fig. 3 for TALL MAN (where "$\alpha_{1/2}$" denotes the midpoint of $[B_L, B_U]$).

An immediate implication of the stochastic fuzzy set view of a subjective attribute A is the resolution of a paradox in "generalized fuzzy set theory" [16]. This theory acknowledges the imprecision inherent in the first level of membership M_1, due to the vague nature of A and models this imprecision by putting a second level of membership M_2 on the first. However, this second level is similarly seen to be imprecise and a third level of membership M_3 is necessary. This process continues ad infinitum, yielding the model

$$A \varepsilon \lim_{n\to\infty} M_n^{\cdot^{\cdot^{\cdot^{M_1^{X(\Theta)}}}}}, \quad M_i = M,\ i=1,2,\ldots,n.$$

Stochastic fuzziness suggests a resolution of this infinite regress paradox. There is no need for second, third, ... levels of membership; one dimension of probability on top of the first level is sufficient. Clearly, the density function $p_{\nu_A}(\alpha|x(\theta))$ contains all the information which a subject is able to give in rating how A any θ in Θ is, since any uncertainty he feels about the membership of θ is revealed by this statistical variability in his responses. So, it is unnecessary to view A as an element of the infinite-stage mapping given above, but only of $\mathbb{P}^{M^{X(\Theta)}}$.

Having defined the stochastic fuzzy set model $\mathfrak{M}_{SFS}$ of A, we may now use it to compare the pure probability model $\mathfrak{M}_{PP}$ and the deterministic fuzzy set model $\mathfrak{M}_{DFS}$. The first step is to show how both can be derived from $\mathfrak{M}_{SFS}$ and thus how $\mathfrak{M}_{SFS}$ generalizes and unites them.

5. DERIVING $\mathfrak{M}_{DFS}$ AND $\mathfrak{M}_{PP}$ FROM $\mathfrak{M}_{SFS}$

In the sequel we will, for the sake of brevity, omit writing θ as an argument of x. That is, $x(\theta)$, $P_A(x(\theta))$, $\mu_A(x(\theta))$, $\nu_A(x(\theta))$, and $p_{\nu_A}(\alpha|x(\theta))$ will be denoted x, $P_A(x)$, $\mu_A(x)$, $\nu_A(x)$, and $p_{\nu_A}(\alpha|x)$, respectively, with the argument θ understood

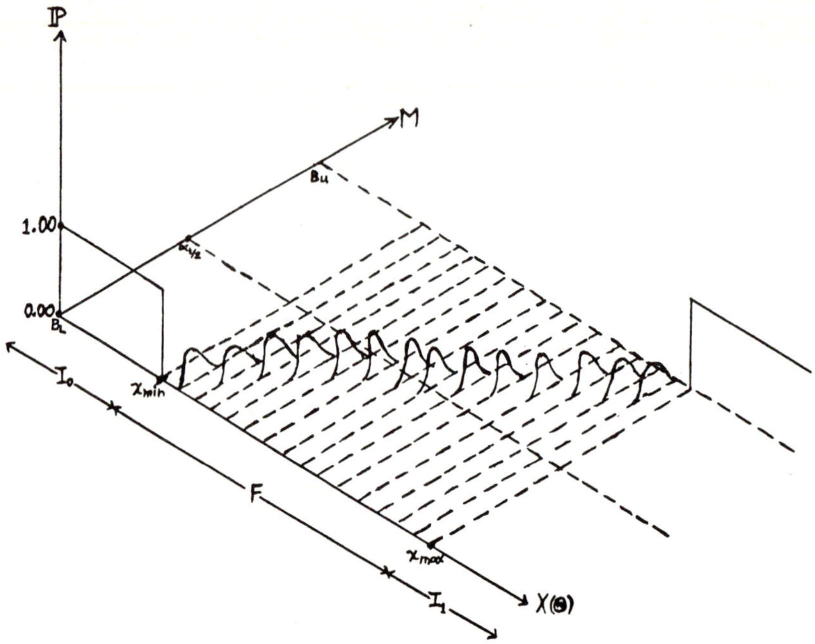

Figure 3.

The derivation of $\mathcal{M}_{DFS}$ from $\mathcal{M}_{SFS}$ follows immediately from the definition of those two models in sections 3 and 4. The deterministic membership function is found by taking the expected value over M of the stochastic membership function:

$$\mu_A(x) = \int_{\alpha \epsilon M} \alpha \, p_{\nu_A}(\alpha|x)d\alpha = \bar{\nu}_A(x).$$

This operation is equivalent, in Fig. 3, to taking all the probability under $p_{\nu_A}(\alpha|x)$ and aggregating it over the mean value of $\nu_A(x)$ in M, creating the deterministic quantity $\bar{\nu}_A(x)$ shown in Fig. 4. The ℙ-dimension is now, however, degenerate and may be ignored. This is done by "looking down" the ℙ-axis from above the X x M plane, with the resulting view being that given in Fig. 2 of the membership function of the fuzzy set literature (but now, of course, with bounds B_L and B_U instead of 0 and 1, due to the interval scale property of membership).

The derivation of $\mathcal{M}_{PP}$ from $\mathcal{M}_{SFS}$ may be performed if an assumption is made about the relation of the continuous direct ratings $\alpha \epsilon M = [B_L, B_U]$ which yield $\mathcal{M}_{SFS}$ to the binary direct ratings $\beta \epsilon M_B \stackrel{\Delta}{=} \{B_L, B_U\} \equiv \{\text{"no", "yes"}\}$ which yield $\mathcal{M}_{PP}$.

<u>Axiom 1</u>: $\alpha \geq \alpha_{1/2} \iff \beta = B_U$ (i.e. "yes, x is A");

$\alpha < \alpha_{1/2} \iff \beta = B_U$ (i.e. "no, x is not A").

Axiom 1 states that if a subject, on any trial of continuous direct rating assigns a value above the midpoint $\alpha_{1/2}$ of M, then if s/he had been asked instead to give a binary direct rating, then β would have taken on the value of the nearer (in this case, upper) bound B_U -- that is, the subject would have replied "yes, θ is A" rather than "no, θ is not A". Similarly, a continuous rating α below the midpoint $\alpha_{1/2}$ would have become a "no" reply under binary rating, which is equivalent to again assigning β the value of the nearer (in this case lower) bound B_L. Now let "$\eta_A(x)$" denote the random variable taking on a value β on any particular binary trial.

<u>Theorem 1</u>: If Axiom 1 holds, then

$$P_A(x) = \int_{\alpha \geq \alpha_{1/2}} p_{\nu_A}(\alpha|x)d\alpha.$$

<u>Proof</u>: If ($\alpha \geq \alpha_{1/2} \iff \beta = B_U$) on any one direct rating trial,

then $\Pr(\nu_A(x) \geq \alpha_{1/2}) = \Pr(\eta_A(x) = B_U)$

over all direct rating trials.

But $\Pr(\nu_A(x) \geq \alpha_{1/2}) = \int_{\alpha \geq \alpha_{1/2}} p_{\nu_A}(\alpha|x)d\alpha.$

and $P_A(x) = \Pr(\eta_A(x) = B_U)$,

so $P_A(x) = \int_{\alpha \geq \alpha_{1/2}} p_{\nu_A}(\alpha|x)d\alpha.$

<u>Corollary</u>: Let "¬" denote the complement, "not". Then,

$$P_{\neg A}(x) = \int_{\alpha < \alpha_{1/2}} p_{\nu_A}(\alpha|x)d\alpha = 1 - P_A(x).$$

Thus, the process of binary rating may be viewed as one of first "splitting" the stochastic

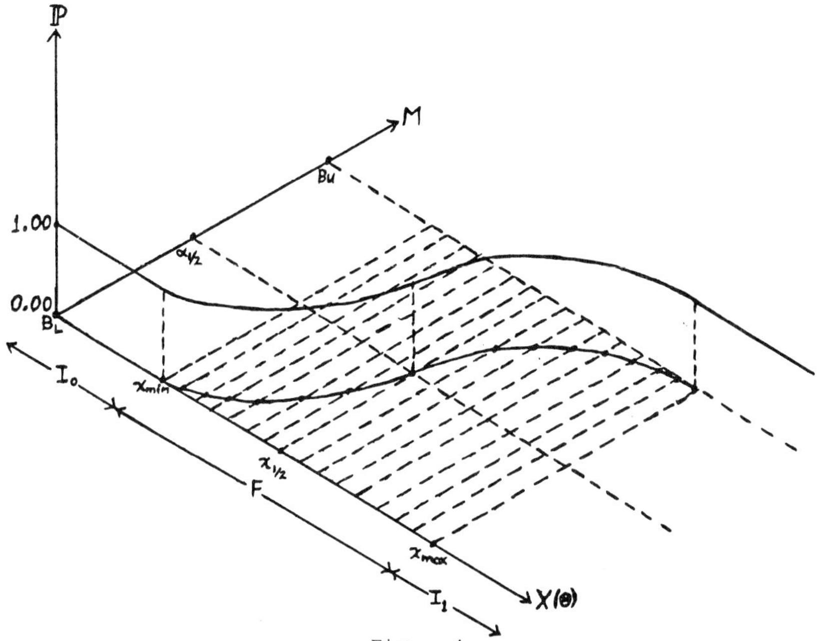

Figure 4.

membership function surface created by continuous direct rating, along the line $\alpha_{\frac{1}{2}}$ in M for all x and then aggregating all of the probability under $p_{\nu_A}(\alpha|x)$ for $\alpha \geq \alpha_{\frac{1}{2}}$ at the upper boundary B_U and aggregating all the probability for $\alpha < \alpha_{\frac{1}{2}}$ at the lower boundary B_L. This process creates a family of Bernoulli random variables $\{\eta_A(x)\}_{x \in X}$ such that

$$\eta_A(x) = \begin{cases} B_U & \text{with probability } P_A(x) \\ B_L & \text{with probability } 1 - P_A(x) \end{cases}$$

The result is that the stochastic membership function surface of Fig. 3 becomes the two-branch surface of Fig. 5 created by this family of Bernoulli density functions. The M-dimension is now degenerate, since the $\eta_A(x) = B_U$ branch of the surface implies the form of the $\eta_A(x) = B_L$ branch. So we may ignore the M-dimension by "looking down" the M-axis from below the X x $\mathbb{P}$ plane at the $\eta_A(x) = B_U$ branch alone. The resulting view is just the classical probability function given in Fig. 1.

Thus, not only the deterministic fuzzy set model $\mathcal{M}_{DFS}$ but also the pure probability model $\mathcal{M}_{PP}$ of a subjective attribute may be obtained from $\mathcal{M}_{SFS}$, so that the stochastic fuzzy set model is seen to generalize each and unite both. We are now in a position to compare $\mathcal{M}_{DFS}$ with $\mathcal{M}_{PP}$ mathematically and philosphically.

6. COMPARING $\mathcal{M}_{DFS}$ WITH $\mathcal{M}_{PP}$ VIA $\mathcal{M}_{SFS}$

Since $\mu_A(x)$ is the mean value of $\nu_A(x)$, $\mathcal{M}_{DFS}$ contains only locational information and no variational information about $p_{\nu_A}(\alpha|x)$ -- specifically, it indicates the "central tendency" of $p_{\nu_A}(\alpha|x)$. On the other hand, $\mathcal{M}_{PP}$ contains some locational as well as some variational information about $p_{\nu_A}(\alpha|x)$-- specifically, it indicates the fraction of $p_{\nu_A}(\alpha|x)$ supported by points in M which are at least as large as the split-point $\alpha_{\frac{1}{2}}$, so that it may be said to indicate the "degree of overlap" of $p_{\nu_A}(\alpha|x)$ with $\alpha_{\frac{1}{2}}$. The value of $P_A(x)$ reflects a combination of information about the mean of $\nu_A(x)$ in M and information about its spread over M. Thus, it is clear that, although $\mathcal{M}_{DFS}$ and $\mathcal{M}_{PP}$ can both be derived from $\mathcal{M}_{SFS}$, neither can be derived from the other, since the mean value $\mu_A(x)$ of $\nu_A(x)$ does not imply, nor is it implied by, the value of its degree of overlap with the point $\alpha_{\frac{1}{2}}$. $\mathcal{M}_{DFS}$ and $\mathcal{M}_{PP}$ therefore model related but different aspects of fuzziness.

We have so far used the interrelation given in Axiom 1 between continuous and binary direct ratings to show that $\mathcal{M}_{PP}$ is subsumed by $\mathcal{M}_{SFS}$: the continuous ratings form the random variable $\nu_A(x)$ with density function $p_{\nu_A}(\alpha|x)$ and the binary ratings form the Bernoulli variable $\eta_A(x)$ whose density function is obtained by splitting that of $\nu_A(x)$ at $\alpha_{\frac{1}{2}}$ in M and which reduces to the equivalent representation $P_A(x)$. However, we can also use the interrelation between the continuous direct and reverse rating procedures

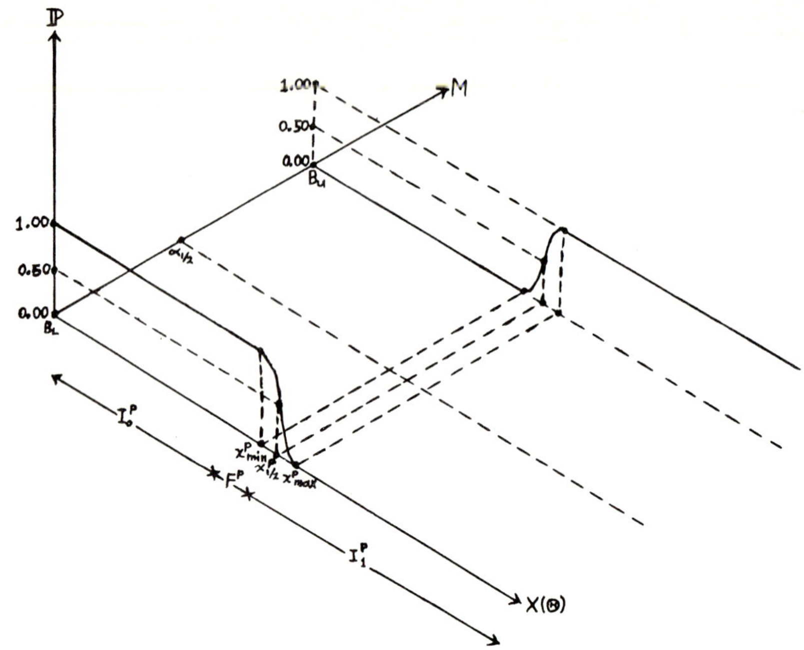

Figure 5.

to give further insight into the relationship between $\mathcal{M}_{DFS}$ and $\mathcal{M}_{PP}$.

Let x_α denote the value in X(Θ) corresponding to the object θ chosen from Θ by the subject in a trial of reverse rating when s/he is presented with α in M. Then x_α is the value, on one trial, of the random variable denoted "X_α". If $\alpha = \alpha_{1/2}$, then we write $x_{\alpha_{1/2}}$ as simply "$x_{1/2}$"; if $\alpha = B_L$ we write x_{B_L} as "x_{min}"; and if $\alpha = B_U$ we write x_{B_U} as "x_{max}". Then the reverse-rated distribution when α is given is denoted $p_{X_\alpha}(x|\alpha)$.

Lastly, let α_x denote the continuous direct rating of a given object θ whose corresponding value in X(Θ) is x (for convenience, the subscript "x" has so far been omitted and will be again after Theorem 2 is proved). Now, the reverse and direct procedures yield the same membership function and are therefore equivalent, as the following axiom states:

Axiom 2: $x_{1/2} \leq x \Longleftrightarrow \alpha_x \geq \alpha_{1/2}$.

Axiom 2 states that if any particular point x in X is at least as large as $x_{1/2}$ (the reverse-rated response when membership value $\alpha_{1/2}$ is presented to the subject on a trial), then if the subject had been asked, instead, to direct rate that particular x, then the resulting membership rating α_x would have been at least as large as $\alpha_{1/2}$ (the direct-rated value of the membership of $x_{1/2}$). So, in Axiom 2, "$x_{1/2}$" and "α_x" are random variable values, whereas "x" and "$\alpha_{1/2}$" are fixed values.

Theorem 2: If Axioms 1 and 2 hold, then

$$P_A(x) = CDF_{X_{1/2}}(x).$$

Proof: $x_{1/2} \leq x \Longleftrightarrow \alpha_x \geq \alpha_{1/2}$ from Axiom 2

Then $\Pr(X_{1/2} \leq x) = \Pr(\nu_A(x) \geq \alpha_{1/2})$

But $\Pr(X_{1/2} \leq x) = CDF_{X_{1/2}}(x)$ $(= \int_{x' \leq x} p_{X_{1/2}}(x'|\alpha_{1/2})dx')$

Also, $\Pr(\nu_A(x) \geq \alpha_{1/2}) = \Pr(\eta_A(x) = B_U)$ by Axiom 1

But $P_A(x) = \Pr(\eta_A(x) = B_U)$

So, $P_A(x) = CDF_{X_{1/2}}(x)$

In Fig. 6 are shown, for the example of TALL MAN, the deterministic membership function in the X x M plane as well as, in the X x ℙ plane at the lower bound of M, both the reverse rating distribution $p_{X_{1/2}}(x|\alpha_{1/2})$ and its associated cumulative density function $CDF_{X_{1/2}}(x)$. Moreover, the direct rating distribution $p_{\nu_A}(\alpha|x)$ is drawn for several points in X. Also, the area under each direct-rated distribution for $\alpha \geq \alpha_{1/2}$ is shaded and the resulting function $P_A(x)$, equal in value to this shaded area, is graphed in the X x ℙ plane at the upper bound of M. Theorem 2 can therefore be illustrated by visually comparing the shaded area under $p_{\nu_A}(\alpha|x)$ with that under $p_{X_{1/2}}(x|\alpha_{1/2})$ to the left of the given x -- that is, by comparing in Fig. 6 the value of $P_A(x)$ with the value of $CDF_{X_{1/2}}(x)$ for that x.

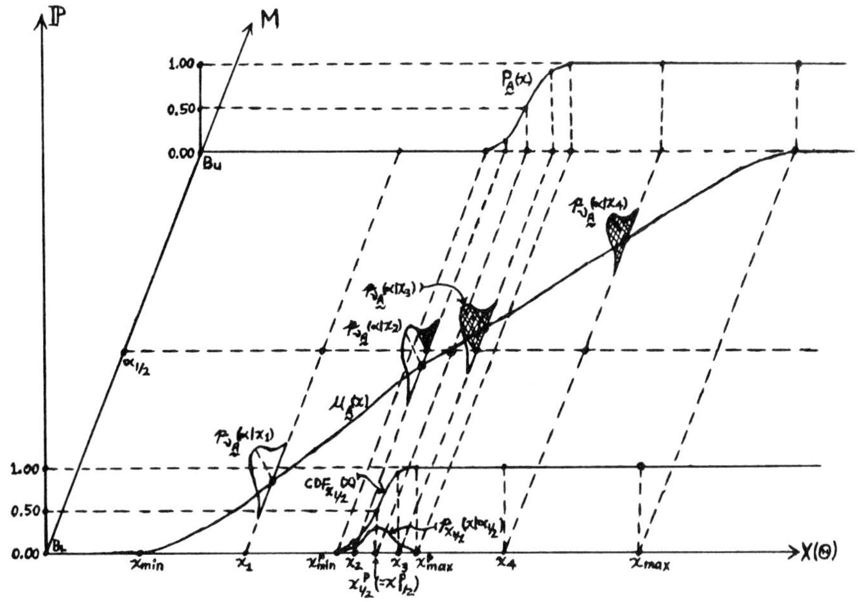

Figure 6.

Essentially then, $P_A(x)$ is generated by a subject trying to locate a split-point $x_{1/2}$ in X which corresponds to the split point $\alpha_{1/2}$ in M. If, on a given trial of binary direct rating to get $P_A(x)$, s/he feels x is greater than $x_{1/2}$, s/he replies, "yes, x is A" whereas if s/he feels x is less than $x_{1/2}$, s/he replies, "no x is not A". Thus, the generation of the binary direct ratings which lead to $P_A(x)$ can be viewed not only, through Theorem 1, as due to a splitting in M of continuous direct ratings of membership, but also, through Theorem 2, as due to a splitting in X of reverse rated values of membership. This means that F^P (the subset of X viewed by $\mathfrak{M}_{PP}$ as the region of semantic uncertainty in the meaning of A) is created only by uncertainty in the location of a single point $x_{1/2}$ resulting from the reverse rating of the one point $\alpha_{1/2}$ in M; that is, we get directly from Theorem 2:

$$F^P = \text{Support}\ (p_{X_{1/2}}(x|\alpha_{1/2})).$$

But F (the subset of X viewed by $\mathfrak{M}_{SFS}$ and $\mathfrak{M}_{DFS}$ as the region of semantic uncertainty) is created by reverse rating to find the location of points x_α for <u>every</u> α in M, that is,

$$F = \bigcup_{\alpha\in M} \text{Support}\ (p_{X_\alpha}(x|\alpha)).$$

Clearly, $F \supseteq F^P$ so that $|F| \geq |F^P|$. If we define $R \triangleq |F^P|/|F|$, then $0 \leq R \leq 1$.

So $\mathfrak{M}_{PP}$ assigns to $P_A(x)$ a value of 0 (i.e. to $\bar{\eta}_A(x)$ a value of B_L) whenever x is in I_0^P and to $P_A(x)$ a value of 1 (i.e. to $\bar{\eta}_A(x)$ a value of B_U) whenever x is in I_1^P. $\mathfrak{M}_{PP}$ therefore threats A as an objective attribute in $I_0^P \cup I_1^P$, which contains the region $F-F^P$. Yet $\mathfrak{M}_{SFS}$ and $\mathfrak{M}_{DFS}$ both clearly show that semantic uncertainty does exist in $F-F^P$, since $\bar{\nu}_A(x)$ (i.e. $\mu_A(x)$) $\notin \{B_L, B_U\}$ in this region. As can be seen from the stochastic membership function surface formed by direct rating (Fig. 4), only when $\bar{\nu}_A = B_L$ (i.e. the subject rates $\alpha = B_L$ on all trials) or when $\bar{\nu}_A = B_U$ (i.e. the subject rates $\alpha = B_U$ on all trials) is there no semantic uncertainty; both $\mathfrak{M}_{SFS}$ and $\mathfrak{M}_{DFS}$ then treat A as an objective attribute by placing x in I_0 or I_1, respectively.

Thus, through the use of stochastic fuzziness, we have shown that $\mathfrak{M}_{PP}$ misrepresents the subject's perception of the subjective attribute A, by making it appear as an objective attribute in $F-F^P$. If we use the ratio R as a quantitative measure of this objectification, then larger values (i.e. close to 1) of R may be said to indicate that $\mathfrak{M}_{PP}$ is a good approximation to $\mathfrak{M}_{DFS}$ but smaller values (i.e. close to 0) may be said to indicate that it is a poor approximation.

We have therefore shown the relation between $\mathfrak{M}_{PP}$ and $\mathfrak{M}_{DFS}$ in the X-dimension. However, we can also compare them in the M-dimension, by deriving a relation involving the values of the functions $P_A(x)$ and $\mu_A(x)$. Now, $P_A(x)$ takes on values in the range $[0,1]$, whereas $\mu_A(x)$ takes on values in the arbitrary-bounded range $[B_L, B_U]$. So in order to compare the two functions, we must put them on the same interval. This is done by recalling that $P_A(x)$ is equivalent to the Bernoulli variable $\eta_A(x)$, from which it was obtained in section 5 through the degeneracy of the M-dimension. Thus, we are able to regard

$P_A(x)$ as equivalent to the mean value in M of $\eta_A(x)$:

$$\bar{\eta}_A(x) = B_U \cdot P_A(x) + B_L \cdot (1 - P_A(x))$$

$$= (B_U - B_L) \cdot P_A(x) + B_L$$

$$= k_1 \cdot P_A + k_2 ,$$

where k_1 and k_2 are fixed constants once the arbitrary constants B_L and B_U are chosen.

Under very general assumptions about the form of the density function $p_{\nu_A}(\alpha|x)$, the following result can be proved.

Theorem 3: $|\bar{\nu}_A(x) - \alpha_{\frac{1}{2}}| \leq |\bar{\eta}_A(x) - \alpha_{\frac{1}{2}}| \; \forall \; x \in X.$

This means that $\mu_A(x)$ is always as close to the split-point $\alpha_{\frac{1}{2}}$ in M as $\bar{\eta}_A(x)$ is. Equality only holds if x is in $I_0^P \cup \{x_{\frac{1}{2}}\} \cup I_0^P$, so that the two functions only cross at membership value $\alpha_{\frac{1}{2}}$. The situation for the example of TALL MAN is illustrated in Fig. 7.

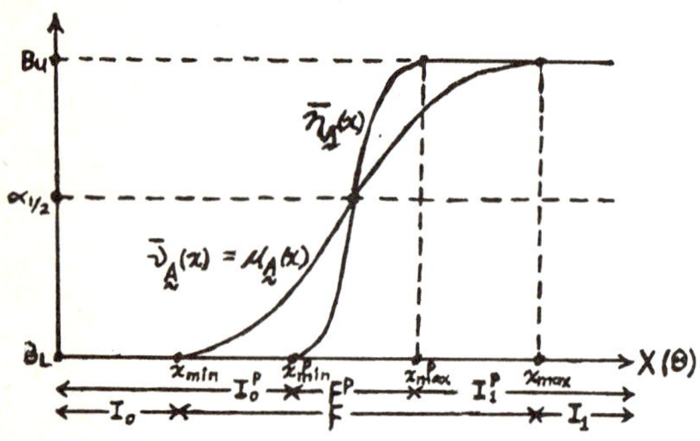

Figure 7.

Having mathematically compared $\mathcal{M}_{SFS}$ and $\mathcal{M}_{DFS}$ with $\mathcal{M}_{PP}$, we are now in a position to compare them philosophically, by explaining and contrasting the psychological processes which lead, on the one hand, to the functions $\nu_A(x)$ and $\mu_A(x)$, and on the other hand, to the function $P_A(x)$ in the mind of a subject. These processes can in fact be inferred by reconsidering Axiom 1, in which a rating α for $\mu_A(x)$ on any continuous direct rating trial is identified with a binary rating $\beta = B_U$ (i.e. "yes, x is A") if α is at least $\alpha_{\frac{1}{2}}$ in value, but with $\beta = B_L$ (i.e. "no, x is not A") if α is less than $\alpha_{\frac{1}{2}}$. Let "$\neg\alpha$" denote the value the subject gives to a continuous direct rating of the complementary subjective attribute "not-A" when s/he is asked to construct $\mu_{\neg A}(x)$.

There are several possible assumptions which may be made about the quantitative relation between the ratings α and $\neg\alpha$. These will be discussed in a forthcoming paper which describes the various relations found in an empirical study. For example, if the subject follows the complementation law on M, then

$$B_U - \alpha = \neg\alpha - B_L.$$

However, regardless of the particular relation which is used, it is demonstrable that Axiom 1 for the generation of the binary rating β may be rewritten as a comparison not of α with $\alpha_{\frac{1}{2}}$ but of α with $\neg\alpha$ (where the mathematical form of this comparison is generated by that particular relation).

Now, when a subject gives direct ratings α and $\neg\alpha$ on the continuous interval $[B_L, B_U]$, for attributes A and not-A, s/he is assessing the "A-ness" and "not-A-ness" of x (i.e. the degree to which x possesses the attributes A and not-A) in the most general or fundamental way possible. For this reason, direct and reverse rating are both called techniques of "fundamental measurement" in the literature of mathematical psychology. Let us therefore say that these continuous ratings α and $\neg\alpha$ measure "fundamental A-ness" and "fundamental not-A-ness". Thus, when the subject gives a binary rating β by comparing α and $\neg\alpha$, s/he is comparing the amount of fundamental A-ness <u>relative</u> to the amount of fundamental not-A-ness.

So the function $P_A(x)$ derived from these β ratings, since it results from the perception of the attribute A, does reflect A-ness, but not the fundamental A-ness $\nu_A(x)$ and $\mu_A(x)$ measure. Rather, it is a measurement derived from $\nu_A(x)$, one which measures the A-ness of x relative to the not-A-ness of x, and so will be said to measure the "relative" A-ness of x. Therefore, we may say that if F is the region in X of "fundamental semantic uncertainty" in the meaning of attribute A, then F^P is the region in X where only "relative semantic uncertainty" in the meaning of A is present (i.e. in the meaning of A relative to the meaning of the complementary attribute not-A).

So $\mathcal{M}_{SFS}$ and $\mathcal{M}_{DFS}$ both model the basic, most detailed perception of a vague or ambiguous linguistic term A by a subject, while $\mathcal{M}_{PP}$ models a simpler perceptual process. The former two models measure the degree of the attribute A possessed by any object in the domain of discourse in a manner which is fundamental in both the sense of the theory of measurement and psychophysical scaling and in the sense that what the latter model measures is derived from it.

Having compared all three models of a subjective attribute mathematically and philosphically, we may summarize the structural interrelationships amoung the four models -- $\mathcal{M}_{OS}$, $\mathcal{M}_{PP}$, $\mathcal{M}_{DFS}$, and $\mathcal{M}_{SFS}$ -- presented in this paper. This is done in Fig. 8.

The table has row dimension "$\mathcal{M}$" and column dimension "$\mathcal{P}$". The $\mathcal{M}$-dimension indicates how direct ratings are assigned by the subject:

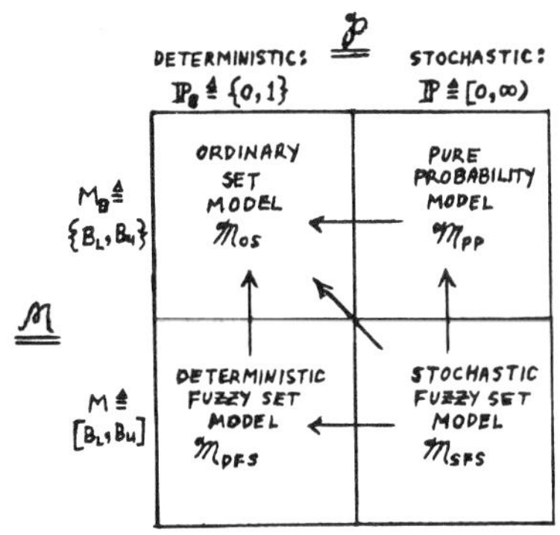

Figure 8. Taxonomy of models of a subjective attribute.

$\mathcal{M} = M_B \triangleq \{B_L, B_U\}$ means that binary "yes/no" ratings are done, whereas $\mathcal{M} = M \triangleq [B_L, B_U]$ means that continuous ratings are done. The $\mathcal{P}$-dimension indicates how the ratings in the $\mathcal{M}$-dimension are distributed: $\mathcal{P} = \mathbb{P}_B \triangleq \{0,1\}$ means that the resulting model is deterministic, since the probability density function takes on a value in $\mathbb{P}_B$ for each point in the $\mathcal{M}$-dimension, whereas $\mathcal{P} = \mathbb{P} \triangleq [0,\infty)$ means that the resulting model is stochastic, since the probability density function takes on a value in $\mathbb{P}$ for each point in the $\mathcal{M}$-dimension. The most general model, $\mathfrak{m}_{SFS}$, occurs when $\mathcal{M} = M$ and $\mathcal{P} = \mathbb{P}$. As shown in section 5, if $\mathcal{M} = M$ and $\mathcal{P} = \mathbb{P}_B$, then the $\mathcal{P}$-dimension is degenerate, yielding $\mathfrak{m}_{DFS}$, whereas if $\mathcal{M} = M_B$ and $\mathcal{P} = \mathbb{P}$, then the $\mathcal{M}$-dimension is degenerate, yielding $\mathfrak{m}_{PP}$. If $\mathcal{M} = M_B$ and $\mathcal{P} = \mathbb{P}_B$, then both the $\mathcal{M}$- and $\mathcal{P}$-dimensions are degenerate, so that $\mathfrak{m}_{OS}$ results. Arrows have also been drawn between some boxes in Fig. 8 to indicate the hierarchy which exists among the four models, since the structure at the point of an arrow is contained in and derivable from (by a transformation given in section 5) the structure at the tail.

7. CONCLUSIONS

In this paper, we have defined a new model, $\mathfrak{m}_{SFS}$, of a subjective attribute (i.e. vague or ambiguous linguistic term) A. This stochastic fuzzy model is contructed by preserving the variability which occurs when any classical psychophysical scaling technique is used to measure a human being's perception of the meaning of A with respect to objects in an empirical domain of discourse Θ (which is represented by a corresponding numerical domain $X(\Theta)$). The model views a fuzzy set as a family of random variables whose density functions are estimated by that stochasticity. This picture of fuzziness has the immediate benefit of eliminating the infinite regress paradox of generalized fuzzy set theory.

Moreover, both of the models of A in current usage, the purely probabilistic model $\mathfrak{m}_{PP}$ and the deterministic fuzzy set model $\mathfrak{m}_{DFS}$, are derivable from $\mathfrak{m}_{SFS}$. $\mathfrak{m}_{SFS}$ also enables us to compare the other two models mathematically and philosophically. We have shown in this paper that $\mathfrak{m}_{SFS}$ and $\mathfrak{m}_{DFS}$ both capture semantic uncertainty or fuzziness at least as well as $\mathfrak{m}_{PP}$, since the fuzzy region F of the former two is at least as large as the fuzzy region F^P of the latter. In fact, our empirical work shows that the ratio $R = |F^P|/|F|$ is in actual practice much closer to 0 than to 1, so that the region $F-F^P$ of $X(\Theta)$ where $\mathfrak{m}_{PP}$ erroneously makes A appear as an objective attribute is often quite large. Thus, semantic uncertainty as embodied by both fuzzy models is not the same as that embodied by the purely probabilistic model $\mathfrak{m}_{PP}$.

It has also been demonstrated that the degree of the attribute A possessed by any θ, and so by any $x(\theta)$, as measured by the two fuzzy models is quite different from that measured by $\mathfrak{m}_{PP}$. $\mathfrak{m}_{SFS}$ and $\mathfrak{m}_{DFS}$ measure "fundamental" A-ness -- the attribute A as perceived in its most general sense (through responses on a continuous interval) by a subject. By contrast, $\mathfrak{m}_{PP}$ measures "relative" A-ness -- the attribute A as perceived in its least general sense (through responses on a binary lattice) and this type of perception is generated by assessing only the <u>relative</u> relation between the fundamental A-ness and the fundamental not-A-ness of θ, and so of $x(\theta)$.

Finally, it has been shown that $\mathfrak{m}_{SFS}$ not only enables us to compare $\mathfrak{m}_{DFS}$ and $\mathfrak{m}_{PP}$ but that the function $\nu_A(x)$ generalizes $\mu_A(x)$ and $P_A(x)$ by uniting the two. The stochastic membership function is the most informative of these three models of a subjective attribute since it uses the most detailed form of both the membership and probability dimensions.

Our experiments have confirmed both the existence of stochastic fuzziness and also the theoretical results which follow from it, as given in sections 5 and 6. It should be mentioned that the theory can be easily generalized to account for a subject using any point in the membership interval M -- not just the midpoint $\alpha_{\frac{1}{2}}$ -- as the split-point for deriving $P_A(x)$ from $\nu_A(x)$. In fact, subjects have been found who do use split-points other than $\alpha_{\frac{1}{2}}$.

Stochastic fuzziness also is useful not only in studying issues within the foundations of fuzzy set theory, but also in designing particular applications of fuzzy sets. In general, if a fuzzy set is no longer regarded as a family of deterministic scalars but rather as a family of random variables, then all the structures of probability theory as well as all the tools of statistics can be utilized in applying fuzzy sets. The authors are currently engaged in designing such applications of stochastic fuzziness as well as in using it to resolve further issues in the foundations of fuzzy set theory.

ACKNOWLEDGEMENTS

This work was supported by Natural Science and Engineering Council of Canada, under grant A7698.

REFERENCES

[1] Zadeh, L.A., Fuzzy Sets, Information and Control. 8 (1965) 338-353.

[2] Gaines, B.R., Fuzzy reasoning and the logic of uncertainty, Proceedings of the Sixth International Symposium on Multiple-Valued Logic (IEEE, 1976) 176-188.

[3] Giles, R., Lukasiewicz logic and fuzzy set theory, International Journal of Man-Machine Studies, 8(3), (1976) 313-327.

[4] Norwich, A.M. and Turksen, I.B., The membership function of fuzzy set theory: representation, uniqueness, and construction, WP #78-011, Dept. of Industrial Engineering, University of Toronto (1978).

[5] Norwich, A.M. and Turksen, I.B., Measurement and scaling of membership functions, in Lasker, G.E. (ed.), Proceedings of International Conference on Applied Systems and Cybernetics, Vol. VI, Acapulco, Mexico, December, 1980, (Pergamon Press, New York, 1981) 2851-2858.

[6] Norwich, A.M. and Turksen, I.B., The fundamental measurement of fuzziness, in Yager, R. (ed.), Recent Developments in Fuzzy Set and Possibility Theory (to appear).

[7] Norwich, A.M. and Turksen, I.B., The construction of membership functions, in Yager, R. (ed.), Recent Developments in Fuzzy Set and Possibility Theory (to appear).

[8] Norwich, A.M. and Turksen, I.B., Meaningulness in fuzzy set theory, in Yager, R. (ed.), Recent Developments in Fuzzy Set and Possibility Theory (to appear).

[9] Norwich, A.M. and Turksen, I.B., A model for the measurement of membership functions and the consequences of its empirical implementation, WP #81-003, Dept. of Industrial Engineering, University of Toronto (1981).

[10] Krantz, D.H., Luce R.D., Suppes, P. and Tversky, A., Foudnations of Measurement, Vol. 1 (Academic Press, New York, 1971).

[11] Suppes, P. and Zinnes, J.L., Basic measurement theory, in Luce, R.D., Bush, R.R., and Galanter, E., (eds.), Handbook of Mathematical Psychology (John Wiley, New York, 1963).

[12] Coombs, C.H., Dawes, R.M. and Tversky, A., Mathematical Psychology (Prentice-Hall, Englewood Cliffs, New Jersey, 1970).

[13] Torgerson, W.S., Theory and Methods of Scaling (John Wiley, New York, 1958).

[14] Guilford, J.P., Psychometric Methods, 2nd ed. (McGraw-Hill, New York, 1954).

[15] Nunnally, J.M., Psychometric Theory, 2nd ed. (McGraw-Hill, New York, 1978).

[16] Watanabe, S., A generalized fuzzy set theory, IEEE Transactions on Systems, Man, Cybernetics, 8 (1978) 756-760.

Approximate Reasoning in Decision Analysis
M.M. Gupta and E. Sanchez (eds.)

MEMBERSHIP DEGREES DETERMINATION FROM SAATY MATRIX TOTALITIES

V.V. Fedorov, V.B. Kuz'min and A.I. Vereskov

Institute for Systems Studies
Moscow, USSR

Estimating the membership degrees w_i is considered for the case where the ratios w_i/w_j are evaluated by n (n≥1) experts. A numerical algorithm is suggested for computing the estimates w_i which relies on a model of the form $y_{ij}^k = w_i/w_j + \psi(w_i,w_j)\varepsilon_{ij}^k$ where y_{ij}^k is a evaluation of the ratio w_i/w_j by the k-th expert, ε_{ij}^k is a random variable with zero mean and unit variance and $\psi(w_i,w_j)$ is a function which describes the errors of the expert in evaluating w_i/w_j. What is important is that there should be at least m-1 relations w_i/w_j to be evaluated by experts. Assuming compatibility of the "true" Saaty matrix the proposed estimates are shown to be consistent and asymptotically normally distributed. Simulating experiments and specifics of the method are discussed.

Keywords: membership degree, Saaty's matrix

1. INTRODUCTION

Estimating the values w_i is the major topic in applications of fuzzy set theory. It is a and z of every applied activity in this field.

Saaty [1,2] has described a possible solution. Yager [3] has applied his approach to determine subjective probabilities. Kalaba and Spingarn [4] first improved the computing tools of the Saaty method and then, in coauthorship with Chu [5] , have developed their own method whereby a certain functional is minimized which is quadratically dependent on the parameters to be estimated. Jonson et al. have shown that if the potential of Saaty approach is used better, then in almost every case two equel but different solutions can be obtained.

In this paper a modification of the method of least squares is applied to solve the Saaty problem for the case where 1) the submitted data are presented by a group of k≥1 experts and 2) each expert probably submits the initial data in an amount smaller than in any of the above References.

2. A SYMMETRICAL INVERSE MATRIX OF PAIRWISE COMPARISONS

Let there be m objects with membership degrees w_i, $w_i>0$, i= 1,2,...,m. It is assumed that w_i cannot be measured directly but experts can compare subjective perception of the membership degrees w_i and w_j of two different objects i and j specifically, the ratios $w_{ij} = w_i/w_j$ (i,j=1,2,...,m) can be evaluated.

Let all w_i, i=1,2,...,m be known. Compose a matrix A of ratios w_{ij}, $w_{ij}>0$, i,j= 1,...,m. The elements of this matrix are symmetrically inverse, $w_{ji}=1/w_{ij}$ and the consistence condition $w_{ij}= w_{il} \times w_{lj}$ i,l,j=1,...,m is met for them. Saaty has noted that the vector $\bar{w}=(w_1, w_2,...,w_m)^T$ is the eigen vector of the matrix A which, corresponds to the main eigen value λ=m of the consistent matrix A.

If w_i are unknown and there are estimates w'_{ij} of the ratios w_{ij}, then the consistence condition is violated in the general case. To find an estimate of the vector $\bar{w}$ Saaty has suggested obtaining a right-hand eigen vector which is associated with the maximal eigen value of the matrix $A'=(w'_{ij})$, or solving a matrix equation $(A' - mI)w'=0$, which is done by solving a set of uniform linear equations.

3. SIMPLEST MODELS OF COMPARISON

Now let us proceed to a method for estimating the vector which is ideologically and computationally very much akin to the least squares method. This is very important in practice because well developed routine algorithms can be used. In further discussion let us consider two basic models of the object - expert system

$$\ln y_{ijk} = \ln w_{it} - \ln w_{jt} + \psi_1(w_{it}, w_{jt})\varepsilon_{ijk} \qquad i,j=1,2,\ldots,m;\ k=1,2,\ldots,n \quad (1)$$

$$y_{ijk} = \frac{w_{it}}{w_{jt}} + \psi_2(w_{it}, w_{jt})\varepsilon_{ijk} \quad (2)$$

The subscript k denotes the expert's number; the subscript t denotes the true values of quantities; $\psi_1(x,z)$ and $\psi_2(x,z)$ are given functions which are positive with $x>0$ and $z>0$; the random errors ε_{ijk} have a zero means $E[\varepsilon_{ijk}] = 0$, unit variances $E[\varepsilon^2_{ijk}]=1$ and are uncorrelated $E[\varepsilon_{ijk}, \varepsilon_{i',j',k'}] = \delta_{ii'} \times \delta_{jj'}, \delta_{kk'}$. Introduction of random errors of a more complex structure (which would, for instance, allow for the fact that the responses of each expert are biased, $E[\varepsilon_{ijk} \mid k=k^*] = \alpha_{k^*} \neq 0$) is not essentially difficult and the generalization is straightforward but would make the final results more involved technically and will not be considered in this paper.

The model (2) is preferable from statistician point of view but permits negative values of y_{ijk} which is in conflict with the problem at hand, for the experts can give only positive y_{ijk}. This fact should be remembered in processing the results.

4. A LINEARIZED MODEL

Consider the model (1). It can be rearranged into

$$z_{ijk} = u_{it} - u_{jt} + \varphi(u_{it}, u_{jt})\varepsilon_{ijk} \quad (3)$$

where the newly introduced variable are obviously connected with the initial ones. Each expert k is associated with a matrix where the element $\pi_{ijk}=1$ if the expert compared the i-th and the j-th objects and $\pi_{ijk}=0$ otherwise. If the objects are shown in pairs then the elements π_{ijk} with $i<j$ are nonzero. The matrix π_k will be assumed known.

Under very weak constraints the estimators (see e.g. Ref.[7])

$$\bar{u} = \operatorname{Arg}\min_{\bar{u}} \sum_{i,j,k} \omega_{ijk}\pi_{ijk}(z_{ijk} - u_i + u_j)^2, \quad \bar{u}=(u_1,\ldots,u_m)^T \quad (4)$$

are best linear unbiased. It is obvious from (4) that in the initial problem all components of the vector $\bar{u}=(u_1,\ldots \ldots u_m)^T$ are not estimable, and additional conditions should be imposed. In Saaty's paper it is required that $\sum_{\alpha=0}^{m} u_\alpha = 1$. We will suggest that $u_0=0$.

The variance matrix of the estimator depends on the weights ω_{ijk}. From the Gauss-Markov theorem it follows that this matrix is minimal (in the sense of positive semidefinite matrices ordering) when $\omega_{ijk} = \varphi^{-2}(u_{it}, u_{jt})$. The true values of u_t are naturally unknown in advance. However, one can substitute into (4) weights close to ω^t_{ijk}. In this way estimators of the following form are obtained

$$\hat{\bar{u}} = \lim_{s\to\infty} \bar{u}^s \quad (5)$$

$$\left.\begin{aligned} \bar{u}^{s+1} &= \operatorname{Arg}\min \sum_{i,j=0}^{m} \sum_{k=1}^{n} \omega^s_{ij}\pi_{ijk}(z_{ijk} - u_i + u_j)^2 \\ \omega^s_{ij} &= \varphi^{-2}(u^s_i, u^s_j) \end{aligned}\right\} \quad (6)$$

For s=1 one can choose $\varphi^{-2}(u^1_i, u^1_j)=1$.

The solution of the extremal problem (6) is

$$\bar{u}^{s+1} = M^{-1}_s Y_s \quad (7)$$

where elements of the matrix M_s are defined by the formulae

$$M_{s\alpha\beta} = M \quad = -n(\omega^s_{\alpha\beta}p_{\alpha\beta} + \omega^s_{\beta\alpha}p_{\beta\alpha}), \quad \alpha\neq\beta; \quad (8)$$

$$M_{s\alpha\alpha} = n\Big[\sum_{\beta=0}^{m}(\omega^s_{\alpha\beta}p_{\alpha\beta} + \omega^s_{\beta\alpha}p_{\beta\alpha}) - 2\omega^s_{\alpha\alpha}p\Big], \quad p_{ij} = n^{-1}\sum_{k=0}^{n} \quad ijk \quad (9)$$

The matrix $P=\{p_{ij}\}^m_0$ will be referred to as the design of an experiment. A design is regular if each of the numbers occurs at least once among the subscripts i and j taken together.

The vector Y_s has a structure

$$Y = \sum_{i=0}^{m}\sum_{k=1}^{n}(\omega^s_{\alpha i}\pi_{\alpha ik}z_{\alpha ik} - \omega^s_{i\alpha}\pi_{i\alpha k}z_{i\alpha k}). \quad (10)$$

Not unexpectedly, the matrices M_s and Y_s are independent of the diagonal elements of the matrices P or $z_k = \{z_{ijk}\}^m_{i,j=0}$. Formulae (8), (9) and (10) can be easily obtained if (6) is represented in the form

$$\bar{u}^{s+1} = \text{Arg}\min_{\bar{u}} \sum_{i,j=0}^{m} \sum_{k=1}^{n} \omega^s_{ij}\pi_{ijk}\left[z_{ijk} - \bar{u}^T f(i,j,k))\right]^2,$$

where $f(i,j,k)=\left(f_1(i,j,k),\dots,f_m(i,j,k)\right)^T$

$$f\,(i,j,k)=\delta_{i\alpha}-\delta_{j\alpha}$$

and δ_{ij} is the Kronecker symbol. Indeed, using the well-known formulae for M_s and Y_s (see Ref. [7]) yields:

$$M_s = \sum_{i,j=0}^{m} \sum_{k=1}^{n} \omega^s_{ij}\pi_{ijk} f(i,j,k) f^T(i,j,k)$$

and

$$Y_s = \sum_{i,j=0}^{m} \sum_{k=1}^{n} \omega^s_{ij}\pi_{ijk} f(i,j,k) z_{ijk}$$

and, following primitive algebraical transformations we arrive at (8), (9), and (10). Though apparently cumbersome, (8) - (10) can be easily computed even manually. The calculation starts with construction of matrices

$$Q=\{\omega^s_{ij}P_{ij}\}^m_{i,j=0}, \quad R_k=\{\omega^s_{ij}\pi_{ijk}z_{ijk}\}^m_{i,j=0},$$

$$R = \sum_{k=1}^{n} R_k .$$

Nondiagonal elements of the matrix M_s are computed in an obvious way. As for the diagonal element with a subscript α it is equal to the sum of elements of the α-th row (without the diagonal element) of the matrix Q and the sum of elements of the α-th column (without the diagonal element) of the same matrix. The α-th component of the vector Y is equal to the α-th row of the matrix R minus the α-th column of the same matrix.

EXAMPLE 1. Let us consider an experiment with (u , u ,) = . In this case the estimates are found in one stage. Assume also that for comparison all possible pairs of objects are offered and the responces are independent of the oreder of offering, or $\pi_{ij}=1, i<j; \pi_{ij}=0, i\geq j$. Then

$$Q=\sigma^{-2}n\begin{pmatrix} 0 & 1 & 1 & \dots & 1\\ 0 & 0 & 1 & \dots & 1\\ \dots & & & & \\ 0 & 0 & 0 & \dots & 1\end{pmatrix}, \quad R=\sigma^{-2}n\ \times$$

$$\times\begin{pmatrix} 0 & z_{01} & z_{02} & \dots & z_{0m}\\ 0 & 0 & z_{12} & \dots & z_{1m}\\ \dots & & & & \\ 0 & 0 & 0 & \dots & 0\end{pmatrix}, \quad z_{ij}=n^{-1}\sum_{k=1}^{n} z_{ijk}.$$

Hence, following the above mentioned rule of computing the elements of the matrix M, we have

$$M=\sigma^{-2}n\begin{pmatrix} m & -1 & -1 & \dots & -1\\ -1 & m & -1 & \dots & -1\\ \dots & & & & \\ -1 & -1 & -1 & \dots & m\end{pmatrix}$$

It is easy to verify that

$$M^{-1}=\sigma^2 n^{-1}(m+1)^{-1}\begin{pmatrix} 2 & 1 & 1 & \dots & 1\\ 1 & 2 & 1 & \dots & 1\\ \dots & & & & \\ 1 & 1 & 1 & \dots & 1\end{pmatrix} \qquad (11)$$

and

$$\hat{u} = (m+1)^{-1}\left[\sum_{\beta=1}^{m} Y_\beta + Y_\alpha\right].$$

Note that (see Ref. [7]) the matrix M^{-1} is the variance matrix of $\hat{u}$. The vector Y is also easily computed

$$Y = \sigma^{-2}\left[\sum_{i=\alpha+1}^{m} z_{\alpha i} - \sum_{i=0}^{\alpha-1} z_{i\alpha}\right].$$

Numerical examples which illustrate computation by these formulae will be discussed at the end of the paper.

5. ASYMPTOTIC PROPERTIES OF THE ESTIMATES

Let the elements of the matrix $\mathfrak{M}$ be described by formulae analogous with (8) and (9)

$$\mathfrak{M}_{\alpha\beta} = -(\omega_{\alpha\beta}P_{\alpha\beta} + \omega_{\beta\alpha}P_{\beta\alpha}), \alpha \neq \beta, \qquad (12)$$

$$\mathfrak{M}_{\alpha\alpha} = \sum_{\beta=0}^{m}(\omega_{\alpha\beta}P_{\alpha\beta} + \omega_{\beta\alpha}P_{\beta\alpha}) - 2\omega_{\alpha\alpha}P_{\alpha\alpha}. \qquad (13)$$

LEMMA 1. If $0 < c_1 \leq \omega_{\alpha\beta} \leq c_2 < \infty$, then the necessary and sufficient condition for regularity of the matrix $\mathfrak{M}$ is regularity of the design P.

PROOF. Consider the quadratic form $x^T\mathfrak{M}x$. From (12) and (13) it follows that

$$x^T\mathfrak{M}x = -2\sum_{\alpha=1}^{m}\sum_{\beta>\alpha}^{m}(\omega_{\alpha\beta}P_{\alpha\beta}+\omega_{\beta\alpha}P_{\beta\alpha})x_\alpha x_\beta + \sum_{\alpha=1}^{m}\sum_{\beta=0}^{m}(\omega_{\alpha\beta}P_{\alpha\beta}+\omega_{\beta\alpha}P_{\beta\alpha})x_\alpha^2 - 2\sum_{\alpha=1}^{m}\omega_{\alpha\alpha}P_{\alpha\alpha}x_\alpha^2 = \qquad (14)$$

$$=\sum_{\alpha=1}^{m}\sum_{\beta>\alpha}^{m}(\omega_{\alpha\beta}P_{\alpha\beta}+\omega_{\beta\alpha}P_{\beta\alpha})(x_\alpha - x_\beta)^2 + \sum_{\alpha=1}^{m}(\omega_{\alpha 0}P_{\alpha 0}+\omega_{0\alpha}P_{0\alpha})x_\alpha^2 .$$

Let the design be regular. Then the first sum of (14) is sure to contain terms of the form $q_{\alpha\beta}(x_\alpha - x_\beta)^2$ and the subscripts α and β, taken together, should contain at least once each of the numbers 1,2,...,m and the second sum will contain at least one term of form $q_{\alpha 0}x_\alpha^2$. For any vector x with a nonzero norm ($\|x\| > 0$) $x^T\mathfrak{M}x > 0$, i.e.

the matrix $\mathcal{M}$ is positive definite. Sufficiency has thus been proved.

Necessity of the condition is obvious because of for any singular design at least one of the columns of the matrix $\mathcal{M}$ consists of zeros alone.

Let us fix the number of objects to be compared. The subscript n will indicate hereafter dependence of the number of experts involved in the experiment.

Let

a) a limit design Φ : $\Phi_{ij} = \lim_{n\to\infty} p^n_{ij}$;

  $i,j=0,1,\ldots,m$ exist and be regular;

b) the function $\varphi(x,y)$ be continuous and $0<c_1\leqslant\varphi(x,y)\leqslant c_2<\infty$.

Let
$$\mathcal{M}_t = \lim_{n\to\infty} n^{-1} M^n_t$$

where elements of the matrix M^n_t are given by formulae (8) and (9) in which ω^s_{ij} is replaced by ω^t_{ij} ;

$M^n = \lim_{s\to\infty} M^n_s$;

D^n is a variance matrix of the best linear unbiased estimates (see comment of (4)) ;

P_n is the probability that the iterative procedure (5) converges for a specified sample size n.

THEOREM 1. If the conditions a) and b) hold, then

1) the estimates (5) are strongly consistent, or almost surely
$$\hat{u} \to \bar{u}_t$$
and are asymptotically normally distributed:
$$F\left[\sqrt{n}\,(\hat{\bar{u}} - \bar{u}_t)\right] \to N(0, \mathcal{M}^{-1}_t).$$

2) $\mathcal{M}^{-1}_t = \lim_{n\to\infty} n\cdot D^n$

with $n^{-1}M^n$ being a strongly consistent estimator of the matrix $\mathcal{M}_t$; and

3) $\lim_{n\to\infty} P_n = 1$.

PROOF. Existence of the limit $\mathcal{M}_t = \lim_{n\to\infty} n^{-1} M^n$ follows from existence of limits of $\bar{p}_{ij}$ and the condition (6). By virtue of Lemma 1 and condition a) matrix $\mathcal{M}_t$ is regular. This enables using the well-known results in regression analysis (see [8,9]) from which the Theorem follows as a particular case.

Let us consider the asymptotic properties of the estimators $\hat{\bar{u}}$ with increasing number of objects to be compared and a fixed number of experts. The subscript m indicates dependence of the quantities on the number of objects to be compared.

Let us first consider the case of Example 1. The variance of any component of the vector $\hat{u}$ is seen from (11) to be equal to
$$D_m(\hat{\bar{u}}_\alpha) = 2\sigma^2 n^{-1}(m+1)^{-1}.$$
Since $\lim_{m\to\infty} D_m(\hat{\bar{u}}_\alpha) = 0$, by virtue of the Tchebyshev inequality the estimator $\hat{u}$ converges in probability to $\bar{u}_{\alpha t}$, or the estimator $\hat{\bar{u}}_\alpha$ is consistent.

Assume that errors are normally distributed. Then the random variable $\Delta^T_m M_m \Delta_m$ where $\Delta_m = \hat{\bar{u}}_m - \bar{u}_{mt}$ has a chi-squared distribution with m degrees of freedom, or
$$P(\Delta^T_m M_m \Delta_m \leqslant \delta^2_m) = {}^2_m(x)\,dx.$$
It is easily verified that
$$\Delta^T_m M_m \Delta_m = \sigma^{-2} n\left[(m+1)\Delta^T_m \Delta_m - \Delta^T_m \ell_m \ell^T_m \Delta_m\right.$$
where 1_m is a column vector of size m which consists of unities. Let us find out $\max \Delta^T_m \Delta_m$ under the constraint
$$(m-1)\Delta^T_m\Delta_m - \Delta^T_m \ell_m \ell^T_m \Delta_m = \sigma^2\delta^2_m n^{-1} = c_m.$$
The solution of this extremal problem is the vector $\Delta^*_m = \sqrt{\frac{c_m}{m}}\, 1_m$ the maximal distance between the boundary of the confidence region and point $\bar{u}_t$ is equal to $r_* = \sqrt{\delta^2_m \sigma^2 n^{-1}}$. Let the confidence level be fixed and equal to γ. From the definition of chi-squared distribution it follows that δ^2_m is the solution of the equation
$$\int_0^{\delta^2_m} \chi^2_m(x)\,dx = \gamma$$
and tends to ∞ as $m\to\infty$. Thus $r_*\to\infty$. Consequently, even thought the variance of each component of the vector $\hat{\bar{u}}_m$ tends to zero, the size of the confidence region of any level, given in advance, grows infinitely.

The result thus obtained can be extended to more general cases.

THEOREM 2. For any design P_m the maximal distance r_* between the boundary of the confidence region with a given significance level and the point $\bar{u}_t$ tends to infinity.

PROOF. From the condition (6) it follows that any matrix M_m can be bounded above (in the sense of positive semidefiniteness) by the matrix $\bar{M}_m$ which represents an experiment where all comparisons were incorporated and where all comparisons were incorporated and where $w_{ij} = \min_{i,j} \varphi(u_i, u_j)$. It is obvious that $r_*(M_m) > r_*(\bar{M}_m)$. The structure of the matrix $\bar{M}_m$ is the same as in Example 1 and so $r_*(\bar{M}_m) \to \infty$, that proves the Theorem.

6. A NONLINEAR MODEL OF COMPARISONS

Let us now consider simplified version of the nonlinear model (2) :

$$y_{ijk} = \frac{w_{it}}{w_{jt}} + \varphi_2(w_{it}, w_{jt})\, \varepsilon_{ijk} \qquad (15)$$

The unknown parameters in the model (15) can be estimated by the method of least squares

$$\hat{w} = \operatorname{Arg}\min_{\bar{w}} \sum_{i,j,k} \omega_{ijk} \pi_{ijk}(y_{ijk} - \frac{w_i}{w_j})^2, \quad \bar{w} = (w_1, \ldots, w_m)^T . \qquad (16)$$

In analogy with (4) the variance matrix of estimators $\hat{w}$ is minimal with $\omega^t_{ijk} = \varphi_2^{-2}(w_{it}, w_{jt})$ where $\bar{w}_t$ are unknown true values of the parameters. In this way we can construct the estimator

$$\hat{w} = \lim_{s\to\infty} \bar{w}^s , \qquad (17)$$

$$\bar{w}^{s+1} = \operatorname{Arg}\min_{\bar{w}} \sum_{i,j=0}^{m} \sum_{k=1}^{n} \omega^s_{ij} \pi_{ijk}(y_{ijk} - \frac{w_i}{w_j})^2, \qquad (18)$$

$$\omega^s_{ij} = \varphi^{-2}(w^s_i, w^s_j).$$

The problem (18) can be solved for instance by the Gauss - Newton algorithm :

$$\bar{w}^{r+1} = \bar{w}^r + M_s^{-1}(\bar{w}^r)\, Y_s(\bar{w}^r) . \qquad (19)$$

The elements of M_s are computed by the formulae

$$M_{s\alpha\beta}(\bar{w}) = M_{s\beta\alpha}(\bar{w}) = n(\omega^s_{\alpha\beta} P_{\alpha\beta} \frac{w_\alpha}{w^3_\beta} + \omega^s_{\beta\alpha} P_{\beta\alpha} \frac{w_\beta}{w^3_\alpha}), \ \alpha \neq \beta \qquad (20)$$

$$M_{s\alpha\alpha}(\bar{w}) = n \sum_{\beta=0}^{m} (\omega_{\alpha\beta} P_{\alpha\beta} \frac{1}{w^2_\beta} + \omega^s_{\beta\alpha} P_{\beta\alpha} \frac{w^2_\beta}{w^4_\alpha}) \qquad (21)$$

The α-th coordinate of the vector Y_s is computed by the formula

$$Y_{s\alpha}(\bar{w}) = \sum_{i=0}^{m} \sum_{k=1}^{n} (\omega^2_{\alpha i} \pi_{\alpha i k} z_{\alpha i k} \frac{1}{w_i} + \omega^2_{i\alpha} \pi_{i\alpha k} z_{i\alpha k} \frac{w_i}{w^2_\alpha}) . \qquad (22)$$

Formulae (20) - (22) are obtained from well-known formulae for M_s and Y_s bearing in mind that for the model (15) $f_\alpha(i,j,k) = \delta_{i\alpha} \frac{1}{w_j} - \delta_{ij} \frac{w_i}{w_j^2}$ (see comment on formulae (8) - (10)).

Let us consider asymptotic properties of the estimators (17). Note that for any model (15) it is important that $w_i > 0$, $i=0,1,\ldots,m$ and one of the parameters is fixed, to be specific, for instance, $w_0=1$. For the model (15) Lemma 1 holds. The proof is similar to that given above. Therefore Theorem 1 is automatically extended to the estimators (17).

Note that the models (1) and (2) are extendible; for instance one can take up models of the form

$$y_{ijk} = \eta(w_{it}, w_{jt}) + \psi_3(w_{it}, w_{jt}, \theta_t) \qquad (23)$$
$$i,j=0,1,\ldots,m; \ k=1,2,\ldots,n ;$$

in which the experts estimate the value of some function of two arguments $\eta(w_{it}, w_{jt})$. Consequently, the models (1) and (2) are particular cases of the model (23) to which the modifications of method of least squares [8,9] can be applied. The formulae for computing the estimates are analogous with those given above. Note also that if the form of the function $\psi(w_i, w_j)$ is unknown, in all the above computing formulae it can be assumed that $\psi(w_i, w_j)=1$ and $\omega_{ijk}=1$. The estimators will be also strongly consistent but they will have worse asymptotical variance matrices.

7. EXAMPLES

To illustrate the method, consider several examples.

EXAMPLE 2. Let m=4 and $\bar{w}$ = (12,6,4,3) be true values of object parameters. The values of w_i/w_j were modeled by formula (2) where

$$\Psi_2(w_{it}, w_{jt}) = |w_{it} - w_{jt}|$$

and ε_{ijk} was generated as a random value on [-0.05;0.05] by random number generator. The modeling was done for k= 1,10 and 20, or for groups of 1, 10 and 20 experts. For each k the set of matrices (y_{ijk}) was generated 400 times independently and 400 independent estimates were obtained. The results are illuminated by histograms (Figure 1) for w_4 (w_1 was fixed and assumed equal to 12) with k=1,10 and 20.

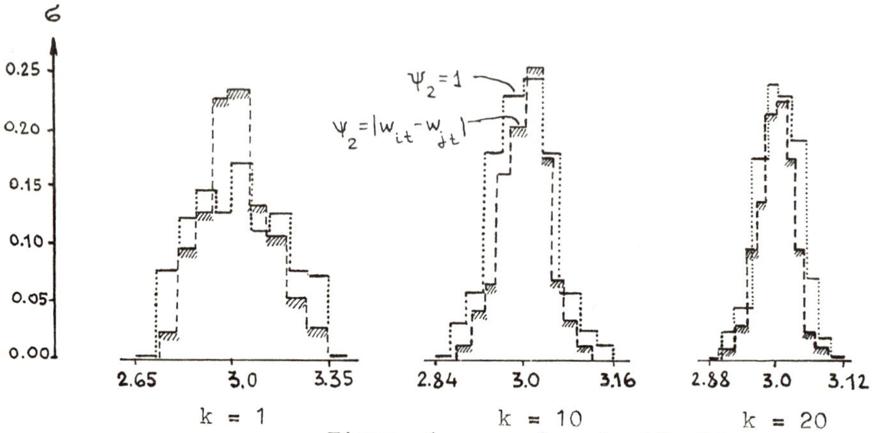

Figure 1. w_4 , k = 1, 10, 20.

These histograms confirm the property of consistenc and asymptotical normality of the estimators. Even though the estimates obtained from (2) are not, as can be shown theoretically, unbiased, the histograms show that in this experiment the bias is negligible.

The same data was processed without regard form the structute of the function Ψ_2, namely, it was assumed that Ψ_2 =1. For comparison with earlier results Fig. 1 shows the histograms for w_4 with k=1, 10, and 20.

Figure 1 shows that the results of computing w with the structure of the weighting function Ψ_2 neglected have worse statistical properties that confirm the theoretical predictions.

Computation in the frame of the model (2) for the same data with $\Psi_2 = |w_i/w_j|$ have yielded results which lead to the same conclusions.

EXAMPLE 3. The data of Table 7 p.255 from Saaty (1977) were processed in the models (1) and (2), see Table 1. Each

Table 1

NO.	Item true values	Vector of eigen values	Model (1)		Model (2)					
			$\Psi = 1$	$\sigma_{\ln w_i}$	$\Psi = 1$	σ_{w_i}	$\Psi = \lvert w_i - w_j\rvert$	σ_{w_i}	$\Psi = \lvert \frac{w_i}{w_j}\rvert$	σ_{w_i}
1	.413	.429	.422	-	.386	-	.383	-	.447	-
2	.225	.231	.232	.28	.287	.030	.262	.090	.229	.054
3	.043	.021	.021	.28	.042	.004	.032	.009	.021	.005
4	.069	.053	.052	.28	.061	.008	.059	.016	.051	.012
5	.055	.053	.052	.28	.061	.008	.059	.016	.051	.012
6	.104	.119	.127	.28	.088	.015	.122	.100	.120	.029
7	.091	.095	.094	.28	.075	.011	.083	.088	.081	.019

column with values of w_i is followed with a column which contains theoretical values of standard deviations

Let us discusse the results obtained from the model (2) with $\psi = |w_i - w_j|$. At the first glance the estimates w_6 and w_7 are unsatisfactory because their standard deviations are comparable with the estimates themselves. The cause of this is either the fact that this weighting function is ill-suited for the initial data or the fact that the function $\psi = |w_i - w_j|$ with close values of w_i and w_j is near-zero, which reduces regularity of the least square problem.

Table 1 shows that the results closest to the true data were obtained in the model (1). This Table gives, however, more of a qualitative idea of the values of the estimates to be compared than of an accurate statistical comparison which cannot be performed unless some appriori information on the "observations" is avaible, for instance, on the nature of errors in these observations. Thus the estimates obtained for $\psi = |w_i - w_j|$ from the model (2) should not be regarded as the worst. They probably give a true reflection of the situation and do not make the values of errors unduly low and so make investigations more close to reality. With data in such short supply several methods and models should be used and robust indices regarded as the answer.

Table 2 describes the estimates of membership degrees and their standard deviations which are obtained from the Saaty matrix Table 7, p. 255 Ref.1 where only the elements (1,3), (1,4), (1,7), (2,5), (4,5), (5,6) and (6,7) were left.

Table 2

No.	Model (1)		Model (2)					
	$\psi = 1$	$\sigma_{\ln w_i}$	$\psi = 1$	σ_{w_i}	$\psi = \|w_i - w_j\|$	σ_{w_i}	$\psi = \|\frac{w_i}{w_j}\|$	σ_{w_i}
1	.355	-	.349	-	.346	-	.353	-
2	.263	.150	.281	.02400	.287	.0210	.267	.0450
3	.039	.100	.039	.00039	.039	.0015	.040	.0045
4	.058	.089	.059	.00087	.057	.0030	.057	.0057
5	.053	.110	.057	.00470	.057	.0030	.054	.0067
6	.160	.110	.144	.00660	.143	.0098	.155	.0190
7	.072	.089	.071	.00130	.071	.0042	.074	.0076

8. CONCLUSIONS

The Saaty method of estimating the membership degrees of an object in a set has long been attractive to investigators. The remarkable properties of nonnegative matrices as formulated in the widely known Perron - Frobenius theory are extensively used for solution of real life problems and in theoretical studies ([10-13]; for other References see [1]). The merits of the method are above all in that: 1) the necessary initial information, viz. pairwise comparisons, are rather easy to obtain either from experts or from statistical data (for instance as the fraction of the number of preferences of the i-th object over the j-th object in the total number of comparisons of these objects) and 2) many methods are available for finding the vector of eigen values of which some are certain to be incorporated in application program packages.

Still, some practical and procedural questions which arise in using the method of the principal vector of eigen values remain unresolved, in particular direct obtaining of group (averaged) estimators of decomposition degrees, accuracy of the resultant estimates, "decomposition" of the complete matrix of pairwise comparisons into plans of expert interrogation such that would both maximally reduce the load of each expert and improve accuracy of group estimates of membership degrees.

To reduce the load of experts, Saaty suggests that objects be compared on those (n - 1) pairs which make a kind of frame of the complete graph of pairwise comparisons while the remaining estimates are obtained with compatibility conditions valid. This tool leads to a complete matrix necessary for obtaining the main vector of eigen values. However, the computed matrix elements do not contain additional data but can significantly distort the resulte because of multiple repetition and recognition of errors in the initial estimates.

References [1,2] suggest using the right-hand principal vector of eigen values for solution of this problem. But as shown in Ref.[6], the left-hand vector can lead to another, equivalent solution which, in the case of incompatible matrix of pairwise comparisons, may feature ordering of membership degrees as wellas their values. Choice of the vector remains an open question.

Relation of the main vector of eigen values with real values of membership degrees has been thoroughly discussed by Yager[3] but the fact should be noted that in determining the membership degrees by experts, even if the true values are available, it would be more accurate to speak of the closeness of perseption in different individuals rather than of agreement of computed estimates and true values.

This paper has solved the problem of determining the membership degree both for the case of a single matrix of pairwise comparisons and of several such matrices. Consistence and asymptotically normal distribution of the resultant estimates in the number of objects to be compared and the number of experts has been proved.The modified method of least squares recognizes the dependence of numerical characteristics of the error distribution pattern on the desired parameters w_i, which is especially important in processing psychophysical measurements and in expert methods.

The possibility of finding the parameters of w_i by using sparse matrices reduces the load of an expert and permits to discuss the problem of optimal plans of interrogation for the group of experts. Further research of the writers will concentrate on solution of this problem in several original statements.

REFERENCES

[1] Saaty,T.L., A Scaling Method for Priorities in Hierarchical Structures. Jrnl. of Mathematical Psychology. 15 (1977) 234-281.

[2] Saaty,T.L., Exploring the Interface between Hierarchies, Multiple Objects and Fuzzy Sets. Fuzzy Sets and Systems.1 (1978) 57-68.

[3] Yager, R.R., An Eigenvalue Method of Obtaining Subjective Probabilities, Behavioral Science. 24 (1979) 382-387.

[4] Kalaba, R.E., Spingarn, K., Numerical Approaches to the Eigenvalues of Saaty's Matrices for Fuzzy Sets, Comp.&Maths. with Appls.,4 (1979) 369-375.

[5] Chu, A.T.W., Kalaba, R.E. and Springarn, K., A Comparison of Two Methods for Determining the Weights of Belonging to Fuzzy Sets, Jrnl of Optimization Theory and Applications. 27 (1979) 531-538.

[6] Jonson, C.R, Beine, W.B. and Wang, T.J., Right - Left Asymmetry in an Eigenvector Ranking Procedure. Jrnl of Mathematical Psychology. 19 (1979) 61-64.

[7] Rao, C.R., Linear Statistical Inference and its Applications (2 ed., Wiley, N.Y., 1973).

[8] Fedorov, V.V., Regression Problems with Controllable Variables Subject to Error, Biometrika. 61 (1980) 114-56.

[9] Malyutov, M.B., Martinez Crespo, C. J., Otsenivanie Trenda i Komponent Dispersii Lineynoy Regressionnoy Modeli (Estimating the Trend and Variance Components in a Linear Regression Model. Statisticheskie metody. Sbornik. Perm (1980) 114-134.

[10] Bruk, B.N., Burkov, V.N., Metody ekspertnykh otsenok v zadachakh uporyadocheniya ob"ektov (Expert Evaluation Methods in Object Ordering Problems). Izvestiya AN SSSR, Tekhnicheskaya kibernetika, No. 6 (29-39.

[11] Chernous'ko, F.L., O vesovykh koeffitsientakh v ekspertnykh otsenlakh (On Weighting Coefficients in Expert Evaluations). Kibernetika, No. 6, (1972) 128-130.

[12] Vasil'ev, Y.L., Dmitriev, A.N., Spektralnyi podkhod k sravneniyu ob"ektov, okharakterizovannykh naborom priznakov (A Spectral Approach to Comparison of Objects Characterized in Terms of a Set of Features). DAN SSSR, 206, No. 6 (1972) 1309-1312.

[13] Kiselyov, Y.V., Otsenka vazhnosti programm metodom parnykh sravneniy (Estimation of Programm Importance by the Method of Pairwise Comparisons). Izvestiya AN SSSR, Tekhnicheskaya kibernetika,No.4 (1971) 41-47.

PART TWO

COMPOSITE FUZZY RELATIONS

Approximate Reasoning in Decision Analysis
M.M. Gupta and E. Sanchez (eds.)

METHOD OF SOLVING THE POLYNOMIAL FORM OF COMPOSITE FUZZY RELATION EQUATIONS AND ITS APPLICATION TO A GROUP DECISION PROBLEM

Ario Ohsato and Takashi Sekiguchi

Department of Computer Engineering
Faculty of Engineering
Yokohama National University
Yokohama, Japan

A new method to solve the polynomial form of composite fuzzy relation equations is proposed. First, the direct product operation of fuzzy relation matrices is introduced. Second, we show the method by which we can transform the polynomial form of composite fuzzy relation equations into the equivalent monomial form by applying the direct product operation. Third, the method for obtaining the solutions to the polynomial form is newly proposed on the basis of Sanchez's method of inverse operations, with some theorems and numerical examples. Finally, we discuss the problem of finding a fuzzy consensus decision rule in a group nursing diagnostic decision constrained by the other decision maker, and an application of the method to the group decision problem is shown.

Keywords: Composite fuzzy relation; relation equation; polynomial form; direct product operation; group decision; nursing diagnosis.

1. INTRODUCTION

Since the concept of a fuzzy set was introduced in 1965 by L.A. Zadeh [1], the fuzzy set theory has made it possible to handle the vagueness arising from the subjectivity which is inherent in human judgement, and the various pioneering researches have been presented [2, 3]. In particular, the method using the fuzzy relation which characterizes the vague relationship between the two non-empty sets has been fully giving the high availabilities to the various fields of practical applications, such as the pattern classification [4], the fuzzy control problem [5], the fuzzy diagnosis [6], the fuzzy information processing [7] and so on.

On the other hand, the problem of solving the composite fuzzy relation equations, in which the unknown fuzzy relation is included, is important in analysis and synthesis of a fuzzy system. R.M. Tong [5, 8] discussed a fuzzy control problem in the fuzzy system represented by the finite discrete fuzzy relation equation $R = R_c \circ R_p$. Several methods have been developed by E. Sanchez [9, 13] and Y. Tsukamoto [10] to solve the monomial form of composite fuzzy relation equations, which is represented in a generalized form of $A * X = Q$ for the unknown fuzzy relation X, where A, Q are the known fuzzy relations or fuzzy sets and $*$ denotes an operator of composition. In application to the medical fields, E. Sanchez [11] presented the fuzzy reasoning method in medical diagnosis in which the medical diagnosis process was formulated by the composite fuzzy relation equation $T = R \circ Q$. In application to the computer system to assist the nurses, A. Ohsato [7] proposed a practical method of information processing for nursing by fuzzy relation. In these researches, the form of composite fuzzy relation equations has been restricted to the monomial form. However, when we approach to the more complex fuzzy system and represent the system more in detail, we are necessarily confronted with the polynomial form of composite fuzzy relation equations, which is represented in the form of $\bigcup_i (A^{(i)} \circ X \circ B^{(i)}) = C$ or $\bigcap_i (A^{(i)} \,\Delta\, X \,\Delta\, B^{(i)}) = C$ for the unknown fuzzy relation X, where the symbols $\circ$, Δ denote the max-min, the min-max compositions respectively, and $A^{(i)}$, $B^{(i)}$, C are the known fuzzy relations. Then it arises that the previous methods of solving the monomial form can not directly be applied to the method of solving the polynomial form. Consequently, in order to overcome the difficulty, in this paper we make a strategy of transforming the polynomial form of composite fuzzy relation equations into the equivalent monomial form.

First, we introduce the direct product operation of fuzzy relation matrices by using the $\wedge$ (min) and the $\vee$ (max) operators. Second, we propose the method to transform the polynomial form of composite fuzzy relation equations into the equivalent monomial form, $G * x = c$, by applying the direct product operation, and it is also shown that the complex problem of solving the polynomial form can be decomposed into the several simple problems of resolving the monomial form [12]. The method to obtain the solutions of the polynomial form of composite fuzzy relation equations is newly proposed on the basis of Sanchez's method of inverse operations, with some theorems and numerical examples.
Third, we show also several fundamental theorems on existence of the solutions to the polynomial form of composite fuzzy relation equations.

Finally, as an application example of the method, we discuss the problem to obtain a fuzzy consensus decision rule in a group decision making constrained by the other decision maker. An application to a new kind of modelling is proposed for the group nursing diagnosis problem, and it is shown that the problem of finding the nurses' fuzzy diagnostic consensus decision rule constrained by the physician or the nursing supervisor will be solved by applying the method.

2. PRELIMINARIES

We consider the finite fuzzy relations and the fuzzy sets which are defined on the finite non-empty sets. Let N and S be the non-empty finite sets whose general elements are denoted by N_i and S_j,

$$N = \{N_i | i=1, 2, \cdots, \bar{n}\},$$

$$S = \{S_j | j=1, 2, \cdots, \bar{s}\}$$

and let [0, 1] be the closed interval of the real line. A fuzzy set n on N, a fuzzy set s on S and a fuzzy relation X on a Cartesian product N × S are defined to be the following functions,

$$n : N \rightarrow [0, 1]$$

$$s : S \rightarrow [0, 1]$$

$$X : N \times S \rightarrow [0, 1]$$

The values of the above functions, $n(N_i)=n_i$, $s(S_j)=s_j$, $X(N_i, S_j)=X_{ij}$, signify the grades of membership of N_i, S_j, (N_i, S_j), respectively. Hereinafter, we denote conventionally the fuzzy set s and the fuzzy relation X by the following matrix-representation,

$$s = \begin{bmatrix} s_1 \\ s_2 \\ \cdot \\ \cdot \\ \cdot \\ s_{\bar{s}} \end{bmatrix}, \quad X = \begin{bmatrix} X_{11} & X_{12} & \cdots & X_{1\bar{s}} \\ X_{21} & \cdot & & \cdot \\ \cdot & & \cdot & \cdot \\ \cdot & & & \cdot \\ \cdot & & & \cdot \\ X_{\bar{n}1} & \cdot & \cdots & X_{\bar{n}\bar{s}} \end{bmatrix}$$

and refer to fuzzy set and fuzzy relation as fuzzy vector and fuzzy relation matrix. We will denote by $\Phi(N)$ the class of all fuzzy vectors on N and by $\Phi(N \times S)$ the class of all fuzzy relation matrices on N × S.

Equivalence of the fuzzy relation matrix $X \in \Phi(N \times S)$ to the fuzzy vector x is defined as follows,

$$X \doteq x, \text{ iff } X_{ij} = x_{(i-1)\bar{s}+j}$$

$$\text{for all } (N_i, S_j) \in N \times S$$

and we denote the x by the following representation,

$$x = [X_{1*} \; X_{2*} \; \cdots \; X_{\bar{n}*}]^T$$

where X_{i*} denotes the i-th row vector of X, and the symbol T signifies the transpose. Then we say that X is equivalent to x.

The transpose of $X \in \Phi(N \times S)$, X^T, is the inverse fuzzy relation of X and is defined by

$$X^T \in \Phi(S \times N) \text{ and } X^T(S_j, N_i) = X(N_i, S_j)$$

$$\text{for all } (S_j, N_i) \in S \times N.$$

Let $A \in \Phi(M \times N)$ and $X \in \Phi(N \times S)$ be two fuzzy relation matrices.

[Definition 1] The O-composite (max-min composite) fuzzy relation matrix of A and X, $A \circ X \in \Phi(M \times S)$, is defined by

$$(A \circ X)(M_i, S_j) = (A \circ X)_{ij} = \bigvee_{k=1}^{\bar{n}} (A_{ik} \wedge X_{kj})$$

$$\text{for all } (M_i, S_j) \in M \times S.$$

[Definition 2] The Δ-composite (min-max composite) fuzzy relation matrix of A and X, $A \,\Delta\, X \in \Phi(M \times S)$, is defined by

$$(A \,\Delta\, X)(M_i, S_j) = (A \,\Delta\, X)_{ij} = \bigwedge_{k=1}^{\bar{n}} (A_{ik} \vee X_{kj})$$

$$\text{for all } (M_i, S_j) \in M \times S.$$

As the notations shown in the above, we do not use the notation $X * A$ to denote the composition of $A \in \Phi(M \times N)$ and $X \in \Phi(N \times S)$ but use the notation $A * X$ from the point of view of the easiness of manipulating the matrix operations.

Let us define the monomial form and the polynomial form of composite fuzzy relation equations as follows.

[Definition 3] The monomial form of composite fuzzy relation equations is defined to be the equation which represents that a composite fuzzy relation matrix (or a composite fuzzy vector) including an unknown fuzzy relation matrix or an unknown fuzzy vector is equal to a known fuzzy relation matrix (or a known fuzzy vector).

[Example 1] The following equations show some examples of the monomial form of composite fuzzy relation equations which have appeared in the previous researches.

$$A \circ X = Q, \tag{1}$$

$$A \Delta X = Q, \tag{2}$$

$$X \circ s = n, \tag{3}$$

$$A \circ X \circ B = C, \tag{4}$$

$$A \Delta X \Delta B = C \tag{5}$$

where $A \in \Phi(M \times N)$, $X \in \Phi(N \times S)$, $Q \in \Phi(M \times S)$, $B \in \Phi(S \times T)$, $n \in \Phi(N)$, $s \in \Phi(S)$ and $C \in \Phi(M \times T)$. In the above equations, when A, Q, s, n, B and C are given and X is unknown, the problems of finding X have been solved [9, 10, 13] and discussed [5, 8] in the previous pioneering researches.

[Definition 4] The polynomial form of composite fuzzy relation equations is defined to be the equation which represents that the union or the intersection of several composite fuzzy relation matrices (or several composite fuzzy vectors), each of which includes an unknown fuzzy relation matrix or an unknown fuzzy vector, is equal to a known fuzzy relation matrix (or a known fuzzy vector).

[Example 2] The following equations show some examples of the polynomial form of composite fuzzy relation equations,

$$(A^{(1)} \circ X) \cup (A^{(2)} \circ X) = C,$$

$$(A^{(1)} \Delta X) \cap (A^{(2)} \Delta X) = C,$$

$$(A^{(1)} \circ X \circ B^{(1)}) \cup (A^{(2)} \circ X \circ B^{(2)}) = C.$$

In this paper, we consider the following two kinds of the polynomial form of composite fuzzy relation equations.

$$\bigcup_{i=1}^{I} (A^{(i)} \circ X \circ B^{(i)}) = C, \tag{6}$$

$$\bigcap_{i=1}^{I} (A^{(i)} \Delta X \Delta B^{(i)}) = C \tag{7}$$

where $A^{(i)} \in \Phi(M \times N)$, $B^{(i)} \in \Phi(S \times T)$, $i=1, 2, \dots, I$, $C \in \Phi(M \times T)$ are the known fuzzy relation matrices and $X \in \Phi(N \times S)$ is the unknown fuzzy relation matrix.

Our main aim is to make it possible to solve the equations (6) and (7) for X.

3. ON SOLUTION OF THE MONOMIAL FORM OF COMPOSITE FUZZY RELATION EQUATIONS

The method of solving the monomial form of composite fuzzy relation equations was initiated in 1976 by E. Sanchez [9]. In the equations (1) and (2), E. Sanchez [9, 13] showed the inverse operations, Ⓐ and Ⓔ, by which we can obtain the greatest element of the solution set of (1) and the smallest element of the solution set of (2), if there exist the solutions. This method is effective because its solving procedure is simple and analytic. Consequently, we pay our attention to the Sanchez's method and try to extend it to the method of solving the polynomial form of composite fuzzy relation equations.

Let us recall some useful definitions and theorems in Sanchez's method [9].

Let $D \in \Phi(N \times M)$ and $Q \in \Phi(M \times S)$ be two fuzzy relation matrices.

[Definition 5] The Ⓐ -composite fuzzy relation matrix of D and Q, D Ⓐ $Q \in \Phi(N \times S)$, is defined by

$$(D \circledA Q)_{kj} = \bigcap_{i=1}^{\bar{m}} (D_{ki} \ \alpha \ Q_{ij})$$

for all $(N_k, S_j) \in N \times S$

where the α operation is defined as follows,

$$\begin{cases} d \ \alpha \ q = 1, \text{ if } d \le q, \\ d \ \alpha \ q = q, \text{ if } d > q \end{cases}$$

for any given elements d and q in [0, 1].

[Definition 6] The Ⓔ -composite fuzzy relation matrix of D and Q, D Ⓔ $Q \in \Phi(N \times S)$, is defined by

$$(D \circledE Q)_{kj} = \bigcup_{i=1}^{\bar{m}} (D_{ki} \ \varepsilon \ Q_{ij})$$

for all $(N_k, S_j) \in N \times S$

where the ε operation is defined as follows,

$$\begin{cases} d \ \varepsilon \ q = q, \text{ if } d < q, \\ d \ \varepsilon \ q = 0, \text{ if } d \ge q \end{cases}$$

for any given elements d and q in [0, 1].

We can see that the Ⓔ-composition is the dual composition of the Ⓐ-composition.

Next, we pay our attention to the two important theorems in Sanchez's method [9] and let us rewrite legibly as follows.

Let $A \in \Phi(M \times N)$ and $Q \in \Phi(M \times S)$ be two fuzzy relation matrices and $X \in \Phi(N \times S)$ be an unknown fuzzy relation matrix.

[Theorem 1] Let $\Omega_1(X)$ be the solution set of fuzzy relation matrices X such that $A \circ X = Q$, then the following three conditions are equivalent to one another,

1) $\Omega_1(X) \neq \phi$,

2) $A^T \text{ⓐ} Q \in \Omega_1(X)$,

3) $A^T \text{ⓐ} Q$ is the greatest element in $\Omega_1(X)$,

where ϕ denotes the empty set.

[Theorem 2] Let $\Omega_2(X)$ be the solution set of fuzzy relation matrices X such that $A \Delta X = Q$, then the following three conditions are equivalent to one another,

1) $\Omega_2(X) \neq \phi$,

2) $A^T \text{ⓔ} Q \in \Omega_2(X)$,

3) $A^T \text{ⓔ} Q$ is the smallest element in $\Omega_2(X)$.

From the above theorems, to known whether there exists a fuzzy relation matrix X such that $A \circ X = Q$ or X such that $A \Delta X = Q$, it is sufficient to check that

$$A \circ (A^T \text{ⓐ} Q) = Q, \tag{8}$$

$$A \Delta (A^T \text{ⓔ} Q) = Q. \tag{9}$$

If the above equations are not verified, there exists neither X such that $A \circ X = Q$ nor X such that $A \Delta X = Q$ [9, 13].

To obtain $A^T \text{ⓐ} Q$ is to resolve $A \circ X = Q$ for X by the ⓐ-composition. Similarly, to obtain $A^T \text{ⓔ} Q$ is to resolve $A \Delta X = Q$ for X by the ⓔ-composition. It should be noted that $A^T \text{ⓐ} Q$ and $A^T \text{ⓔ} Q$ obtained by resolving $A \circ X = Q$ and $A \Delta X = Q$ are not always the solutions to the equations $A \circ X = Q$ and $A \Delta X = Q$.

[Example 3] Let us solve the monomial form of composite fuzzy relation equations (4) and (5) by using Theorem 1 and Theorem 2.

If we resolve (4) and (5) for X by the ⓐ-composition and the ⓔ-composition respectively, we can obtain the following two fuzzy relation matrices.

$$X_1 = (B \text{ⓐ} (A^T \text{ⓐ} C)^T)^T \tag{10}$$

$$X_2 = (B \text{ⓔ} (A^T \text{ⓔ} C)^T)^T \tag{11}$$

Of course, the above fuzzy relation matrices are not always the solutions to (4) and (5). However, if (4) and (5) have the solutions, X_1 is the greatest solution to (4) and X_2 is the smallest solution to (5).

4. METHOD OF SOLVING THE POLYNOMIAL FORM OF COMPOSITE FUZZY RELATION EQUATIONS

4.1 Definition of Direct Product Operations of Fuzzy Relation Matrices

The direct product operations of fuzzy relation matrices by using the $\wedge$(min) and the $\vee$(max) operations are defined by generalizing the ordinary direct product between two non-fuzzy matrices [12, 14].

Let $A \in \Phi(M \times N)$ and $B \in \Phi(S \times T)$ be two fuzzy relation matrices.

[Definition 7] The min-direct product of A and B by the $\wedge$(min) operation, $A \bigotimes B \in \Phi(M \times N \times S \times T)$, is defined to be the following partitioned fuzzy relation matrix,

$$A \bigotimes B = \begin{bmatrix} A_{11} \wedge B & A_{12} \wedge B & \cdots & A_{1\bar{n}} \wedge B \\ A_{21} \wedge B & \cdot & & \cdot \\ \vdots & & \ddots & \vdots \\ A_{\bar{m}1} \wedge B & \cdot & \cdots & A_{\bar{m}\bar{n}} \wedge B \end{bmatrix}$$

where $A_{ij} \wedge B \in \Phi(S \times T)$ is defined by $(A_{ij} \wedge B)_{kp} = A_{ij} \wedge B_{kp}$.

[Definition 8] The max-direct product of A and B by the $\vee$(max) operation, $A \bigovee B \in \Phi(M \times N \times S \times T)$, is defined to be the following partitioned fuzzy relation matrix,

$$A \bigovee B = \begin{bmatrix} A_{11} \vee B & A_{12} \vee B & \cdots & A_{1\bar{n}} \vee B \\ A_{21} \vee B & \cdot & & \cdot \\ \vdots & & \ddots & \vdots \\ A_{\bar{m}1} \vee B & \cdot & \cdots & A_{\bar{m}\bar{n}} \vee B \end{bmatrix}$$

where $A_{ij} \vee B \in \Phi(S \times T)$ is defined by $(A_{ij} \vee B)_{kp} = A_{ij} \vee B_{kp}$.

From the above definitions, we can obtain the following properties of the transpose.

$$(A \bigotimes B)^T = A^T \bigotimes B^T$$

$$(A \bigovee B)^T = A^T \bigovee B^T$$

4.2 Transformation of the Polynomial Form of Composite Fuzzy Relation Equations into the Equivalent Monomial Form

First, we show that the monomial form of composite fuzzy relation equations shown by the equations (4) and (5) can easily be simplified into the form of $G * x = c$ by using the direct product operations.

Let $A \in \Phi(M \times N)$, $B \in \Phi(S \times T)$ and $C \in \Phi(M \times T)$ be the known fuzzy relation matrices and $X \in \Phi(N \times S)$ be an unknown fuzzy relation matrix.

[Theorem 3] $\tilde{X} \in \Phi(N \times S)$ belongs to the set of fuzzy relation matrices X such that

$$A \circ X \circ B = C, \tag{12}$$

iff $\tilde{x}$ equivalent to $\tilde{X}$ belongs to the set of fuzzy vectors x such that

$$G \circ x = c \tag{13}$$

where
$$G = A \owedge B^{T}, \tag{14}$$

$$\tilde{x} = [\tilde{X}_{1*} \quad \tilde{X}_{2*} \quad \ldots \quad \tilde{X}_{\bar{n}*}]^{T} \doteq \tilde{X}, \tag{15}$$

$$c = [C_{1*} \quad C_{2*} \quad \ldots \quad C_{\bar{m}*}]^{T} \doteq C. \tag{16}$$

Proof. If $\tilde{X} \in \Phi(N \times S)$ is a fuzzy relation matrix such that $A \circ \tilde{X} \circ B = C$, then from (12) we have

$$C_{rj} = \bigvee_{p=1}^{\bar{s}} \bigvee_{k=1}^{\bar{n}} (A_{rk} \wedge \tilde{X}_{kp} \wedge B_{pj})$$

$$\text{for all } (M_r, T_j) \in M \times T. \tag{17}$$

From (14), (15) and (17) we have

$$C_{rj} = \bigvee_{k=1}^{\bar{n}} \bigvee_{p=1}^{\bar{s}} (A_{rk} \wedge B_{pj} \wedge \tilde{X}_{kp})$$

$$= \bigvee_{k=1}^{\bar{n}} ((A_{rk} \wedge (B^{T})_{j*}) \circ (\tilde{X}_{k*})^{T})$$

$$\equiv G_{((r-1)\bar{t}+j)*} \cup \tilde{x} \tag{18}$$

where $G_{((r-1)\bar{t}+j)*}$ denotes the $((r-1)\bar{t}+j)$-th row vector of G.

From (16) and (18) we have

$$c_{(r-1)\bar{t}+j} = G_{((r-1)\bar{t}+j)*} \circ \tilde{x}$$

$$\text{for all } (M_r, T_j) \in M \times T. \tag{19}$$

Thus from (19) it is shown that $G \circ \tilde{x} = c$. Conversely, if $\tilde{x} \in \Phi(N \times S)$ is a fuzzy vector such that $G \circ \tilde{x} = c$, then from (19), (18), (17), (16) and (15), we obtain the following equation,

$$A \cup \tilde{X} \cup B = C.$$

[Theorem 4] $\tilde{X} \in \Phi(N \times S)$ belongs to the set of fuzzy relation matrices X such that

$$A \mathbin{\Delta} X \mathbin{\Delta} B = C, \tag{20}$$

iff $\tilde{x}$ equivalent to $\tilde{X}$ belongs to the set of fuzzy vectors x such that

$$G \mathbin{\Delta} x = c \tag{21}$$

where $G = A \ovee B^{T}$, and $\tilde{x}$, c are defined by (15), (16), respectively.

The proof of Theorem 4 is dually analogous to the proof of Theorem 3.

Consequently, applying the $\textcircled{\alpha}$-composition and the $\textcircled{\varepsilon}$-composition to (13) and (21), we can obtain the solutions to (12) and (20) as follows (if there exist the solutions),

$$x_{1} = (A^{T} \owedge B) \textcircled{\alpha} C, \tag{22}$$

$$x_{2} = (A^{T} \ovee B) \textcircled{\varepsilon} C. \tag{23}$$

Then the solutions (22) and (23) are equivalent to (10) and (11), respectively.

Next, we propose the method of transforming the polynomial form of composite fuzzy relation equations into the equivalent monomial form by showing the following two theorems.

Let $A^{(i)} \in \Phi(M \times N)$, $B^{(i)} \in \Phi(S \times T)$, $i=1, 2, \ldots, I$, and $C \in \Phi(M \times T)$ be the known fuzzy relation matrices and $X \in \Phi(N \times S)$ be the unknown fuzzy relation matrix.

[Theorem 5] Let $\tilde{X} \in \Phi(N \times S)$ be a fuzzy relation matrix and $\tilde{x}$ be the equivalent fuzzy vector to $\tilde{X}$, then

$$\tilde{X} \in \Omega_{3}(X) = \{X \mid \bigcup_{i=1}^{I} (A^{(i)} \circ X \circ B^{(i)}) = C\},$$

$$\text{iff } \tilde{x} \in \Omega_{3}(x) = \{x \mid G \circ x = c\} \tag{24}$$

where
$$G = \bigcup_{i=1}^{I} (A^{(i)} \owedge B^{(i)^{T}}), \tag{25}$$

$$\tilde{x} = [\tilde{X}_{1*} \quad \tilde{X}_{2*} \quad \ldots \quad \tilde{X}_{\bar{n}*}]^{T}, \tag{26}$$

$$c = [C_{1*} \quad C_{2*} \quad \ldots \quad C_{\bar{m}*}]^{T} \tag{27}$$

Proof. Let us assume that $\tilde{X} \in \Omega_{3}(X)$, then we have

$$\bigcup_{i=1}^{I} (A^{(i)} \circ \tilde{X} \circ B^{(i)}) = C. \tag{28}$$

From (28) we have

$$C_{rj} = \bigvee_{i=1}^{I} \bigvee_{p=1}^{\bar{s}} \bigvee_{k=1}^{\bar{n}} (A^{(i)}_{rk} \wedge \tilde{X}_{kp} \wedge B^{(i)}_{pj}). \tag{29}$$

From (25), (26) and (29) we have

$$C_{rj} = \bigvee_{i=1}^{I} \bigvee_{k=1}^{\bar{n}} \bigvee_{p=1}^{\bar{s}} (A^{(i)}_{rk} \wedge B^{(i)}_{pj} \wedge \tilde{X}_{kp})$$

$$= \bigvee_{i=1}^{I} (\bigvee_{k=1}^{\bar{n}} ((A^{(i)}_{rk} \wedge (B^{(i)T})_{j*}) \circ (\tilde{X}_{k*})^{T}))$$

$$= \bigvee_{i=1}^{I} ((A^{(i)} \circledwedge B^{(i)T})_{((r-1)\bar{t}+j)*} \circ \tilde{x})$$

$$= (\bigcup_{i=1}^{I} (A^{(i)} \circledwedge B^{(i)T})_{((r-1)\bar{t}+j)*}) \circ \tilde{x}$$

$$= G_{((r-1)\bar{t}+j)*} \circ \tilde{x}. \tag{30}$$

From (27) and (30) we have

$$c_{(r-1)\bar{t}+j} = G_{((r-1)\bar{t}+j)*} \circ \tilde{x}$$

$$\text{for all } (M_r, T_j) \in M \times T. \tag{31}$$

Thus from (31) it is shown that $G \circ \tilde{x} = c$. Consequently, it is proved that if $\tilde{X} \in \Omega_3(X)$, then $\tilde{x} \in \Omega_3(x)$.

Conversely, let us assume that $\tilde{x} \in \Omega_3(x)$, then we have

$$G \circ \tilde{x} = c. \tag{32}$$

From (32), (31), (27), (25), (30) and (29) we have

$$\bigcup_{i=1}^{I} (A^{(i)} \circ \tilde{X} \circ B^{(i)}) = C.$$

Consequently, it is proved that if $\tilde{x} \in \Omega_3(x)$, then $\tilde{X} \in \Omega_3(X)$.

It follows from Theorem 5 that the solution set of fuzzy relation matrices X such that $\bigcup_i (A^{(i)} \circ X \circ B^{(i)}) = C$ coincides with the solution set of fuzzy vectors x such that $G \circ x = c$. Therefore the problem of solving the polynomial form of composite fuzzy relation equations mentioned above is completely equivalent to the problem of solving the monomial form $G \circ x = c$. Consequently, applying the Ⓐ-composition, we can obtain the following solution,

$$x = G^{T} \circledAt c$$

$$= (\bigcup_{i=1}^{I} (A^{(i)T} \circledwedge B^{(i)})) \circledAt c.$$

[Theorem 6] Let $\tilde{X} \in \Phi(N \times S)$ be a fuzzy relation matrix and $\tilde{x}$ be the equivalent fuzzy vector to $\tilde{X}$, then

$$\tilde{X} \in \Omega_4(X) = \{X | \bigcap_{i=1}^{I} (A^{(i)} \Delta X \Delta B^{(i)}) = C\},$$

$$\text{iff } \tilde{x} \in \Omega_4(x) = \{x | G \Delta x = c\} \tag{33}$$

where

$$G = \bigcap_{i=1}^{I} (A^{(i)} \circledvee B^{(i)T}), \tag{34}$$

$$\tilde{x} = [\tilde{X}_{1*} \quad \tilde{X}_{2*} \quad \cdots \quad \tilde{X}_{\bar{n}*}]^{T} \doteq \tilde{X},$$

$$c = [C_{1*} \quad C_{2*} \quad \quad C_{\bar{m}*}]^{T} \doteq C.$$

The proof of Theorem 6 is dually analogous to the proof of Theorem 5.

Similarly it follows from Theorem 6 that the solution set of fuzzy relation matrices X such that $\bigcap_i (A^{(i)} \Delta X \Delta B^{(i)}) = C$ coincides with the solution set of fuzzy vectors x such that $G \Delta x = c$. Consequently, applying the Ⓔ-composition, we can obtain the following solution,

$$x = G^{T} \circledE c$$

$$= (\bigcap_{i=1}^{I} (A^{(i)T} \circledvee B^{(i)})) \circledE c.$$

Theorem 5 and Theorem 6 give us an operational law of fuzzy relation matrices to transform the polynomial form of composite fuzzy relation equations into the equivalent monomial form.

4.3 On Solution to the Polynomial Form of Composite Fuzzy Relation Equations by Using the Ⓐ-composition and Ⓔ-composition

First, we provide preliminarily the following properties [9, 12].

$$X \subseteq A^{T} \circledAt (A \circ X), \tag{35}$$

$$A \circ (A^{T} \circledAt Q) \subseteq Q, \tag{36}$$

$$(\bigcup_{i=1}^{I} D^{(i)}) \circledAt Q = \bigcap_{i=1}^{I} (D^{(i)} \circledAt Q), \tag{37}$$

$$(B \circledAt (A^{T} \circledAt C)^{T})^{T} \doteq (A^{T} \circledwedge B) \circledAt c, \tag{38}$$

$$X \supseteq A^{T} \circledE (A \Delta X), \tag{39}$$

$$A \Delta (A^{T} \circledE Q) \supseteq Q \tag{40}$$

$$(\bigcap_{i=1}^{I} D^{(i)}) \circledE Q = \bigcup_{i=1}^{I} (D^{(i)} \circledE Q), \tag{41}$$

$$(B \circledcirc\!\!\varepsilon\, (A^{T} \circledcirc\!\!\varepsilon\, C)^{T})^{T} \doteq (A^{T} \circledvee B) \circledcirc\!\!\varepsilon\, c, \tag{42}$$

where $\subset$ is the symbol of containment.

In the above equations, we can see that (39), (40), (41) and (42) are the dual results of (35), (36), (37) and (38), respectively.

On existence of the solutions to the polynomial form of composite fuzzy relation equations, we can now state the two fundamental theorems.

[Theorem 7] The following three conditions are equivalent to one another,

1) $\Omega_3(X) \neq \phi$,

2) $\bigcap_{i=1}^{I} (B^{(i)} \circledcirc\!\!\alpha\, (A^{(i)T} \circledcirc\!\!\alpha\, C)^{T})^{T} \in \Omega_3(X)$,

3) $\bigcap_{i=1}^{I} (B^{(i)} \circledcirc\!\!\alpha\, (A^{(i)T} \circledcirc\!\!\alpha\, C)^{T})^{T}$ is the greatest element in $\Omega_3(X)$,

where $\Omega_3(X) = \{X | \bigcup_{i=1}^{I} (A^{(i)} \circ X \circ B^{(i)}) = C\}$.

Proof. Let us prove only the non-trivial implications. If $\Omega_3(X) \neq \phi$, we can consider a fuzzy relation matrix $\tilde{X}$ such that

$$\bigcup_{i=1}^{I} (A^{(i)} \circ \tilde{X} \circ B^{(i)}) = C.$$

Let $\tilde{x}$ be the equivalent fuzzy vector to $\tilde{X}$. From Theorem 5 we have

$$G \circ \tilde{x} = c \tag{43}$$

where $G = \bigcup_{i=1}^{I} (A^{(i)} \circledwedge B^{(i)T})$.

From (35) and (43) we have

$$\tilde{x} \subseteq G^{T} \circledcirc\!\!\alpha\, (G \circ \tilde{x}), \quad \text{i.e. } \tilde{x} \subseteq G^{T} \circledcirc\!\!\alpha\, c. \tag{44}$$

On the other hand, using the general properties shown by (37) and (38), $G^{T} \circledcirc\!\!\alpha\, c$ can equivalently be represented as follows,

$$\begin{aligned} G^{T} \circledcirc\!\!\alpha\, c &= (\bigcup_{i=1}^{I} (A^{(i)} \circledwedge B^{(i)T}))^{T} \circledcirc\!\!\alpha\, c \\ &= \bigcap_{i=1}^{I} ((A^{(i)T} \circledwedge B^{(i)}) \circledcirc\!\!\alpha\, c) \\ &\doteq \bigcap_{i=1}^{I} (B^{(i)} \circledcirc\!\!\alpha\, (A^{(i)T} \circledcirc\!\!\alpha\, C)^{T})^{T}. \end{aligned} \tag{45}$$

From (44) and (45) we have

$$\tilde{X} \subseteq \bigcap_{i=1}^{I} (B^{(i)} \circledcirc\!\!\alpha\, (A^{(i)} \circledcirc\!\!\alpha\, C)^{T})^{T}. \tag{46}$$

From the $\circ$-composition of G with (44) we have

$$G \circ \tilde{x} \subseteq G \circ (G^{T} \circledcirc\!\!\alpha\, c),$$

$$\text{i.e. } c \subseteq G \circ (G^{T} \circledcirc\!\!\alpha\, c). \tag{47}$$

By applying (36) to G and c, we have

$$G \circ (G^{T} \circledcirc\!\!\alpha\, c) \subseteq c. \tag{48}$$

From (47) and (48) we have

$$G \circ (G^{T} \circledcirc\!\!\alpha\, c) = c, \text{ i.e. } G^{T} \circledcirc\!\!\alpha\, c \in \Omega_3(x). \tag{49}$$

Thus we have

$$\bigcap_{i=1}^{I} (B^{(i)} \circledcirc\!\!\alpha\, (A^{(i)T} \circledcirc\!\!\alpha\, C)^{T})^{T} \in \Omega_3(X). \tag{50}$$

Consequently, it is proved that if the condition 1) is satisfied, then the condition 2) is always satisfied. On the other hand, as the equation (46) is always satisfied for an arbitrary solution $\tilde{X}$, it is evident that $\bigcap_i (B^{(i)} \circledcirc\!\!\alpha\, (A^{(i)T} \circledcirc\!\!\alpha\, C)^{T})^{T}$ is the greatest element in $\Omega_3(X)$, if $\Omega_3(X) \neq \phi$.

[Theorem 8] The following three conditions are equivalent to one another,

1) $\Omega_4(X) \neq \phi$,

2) $\bigcup_{i=1}^{I} (B^{(i)} \circledcirc\!\!\varepsilon\, (A^{(i)T} \circledcirc\!\!\varepsilon\, C)^{T})^{T} \in \Omega_4(X)$,

3) $\bigcup_{i=1}^{I} (B^{(i)} \circledcirc\!\!\varepsilon\, (A^{(i)T} \circledcirc\!\!\varepsilon\, C)^{T})^{T}$ is the smallest element in $\Omega_4(X)$,

where $\Omega_4(X) = \{X | \bigcap_{i=1}^{I} (A^{(i)} \Delta X \Delta B^{(i)}) = C\}$.

The proof of Theorem 8 is dually analogous to the proof of Theorem 7.

From Theorems 5, 6, 7 and 8 we can obtain the following equivalences,

$$\begin{aligned} &\bigcap_{i=1}^{I} (B^{(i)} \circledcirc\!\!\alpha\, (A^{(i)T} \circledcirc\!\!\alpha\, C)^{T})^{T} \\ &\doteq (\bigcup_{i=1}^{I} (A^{(i)T} \circledwedge B^{(i)})) \circledcirc\!\!\alpha\, c, \end{aligned} \tag{51}$$

$$\bigcup_{i=1}^{I} (B^{(i)} \circledS (A^{(i)T} \circledS C)^T)^T$$

$$\doteq (\bigcap_{i=1}^{I} (A^{(i)T} \oslash B^{(i)})) \circledS c. \tag{52}$$

Consequently, from Theorems 7 and 8 we can derive the following properties,

P1) To know whether there exists a fuzzy relation matrix X such that

$$\bigcup_{i=1}^{I} (A^{(i)} \circ X \circ B^{(i)}) = C, \tag{53}$$

it is sufficient to check that

$$\bigcup_{i=1}^{I} (A^{(i)} \circ \check{X} \circ B^{(i)}) = C \tag{54}$$

where $\check{X} = \bigcap_{i=1}^{I} (B^{(i)} \circledast (A^{(i)T} \circledast C)^T)^T$

$$\text{or } G \circ \check{x} = c \tag{55}$$

where $G = \bigcup_{i=1}^{I} (A^{(i)} \otimes B^{(i)T})$,

$\check{x} = G^T \circledast c$,

$c \doteq C$.

P2) To know whether there exists a fuzzy relation matrix X such that

$$\bigcap_{i=1}^{I} (A^{(i)} \Delta X \Delta B^{(i)}) = C, \tag{56}$$

it is sufficient to check that

$$\bigcap_{i=1}^{I} (A^{(i)} \Delta \hat{X} \Delta B^{(i)}) = C, \tag{57}$$

where $\hat{X} = \bigcup_{i=1}^{I} (B^{(i)} \circledS (A^{(i)T} \circledS C)^T)^T$

$$\text{or } G \Delta \hat{x} = c \tag{58}$$

where $G = \bigcap_{i=1}^{I} (A^{(i)} \oslash B^{(i)T})$,

$\hat{x} = G^T \circledS c$,

$c \doteq C$.

On the other hand, the following composite fuzzy relation matrices in $\check{X}$ and $\hat{X}$,

$$(B^{(i)} \circledast (A^{(i)T} \circledast C)^T)^T, \tag{59}$$

$$(B^{(i)} \circledS (A^{(i)T} \circledS C)^T)^T \tag{60}$$

are the fuzzy relation matrices $X^{(i)}$ obtained by the resolution of the following monomial forms of composite fuzzy relation equations by applying the ⓐ-composition and the ⓔ-composition, respectively.

$$A^{(i)} \circ X^{(i)} \circ B^{(i)} = C,$$

$$A^{(i)} \Delta X^{(i)} \Delta B^{(i)} = C.$$

From P1), P2) and the above discussion, consequently, we can obtain the following two properties,

P3) The complex problem of solving the polynomial form of composite fuzzy relation equation,

$$\bigcup_{i=1}^{I} (A^{(i)} \circ X \circ B^{(i)}) = C, \tag{61}$$

is decomposed into the equivalent I simple problems of resolving the following monomial forms of composite fuzzy relation equations for $X^{(i)}$ by applying the ⓐ-composition,

$$A^{(i)} \circ X^{(i)} \circ B^{(i)} = C, \quad i=1, 2, \cdots, I. \tag{62}$$

Thus a solution to (61) can be obtained by

$$X = \bigcap_{i=1}^{I} X^{(i)}, \tag{63}$$

if it exists.

P4) The complex problem of solving the polynomial form of composite fuzzy relation equation,

$$\bigcap_{i=1}^{I} (A^{(i)} \Delta X \Delta B^{(i)}) = C, \tag{64}$$

is decomposed into the equivalent I simple problems of resolving the following monomial forms of composite fuzzy relation equations for $X^{(i)}$ by applying the ⓔ-composition,

$$A^{(i)} \Delta X^{(i)} \Delta B^{(i)} = C, \quad i=1, 2, \cdots, I. \tag{65}$$

Thus a solution to (64) can be obtained by

$$X = \bigcup_{i=1}^{I} X^{(i)},$$

if it exists.

We can see that P1), P2), P3) and P4) give us the effective method to solve the polynomial form of composite fuzzy relation equations.

4.4 Numerical Examples

[Example 4] Let us consider the problem of finding X such that

$$(A^{(1)} \circ X \circ B^{(1)}) \cup (A^{(2)} \circ X \circ B^{(2)}) = C \tag{66}$$

where $A^{(1)} = \begin{bmatrix} 0.2 & 0.5 \\ 0.6 & 0.9 \end{bmatrix}$, $A^{(2)} = \begin{bmatrix} 0.3 & 0.2 \\ 0.7 & 0.8 \end{bmatrix}$

$B^{(1)} = \begin{bmatrix} 0.4 & 0.9 \\ 0.7 & 0.4 \end{bmatrix}$, $B^{(2)} = \begin{bmatrix} 0.8 & 0.7 \\ 0.6 & 0.8 \end{bmatrix}$

$C = \begin{bmatrix} 0.4 & 0.5 \\ 0.6 & 0.7 \end{bmatrix}$, $X = \begin{bmatrix} X_{11} & X_{12} \\ X_{21} & X_{22} \end{bmatrix}$

Applying the min-direct product operation of $A^{(i)}$ and $B^{(i)}$ to (66), we can transform (66) into the following equivalent monomial form,

$$G \circ x = c \tag{67}$$

where $G = (A^{(1)} \bigotimes B^{(1)^{\mathrm{T}}}) \cup (A^{(2)} \bigotimes B^{(2)^{\mathrm{T}}})$

$$= \begin{bmatrix} 0.3 & 0.3 & 0.4 & 0.5 \\ 0.3 & 0.3 & 0.5 & 0.4 \\ 0.7 & 0.6 & 0.8 & 0.7 \\ 0.7 & 0.7 & 0.9 & 0.8 \end{bmatrix},$$

$$x = [X_{11} \quad X_{12} \quad X_{21} \quad X_{22}]^{\mathrm{T}},$$

$$c = [0.4 \quad 0.5 \quad 0.6 \quad 0.7]^{\mathrm{T}}.$$

Resolving (67) for x by use of the ⓐ-composition, we have the following fuzzy vector,

$$\check{x} = G^{\mathrm{T}} ⓐ\, c$$

$$= [0.6 \quad 1.0 \quad 0.6 \quad 0.4]^{\mathrm{T}}. \tag{68}$$

As $\check{x}$ satifies (67), $\check{x}$ is a solution to (66).

On the other hand, let us consider the two simple problems of resolving the following monomial forms of composite fuzzy relation equations for $X^{(1)}$ and $X^{(2)}$ by use of the ⓐ-composition,

$$\left.\begin{aligned} A^{(1)} \circ X^{(1)} \circ B^{(1)} &= C, \\ A^{(2)} \circ X^{(2)} \circ B^{(2)} &= C. \end{aligned}\right\} \tag{69}$$

Then we have

$$\check{X}^{(1)} = (B^{(1)} ⓐ (A^{(1)^{\mathrm{T}}} ⓐ\, C)^{\mathrm{T}})^{\mathrm{T}}$$

$$= \begin{bmatrix} 1.0 & 1.0 \\ 0.7 & 0.4 \end{bmatrix},$$

$$\check{X}^{(2)} = (B^{(2)} ⓐ (A^{(2)^{\mathrm{T}}} ⓐ\, C)^{\mathrm{T}})^{\mathrm{T}}$$

$$= \begin{bmatrix} 0.6 & 1.0 \\ 0.6 & 0.7 \end{bmatrix},$$

$$\check{X} = \check{X}^{(1)} \cap \check{X}^{(2)}$$

$$= \begin{bmatrix} 0.6 & 1.0 \\ 0.6 & 0.4 \end{bmatrix}. \tag{70}$$

From the above results, we can see that $\check{X}$ is equivalent to $\check{x}$, and, of course, $\check{X}$ is also a solution to (66).

[Example 5] Let us consider the problem of finding X such that

$$(A \,\Delta\, X) \cap (X \,\Delta\, B) = C \tag{71}$$

where $A = \begin{bmatrix} 0.2 & 0.5 \\ 0.6 & 0.9 \end{bmatrix}$, $B = \begin{bmatrix} 0.4 & 0.9 \\ 0.7 & 0.4 \end{bmatrix}$,

$C = \begin{bmatrix} 0.2 & 0.3 \\ 0.5 & 0.4 \end{bmatrix}$.

Let us introduce a fuzzy identity matrix $\hat{I}$ relating to the Δ-compositional operation as follows,

$$\hat{I} = \begin{bmatrix} 0.0 & 1.0 \\ 1.0 & 0.0 \end{bmatrix},$$

then $\hat{I}$ is the fuzzy relation matrix such that

$$\hat{I} \,\Delta\, X = X \quad \text{and} \quad X \,\Delta\, \hat{I} = X$$

for an arbitrary fuzzy relation matrix X.

By using $\hat{I}$, we have the following equation which is equivalent to (71),

$$(A \,\Delta\, X \,\Delta\, \hat{I}) \cap (\hat{I} \,\Delta\, X \,\Delta\, B) = C. \tag{72}$$

Using the max-direct product operation, we can

transform (72) into the following equivalent monomial form,

$$G \wedge x = c$$

where $G = (A \circledvee \hat{I}) \cap (\hat{I} \circledvee B^T)$

$$= \begin{bmatrix} 0.2 & 0.7 & 0.5 & 1.0 \\ 0.9 & 0.2 & 1.0 & 0.5 \\ 0.6 & 1.0 & 0.4 & 0.7 \\ 1.0 & 0.6 & 0.9 & 0.4 \end{bmatrix},$$

$$c = [0.2 \quad 0.3 \quad 0.5 \quad 0.4]^T.$$

Applying the Ⓔ-composition, we have

$$x = G^T \circledE c$$

$$= [0.0 \quad 0.3 \quad 0.5 \quad 0.0]^T,$$

$$\hat{X} = (\hat{I} \circledE (A^T \circledE c)^T)^T \cup (B \circledE (\hat{I} \circledE c)^T)^T$$

$$= \begin{bmatrix} 0.0 & 0.3 \\ 0.5 & 0.0 \end{bmatrix}.$$

$\hat{X}$ is a solution which satisfies (71).

5. APPLICATION TO A GROUP DECISION PROBLEM

Considering a practical application to the real problems, we find that the fuzzy relation is one of the most important concepts in the fuzzy set theory. Recently, it has been suggested that the fuzzy relation method may play an important role in decision problem [15, 16]. A strategy of representing a decision problem by the notion of fuzzy relation is practically effective because the fuzzy relation possesses the operational role as a mapping and a function.

In this section, an application of the proposed method to a group decision problem is discussed. We consider the problem of finding a fuzzy diagnostic consensus decision rule in a group nursing diagnosis decision constrained by the other decision maker, such as the physician or the nursing supervisor (head nurse).

It is assumed that a fuzzy decision rule is a fuzzy mapping from a certain finite set to the other finite set or a mapping from a certain family of fuzzy sets to the other family of fuzzy sets.

[Definition 9] Let S and D be two non-empty sets, then a fuzzy relation $X \in \Phi(S \times D)$ is a mapping,

$$X : \Phi(S) \to \Phi(D).$$

For example, if we denote by S a set of symptoms and by D a set of medical diagnoses, then $X \in \Phi(S \times D)$ is a fuzzy diagnostic decision rule from S to D. When X and $s \in \Phi(S)$ are given, we can induce a fuzzy set $d \in \Phi(D)$ by using the O-composition as follows,

$$d = X \circ s.$$

The above equation shows that X is a mapping which associates to each element of $\Phi(S)$ a unique element of $\Phi(D)$.

Let us consider the group nursing care by N nurses for a set of patients. Generally speaking, the nurses' various decision rules in the actual cares are not deterministic and depend on the nurses' own subjective uncertainty, and that is fuzziness.

We assume the following finite sets.

P : a set of specific patients (patient space)

S : a set of symptoms (symptom space)

D : a set of nursing diagnoses (nursing diagnosis space)

G : a set of goals in nursing care (care goal space)

Let us assume the N nurses' individual fuzzy decision rules between the above sets as follows,

$$A^{(i)} : \Phi(P) \to \Phi(S),\ i=1, 2, \cdots, N \qquad (73)$$

$$X^{(i)} : \Phi(S) \to \Phi(D),\ i=1, 2, \ldots, N \qquad (74)$$

$$B^{(i)} : \Phi(D) \to \Phi(G),\ i=1, 2, \ldots, N \qquad (75)$$

where $A^{(i)} \in \Phi(P \times S)$ is the i-th nurse's fuzzy observation decision rule from P to S, $X^{(i)} \in \Phi(S \times D)$ is the i-th nurse's fuzzy diagnostic decision rule from S to D, and $B^{(i)}$ is the i-th nurse's fuzzy partial assessment decision rule from D to G.

Next, we assume the following fuzzy decision rule C by which the above decision rules are constrained,

$$C : \Phi(P) \to \Phi(G) \qquad (76)$$

where $C \in \Phi(P \times G)$ is the physician's or the nursing supervisor's fuzzy total assessment decision rule from the patient space P to the care goal space G.

Let us assume the O-composition of the fuzzy decision rules, then the N nurses' individual fuzzy total assessment decision rules from P to G can be represented by

$$A^{(i)} \circ X^{(i)} \circ B^{(i)} \in \Phi(P \times G),$$
$$i=1,\ 2,\ \cdots,\ N. \quad (77)$$

If there exists a fuzzy decision rule $X^{(i)}$ such that

$$A^{(i)} \circ X^{(i)} \circ B^{(i)} = C,$$

then $X^{(i)}$ is the i-th nurse's individual fuzzy diagnostic decision rule from S into D subject to the constraint of the physician's C.

On the other hand, the problem of finding the fuzzy diagnostic consensus decision rule, $X \in \Phi(S \times D)$, in a group nursing diagnosis of N nurses must inevitably be more complicated. Figure 1 shows a schematic diagram of a new kind of modelling method for the problem. In Fig. 1, the solid curves with arrows denote the mapping directions of fuzzy decision rule, $A^{(i)}$, $B^{(i)}$, X and C.

First, let us represent the problem as follows,

Problem 1 :

$$A^{(i)} \circ X \circ B^{(i)} = C,\ i=1,\ 2,\ \cdots,\ N \quad (78)$$

where it is assumed that $A^{(i)}$, $B^{(i)}$ are given by the N nurses, C is given by the physician or the nursing supervisor, and X is the unknown fuzzy diagnostic consensus decision rule.

In general, however, it is very difficult to obtain X satisfying simultaneously the above N equations because there exists no solution in most cases by reason of the strict constraint of the equation (78).

Second, if it may be permitted to loosen slightly the strictness of *Problem 1*, we can consider the following problem instead of it.

Problem 2 :

$$X = \bigcap_{i=1}^{N} X^{(i)} \quad (79)$$

subject to

$$A^{(i)} \circ X^{(i)} \circ B^{(i)} = C,$$
$$i=1,\ 2,\ \cdots,\ N. \quad (80)$$

On *Problem 2*, if there exist the N solutions $X^{(i)}$ satisfying (80), a fuzzy diagnostic consensus decision rule X can be ontained as follows,

$$X = \bigcap_{i=1}^{N} (B^{(i)} \circleda (A^{(i)T} \circleda C)^{T})^{T}. \quad (81)$$

Finally, if it may be further permitted to reformulate more loosely *Problem 1* and *Problem 2*,

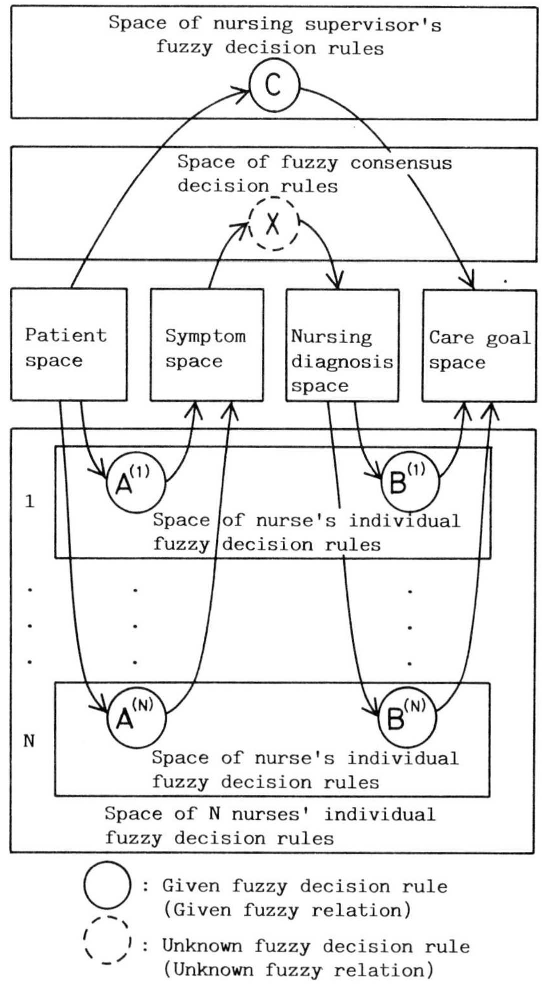

Figure 1 : A schematic diagram of a modelling for the group decision problem to find a fuzzy diagnostic consensus decision rule in a group nursing diagnosis constrained by the physician or the nursing supervisor

then we have the following problem,

Problem 3 :

$$\bigcup_{i=1}^{N} (A^{(i)} \circ X \circ B^{(i)}) = C. \quad (82)$$

Namely, from the above formulation we can see that *Problem 3* is to find X such that every $A^{(i)} \circ X \circ B^{(i)}$ is contained in C and the maximum value of $(A^{(i)} \circ X \circ B^{(i)})_{rj}$ for i=1, 2, $\cdots$, N, coincides with C_{rj} for every (r, j)

Therefore *Problem 3* is more solvable than *Problem 1* and *Problem 2*, and it stands for a good possibility of existence of solutions.

If the solution set of *Problem 3* is not empty, then from the properties P1) and P3) we can obtain the following solution,

$$X = \bigcap_{i=1}^{N} (B^{(i)} \circledast (A^{(i)^T} \circledast C)^T)^T$$

which is nothing but a fuzzy diagnostic consensus decision rule in a group nursing diagnosis of N nurses.

6. CONCLUDING REMARKS

A notion of representing the fuzzy decision processes by means of the fuzzy relation is fully supported in a practical application to the real problems. Especially, further development of the methods to solve the various forms of composite fuzzy relation equations will bring about the effective approaches to the various types of fuzzy decision processes.

In this study, we have paid our attention to the polynomial form of composite fuzzy relation equations, and put stress upon the method of solving it. By applying the min- and the max-direct product operations between two fuzzy relation matrices, it has been shown that the polynomial form can be easily transformed into the equivalent monomial form, and that the complex problem of solving the polynomial form can be decomposed into the several simple problems of resolving the monomial form. The transformation and the decomposition have made it possible to solve the polynomial form of composite fuzzy relation equations by using the existing methods of solving the monomial form.

However, the polynomial form considered in this paper is only one type of complex forms of composite fuzzy relation equations, and therefore when we are confronted with the problem of solving the different type of complex forms, we must newly develop the method to solve it.

In the present study, we applied the proposed method to a new kind of modelling for the fuzzy consensus decision rule problem in a group nursing diagnostic decision constrained by the physician or the nursing supervisor. It has been shown that this decision problem can be formulated by the polynomial form of composite fuzzy relation equations and can be easily solved by the method proposed in this study. The fuzzy diagnostic consensus decision rule in a group of nurses is useful in establishing the practical nursing care plan and may induce a generalized valid nursing assessment rule. Moreover, the obtained diagnostic consensus decision rule will be available to a computerized information processing for assisting the nurses. Furthermore, the results obtained in this paper will be useful to the other application fields, such as a control problem of complicated fuzzy system and so on.

REFERENCES

[1] Zadeh, L.A., Fuzzy sets, Information and Control 8 (1965) 338-353.

[2] Gupta, M.M., Saridis, G.N. and Gaines, B.R. (eds.), Fuzzy Automata and Decision Processes (North-Holland, Amsterdam, 1977).

[3] Gupta, M.M., Ragade, R.K. and Yager, R.R. (eds.), Advances in Fuzzy Set Theory and Applications (North-Holland, Amsterdam, 1979).

[4] Tamura, S., Higuchi, S. and Tanaka, K., Pattern classification based on fuzzy relations, IEEE Trans. on Systems, Man and Cybernetics SMC-1-1 (1971) 61-66.

[5] Tong, R.M., Analysis and control of fuzzy systems using finite relations, Int. J. of Control 27-3 (1978) 431-440.

[6] Terano, T., Tsukamoto, Y., Kurosu, K., Murayama, Y. and Inasaka, F., Diagnosis of engine trouble by fuzzy logic, Proc. of IFAC 7th World Congress (1978) 1621-1628.

[7] Ohsato, A., Sekiguchi, T., Nakai, T. and Yamazaki, K., Information processing for nursing by fuzzy relation, Proc. of The 3rd World Conference on Medical Informatics Part 1 (1980) 62-66.

[8] Tong, R.M., Some properties of fuzzy feedback systems, IEEE Trans. on Systems, Man and Cybernetics SMC-10-6 (1980) 327-330.

[9] Sanchez, E., Resolution of composite fuzzy relation equations, Information and Control 30 (1976) 38-48.

[10] Tsukamoto, Y. and Tashiro, T., Method of solution to fuzzy inverse problem, Trans. of the Society of Instrument and Control Engineers (Japan) 15-1 (1979) 21-25 (in Japanese).

[11] Sanchez, E., Medical diagnosis and composite fuzzy relations, in Gupta, M.M., Ragade, R.K. and Yager, R.R. (eds.), Advances in Fuzzy Set Theory and Applications (North-Holland, Amsterdam, 1979) 437-447.

[12] Ohsato, A. and Sekiguchi, T., Methods of solving the polynomial form of composite fuzzy relation equations, Trans. of the Society of Instrument and Control Engineers (Japan) 17-7 (1981) 756-763 (in Japanese).

[13] Sanchez, E., Solutions in composite fuzzy relation equations : Application to medical diagnosis in Brouwerian logic, in Gupta, M.M., Saridis, G.N. and Gaines, B.R.

(eds.), Fuzzy Automata and Decision Processes (North-Holland, Amsterdam, 1977) 221-234.

[14] Lancaster, P., Theory of Matrices (Academic Press, New York and London, 1969).

[15] Blin, J.M., Fuzzy relations in group decision theory, J. of Cybernetics 4-2 (1974) 17-22.

[16] Bezdek, J.C., Spillman, B. and Spillman, R., A fuzzy relation space for group decision theory, Fuzzy Sets and Systems 1 (1978) 255-268.

Approximate Reasoning in Decision Analysis
M.M. Gupta and E. Sanchez (eds.)

AN ALGORITHM TO SOLVE THE MAX-MIN COMPOSITE FUZZY RELATIONAL EQUATIONS

Wen-Li Xu, Chiu-feng Wu, Wei-min Cheng

Department of Automation, Tsinghua University
Beijing, China

The composite fuzzy relational equations and their applications were first put forward by E. sanchez[1]. Afterwards C.P. Pappis and M. Sugeno investigated such a particular case "given a fuzzy relation $R \subset X \times Y$ and a fuzzy subset $B \subset Y$, find all $A \subset X$ such that $A \circ R = B$." C.P. Pappis et al. have proposed an analytical method to obtain all solutions of the above problem[3]. Recently Y. Tsukamoto has given another algorithm and has applied it to failure diagnosis[4].
In this paper, a new algorithm for the determination of the solutions which is called S array selective reading method is developed. This method is not only much simpler than others, but also can obtain all minimal solutions directly.

Keywords: Fuzzy relational equation, maximal solution, minimal solution

1. Introduction

In this paper, the basic problem to be discussed is: find all X such that $X \circ R = T$,

$$X = (x_i)_m,\ T = (t_j)_n,\ R = (r_{ij})_{m\times n}$$

$$x_i,\ t_j,\ r_{ij} \in [0,1] \quad \text{for all } i,j$$

$$X \circ R = T \iff \bigvee_{i=1}^{m} (x_i \wedge r_{ij}) = t_j \quad j = 1,\dots,n$$

If the solutions of the equation exist, generally speaking, they are not unique. It is known that there are several minimal solutions and only one maximal solution in the problem, and that any fuzzy vector which is between the maximal solution and any minimal one is the solution of the equation too. Therefore, the key to the problem is to determine the maximal solution and all minimal solutions.

The main steps of the algorithm introduced in this paper are: first making a matrix S under the name of minimal solution reading array which can be made easily. Then using two selecting rules to read out all of the minimal solutions. In the following, this method is introduced but the proofs are omitted.

2. Minimal Solution Reading Array

Definition 1: α, δ operator

If $r \in [0,1]$ $\quad t \in [0,1]$

$$r\ \alpha\ t \triangleq \begin{cases} t & r > t \\ 1 & r \leqslant t \end{cases} \tag{1}$$

$$r\ \delta\ t \triangleq \begin{cases} 1 & r \geqslant t \\ 0 & r < t \end{cases} \tag{2}$$

Definition 2: Normal arrangement

In the equation $X \circ R = T$, if the elements of T are arranged in the order from large to small ($t_1 \geqslant t_2 \geqslant t_3 \geqslant \dots \geqslant t_n$) and the relevent columns in R are also interchanged accordingly, then it is called normal arrangement.

Example 1:

$$T = (.7\ \ .9\ \ .3) \qquad\qquad T = (.9\ \ .7\ \ .3)$$

$$R = \begin{bmatrix} .6 & 1 & .9 \\ .8 & .5 & .3 \\ .4 & .2 & .1 \end{bmatrix} \qquad R = \begin{bmatrix} 1 & .6 & .9 \\ .5 & .8 & .3 \\ .2 & .4 & .1 \end{bmatrix}$$

original arrangement — normal arrangement

Evidently, the solutions of the normally arranged equation are the same as the solutions of the original equation.

Definition 3: Minimal solution reading array

For the equation $X \circ R = T$, if T, R are in normal arrangement, we can define X^u and a minimal solution reading array S as follows:

$$X^u \triangleq (x_i^u)_m \tag{3}$$

$$x_i^u \triangleq \bigwedge_j (r_{ij}\ \alpha\ t_j) \tag{4}$$

$$S \triangleq (s_{ij})_{m\times n} \tag{5}$$

$$s_{ij} \triangleq (r_{ij} \wedge x_i^u)\ \delta\ t_j \tag{6}$$

The practical procedures of constructing X^u and S are: (see Example 2)

(1) Compare the elements of the ith row in R with those of T from right to left. Once $r_{ij} > t_j$ (the r_{ij} is marked by •), put $x_i^u = t_j$. If $r_{ij} \leq t_j$ for all j, put $x_i^u = 1$.

(2) In the process of determining $x_i^u = t_j$, set $s_{ik} = 1$ if $r_{ik} = t_k$ for $k > j$. Set s_{ij} and all successive s_{ik} equal to one so long as $t_k = t_j$ and $r_{ik} \geq t_k$. All remaining $s_{ik} = 0$.

Example 2:

Given R and T in normal arrangemet, determine X^u and S.

$$T = (.9 \quad .7 \quad .5 \quad .5 \quad .3)$$

$$R = \begin{pmatrix} .5 & .8 & .9 & .6 & .5^{\bullet} \\ .7 & .9 & .8 & .7^{\bullet} & .3 \\ 1^{\bullet} & .7 & .4 & .5 & .2 \\ .5 & .6 & .5 & .4 & .1 \end{pmatrix} \quad \begin{matrix} .3 \\ .5 \\ .9 \\ 1 \end{matrix}$$

$$S = \begin{pmatrix} 0 & 0 & 0 & 0 & 1 \\ 0 & 0 & 1 & 1 & 1 \\ 1 & 1 & 0 & 1 & 0 \\ 0 & 0 & 1 & 0 & 0 \end{pmatrix}$$

$$X^u = (.3 \quad .5 \quad .9 \quad 1)$$

The above method agrees with the formulas defined by (3) $\sim$(6), therefore X^u and S can be made up very easily.

It can be proved that the sufficient and neccessary condition of the existence of the solution for X o R = T is:

$$\forall j, \ \exists i; \ s_{ij} = 1 \qquad (7)$$

If this condition is satisfied, then the maximal solution is X^u, and all minimal solutions can be obtained from S by two selecting rules which are described below.

3. Selecting Rules

Selecting rule I:

(1) In the first column of S, choose arbitrarily a "1" element which is called "selected". Let its row index be M.

(2) Along the selected row go from left to right. Stop at the jth column where $s_{ij}=0$ for all $i \in M$. Choose a "selected" again in the jth column and modify M so that it consists of all "selected" row indexes

(3) To complete one scheme, repeat step(2) until the last column of S is reached or selected.

Make up all possible schemes by the selecting rule I, then any scheme can construct a solution X:

$$x_i = \begin{cases} t_j & s_{ij} \text{ is "selected"} \\ 0 & \text{otherwise} \end{cases} \qquad (8)$$

Theorem 1:

Any solution constructed by the selecting rule I is a minimal solution, if there are no same non-zero elements in it.

Theorem 2:

If there are no same non-zero elements in T, then all solutions constructed by the selecting rule I are just all of the minimal solutions of the equation.

In example 3, according to theorem 1, $X^1 = (0 \ .5 \ .9 \ \ 0)$ is a minimal solution, so are X^2 and X^3.

Sometimes selecting rule II must be added in order to obtain all minimal solutions and avoid unnecessary repetition. Before stating this rule, let us define some terminologies as follows:

(1) Let M be a row index set of S. Let k and l be two column indexes, $k \leq l$. If $\forall j \in [k,l]$, $\exists i \in M$; $s_{ij}=1$, then it is represented as $M \twoheadrightarrow [k,l]$.

(2) If $i \in M$, we use a symbol $\{M - i\}$ to represent the row index set M without i.

Selecting rule II.

In the process of constructing a scheme by selecting rule I, suppose s_{ij} is just "selected" and M represents the "selected" row index set (including S_{ij}), besides, $K \triangleq \{k \mid t_k = t_j,\ k < j,\ s_{i_k k} \text{ is a "selected"}\}$. If $\exists k \in K$; $\{M - i_k\} \twoheadrightarrow [k, j-1]$, then this scheme must be abandoned.

Theorem 3

If not all elements in T are zero, then the solutions constructed by both selecting rule I and II constitute the whole minimal solutions of the equation.

Example 4 is an illustrative example in which the rule I and II are made use of.

Example 3:

$$T = (.9 \quad .7 \quad .5 \quad .5 \quad .3)$$

$$S = \begin{pmatrix} 0 & 0 & 0 & 0 & 1 \\ 0 & 0 & 1^{*} & 1 & 1 \\ 1^{*} & 1 & 0 & 1 & 0 \\ 0 & 0 & 1 & 0 & 0 \end{pmatrix}$$

scheme number	"selected" (row,column)	minimal solutions
1	(3,1)⟶(2,3) marked by *	X^1 = (0 .5 .9 0)
2	(3,1)⟶(4,3)⟶(1,5)	X^2 = (.3 0 .9 .5)
3	(3,1)⟶(4,3)⟶(2,5)	X^3 = (0 .3 .9 .5)

Example 4:

$$T = (.8 \quad .8 \quad .6 \quad .6 \quad .6 \quad .6 \quad .4 \quad .4)$$

$$S = \begin{pmatrix} 1^{*} & 1 & 0 & 1 & 0 & 0 & 0 & 0 \\ 1 & 0 & 1^{*} & 0 & 1 & 0 & 1 & 0 \\ 0 & 0 & 1 & 1 & 0 & 1 & 0 & 0 \\ 1 & 1 & 1 & 0 & 1 & 1^{*} & 0 & 1 \end{pmatrix}$$

scheme number	"selected" (row,column)	minimal solutions
1	(1,1)⟶(2,3)⟶(3,6)⟶(4,8)	X^1 = (.8 .6 .6 .4)
×	(1,1)⟶(2,3)⟶(4,6) marked by *	
×	(1,1)⟶(3,3)⟶(2,5)	
×	(1,1)⟶(3,3)⟶(4,5)	
2	(1,1)⟶(4,3)⟶(2,7)	X^2 = (.8 .4 0 .6)
×	(2,1)⟶(1,2)	
×	(2,1)⟶(4,2)	
3	(4,1)⟶(1,4)⟶(2,7)	X^3 = (.6 .4 0 .8)
4	(4,1)⟶(3,4)⟶(2,7)	X^4 = (0 .4 .6 .8)

In the table of this example, the schemes marked by × are abandoned by rule II. $X^1 \sim X^4$ are just all of the minimal solutions of the original equation.

The complete steps for solving X o R = T which is called S array selective reading method are summarised as follows:

(1) Put T and R into normal arrangement.

(2) Construct X^u and S. If and only if $\forall j, \exists i;\ s_{ij}=1$, then the solutions exist and X^u is the maximal solution of the equation.

(3) Use selecting rule I with the additional use of rule II to construct all of the schemes. For the kth scheme, the corresponding minimal solution is:

$$X^k = (X_i^k)_m$$

$$x_i^k = \begin{cases} t_j & s_{ij} \text{ is "selected"} \\ 0 & \text{otherwise} \end{cases}$$

4. Conclusion

The new algorithm is not only much simpler than others, but also can obtain all minimal solutions directly. This point is peculiar to the algorithm.

References:

[1] Sanchez, E., Resolution of Composite Fuzzy Relation Equations, Information and Control, 30(1976) 38-48

[2] Sanchez, E., Medical Diagnosis and Composite Fuzzy Relations, Advances in Fuzzy Set Theory and Applications (1979) 437-444

[3] Pappis, C.P. and Sugeno, M., Fuzzy Relational Equations and the Inverse Problem, Internal Report, Queen Mary College, London (1976)

[4] Terano, T., Tsukamoto, Y. et al., Diagnosis of Engine Trouble by Fuzzy logic, Proc. of IFAC 7th World Congress (1978) 1621-1628

Approximate Reasoning in Decision Analysis
M.M. Gupta and E. Sanchez (eds.)

LSG POWERS OF AN L-FUZZY MATRIX

Shih-pe Lou and Zhengxiang Tong

Research Section of Multivalued Logic & Fuzzy System,
Shanghai Railway Institute, Shanghai, China

Following J.A.Goguen [1] and M.G.Thomason [2] , this paper develops the concepts of LSG powers, its convergence and the LSG closure of an L-fuzzy matrix. An algorithm for finding the LSG transitive closure of an L-fuzzy matrix is also given in this paper.

KEYWORDS: L-fuzzy set, L-fuzzy relation, LSG operator, LSG product, LSG power, Convergence, LSG transitive closure

1. LSG PRODUCT OF L-FUZZY RELATIONS

Let X and Y be sets, L a complete lattice. The mapping $R: X \times Y \to L$ is called an L-fuzzy relation between X and Y. The family of all L-fuzzy relations between X and Y is denoted by $\mathcal{L}(X \times Y)$.

DEFINITION 1.1. Let $R_1, R_2 \in \mathcal{L}(X \times Y)$. If

$$R_1(x,y) \leq R_2(x,y) \qquad \forall (x,y) \in X \times Y$$

then we say $R_1 \preccurlyeq R_2$.

It is well known that " $\preccurlyeq$ " is a partial order in $\mathcal{L}(X \times Y)$ and $\mathcal{L}(X \times Y)$ constitutes a complete lattice with the order " $\preccurlyeq$ ".

DEFINITION 1.2. Let $*$ be a binary operation in L. If $*$ satisfies the following conditions:

1. Associative Law

$$(a * b) * c == a * (b * c) \qquad \forall a,b,c \in L$$

2. Distributive Law to '$\vee$'

$$b * \bigvee_{i \in T} a_i == \bigvee_{i \in T} b * a_i$$

$$(\bigvee_{i \in T} a_i) * b == \bigvee_{i \in T} (a_i * b)$$

where T is an index set, then $*$ is called an LSG operator in L.

PROPOSITION 1.1. If $*$ is an LSG operator in L, then it possesses the property of preserving order, namely,

$$a \leq b,\ c \leq d \Longrightarrow a * c \leq b * d$$

PROOF From De. 1.2., it is clear that

$$\begin{aligned} b * d &== (a \vee b) * (c \vee d) \\ &== (a \vee b) * c \vee (a \vee b) * d \\ &\geqslant (a \vee b) * c \\ &== a * c \vee b * c \\ &\geqslant a * c \end{aligned}$$

Q.E.D.

DEFINITION 1.3. Let $R \in \mathcal{L}(X \times Y)$, $Q \in \mathcal{L}(Y \times Z)$, $T \in \mathcal{L}(X \times Z)$, and $*$ be a LSG operator in L. If

$$T(x,z) == \bigvee_{y \in Y} R(x,y) * Q(y,z)$$

holds for any $(x,z) \in X \times Z$, then we call T the LSG product (or LSG composition) of R and Q, denoted by $T == R \overset{\circ}{*} Q$.

THEOREM 1.1. Let X be a non-empty set, L a complete lattice and $*$ an LSG operator in L, then $\overset{\circ}{*}$ is an LSG operator in $\mathcal{L}(X \times X)$.

PROOF Let $T, R_i, Q_i \in \mathcal{L}(X \times X)$, $i \in I$ and $R_1 \preccurlyeq R_2$, $Q_1 \preccurlyeq Q_2$. It follows from De.1.3. that for any $(y,z) \in X \times X$,

$$\begin{aligned} (R_1 \overset{\circ}{*} Q_1)(y,z) &== \bigvee_{x \in X} R_1(y,x) * Q_1(x,z) \\ &\leq \bigvee_{x \in X} R_2(y,x) * Q_2(x,z) \\ &== (R_2 \overset{\circ}{*} Q_2)(y,z) \end{aligned}$$

$$((R \overset{\circ}{*} Q) \overset{\circ}{*} T)(y,z) == \bigvee_{x_2 \in X} (R \overset{\circ}{*} Q)(y,x_2) * T(x_2,z)$$

$$= \bigvee_{x_2\in X}(\bigvee_{x_1\in X}(R(y,x_1) * Q(x_1,x_2))) * T(x_2,z))$$

$$= \bigvee_{x_2\in X}\bigvee_{x_1\in X}((R(y,x_1) * Q(x_1,x_2)) * T(x_2,z))$$

$$= \bigvee_{x_2\in X}\bigvee_{x_1\in X}(R(y,x_1) * (Q(x_1,x_2) * T(x_2,z)))$$

$$= \bigvee_{x_1\in X}(R(y,x_1) * \bigvee_{x_2\in X}(Q(x_1,x_2) * T(x_2,z)))$$

$$= \bigvee_{x_1\in X}(R(y,x_1) * (Q \mathring{*} T)(x_1,z))$$

$$= (R \mathring{*} (Q \mathring{*} T))(y,z)$$

$$(T \mathring{*} \bigvee_{i\in I} R_i)(y,z) = \bigvee_{x\in X} T(y,x) * (\bigvee_{i\in I} R_i)(x,z)$$

$$= \bigvee_{x\in X} T(y,x) * (\bigvee_{i\in I} R_i(x,z))$$

$$= \bigvee_{x\in X}\bigvee_{i\in I}(T(y,x) * R_i(x,z))$$

$$= \bigvee_{i\in I}\bigvee_{x\in X}(T(y,x) * R_i(x,z))$$

$$= \bigvee_{i\in I}(T \mathring{*} R_i)(y,z)$$

Analogously, we can prove that

$$((\bigvee_{i\in I} R_i) \mathring{*} T)(y,z) = \bigvee_{i\in I}(R_i \mathring{*} T)(y,z)$$

Corresponding to De.1.2., we know that $\mathring{*}$ is an LSG operator in $\mathcal{L}(X \times X)$.

DEFINITION 1.4. Let $R \in \mathcal{L}(X \times X)$. If

$$R(x,y) = R(y,x) \qquad \forall (x,y) \in X \times X$$

then R is called a symmetric L-fuzzy relation on X.

THEOREM1.2. Let $*$ be a commutative LSG operator in L. If R is a symmetric L-fuzzy relation on X, then so is $R \mathring{*} R$.

PROOF Given any $(x,y) \in X \times X$, we have

$$(R \mathring{*} R)(x,y) = \bigvee_{z\in X} R(x,z) * R(z,y)$$

$$= \bigvee_{z\in X} R(z,x) * R(y,z)$$

$$= \bigvee_{z\in X} R(y,z) * R(z,x)$$

$$= (R \mathring{*} R)(y,x) \qquad \text{Q.E.D.}$$

DEFINITION1.5. Let $R \in \mathcal{L}(X \times X)$, $*$ be an LSG operator in L, and k a non-negative integer. The R's LSG power of order k, say R^k, is defined as follows

$$R^k = \begin{cases} R & k = 1 \\ R^{k-1} \mathring{*} R & k > 1 \\ I & k = 0 \end{cases}$$

where I is such an L-fuzzy relation on X that

$$I(x,y) = \begin{cases} 1 & x = y \\ 0 & x \neq y \end{cases}$$

DEFINITION1.6. Let $*$ be an LSG operator in L. If it satisfies the following conditions:

$$I * a = a * I = a$$

$$0 * a = a * 0 = 0$$

where a is any element in L, then $*$ is called a regular LSG operator in L.

THEOREM1.3. If $R \in \mathcal{L}(X \times X)$ and is a regular LSG operator in L, then for any non-negative integers k and p, we have

$$R^{k+p} = R^k \mathring{*} R^p$$

PROOF Since $\mathring{*}$ is an LSG operator in $\mathcal{L}(X \times X)$ and possesses the property of associative law, the conclusion is true in the case $k > 0$ and $p > 0$. In another case, without loss of generality, supposing k=0, the conclution remains true because the following formula holds for any regular LSG operator $*$ in L

$$I \mathring{*} Q = Q \mathring{*} I = Q \qquad \forall Q \in \mathcal{L}(X \times X)$$

2. CONVERGENCE OF LSG POWERS OF AN L-FUZZY MATRIX

If X is a set with n elements, denoted $\{x_1, \cdots x_n\}$, then the L-fuzzy relation R on X is called an n×n L-fuzzy matrix, denoted $R=(a_{ij})$, where $a_{ij} = R(x_i, x_j)$. Let $S(a_{ij}, *, \vee)$ denote the set whose elements can be obtained by the elements of the set $\{a_{ij}\}$ with finite operations of $*$ and $\vee$.

DEFINITION2.1. Let $\{R_m\}$ be a sequence of n×n L-fuzzy matrices. If there are such positive integers T and M that the following formula holds whenever $m > M$

$$R_m = R_{m+T}$$

then $\{R_m\}$ is called a periodically oscillating sequence of $n \times n$ L-fuzzy matrices. If T=1, then $\{R_m\}$ is called a convergent sequence.

THEOREM2.1. Let $R=(a_{ij})$ be an $n \times n$ L-fuzzy matrix, $*$ an LSG operator in L. If $S(a_{ij}, *, \vee)$ is a finite set, then the sequence $\{R^m\}$ of R's LSG powers is either convergent or periodically oscillating.

PROOF Let $S(a_{ij}, *, \vee)$ consists of N elements. Then there are at most N^{n^2} different matrices in $\{R^m\}$. In other words, there must be two positive integers M and T,

$$R^M = R^{M+T}$$

Furthermore, it follows from Th.1.3 that for any positive integer $m > M$,

$$\begin{aligned} R^{m+T} &= R^{(m-M)+M+T} \qquad (m-M>0) \\ &= R^{M+T} \mathring{*} R^{m-M} \\ &= R^{M} \mathring{*} R^{m-M} \\ &= R^{M+m-M} \\ &= R^{m} \end{aligned}$$

Of course, the sequence $\{R^m\}$ oscillates periodically and converges in the case T=1.

Q.E.D.

COROLLARY2.1.1 Under the assumption of Th.2.1., $\{R^m\}$ converges iff there is such a positive integer M that $R^M = R^{M+1}$.

COROLLARY2.1.2 Under the assumption of Th.2.1, $\{R^m\}$ converges iff there is such a positive integer M that either $R^M \preccurlyeq R^{M+1}$ or $R^M \succcurlyeq R^{M+1}$ holds.

PROOF Without loss of generality, we suppose that $R^M \preccurlyeq R^{M+1}$. From Prop.1.1., it is clear that

$$R^M \preccurlyeq R^{M+1} \preccurlyeq R^{M+2} \preccurlyeq \cdots$$

Corresponding to Th.2.1, there are such positive integers P and T, $P > M$, that

$$R^P = R^{P+T}$$

Hence

$$R^P = R^{P+1} = \cdots = R^{P+T}$$

It shows that the sequence $\{R^m\}$ converges.

EXAMPLE Let $R=(a_{ij})$, where a_{ij} are rational numbers in the interval [0,1], and $*$ be the bounded product $\otimes$. It is easy to show that $*$ is an LSG operator in [0,1] and $S(a_{ij}, *, \vee)$ is a finite set. So $\{R^m\}$, the sequence of the R's LSG powers, either converges or periodically oscillates. The kind of this powers is called $\vee - \textcircled{\cap}$ power [4].

EXAMPLE Let $R=(a_{ij})$, $a_{ij} \in [0,1]$ and $*$ the min operator $\wedge$. If

$$a_{ij} \le a_{ii} \vee a_{jj} \qquad \forall i,j,\ 0 < i,j \le n$$

then $\{R^m\}$ converges. In fact, $*$ is a regular LSGoperator in [0,1] and $S(a_{ij}, *, \vee) = \{a_{ij}\}$. Furthermore, for any i, j, $0 < i, j \le n$,

$$\begin{aligned} \bigvee_{k=1}^{n} a_{ik} \wedge a_{kj} &\geq a_{ii} \wedge a_{ij} \vee a_{ij} \wedge a_{jj} \\ &= (a_{ii} \vee a_{jj}) \wedge a_{ij} \\ &= a_{ij} \end{aligned}$$

so $R \preccurlyeq R^2$. By Coro.2.1.2., it shows that $\{R^m\}$ converges.

3. THE LSG TRANSITIVE CLOSURE OF A L-FUZZY MATRIX

DEFINITION3.1. Let $R=(a_{ij})$ and $*$ an LSG operator in L. If $R \mathring{*} R \preccurlyeq R$, then R is called an $n \times n$ transitive L-fuzzy matrix.

THEOREM3.1. Let T be an index set. If $\{R_t | t \in T\}$ is a family of $n \times n$ transitive L-fuzzy matrices then $\bigwedge_{t \in T} R_t$ is also an $n \times n$ transitive L-fuzzy matrix.

PROOF Let $R_t = (a^t_{ij})$, $(\bigwedge_{t \in T} R_t)^2 = (b_{ij})$. For any $t \in T$, we have

$$\begin{aligned} b_{ij} &= \bigvee_{k=1}^{n} (\bigwedge_{t \in T} a^t_{ik}) * (\bigwedge_{t \in T} a^t_{kj}) \\ &\le \bigvee_{k=1}^{n} (a^t_{ik} * a^t_{kj}) \\ &\le a^t_{ij} \end{aligned}$$

Hence $b_{ij} \le \bigwedge_{t \in T} a^t_{ij}$, which shows that

$$(\bigwedge_{t \in T} R_t)^2 \preccurlyeq \bigwedge_{t \in T} R_t$$

DEFINITION3.2. Let R,Q be $n \times n$ L-fuzzy matrices and $*$ an LSG operator in L. If Q satisfies the following conditions:

1. $Q \succcurlyeq R$

2. Q is a transitive L-fuzzy matrix

3. If there is an n n transitive L-fuzzy matrix S and $S \succcurlyeq R$, then $S \succcurlyeq Q$,

then Q is called the LSG transitive closure of R, denoted by $\hat{R}$.

THEOREM 3.2. If R is an n×n L-fuzzy matrix, then

$$\hat{R}=\bigvee_{m=1}^{\infty} R^m$$

PROOF It is similar to that of the classical theorem.

THEOREM 3.3. If R is an n×n L-fuzzy matrix and $*$ a regular LSG operator in L, then

$$\hat{R}=\bigvee_{k=1}^{n} R^k$$

PROOF Corresponding to Th.3.2., we need only to show that for any m>n,

$$R^m \preccurlyeq \bigvee_{k=1}^{n} R^k$$

Let $R=(a_{ij})$, $R^m=(a_{ij}^{(m)})$. Evidently,

$$a_{ij}^{(m)} = \bigvee_{(k_1,\cdots,k_{m-1})} a_{ik_1} * a_{k_1k_2} * \cdots * a_{k_{m-1}j}$$

$$\forall\, i,j,\ 1 \le i,j \le n$$

Consider any given term $a_{ik_1} * a_{k_1k_2} * \cdots * a_{k_{m-1}j}$. Since all the numbers $k_1, k_2, \cdots, k_m$ (we denote j by k_m) are elements of the set $\{1,2,\cdots,n\}$, there must be some numbers, say $k_{p_1}, k_{p_2}, k_{p_3}, k_{p_4}, \cdots, k_{p_{2r-1}}, k_{p_{2r}}$, which satify the following conditions:

1. $k_{p_1}=k_{p_2},\ k_{p_3}=k_{p_4}, \cdots, k_{p_{2r-1}}=k_{p_{2r}}$

2. the numbers in the set $S=\{k_1, k_2, \cdots, k_{p_1}, k_{p_2+1}, \cdots, k_{p_3}, k_{p_4+1}, \cdots, k_{p_5}, k_{p_6+1}, \cdots, k_{p_{2r-1}}, k_{p_{2r}+1}, \cdots, k_n\}$ are different to each another.

Suppose the set S contains M elements. By the pigeonhole principle, $M \le n$. Then, we have

$$\begin{aligned} & a_{ik_1} * a_{k_1k_2} * \cdots * a_{k_{m-1}j} \\ \le\ & a_{ik_1} * \cdots * a_{k_{p_1}k_{p_2+1}} * \cdots * a_{k_{m-1}j} \\ \le\ & a_{ij}^{(M)} \\ \le\ & \bigvee_{k=1}^{n} a_{ij}^{(k)} \end{aligned}$$

By the arbitrality of the term $a_{ik_1} * a_{k_1k_2} * \cdots * a_{k_{m-1}j}$, we obtain

$$a_{ij}^{(m)} \le \bigvee_{k=1}^{n} a_{ij}^{(k)}$$

It follows that

$$R^m \preccurlyeq \bigvee_{k=1}^{n} R^k \qquad \text{Q.E.D.}$$

THEOREM 3.4. Let $*$ be a regular LSG operator in L, $R=(a_{ij})$ and $R_k=(a_{ij}^{(k)})$ be n×n L-fuzzy matrices. If

$$a_{ij}^{(k)} = \begin{cases} a_{ij} & k=0 \\ a_{ij}^{(k-1)} \vee a_{ik}^{(k-1)} * a_{kj}^{(k-1)} & 1 \le k \le n \end{cases}$$

then $R_n=\hat{R}$.

PROOF Let P_k be the multi-set $\{\infty\cdot 1, \infty\cdot 2, \cdots, \infty\cdot k\}$, $\mathcal{P}_k$ the set which consists of all permutations p in P_k, p(t) the permutation in P_k which contains the element t, $\mathcal{P}_k^{(t)}$ the set of all p(t), ipj denote $a_{ip_1} * a_{p_1p_2} * \cdots * a_{p_mj}$, where $p=(p_1, p_2, \cdots, p_m) \in \mathcal{P}_k$, $i\mathcal{P}_kj$ denote $\bigvee_{p\in\mathcal{P}_k} ipj$ and $i\mathcal{P}_k^{(t)}j$ denote $\bigvee_{p\in\mathcal{P}_k^{(t)}} ipj$.

First we can show that for any k, $1 \le k \le n$

$$i\mathcal{P}_k^{(k)}j = i\mathcal{P}_{k-1}k * k\mathcal{P}_{k-1}j$$

In fact, given any $p \in \mathcal{P}_k^{(k)}$, it can be denoted by $(p_1, \cdots, p_m, k, \cdots, k, q_1, \cdots, q_l)$, where $p_1, \cdots, p_m, q_1, \cdots, q_l \in \{1,2,\cdots,k-1\}$. Since $*$ is a regular LSG operator, we have

$$\begin{aligned} ipj &\le i(p_1, \cdots, p_m)k * k(q_1, \cdots, q_l) \\ &\le i\mathcal{P}_{k-1}k * k\mathcal{P}_{k-1}j \end{aligned}$$

Considering the arbitrariness of p, we have

$$i\mathcal{P}_k^{(k)}j \le i\mathcal{P}_{k-1}k * k\mathcal{P}_{k-1}j$$

To obtain another inequality, we consider any given permutations $p=(p_1, \cdots, p_m) \in \mathcal{P}_{k-1}'$, $q=(q_1, \cdots, q_l) \in \mathcal{P}_{k-1}$. Evidently,

$$r=(p_1, \cdots, p_m, k, q_1, \cdots, q_l) \in \mathcal{P}_k^{(k)}$$

Hence,

$$ipk * kqj = irj \le i\mathcal{P}_k^{(k)}j$$

Considering the arbitrariness of p and q, we have

$$i\mathcal{P}_{k-1}k * k\mathcal{P}_{k-1}j = \bigvee_{\substack{p\in\mathcal{P}_{k-1} \\ q\in\mathcal{P}_{k-1}}} ipk * kqj \le i\mathcal{P}_k^{(k)}j$$

Then

$$i\mathcal{P}_k^{(k)}j = i\mathcal{P}_{k-1}k * k\mathcal{P}_{k-1}j$$

Let $R=(\hat{a}_{ij})$. By Th.3.2., we hwve $\hat{a}_{ij} = i\mathcal{P}_n j$ Therefore, the conclusion of this theorem will be proved if we can show that for any k, $1\le k\le n$,

$$a_{ij}^{(k)} = i\mathcal{P}_k j$$

We prove this assfollows. As k=1,

$$a_{ij}^{(1)} = a_{ij} \vee (a_{i1} * a_{1j}) = i\mathcal{P}_1 j$$

Assume that $a_{ij}^{(k)} = i\mathcal{P}_k j$. Since

$$\begin{aligned} i\mathcal{P}_{k+1} j &= i\mathcal{P}_k j \vee i\mathcal{P}_{k+1}^{(k+1)} j \\ &= i\mathcal{P}_k j \vee i\mathcal{P}_k (k+1) * (k+1)\mathcal{P}_k j \\ &= a_{ij}^{(k)} \vee a_{i(k+1)}^{(k)} * a_{(k+1)j}^{(k)} \\ &= a_{ij}^{(k+1)} \end{aligned}$$

it is clear that for any k, $1\le k\le n$,

$$a_{ij}^{(k)} = i\mathcal{P}_k j \qquad \text{Q.E.D.}$$

When $L=[0,1]$, $* = \wedge$, this theorem gives an algorithm [3] for finding the transitive closure of a fuzzy matrix, which is superior to Tamura algorithm and can be applied to fuzzy clursting. If $*$ is other fuzzy operator and L other lattice, the theorem will be applied to other different area.

REFERENCES

[1] J.A.Goguen, L-fuzzy Sets, J. Math. Anal. Appl., 18(1967), 145-174.

[2] M.G.Thomason, Convergences of Power of a Fuzzy Matrix, J. Math. Anal. Appl. 57(1977), 476-480

[3] S.P.Lou & Z.X.Tong, An Algorithm for Finding the Transitive Closure of a Fuzzy Matrix, Journal of Shanghai Railway Institute, 1(1981), 37-42,(in Chinese).

[4] D.Dubois & H.Prade, Outline of Fuzzy Theory: An Introduction, Advances in Fuzzy Set Theory and Applications, 1981,27-48.

S.P.Lou graduated from Nanking University in 1962. He is the director of Multivalue Logic and Fuzzy System Research Section, Shanghai Railway Institute, Shanghai, China. Sinve 1981, he has been the Editor-in-chief of the journal of "Fuzzy Mathematics", His forty ahese and three works on Fuzzy Mathematics, Multivalue Logic and Graph Theory have been pulished. He was given the Invention Achievement Award of the first grade by the Ministry of Railway of China in 1978.

Z.X.Tong graduated from Nanking University in 1966. He is the editor of the journal of "Fuzzy Mathematics" published in china. He has been working on various topics in pure and applied mathematics, such as functions of complex variables, functional analysis, number theory, combinatorial mathematics, probability theory, fuzzy mathematics and combinatorial algorithm.

Approximate Reasoning in Decision Analysis
M.M. Gupta and E. Sanchez (eds.)

GENERALIZED INVERSES OF FUZZY MATRIX

Luo Cheng - Zhong

Dept. of Mathematics
Beijing Normal University
China

K.H. Kim and F.W. Roush have described the concepts of regularity and the generalized inverses of the fuzzy matrix[1]. In this paper a method of determining all the generalized inverses of a given regular fuzzy matrix over the fuzzy algebra L = [0, 1] is given. There exists a largest generalized inverse and some minima for a regular fuzzy matrix.

KEYWORDS: fuzzy matrix, generalized inverse, regular, fuzzy relation, maximum, quasi-minimum

1. INTRODUCTION

Let A, where

$$A = \begin{pmatrix} a_{11} & a_{12} \cdots & a_{1m} \\ a_{21} & a_{22} \cdots & a_{2m} \\ \cdots & \cdots & \cdots \\ a_{n} & a_{n} \cdots & a_{nm} \end{pmatrix}, \quad o \le a_{ij} \le 1$$

be a n x m fuzzy matrix over L = [o, 1] and let Bm x 1. C = AoB is the resultant of A into B if

$$C_{ij} = \bigvee_{k=1}^{m} (a_{ik} \wedge b_{kj}) \quad (i = 1, 2, \ldots, n;\ j = 1, 2, \ldots, 1)$$

"$\bigvee$ = sup $\bigwedge$ = inf"

Given two n x m fuzzy matrices A and B, then $A \subseteq B$ if and only if

$$a_{ij} \le b_{ij} \quad (i = 1, 2, \ldots, n;\ j = 1, 2, \ldots, m)$$

Evidently, if $A \subseteq B$

$AoC \subseteq BoC$ $\quad$ $DoA \subseteq DoB$

Given a n x m fuzzy matrix A. A is regular if and only if there exists a m x m fuzzy matrix B such that

AoBoA = A

and B is a generalized inverse of A.

2. GENERALIZED INVERSE

Given a fuzzy matrix $A_{n \times m}$,

Let $\bar{X} = (\bar{x}_{ik})$

where

$$\bar{x}_{ik} = \bigwedge_{a_{st} < (a_{sj} \wedge a_{kt})} (a_{st})$$

$$i = 1, 2, \ldots, m;\ k = 1, 2, \ldots, n$$

Let

$$g_{il} = \{g_{il} = (j_{il}, k_{il}) \mid a_{ij_{il}} \wedge x_{j_{il}k_{il}} \wedge a_{k_{il}l} = a_{il}\}$$

$$g = \{n \times m \text{ matrix } G = (g_{il}) \mid g_{il} \in g_{il}\}$$

if $g \ne \phi$, for $\forall$ $G \in g$, let X_G be m x n fuzzy matrix such that

$$x_{G_{jk}} = \bigvee_{(j_{il}, k_{il}) = (j,k)} (a_{il})$$

$$j = 1, 2, \ldots, m;\ k = 1, 2, \ldots, n$$

(In this paper, it is assumed that the infimum of the empty set is 1 and the supremum is 0).

Theorem. The matrix A is regular if and only if $g \ne \phi$. When $g \ne \phi$ the generalized inverse set of A is

$$\mathfrak{X} = \{X \mid X_G \subseteq X \subseteq \bar{X},\ G \in g\}$$

Proof. 1. Suppose that A is any generalized inverse of A

AoXoA = A

This means that for $\forall$ (i, 1)

$$\bigvee_k [(\bigvee_j (a_{ij} \wedge x_{jk})) \wedge a_{kl}] = a_{il}$$

$$\rightarrow \bigvee_k \bigvee_j (a_{ij} \wedge x_{jk} \wedge a_{kl}) = a_{il}$$

$$\rightarrow \forall (k,j),\ (a_{ij} \wedge a_{kl}) \wedge x_{jk} \le a_{il}$$

$$\rightarrow \forall (k,j),\ \begin{cases} o \le x_{jk} \le 1 \text{ when } a_{ij} \wedge a_{kl} \le a_{il} \\ o \le x_{jk} \le a_{il} \text{ when } a_{ij} \wedge a_{kl} > a_{il} \end{cases}$$

Thus,

$o \le x_{jk} \le \bigwedge (a_{st}) = \bar{x}_{jk}$ for $\forall (j,k)$

$a_{st} < (a_{st} \wedge a_{kt})$

This means that $X \subseteq \bar{X}$ and

$Ao\bar{X}oA \supseteq AoXoA = A$

On the other hand, for $\forall (i, l)$ $\exists (j_{il}, k_{il})$ such that

$$a_{ij_{il}} \wedge x_{j_{il}k_{il}} \wedge a_{k_{il}l} = a_{il}$$

$\rightarrow \exists g_{il} = (j_{il}, k_{il})$ such that

$$a_{ij_{il}} \wedge x_{j_{il}k_{il}} \wedge a_{k_{il}l}$$

$$\ge a_{ij_{il}} \wedge x_{j_{il}k_{il}} \wedge a_{k_{il}l} = a_{il}$$

For $\forall (i, l)$ $\forall (j, k)$ if $a_{il} < (a_{ij} \wedge a_{kl})$.

$$a_{ij} \wedge \bar{x}_{jk} \wedge a_{kl} \le \bar{x}_{jk} = \bigwedge_{a_{st} < (a_{sj} \wedge a_{kt})} (a_{st}) \le a_{il}$$

and if $a_{il} \ge (a_{ij} \wedge a_{kl})$,

$$a_{ij} \wedge \bar{x}_{jk} \wedge a_{kl} \le a_{ij} \wedge a_{kl} \le a_{il}$$

Hence, for $\forall (j, k)$

$$a_{ij} \wedge \bar{x}_{jk} \wedge a_{kl} \le a_{il}$$

Thus,

$$a_{ij_{il}} \wedge \bar{x}_{j_{il}k_{il}} \wedge a_{k_{il}l} = a_{il} \text{ for } \forall (i, l)$$

which means $\exists G = (g_{il}) \in \mathcal{g}$. Then $\mathcal{g} \ne \phi$.

Let

$$x_{G_{jk}} = \bigvee_{(j_{il}, k_{il}) = (j, k)} (a_{il})$$

For $\forall (j, k)$, if some $(j_{il}, k_{il}) = (j, k)$, by

$$a_{ij_{il}} \wedge x_{j_{il}k_{il}} \wedge a_{k_{il}l} = a_{il}$$

$$x_{jk} = x_{j_{il}k_{il}} \ge a_{il} \text{ for } \forall (j_{il}, k_{il}) = (j, k)$$

Thus,

$$x_{G_{jk}} = \bigvee_{(j_{il}, k_{il}) = (j, k)} (a_{il}) \le x_{jk}$$

and if $(j_{il}, k_{il}) \ne (j, k)$ for $\forall (i, l)$

$$x_{G_{jk}} = \bigvee \phi = o \le x_{jk}$$

This means that $X_G \subseteq X \subseteq \bar{X}$. Hence $X \in \mathcal{X}$.

2. If $\mathcal{g} \ne \phi$, for $\forall G = (g_{il}) \in \mathcal{g}$,

$$a_{ij_{il}} \wedge \bar{x}_{j_{il}k_{il}} \wedge a_{k_{il}l} = a_{il}$$

for $\forall (i, l)$

By $x_{G_{j_{il}k_{il}}} = \bigvee_{(j_{st}, k_{st}) = (j_{il}, k_{il})} (a_{st}) \ge a_{il}$

$$a_{ij_{il}} \wedge x_{G_{j_{il}k_{il}}} \wedge a_{k_{il}k} \ge a_{il}$$

$$\rightarrow \bigvee_k \bigvee_j (a_{ij} \wedge x_{G_{jk}} \wedge a_{kl}) \ge a_{il} \text{ for } \forall (i, l)$$

Thus,

$AoX_GoA \supseteq A$

Since for $\forall (i,l)$, $\forall (j,k)$

$$a_{ij} \wedge \bar{x}_{jk} \wedge a_{kl} \le a_{il}$$

and $\bigvee_j \bigvee_k (a_{ij} \wedge \bar{x}_{jk} \wedge a_{kl}) \le a_{il}$ for $\forall (i, l)$

Hence,

$Ao\bar{X}oA \subseteq A$

On the other hand, for $\forall (i,l)$ if some $(j_{il}, k_{il}) = (j, k)$

$$\bar{x}_{jk} = \bar{x}_{j_{il}k_{il}} \ge a_{ij_{il}} \wedge \bar{x}_{j_{il}k_{il}} \wedge a_{k_{il}l} = a_{il}$$

Thus,

$$x_{G_{jk}} = \bigvee_{(j_{il}, k_{il}) = (j, k)} (a_{il}) \le \bar{x}_{jk}$$

and if $(j_{il}, k_{il}) \ne (j, k)$ for all (i, l)

$$x_{G_{jk}} = \bigvee \phi = o \le \bar{x}_{jk}$$

Thus,

$$x_{G_{jk}} \le \bar{x}_{jk} \quad \text{for} \quad \forall (j, k)$$

and

$X_G \subseteq \bar{X}$

Hence,

$A \subseteq AoX_GoA \subseteq Ao\bar{X}oA \subseteq A$

It can be said, therefore, that all m x n fuzzy matrices such that $X_G \subseteq X \subseteq \bar{X}$ are the generalized inverses of A.

$\bar{X}$ is the largest generalized inverse of A.

X_G is called the quasi-mimimun of the generalized inverse set of A associated with $G \in \mathcal{g}$.

This theorem gives a method of finding the

generalized inverse set. This procedure may be summarized by the following table and discussion:

	$\bar{x}_{11} \ldots \bar{x}_{1n}\ \bar{x}_{21} \ldots \bar{x}_{2n} \ldots \bar{x}_{m1} \ldots \bar{x}_{mn}$
a_{il}	Table I
$\bar{X}$	$\bar{x}_{11} \ldots \bar{x}_{1}\ \bar{x}_{21} \ldots \bar{x}_{2n} \ldots \bar{x}_{m1} \ldots \bar{x}_{mn}$
$\underline{\mathcal{X}}$	Table II

where:

1. The larger a_{il} is placed below the smaller one.
2. By

$$\bar{x}_{jk} = \bigwedge_{a_{st} < (a_{sj} \wedge a_{kt})} (a_{st})$$

   $\bar{X}$ is calculated.

3. In table (I) for $\forall$ (i, l) $\forall$ (j, k), if

$$a_{il} \leq (a_{ij} \wedge a_{kl})$$

   a_{il} is placed at the intersection of the row containing a_{il} with the column containing x_{jk}. Zeros are placed in the other places in table (I).

4. In every column of table (I), the elements which are larger than $\bar{x}_{jk}$ are eliminated.
5. A is regular if and only if every row in the table (I) is non-empty.
6. An element in every row of the table (I) is selected and the supremum of every column worked out. It is evident that those supremums make a quasi-minimum of the generalized inverse set.
7. If one of the quasi-minimum contains others, then the larger one is eliminated. Thus, the minima of the generalized inverse set is obtained. The minima in table (II) is then

Example 3 $\quad A = \begin{pmatrix} 0.5 & 0.5 & 0.3 \\ 0.4 & 0.4 & 0.3 \\ 0.2 & 0.2 & 0.2 \end{pmatrix}$

By

$$\bar{x}_{jk} = \bigwedge_{a_{st} < (a_{sj} \wedge a_{kt})} (a_{st})$$

We obtain

$$\bar{X} = \begin{pmatrix} 1 & 1 & 0.3 \\ 1 & 1 & 0.3 \\ 0.2 & 0.2 & 1 \end{pmatrix}$$

According to the above-mentioned procedure

	x_{11}	x_{12}	x_{13}	x_{21}	x_{22}	x_{23}	x_{31}	x_{32}	x_{33}
$a_{31}=0.2$	0.2	0.2	0.2	0.2	0.2	0.2	0.2	0.2	0.2
$a_{32}=0.2$	0.2	0.2	0.2	0.2	0.2	0.2	0.2	0.2	0.2
$a_{13}=0.3$	0.3	0.3	0.3	0.3	0.3	0.3	0/3	0/3	0.3
$a_{23}=0.3$	0.3	0.3	0.3	0.3	0.3	0.3	0/3	0/3	0.3
$a_{21}=0.4$	0.4	0.4		0.4	0.4				
$a_{22}=0.4$	0.4	0.4		0.4	0.4				
$a_{11}=0.5$	0.5			0.5					
$a_{12}=0.5$	0.5			0.5					
$a_{33}=0.5$									0.5
$\bar{X}$	1	1	0.3	1	1	0.3	0.2	0.2	1
$\underline{\mathcal{X}}$	0.5	0	0	0	0	0	0	0	0.5
	0	0	0	0.5	0	0	0	0	0.5

The generalized inverse set consists of the following:

$$\begin{pmatrix} [0.5,1] & [0,1] & [0,0.3] \\ [0,1] & [0,1] & [0,0.3] \\ [0,0.2] & [0,0.2] & [0.5,1] \end{pmatrix} \begin{pmatrix} [0,1] & [0,1] & [0,0.3] \\ [0.5,1] & [0,1] & [0,0.3] \\ [0,0.2] & [0,0.2] & [0.5,1] \end{pmatrix}$$

There are two elements in table (I) at the 8th row. Each of these must be selected respectively. In the 7th row, there are also two elements. If we select the 1st column element in 8th row, we must only select the 1st column element in the 7th row, because other selections give a quasi-minimum which is not the minimum.

Example 2. Let $A = \begin{pmatrix} 0.7 & 0.1 & 0.3 \\ 0.2 & 0.5 & 0.4 \end{pmatrix}$

By

$$\bar{X} = \begin{pmatrix} 1 & 0.1 \\ 0.2 & 1 \\ 0.2 & 0.1 \end{pmatrix}$$

	x_{11}	x_{12}	x_{21}	x_{22}	x_{31}	x_{32}
$a_{12}=0.1$	0.1	0.1	0.1	0.1	0.1	0.1
$a_{21}=0.2$	0.2	0/2	0.2	0.2	0.2	0/2
$a_{13}=0.3$	0.3	0/3			0/3	0/3
$a_{23}=0.4$				0.4		0/4
$a_{22}=0.5$				0.5		
$a_{11}=0.7$	0.7					
$\bar{X}$	1	0.1	0.2	1	0.2	0.1
$\underline{X}$	0.7	0	0	0.5	0	0

The generalized inverse set is then

$$\begin{bmatrix} [0.7,1] & [0,0.1] \\ [0,0.2] & [0.5,1] \\ [0,0.2] & [0,0.1] \end{bmatrix}$$

REFERENCES

[1] K.H. Kim and F.W. Roush, "Generalized fuzzy matrices", Fuzzy Sets and Systems 4, 1980.

[2] Luo Cheng-Zhong, "Fuzzy relations on finite sets", Selected papers on fuzzy subsets, Dept. of Math., Beijing Normal University, 1981.

Approximate Reasoning in Decision Analysis
M.M. Gupta and E. Sanchez (eds.)

THE EIGEN FUZZY SETS OF A FUZZY MATRIX

Cao Zhi-qiang

Institute of Automation, Academia Sinica
P.O. 2728
Beijing, China

In this paper, we propose an algorithm for obtaining all the eigen fuzzy sets of a fuzzy matrix and show that the set of all eigen fuzzy sets of an n x n matrix is a module generated by m elements ($m \leq n$). The results derived in this paper are also true for distributive lattice matrices.

KEYWORDS: Eigen fuzzy set, Fuzzy matrix, Lattice matrix, Lattice module-homomorphism, Finitely generated module over a lattice.

1. INTRODUCTION

The resolution problem of eigen fuzzy sets equations was first proposed by Elie Sanchez. He gave three methods for computing the greatest eigen fuzzy set (GEFS) associated with a given fuzzy relation and discussed its medical applications [1].

In this paper, we discuss the problem of the eigen vectors of a matrix over a distributive lattice and give an algorithm for obtaining all the eigen vectors of a matrix. Of course, the eigen fuzzy sets problem is only a particular case of the problem discussed here. It is important to note that in this paper we refer a matrix over a lattice to a lattice module-homomorphism. We also show that the set of all eigen vectors of a lattice matrix is but a finitely generated submodule of a finitely generated free module over the lattice.

The results obtained in this paper can be applied to the discussion of some fuzzy controllers and systems described by fuzzy dynamic equations, e.g., some psychological phenomena discussed by the author in [2], as well as to medical diagnosis.

2. DEFINITIONS

For convenience of the presentation, we give the definitions below. In this paper, we deal only with distributive lattice. Note that we denote $a+b = a\vee b$ and $a \cdot b = a\wedge b$ where $\vee$ and $\wedge$ are the operations join and meet on a lattice.

Definition 2.1 A module M over a lattice L is a commutative semigroup (M,+) together with a map $(a,x) \to ax$ of L x M into M such that for any $x,y \in M$; $a,b \in L$

(1) $a(x+y) = ax + ay$, (2) $a(bx) = (a \cdot b)x$,
(3) $(a+b)x = ax + bx$, (4) $1x = x$,
(5) $0x = \theta$

where θ is the additive identity of M, and 1, 0 are the greatest, and the least elements of L, respectively.

Example 2.1 Denote $Mm = ([0,1], \vee, \wedge)$. Obviously, Mm is a distributive lattice with the least and greatest elements. Denote $MmV_2 = (\{(a,b): a,b \in Mm\},+)$ with $(a_1,b_1) + (a_2,b_2) = (a_1 \vee a_2, b_1 \vee b_2)$ and $c(a,b) = (c\wedge a, c\wedge b)$. MmV_2 is a module over Mm. Obviously, MmV_2 also is the set of all fuzzy sets of a set consisting of two elements.

Proposition 2.1 Let M be a module over L. Then
(1) $ax + x = x$ (2) $a\theta = \theta$,
(3) If $x + y = \theta$, then $x = y = \theta$
hold for all $a \in L$ and $x,y \in M$.

Corollary A module, as a commutative semi-group, is a semi-lattice and a partially ordered set.

Definition 2.2 A finite subset $\{s_i\}$ of a module over L is independent iff for all $a_j \in L$ and all $s_i \in \{s_i\}$

$$s_i \neq \sum_{j \neq i} a_j s_i .$$

Definition 2.3 A module M is finitely generated iff there exists a finite set $\{s_i\}$ such that for any $x \in M$ the set $X = \{(a_1,a_2,\ldots,a_n): x = \Sigma a_i s_i, a_i \in L\}$ is non-empty. If for every $x \in M$, the set X has a unique element, then the module M is called as finitely generated free, and the set $\{s_i\}$ is called as a basis of M.

Definition 2.4 A map H is a homomorphism from M to N iff $H(x+y) = H(x) + H(y)$ and $H(ax) = aH(x)$ for any $x,y \in M$ and $a \in L$ where both M and N are modules over L.

Note that every element of a finitely generated free module can be represented as a vector under a certain basis, while every module-homomorphism as a matrix. Conversely, every lattice matrix is just a lattice module-homomorphism.

Some properties of lattice matrices were discussed in [3]. The author gave more properties of matrices and module over another algebraic system--slope in [2][4], and a distributive lattice is just a particular slope.

3. EQUATION Ax = x

Lemma 3.1 For any square matrix A over a distributive lattice, the sequence $A, A^2, A^3, \ldots$ is ultimately periodic [3].

Theorem 3.1 (Main Theorem) For any n x n matrix A over a distributive lattice the set $U(A) = \{x: Ax = x\}$ is a finitely generated module over the lattice, whose spanning set is the columns vectors of an n x n matrix determined by A.

Proof By Lemma 3.1, for the matrix A, there exist p and q such that the sequence $A, A^2, A^3, \ldots$ has the form: $A, A^2, \ldots, A^{p-1}, A^p, \ldots, A^q, A^p, \ldots, A^q, A^p, \ldots$. Denote $A^p + A^{p+1} + \ldots + A^q = M$. We will show that the set $U(A) = \langle M \rangle$, where $\langle M \rangle$ denotesthe module generated by the columns of M.

First suppose that x is an element of U(A). From Ax = x, we have $A^k x = x$ for any natural number k, hence, $A^p x + \ldots + A^q x = x$; that is, Mx = x and $x \in \langle M \rangle$. Conversely, suppose $x \in \langle M \rangle$. Then there exists an element y such that My = x. Note $A^{q+1} = A^p$ and AM = M. We have Ax = AMy = My = x; that is $x \in U(A)$.

Corollary If $A^2 = A$, then $U(A) = \langle A \rangle$.

In fact, Theorem 3.1 provides an algorithm for obtaining all the eigen vectors of a lattice matrix.

In some applications, it is necessary to know the relationship between U(A) and $U(A^k)$. The following theorem shows that there exists a matrix T such that $U(A) = TU(A^k)$.

Lemma 3.2 $U(A) \subseteq U(A^k)$ for any natural number k.

Theorem 3.2 For any square matrix A and natural number k, $(I + A + \ldots + A^{k-1})U(A^k) = U(A)$.

Proof Suppose $x \in U(A)$. Since Ax = x, $A^2x = A^3x = \ldots = A^k x = x$. Hence, $x \in U(A^k)$ and $(I + A + \ldots + A^{k-1})x = x$; that is, $x \in (I + A + \ldots + A^{k-1})U(A^k)$.

Conversely, suppose $x \in U(A^k)$. Then $y = (I + A + \ldots + A^{k-1})x$, $Ay = Ax + A^2x + \ldots + A^k x = Ax + A^2x + \ldots + A^{k-1}x + Ix = y$; that is, $(I + A + \ldots + A^{k-1})U(A^k) \subseteq U(A)$. This proves the theorem.

Lemma 3.3 Every lattice module-homomorphism is a monotone mapping.

Proof Let H be a lattice module-homomorphism. Since $H(x + y) = H(x) + H(y)$, when $x \geq y$; that is $x + y = x$. Then $H(x + y) = H(x) = H(x) + H(y)$; that is, $H(x) \geq H(y)$.

Lemma 3.4 For the sequence $Ae, A^2e, \ldots$, there exists an p such that $A^pe = A^{p+1}e = A^{p+2}e = \ldots$, where e = (1, 1, ..., 1).

Proof Since e Ae, than Ae A^2e A^3e .... By Lemma 3.1 there exists a p such that $A^pe = A^{p+1}e = A^{p+2}e = \ldots$.

Theorem 3.3 For any square matrix A there exists a p such that A^pe is the greatest eigen vector of the matrix.

Proof By Lemma 3.4 for some p A^pe is an eigen vector. For any $x \in U(A)$, $e \geq x$. Hence, $Ae \geq Ax$ and $A^pe \geq A^px = x$, that is, A^pe is the greatest eigen vector.

Elie Sanchez's Algorithm is just based on this property of fuzzy matrices.

Theorem 3.4 Let AB = BA. Then $U(A) \cap U(B) = \langle MN \rangle$, where $M = A^p + A^{p+1} + \ldots + A^q$ and $A^{q+1} = A^p$; $N = B^r + B^{r+1} + \ldots + B^t$ and $B^{t+1} = B^r$.

Proof It is obvious that for every $x \in U(A) \cap U(B)$, that is $Ax = Bx = x$, $A^iB^jx = x$. Hence, $(A^p + \ldots + A^{q-1} + A^q)(B^r + \ldots + B^{t-1} + B^t)x = x$. This means that $x \in \langle MN \rangle$. Conversely, suppose $x \in \langle MN \rangle$. Since AMN = MN and BMN = MN, we see that $x \in U(A) \cap U(B)$.

4. CONCLUDING REMARKS

In this paper, the structure of the eigen fuzzy sets associated with a fuzzy relation has been explained and an algorithm given for all the eigen fuzzy sets. These results are very important for practical applications. For example, by means of the above algorithm, a fuzzy logic controller can automatically analyze its stability and determine its stable region [15].

The theoretical important of these results is obvious. The resolution problem of the eigen fuzzy sets has been solved. An interesting result is that this work associates the resolution of a fuzzy relation equation with the resolution of a eigen fuzzy sets equation. In fact, an element x is a solution of Ax = x iff the fuzzy relation equation My = x determined by A is solvable.

ACKNOWLEDGEMENT

This research was encouraged by Dr. Elie Sanchez during his visit to China. I wish also to thank my friend Liu Jia-quan of the Institute of Systems Science and Mathematical Sciences, Academia Sinica. I benefited greatly from many discussions with him during the preparation of this paper.

REFERENCES

[1] Sanchez, E., Resolution of eigen fuzzy sets equations, Fuzzy Sets and Systems 1 (1978), 69-74.

[2] Cao Zhi-qiang, Modern control theory of psychological phenomena, in Proceedings of

CAA-IEEE Bilateral Meeting on Control Systems, Shanghai China (August 1981).

[3] Give'on, Y., Lattice matrices, Information and Control 7 (1964), 477-484.

[4] Cao Zhi-qiang, An algebraic system generalizing the fuzzy sets of a set, in Paul P. Wang (Ed.) Advances in Fuzzy Set Theory and Applications (Plenum Publishing Corporation, New York, 1982).

[5] Kickert, W.J.M., and Mamdani, E.H., Analysis of a fuzzy logic controller, Fuzzy Sets and Systems 1 (1978), 29-44.

PART THREE

FUZZY LOGIC AND INFERENCE

Approximate Reasoning in Decision Analysis
M.M. Gupta and E. Sanchez (eds.)

FUZZY INFERENCE USING MAX-Δ COMPOSITION IN THE COMPOSITIONAL RULE OF INFERENCE

Masaharu MIZUMOTO

Information Science Center
Osaka Electro-Communication University
Neyagawa, Osaka, 572 Japan

This paper shows that most of fuzzy inference methods for fuzzy conditional "If x is A then y is B" with A and B being fuzzy concepts can infer quite reasonable consequences which fit our intuition with respect to several criteria such as modus ponens and modus tollens, if a new composition called "max-Δ composition" is used in the compositional rule of inference, though, as was pointed out before, reasonable consequences can not always be obtained when using the max-min composition which is used usually in the compositional rule of inference. Moreover, it is shown that a syllogism holds for most of the methods under the max-Δ composition, though they do not always satisfy the syllogism under the max-min composition.

Keywords: Fuzzy conditional inference, Compositional rule of inference, Fuzzy modus ponens, Fuzzy modus tollens, Max-Δ composition, Syllogism

1. INTRODUCTION

In our daily life we often make such an inference of the form:

Ant 1:	If x is A then y is B
Ant 2:	x is A'
Cons:	y is B'

where A, A', B and B' are fuzzy concepts. In order to make such an inference with fuzzy concepts, Zadeh [1] suggested an inference rule called "compositional rule of inference" which infers B' of Cons from Ant 1 and Ant 2 by taking the max-min composition of A' and the fuzzy relation which is translated from a fuzzy conditional proposition "If x is A then y is B." In this connection, he [1], Mamdani [2] and Mizumoto et al. [3-6] suggested several translating rules for translating the fuzzy proposition "If x is A then y is B" into a fuzzy relation.

In [4-6] we pointed out that the consequences inferred by Zadeh's and Mamdani's methods do not always fit our intuition, and suggested some new methods which get the consequences coinciding with our intuition with respect to several criteria such as modus ponens and modus tollens. Moreover, we have proposed in [7] a number of translating rules which are obtained by introducing implication rules of many-valued logic systems, but they were found not to infer reasonable consequences.

In this paper, on the contrary, we show that almost all the methods proposed before can infer quite reasonable consequences if, instead of the max-min composition usually used in the compositional rule of inference, we use a new composition called "max-Δ composition" in the compositional rule of inference, where Δ is the operation of "drastic product" introduced by Dubois [8]. Moreover, it is shown that the syllogism holds for most of these methods when using the max-Δ composition, though they do not satisfy the syllogism under the max-min composition [7].

2. FUZZY INFERENCE METHODS

We shall first consider the following form of inference in which a fuzzy conditional proposition is contained.

Ant 1:	If x is A then y is B	
Ant 2:	x is A'	(1)
Cons:	y is B'	

where x and y are the names of objects, and A, A', B and B' are fuzzy concepts represented by fuzzy sets in universes of discourse U, U, V and V, respectively. This form of inference may be viewed as a fuzzy modus ponens which reduces to the classical modus ponens when A' = A and B' = B.

Moreover, the following form of inference is also possible which also contains a fuzzy conditional proposition.

Ant 1:	If x is A then y is B	
Ant 2:	y is B'	(2)
Cons:	x is A'	

This inference can be considered as a fuzzy modus tollens which reduce to modus tollens when B' = not B and A' = not A.

The Ant 1 of the form "If x is A then y is B" in (1) and (2) may represent a certain relationship between A and B. From this point of view, several methods were proposed for the form of fuzzy conditional proposition "If x is A then y is B."

Let A and B be fuzzy sets in U and V, respectively, which are represented as

$$A = \int_U \mu_A(u)/u \; ; \qquad B = \int_V \mu_B(v)/v$$

and let $\times$, $\cup$, $\cap$, $\neg$ and $\oplus$ be cartesian product, union, intersection, complement and bounded-sum for fuzzy sets, respectively. Then the following fuzzy relations in U x V can be derived from the proposition "If x is A then y is B." The fuzzy relation Rm and Ra were proposed by Zadeh [1], Rc by Mamdani [2], and the others are by Mizumoto et al. [3-7] by introducing the implications of many-valued logic systems [9-11].

$$\begin{aligned} Rm &= (A \times B) \cup (\neg A \times V) \\ &= \int_{U\times V} (\mu_A(u) \wedge \mu_B(v)) \vee (1-\mu_A(u)) \,/\, (u,v). \end{aligned} \tag{3}$$

$$\begin{aligned} Ra &= (\neg A \times V) \oplus (U \times B) \\ &= \int_{U\times V} 1 \wedge (1-\mu_A(u)+\mu_B(v)) \,/\, (u,v). \end{aligned} \tag{4}$$

$$\begin{aligned} Rc &= A \times B \\ &= \int_{U\times V} \mu_A(u) \wedge \mu_B(v) \,/\, (u,v). \end{aligned} \tag{5}$$

$$\begin{aligned} Rs &= A \times V \underset{s}{\Longrightarrow} U \times B \\ &= \int_{U\times V} [\mu_A(u) \underset{s}{\rightarrow} \mu_B(v)] \,/\, (u,v), \end{aligned} \tag{6}$$

where

$$\mu_A(u) \underset{s}{\rightarrow} \mu_B(v) = \begin{cases} 1 & \ldots \ \mu_A(u) \leqq \mu_B(v), \\ 0 & \ldots \ \mu_A(u) > \mu_B(v). \end{cases}$$

$$\begin{aligned} Rg &= A \times V \underset{g}{\Longrightarrow} U \times B \\ &= \int_{U\times V} [\mu_A(u) \underset{g}{\rightarrow} \mu_B(v)] \,/\, (u,v), \end{aligned} \tag{7}$$

where

$$\mu_A(u) \underset{g}{\rightarrow} \mu_B(v) = \begin{cases} 1 & \ldots \ \mu_A(u) \leqq \mu_B(v), \\ \mu_B(v) & \ldots \ \mu_A(u) > \mu_B(v). \end{cases}$$

$$\begin{aligned} Rsg &= (A \times V \underset{s}{\Longrightarrow} U \times B) \cap (\neg A \times V \underset{g}{\Longrightarrow} U \times \neg B) \\ &= \int_{U\times V} [\mu_A(u) \underset{s}{\rightarrow} \mu_B(v)] \wedge [1-\mu_A(u) \underset{g}{\rightarrow} 1-\mu_B(v)] / (u,v). \end{aligned} \tag{8}$$

$$\begin{aligned} Rgg &= (A \times V \underset{g}{\Longrightarrow} U \times B) \cap (\neg A \times V \underset{g}{\Longrightarrow} U \times \neg B) \\ &= \int_{U\times V} [\mu_A(u) \underset{g}{\rightarrow} \mu_B(v)] \wedge [1-\mu_A(u) \underset{g}{\rightarrow} 1-\mu_B(v)] / (u,v). \end{aligned} \tag{9}$$

$$\begin{aligned} Rgs &= (A \times V \underset{g}{\Longrightarrow} U \times B) \cap (\neg A \times V \underset{s}{\Longrightarrow} U \times \neg B) \\ &= \int_{U\times V} [\mu_A(u) \underset{g}{\rightarrow} \mu_B(v)] \wedge [1-\mu_A(u) \underset{s}{\rightarrow} 1-\mu_B(v)] / (u,v). \end{aligned} \tag{10}$$

$$\begin{aligned} Rss &= (A \times V \underset{s}{\Longrightarrow} U \times B) \cap (\neg A \times V \underset{s}{\Longrightarrow} U \times \neg B) \\ &= \int_{U\times V} [\mu_A(u) \underset{s}{\rightarrow} \mu_B(v)] \wedge [1-\mu_A(u) \underset{s}{\rightarrow} 1-\mu_B(v)] / (u,v). \end{aligned} \tag{11}$$

$$\begin{aligned} Rb &= (\neg A \times V) \cup (U \times B) \\ &= \int_{U\times V} (1-\mu_A(u)) \vee \mu_B(v) \,/\, (u,v). \end{aligned} \tag{12}$$

$$\begin{aligned} R_\Delta &= A \times V \underset{\Delta}{\Longrightarrow} U \times B \\ &= \int_{U\times V} [\mu_A(u) \underset{\Delta}{\rightarrow} \mu_B(v)] \,/\, (u,v), \end{aligned} \tag{13}$$

where

$$\mu_A(u) \underset{\Delta}{\rightarrow} \mu_B(v) = \begin{cases} 1 & \ldots \ \mu_A(u) \leqq \mu_B(v), \\ \dfrac{\mu_B(v)}{\mu_A(u)} & \ldots \ \mu_A(u) > \mu_B(v). \end{cases}$$

$$\begin{aligned} R_\blacktriangle &= A \times V \underset{\blacktriangle}{\Longrightarrow} U \times B \\ &= \int_{U\times V} [\mu_A(u) \underset{\blacktriangle}{\rightarrow} \mu_B(v)] \,/\, (u,v), \end{aligned} \tag{14}$$

$$\begin{aligned} &\mu_A(u) \underset{\blacktriangle}{\rightarrow} \mu_B(v) \\ &\quad = [\mu_A(u) \underset{\Delta}{\rightarrow} \mu_B(v)] \wedge [1-\mu_B(v) \underset{\Delta}{\rightarrow} 1-\mu_A(u)] \\ &\quad = \begin{cases} 1 \wedge \dfrac{\mu_B(v)}{\mu_A(u)} \wedge \dfrac{1-\mu_A(u)}{1-\mu_B(v)} & \ldots \ \mu_A(u)>0,\ 1-\mu_B(v)>0, \\ 1 & \ldots \ \mu_A(u)=0 \text{ or } 1-\mu_B(v)=0. \end{cases} \end{aligned}$$

$$\begin{aligned} R_* &= A \times V \underset{*}{\Longrightarrow} U \times B \\ &= \int_{U\times V} [\mu_A(u) \underset{*}{\rightarrow} \mu_B(v)] \,/\, (u,v), \\ &\mu_A(u) \underset{*}{\rightarrow} \mu_B(v) = 1 - \mu_A(u) + \mu_A(u)\mu_B(v). \end{aligned} \tag{15}$$

$$\begin{aligned} R_\# &= A \times V \underset{\#}{\Longrightarrow} U \times B \\ &= \int_{U\times V} [\mu_A(u) \underset{\#}{\rightarrow} \mu_B(v)] \,/\, (u,v), \end{aligned} \tag{16}$$

$$\begin{aligned} &\mu_A(u) \underset{\#}{\rightarrow} \mu_B(v) \\ &= (\mu_A(u) \wedge \mu_B(v)) \vee (1-\mu_A(u) \wedge 1-\mu_B(v)) \vee (\mu_B(v) \wedge 1-\mu_A(u)) \\ &= (1-\mu_A(u) \vee \mu_B(v)) \wedge (\mu_A(u) \vee 1-\mu_A(u)) \wedge (\mu_B(v) \vee 1-\mu_B(v)). \end{aligned}$$

$$\begin{aligned} R_\square &= A \times V \underset{\square}{\Longrightarrow} U \times B \\ &= \int_{U\times V} [\mu_A(u) \underset{\square}{\rightarrow} \mu_B(v)] \,/\, (u,v), \end{aligned} \tag{17}$$

$$\mu_A(u) \underset{\square}{\rightarrow} \mu_B(v) = \begin{cases} 1 & \ldots \ \mu_A(u)<1 \text{ or } \mu_B(v)=1, \\ 0 & \ldots \ \mu_A(u)=1,\ \mu_B(v)<1. \end{cases}$$

In order to define a new composition "max-$\hat{\wedge}$ composition" which will be used in the compositional rule of inference, we shall introduce a new binary operation $\hat{\wedge}$ called "drastic product" which is the operation Tw(x,y) by Dubois [8].

For $x,\ y \in [0,1]$,

$$x \,\hat{\wedge}\, y = Tw(x,y) = \begin{cases} x & \ldots \ y = 1, \\ y & \ldots \ x = 1, \\ 0 & \ldots \ x,\ y < 1. \end{cases} \tag{18}$$

Using this operation, we can easily define a new composition of "max-$\hat{\wedge}$ composition" of a fuzzy set A in U and a fuzzy relation R in UxV.

Max-▲ Composition:

$$\mu_{A▲R}(v) = \bigvee_u \{\mu_A(u) \mathbin{▲} \mu_R(u,v)\}. \quad (19)$$

From the definition of max-▲ composition "▲" we can have the following properties which will be useful to discuss the fuzzy conditional inference. The more detailed properties of max-▲ composition ▲ and drastic product ▲ are found in [8,12].

Let A, A_1 and A_2 be fuzzy sets in U, and R, R_1 and R_2 be fuzzy relations in U x V, then

$$A ▲ (R_1 \cup R_2) = (A ▲ R_1) \cup (A ▲ R_2), \quad (20)$$

$$(A_1 \cup A_2) ▲ R = (A_1 ▲ R) \cup (A_2 ▲ R), \quad (21)$$

$$A ▲ (R_1 \cap R_2) \subseteq (A ▲ R_1) \cap (A ▲ R_2), \quad (22)$$

$$(A_1 \cap A_2) ▲ R \subseteq (A_1 ▲ R) \cap (A_2 ▲ R). \quad (23)$$

Now, we shall begin with the fuzzy modus ponens in (1). Using the max-▲ composition (19), we can deduce the consequence B' of Cons in (1) from Ant 1 and Ant 2 by taking the max-▲ composition "▲" of the fuzzy set A' and the fuzzy relation given in (3)-(17). For example, we can have for the method Rm of (3)

$$Bm' = A' ▲ Rm$$

$$= A' ▲ [(A \times B) \cup (\neg A \times V)]. \quad (24)$$

The membership function of the fuzzy set Bm' in V is given as

$$\mu_{Bm'}(v) = \bigvee_u \{\mu_{A'}(u) \mathbin{▲} \mu_{Rm}(u,v)\} \quad (25)$$

$$= \bigvee_u \{\mu_{A'}(u) \mathbin{▲} [(\mu_A(u) \wedge \mu_B(v)) \vee (1-\mu_A(u))]\}.$$

In the same way, we have

$$Ba' = A' ▲ Ra = A' ▲ [(\neg A \times V) \oplus (U \times B)]. \quad (26)$$

$$Bc' = A' ▲ Rc = A' ▲ (A \times B). \quad (27)$$

$$Bs' = A' ▲ Rs = A' ▲ [A \times V \underset{s}{\Longrightarrow} U \times B]. \quad (28)$$

$$\vdots$$

Similarly, in the fuzzy modus tollens of (2), the consequence A' in Cons can be deduced using the composition "▲" of the fuzzy relation and the fuzzy set B'. Namely,

$$Am' = Rm ▲ B'$$

$$= [(A \times B) \cup (\neg A \times V)] ▲ B' \quad (29)$$

$$= \int_U \bigvee_v \{[(\mu_A(u) \wedge \mu_B(v)) \vee (1-\mu_A(u))] \mathbin{▲} \mu_{B'}(v)\}/u.$$

$$Aa' = Ra ▲ B' = [(\neg A \times V) \oplus (U \times B)] ▲ B'. \quad (30)$$

$$Ac' = Rc ▲ B' = (A \times B) ▲ B'. \quad (31)$$

$$As' = Rs ▲ B' = [A \times V \underset{s}{\Longrightarrow} U \times B] ▲ B'. \quad (32)$$

$$\vdots$$

3. COMPARISON OF FUZZY INFERENCE METHODS UNDER MAX-▲ COMPOSITION

In this section we shall make comparison of the fuzzy inference methods obtained above by applying 15 fuzzy relations (3)-(17) to the fuzzy modus ponens (1) and the fuzzy modus tollens (2).

In the fuzzy modus ponens, we shall show what the consequences Bm', Ba', Bc', ... will be when using the max-▲ composition of the fuzzy set A' and the fuzzy relation, where the fuzzy set A' is

$$A' = A = \int_U \mu_A(u)/u,$$

$$A' = \underline{\text{very}}\ A = A^2 = \int_U \mu_A(u)^2/u,$$

$$A' = \underline{\text{more or less}}\ A = A^{0.5} = \int_U \mu_A(u)^{0.5}/u,$$

$$A' = \underline{\text{not}}\ A = \neg A = \int_U 1-\mu_A(u)/u,$$

which are typical examples of A'.

Similarly, in the fuzzy modus tollens we shall show the consequences Am', Aa', Ac', ... under the max-▲ composition (as in (29)-(32)) of the fuzzy relation and the fuzzy set B', where B' is

$$B' = \underline{\text{not}}\ B = \neg B = \int_V 1-\mu_B(v)/v,$$

$$B' = \underline{\text{not very}}\ B = \neg B^2 = \int_V 1-\mu_B(v)^2/v,$$

$$B' = \underline{\text{not more or less}}\ B = \neg B^{0.5}$$

$$= \int_V 1-\mu_B(v)^{0.5}/v,$$

$$B' = B = \int_V \mu_B(v)/v.$$

We shall begin with the fuzzy modus ponens in (1). We assume in the discussion of fuzzy modus ponens that $\mu_A(u)$ takes all values in [0,1] according to u varying all over U, that is, μ_A is a function onto [0,1]. Clearly, from this assumption, the fuzzy set A is a normal fuzzy set.

We shall first discuss Rm and obtain Bm' of (24). From the above assumption, the expression (25) can be rewritten as

$$b_{m'} = \bigvee_x \{x' \mathbin{▲} [(x \wedge b) \vee (1-x)]\}, \quad (33)$$

and $f(x) = x' \mathbin{▲} [(x \wedge b) \vee (1-x)]$, (34)

by letting

$$\mu_A(u) = x,\ \mu_{A'}(u) = x',\ \mu_B(v) = b,\quad \mu_{Bm'}(v) = b_{m'}. \quad (35)$$

The expression $(x \wedge b) \vee (1-x)$ in (33) can be shown in Fig.1(a) by using a parameter b.

When A' is A, x' becomes x. Thus, f(x) of (34) is

$$f(x) = x \mathbin{▲} [(x \wedge b) \vee (1-x)].$$

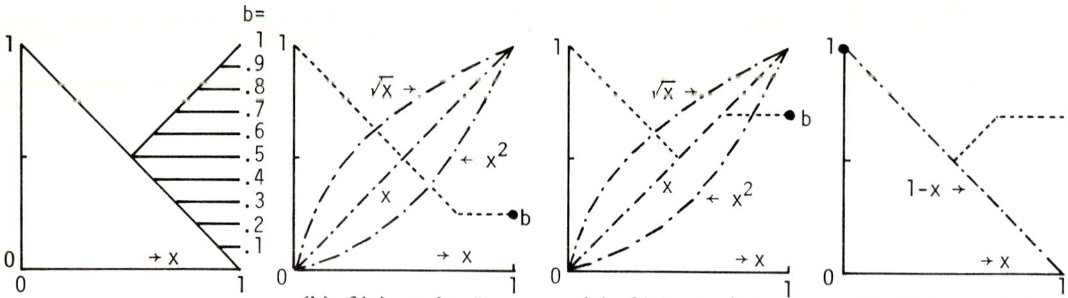

(a) (x∧b)∨(1-x) (b) f(x) at b≦.5 (black circle) (c) f(x) at b≧.5 (black circle) (d) f(x) at x'=1-x (black circle)

Fig.1 $f(x) = x' \wedge [(x \wedge b) \vee (1-x)]$ of (34) at $x' = x, x^2, \sqrt{x}$ and $1-x$

For example, at $b \leqq 0.5$, $f(x)$ is shown by the black circle in Fig.1(b), i.e.,

$$f(x) = \begin{cases} b & \dots\ x = 1, \\ 0 & \dots\ x < 1. \end{cases}$$

Hence,

$$b_{m'} = \bigvee_x f(x) = b.$$

In the same way, at $b \geqq 0.5$, $f(x)$ is shown by the black circle in Fig.1(c). Thus,

$$b_{m'} = \bigvee_x f(x) = b.$$

In general, we can obtain $b_{m'} = b$ for any b. In other words, we have $b_{m'} = b$ when $x' = x$, which leads to $Bm' = B$ at $A' = A$. Hence, from (24) the following is obtained. This shows that the so-called modus ponens is satisfied under the max-$\wedge$ composition "▲". Note that modus ponens does not hold for the max-min composition [4].

$$Bm' = A \blacktriangle Rm = B. \tag{36}$$

Similarly, at A' = very A (i.e., $x' = x^2$) and A' = more or less A (i.e., $x' = \sqrt{x}$), we can have $b_{m'} = b$ for any b from Fig.1(b) and (c). Therefore,

$$Bm' = \text{very } A \blacktriangle Rm = B, \tag{37}$$

$$Bm' = \text{more or less } A \blacktriangle Rm = B. \tag{38}$$

Finally, when A' = not A (i.e., $x' = 1-x$), $f(x)$ of (34) is

$$f(x) = (1-x) \wedge [(x \wedge b) \vee (1-x)]$$

and given from Fig.1(d) by

$$f(x) = \begin{cases} 1 & \dots\ x = 0, \\ 0 & \dots\ x > 0, \end{cases}$$

for any b. Thus,

$$b_{m'} = \bigvee_x f(x) = 1,$$

which leads to $b_{m'} = 1$ at $x' = 1-x$, that is, Bm' = unknown at A' = not A. Therefore,

$$\text{not } A \blacktriangle Rm = \text{unknown}. \tag{39}$$

We can obtain the consequences Ba', Bc', Bs', ..., $B_\square'$ in the same way as Bm', and thus we omit the ways of how to obtain them. Table I summarizes the consequences inferred by all the fuzzy inference methods (3)-(17).

We shall next discuss the fuzzy modus tollens in (2). In the case of fuzzy modus tollens, we shall assume that μ_B is a function onto [0,1]. We shall investigate only the case of R_Δ of (13) because of the limitation of space.

The consequence A_Δ' is obtained by

$$A_\Delta' = R_\Delta \blacktriangle B',$$

$$\mu_{A_\Delta'}(u) = \bigvee_v \{[\mu_A(u) \underset{\Delta}{\rightarrow} \mu_B(v)] \wedge \mu_{B'}(v)\}. \tag{40}$$

From the assumption, this expression can be re-written as

$$a_\Delta' = \bigvee_x [a \underset{\Delta}{\rightarrow} x] \wedge x', \tag{41}$$

$$g(x) = [a \underset{\Delta}{\rightarrow} x] \wedge x', \tag{42}$$

where

$$x = \mu_B(v), \quad x' = \mu_{B'}(v), \quad a = \mu_A(u),$$

$$a_\Delta' = \mu_{A_\Delta'}(u),$$

$$a \underset{\Delta}{\rightarrow} x = \begin{cases} 1 & \dots\ a \leqq x, \\ \frac{x}{a} & \dots\ a > x. \end{cases} \tag{43}$$

The expression (43) with parameter a is depicted in Fig.2(a).

When B' is not B, x' becomes $1-x$. Thus, $g(x)$ of (42) becomes

$$g(x) = [a \underset{\Delta}{\rightarrow} x] \wedge (1-x)$$

and is obtained from Fig.2(b) as

$$g(x) = \begin{cases} 1-x & \dots\ a \leqq x \leqq 1, \\ 0 & \dots\ \text{otherwise}. \end{cases}$$

Table I Inference results by each method (Case of fuzzy modus ponens)

	A	very A	more or less A	not A
Rm	B	B	B	unknown
Ra	B	B	more or less B	unknown
Rc	B	B	B	$\emptyset$
Rs	B	very B	more or less B	unknown
Rg	B	B	more or less B	unknown
Rsg	B	very B	more or less B	not B
Rgg	B	B	more or less B	not B
Rgs	B	B	more or less B	not B
Rss	B	very B	more or less B	not B
Rb	B	B	B	unknown
$R_\triangle$	B	B	more or less B	unknown
$R_\blacktriangle$	B	very B	more or less B	unknown
R_*	B	B	B	unknown
$R_\#$	B	B	B	B ∪ not B
$R_\square$	unknown	unknown	unknown	unknown

Table II Inference results by each method (Case of fuzzy modus tollens)

	not B	not very B	not more or less B	B
Rm	not A	not A	not A	A ∪ not A
Ra	not A	not very A	not A	unknown
Rc	$\emptyset$	$\emptyset$	$\emptyset$	A
Rs	not A	not very A	not more or less A	unknown
Rg	not A	not very A	not more or less A	unknown
Rsg	not A	not very A	not more or less A	A
Rgg	not A	not very A	not more or less A	A
Rgs	not A	not very A	not more or less A	A
Rss	not A	not very A	not more or less A	A
Rb	not A	not A	not A	unknown
$R_\triangle$	not A	not very A	not more or less A	unknown
$R_\blacktriangle$	not A	not very A	not more or less A	unknown
R_*	not A	not A	not A	unknown
$R_\#$	not A	not A	not A	A ∪ not A
$R_\square$	$\{^{1 .. \mu_A<1}_{0 .. \mu_A=1}$	$\{^{1 .. \mu_A<1}_{0 .. \mu_A=1}$	$\{^{1 \ldots \mu_A<1}_{0 \ldots \mu_A=1}$	unknown

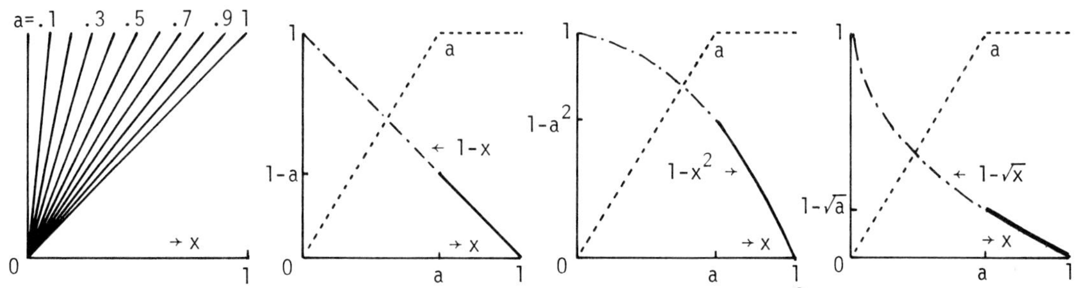

(a) $a \underset{\triangle}{\rightarrow} x$ (b) g(x) at x'=1-x (c) g(x) at $x'=1-x^2$ (d) g(x) at $x'=1-\sqrt{x}$

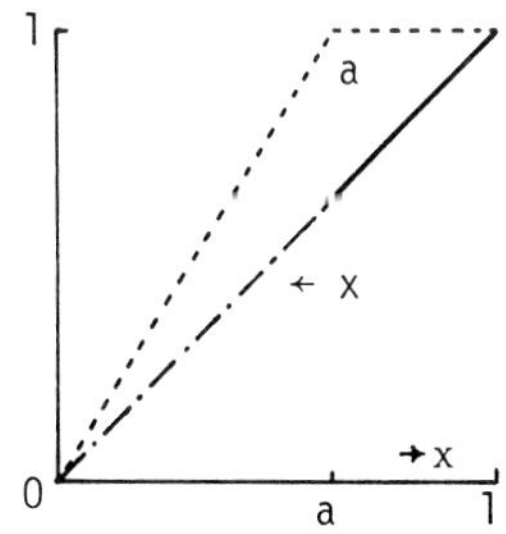

(e) g(x) at x'=x

Fig.2 $g(x) = [a \underset{\triangle}{\rightarrow} x] \blacktriangle x'$ of (42) (solid line)

Hence,

$$a_\triangle' = \bigvee_x g(x) = \bigvee_{x\varepsilon[a,1]} 1-x = 1-a$$

for any a. Therefore, $a_\triangle' = 1-a$ at $x' = 1-x$, that is, $A_\triangle' =$ not A at B' = not B. Stated alternatively,

$$A_\triangle' = R_\triangle \blacktriangle \text{ not } B = \text{not } A. \quad (44)$$

When B' = not very B (i.e., $x' = 1 - x^2$), g(x) of (42) will be

$$g(x) = \begin{cases} 1 - x^2 & \ldots \ a \leqq x \leqq 1, \\ 0 & \ldots \ \text{otherwise}, \end{cases}$$

from Fig.2(c). Thus,

$$a_\triangle' = \bigvee_x g(x) = \bigvee_{x\varepsilon[a,1]} 1 - x^2 = 1 - a^2.$$

Therefore, we have $a_\triangle' = 1 - a^2$ at $x' = 1 - x^2$. Namely,

$$A_\triangle' = R_\triangle \blacktriangle \text{ not very } B = \text{not very } A. \quad (45)$$

At B' = not more or less B ($x' = 1 - \sqrt{x}$), g(x) is given by

Table III Relations between Ant 2 and Cons under Ant 1 for the fuzzy modus ponens in (1)

	x is A'	y is B'
Relation I (modus ponens)	x is A	y is B
Relation II-1	x is very A	y is very B
Relation II-2	x is very A	y is B
Relation III-1	x is more or less A	y is more or less B
Relation III-2	x is more or less A	y is B
Relation IV-1	x is not A	y is unknown
Relation IV-2	x is not A	y is not B

Table IV Relations between Ant 2 and Cons under Ant 1 for the fuzzy modus tollens in (2)

	y is B'	x is A'
Relation V (modus tollens)	y is not B	x is not A
Relation VI-1	y is not very B	x is not very A
Relation VI-2	y is not very B	x is not A
Relation VII-1	y is not more or less B	x is not more or less A
Relation VII-2	y is not more or less B	x is not A
Relation VIII-1	y is B	x is unknown
Relation VIII-2	y is B	x is A

$$g(x) = \begin{cases} 1 - \sqrt{x} & \ldots \quad a \leqq x \leqq 1, \\ 0 & \ldots \quad \text{otherwise}, \end{cases}$$

and

$$a_\Delta' = \bigvee_{x \in [a,1]} 1 - \sqrt{x} = 1 - \sqrt{a}.$$

Therefore,

$$A_\Delta' = R_\Delta \blacktriangle \underline{\text{not more or less}}\ B = \underline{\text{not more or less}}\ A. \tag{46}$$

Finally, at B' = B (x' = x)

$$g(x) = \begin{cases} x & \ldots \quad a \leqq x \leqq 1, \\ 0 & \ldots \quad \text{otherwise}. \end{cases}$$

$$a_\Delta' = \bigvee_{x \in [a,1]} x = 1.$$

Therefore,

$$A_\Delta' = R_\Delta \blacktriangle B = \underline{\text{unknown}}. \tag{47}$$

We can obtain the consequences Am', Aa', Ac', ..., $A_\square$' in the same way as R_Δ'. In Table II the inference results by all the methods are listed.

In the forms of fuzzy conditional inferences (1) and (2), it seems according to our intuition that the relations between A' in Ant 2 and B' in Cons of the fuzzy modus ponens (1) ought to be satisfied as shown in Table III (cf. [4,5]). Similarly, the relations between B' in Ant 2 and A' in Cons of the fuzzy modus tollens (2) ought to be satisfied as in Table IV.

In Table V, the satisfaction (O) or failure (X) of each relation in Tables III and IV under each fuzzy inference method is indicated by using the consequence results of Tables I and II. In order to compare the inference results under the max-△ composition and the max-min composition, the inference results under the max-min composition is listed in Table VI [7].

From Tables I, II and V it follows that all the inference methods except $R_\square$ can satisfy the so-called modus ponens under the max-△ composition, but only the methods Rc, Rs, ..., Rss can satisfy the modus ponens under the max-min composition. The same holds for modus tollens. Moreover, it is found that almost all the methods can infer quite reasonable consequences under the max-△ composition, though we can not always get reasonable consequences under the max-min composition as shown in Table VI.

4. SYLLOGISM BY EACH METHOD UNDER MAX-△ COMPOSITION

In this section we shall investigate a syllogism by each fuzzy inference method under the max-△ composition.

Let P_1, P_2 and P_3 be fuzzy conditional propositions such as

P_1: If x is A then y is B

P_2: If y is B then z is C

P_3: If x is A then z is C

where A, B and C are fuzzy sets in U, V and W, respectively. If the proposition P_3 is deduced from the propositions P_1 and P_2, that is, the following holds:

P_1: If x is A then y is B
P_2: If y is B then z is C
―――――――――――――
P_3: If x is A then z is C

then it is said that a syllogism holds.

Let R(A,B), R(B,C) and R(A,C) be fuzzy relations in UxV, VxW and UxW, respectively, which are obtained from the propositions P_1, P_2 and P_3, respectively. If the following equality holds, the syllogism holds under the max-△ composition.

$$R(A,B) \blacktriangle R(B,C) = R(A,C). \tag{48}$$

That is to say,

P_1: If x is A then y is B ⟶ R(A,B)
P_2: If y is B then z is C ⟶ R(B,C) (49)
――――――――――――――――――――
P_3: If x is A then z is C ⟵ R(A,B)▲R(B,C)

where "▲" is the max-△ composition of R(A,B) and R(B,C), and the membership function of R(A,B) ▲ R(B,C) is given by

Table V Satisfaction of each relation in Tables III and IV under each method
(The case of max-$\wedge$ composition)

	Ant 2	Cons	Rm	Ra	Rc	Rs	Rg	Rsg	Rgg	Rgs	Rss	Rb	$R_{\triangle}$	$R_{\blacktriangle}$	R_{*}	$R_{\#}$	$R_{\square}$
Relation I (modus ponens)	A	B	O	O	O	O	O	O	O	O	O	O	O	O	O	O	X
Relation II-1	very A	very B	X	X	X	O	X	O	X	X	O	X	X	O	X	X	X
Relation II-2	very A	B	O	O	O	X	O	X	O	O	X	O	O	X	O	O	X
Relation III-1	more or less A	more or less B	X	O	X	O	O	O	O	O	O	X	O	O	X	X	X
Relation III-2	more or less A	B	O	X	O	X	X	X	X	X	X	O	X	X	O	O	X
Relation IV-1	not A	unknown	O	O	X	O	O	X	X	X	X	O	O	O	O	X	O
Relation IV-2	not A	not B	X	X	X	X	X	O	O	O	O	X	X	X	X	X	X
Relation V (modus tollens)	not B	not A	O	O	X	O	O	O	O	O	O	O	O	O	O	O	X
Relation VI-1	not very B	not very A	X	O	X	O	O	O	O	O	O	X	O	O	X	X	X
Relation VI-2	not very B	not A	O	X	X	X	X	X	X	X	X	O	X	X	O	O	X
Relation VII-1	not more or less B	not more or less A	X	X	X	O	O	O	O	O	O	X	O	O	X	X	X
Relation VII-2	not more or less B	not A	O	O	X	X	X	X	X	X	X	O	X	X	O	O	X
Relation VIII-1	B	unknown	X	O	X	O	O	X	X	X	X	O	O	O	O	X	O
Relation VIII-2	B	A	X	X	O	X	X	O	O	O	O	X	X	X	X	X	X

Table VI Satisfaction of each relation in Tables III and IV under each method
(The case of max-min composition) (cf. [7])

	Ant 2	Cons	Rm	Ra	Rc	Rs	Rg	Rsg	Rgg	Rgs	Rss	Rb	$R_{\triangle}$	$R_{\blacktriangle}$	R_{*}	$R_{\#}$	$R_{\square}$
Relation I (modus ponens)	A	B	X	X	O	O	O	O	O	O	O	X	X	X	X	X	X
Relation II-1	very A	very B	X	X	X	O	X	O	X	X	O	X	X	X	X	X	X
Relation II-2	very A	B	X	X	O	X	O	X	O	O	X	X	X	X	X	X	X
Relation III-1	more or less A	more or less B	X	X	X	O	O	O	O	O	O	X	X	X	X	X	X
Relation III-2	more or less A	B	X	X	O	X	X	X	X	X	X	X	X	X	X	X	X
Relation IV-1	not A	unknown	O	O	X	O	O	X	X	X	X	O	O	O	O	X	O
Relation IV-2	not A	not B	X	X	X	X	X	O	O	O	O	X	X	X	X	X	X
Relation V (modus tollens)	not B	not A	X	X	X	O	X	O	X	X	O	X	X	X	X	X	X
Relation VI-1	not very B	not very A	X	X	X	O	X	O	X	X	O	X	X	X	X	X	X
Relation VI-2	not very B	not A	X	X	X	X	X	X	X	X	X	X	X	X	X	X	X
Relation VII-1	not more or less B	not more or less A	X	X	X	O	X	O	X	X	O	X	X	X	X	X	X
Relation VII-2	not more or less B	not A	X	X	X	X	X	X	X	X	X	X	X	X	X	X	X
Relation VIII-1	B	unknown	X	O	X	O	O	X	X	X	X	O	O	O	O	X	O
Relation VIII-2	B	A	X	X	O	X	X	X	X	O	O	X	X	X	X	X	X

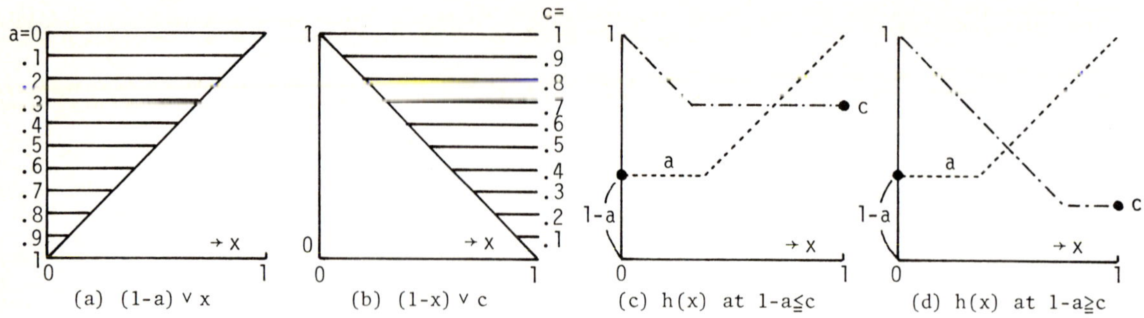

Fig.3 $h(x) = [(1-a) \vee x] \vartriangle [(1-x) \vee c]$ of (52) (black circles)

$$\mu_{R(A,B)\blacktriangle R(B,C)}(u,w) = \bigvee_v \{\mu_{R(A,B)}(u,v) \vartriangle \mu_{R(B,C)}(v,w)\}. \quad (50)$$

Now we shall obtain $R(A,B) \blacktriangle R(B,C)$ under each fuzzy inference method and show whether the syllogism holds or not. In the discussion of the syllogism it is assumed that the membership function μ_B of the fuzzy set B is a function onto [0,1].

We shall discuss only the case of Rb of (12). The fuzzy relations Rb(A,B) and Rb(B,C) are obtained from the propositions P_1 and P_2 by using (12).

$$Rb(A,B) = (\neg A \times V) \cup (U \times B),$$

$$Rb(B,C) = (\neg B \times W) \cup (V \times C).$$

Thus, the max-$\vartriangle$ composition of Rb(A,B) and Rb(B,C) will be

$$Rb(A,B) \blacktriangle Rb(B,C) = [(\neg A \times V) \cup (U \times B)] \blacktriangle [(\neg B \times W) \cup (V \times C)]$$

and its membership function is as follows.

$$\mu_{Rb(A,B)\blacktriangle Rb(B,C)}(u,w) = \bigvee_v \{[(1-\mu_A(u)) \vee \mu_B(v)] \vartriangle [(1-\mu_B(v)) \vee \mu_C(w)]\}.$$

Moreover, this expression can be rewritten as

$$d = \bigvee_x \{[(1-a) \vee x] \vartriangle [(1-x) \vee c]\}, \quad (51)$$

$$h(x) = [(1-a) \vee x] \vartriangle [(1-x) \vee c] \quad (52)$$

under the above assumption that μ_B is a function onto [0,1], where

$$d = \mu_{Rb(A,B)\blacktriangle Rb(B,C)}(u,w), \quad a = \mu_A(u),$$

$$x = \mu_B(v), \quad c = \mu_C(w).$$

The expression $(1-a) \vee x$ of (52) can be depicted in Fig.3(a) by using parameter a, and the expression $(1-x) \vee c$ is shown by using parameter c as in Fig.3(b).

When $1-a \leq c$, the function h(x) of (52) is given by the black circles in Fig.3(c), i.e.,

$$h(x) = \begin{cases} 1-a & \ldots \; x = 0, \\ c & \ldots \; x = 1, \\ 0 & \ldots \; \text{otherwise}. \end{cases}$$

Thus, d of (51) is obtained by

$$d = \bigvee_x h(x) = c \quad \ldots \text{ at } 1-a \leq c. \quad (53)$$

On the other hand, when $1-a \geq c$, h(x) is given by the black circles in Fig.3(d). Thus,

$$d = 1 - a \quad \ldots \text{ at } 1-a \geq c. \quad (54)$$

Therefore, from (53) and (54) we have

$$d = (1-a) \vee c$$

for any a and c, i.e.,

$$\mu_{Rb(A,B)\blacktriangle Rb(B,C)}(u,w) = (1 - \mu_A(u)) \vee \mu_C(w), \quad (55)$$

which indicates

$$Rb(A,B) \blacktriangle Rb(B,C) = Rb(A,C). \quad (56)$$

Therefore, the syllogism holds for Rb under the max-$\vartriangle$ composition "$\blacktriangle$". Note that the syllogism does not hold under the max-min composition [7].

In the same way, we can obtain $R(A,B) \blacktriangle R(B,C)$ by the other fuzzy inference methods and thus we shall list the results in the following.

$$Rm(A,B) \blacktriangle Rm(B,C) = \int_{U\times W} f(\mu_A(u),\mu_C(w)) \,/\, (u,w) \quad (57)$$

$$\neq Rm(A,C) \; \left(= \int_{U\times W} (\mu_A(u) \wedge \mu_C(w)) \vee (1-\mu_A(u)) / (u,w)\right)$$

where

$$f(\mu_A(u),\mu_C(w)) = \begin{cases} \mu_C(w) & \ldots \; \mu_A(u)=1, \\ \mu_A(u) \vee (1-\mu_A(u)) & \ldots \; \mu_C(w)=1, \\ 0 & \ldots \; \text{otherwise}. \end{cases}$$

Table VII Satisfaction of syllogism under the max-$\blacktriangle$ composition and max-min composition

	Rm	Ra	Rc	Rs	Rg	Rsg	Rgg	Rgs	Rss	Rb	$R_\triangle$	$R_\blacktriangle$	R_*	$R_\#$	$R_\square$
Max-$\blacktriangle$ composition	X	0	X	0	0	0	0	0	0	0	0	0	X	X	0
Max-min composition	X	X	0	0	0	0	0	0	0	X	X	X	X	X	0

$$Ra(A,B) \blacktriangle Ra(B,C) = \int_{U\times W} 1 \wedge (1 - \mu_A(u) + \mu_C(w)) / (u,w) = Ra(A,C). \quad (58)$$

$$Rc(A,B) \blacktriangle Rc(B,C) = \int_{U\times W} f(\mu_A(u),\mu_C(w)) / (u,w) \neq Rc(A,C) \ (= \int_{U\times W} \mu_A(u) \wedge \mu_C(w) / (u,w)), \quad (59)$$

where

$$f(\mu_A(u),\mu_C(w)) = \begin{cases} \mu_C(w) & \ldots \ \mu_A(u) = 1, \\ \mu_A(u) & \ldots \ \mu_C(w) = 1, \\ 0 & \ldots \ \text{otherwise.} \end{cases}$$

$$Rs(A,B) \blacktriangle Rs(B,C) = \int_{U\times W} \mu_A(u) \underset{s}{\rightarrow} \mu_C(w) / (u,w) = Rs(A,C). \quad (60)$$

$$Rg(A,B) \blacktriangle Rg(B,C) = \int_{U\times W} \mu_A(u) \underset{g}{\rightarrow} \mu_C(w) / (u,w) = Rg(A,C). \quad (61)$$

$$Rsg(A,B) \blacktriangle Rsg(B,C) = \int_{U\times W} [\mu_A(u) \underset{s}{\rightarrow} \mu_C(w)] \wedge [1-\mu_A(u) \underset{g}{\rightarrow} 1-\mu_C(w)]/(u,w) = Rsg(A,C). \quad (62)$$

$$Rgg(A,B) \blacktriangle Rgg(B,C) = \int_{U\times W} [\mu_A(u) \underset{g}{\rightarrow} \mu_C(w)] \wedge [1-\mu_A(u) \underset{g}{\rightarrow} 1-\mu_C(w)]/(u,w) = Rgg(A,C). \quad (63)$$

$$Rgs(A,B) \blacktriangle Rgs(B,C) = \int_{U\times W} [\mu_A(u) \underset{g}{\rightarrow} \mu_C(w)] \wedge [1-\mu_A(u) \underset{s}{\rightarrow} 1-\mu_C(w)]/(u,w) = Rgs(A,C). \quad (64)$$

$$Rss(A,B) \blacktriangle Rss(B,C) = \int_{U\times W} [\mu_A(u) \underset{s}{\rightarrow} \mu_C(w)] \wedge [1-\mu_A(u) \underset{s}{\rightarrow} 1-\mu_C(w)]/(u,w) = Rss(A,C). \quad (65)$$

$$Rb(A,B) \blacktriangle Rb(B,C) = \int_{U\times W} (1 - \mu_A(u)) \vee \mu_C(w) / (u,w) = Rb(A,C). \quad (66)$$

$$R_\triangle(A,B) \blacktriangle R_\triangle(B,C) = \int_{U\times W} \mu_A(u) \underset{\triangle}{\rightarrow} \mu_C(w) / (u,w) = R_\triangle(A,C). \quad (67)$$

$$R_\blacktriangle(A,B) \blacktriangle R_\blacktriangle(B,C) = \int_{U\times W} \mu_A(u) \underset{\blacktriangle}{\rightarrow} \mu_C(w) / (u,w) = R_\blacktriangle(A,C). \quad (68)$$

$$R_*(A,B) \blacktriangle R_*(B,C) = \int_{U\times W} (1 - \mu_A(u)) \vee \mu_C(w) / (u,w) \quad (69)$$

$$\neq R_*(A,C) \ (= \int_{U\times W} 1-\mu_A(u)+\mu_A(u)\mu_C(w)/(u,w)).$$

$$R_\#(A,B) \blacktriangle R_\#(B,C) = \int_{U\times W} f(\mu_A(u),\mu_C(w)) / (u,w)$$

$$\neq R_\#(A,C) \quad (70)$$

$$(= \int_{U\times W} (1-\mu_A(u) \vee \mu_C(w)) \wedge (\mu_A(u) \vee 1-\mu_A(u)) \wedge (1-\mu_C(w) \vee \mu_C(w)) / (u,w)),$$

where

$$f(\mu_A(u),\mu_C(w)) = \begin{cases} \mu_C(w) \vee (1-\mu_C(w)) & \ldots \ \mu_A(u) = 0, \\ \mu_C(w) & \ldots \ \mu_A(u) = 1, \\ 1 - \mu_A(u) & \ldots \ \mu_C(w) = 0, \\ \mu_A(u) \vee (1-\mu_A(u)) & \ldots \ \mu_C(w) = 1, \\ 0 & \ldots \ \text{otherwise.} \end{cases}$$

$$R_\square(A,B) \blacktriangle R_\square(B,C) = \int_{U\times W} \mu_A(u) \underset{\square}{\rightarrow} \mu_C(w) / (u,w) = R_\square(A,C). \quad (71)$$

Using these results, the satisfaction (0) or failure (X) of the syllogism by each method under the max-▵ composition is listed in Table VII. This table also contains the results under the max-min composition (cf. [7]).

It follows from Table VII that the methods Ra, Rb, R_Δ and $R_\blacktriangle$ can satisfy the syllogism under the max-▵ composition, though they do not satisfy it under the max-min composition. But the converse holds for Rc.

5. CONCLUSION

We have shown that, when the max-▵ composition is used in the compositional rule of inference, most of the fuzzy inference methods can get quite reasonable consequences which coincide with our intuition with respect to several criteria such as modus ponens, modus tollens and syllogism.

It will be of interest to apply the max-▵ composition to fuzzy inferences which are of the more complicated form such as

If x is A then y is B else y is C.
x is A'.
―――――――――――――――
y is D.

If x is A_1 then y is B_1 else
If x is A_2 then y is B_2 else
⋮
If x is A_n then y is B_n.
x is A'.
―――――――――――――――
y is B'.

These results will be presented in subsequent papers.

Acknowledgment

This work was attained during the author's stay (Nov. 1980-Aug. 1981) at RWTH Aachen, West Germany, with the assistance of the Alexander von Humboldt Foundation. He acknowledges the invaluable help of Prof.Dr. H.-J. Zimmermann and the members of fuzzy research group at RWTH Aachen.

REFERENCES

[1] Zadeh, L.A., Calculus of fuzzy restriction, in Zadeh, L.A., Fu, K.S., Tanaka, K. and Shimura, M. (eds.), Fuzzy Sets and Their Applications to Cognitive and Decision Processes (Academic Press, New York, 1975), 1-39.

[2] Mamdani, E.H., Application of fuzzy logic to approximate reasoning using linguistic systems, IEEE Trans. on Computer c-26 (1977) 1182-1191.

[3] Mizumoto, M., Fukami, S. and Tanaka, K., Fuzzy conditional inference and fuzzy inference with fuzzy quantifiers, Proc. of 6th Int. Conf. on Artificial Intelligence (Tokyo, Aug. 20-23, 1979), pp.589-591.

[4] Mizumoto, M., Fukami, S. and Tanaka, K., Some methods of fuzzy reasoning, in Gupta, M.M., Ragade, R.K. and Yager, R.R. (eds.), Advances in Fuzzy Set Theory and Applications (North-Holland, Amsterdam, 1979), pp.117-136.

[5] Mizumoto, M., Fukami, S. and Tanaka, K., Several methods for fuzzy conditional inference, Proc. of IEEE Conf. on Decision and Control (Florida, Dec. 12-14, 1979), pp.777-782.

[6] Fukami, S., Mizumoto, M. and Tanaka, K., Some considerations on fuzzy conditional inference, Fuzzy Sets and Systems 4 (1980) 243-273.

[7] Mizumoto, M. and Zimmermann, H.J., Comparison of fuzzy reasoning methods, Fuzzy Sets and Systems (in Press).

[8] Dubois, D., Quelques classes d'operateurs remarquables pour combiner des ensembles flous, Busefal No.1 (1979) 29-35.

[9] Rescher, N., Many Valued Logic (McGraw-Hill, New York, 1969).

[10] Bandler, W. and Kohout, L., Fuzzy power sets and fuzzy implication operators, Fuzzy Sets and Systems 4 (1980) 13-30.

[11] Willmott, R., Two fuzzier implication operators in the theory of fuzzy power sets, Fuzzy Sets and Systems 4 (1980) 31-37.

[12] Mizumoto, M., Fuzzy sets under various operations (Part 2), Busefal No.7 (1981) 32-44.

Approximate Reasoning in Decision Analysis
M.M. Gupta and E. Sanchez (eds.)
© North-Holland Publishing Company, 1982

SOFT DEDUCTION RULES IN MEDICAL DIAGNOSTIC PROCESSES

G. Soula and E. Sanchez*

Service Universitaire de Biomathématiques
Faculté de Médecine, Marseille, France

The methodology we propose for medical decision making is based on possibility theory and fuzzy logic. Three types of imprecise concepts involved in medical diagnosis processes are taken into account: evaluation of diagnostic indicators, medical knowledge and computed results. Moreover, this method allows the setting of a hierarchy among diagnostic indicators by means of what we call the suggestion value and the disconfirmation value associated with each diagnosis. Two soft deduction rules are proposed, that, in some sense, may be viewed as extensions of Modus Ponens and Modus Tollens. These rules act on fuzzy propositions and yield fuzzy degrees of presence and absence of a diagnosis which are then simultaneously interpreted. A concrete application to the classification of hyperlipoproteinemias, currently used in a conversational mode, is finally described.

Keywords: possibility distributions, fuzzy logic, deduction rules, suggestion, disconfirmation, medical diagnosis, classification.

1. INTRODUCTION

In medical reasoning, it is common to encounter qualitative descriptions of symptoms, diagnoses and pathological situations. In fact, many propositions state properties of attributes that may be viewed as labels of fuzzy sets because of vague boundaries, subjectivity, linguistic relationships, approximate descriptions, etc. Fuzziness appears to be inherent in most concept-formation and human reasoning processes, especially in the setting of some classes of medical diagnoses. Thus, handling of thresholds in biological tests is a difficult task for, in automatic procedures, acceptance or disconfirmation of a result can be a close decision in borderline cases. Can one say that a patient with a glycemia of 1.21 g/ℓ. is diabetic and that he/she is healthy with a glycemia of 1.19 g/ℓ? Another common example of imprecision is a patient's condition which is not either a healthy or a pathological state; instead there exists a gradual transition between these two states.

A sentence like "cholesterol is slightly increased" can be considered as a fuzzy proposition, of the form "X is A", inducing a possibility distribution $\Pi_X = A$. The theory of possibility distributions introduced by Zadeh is a simple and well adapted tool for handling such imprecise propositions. We shall widely use it in this paper to describe some deduction methods in fuzzy reasoning.

Our exposition is divided into three sections.

First, we propose two soft deduction rules for inference from fuzzy propositions. These rules are referred to as "Extended Modus Ponens" (EMP) and "Extended Modus Tollens" (EMT). Each is decomposed into two steps: matching (or not) of attributes by means of possibility measures, and final computation of the result by means of the bounded sum. A basic idea which we use throughout this paper involves the use of a functional correspondence between numbers in [0, 1] and possibility distributions of fuzzy subsets of [0, 1].

Second, the two soft deduction rules are employed as a basis for a methodology of computer-assisted medical decision-making. In particular, two notions of suggestion and disconfirmation which relate diagnostic indicators and diagnosis are introduced. These notions allow the setting of a hierarchy among diagnostic indicators, which relates to their importance with respect to the presence or absence of diagnoses. Suggestion and disconfirmation concepts are treated simultaneously to obtain a result.

Finally, a concrete application of this methodology to the classification of hyperlipoproteinemias is presented, an application which is simple to use with a computer in a conversational mode. Parameters defining fuzzy membership functions can be easily modified and the computed results are very informative.

2. SOFT DEDUCTION RULES

Let us first recall two basic concepts and definitions in possibility theory, Zadeh [21], namely possibility distribution and possibility measure.

*Visiting Research Associate, Department of EECS, Computer Science Division, University of California, Berkeley.

Let X be available which takes values in a universe of discourse U and let A be a fuzzy subset of U; then the proposition "X is A" associates a possibility distribution, Π_X, with X which is postulated to be equal to A. Instead of the possibility assignment equation "$\Pi_X = A$", we here simply write Π^A, i.e.

$$X \text{ is } A \rightarrow \Pi^A,$$

where, on the right hand side, the variable X_A is implicit, and the symbol "→" indicates that Π^A is induced by "X is A."

Manipulation of possibility distributions is then derived from the basic operations in fuzzy set theory and fuzzy logic, e.g. if B is a fuzzy subset of U, then

$$X \text{ is } A \text{ and } X \text{ is } B \rightarrow \Pi^{A\cap B},$$

if

$$X \text{ is } B \rightarrow \Pi^B.$$

Assume now that Π^B is a reference possibility distribution in the sense that it will serve as a basis for characterizing a pattern with which other possibility distributions may be compared. Then, the possibility measure, $\pi(A)$, of A is defined as a number in [0, 1] given by[(1)]

$$\pi(A) \triangleq \sup_{u\in U} \mu_A(u) \wedge \mu_B(u),$$

where μ_A and μ_B are the respective membership functions of A and B.

We recall now that $\pi(A)$ expresses "the possibility that X is A given X is B," which we denote by $\pi(A|B)$, yielding

$$\pi(A|B) \triangleq \sup \Pi^{A\cap B},$$

where, equivalently, the right hand side is expressed in terms of compound possibility distributions.

In this definition, A and B are fuzzy sets in the same universe of discourse, U, so that they can be directly be compared in regard to their meaning.

Let us now introduce two new deduction rules, (I) and (II), involving fuzzy propositions.

$$(\text{I}) \quad \left\{ \begin{array}{l} p_1 \triangleq X \text{ is } A \\ q_1 \triangleq \text{If } X \text{ is } B \text{ then } Y \text{ is } C \\ \hline r_1 \triangleq Y \text{ is } D \end{array} \right.$$

where X and Y are variables that take values in the universes of discourse U and V, respectively; A and B are fuzzy subsets of U; C and D are fuzzy subsets of V.

Several authors, e.g. Bellman and Zadeh [3], Mizumoto et al. [11], Baldwin [2], proposed and investigated methods to handle (I), i.e. how to derive proposition r_1 from the knowledge of propositions p_1 and q_1. The deduction rules we present here (see [17] for a more detailed description) are different; they are in fact very much oriented towards applications in the spirit of the one shown at the end of this paper. They involve normal[(2)] fuzzy sets either expressing concepts like "around a" where a is a number (or an interval), or fuzzy subsets of the unit interval [0, 1] expressing truth-values.

Strictly speaking, q_1 does not correspond to a logical implication, rather it expresses some dependence of C from X that emphasizes the "importance" of "X is B" in connection with a characterization of Y. For example, q_1 may have the form "If X is B_Y then Y is C_X," which means "If X is B (for a given Y) then Y is C (where C is defined in connection with X)." Further interpretations will be given with an application in this paper.

Returning now to (I), here is what we require in the deduction process. If A matches B, in the sense of $\pi(A|B) = 1$ (A not being necessarily equal to B, instead we may have $A \subseteq B$), then the inferred D is precisely C. In the particular particular case where A = B, (I) can be written as follows:

$$\left\{ \begin{array}{l} X \text{ is } A \\ \text{If } X \text{ is } A \text{ then } Y \text{ is } C \\ \hline Y \text{ is } C \end{array} \right.$$

which explains the reference to (I) as the "extended Modus Ponens" or EMP, for short.

Before defining C, let us turn to (II) which will be referred to as "Extended Modus Tollens" or EMT.

---

(1) The symbol $\triangleq$ stands for "denotes" or "is equal by definition to."

(2) A fuzzy subset A of U is said normal iff $\sup_{u\in U} \mu_A(u) = 1$. Moreover, in our examples, the supremum is attained.

$$
\text{(II)} \quad \begin{cases} p_2 \triangleq X \text{ is } A \\ q_2 \triangleq \text{If } Y \text{ is } C \text{ then } X \text{ is } B \\ \hline r_2 \triangleq Y \text{ is } D . \end{cases}
$$

As in (I), X and Y are variables that take values in U and V, respectively; A and B are fuzzy subsets of U; C and D are fuzzy subsets of V. q_2 is interpreted in the same spirit as q_1. But here is now what we required in the deduction process. If A does not match B, i.e., if A is totally disjoint from B (A not being necessarily related to the complement B' of B) in the sense of $\pi(A|B) = 0$, then the inferred D in r_2 is precisely the complement C' of C.

In order to define fuzzy sets D in r_1 and in r_2, let us recall some definitions of fuzzy truth values.

In fuzzy logic [3], a fuzzy truth value is a fuzzy subset of [0, 1], where [0, 1] in association with the logical connectives constitutes the base logic.

Fuzzy truth values true and false are defined as follows, Zadeh [20], as in the work of Baldwin [2], Tsukamoto [18].

$$\forall x \in [0,1], \ \mu_{\underline{true}}(x) = x, \ \mu_{\underline{false}}(x) = 1-x.$$

From these fuzzy truth values, by using linguistic modifiers such as fairly, very, other fuzzy truth values are defined. For example, $\forall x \in [0,1]$,

$$\mu_{\underline{very\ true}}(x) = x^2, \ \mu_{fairly\ true}(x) = x^{1/2},$$

$$\mu_{\underline{very\ false}}(x) = (1-x)^2, \text{ etc.}$$

Moreover, the fuzzy truth values absolutely true (τ) and absolutely false (ϕ) are defined as:

$$\mu_\tau(x) = \begin{cases} 1 & \text{if } x = 1 \\ 0 & \text{otherwise} \end{cases} ; \ \mu_\phi(x) = \begin{cases} 1 & \text{if } x = 0 \\ 0 & \text{otherwise} \end{cases}$$

a fuzzy truth value T does not provide a precise characterization of the truth value of a proposition; rather it yields a possibility distribution Π^T of this truth value, which allows to take into account the imprecision in the assignment of a truth value to a proposition.

In this paper we treat separately two families of truth values: T associated with TRUTH, and F associated with FALSEHOOD as illustrated in Fig. 1.

When two fuzzy truth values A and B either both belong to T or either both belong to F, and only in these two cases, we here use the distance

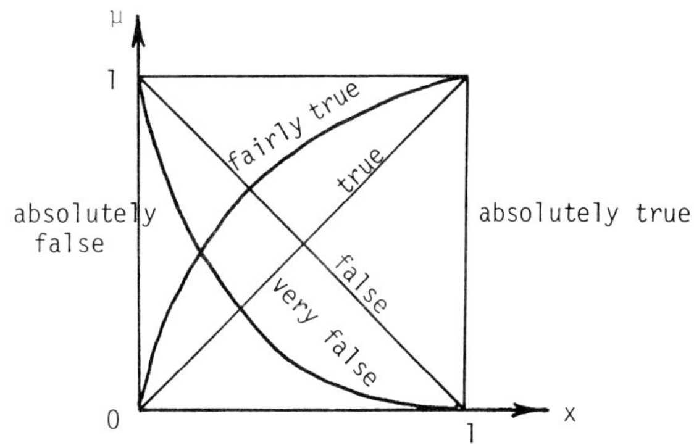

Fig. 1. Possibility distributions of fuzzy truth and fuzzy falsehood values.

d, [10], defined on possibility distributions as follows.

$$d(\Pi^A,\Pi^B) = \int_0^1 |\mu_A(x)-\mu_B(x)|\,dx .$$

In particular, if $A \in T$, $d(\Pi^A,\Pi^\tau) = \int_0^1 \mu_A(x)dx$ $= a \in [0,1]$; if $B \in F$, $d(\Pi^B,\Pi^\phi) = \int_0^1 \mu_B(x)dx$ $= b \in [0,1]$.

From now on, we shall assume that for all $\alpha \in [0, 1]$, there exists one and only one $A \in T$ and, one and only one, $B \in F$ such that

$$\alpha = d(\Pi^A,\Pi^\tau) = d(\Pi^B,\Pi^\phi).$$

This functional correspondance between numbers in [0, 1] and possibility distributions in T (or in F) is a basic assumption in the sequel. For example, the elements of T (or of F) can be defined as being generated by powers of true (or of false) but we do not have to impose, here, precise definitions of the elements of T (or of F).

We are now able to define the fuzzy sets D in r_1 (I) and in r_2 (II). In (I) as well as in (II) two steps are needed to compute the corresponding D's. In all cases it is of course assumed that fuzzy propositions induce corresponding possibility distributions.

(I) EMP - Step 1. Matching of A and B.

Define $M \in T$ such that $d(\Pi^M,\Pi^\tau) = 1-\pi(A|B)$. Thus, comparison of A with B by means of a possibility measure, yields a truth value M in the family T, as illustrated in Figure 2.

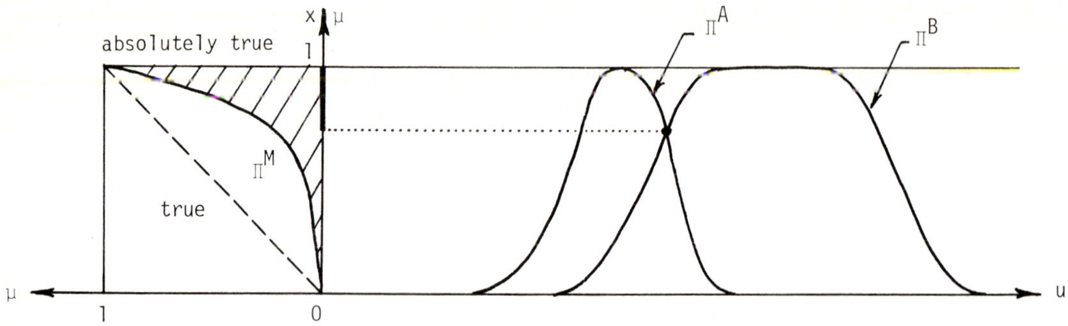

Fig. 2. Illustrative example of matching for A and B

Note that if $\pi(A|B) = 1$, e.g. when $A \subseteq B$, then $M = \tau$, i.e., absolutely true.

(I) EMP - Step 2. Definition of D.

$$\forall v \in V,\ \mu_D(v) \triangleq \mu_C(v) \oplus \mu_M(\mu_C(v)),$$

where for a and b in [0, 1], $a \oplus b = \min(a+b,1)$, i.e., $\oplus \triangleq$ bounded sum. See in Fig. 3 an illustration for the deduction of D in EMP.

Note that in all cases, deduction by EMP yields a fuzzy set D such that $C \subseteq D$.

Moreover, if A = B then C = D, for when A = B, $\pi(A|A) = 1$ (recall that fuzzy sets are assumed to be normal), $M = \tau$, $\mu_D(v) = \mu_C(v) \oplus 0$ (if $\mu_C(v) < 1$) or $\mu_D(v) = \mu_C(v) \oplus 1 = 1$ (if $\mu_C(v) = 1$).

SPECIAL CASE. When the C's belong to a family with a structure akin to the families of truth values, deduction processes can be defined in a slightly different, but more homogeneous form. This is the case when Y takes values in [0, 1] to handle concepts like beauty, pain, etc. All C's are then generated from a basic term and its antonym like true and false, for example handsome and ugly in the case of beauty, presence and absence in the case of pain. Moreover, all C's are characterized by the distance of their respective possibility distributions to the extremal possibility distribution ($\Pi^{\text{absolutely handsome}}$, for example) which we generally denote by Π^E. In the deduction process, first step is unchanged but, in second step, D, or equivalently Π^D, is now defined as follows.

$$d(\Pi^D,\Pi^E) = d(\Pi^M,\Pi^\tau) \oplus d(\Pi^C,\Pi^E).$$

(II) EMT - Step 1. "Nonmatching" of A and B.

The goal here is to determine to what extent A does not match B. The result of the comparison is $N \in F$ such that

$$d(\Pi^N,\Pi^\phi) = \pi(A|B),$$

as illustrated in Fig. 4.

Note that if $\pi(A|B) = 0$, then $N = \phi$, i.e., absolutely false.

(II) EMT - Step 2. Definition of D.

$$\forall v \in V,\ \mu_D(v) \triangleq \mu_{C'}(v) \oplus \mu_N(\mu_C(v)),$$

where we recall that $\mu_{C'}(v) = 1-\mu_C(v)$ and $\oplus$ is the bounded sum. See in Fig. 5 an illustration for the deduction of D in EMT.

Note that in all cases, deduction by EMT yields a fuzzy set D such that $C' \subseteq D$.

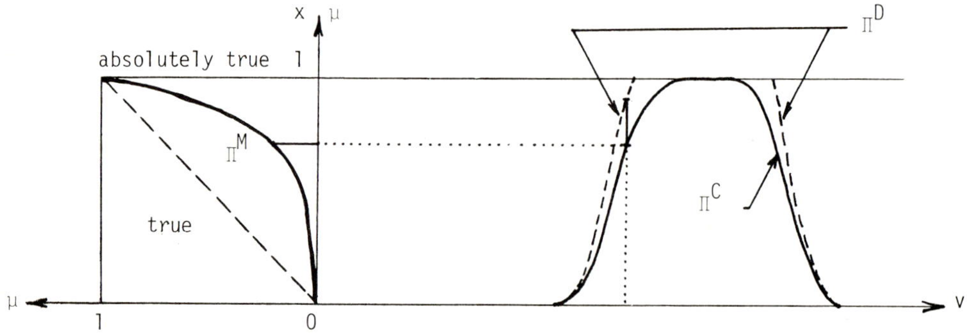

Fig. 3. Illustrative example for deducing D in EMP.

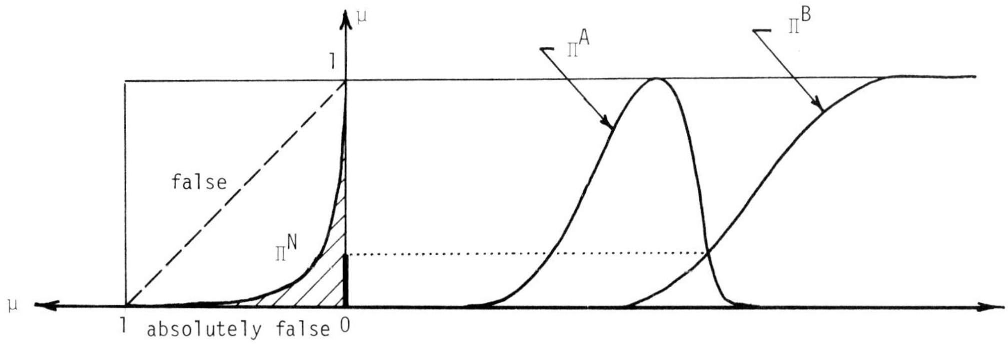

Fig. 4. Illustrative example of "nonmatching" for A and B.

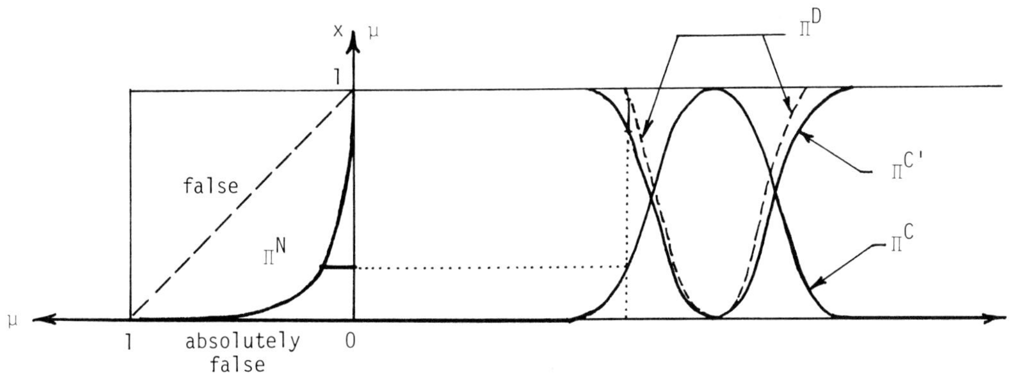

Fig. 5. Illustrative example for deducing D in EMT.

Moreover, if A is totally disjoint from B, in the sense of $\pi(A|B) = 0$, then $N = \phi$, $\mu_D(v) = \mu_{C'}(v) \oplus 0$ (if $\mu_C(v) > 0$) or $\mu_D(v) = \mu_{C'}(v) \oplus 1 = 1$ (if $\mu_C(v) = 0$, i.e., $\mu_{C'}(v) = 1$), hence $D = C'$.

<u>SPECIAL CASE</u>. When the C's belong to a family with a structure akin to the families of truth values, deduction processes can again be defined in a slightly different, but more homogeneous form. If we still denote by Π^E the extremal possibility distribution like in (I), the first step is unchanged but, in the second step, D, or equivalently, Π^D, is now defined as follows.

$$d(\Pi^D,\Pi^E) = d(\Pi^N,\Pi^\phi) \oplus d(\Pi^{C*},\Pi^E),$$

where $\forall v \in [0, 1]$, $\mu_{C*}(v) = \mu_C(1-v)$.

3. MEDICAL DECISION PROCESSES

The methodology we propose for computer-assisted medical decision making is based on the two soft deduction rules EMP and EMT which we have introduced in the preceding section. It can also be applied in other domains to fault diagnosis or to fuzzy logic controllers, for example.

Within a given pathology we consider a set of diagnostic indicators or symptoms and a set of diagnoses (or groups, or types, or syndromes, etc.). Fuzziness will be considered in the three domains of evaluation of diagnostic indicators, medical knowledge representation, and computation of results.

i) <u>Evaluation of diagnostic indicators</u>. In most cases, subjectivity and imprecision are associated with evaluation of diagnostic indicators for some of the following reasons.

- Difficulty in quantifying symptoms like "pain" for example.
- Errors due to technical measurement procedures.
- Poor conditions of observation.
- Change in symptoms in the course of a disease.

In all cases, the imprecision in the evaluation of a diagnostic indicator will be interpreted by means of a fuzzy proposition of the form: The diagnostic indicator is <u>around</u> a or <u>close to</u> a where a is a numerical value. A fuzzy set labeled around a will be denoted by $\tilde{a}$, and it will be assumed that fuzzy propositions translate into corresponding possibility distributions. For example,

John's triglycerides are 6.3 mmol/ℓ is transformed into

Triglycerides (John) = $\widetilde{6.3}$
which translates into a possibility distribution of the type shown in Figure 9, with $a_j = 6.3$.

ii) Medical knowledge. Three concepts are taken into account by means of finite matrices expressing relationships between diagnoses (rows) and diagnostic indicators (columns).

The pattern matrix G is such that its entries express the theoretical nature of diagnostic indicators associated with diagnoses. For examples, in the case of poorly defined dosage thresholds, G reflects fuzzy propositions such as (in the context of a given diagnosis) diagnostic indicator is slightly higher than ..., or clearly lower than ...

The suggestion matrix H is such that its suggestive values reflect the subjectivity associated with each diagnostic indicator in relation to the corresponding diagnoses. This matrix allows the setting of a hierarchy among signs to induce a diagnosis. The entries stand for properties like high suggestive value or low suggestion value, etc.

The disconfirmation matrix J is such that its entries represent how subjectively the diagnostic indicators disconfirm diagnoses in order to eliminate them in the deduction process. This matrix also allows a setting of a hierarchy among diagnostic indicators, but to reject diagnoses. Entries are exemplified by translation of properties like low disconfirmation value of very low disconfirmation value, etc.

These matrices, G, H, J, are filled up by physicians according to their experience and how subjectively they feel about the different relationships. They can be modified after some training and further experience.

iii) Computed results. With the exception of specific cases, it is uncommon for the combination of observed diagnostic indicators over patients and medical knowledge to yield precise results. The yes-or-no membership of a patient in relation to a pathological condition is less often encountered than a graded membership which represents a transition stage between a normal and a pathological condition. Hence, each patient is characterized by a graded membership in each possible decision which reflects both suggestion and disconfirmation values.

ALGORITHM. Each observed diagnostic indicator on a patient is first transformed into a possibility distribution, and compared with each entry in G (a possibility distribution) by means of the possibility measure which yields the possibility distributions of matching and non-matching fuzzy sets, i.e., Π^M and Π^N respectively. These possibility distributions -- which determine whether or not the patient matches the theoretical pattern G -- are respectively combined with each entry in the suggestion matrix H by EMP, and with each entry in the disconfirmation matrix J by EMT (see Figure 7). Let us rewrite the deduction rules in terms suited for medical applications, assuming that diagnoses are characterized over [0, 1] (cf. V).

Let S_j be a diagnostic indicator or symptom taking values in a set U_j (usually a real interval) and let $\mathcal{D}_i$ be a diagnosis taking values in V = [0, 1]; S_j and $\mathcal{D}_i$ are viewed as variables (cf. X and Y, respectively).

$G_{ij} \triangleq$ fuzzy subset of U_j expressing a (reference) relationship between $\mathcal{D}_i$ and S_j; it is the (i,j)-th entry in the pattern matrix G (cf. B in (I) and (II)).

$H_{ij} \triangleq$ fuzzy subset of V expressing how $\mathcal{D}_i$ is suggested by S_j; it is the (i,j)-th entry in the suggestion matrix H (cf. C in (I)).

$J_{ij} \triangleq$ fuzzy subset of V expressing how $\mathcal{D}_i$ is disconfirmed by S_j; it is the (i,j)-th entry in the disconfirmation matrix J (cf. C in (II)).

Assume now that a measurement of S_j in U_j yields a value "a_j" which is then transformed into $\tilde{a}_j$ (cf. A in (I) and (II)), expressing "around a." By EMP, a fuzzy subset D^I_{ij} of V is inferred and, by EMT, a fuzzy subset D^{II}_{ij} of V is also inferred.

(I) or EMP

S_j is $\tilde{a}_j$	: observed diagnostic indicator
If S_j is G_{ij} then $\mathcal{D}_i$ is H_{ij}	: medical knowledge (pattern & suggestion)
$\mathcal{D}_i$ is D^I_{ij}	: fuzzy degree of presence

D^I_{ij} will be determined by a possibility distribution characterized by the distance

$d(\Pi^{D^I_{ij}}, \Pi^{AP})$ (cf. $d(\Pi^D, \Pi^E)$), where AP $\triangleq$ absolutely present, see Figure 6 for illustration.

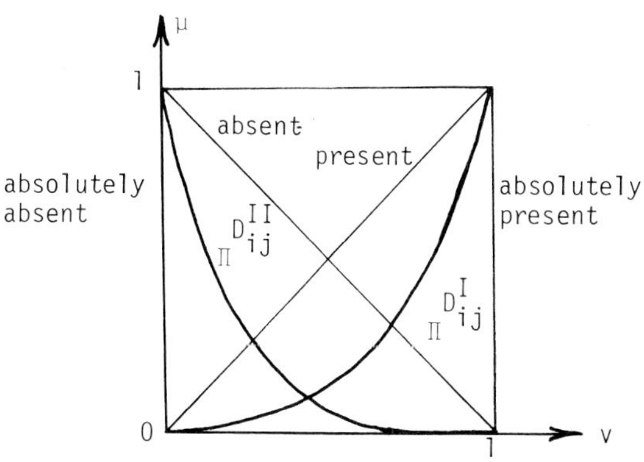

Fig. 6. Possibility distributions of fuzzy presence and fuzzy absence values.

We briefly recall definition of D^{I}_{ij}, or, equivalently, its possibility distribution (cf. special case, in (I)).

$$d(\Pi^{D^{I}_{ij}}, \Pi^{AP}) = (1-\pi(\underset{\sim}{a}_j | G_{ij})) \oplus d(\Pi^{H_{ij}}, \Pi^{AS}),$$

where AS $\triangleq$ absolutely suggestive

(recall that $M \in \mathcal{T}$ is defined by $d(\Pi^{M}, \Pi^{\tau}) = 1 - \pi(\underset{\sim}{a}_j | G_{ij})$).

(II) or EMT.

S_j is $\underset{\sim}{a}_j$	observed diagnostic indicator
If $\mathcal{D}_i$ is J_{ij} then S_j is G_{ij} :	medical knowledge (pattern & disconfirmation)
$\mathcal{D}_i$ is D^{II}_{ij} :	fuzzy degree of absence

D^{II}_{ij} will now be determined by the distance $d(\Pi^{D^{II}_{ij}}, \Pi^{AA})$, where AA $\triangleq$ absolutely absent, see Figure 6 for illustration.

Let us briefly recall, too, the definition of D^{II}_{ij}, or, equivalently, its possibility distribution (cf. special case, in (II)).

$$d(\Pi^{D^{II}_{ij}}, \Pi^{AA}) = \pi(\underset{\sim}{a}_j | G_{ij}) \oplus d(\Pi^{J^{*}_{ij}}, \Pi^{AD}),$$

where $\forall v \in [0, 1]$, $\mu_{J^{*}_{ij}}(v) = \mu_{J_{ij}}(1-v)$ and AD $\triangleq$ absolutely disconfirmed (recall that $N \in \mathcal{F}$ is defined by $d(\Pi^{N}, \Pi^{\phi}) = \pi(\underset{\sim}{a}_j | G_{ij})$).

For each patient, the entries in the two computed matrices D^{I} and D^{II} are fuzzy degrees of presence (D^{I}) and fuzzy degrees of absence (D^{II}) for each possible diagnosis $\mathcal{D}_i$. The elements of D^{I} and D^{II} are finally combined by means of aggregation operators whose choice is application-dependent. Here, we have chosen the minimum operator acting on possibility distributions. For each $\mathcal{D}_i$, then, we obtain two possibility distributions Π^{P_i} and Π^{A_i} which express a fuzzy degree of presence and a fuzzy degree of absence of $\mathcal{D}_i$. They are defined and combined as follows, [17].

$$d(\Pi^{P_i}, \Pi^{AP}) \triangleq \min_j d(\Pi^{D^{I}_{ij}}, \Pi^{AP}) = \alpha_i,$$

$$d(\Pi^{A_i}, \Pi^{AA}) \triangleq \min_j d(\Pi^{D^{II}_{ij}}, \Pi^{AA}) = \beta_i.$$

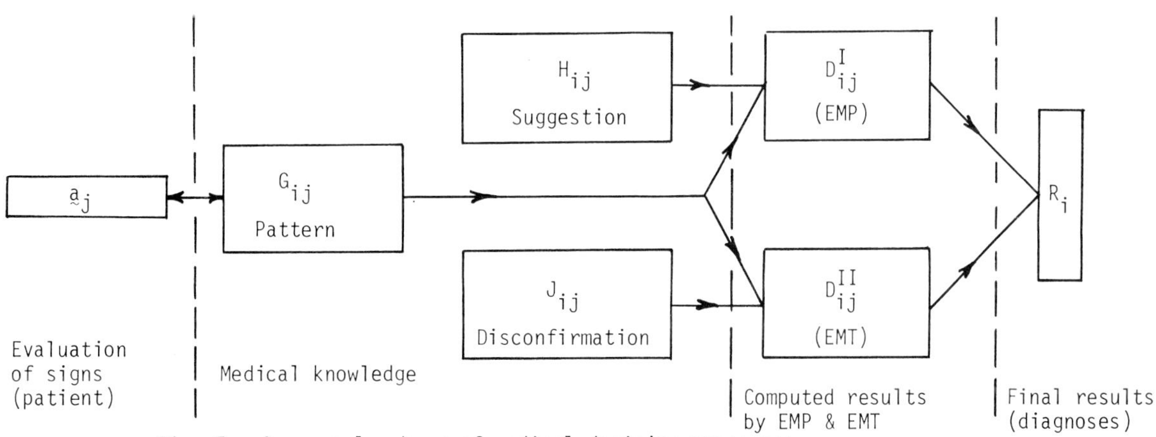

Fig. 7. A general schema of medical decision processes.

For each diagnosis $\mathcal{D}_i$, the solution R_i is derived from a simultaneous analysis of the fuzzy degree of presence and the fuzzy degree of absence. We express it by the variation range $[1-\alpha_i,\beta_i]$ or $[\alpha_i',\beta_i]$, when $\alpha_i' \leq \beta_i$, which is the condition of existence of a solution. This condition of existence expresses consistency and homogeneity in the observed diagnostic indicators on a patient. Homogeneity depends on both suggestion diagnostic indicators and disconfirmation diagnostic indicators in relation to a diagnosis $\mathcal{D}_i$.

If condition of existence for a diagnosis $\mathcal{D}_i$ is not satisfied, it is defined as a degree of heterogeneity $h_i \triangleq \alpha_i'-\beta_i$.

In summary, for each diagnosis $\mathcal{D}_i$, we specify either a variation range $[\alpha_i',\beta_i]$ or the value of β_i, associated with a heterogeneity degree h_i.

4. APPLICATION TO THE CLASSIFICATION OF HYPERLIPOPROTEINEMIAS

Hyperlipoproteinemias are a major metabolic perturbation and their etio-pathogenic role on vascular atherosclerosis has been documented during the past years. A synthesis of these abnormalities was first given by Fredrickson and, later on, a classification was proposed by the W.H.O. [22]. This classification relies upon respective values of lipidemia, cholesterolemia, triglyceridemia, electrophoresis and/or electrocentrifugation of lipoproteins.

Description of these abnormalities and criteria for their classification remain imprecise; they are expressed by means of propositions such as "Plasma cholesterol is normal or increased," "β-lipoproteins markedly decreased," "triglycerides are clearly increased," "broad band suspected on electrophoresis" [22]. There is no information on thresholds in these propositions, which are fuzzy indeed, so that a wide and subjective interpretation is permissible.

Moreover, there exists a hierarchy among the variables entering in the classification, according to their degree of importance. For example, total cholesterol and triglycerides are basic factors in the definition of what we call primary classes (they play the role of "diagnoses" in the general study), i.e. the "normal" class and classes II_a, II_b and IV. To the contrary, the three remaining variables entering in this classification, i.e., percentage of β lipoproteins, percentage of pre-β lipoproteins and total lipidemia, are less important and their presence confirms membership of a patient in a class or determines so-called minor classes, i.e., minor II_a, minor II_b and minor IV.

In the present application, classes I, III, and V that appear in the international classification are not introduced since they correspond to uncommon genetic abnormalities and they are determined by specific variables, i.e., by the conjunction of presence, or absence of chylomicrons and/or broad β lipoproteins suspected on electrophoresis. Moreover, percentage of α lipoproteins is not taken into account since it follows from the constraint $\alpha + \beta + \text{pre } \beta = 100$ and it does not provide additional information regarding the classification.

In summary, this application deals only with seven classes: Normal, II_a, minor II_a, II_b, minor II_b, IV and minor IV. These classes are characterized by the variations of five variables (diagnostic indicators): total lipids, total cholesterol, triglycerides, β lipoproteins and pre-β lipoproteins.

In practice, the method runs in a conversational mode and comprises two stages, initialization and computation, as follows

INITIALIZATION. In this first stage, the three components of the medical knowledge are determined.

The pattern matrix G reflects the theoretical description of the W.H.O. classification, derived from fuzzy propositions taking into account the constructed classes and giving the possible values of the five biological tests. Here are some examples of fuzzy propositions, the corresponding fuzzy sets are to be seen in Table I. "In class IIa ($\mathcal{D}_i$), cholesterol (S_j) is markedly increased (G_{ij})," "In class minor IIa, triglycerides are normal," "In class IV, lipids are very increased," etc. Fuzzy sets in Table I are built from one of the two types of parametrized curves shown in Figure 8; they are derived from the S-membership function [3] which is piece-wise quadratic.

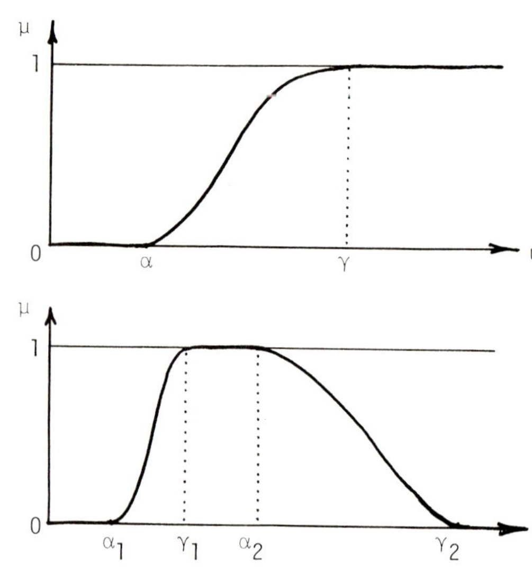

Fig. 8. The two types of curves used in G.

Suggestion matrix H and disconfirmation matrix J are also specified by the biologist to introduce the notion of hierarchy into diagnostic indicators, either to determine the membership (using H) or the non-membership (using J) of a patient in a class. Suggestion and disconfirmation values are, of course, imprecise and based on the biologist's experience. They reflect fuzzy properties like very suggestive value or weakly suggestive value, by possibility distributions in the universe of discourse [0, 1]. Such possibility distributions are characterized by their respective distances to the possibility distribution of absolutely suggestive. As the suggestion value increases, the distance decreases and conversely, so that the biologist determines the suggestion (and the disconfirmation) values with respect to the associated distances. Suggestion matrix and disconfirmation matrix are respectively reproduced in Table II and Table III where, for the sake of simplicity, the entries stand not for the value of a distance but for the complement of this value. For example, the higher the suggestion value, the higher the entry in the matrix (the corresponding distance has a low value).

Finally, the imprecision attached to the result "a_j" of a biological test is translated into fuzzy propositions such as "percentage of pre-β lipoproteins (S_j) is around a_j." Every test performed on a patient will be defined by a curve, which is a combination of an S and an S' = (1-S)-membership functions, and which depends on two parameters a_j (the measured value) and, b_j that depends only on the nature of S_j and not on the measured values, and take into account the fuzziness of "around" (see Figure 9). In our application, the b_j's we use are reproduced in Table IV.

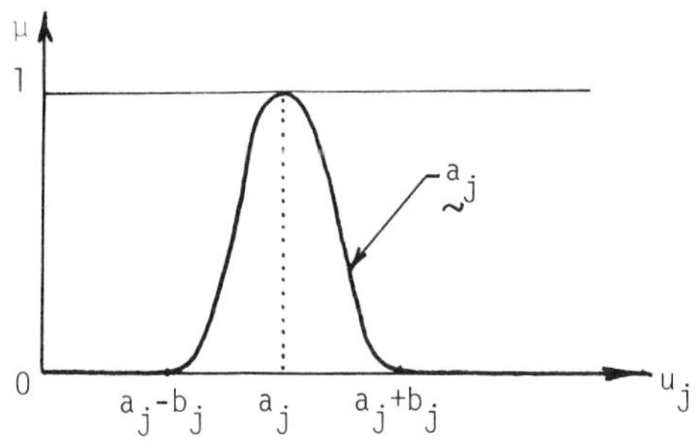

Fig. 9. Representation of the result of a biological test S_j.

COMPUTATION. The application of the proposed method to a classification process which depends on the biological tests performed on a patient presents no difficulty. It is necessary only to provide the computer with the results of five tests. The method yields intervals (cf. $[\alpha_i', \beta_i]$) associated with each of the seven predetermined classes (the D_i's). The boundaries and the range of the intervals represent the membership of a patient in a class. If necessary, heterogeneity degrees are determined on request.

If the condition of existence of a solution is satisfied (cf. $\alpha_i' \leq \beta_i$), the variation ranges are interpreted as follows.

Two bounds close to 1 indicate full membership to a group, e.g. [0.9, 1];

Two bounds close to 0 indicate non membership to a group, e.g. [0, 0.1];

The narrower the variation range, the more accurate the result;

The larger the variation range, the more inaccurate the result (the limit case is [0, 1]).

An example with some results is shown in Table V.

5. CONCLUSION

In practive, clinicians and biologists were substantially satisfied with the classification of patients in the different classes, and by now more than a thousand patients have been examined by means of this methodology. To summarize, the application of the method to the classification of hyperlipoproteinemias yields:

A clinician's personal and clearer perception of the definition of more or less subjective classes of medical knowledge;

Similar and stable results of the same tests; this prevents misclassifications due to a collaborator's lack of experience and prevents any evolution of the subjectivity inherent to the interpretation;

A graded classification in many classes allowing a gradation of lipid analyses. In particular, the existence of intermediate classes allows one to assume, in absence of any prevention or therapy, a final evolution towards a crisper class. This is of great interest in epidemiologic studies.

Finally, let us mention that, in our Department, fuzzy set theory has been applied in problems of thyroid patholody, of cardiac insufficiency [9], of anemias and of the classification of some icterias [15], and is now used in the treatment of diabetes.

Table I. Classification of hyperlipoproteinemias: Pattern matrix G.

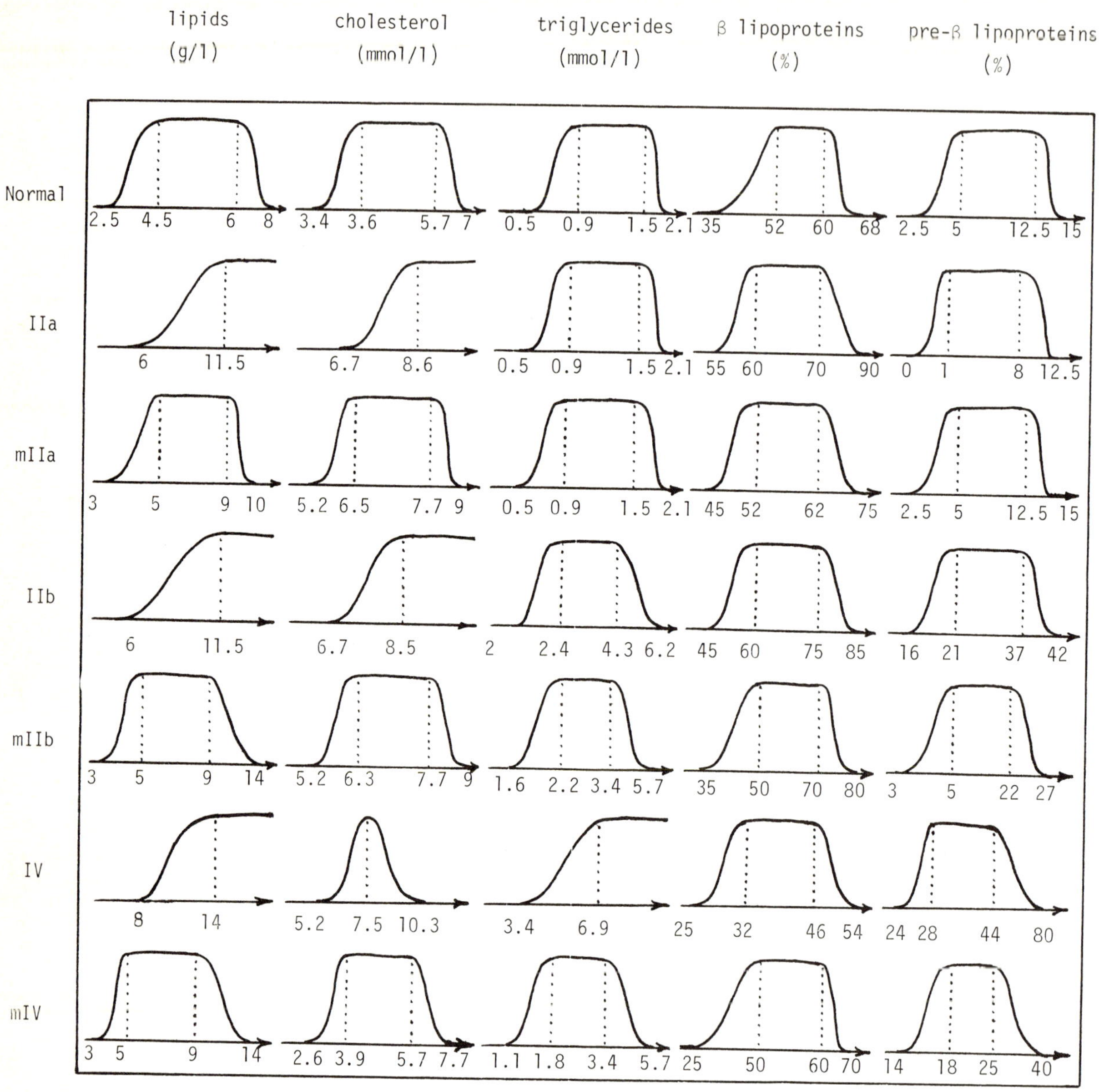

Table II. Suggestion values.

	Lipids	Chol.	Trigl.	β-lip.	pre-β lip.
Normal	0.7	1	1	0	0
IIa	0	1	0	0.9	0
mIIa	0	1	0	0.9	0
IIb	0	1	1	0.8	0.8
mIIb	0	1	1	0.8	0.8
IV	0.7	0	1	0	0.9
mIV	0.5	0	1	0	0.9

Table III. Disconfirmation values.

	Lipids	Chol.	Trigl.	β-lip	pre-β lip.
Normal	0.8	0.9	0.9	1	1
IIa	0.5	0.8	0.7	0.9	0.6
mIIa	0.5	0.8	0.7	0.9	0.7
IIb	0.5	0.9	0.8	0.7	0.8
mIIb	0.5	0.9	0.9	0.7	0.7
IV	0.6	0.5	0.8	0.6	0.9
mIV	0.5	0.9	0.8	0.9	0.7

Table IV. Fuzziness attached to the biological tests.

S_j	Lipids	Chol.	Trigl.	β-lip.	pre-β lip.
b_j	1.8 g/ℓ	1.5 mmol/ℓ	0.6 mmol/ℓ	10%	10%

Table V. Examples of Classification.

Results of biological tests on patients

patients	lipids	cholesterol	triglycerides	β	pre-β
1	9	7.5	1.6	75	6
2	12	5.93	3	39	38
3	4.3	3.3	0.6	53	11
4	12	5.93	3	39	42
5	15	7.7	4.8	60	32

Final Results

patients	N	IIa	mIIa	IIb	mIIb	IV	mIV
1	β=0.1 h=0.9	[0.8,1]	β=0.5 h=1	β=0.2 h=0.6	β=0.6 h=0.4	[0,0.1]	β=0.2 h=0.8
2	β=0 h=1	[0.1,0.1]	β=0.2 h=0.7	β=0.2 h=0.8	β=0.3 h=0.7	β=0.2 h=0.7	β=0.8 h=0.2
3	[0.9,0.9]	β=0.2 h=0.3	β=0.2 h=0.7	β=0.1 h=0.5	β=0.1 h=0.7	[0,0.1]	β=0.2 h=0.2
4	β=0 h=1	[0.1,0.1]	β-0.2 h=0.7	β=0.2 h=0.8	β=0.3 h=0.7	β-0.2 h=0.7	β=0.5 h=0.5
5	β=0 h=0.1	β=0.3 h=0.6	β=0.3 h=0.7	[0.9,1]	β=0.5 h=0.5	β=0.5 h=0.4	β=0.4 h=0.3

ACKNOWLEDGEMENT

The authors wish to acknowledge the helpful comments of Professor L. A. Zadeh on an earlier draft of this paper.

REFERENCES

[1] Adlassnig, K.P., (1980), "A fuzzy logical model of computer-assisted medical diagnosis," Methods of Information in Medicine, 18, 3, pp. 141-148.

[2] Baldwin, J.F., (1979) "A new approach to approximate reasoning using a fuzzy logic, Fuzzy Sets and Systems, 2, 4, pp. 309-325.

[3] Bellman, R.E., and Zadeh, L.A., (1976) "Local and fuzzy logics, Electronics Research Laboratory Memorandum M-584, University of California, Berkeley.

[4] Bonifay, B., (1981), "Approche floue de caractérisation des principaux types d'anémies rencontrés en médecine interne, Medical Thesis, Marseille.

[5] Blanc, P., (1981) Presentation d'une méthode originale de classification automatique des hyperlipoprotéinémies par l'utilisation de la théorie des sous-ensembles flous à propos de 1000 bilans lipidiques, Medical Thesis, Marseille.

[6] Esogbue, A.O., and Elder, R.C., ((1979) "Fuzzy sets and the modelling of physician decision processes, part I: the initial interview-information gathering session, Fuzzy Sets and Systems, 2, 4, pp. 279-291.

[7] Esogbue, A.O., and Elder, R.C., (1980), "Fuzzy sets and the modelling of physician decision processes, part II: Fuzzy diagnosis decision models, Fuzzy Sets and Systems, 3, 1, pp. 1-9.

[8] Fredrickson, D.S., (1975), "It's time to be practical," Circulation, 51, pp. 209-211.

[9] Joly, H., Sanchez, E., Gouvernet, J., and Valty, T., (1980), "Application of fuzzy set theory to the evaluation of cardiac function, Medinfo 80, Tokyo, Proc. North-Holland I, pp. 91-95.

[10] Kaufmann, A., (1975), Introduction to the theory of fuzzy subsets, vol. 1, Fundamental Theoretical Elements, Academic Press, New York.

[11] Mizumoto, M., Fukami, S. and Tanaka, K., (1979), Some Methods of Fuzzy Reasoning, in Advances in Fuzzy Set Theory and Applications, Gupta, M.M., Ragade, R.K., and Yager, R.R. (eds.), North-Holland, Amsterdam, pp. 117-136.

[12] Rescher, N., (1969), Many Valued Logic, McGraw-Hill, New York.

[13] Sanchez, E., (1979) Medical Diagnosis and composite Fuzzy Relations," in Advances in Fuzzy Set Theory and Applications, Gupta, M.M., Ragade, R.K., and Yager, R.R. (Eds.), North-Holland, Amsterdam pp. 437-444.

[14] Sanchez, E., (1980), "Fuzzy logics with application to medical diagnosis, Proc. J.A.C.C., San Francisco.

[15] Sanchez, G., (1982), "Application de la théorie des ensembles flous à la classification de certains ictères, Medical Thesis, Marseille.

[16] Soula, G., Gouvernet, J., Barré, A., and San Marco, J.L., (1980) "Application of fuzzy relations to medical decision making," Medinfo 80, Tokyo, Proc. North-Holland II, pp. 844-848.

[17] Soula, G., (1981), Aide à la decision en logique floue: Application en médecine These d'Etat en Biologie Humaine, Faculté de Médecine, Marseille.

[18] Tsukamoto, Y., (1979), "Fuzzy logic based on Lukaciewicz logic and its applications to diagnosis and control," Ph.D. Thesis, Tokyo Institute of Technology.

[19] Zadeh, L.A., (1977), "A theory of approximate reasoning (AR)," Electronics Research Laboratory Memorandum M77/58; University of California, Berkeley.

[20] Zadeh, L.A., (1975), "The concept of a linguistic variable and its application to approximate reasoning, Part I, Information Sciences, 8, pp. 199-249; Part II, Information Sciences, 8, pp. 301-357; Part III, Information Sciences, 9, pp. 43-80.

[21] Zadeh, L.A., (1978), "Fuzzy sets as a basis for a theory of possibility," Fuzzy Sets and Systems, 1, pp. 3-28.

[22] World Health Organization, (1970), Classification of hyperlipidemias and hyperlipoproteinemias, Bulletin WHO, 43 pp. 891-915.

Research sponsored in part by the National Science Foundation Grants MCS79-06543/IST-801896.

Approximate Reasoning in Decision Analysis
M.M. Gupta and E. Sanchez (eds.)

IMPRECISE DECISION TABLES AND THEIR OPTIMIZATION

J. M. Francioni, A. Kandel and C. M. Eastman

Department of Mathematics and Computer Science
Florida State University
Tallahassee, Florida 32306 U.S.A.

Decision tables have been used for many years in the form of tax rate tables and rate books of insurance salesmen. The formal usage of decision tables, however, did not come about until the early sixties when they were used to determine complex conditionals. These decision tables can be used only when dealing with deterministic conditions. Using fuzzy set theory, decision tables can be modified to deal with imprecise conditions. Just as deterministic decision tables can be represented as Boolean functions, it is also possible to represent imprecise decision tables as fuzzy functions. Once the decision rules are reduced to fuzzy functions, then these same functions can be compacted using a fuzzy minimization technique which will result in an optimal decision table. Such optimal decision tables are the result of this investigation.

Keywords: Decision Tables, Fuzzy Switching Function, Fuzzy Sets, Minimization, Compactification of Fuzzy Functions.

1. INTRODUCTION

Decision tables provide a mechanism to help in the processing of decisions based on precise conditions. Utilizing the concepts of fuzzy set theory, decision tables can be modified to deal with processing decisions based on imprecise conditions. Such modified decision tables are able to incorporate the use of fuzzy functions, just as a deterministic decision table incorporates the use of Boolean functions. Using fuzzy minimization techniques, a fuzzy decision table can itself be minimized.

In Section 2, deterministic decision tables are briefly summarized. Section 3 summarizes the fuzzy concepts used later. These two sections are intended to provide a quick review and may be skipped by a reader familiar with the concepts. In Section 4, deterministic decision tables are modified to express imprecise data. In Section 5, mixed decision tables which use both Boolean and fuzzy variables are described. Section 6 outlines the steps involved in setting up a fuzzy decision table. In Section 7 examples of fuzzy decision tables are given. Section 8 discusses the implementation of fuzzy decision tables. Section 9 provides a summary.

2. DECISION TABLES

A decision table is a special form of a table that determines a set of decision rules based on a clearly identified set of conditions and resulting action. Decision tables provide a means for organizing and clarifying the conditions behind alternative actions and communicating this logic. Decision tables and procedures for handling them are described in [4], [6], [7], [13], [16], [17], [18], and [20].

Decision tables are made up of four specific parts. They are the condition stub, the condition entry, the action stub and the action entry. Figure 1 illustrates their positions in a decision table.

Condition Stub	Condition Entry
Action Stub	Action Entry

FIGURE 1. Decision Table Nomenclature

The condition stub names logical variables, each of which can be evaluated as true or false at any given time. The true and false values are placed in the condition entry area. The action stub names action variables. Sequences of values for the action variables are listed in the action entry area. A column of values from the condition entry is associated with a sequence of actions from the action entry. These associations are called rules. A rule can be interpreted as "If C_1 and C_2 and ..., then A_1 and A_2 and ..." where C_i is the condition, either true or false as specified by the condition entry, and A_i is the action to be taken as specified in the action entry.

A decision table for deciding about playing tennis is shown in Figure 2. Rule 1 can be interpreted as "If the courts are dry and a partner is available and you have tennis balls, then play tennis outside." Rule 5 can be interpreted as "If a partner is not available and you have tennis balls, then read a book."

	1	2	3	4	5	6	7	8
Tennis courts dry	T	T	F	F	T	T	F	F
Partner Available	T	T	T	T	F	F	F	F
Have tennis balls	T	F	T	F	T	F	T	F
Play tennis outside	X	X	-	-	-	-	-	-
Play tennis inside	-	-	X	X	-	-	-	-
Buy tennis balls	-	X	-	X	-	-	-	-
Read a book on tennis	-	-	-	-	X	X	X	X

FIGURE 2. Decision Table on Playing Tennis

When the rules described in the decision table are exhaustive and mutually exclusive, then for any possible input, one and only one rule will be selected. To process such a decision table the following is done:

1. Enter the table with input;
2. select a single appropriate rule;
3. execute the actions implied by the rule; and
4. exit from the table.

An important consideration in the use of decision tables is their efficient implementation. Decision tables may be simplified by using techniques such as rule merging and sequential testing procedures. Simplification techniques are described in [16,], [17], [18], [20], [21], and [22].

Rule merging simplifies the table by combining rules which imply the same action set. If two rules have the same action set and their condition entries differ only in one condition row, then they may be combined into one rule with a "don't care" for the condition entry in which they differed. Figure 3 shows the tennis decision table after rule merging has been applied. Since the original rules 5, 6, 7 and 8 have the same action set, they can be collapsed into one rule.

Sequential testing procedures are treelike structures which are generated when a limited-entry decision table is converted into a computer program. Many decision table optimization techniques are directed at finding efficient sequential testing procedures. For example, in the tennis decision table one might want to check for a partner before checking the other two conditions. If a partner is not available, the other conditions need not be checked.

	1	2	3	4	5
Tennis court dry	T	T	F	F	-
Partner available	T	T	T	T	F
Have tennis balls	T	F	T	F	-
Play tennis outside	X	X	-	-	-
Play tennis inside	-	-	X	X	-
Buy tennis balls	-	X	-	X	-
Read a book on tennis	-	-	-	-	X

FIGURE 3. Tennis Decision Table After Rule Merging

3. SOME FUZZY CONCEPTS

Since the introduction of fuzzy set theory by Zadeh [26], its implications and applications have been extensively studied. A recent general discussion of fuzzy theory may be found in [12]. A brief summary of the terminology and concepts used later on in this paper is included in this section.

Intuitively, a fuzzy set is a class which admits the possibility of partial membership. Let $X = \{x\}$ denote a space of objects. Specifically, a fuzzy set A in X is a set of ordered pairs $(x,\mu(x))$ where x is an object and $\mu(x)$ is the grade of membership of x in A. Symbolically, $A = \{(x,\mu(x))\}, \forall x \in X$. Generally, it is assumed that $\mu(x)$ is a number in the interval [0,1]. 0 represents non-membership in the fuzzy set while 1 represents full membership. For simplicity, the term "membership grade" of a variable in a set will be replaced by the term "fuzzy variable." In other words, the fuzzy variable (x) will imply $\mu(x)$.

This paper uses the common fuzzy algebra defined by the system $\sum = \langle[0,1],+,*,-\rangle$. + will be interpreted as max, $*$ will be interpreted as min and - will be interpreted as complement where $\mu(\bar{x}) = 1 - \mu(x)$, $\mu(x) \in [0,1]$. The unique identities e_+ and e_* are 0 and 1 respectively. Conventionally, $x * y$ is written simply as xy.

The fuzzy decision tables to be defined in the next section depend upon the use of fuzzy functions. Informally, a fuzzy function may be defined as a form containing fuzzy variables combined with the operations + and $*$. For example, $x_1\bar{x}_2 + \bar{x}_1x_3$ is a fuzzy function. An extensive discussion of fuzzy functions may be found in [8] and [10].

Fuzzy functions may be implemented more efficiently if they can be simplified. For example, the function $x_1\bar{x}_1\bar{x}_2 + x_1\bar{x}_1\bar{x}_3x_4 + x_1\bar{x}_1x_4 +$ $+ x_1\bar{x}_1x_2x_3x_4$ may be simplified to $x_1\bar{x}_1$. The minimization of fuzzy functions has been extensively studied, and detailed descriptions of appropriate algorithms may be found in [2], [5], [8], [9], [10], [11], [14], [23], and [24].

4. FUZZY DECISION TABLES

Traditional decision tables handle Boolean conditions well. But many real conditions are imprecise and are better represented using fuzzy techniques. If a decision table can be modified to be a fuzzy decision table, then it can handle such fuzzy conditions. Fuzzy decision tables can be defined in a manner parallel to Boolean decision tables.

Definition 1: A fuzzy decision table is a decision table where

1. the variables in the condition stub are fuzzy variables,
2. the values in the condition entry are either x_i, $\bar{x}_i$, $x_i\bar{x}_i$, or $x_i + \bar{x}_i$, and
3. the values in the action entry are intervals for accepted grades of membership.

A specific action is taken if the value of the fuzzy function associated with the rules of the fuzzy decision table is within the interval specified in the action entry.

Consider the tennis decision table given previously. The conditions given there were represented as Boolean variables. However, even conditions like these can be regarded as fuzzy. The tennis courts can be completely flooded, completely dry, or some intermediate degree of dryness. Or one could have very old tennis balls on hand that are not really good enough to play with.

Figure 4 gives a fuzzy version of the tennis decision table. Here three fuzzy variables are used: The variable x_1 represents the condition of the courts; a value of 1 is completely dry, and a value of 0 is completely wet. The variable x_2 represents the availability of a partner. A value of 0 indicates that no partner is available, a value of 1 indicates that an ideal partner is available, and an intermediate value indicates that a less than ideal partner is available. The variable x_3 represents the condition of the balls. A value of 0 indicates no balls, a value of 1 indicates brand new balls, and an intermediate value indicates old balls.

	1	2	3	4	5	6	7	8
Tennis courts dry enough	x_1	x_1	$\bar{x}_1$	$\bar{x}_1$	x_1	x_1	$\bar{x}_1$	$\bar{x}_1$
Suitable partner available	x_2	x_2	x_2	x_2	$\bar{x}_2$	$\bar{x}_2$	$\bar{x}_2$	$\bar{x}_2$
Tennis balls in good condition	x_3	$\bar{x}_3$	x_3	$\bar{x}_3$	x_3	$\bar{x}_3$	x_3	$\bar{x}_3$
Play tennis outside	0.7-1.0	0.7-1.0						
Play tennis inside			0.7-1.0	0.7-1.0				
Buy tennis balls		0.7-1.0		0.7-1.0				
Read a book on tennis					0.7-1.0	0.7-1.0	0.7-1.0	0.7-1.0

FIGURE 4. Fuzzy Decision Table On Playing Tennis

One can specity 8 possible rules corresponding to the 8 Boolean rules. Consider the situation where $x_1 = 0.9$ (almost dry), $x_2 = 0.8$ (good partner), and $x_3 = 1.0$ (new balls). The values evaluated for the functions representing each of the condition rules for this case and the following rules are shown in Figure 5. The value evaluated for the Rule 1 function ($x_1x_2x_3$) is 0.8; this value falls within the range specified for the action "play tennis outside" so that action is taken. None of the other rules yield values within the designated ranges so no actions result there.

Rule	Function	$x_1 = 0.9$ $x_2 = 0.8$ $x_3 = 1.0$	$x_1 = 0.8$ $x_2 = 0.0$ $x_3 = 0.7$	$x_1 = 0.9$ $x_2 = 0.0$ $x_3 = 0.4$
1	$x_1x_2x_3$	0.8*	0.0	0.0
2	$x_1x_2\bar{x}_3$	0.0	0.0	0.0
3	$\bar{x}_1x_2x_3$	0.1	0.0	0.0
4	$\bar{x}_1x_2\bar{x}_3$	0.0	0.0	0.0
5	$x_1\bar{x}_2x_3$	0.2	0.7*	0.6
6	$x_1\bar{x}_2\bar{x}_3$	0.0	0.3	0.6
7	$\bar{x}_1\bar{x}_2x_3$	0.1	0.2	0.1
8	$\bar{x}_1\bar{x}_2\bar{x}_3$	0.0	0.2	0.1

FIGURE 5. Some Examples Using The Fuzzy Tennis Decision Table

Consider a second situation in which $x_1 = 0.8$ (pretty dry, $x_2 = 0.0$ (no partner) and $x_3 = 0.7$

(acceptable balls). Here the function for Rule 5 evaluates to 0.7; all others fall outside the indicated ranges. So the fourth action (read a book) is taken.

Consider yet another case. Suppose that x_1 = 0.9 (almost dry), x_2 = 0.0 (no partner) and x_3 = 0.4 (mediocre balls). Here the functions for all rules yield values which fall outside the ranges for action. So no action is taken. This situation illustrates that it is possible to set up a fuzzy decision table in which none of the rules result in an action. As for any decision table, care must be taken that the table is both complete and consistent.

Simplifications and optimizations can be applied to fuzzy decision tables. For this fuzzy tennis table, the last four rules all result in the same action. So these rules can be merged into a single rule. This rule can then be represented by a single fuzzy switching function:

$$x_1\bar{x}_2x_3 + x_1\bar{x}_2\bar{x}_3 + \bar{x}_1\bar{x}_2x_3 + \bar{x}_1\bar{x}_2\bar{x}_3$$

This function can obviously be simplified to a single rule which tests only for x_2 and in which x_1 and x_3 are "don't care" cases. This decision table is shown in Figure 6.

The decision table can be organized for efficient evaluation. For example, the rule resulting from merging the last four should be checked first. If no suitable partner is available, one cannot play tennis at all and the other rules need not be checked.

	1	2	3	4	5
Tennis courts dry enough	x_1	x_1	$\bar{x}_1$	$\bar{x}_1$	-
Suitable partner available	x_2	x_2	x_2	x_2	$\bar{x}_2$
Tennis balls in good condition	x_3	$\bar{x}_3$	x_3	$\bar{x}_3$	-
Play tennis outside	0.7-1.0	0.7-1.0			
Play tennis inside			0.7-1.0	0.7-1.0	
Buy tennis balls		0.7-1.0		0.7-1.0	
Read a book on tennis					0.7-1.0

FIGURE 6. Fuzzy Decision Table On Playing Tennis After Rule Merging

5. MIXED DECISION TABLES

It is possible to define a mixed decision table in which some variables are fuzzy and others Boolean.

Definition 2: A mixed decision table is a decision table where

1. the variables in the condition stub are either fuzzy variables or Boolean variables,

2. the values in the condition entry for a Boolean variable are either T or F,

3. the values in the condition entry for a fuzzy variable are either x_i, $\bar{x}_i$, $x_i\bar{x}_i$, or $x_i + \bar{x}_i$, and

4. the values in the action entry are intervals for accepted grades of membership.

The Boolean variables narrow down the possible rules. Then a specific action is taken if the value of the fuzzy function associated with a rule is within the interval specified in the action entry.

The tennis situation can be handled with a mixed decision table as shown in Figure 7. Here fuzzy variables are used to represent the condition of the courts and of the balls and a Boolean variable is used to represent the availability of a partner.

Tennis courts dry enough	x_1	x_1	$\bar{x}_1$	$\bar{x}$	-
Partner available	T	T	T	T	F
Tennis balls in good condition	x_3	$\bar{x}_3$	x_3	$\bar{x}_3$	-
Play tennis outside	0.7-1.0	0.7-1.0			
Play tennis inside			0.7-1.0	0.7-1.0	
Buy tennis balls		0.7-1.0		0.7-1.0	
Read a book on tennis					0.7-1.0

FIGURE 7. Mixed Tennis Decision Table

From a theoretical point of view, a mixed decision table is no more powerful than a fuzzy decision table. However, it might be seen as a better conceptual model for some situations.

6. DEVELOPMENT AND USE OF FUZZY DECISION TABLES

The steps involved in the use of fuzzy decision tables are outlined in this section. The problem must be specified, and then the decision table can be developed, checked for problems and optimized.

(a) Specify the Problem

The task that the fuzzy decision table is to be used for must be specified. The variables of interest need to be determined; a decision needs to be made about which should be handled as Boolean variables and which as fuzzy variables. Appropriate membership functions for the fuzzy variables should be defined.

(b) Define the Decision Table

The decision table must be defined by specifying the condition variables, the possible actions, and the rules. The decision table at this point may not be in the best format.

(c) Check for Inconsistencies and Omissions

If two rules have the same condition entries but different action entries, they are inconsistent and this inconsistency should be resolved. If some possible assignments of values to the variables result in no action being selected, it should be sure that this is intended.

(d) Merge Appropriate Rules

If two rules have the same action entries but different condition entries, the rules may be merged. This rule merger results in a specification of the merged condition entries in the form of a fuzzy function.

(e) Minimize Any Fuzzy Functions Resulting From Mergers

The fuzzy functions resulting from the previous step may be minimized using the techniques referenced in Section 3.

(f) Order The Rules

The remaining rules in a fuzzy decision table may be ordered for execution purposes using the same basic principles used for Boolean decision tables. These include the number of "don't care" variables and the frequency with which a rule is expected to be selected.

7. EXAMPLES OF FUZZY DECISION TABLES

In this section two examples of fuzzy decision tables are given. Both are used to represent decision rules in realistic situations where the variables of interest are inherently fuzzy. The first involves medical diagnosis, and the second involves the task assignments in a sheltered workshop for mentally retarded children.

Consider the field of medical diagnostics. The symptoms of an illness are usually fuzzy. For example, it is very difficult to describe pain in exact and precise terms. Other symptoms, such as discoloration and swelling, have no exact definition in relation to appearance. The doctor, however, must decide on specific tests to be administered or specific medication to be prescribed based on fuzzy symptoms. For example, the symptoms of monomucleosis and the symptoms of strept throat are similar. A person with mononucleosis often has a low fever, slight throat pain, and is very tired. A person with strept throat is not necessarily tired but often has a high fever and severe throat pain. In this example, it can easily be seen that the conditions of interest are definitely not Boolean. Not having a low fever does not imply having a high fever. Fever, degree of throat pain and level of energy can be considered as fuzzy variables in a fuzzy decision table.

In order to use these fuzzy variables in a fuzzy decision table, degrees of membership must be defined. Degree of throat pain and level of energy are inherently subjective. They might be rated by the patient on a scale of 1 to 10 which is then mapped onto the interval 0 - 1 to define membership functions. An alternative approach would be to use related measures which are less subjective. For example, one might use the degree of throat inflammation as measured by medical personnel and the amount of extra time spent sleeping recently. Body temperature can be measured directly and then mapped onto the 0 - 1 interval. These three fuzzy variables can be referred to as x_1 (degree of throat pain), x_2 (level of energy), and x_3 (fever). In each case the values near 1 represent the more severe symptoms, although this need not be the case.

A person who has classic severe symptoms for strept throat should obviously be given the test for the strept throat. A person who has classic mono symptoms should be given the test for mononucleosis. A person with no symptoms should not be given any tests. People with intermediate or mild symptoms present more of a problem.

A possible fuzzy decision table for this situation is shown in Figure 8. There are three conditions and two possible actions. It is acceptable not to select any action. Rule 1 indicates that if the person has severe throat pain and high fever, a test for strept throat should be given no matter how tired the patient is. Rule 2 indicates that if the patient has been rather tired recently that a test for mono is given. Rule 3 indicates that if the patient has severe throat pain, a test for strept throat is given. If the patient has a high fever, then a test for strept throat is also given according to Rule 4.

	1	2	3	4
Throat pain	x_1	-	$\bar{x}_1$	-
Level of energy	-	x_2	-	-
Fever	x_3	-	-	x_3
Test for mononucleosis		0.5-1.0		
Test for strept throat	0.5-1.0		0.6-1.0	0.6-1.0

FIGURE 8. A Simple Diagnostic Fuzzy Decision Table

Consider a person who has classic strept throat symptoms. The fuzzy variable here might be x_1 = 0.9 (intense throat pain), x_2 = 0.3 (moderately tired), and x_3 = 0.9 (high fever). Evaluation of the first rule gives a value of 0.7. The value of 0.7 falls in the range associated with the test for strept throat, so that test is done. Evaluation of the second rule gives a value of 0.3, so no test for monomucleosis is given.

Since Rules 3 and 4 have the same action entries they can be merged. The fuzzy function for the merged rule is $\bar{x}_1 + x_3$. So there are now three rules represented by fuzzy functions, x_1x_3, x_2, and $x_1 + x_3$. Rule 1 also selects for the strept throat test, but it is not merged since the range specified to choose the action is different. (If both severe throat pain and high fever are present, they do not need to be as bad before a test is called for.)

It is possible to select more than one rule in this table. Consider a person who has a bad sore throat (x_1 = 0.9), is very tired (x_2 = 0.9), and has a high fever (x_3 = 0.9). All four rules would be selected, and both tests would be given.

Another example is job assignments in a Sheltered Workshop for mentally retarded clients. Deciding which client can do which job depends on a number of subjective conditions. Some of these conditions to be considered are a client's gross motor and fine motor skills, a client's eye-hand coordination, a client's attention span, and even a client's ability to work with other clients assigned to the same job. The conditions are imprecise. For example, a person does not either have or not have eye-hand coordination, rather he or she has a degree of eye-hand coordination. This lends itself very well to the idea of a fuzzy variable where coordination is measured as a grade of membership. The same is true for motor skills, attention span and the ability to work with others.

As can be seen by the two preceeding examples, very often the conditions to be considered are naturally fuzzy. Modifying these conditions to fit a traditional decision table could result in losing important levels of distinction. The only way to keep the necessary levels of distinction in a deterministic table is to include conditions for every possible value of each variable being considered. For example, consider a variable for a person's eye-hand coordination. If eye-hand coordination is measured on a scale of one to five, then instead of one condition row for eye-hand coordination, a deterministic decision table would need five condition rows as follows:

1. Eye-hand coordination is 1;

2. Eye-hand coordination is 2;

3. Eye-hand coordination is 3;

4. Eye-hand coordination is 4; and

5. Eye-hand coordination is 5.

Having five condition rows instead of one also increases the number of rules to be considered since the number of possible combinations has increased. If eye-hand coordination is measured on a scale of one to one hundred, then it is possible that one hundred condition rows would be necessary instead on one condition row. Since the number of combinations to be considered becomes extremely large, the table itself becomes too large to work with, with any assurance of completeness. As the number of conditions and rules increases, the chance for error and incompleteness also increases. When a fuzzy variable is used in a condition, this large number of condition rows is not necessary. Since a fuzzy variable represents a grade of membership, only one condition row is necessary to test the value of the eye-hand coordination variable whether the scale for eye-hand coordination is one to five or one to one million.

One possible project in such a sheltered workshop is the production of key chains. The steps associated with this project can be broken down into a number of more specific tasks. For example, a possible subdivision of tasks associated with this project would be:

a. attach chain,

b. count a batch of 200,

c. fill a bag,

d. seal the bag.

The abilities required are not the same for each task. For example, attaching a chain requires more eye-hand coordination than does filling the bag. Three of the many abilities which could be considered in job assignments are eye-hand coordination, finger dexterity, and ability to follow instructions. Each of these could be rated on an appropriate scale and then mapped to a 0 - 1 membership grade. Fuzzy variables can be used for these three conditions: x_1 for eye-hand coordination, x_2 for finger dexterity, and x_3 for ability to follow instructions.

A possible decision table for this situation is shown in Figure 9. Rule 1 indicates that if eye-hand coordination, finger dexterity, and the ability to follow instructions are all high, an assignment to attach chains is reasonable. Counting a batch of 200 requires less desterity and coordination, but still requires an ability to follow instructions; this is covered in Rule 2. Filling and sealing the bag are not very complicated and require only a moderate amount of dexterity; again this situation is covered by Rule 1. Not everyone can be assigned to a task by this decision table because at least a minimum skill level is required to accomplish each task.

Eye-hand coordination	x_1	$\bar{x}_1$
Finger dexterity	x_2	$\bar{x}_2$
Ability to follow instructions	x_3	$\bar{x}_3$
Attach chain	0.7-1.0	
Count a batch of 200		0.5-0.8
Fill a bag	0.2-0.5	
Seal the bag	0.2-0.5	

FIGURE 9. A Fuzzy Decision Table For Job Assignments

8. IMPLEMENTATION OF FUZZY DECISION TABLES

If a decision table is small, as all the examples have been, implementation considerations are relatively unimportant. But this is not the case for the larger fuzzy decision tables which might be of interest in a realistic situation.

Techniques for the optimization of fuzzy decision tables in large part parallel those for Boolean decision tables. Rules can be merged and conditions can be sorted. So the original table can often be reduced in size.

Each rule can be represented as a fuzzy function in disjunctive normal form. The space required depends on the number of rules, the number of variables, and the number of terms in each rule. It takes a minimum of two bits to represent each variable in a term since there are four possibilities (x_1, $\bar{x}_1$, $x\bar{x}_1$, and not present). So, if there are n variables, each term can be represented with 2n bits. Selected action entries are represented by a range of values for membership grades. So a selected action entry requires relatively more space to represent than a rule.

More information is retained in a fuzzy decision table than would be the case in a parallel Boolean table. So it is not to be expected that the fuzzy table could be represented as compactly or processed as quickly. A decision as to the desired tradeoff in processing efficiently as opposed to depth in representation must be made. It should also be remembered that use of a Boolean table might force more complex decisions to be made before entering the table rather than after.

9. SUMMARY AND CONCLUSIONS

The concept of a fuzzy decision table was introduced. Such fuzzy decision tables are based upon the use of fuzzy variables rather than Boolean variables, and they can thus be used in realistic situations where the factors of interest are imprecise. Several examples of fuzzy decision tables were presented and the steps necessary to set up a fuzzy decision table were outlined.

Such fuzzy decision tables have potential, but they need to be developed in more detail. More work could be done on implementation, tests for consistency and completeness, and methods for transforming a problem into a fuzzy decision table. Fortunately, some of the primarily theoretical work in the fuzzy area can be called upon to aid in this task. For example, it has been noted that minimization techniques for fuzzy switching functions, which have been well studied, can be of use in optimizing fuzzy decision tables.

It may well be that a fuzzy decision table could be used as a model of a situation even if it is not used in a final implementation of a computer algorithm. It could serve as an intermediate stage for purposes of design and perhaps be transformed into another form (perhaps a Boolean decision table) to allow more efficient processing.

BIBLIOGRAPHY

[1] Bellman, R. E. & Giertz, M. On the analytic formalism of the theory of fuzzy sets. Information Sciences, 1973, 149-156.

[2] Ben-David, M. On the properties of fuzzy switching functions. Masters Thesis, Department of Computer Science, New Mexico Institute of Mining and Technology, Socorro, New Mexico, August, 1978.

[3] Black, M. Reasoning with loose concepts. Dialogue, 1973, 2, 1-12.

[4] Cantrell, H. N., King, J., & King, F. E. H. Logic structure tables. Communications of the ACM, 1961, 4, 272-275.

[5] Das, S. R., & Khabra, N. S. Clause-column table approach for generating all the prime implicants of switching functions. Technical Report No. 72-4, Department of Electrical Engineering, Faculty of Science and Engineering, University of Ottawa, Ottawa, Canada, 1972.

[6] Decision tables: A system analysis and documentation technique. IBM General Information Manual F20-8102, IBM Corp., White Plains, New York, 1962.

[7] Humby, E. Programs from decision tables. New York: Amer. Elsevier, 1973.

[8] Kandel, A. On minimization of fuzzy functions, IEEE Transactions on Computers, 1973, C-22(9), 826-832.

[9] Kandel, A. On minimization on incompletely specified fuzzy functions, Information and Control, 1974, 26(2), 141-153.

[10] Kandel, A. On the properties of fuzzy switching functions, Journal of Cybernetics, 1974, 4(1), 119-126.

[11] Kandel, A. A note on the simplification of fuzzy switching functions, Information Sciences, 1977, 13, 91-94.

[12] Kandel, A., & Lee, S. C. Fuzzy switching and automata: Theory and applications, New York: Crane, Russak & Company, Inc., 1979.

[13] Kavanagh, T. F. TABSOL--The language of decision making, Computers and Automation, 1961, 10(9:15), 18-22.

[14] Lee, R. C. T., & Chang, C. L. Some properties of fuzzy logic, Information and Control, 1971, 19, 417-431.

[15] Mendelson, E. Introduction to mathematical logic, Princeton, New Jersey: D. Van Nostrand Company, Inc., 1964.

[16] Metzner, J. R., & Barnes, B. H. Decision table language and systems, New York: Academic Press, 1977.

[17] Montalbano, M. Tables, flow charts, and program logic, IBM System Journal, 1962, 51-63.

[18] Montalbano, M. Decision Tables, Chicago: Science Research Associates, Inc., 1974.

[19] Myers, H. J. Compiling optimized code from decision tables. IBM Journal of Research and Development, 1972, 16(5).

[20] Pollack, S. L., Hicks, H. T., & Harrison, W. J. Decision tables: Theory and practice, New York: Wiley (Interscience), 1971.

[21] Reinwald, L. T., & Soland, R. M. Conversion of limited-entry decision tables to optimal computer programs I: Minimum average processing time, Journal of the ACM, 1966, 339-358.

[22] Reinwald, L. T., & Soland, R. M. Conversion of limited-entry decision tables to optimal computer programs II: Minimum storage requirement, Journal of the ACM, 1967, 742-755.

[23] Richman, S. M., & Kandel, A. Column table approach for the minimization of fuzzy functions, Information Sciences, 1977, 12, 111-128.

[24] Siy, P., & Chen, C. S. Minimization of fuzzy functions, IEEE Transactions on Computers, 1972, C-21, 100-102.

[25] Veitch, E. W. A chart method for simplifying truth functions, Proceedings of the ACM National Conference, 1952, 127-134.

[26] Zadeh, L. A. Fuzzy sets, Information and Control, 1965, 8, 338-353.

[27] Zadeh, L. A. A fuzzy-algorithmic approach to the definitions of complex or imprecise concepts, International Journal of Man-Machine Studies, 1976, 8, 249-291.

Approximate Reasoning in Decision Analysis
M.M. Gupta and E. Sanchez (eds.)

NEW CANONICAL FORMS OF FUZZY SWITCHING FUNCTIONS

Masao Mukaidono

Faculty of Engineering
Meiji University

1-1-1 Higashi-mita Tamaku
Kawasaki-shi JAPAN 214

New canonical forms of fuzzy switching functions are proposed and are explained in detail by using simple examples.
The new canonical forms have the advantages of already known canonical forms.

Keywords: Fuzzy switching function, Fuzzy logic, Canonical form.

1. INTRODUCTION

Since L.A.Zadeh[1965] introduced the concept of fuzzy sets as an attempt to treat certain ambiguities, an infinite multiple-valued switching mechanism, entitled fuzzy switching functions or fuzzy logic functions, has been studied by many researchers (see, for example, Kandel and Lee[[1979] and Dubois and Prade [1980]).

Concerning the representation of fuzzy switching functions, Preparata and Yeh[1972] gave the preliminary forms which are composed of a pair of logic formulas. In the paper on B-ternary logic functions, Mukaidono[1970,1972] was the first to provide the canonical forms of fuzzy switching functions which are used at present as standard representations of fuzzy switching functions. The same canonical forms were proposed independently by Davio and Thayse[1973]. These canonical forms, canonical disjunctive form and canonical conjunctive form, of a fuzzy switching function are determined uniquely for any given fuzzy switching function. The proof of the uniqueness of these forms can be found in Mukaidono[1972, 1975]. Kandel[1973] used implicitly these canonical forms for finding minimized fuzzy switching functions.

The present paper proposes new canonical forms of fuzzy switching functions, which are uniquely determined also, based on the properties of already known canonical forms which this paper surveys at first. These new canonical forms have the advantages of existing canonical forms. The new canonical forms are composed of two parts -- the disjunctive and conjunctive parts. While a charactristic of existing canonical form is that they have contradictory phrases or tautological clauses as their factors, the new canonical forms have not. Furthermore, it is shown that the new canonical forms are directly applicable to enumerating the number of distinct fuzzy switching functions.

In general, the term "canonical form", as usually in symbolic logic, refers to a standered type of formula capable of rendering any functional mapping:$C^n \to C$, where C is the carrier, that is, the primitive functions deployed in the canonical formula form a functionally complete system for the functions:$C^n \to C$. In this paper, we use the term "canonical form" as the following meaning: We can represent uniqeuly any fuzzy switching function which is a special kind of continuously function:$[0,1]^n \to [0,1]$, by using the canonical form, that is, the primitive functions deployed in the canonical formula form a functionally complete system for the sub-set, called fuzzy switching functions, of the functions:$[0,1]^n \to [0,1]$, instead of for the functions:$[0,1]^n \to [0,1]$.

2. REPRESENTATIONS OF FUZZY SWITCHING FUNCTIONS

Let a symbol V denote the closed interval [0,1]. A function F from the domeine V^n to the range V is called a n-variable fuzzy function. A fuzzy function expressible by a logic formula is, especially, called a fuzzy switching function.

[Definition 1] (1) 0, 1 and $x_i (i=1,\cdots,n)$ are logic formulae,
(2) if G and H are logic formulae, then G·H, G+H and $\overline{G}$ are logic formulae, respectively,
(3) the only logic formulae are given by (1) and (2).

In the definition of the logic formula, if the variable x_i takes the value of V and the logic operations ·(AND or conjunction), +(OR or disjunction) and $^-$ (NOT or negation) are defined such that:

$$x_i \cdot x_j = \min(x_i, x_j),$$
$$x_i + x_j = \max(x_i, x_j),$$
$$\overline{x}_i = 1 - x_i, \text{ where } x_i \text{ and } x_j \text{ are elements of}$$

V, then a logic formula represents a fuzzy function.

[Definition 2] A fuzzy function represented by a logic formula is called a fuzzy switching function.

Hereafter we will identify a logic formula with the function represented by it and omit the symbol $\cdot$ in the logic formula for simplicity.

[Example 1] $(x_1+x_2\bar{x}_3)(\bar{x}_1+\bar{x}_2+x_3+x_1x_2)+x_2\bar{x}_2x_3$ is a logic formula and represents a fuzzy switching function $F(x_1,x_2,x_3):V^3\to V$. In this case, for example, $F(0.2,0.6,0.5)=(0.2+0.6\cdot(1-0.5))\cdot((1-0.2)+(1-0.6)+0.5+0.2\cdot 0.6)+0.6\cdot(1-0.6)\cdot 0.5=0.5\cdot 0.8+0.4=0.5$.

A literal is a variable x_i or $\bar{x}_i$, the negation of x_i. A phrase is a conjunction of one or more literals and a clause is a disjunction of one or more literals. In the definition of the phrase or clause it is assumed that any repeated literals are removed from it.

A fuzzy switching function F is said to be in a disjunctive form if

$$F=P_1+\cdots+P_m \quad (P_i(1\leq i\leq m) \text{ is a phrase and } P_i\not\subset P_j \text{ if } i\neq j),$$

and is said to be in a conjunctive form if

$$F=C_1\cdot\cdots\cdot C_j \quad (C_i(1\leq i\leq m) \text{ is a clause and } C_i\not\subset C_j \text{ if } i\neq j).$$

In fuzzy logic it is possible to express any fuzzy switching function in both disjunctive and conjunctive form in accordance with the distributive laws, De Morgan's laws and the absorption laws as in the two valued logic except the complementary laws. For any given fuzzy switching function F, in general, the disjunctive form or the conjunctive form of F is not determined uniquely.

[Example 2] The example fuzzy switching function F of Example 1 can be expressed in disjunctive form (1) and in conjunctive form (2) as follow:

$$F=x_1\bar{x}_2+x_1x_2+x_1x_3+\bar{x}_1x_2\bar{x}_3+x_1\bar{x}_1+x_2\bar{x}_2x_3+x_2x_3\bar{x}_3+x_2\bar{x}_2\bar{x}_3 \quad \text{------------(1)}$$

$$=(x_1+x_2)(x_1+\bar{x}_2+\bar{x}_3)(\bar{x}_1+x_2+\bar{x}_2+x_3)(x_1+\bar{x}_1+\bar{x}_2+x_3)(x_1+x_3+\bar{x}_3) \quad \text{------------(2).}$$

In a disjunctive form of a fuzzy switching function, there are two kinds of phrases: one is a phrase, called contradictory phrase or complementary phrase, which contains a factor $x_i\bar{x}_i$ for at least one variable x_i, and the other is a phrase, called simple phrase, which does not contain the above. Similary, a conjunctive form contains two kinds of clauses: a tautological clause which contains a factor $x_i+\bar{x}_i$ for at least one variable x_i, and a simple clause which does not contain it.

[Example 3] In (1) of Example 2, $x_1\bar{x}_2$, x_1x_2, x_1x_3 and $\bar{x}_1x_2\bar{x}_3$ are simple phrases, and $x_1\bar{x}_1$, $x_2\bar{x}_2x_3$ and $x_2x_3\bar{x}_3$ are contradictory phrases. In (2) of Example 2, (x_1+x_2) and $(x_1+\bar{x}_2+\bar{x}_3)$ are simple clauses, and $(\bar{x}_1+x_2+\bar{x}_2+x_3)$, $(x_1+\bar{x}_1+\bar{x}_2+x_3)$ and $(x_1+x_3+\bar{x}_3)$ are tautological clauses.

If a contradictory phrase (a tautological clause) contains all variables as factors, then it is called complete.

In the two valued logic, any phrase (clause) can be expanded into the disjunction (conjunction) of minterms (maxterms) which contain all variables as factors. In the fuzzy logic, it is not true for simple phrases (simple clauses) but true for contradictory phrases (tautological clauses). That is, any contradictory phrase (tautological clause) can be expanded into the disjunction (conjunction) of completed contradictory phrases (completed tautological clauses), because

$$\alpha x_i\bar{x}_i=\alpha x_i\bar{x}_i(x_j+\bar{x}_j)=\alpha x_i\bar{x}_ix_j+\alpha x_i\bar{x}_i\bar{x}_j\leq 1/2$$

$$(\alpha+x_i+\bar{x}_i=\alpha+x_i+\bar{x}_i+x_j\bar{x}_j=(\alpha+x_i+\bar{x}_i+x_j)(\alpha+x_i+\bar{x}_i+\bar{x}_j)\geq 1/2)$$

folds for any i and j, where α is an any phrase (clause).

[Example 4]

$$x_2\bar{x}_2x_3=(x_1+\bar{x}_1)x_2\bar{x}_2x_3=x_1x_2\bar{x}_2x_3+\bar{x}_1x_2\bar{x}_2x_3,$$

$$x_1+x_3+\bar{x}_3=x_1+x_2\bar{x}_2+x_3+\bar{x}_3=(x_1+x_2+x_3+\bar{x}_3)(x_1+\bar{x}_2+x_3+\bar{x}_3).$$

Here, we can obtain the canonical disjunctive form of a fuzzy switching function,which is given by the following algorithm (Davio and Thayse[1973], Mukaidono[1972,1975]):

(1) expand the formula into a disjunctive form;
(2) expand the contradictory phrases into a disjunction of completed contradictory phrases;
(3) suppress redundant phrases using the absorption laws.

In the similar manner we can obtain the canonical conjunctive form of a fuzzy switching function. These canonical forms are determined uniquely for any given fuzzy switching function. We will call the canonical form given by the above algorithm type 1. It is composed of the disjunction of simple phrases and completed contradictory phrases, or of the conjunction of simple clauses and completed tautological clauses.

[Example 5] The following (3) and (4) are the type 1 canonical disjunctive and conjunctive forms of the fuzzy switching function of Example 2.

$$F=x_1\bar{x}_2+x_1x_2+x_1x_3+\bar{x}_1x_2\bar{x}_3+\bar{x}_1x_2\bar{x}_2x_3 \quad \text{-------(3)}$$

$$=(x_1+x_2)(x_1+\bar{x}_2+\bar{x}_3)(\bar{x}_1+x_2+\bar{x}_2+x_3)(x_1+\bar{x}_1+\bar{x}_2+x_3) \quad \text{-------(4)}$$

3. FUNDAMENTAL PROPERTIES OF FUZZY SWITCHING FUNCTIONS

Let V_3 be a set of 0, 1 and 1/2. Then, the following theorem is already known as a fundamental properties of fuzzy switching functions:

[Theorem 1] (Preparata and Yeh[1972],Mukaidono[1975])
If fuzzy switching functions F and G satisfy

$F(A)=G(A)$ for all A of V_3^n,

then, F and G are identical fuzzy switching functions, that is,

$F(A)=G(A)$ for all A of V^n.

This theorem shows that a fuzzy switching function is uniquely determined by the values at the elements of V_3^n. Therefore, the question as to whether or not one fuzzy switching function is equal to another is answered in a finite number of steps by testing whether or not it is equal in V_3^n. The above fact was proved by Preparata and Yeh[1972] by means of vector spaces and by Mukaidono[1975] by means of the partial ordered relation describing ambiguity which is defined as follow:

The partial ordered relation that describes ambiguity is ¶ such that: for all a_i and a_j of V, $a_i \P a_j$ if and only if either $1/2 \leq a_i \leq a_j$ or $1/2 \geq a_i \geq a_j$. We have always $1/2 \P a_i$ for all a_i of V. Moreover, a_i of (1/2,1] and a_j of [0,1/2) cannot be compared with each other. $a_i \P a_j$ means that a_i is more ambiguous than or equal to a_j. The relation ¶ is extended to V^n as follows: for $A=(a_1,\cdots,a_n)$, $B=(b_1,\cdots,b_n)$, $A \P B$ if and only if $a_i \P a_j$ for all i.

The following theorem shows an important properties of fuzzy switching functions:

[Theorem 2] (Mukaidono[1975])
Let F be a fuzzy switching function. If A¶B, then F(A)¶F(B).

As a consequence of the theorem we have, if $F(A)=1/2$, then $F(B)=1/2$ for all B such as B¶A, and if F(A) is 0 or 1, then F(A)=F(B) for all B such as A¶B.

4. NEW CANONICAL FORMS OF FUZZY SWITCHING FUNCTIONS

Let F be a fuzzy switching function and

$F=F_{sp}+F_{cp}$

be the type 1 canonical disjunctive form and

$F=F_{sc}\cdot F_{cc}$

be the type 1 canonical conjunctive form of F, where F_{sp} (F_{cp}) is a disjunction of simple phrases (completed contradictory phrases) and F_{sc} (F_{cc}) is a conjunction of simple clauses (completed tautological clauses).

[Lemma 1] Let F be a fuzzy switching function and $F=F_{sp}+F_{cp}$, $F=F_{sc}\cdot F_{cc}$ be the type 1 canonical forms of F. Then, the following properties hold:

(1) $F(A)=1$ if and only if $F_{sp}(A)=1$,

(2) $F(A)=0$ if and only if $F_{sc}(A)=0$,

(3) $F(A)=1/2$ if $F_{sp}(A)=1/2$,

(4) $F(A)=1/2$ if $F_{sc}(A)=1/2$,

(5) if $F(A)=1$, then $F_{sc}(A)=1$ and $F_{cc}(A)=1$,

(6) if $F(A)=0$, then $F_{sp}(A)=0$ and $F_{cp}(a)=0$.

(Proof) (1)$\cdots$(4) are derived from the fact $F_{cp}(A)\leq 1/2$ and $F_{cc}(A)\geq 1/2$ for all A of V^n. (5) and (6) are evident by the definition. (Q.E.D.)

For any given fuzzy switching function F, let F_p be the fuzzy switching function which is represented by the disjunction (conjunction) of all prime implicants (prime implicates) of F in the two valued logic sense. That is,

$F_p=P_1+P_2+\cdots+P_m=Q_1\cdot Q_2\cdot\cdots\cdot Q_s$,

where P_i $(1\leq i\leq m)$ is a prime implicant of F and Q_i $(1\leq i\leq s)$ is a prime implicate of F in the two valued logic sense.

[Example 6] For the fuzzy switching function F of our example, F_p is given by the followings:

$F_p=x_1+x_2\bar{x}_3=(x_1+x_2)(x_1+\bar{x}_3)$.

[Lemma 2] (Mukaidono[1972])

(1) $F_{sc}(A)=1$ if and only if $F_p(A)=1$,

(2) $F_{sp}(A)=0$ if and only if $F_p(A)=0$,

(3) if $F(A)=1$, then $F_p(A)=1$,

(4) if $F(A)=0$, then $F_p(A)=0$.

[Lemma 3]

$$F_{sp}=F_p\cdot F_{cc} \qquad \text{--------------------(5)}$$

$$F_{sc}=F_p+F_{cp} \qquad \text{--------------------(6)}$$

(Proof)
It is sufficient if we prove that (5) and (6) are valid for all elements of V_3^n by Theorem 1. If $F_{sp}(A)=1$, then $F(A)=1=F_p(A)=F_{cc}(A)$ (Lemma 1 and Lemma 2). Therefore, (5) holds. If $F_{sp}(A)=1/2$, then $F_p(A)=1/2$ or 1 (Lemma 2). If $F_{sp}(A)=F_p(A)=1/2$, then (5) is valid because $F_{cc}(A)\geq 1/2$ holds always. Suppose $F_{sp}(A)=1/2$ and $F_p(A)=1$. Then $F_{sc}(A)=1$ (Lemma 2) and $F(A)=1/2$ because of $F=F_{sp}+F_{cp}$ and $F_{cp}(A)\leq 1/2$. Therefore, it must be $F_{cc}(A)=1/2$ because $F=F_{sc}\cdot F_{cc}$. Therefore, (5) holds. If $F_{sp}(A)=0$, then $F_p(A)=0$ (Lemma 2). Therefore, (5) is valid. In all cases (5) is valid. In the similar manner we can prove (6). (Q.E.D.)

[Lemma 4]

$$F_{sc}\geq F_p\geq F_{sp}.$$

(Proof) It is evident from Lemma 3. (Q.E.D.)

[Lemma 5]

$$F_{cp} \leq F_{sc} \cdot 1/2 \quad \text{------------------------(7)}$$

$$F_{cc} \geq F_{cp} + 1/2 \quad \text{------------------------(8).}$$

(Proof) It is evident that $F_{cp} \leq 1/2$. We can obtain $F_{cp} \leq F_{sc}$ because $F_{cp}+F_{sc}=F_{cp}+F_{p}+F_{cp}=F_{cp}+F_{p}=F_{sc}$ (Lemma 3). Therefore, we can prove (7). On the other hand, $F_{cc} \geq 1/2$ is evident and $F_{cc} \cdot F_{sp} = F_{cc} \cdot F_{p} \cdot F_{cc} = F_{cc} \cdot F_{p} = F_{sp}$ (Lemma 3) leads to $F_{cc} \geq F_{sp}$. Therefore, we can arrive at (8). (Q.E.D.)

[Lemma 6]

$$1/2 \cdot F_{sc} = 1/2 \cdot F,$$

$$1/2 + F_{sp} = 1/2 + F.$$

(Proof) $1/2 \cdot F = 1/2 \cdot F_{sc} \cdot F_{cc} = F_{sc} \cdot (1/2 \cdot F_{cc}) = F_{sc} \cdot 1/2$, $1/2+F=1/2+F_{sp}+F_{cp}=F_{sp}+(1/2+F_{cp})=F_{sp}+1/2$. (Q.E.D.)

[Lemma 7] (Davio and Thayse[1973],Mukaidono[1975b, 1978])

$$F = F_{p} \cdot F_{cc} + F_{cp}$$

$$= (F_{p} + F_{cp}) \cdot F_{cc}.$$

(Proof) It is evident from the definition and Lemma 3. (Q.E.D.)

The forms of Lemma 7 can be used as canonical forms of fuzzy switching function, which we will call type 2, because F_{p}, F_{cc} and F_{cp} are determined uniquely for any given fuzzy switching function F. The type 2 canonical forms were already known and it was shown that they were applicable to the detection of hazards in combinational switching circuits (Mukaidono[1978]).

[Example 7] For the fuzzy switching function F of our example, F_{cc} and F_{cp} are given by the following:

$$F_{cc} = (\bar{x}_1+x_2+\bar{x}_2+x_3)(x_1+\bar{x}_1+\bar{x}_2+x_3),$$

$$F_{cp} = \bar{x}_1 x_2 \bar{x}_2 x_3.$$

Therefore, the type 2 canonical forms of F are given by

$$F = (x_1+x_2)(x_1+\bar{x}_3)(\bar{x}_1+x_2+\bar{x}_2+x_3)(x_1+\bar{x}_1+\bar{x}_2+x_3) + \bar{x}_1 x_2 \bar{x}_2 x_3$$

$$= (x_1+x_2\bar{x}_3+\bar{x}_1 x_2 \bar{x}_2 x_3)(\bar{x}_1+x_2+\bar{x}_2+x_3)(x_1+\bar{x}_1+\bar{x}_2+x_3)$$

Using the above lemmas, we have new canonical forms of fuzzy switching functions as follows:

[Theorem 3] Let F be a fuzzy switching function, and F_{sp} and F_{sc} be the disjunction of simple phrases and the conjunction of simple clauses of the type 1 canonical forms of F, respectively. Then,

$$F = F_{sp} + 1/2 \cdot F_{sc} \quad \text{-------------------------(9)}$$

$$= (F_{sp} + 1/2) \cdot F_{sc} \quad \text{-----------------------(10).}$$

(Proof) From Lemma 5, we can prove

$$F_{sp} + 1/2 \cdot F_{sc} \geq F_{sp} + F_{cp} = F.$$

On the other hand, $F_{sp}+1/2 \cdot F_{sc} = (F_{sp}+1/2)(F_{sp}+F_{sc})$. Lemma 4 shows that $F_{sp}+F_{sc}=F_{sc}$ holds always. Therefore, Lemma 5 gives $F_{sp}+1/2 \cdot F_{sc} = (F_{sp}+1/2) \cdot F_{sc} \leq F_{cc} \cdot F_{sc} = F$. From the above, we can prove $F = F_{sp}+1/2 \cdot F_{sc}$. In the similar manner, we can prove (10). (Q.E.D.)

For any given fuzzy switching function F, F_{sp} and F_{sc} are determined uniquely. Therefore, we can adopt the formulae (9) and (10) as new canonical forms of fuzzy switching functions. We will call the new canonical forms type 3.

The following is an algorithm to obtain the type 3 canonical form:

(1) expand the formula into the disjunction of simple phrases, F_{sp}, ignoring the contradictory phrases, and suppress redundant phrases using the absorption laws,

(2) expand the formula into the conjunction of simple clauses, F_{sc}, ignoring the tautological clauses, and suppress redundant clauses using the absorption laws,

(3) $F=F_{sp}+1/2 \cdot F_{sc}$ or $F=(F_{sp}+1/2) \cdot F_{sc}$ is the type 3 canonical form.

[Example 8] For the example fuzzy switching function F, F_{sp} and F_{sc} are given by the following:

$$F_{sp} = x_1\bar{x}_2 + x_1 x_2 + x_1 x_3 + \bar{x}_1 x_2 \bar{x}_3,$$

$$F_{sc} = (x_1+x_2)(x_1+\bar{x}_2+\bar{x}_3)$$

Therefore, the type 3 canonical forms of F are given by

$$F = x_1\bar{x}_2 + x_1 x_2 + x_1 x_3 + \bar{x}_1 x_2 \bar{x}_3 + 1/2(x_1+x_2)(x_1+\bar{x}_2+\bar{x}_3)$$

$$= (x_1\bar{x}_2 + x_1 x_2 + x_1 x_3 + \bar{x}_1 x_2 \bar{x}_3 + 1/2)(x_1+x_2)(x_1+\bar{x}_2+\bar{x}_3).$$

In comparison with the existing canonical forms, the type 1 and the type 2, the new canonical forms described here, the type 3, have the following characteristics; that is, they do not include any contradictory phrases and tautological clauses which are unnatural in the two valued logic sense. In addition, it is shown(Mukaidono [1982]) that they are applicable to enumerating the number of n-variable distinct fuzzy switching functions. In fact, the number of 4-variable distinct fuzzy switching functions, 160297985276, was enumerated by using the type 3 canonical forms of fuzzy switching functions (Berman and Mukaidono[1981]).

ACKNOWLEDGEMENT

I would like to thank Honorary Professor M. Goto of Meiji University and Professor L.A. Zadeh of University of California at Berkeley for their continued encouragement and Professor J. Berman of the University of Illinois at Chicago Circle for his discussions on the subject.

REFERENCES

Berman, J. and Mukaidono, M.[1981], The number of fuzzy switching functions in four variables, Abstracts of the American Mathematical Society, Vol.2.

Davio, M. and Thayse, A.[1973], Representations of fuzzy functions, Phillips Res. Reports 28, 93--106.

Dubois, D. and Prade, H.[1980], Fuzzy Sets and Systems, Academic Press, New York.

Kandel, A.[1973], On minimization of fuzzy functions, IEEE Trans. Computer, C-22, 826--832.

Kandel, A. and Lee, S.[1979], Fuzzy Switching and Automata: Theory and Applications, Crame Russak, New York.

Mukaidono, M.[1970]. On B-ternary logical functions, (in Japanese) Paper of Technical Group on Theory and Automata, IECE Japan, A70-73.

Mukaidono, M.[1972], On the B-ternary logical functions--A ternary logic considering ambiguity, Systems·Computers·Controls, 3,No.3, 27--36.

Mukaidono, M.[1975], On some properties of fuzzy logic, Systems·Computers·Controls, 6, No.2, 36--43.

Mukaidono, M.[1975b], An algebraic structure of fuzzy logical functions and its minimal and irredundant forms, Systems·Computers·Controls, 6, No.6.

Mukaidono, M.[1978], The B-ternary logic and its applications to the detection of hazards in combinational switching circuits, International Symposium on Multiple-Valued Logic-8.

Mukaidono, M.[1982], New canonical forms and their applications to enumerating fuzzy switching functions, International Symposium on Multiple-Valued Logic-12.

Preparata, F. and Yeh, R.[1972], Continuously valued logic, J. Computer and Systems Sciences 6, 397--418.

Zadeh, L. A.[1965], Fuzzy sets, Information and Control, 8, 338--353.

Approximate Reasoning in Decision Analysis
M.M. Gupta and E. Sanchez (eds.)

FUZZY SYSTEMS IN CIVIL ENGINEERING

David Blockley

Department of Civil Engineering,
University of Bristol,
Bristol, England

Practising engineers call upon judgement and experience in interpreting theoretical models applied to complex systems. Thus a mathematics is required which can not only handle precise propositions with an associated randomness but also imprecision, vagueness and fuzziness. It is for this reason that some civil engineering researchers have begun to examine the role of fuzzy systems analysis.
In this chapter a review is made of progress principally in the estimation of structural safety and reliability. The first efforts involved the use of fuzzy sets and the use of various entropy measures. The use of Baldwin's fuzzy logic is also described with an example. Finally the development of an expert systems approach is anticipated.

KEYWORDS Civil Engineering, Structures, Safety, Reliability
Fuzzy Sets, Fuzzy Logic, Human Error.

1. INTRODUCTION

Human beings have a number of basic needs which are necessary to ensure emotional security, and one of them is adequate shelter and protection from the elements. It is the civil and structural engineer who provides this shelter, amongst other things, and he has consequently to do it with low risk of structural failure. People's perception of risk is complex and requires much further research work. For example risk which is sort out and is present for only a short time can be stimulating (e.g. mountaineering) and on the other hand there is a tendency for greater public concern about one accident costing 50 lives than 50 accidents costing one life each. Structural failures are fortunately rare but consequently public reaction to the unexpected can be considerable. Clearly it is important that the civil engineer understands and controls the risk of structural failure so that adequate safety levels may be maintained.

Engineering is often described as an applied science, but this is an oversimplification. An eminent engineer Hardy Cross described it thus {1} "Engineering is an old art. It has always demanded ability to weigh evidence, to draw common-sense conclusions, to work out a simple and satisfactory synthesis and then see that the synthesis can be carried out". "Thoughtful engineers weigh the findings presented to them through all or any of these sources (theory, experience, hunches etc.) with a full appreciation of the effect their personal prejudices might have on conclusions drawn from evidence".

Fundamentally, engineering is about making things, and in order to make things it is necessary to decide what is to be done. To decide what is to be done requires information and this is inevitably of variable quality. There is a growing tendency to think of engineering as a management type discipline rather than an applied science because information, whether scientific or non scientific, is a basis for decision and hence action. Illustrative of this more general approach is the recently published report by the International Association for Bridge and Structural Engineering {2} outlining general principles concerning quality assurance for structures and on reliability for structural design.

Information useful to the engineer is varied and complex. It may be both informative and restrictive such as national regulations and specifications; it may be commercial information about available products or it may concern experience from similar work or information about the site. One of the most important sources however, is what might be called professional information and includes engineering knowledge. Engineering knowledge has been classified into three parts {3}; firstly science and mathematics, consisting for structural engineers of deductions based on Newtonian mechanics and tested in laboratory controlled conditions. Secondly the application of science and mathematics (with necessary approximating assumptions) to the design of actual structures and this knowledge is tested by the success or failure of these structures. Thirdly, 'rules of thumb', heuristics, or common sense hypotheses of restricted scope which are also tested by the performance of the structure in service. The last two categories necessarily involve the difficult area of subjective judgement but as scientific knowledge develops so the role of the third category reduces. However there is still a very large requirement for subjective judgement on the basis of an individual engineer's experience. There tends to be, in consequence, two attitudes within engineering; the first is that of the 'engineering scientist' who is dominated by the scientific interest in accuracy and as a result often frowns upon 'rules' as being intellectually inferior; the second is that of the 'practical engineer' who relies heavily on intuition, rules of thumb and experience and tends to mistrust advanced scientific and mathematical research. It has been argued {4} that one of the reasons for this attitude gap is that traditional science and mathematics is literal minded. Mathematics is able to deal successfully with simple situations and only with more complex situations to the extent that they depend upon a few dominant factors. Schwarz {5} is quoted "That form of wisdom which is the opposite of single mindedness, the ability to keep many threads in hand, to draw for an argument from many disparate sources, is quite foreign to mathematics. This inability accounts for much of the difficulty which mathematics experiences in attempting to penetrate the social sciences". Armitage {6} considers the skill of engineering judgement is the ability to gauge the sensitivity of the final outcome to the various influences upon it.

If traditional mathematics is to be extended so that it may have greater impact on problems of complex systems, it must be able to process imprecise data and incorporate the judgement of experts. It necessarily involves more than that uncertainty due to randomness, it concerns imprecision and many to many relationships. It is this sort of thinking which has led some civil engineering researchers to examine fuzzy sets and systems. In this chapter an outline will be given of some of the developments in the use of fuzzy sets and fuzzy logic in civil engineering, chiefly on problems of structural safety and reliability.

2. UNCERTAINTY

The engineer has to make decisions about all aspects of his design solution. He has to ensure that the structure will be constructed successfully and that it will be successfully used for its desired life span. The small, but finite, chance that an accident will happen has to be kept acceptably low. Table 1 shows a classification of the causes of failure. The first group, the limit states of the structure, are those states which the engineer spends most of his calculational effort in avoiding. Various safety measures may be used in these calculations to avoid, for instance, a load effect overcoming a strength effect. Any assessment of safety is based on descriptions of the behaviour of the structure using a theoretical model. The models used vary in accuracy and consequently any assessment of safety must take this into account. Assuming no human error, the system uncertainty arises from the inaccuracy of the theoretical model, given precise input parameters. Alternatively, the parameter uncertainty arises from the uncertain values of the parameters which should be input into the system model in order to solve a particular problem. The second group of hazards is that of external random hazards such as fires, floods and vehicle impact. The third group concerns that human based error which is normally dealt with by trying to ensure good professional practice by all those people involved in a particular project. It has been shown recently by studies of actual structural failures that human error is a major contributory factor to failure {4, 7, 12}.

Table 1 Some Causes of Structural Failure

Limit states	
Overload:	geophysical, dead, wind, earthquake, etc.; man made, imposed, etc.
Understrength:	structure, materials instability
Movement:	foundation settlement, creep, shrinkage, etc.;
Deterioration:	cracking, fatigue, corrosion, erosion, etc.
Random hazards	
Fire	
Floods	
Explosions:	accidental, sabotage
Earthquake	
Vehicle impact	
Human based errors	
Design error:	mistake, misunderstanding of structure behaviour
Construction error:	mistake, bad practice, poor communications

Ordinary reliability theory {8} has been applied to the problem of determining adequate safety factors for use in design. However, it is argued {4} that such calculations can only consider parameter uncertainty and that if the system uncertainty is large (as it often is) or if human error is to be considered them some other method of tackling the problem is required.

3. SYSTEM UNCERTAINTY AND FUZZY SETS

Early work on this problem is typified by Blockley and Ellison {9}. A simplified treatment of the difficult problem of predicting the life of components operating in modern power plant such as nuclear reactors, gas and steam turbines, was used to demonstrate the method. These components are subject to complex loading cycles at elevated temperatures so that combined fatigue/creep damage often occurs. Certain representative service conditions can be simulated in laboratory tests by subjecting the material to plastic strains with suitable dwell periods of, say, 30 minutes at the maximum strain in the cycle. The problem then becomes one of predicting behaviour with say a 16 hour dwell period. The data is very sparse because of the difficulty of performing laboratory tests. The deterministic method utilises curves drawn through experimental data for virgin state creep tests which are then used to find a time to rupture. Experimental data of numbers of cycles to failure for various strain ranges give a value for cycles to failure at a given cyclic strain rate and the predicted life is determined by the use of a linear damage rule for summing up the fatigue creep damage. In order to consider the likely variability in the estimate of this life due both to uncertainties in the relationship between, for example, cyclic strain and peak stress, the experimental curves were reconsidered as fuzzy relations and the linear damage rule as a fuzzy mapping. Instead of a one-to-one relation, therefore, between strain range and peak stress, the relation was a many-to-many mapping with various degrees of belief, on behalf of the experimentalist, about the membership of a particular mapping on the cartesian product. For example fig. 1 shows the relation of cyclic strain with peak stress used in the calculation, details of which are given {9}.

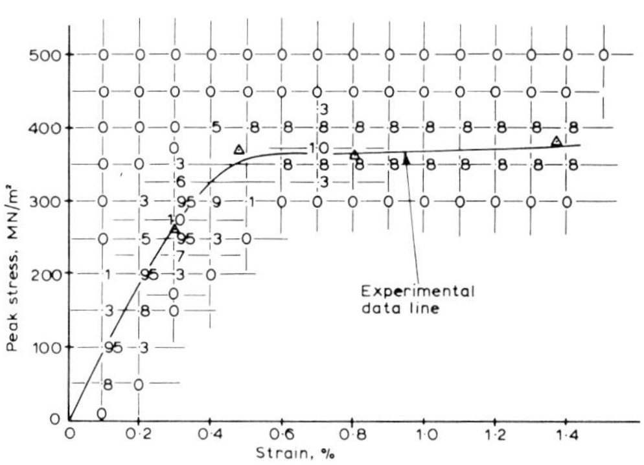

Fig 1 Peak stress vs cyclic strain. Experimental data and membership levels of R

Brown {10} was rather more precise in the separation of objective and subjective information. He clearly separated countable data where uncertainty can be expressed in a frequentist probabilistic sense, from information which derives from the mental process of the engineer and involves experience, understanding, ability and intuition. As an example he discussed a problem concerning the strength of concrete in a structure. As a guide, cylinder tests on samples extracted from concrete poured in the structure are tested after appropriate preservation measures. A frequentist perception is obtained which indicates that the probability of the strength exceeding or equalling θ is p and that being smaller than θ is 1 - p. These are countable data cast in a probabilistic form. However, it is not claimed that the probability of the strength of the concrete in the structure being greater than θ is p. Reported empirical results suggest different values from p and this viewpoint is backed up by the knowledge of the contractor and concrete supplier about weather and curing. It is essential that this perspective is included in a proper interpretation of the data. The problem, as Brown sees it, is to update p to $\hat{p}$ in the light of this mental perception. He obtains p by maximising the information entropy subject to the countable data restraints and then a fuzzy entropy is constructed that is a measure of the imprecision. The sum of the two entropies provides a measure which is utilised to determine the updated $\hat{p}$.

The definition of entropy within fuzzy sets used by Brown was that of De Luca and Termini or

$$G = K \sum_{i=1}^{n} p_i G_i$$

where $G_i = -\chi(x_i) \ln \chi(x_i) - (1 - \chi(x_i)) \ln (1 - \chi(x_i))$

where $\chi(x_i)$ is the fuzzy support for membership in x_i and the combined entropy is

$$F(p_i;\chi) = - \sum_{i=1}^{n} p_i \ln p_i + D \sum_{i=1}^{n} p_i G_i$$

The quantities $\hat{p}_i$ were obtained by Brown by arranging that the information entropy equals the combined entropy so that

$$F(p;\chi) = - \sum_i \hat{p}_i \ln \hat{p}_i$$

Some criterion for the evaluation of D was needed and Brown suggested that when all $\chi(x_i)$ are a half then $\hat{p}_i$ must be $\frac{1}{n}$. Using this

$$D = \frac{1}{\ln 2} (\ln n + \sum p_i \ln p_i)$$

Munro {11} pointed out that this formulation implies that the decision maker abandons the prior statistical knowledge when he is undecided about the relevance of the statistics. He argued that most decision makers would attach some credence to the prior statistical knowledge until convinced of its irrelevance. In order to incorporate this criteria he modified the combined entropy as

$$C = - \sum p_i \ln p_i - \sum \ln \left[\chi(x_i) + c (1 - \chi(x_i)) \right]$$

where c is a scaling constant determined from the criteria that

(i) if all $\chi(x_i) = 0$, all $\hat{p}_i = \frac{1}{n}$

(ii) if all $\chi(x_i) = 1$, then $C = - \sum p_i \ln p_i$

so that $c = \exp \left[\frac{\sum p_i \ln p_i - \ln n}{n} \right]$.

4. HUMAN ERROR

As was noted earlier, recent studies into actual causes of structural failure have shown that human error is a principal factor. The first efforts at tackling this problem using fuzzy sets were by Blockley {12} and by Brown {13}. A checklist of 24 propositions was drawn up which was an attempt to provide some parameters which could be used to measure the complex situation surrounding a structural engineering project. Typical amongst these were the following {12};

1(a) The loads assumed in the design calculations are a good and/or safe representation of the loads the structure will actually experience.

4(a) The materials to be used in the structure are well tried and tested by use in previous structures.

4(e) There is no possible danger of a mode of behaviour of the structure, inadequately understood through existing technology and which has never before been critical with this structural form, now becoming critical.

5(c) The designers are adequately experienced in this type of work.

6(c) The likelihood of construction errors is negligible.

7(b) The general climate surrounding the project design and construction is perfect under each of the following headings: financial, industrial, political, professional.

These 24 parameter statements were assessed subjectively for 23 past structural failures varying from the Tay Bridge of 1879 to the Ronan Point multi-storey flats of 1968. Two assessments were made; the first was the degree of confidence in the truth of the statement and the second was the importance of that statement with respect to failure. These estimates are obviously highly imprecise and it was for this reason that fuzzy linguistic variables were used for the analysis. If for a particular accident j the importance of a parameter statement i is w_{ij} and the degree of confidence in the truth of that statement is r_{ij} then a rating value for any particular accident is

$$\bar{r}_j = \sum_{i=1}^{24} w_{ij}\, r_{ij}, \quad j = 1,2 \ldots\ldots\ldots 23$$

and $$\chi_{\bar{r}_j}(\bar{r}) = \underset{\bar{r}}{\text{MAX}} \left[\text{MIN}\ \chi_w(w),\ \chi_r(r) \right]$$

The worst or "most inevitable" failure will be that with the highest rating $\bar{r}_j$. Thus using these 23 fuzzy sets the accidents were ranked in order of "inevitability". In other words, the failure which had the most number of highly dangerous circumstances surrounding it was ranked first and the least likely failure was ranked last. An alternative way of analysing the fuzzy parameter assessments is to look for their worst combination. There are 24 parameter sets $R_{ij} = w_{ij} r_{ij}$ for each accident. Let ${}^{24}I_m$ be a combination of m of the numbers 1,2. ....24. Let i_k be the kth number in ${}^{24}I_m$. The worst combination is thus

$$P_j = \underset{m}{\text{MAX}}\ \underset{{}^{24}I_m}{\text{MIN}} \left[\bigcap_{k=1}^{m} R_{i_k, j} \right]$$

and the maximum set is that set which has the most concentrated membership levels towards the element value of 1. Fig. 2 shows some results for these operations {4}.

It was then assumed that a structural analysis of the structure under normal assumptions (i.e. not considering the factors covered by the parameter statements) can be performed and an expected value of the probability of failure in some limit state estimated. The influence of estimates such as P is to make the probability of failure p_f much more imprecise or fuzzy. If $p_f = 10^{-n}$ and $E(n) = q$ where q is an element in non-fuzzy sets Q in N and $n \varepsilon N$, N = 1,2.......10, and Q is fuzzified by P by a kernel K(n) to give Q^1

$$Q^1 = \bigcup_n \chi_Q(q) .\ K(q)$$

The fuzzier K(n) is obtained by

$$K(n) = P_o H$$

and H is a fuzzy relation to be calibrated (one may begin by assuming it to be the unit matrix).

Thus Q^1 is the measure which expresses the proneness of a structure to failure.

Brown {13} has also used this idea to develop a safety measure and Yao {14} has used it to consider a damage assessment method for existing structures. Brown was particularly concerned with the gap between predictions of failure probability using reliability theory and those perceived in practice. Ditlevsen {15}, {16}, similarly motivated, has separated the theoretical failure probability p_{th} obtained by ordinary reliability theory from p_{gr} which is some measure of proneness to failure due to gross errors. He argues that for a given lay-

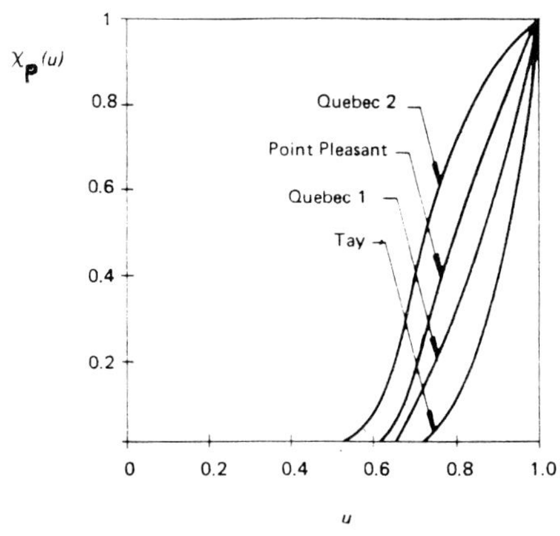

Fuzzy Sets P for some failures

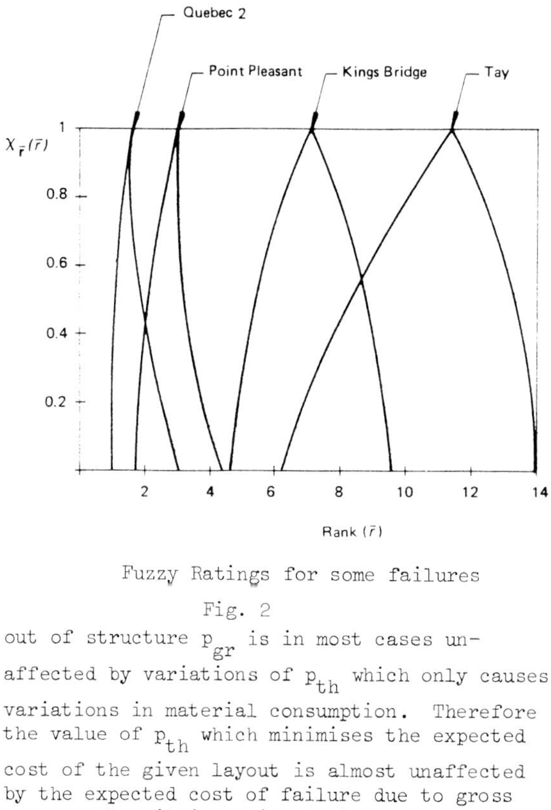

Fuzzy Ratings for some failures

Fig. 2

out of structure p_{gr} is in most cases unaffected by variations of p_{th} which only causes variations in material consumption. Therefore the value of p_{th} which minimises the expected cost of the given layout is almost unaffected by the expected cost of failure due to gross error. Thus it is rational, for each layout, for the designer to choose as a design value that value of p_{th} which minimises the expected cost of the layout. However, when the question is one of choosing between expected layouts the expected cost due to gross errors must be added and this depends on p_{gr}.

5. FUZZY LOGIC ANALYSIS OF STRUCTURAL SAFETY

Any assessment of the quality of a structural design and its safety must depend on the information available and that information will change during the course of the project. This has led to a broader consideration of the problem using Baldwin's fuzzy logic to obtain a dynamic measure. In accordance with the previous discussion three necessary conditions on the safety of a structure have been identified. Firstly the structure should be safe from failure in any given limit state; secondly it should be able to resist any random hazards; thirdly the possibility of human error should be suitably remote. Expressing this in a fuzzy logical form

(the structure is perfectly safe)(S) $\supset$ (the structure has a low probability in the critical limit state)(NP) is absolutely true (τ_{abs})

S $\supset$ (the structure has a low probability of failure due to random hazards) (RH) is τ_{abs}

S $\supset$ (the structure has a low probability of failure due to human error)(HE) is τ_{abs}

It is possible also to write further necessary conditions upon NP, RH and HE and still further necessary conditions upon those conditions in an hierarchical scheme as shown in Fig. 3. Fig. 4 shows the standard definitions of truth restrictions used.

NP $\supset$ (the notional probability of failure (assuming a perfect calculation model (LSM)) is low)(NPF) is very true (τ_{vt})

NP $\supset$ (low likelihood of new presently unknown effect in the material)(MMM) is τ_{vt}

NP $\supset$ (low likelihood of new presently unknown effect due to structural form) (ƐƐƐ) is τ_{vt}

NP $\supset$ (low likelihood of new presently unknown loading effect)(LLL) is τ_{vt}

(the possibility that the calculation model is perfect is high)(LSMP) $\supset$ (the calculated notional probability of failure is perfectly dependable) (NPFR) is τ_{vt}

LSM $\supset$ (the model used for the loads is perfect)(LSML) is τ_{vt}

LSM $\supset$ (the model used for the resistance is perfect)(LSMR) is τ_{vt}

LSML $\supset$ (the system used for the loads is perfect)(LSMLS) is τ_{abs}

LSML $\supset$ (the parameter statistics for the loads are perfect)(LSMLP) is τ_{abs}

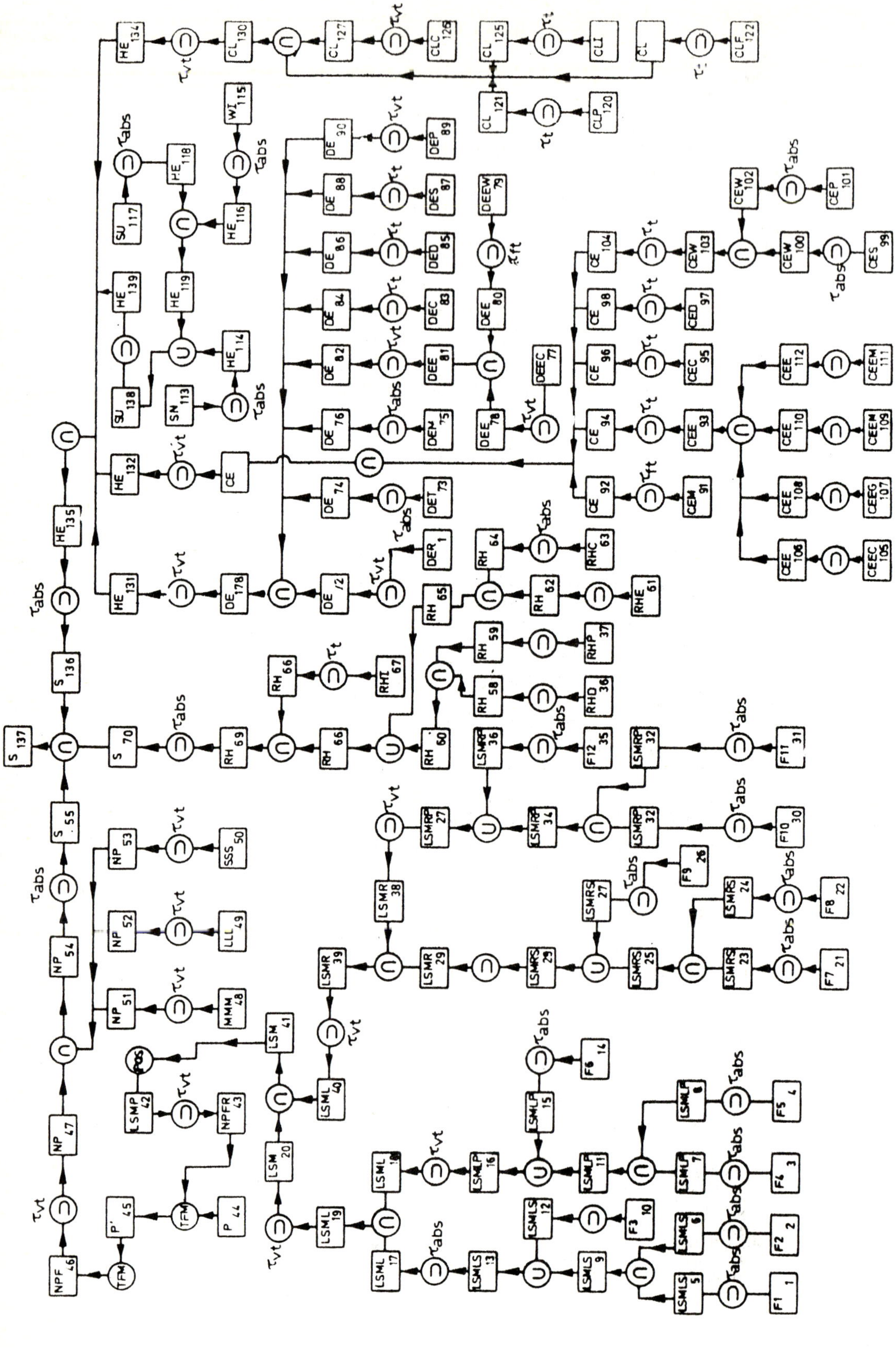

Fig.3 Logical hierarchy for structural safety

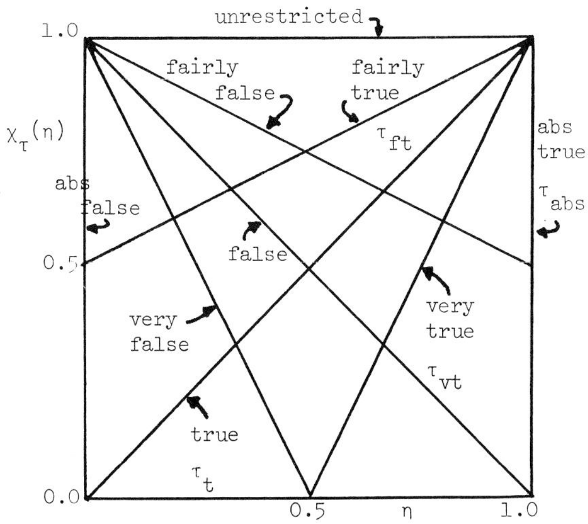

Fig. 4 Some Defined Fuzzy Truth Restrictions

LSMLS $\supset$ [(The model has been used before with no problems (F1) and there is no change between this useage and other previous ones)(F2)] OR (the test data available are perfectly satisfactory)(F3) is τ_{abs}

LSMLP $\supset$ [(the statistics have been used before with no problems)(F4) AND (there is no underlying change between this useage and previous ones) (F5)] OR (data are available which are perfect)(F6) is τ_{abs}

LSMR $\supset$ (the system used for the strength calculation is perfect)(LSMRS) is τ_{abs}

LSMR $\supset$ (the parameter statistics for the strength model are perfect)(LSMRP) is τ_{abs}

LSMRS $\supset$ [(the system model has been used before with no problems)(F7) AND (there is no change in this respect between this problem and other applications)(F8)] OR (test data from, for example, prototype testing are available)(F9) is τ_{abs}

LSMRP $\supset$ [(the parameter statistics have been used before with no problems)(F10) AND (there is no change in this respect between this problem and other applications)(F11)] OR (relevant measurements from sample surveys are available)(F12) is τ_{abs}

RH $\supset$ (all random hazards have been identified) RHI is τ_t

RH $\supset$ [(the experience for this site suggests risk of random hazards is low) RHE

$\cap$ (there is no change in environment to suggest this assessment is wrong) RHC]

$\cup$ [(perfectly adequate established data have been collected RHD $\cap$ (the probability of failure based on these data is low) RHP] is τ_{abs}

HE $\supset$ (No Design Error) DE is τ_{vt}

HE $\supset$ (No Construction Error) CE is τ_{vt}

HE $\supset$ (The 'climate' is perfect) CL is τ_{vt}

HE $\supset$ [(The structure is sensitive to the way it is used) SU $\cap$ (Adequate instruction and warning given to users) WI] $\cup$ (The structure is not sensitive to use) SN is τ_{ft}

DE $\supset$ (No well known mode of failure missed) DEM is τ_{abs}

DE $\supset$ (No calculation errors) DEE is τ_{vt}

DE $\supset$ (Design consultants have adequate experience) DEC is τ_t

DE $\supset$ (Personnel available for design work are suitably experienced) DED is τ_t

DE $\supset$ (Personnel available for site supervision are suitably experienced) DES is τ_t

DE $\supset$ (Specifications are perfectly adequate) DEP is τ_{vt}

DE $\supset$ (Quantity and quality of R & D information is sufficient) DER is τ_{vt}

DE $\supset$ (There is no mode of structural behaviour inadequately understood by existing technology) DET is τ_{abs}

DEE $\supset$ (Checking procedures are adequate) DEEC is τ_{vt}

DEE $\supset$ (Conditions of work and employment are good) DEEW is τ_{ft}

CE $\supset$ (Construction methods to be used are well tried and tested) CEM is τ_{ft}

CE $\supset$ (Likelihood of construction mistakes is low) CEE is τ_t

CE $\supset$ (Construction company has adequate experience) CEC is τ_t

CE $\supset$ (Personnel available for falsework design are adequately experienced) CED is τ_t

CE $\supset$ (Personnel available for site work are adequately experienced) CES $\cap$ (they are able to appreciate technical problems associated with the design) CEP is τ_t

CEE $\supset$ (Record of company is good; mistakes infrequent in past) CEEC $\cap$ (Personnel working in good conditions) CEEG $\cap$ (Good happy relationship between personnel in company) CEEH $\cap$ (Structure is not sensitive to erection method) CEEM is τ_{abs}

CL $\supset$ (Perfectly normal contract procedure) CLC is τ_{vt}

CL $\supset$ (No undue political pressures) CLP is τ_t

CL $\supset$ (No undue industrial pressures) CLI is τ_t

CL $\supset$ (No undue financial pressures) CLF is τ_t

The lowest statements in the hierarchy such as F1, F2, RHD, RHP, CEEC, CES, CLF etc. are such that input truth restrictions may be assessed for them for a particular example. The results of a traditional reliability calculation of a probability of failure which is 'notional' may be input also (see P labelled box 44 Fig. 3). This part of the calculation is described in detail elsewhere {4}. It is important to understand that the input truth values are fuzzy restrictions and that the logical arguments are nearly all modus tollens. Thus they are of the form

$$\frac{\begin{array}{l}(a \text{ is } A) \supset (b \text{ is } B) \text{ is } \tau \\ (b \text{ is } B) \text{ is } \tau_B\end{array}}{v(a \text{ is } A) = I(\tau)_o \tau_B}$$

and using Lukasiewicz implication rule I, truth functionally modified by τ

$$\chi_{v(a \text{ is } A)}(\eta) = \bigvee \left[(\chi_\tau(1 \wedge (1-\eta+\lambda))) \wedge \chi_{\tau_B}(\lambda) \right]$$

The result of the total computation, a whole series of these deductions, is a truth restriction on the proposition (S) 'the structure is perfectly safe' and this is the measure of structural safety adopted. The reason for the use of the word perfectly derives from the fact that the modus tollens leads only to falsification, and so in a comparison of two results for truth restrictions on S the safest will be that which is least false.

In Fig. 3 each box contains a fuzzy proposition and a number which is a truth restriction τ_1, τ_2, τ_3 etc. The circles are fuzzy logical operators of implication, conjunction and disjunction each of which may have an associated fuzzy restriction.

6. AN EXAMPLE

Certain of the basic propositions in the hierarchy of Fig. 3 cannot be assessed at the beginning of a project. For example propositions concerning the contractor cannot be assessed before the contractor is appointed. As a project progresses other assessments may change as information becomes available. At the beginning of a project the information will be the least definite and the capability of changing decisions at its greatest. As the project progresses more and more information becomes available but there is less and less room for manoevre. Thus any measure of safety as has been described will change during the design and construction process and the values may even be influenced by the values of previous assessments. If a project runs into technical or organisational problems and it is appreciated by those involved that this could lead to failure then they will act more cautiously and this will hopefully reduce the risk of failure.

Assessments for the basic propositions of Fig. 3 have been made for an imaginary project at four different stages of its progress: {17}

(1) after detailed design and reliability analysis of the traditional type;

(2) after tender stage when the contract has been let;

(3) midway through contract;

(4) end of contract.

Fig. 5 shows these assessments and the problems introduced into this imaginary project can be appreciated from them. After the contract has been let it was discovered that the model used for the loading (F1) had given some problems in previous projects and during the contract it was similarly discovered that one of the materials also had deficiencies not realised at the time of the design (MMM). It was also thought that all random hazards had been considered at the design stage although there was some degree of doubt, but again during the contract another random hazard was discovered to be possible and this reduced confidence (RHI). Towards the end of the project evidence was discovered which suggested an increased probability of a random hazard (RHE). During the project industrial pressures due to strikes (CLI) and financial (CLF) and political pressures (CLP) were also evident and snags due to the contractual arrangement were thought to be serious midway through the contract but were resolved somewhat by the end (CLC). Even at the design stage the designers felt the need for more research and development information (DER) and it was realised midway through the contract that a form of structural behaviour was possible that they had not really understood (DET). It was also discovered that a fairly well known mode of behaviour had been inadequately catered for although the consulting engineers were very experienced (DEC). Checking procedures for the design calculations were also discovered to be lacking (DEEC) and the specification were suspect (DEP) and this may have been due to inexperienced personnel in the consultant's office (DED).

Proposition	Stage No 1	2	3	4	Proposition	Stage No 1	2	3	4
F1	-	vf	vf	vf	DER	vf	vf	vf	vf
F2	-	-	-	-	DET	ff	f	vf	f
F3	vf	vf	vf	vf	DEM	ff	ff	vf	f
F4	-	-	-	-	DEEC	f	vf	vf	vf
F5	-	-	-	-	DEEW	-	f	f	f
F6	vf	vf	vf	vf	DEC	-	-	ff	-
F7	-	-	-	-	DED	-	-	vf	vf
F8	-	-	-	-	DES	ff	-	abs	vf
F9	abs	abs	abs	abs	DEP	-	-	abs	vf
F10	-	-	-	-					
F11	-	-	-	-	CEM	-	-	vf	-
F12	abs	abs	abs	abs	CEEC	-	-	ff	-
MMM	f	f	vf	vf	CEEG	-	-	vf	vf
SSS	f	f	f	f	CEEH	-	-	vf	vf
LLL	ff	ff	ff	ff	CEEM	-	-	vf	-
					CEC	-	-	f	-
RHD	ff	ff	ff	ff	CED	-	-	abs	-
RHP	-	-	-	-	CES	-	-	abs	vf
RHE	f	f	f	vf	CEP	-	-	abs	abs
RHC	-	-	-	-					
RHI	f	f	vf	vf	SN	-	-	-	-
					SU	abs	abs	abs	vf
CLC	-	-	vf	f	WI	-	-	-	vf
CLP	ff	f	vf	vf					
CLI	-	-	abs	abs					
CLF	f	vf	abs	abs					

Key: abs = absolutely false; vf = very false; f = false;
ff = false; - = unrestricted

Fig. 5 Fuzzy Truth Restrictions Input for the Four Stages of the Example Project

Midway through the contract the contractor got into difficulties but many of them were more or less resolved by completion. The structure was sensitive to the chosen erection method (CEEM) and unfortunately although the company had a good past record (CEEC) the conditions on site and the inexperienced site personnel (DES, CES, CEP) and some friction through personality clashes (CEEH), lead to an increased chance of error. At the end of the project it was felt that the owner was not given adequate warning about the sensitivity of the structure to the way it is used (WI).

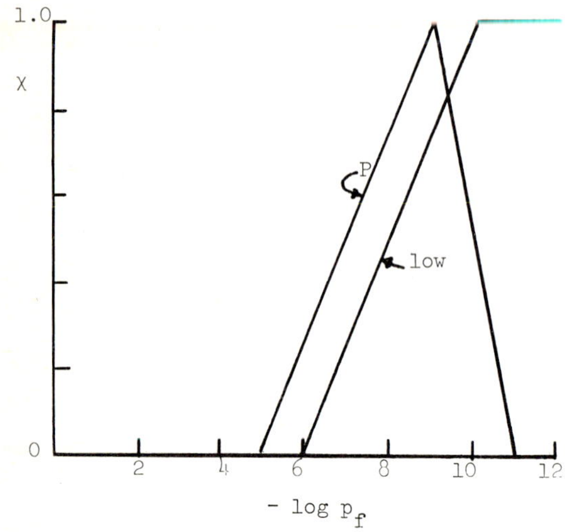

Fig 6 Fuzzy Sets of Probabilities used in Example

Fig. 6 shows a fuzzy 'notional' probability which is the result of differing reliability theory calculations of the traditional kind. This probability is then modified by a process described in Reference {4} which involves the truth restriction on the proposition LSM. The degree by which this can be interpreted as a low probability as defined in Fig. 6 is then calculated as a fuzzy restriction on NP. The final restriction on S from the limit state calculations is τ_{55} (Fig. 3). The restrictions on S at the four stages of the project are shown in Fig. 7. The effect of the input assessments on the restrictions on S from human error (HE)τ_{136}, from random hazards (RH)τ_{70} and from the limit states (NP)τ_{55} can be seen clearly. The difference in τ_{137} for stages 1 and 2 of the project is very small but stage 3 midway through the contract the restriction τ_{137} had moved considerably towards being very false. By completion however the situation had been relieved somewhat although the truth restriction on S was not as good as it was during the design stage. This process can be modelled conceptually on a cusp catastrophe. Fig. 8 shows the path taken by the safety measure in this imaginary example. If at any time the 'pressures' on the safety of the structure became too great then the path would approach the fold of the cusp and any small 'trigger' incident would push the path over the edge and failure would occur. However if it were realised that the situation had become dangerous then remedial action would be taken. In other words the model might well be developed into a management tool used to help avoid serious consequences.

REMARKS

A further development would be to turn the model into an expert system. Yao, Ishizuka and Fu {18} have begun work on this for the damage assessment of existing structures. They use a production system with a certainty factor which is a function of probabilities. The result is a system called SPERIL which is similar to that described in this chapter except that the form of implication is not IF Hypothesis THEN Evidence but IF Evidence THEN Hypothesis. Production rules are expressed for example as

If X THEN there is indication ($C_{h,x}$) that H

If Y THEN there is indication ($C_{h,y}$) that H

and

$$C_{h,x} = \begin{cases} 1 & \text{if } P(H) = 1 \\ \dfrac{P(H/X) - P(H)}{1 - P(H)} & \text{if } P(H/X) \geq P(H) \\ \dfrac{P(H/X) - P(H)}{P(H)} & \text{if } P(H/X) < P(H) \\ -1 & \text{if } P(H) = 0 \end{cases}$$

in particular

IF 1) the diagnosis of stiffness is severe AND

2) the structural material is reinforced concrete THEN

there is considerable indication (0.6) that damage of global nature is severe.

The difference between this approach and the one described earlier is part of the wider debate between the inductive logicians (e.g. Carnap and his followers) and those favouring deductive methods (e.g. Popper). This has been discussed recently {19} on the basis of an argument by Lakatos {20} that the confusion stems from the use of two rival and inconsistent notions, evidential support and betting. According to our betting intuition any conjecture or hypotheses whatever the evidence, is at least as risky as any of the conjuncts (i.e. $p(h/e) \geq p(h\&h^1/e)$). According to our intuition of evidential support the more a proposition says the more evidential support it may aquire (i.e. $c(h/e < c(h\&h^1/e)$, where c is some measure of evidential support). The Carnapian school concentrates on the appraisal of existing knowledge using some probabilistic measure and the Popperian school concentrates on the growth of knowledge and notions such as logical falsifiability and testability.

CONCLUSIONS

1. System uncertainty and the possibility of human error must be considered as part of any estimation of structural safety.

2. Fuzzy sets have been used to represent the subjective assessment of imprecise data

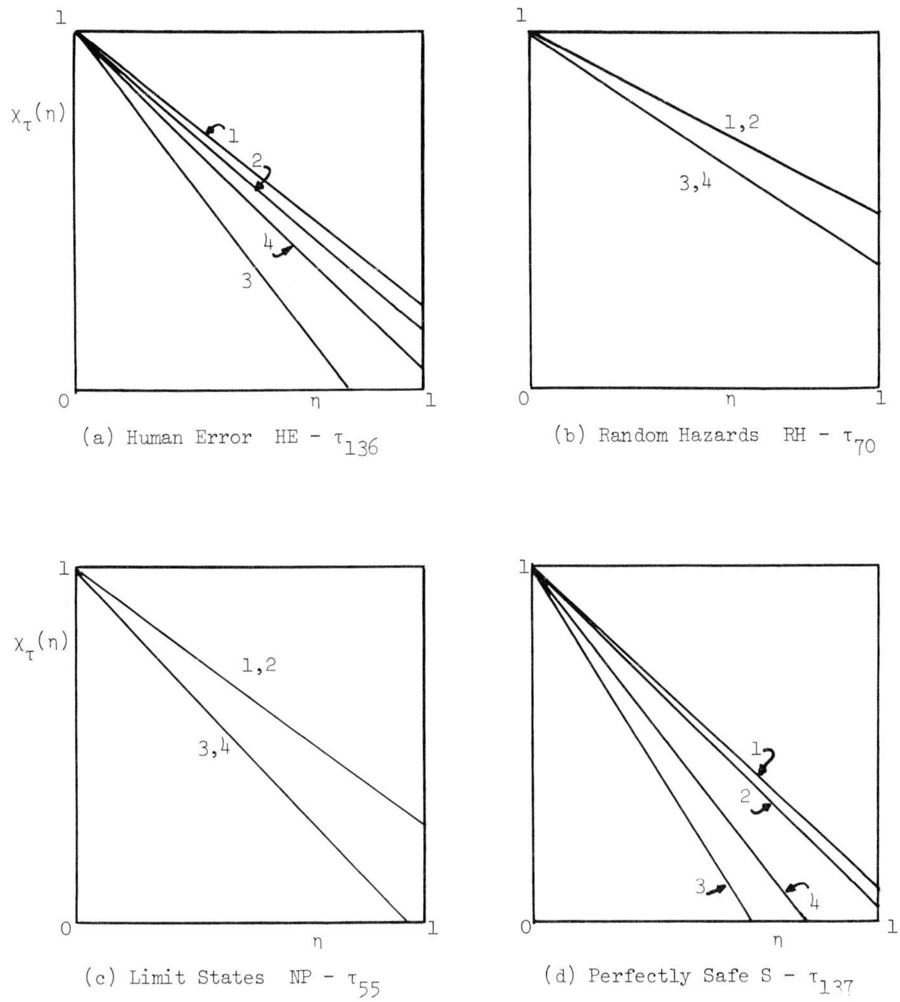

Fig 7 Fuzzy Dependability Restrictions Resulting from the Assessments for Stages 1-4 of Fig 5 (for the positions of τ_{136}, τ_{70}, τ_{55}, τ_{137} see Fig 3)

attempting to utilise the judgement and experience of the engineer. The use of a combined entropy measure of probability and imprecision is presently being examined.

3. A model, based on Baldwin's fuzzy logic, of structural safety incorporating reliability theory, system uncertainty and human error has been developed. It is possible to use this model to follow the changing perception of safety during the execution of a project. It may well be possible to use such a model as a management tool in order to avoid failure when a complex project runs into difficulties.

References

{1} Goodpasture, R.C., "Hardy Cross: Engineers and Ivory Towers", McGraw Hill, 1952.

{2} Joint Committee on Structural Safety, "General Principles on Quality Assurance for Structures, General Principles on Reliability for Structural Design", Int. Assoc. Bridge, Structural Engng., Zurich, April 1981.

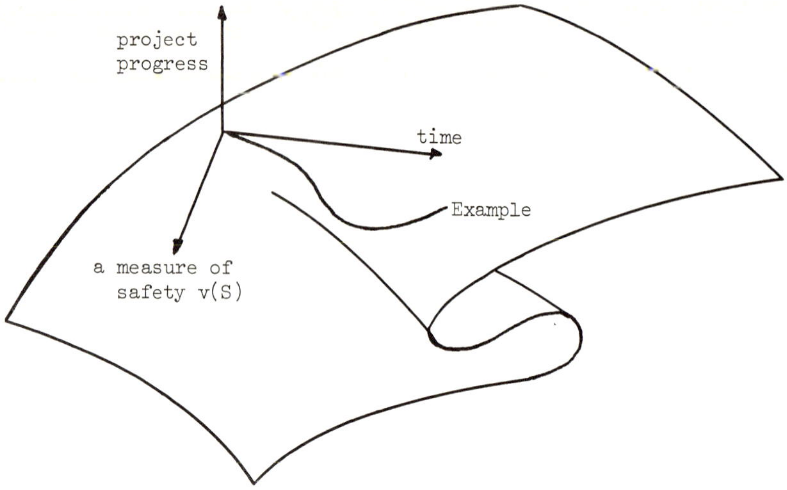

(a) Cusp catastrophe

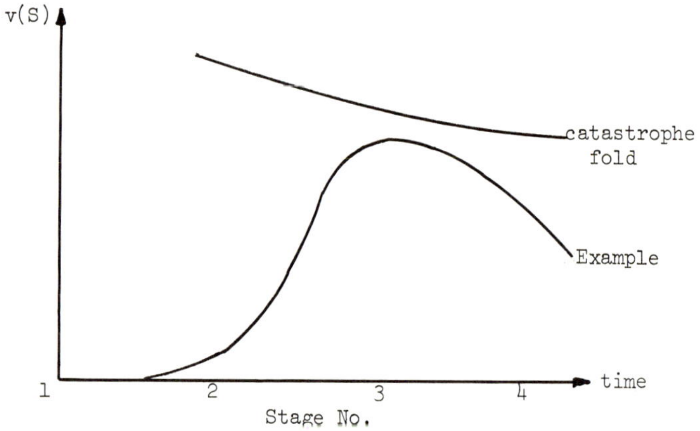

(b) Projection of (a) onto v(S) x time

Fig 8 Catastrophe Theory Model of Structural Safety

{3} Blockley, D.I., Henderson, J.R., "Structural Failures and the Growth of Engineering Knowledge", Proc. Instn. Civ. Engrs., Part 1, 1980, 68, November, 719-728.

{4} Blockley, D.I., "The Nature of Structural Design and Safety", Ellis Horwood, Chichester, England, 1981.

{5} Schwartz, J., "The Pernicious Influence of Mathematics on Science", in Logic, Methodology and Philosophy of Science, Proc. 1960 Int. Congress, Ed. Nagel, E., Suppes, P., Tarski, A., Stanford University Press, 1962.

{6} Armitage, J., "The Anatomy and Exercise of Engineering Judgement", The Structural Engineer, Vol. 59A, No. 5, May 1981, 167-171.

{7} Matousek, M., "Outcomings of a Survey on 800 Construction Failures", Int. Assoc. Bridge Struct. Engng., Colloquium on

Inspection and Quality Control, Cambridge, England, 1977.

{8} "Rationalisation of Safety and Serviceability Factors in Structural Codes", CIRIA Report 63, London, July 1977.

{9} Blockley, D.I., Ellison, E.G., "A New Technique for Estimating System Uncertainty in Design", Proc. Instn. Mech. Engrs., 1979, 193, No. 5, 159-168.

{10} Brown, C.B., "Entropy Constructed Probabilities", Proc. ASCE, Vol. 106, No. EM4, August 1980, 633-640.

{11} Munro, J., "Uncertainty and Fuzziness in Engineering Decision Making", First Canadian Colloquium on Systems Theory for the Civil Engineer, University of Calgary, October 1979, 113-133.

{12} Blockley, D.I., "Analysis of Structural Failures", Proc. Instn. Civ. Engrs., Part 1, 62, February 1977, 51-74.

{13} Brown, C.B., "A Fuzzy Safety Measure", Proc. ASCE, Vol. 105, No. EM5, October 1979, 855-872.

{14} Yao, J.T.P., "Damage Assessment of Existing Structures", Proc. ASCE, Vol. 106, EM4, August 1980, 785-799.

{15} Ditlevsen, O., "Formal Failure Probability and Observed Failure Rate", IABSE Anniversary Congress, Vienna, September 1980.

{16} Ditlevsen, O., "Formal and Real Structural Safety. Influence of Gross Errors", IABSE Periodica 4/1980, November, 185-204.

{17} Blockley, D.I., "Reliability Theory - Incorporating Gross Errors", in Structural Safety and Reliability, Moan, T., Shinozuka, M. (Eds), Elsevier, 1981.

{18} Ishizuka, M., Fu, K.S., Yao, J.T.P., "Inexact Inference for Rule-Based Damage Assessment of Existing Structures", CE-STR-81-5, School of Civil Engineering, Purdue University, Indiana, U.S.A., February 1981.

{19} Blockley, D.I., "Probability, Fuzziness and How Good is a Theory?", ASCE Convention, St. Louis, October 1981.

{20} Lakatos, I., "Mathematics, Science and Epistemology", Philosophical Papers No. 2, Cambridge University Press, 1978.

PART FOUR

CLASSIFICATIONS AND SIMILARITY MEASURES

Approximate Reasoning in Decision Analysis
M.M. Gupta and E. Sanchez (eds.)

CLASSIFICATION IN FUZZY ENVIRONMENTS

V. Kh. Kaipov, A.A. Seliugin

Automation Institute, The Academy of Science,
Kirghiz SSR, Frunze Polytechnical Institute
Frunze, USSR

This paper discusses some aspects of classifying objects that are described in a space of signs some of which are fuzzy variables. The algorithms developed for solving the classification problem are based on the calculation of the proximity measure between the fuzzy vectors.

One of the algorithms was used for determining how the burning regimes of a rotary cement kiln influence the quality of the output.

Keywords: linguistic variables, classification algorithms, proximity measure, distance, fuzzy vectors, rotary cement kiln.

1. INTRODUCTION

This article deals with the problem of classifying objects that are described in a space of signs some of which are fuzzy variables. In this paper these variables are linguistic type. Classification algorithms are suggested for use if:

- the number of classes is prescribed and centers of the classes are determined;
- the number of classes is not prescribed and all the signs are fuzzy;
- the number of classes is not prescribed and some of the signs are simple variables.

The algorithm for solving the first problem operates in accordance with the following rule: The object being classified is referred to the class to which the proximity measure of the object is the maximum. The suggested proximity measure non-obligatory fulfills the distance axioms.

The algorithm for solving the second problem is based upon calculations of the distances between two vectors (i.e. generalization of the Eucledian distance). One of the objects from the complete collection is considered first and the distance from it to the other objects is calculated. The nearest one is then united with the initial one and the process is repeated until the complete sequence of the distances is obtained. Class boundaries are defined by abrupt changes in the sequence of the calculated distances.

The algorithm for solving the third problem is similar to the second one, but in this case the formulae for calculating the distances and those for uniting objects in a group (in regard with the simple variables) are modified using weight coefficients, which take into account the nature of the variables.

One of the algorithms is used for classifying the burning regimes in a rotary kiln for the purpose of investigating their influence upon the quality of the output.

2. FORMULATION OF THE CLASSIFICATION PROBLEM

Classification and pattern recognition problems have been discussed in a large number of works. A number of algorithms, which operate in conditions of various a priori information and are based upon deterministic, statistical, nonparametrical methods, have also been developed. These algorithms have proven useful in process control, plant management, technical and medical diagnostics, and other research works.

However signs, according to which objects are classified or patterns recognized, can not always be measured and evaluated quantitatively. Nevertheless, it is possible to characterize the meaning of such signs or quantities by employing knowledge of the object under investigation and/or man's own experience using for this purpose the natural language and terms that are well known to people.

Typical examples of such terms are: 'The temperature is rather high', 'The flowrate is very small' (on characterizing a process control), 'The pain is not violent', 'Excitability is normal' (in medical diagnostics), etc. Some of sensing elements (sensors-indicators) can measure the quantitative value of a sign with similar accuracy.

The theory of fuzzy sets allows algorithms to be developed for the classification and recognition of patterns on the basis of information received from man. Some of the approaches suggested for solving the above mentioned problems are:

Let

$$X = \{X_1, X_2, \ldots, X_r, \ldots, X_N\} \quad (1)$$

be a collection of signs, each one being in the general case a linguistic variable bearing information about the object under classification (or on it's state). The term-set for the linguistic variable is prescribed as:

$$T(X_r) = \{X_r^1, X_r^2, \ldots, X_r^m, \ldots X_r^M\} \quad (2)$$

where M is the number of terms in $T(X_r)$, depending in the general case on r.

Let the object Z_S that is being classified be a collection of concrete values of signs (1) from their term-sets (2):

$$Z_S = \{X_1^{(S)}, X_2^{(S)}, \ldots, X_r^{(X)}, \ldots, X_N^{(S)}\} \quad (3)$$

where S is the ordinal number of the object from the sequence

$$Z = \{Z_1, Z_2, Z_3, \ldots, Z_S, \ldots\}$$

which is supplied to the classifier (S may sometimes be interpreted as the discrete time). The superscript S in the brackets at X_r means that in Z_S the sign takes on a concrete value for the m-th term from the term-set (2). Each linguistic variable from (1) is defined on a certain universal set L_r:

$$L_r = \{\ell_r^1, \ell_r^2, \ldots, \ell_r^r, \ldots, \ell_r^r\} \quad (4)$$

In the general case R also depends on r and the value of the sign X_r in each vector from (4) represents a fuzzy set of the type:

$$X_r^{(S)} = \{M_{X_r^{(S)}}(\ell_r^1)/\ell_r^1, M_{X_r^{(S)}}(\ell_r^2)/\ell_r^2, \ldots, M_{X_r}^{(S)}(\ell_r^R)/\ell_r^R\} \quad (5)$$

Thus, the vector Z_S is a fuzzy subset of the universal set L, which represents a cartesian of the universal sets:

$$L = L_1 \times L_2 \times \ldots \times L_r \times \ldots L_N \quad (6)$$

Suppose, that the fuzzy sets (5) representing the values of the terms in the vector (3) are preassigned and the support of any fuzzy set coincides with the universal set, i.e. the degrees of membership in (5) are positive everywhere.

The problem of classifying the sequence (4) may be formulated in two ways:

- each of the vectors Z_S is to be referred to one of i classes, which are predetermined a priori (i = 1, 2, ..., I);
- each of the vectors Z_S is to be referred to one of the i classes, the number of which a priori is unknown.

Formulation of the first type is specific for the solution of practical problems, the result of which is preassigned (product rating, alternative decision-making, diagnostics). Formulation of the second type is more specific for solving scientific or research problems.

3. CLASSIFICATION OF FUZZY OBJECTS WITH A PRESCRIBED NUMBER OF CLASSES

Let the vector Z_S, which is characterized by a certain collection of signs from X, accidentally appear in the sequence Z (4) and belong to one of the classes A_i, the number of classes being given a priori upon formulation of the problem.

The user of the algorithm defines the number of classes and selects I of the vectors Z_i from Z, determined as centers of the classes A_i. The classification problem is to refer the newly appeared vector Z_S to the fuzzy set A_i that forms the i-th class for which the proximity characteristics of Z_S to Z_i is higher than any of Z_j, $j \neq i$.

The classification algorithm has the form:

$$Z_S \in A_i \quad (7)$$

if the condition

$$\rho(Z_S, Z_i) > \rho(Z_S, Z_j) \quad (8)$$

is true for all i, j $i \neq j$ where $\rho(Z_S, Z_i)$ is the proximity characteristic of the objects Z_S and Z_i.

Let us determine the characteristic of proximity $\rho(Z_S, Z_i)$ of the object Z_S to the center of the i-th class A_i, which is prescribed by the fuzzy set Z_i. Now select for Z_S r-tuple L_S^0 of the universal set L:

$$L_S^0 = \{\ell_{1S}^0, \ell_{2S}^0, \ldots, \ell_{rS}^0, \ldots, \ell_{NS}^0\} \quad (9)$$

each element of which has the maximum degree of membership to the corresponding term $X_{rr}^{(S)}$ in Z_S. ℓ_{rS}^0 corresponds to that universal variable ℓ_r^r in (5), for which

$$\mu_{X_r}^{(S)}(\ell_r^r) = \max_r \quad (10)$$

that is,

$$\ell_{rs}^0 = \arg\max_r \mu_{X_r}^{(S)}(\ell_r^r)$$

Then L_1^0, in accordance with (10), assumes the form

$$L_1^0 = \arg\max_\mu Z_S \quad (11)$$

and the proximity characteristic of Z_S and Z_i is

$$\rho(Z_S, Z_i) = \mu_{Z_i}(L_S^0).$$

It is possible to consider $\rho(Z_S, Z_i)$ as the degree of the membership of the vector Z; to the class Z_i, calculated as

$$\rho(Z_S, Z_i) = \hat{\mu}_{Z_i}(L_S^0) = \mu_{A_i}(Z_S) = \mu_{X_1}^{(i)}(\ell_{1S}^0) * \mu_{X_2}(i)(\ell_{2S}^0) * \ldots * \mu_{X_N}^{(i)}(\ell_{ns}^0) \quad (12)$$

The symbol * may stand for a min operation, an arithmetical multiplication, an operation of the type

$$\mu_1 \oplus \mu_2 = \mu_1 + \mu_2 - \mu_1\nu_2,$$

or the operation for calculating the Eucledian length of the vector with components:

$$\mu_{X_1}^{(i)}(\ell_{1S}^0),\ \mu_{X_2}^{(i)}(\ell_{2S}^0),\ \ldots,\ \mu_{X_N}^{(i)}(\ell_{NS}^0).$$

Thus, the process of classifying objects with a prescribed number of classes represents a two-stage decision-making procedure:

- the first stage in accordance with the formulae (9) - (12), includes calculating the proximity characteristic of the object Z_S being classified, to all the fuzzy sets Z_i, which define the classes A_i, i = 1, 2, ..., I;
- the second stage includes making the decision for refering Z_S to that class A_i for which $\mu_{A_i}(Z_S)$ is the maximum.

4. CLASSIFICATION OF FUZZY OBJECTS ON THE DISTANCE MEASURING BASIS

The problem of classifying a non-prescribed number of classes may be solved only if the objects under investigation form sufficiently remote groups in the space of fuzzy signs.

In order to evaluate the remoteness of fuzzy sets from each other, the corresponding distances between them have to be estimated. A few distance calculation methods are given in [1]. All of them have a peculiar distinction in that the distances between any disjoint (nonoverlapping) sets are equal. The following formula (an analogue of Eucledian distance) can be used to measure distances between two fuzzy sets:

$$d(X_1, X_2) = \left(\frac{1}{R}\sum_{r=1}^{R}(\mu_{X_1}(\ell_1^2) - \mu_{X_2}(\ell_2^r))\right)^{\frac{1}{2}}.$$

To measure the distance between objects Z_S and Z_K this formula should be generalized to a vector. Define the distance between the objects (vectors) Z_S and Z_K, including fuzzy sets $X_r^{(S)}$ and $X_r^{(R)}$ as their components, by the formula

$$d(Z_S, Z_K) = \left(\sum_{n=1}^{N}(d(X_r^{(S)}, X_r^{(k)})^2\right)^{\frac{1}{2}}, \quad (13)$$

where

$$d(X_r^{(s)}, X_r^{(k)}) = \left(\frac{1}{R}\sum_{r=1}^{R}(\mu_{X_r}^{(S)}(\ell_r^r) - \mu_{X_r}^{(k)}(\ell_r^r))^2\right)^{\frac{1}{2}} \quad (14)$$

By introducing (14) into (13) a formula for calculation of distances between the two objects is obtained:

$$d(Z_S, Z_R^o) = \left(\frac{1}{R}\sum_{A=1}^{N}\sum_{r=1}^{R}(\mu_{X_r}^{(S)}(\ell_r^r) - \mu_{X_r}^{(k)}(\ell_r^r))^2\right)^{\frac{1}{2}} \quad (15)$$

During the classification it is necessary to determine the distances between the next object to be classified and the objects that have already been united into a class

$$d(Z_{S+1}, \hat{Z}_S),$$

where

$$\hat{Z}_S = Z_1 \cup Z_2 \cup \ldots \cup Z_S. \quad (16)$$

A post-subscript at Z in the right-hand part of (16) denotes the order of referring them to the group Z_S which is different from (4) where the objects are labelled arbitrarily.

Let us now calculate the membership functions that define the fuzzy set Z_S:

$$\begin{aligned} \mu_{Z_S}(\ell) &= \mu_{Z_1 \cup Z_2 \cup \ldots \cup Z_S}(\ell) \\ &= \mu_{Z1}(\ell) \cup \mu_{Z_2}(\ell) \cup \ldots \cup \mu_{Z_S}(\ell) \\ &= \mu_{Z1}(\ell)\ V_r \mu_{Z_2}(\ell)\ V_2 \ldots V_2\ \mu_{Z_S}(\ell), \end{aligned} \quad (17)$$

where ℓ is r-tuple of the univeral set L. Then $\hat{Z}_S$ is

$$\hat{Z}_S = \{\mu_{Z_S}(\ell)/\ell\},$$

where

$$\mu_{\hat{Z}_B}(\ell)/\ell = \{\mu_{\hat{X}_1}(S)(\ell_1)/\ell_1,$$

$$\mu_{\hat{X}_2}(S)(\ell_2)/\ell_2, \ldots, \mu_{\hat{X}_N}(S)(\ell_N)/\ell_N\},$$

$$\mu_{\hat{X}_r}(S)(\ell_r) = \{\mu_{\hat{X}_r}(S)(\ell_r^1),$$

$$\mu_{\hat{X}_r}(S)(\ell_r^2), \ldots, \mu_{\hat{X}_r}(S)(\ell_r^R)\},$$

and the membership function $\mu_{X_r}(S)(\ell_r)$ is calculated in the following way:

$$\mu_{\hat{X}_r(S)}(\ell_r) = \{\sum^{R}(\mu_{X_r(1)}(\ell_r^r)\ V\ \mu_{\hat{X}_r(2)}(\ell_r)\ V \ldots V\ \mu_{\hat{X}_r(S)}(\ell_r)\} \quad (18)$$

The symbols Σ and V in (17) and (18) are considered as the maximum and as the union of sets respectively. Using the formulae for calculating the distances and for uniting objects in a group we can classify a certain finite collection of these objects:

$$Z = \{Z_1, Z_2, \ldots, Z_S, \ldots, Z_S\}. \qquad (19)$$

For the classification procedure the algorithms developed for classification of objects that are described by the standard, numerical signs, as in [2] are used. The algorithms for classifying the fuzzy objects will have the following sequence of calculations:

- the vector Z_1(or any other) in (19) is taken as the initial one, and from the remaining vectors S - 1 the one that is the nearest to the first vector according to the formula (15) is taken:

$$\min d(Z_1, Z_j),$$
$$j = 2, 3, \ldots, S$$

This vector is designated as $\tilde{Z}_2$:

- the vectors Z_1 and $\tilde{Z}_2$ are brought together into the group $\hat{Z}_S$ with the use of formula (18)

$$\hat{Z}_S = Z_1 \cup \tilde{Z}_2;$$

- from the remaining S - 2 vectors the one which is the nearest to $\hat{Z}_S$ is taken:

$$\min d(\hat{Z}_S, Z_j),$$
$$j = 3, 4, \ldots, S$$

- the vector calculated in this way is designated as $\tilde{Z}_3$, thus the group $\hat{Z}_S$ is replenished by $\tilde{Z}_3$.

$$\hat{Z}_S = Z_1 \cup \tilde{Z}_2 \cup \tilde{Z}_3 = \hat{Z}_S \cup \tilde{Z}_3$$

By repeating the calculations a new sequence of vectors from Z is obtained.

$$Z = \{Z_1, \tilde{Z}_2, \ldots, \tilde{Z}_S, \ldots, \tilde{Z}_S\}.$$

The next sequence of distances corresponds to the previous one is

$$d(Z_1, \tilde{Z}_2), d(\hat{Z}_1, \tilde{Z}_3), \ldots, d(\hat{Z}_{S-1}, \tilde{Z}_S) \qquad (20)$$

Depending on the classification algorithm in use, formula (20) may be regarded as a sequence of certain functions of distances $f(d(\hat{Z}_S, Z_S))$.

If the a priori assumption of the existence of sufficiently remote groups in a collection of the vectors Z is true, then near the separation boundary of the groups in the sequence (20) the following values

$$D = /d(\hat{Z}_S, \tilde{Z}_{S+1}) - d(\hat{Z}_{S+1}, \tilde{Z}_{S+2})/$$

are noticeably greater than neighbouring ones. By establishing the threshold values for the group separation certain number of classes and the vectors that constitute these classes is obtained. A reverse method is also possible: the required number of classes Z may be prescribed and separated in accordance with sequence (20), with reference to the values D.

5. CLASSIFICATION OF THE MIXED TYPE OBJECTS

The case where, in the vector of the signs (1), there are signs that can be measured exactly will now be examined. Suppose, for instance, that in Z_S the first P of the signs from N are of the same nature mentioned above and all the rest are fuzzy:

$$Z_S = \{Y_1^{(S)}, Y_2^{(S)}, \ldots, Y_p^{(S)}, X_{p+1}^{(S)}, \ldots X_N^{(S)}\}.$$

The distance between non-fuzzy signs is:

$$d(Y_r^{(S)}, Y_r^{(k)}) = Y_r^{(S)} - Y_r^{(k)} \qquad (21)$$

Then

$$d(Z_S, Z_k) = (\sum_{n=1}^{P} (d(Y_r^{(S)}, Y_r^{(k)}))^2 + \sum_{r=P+1}^{N} (d(X_r^{(S)}, X_r^{(k)}))^2)^{\frac{1}{2}}$$

and thus formula (15) for calculating the distances between two objects from Z will be as follows

$$d(Z_S, Z_k) = (\sum_{n=1}^{P} \sigma_n (Y_n^{(S)} - Y_n^{(k)})^2 + \frac{1}{R} \sum_{n=P+1}^{N} \sum_{r-1}^{R} (\mu_{X_r^{(S)}}(\ell_r^r) - \mu_{X_r^{(k)}}(\ell_r^r))^2)^{\frac{1}{2}}.$$

In (22) σ_r - are weighting coefficients which take into account the physical scale of the signs Y_r and X_r according to the meaning of the problem and the user's purposes. After calculating these distances it is necessary to define a method of uniting the vectors in a group. Obviously, forumla (18) cannot be used for this procedure due to the presence of simple variables representing the points on the number axes that define certain physical values.

Suppose as in the previous case that

$$\hat{Z}_S = Z_1 \cup \tilde{Z}_2 \ldots \cup \tilde{Z}_S$$

but in the group Z_S separate the two subsets:

$$\hat{Z}_S = U_p (Y_r^{(1)}, Y_p^{(2)}, \ldots, Y_p^{(3)},$$
$$\sum_{n=P+1}^{N} (X_r^{(1)}, X_r^{(2)}, \ldots, X_r^{(S)}) .$$

The second subset represents a collection of fuzzy signs obtained on performing procedure

(18). The first subset represents a union of non-fuzzy signs in a common sense (i.e. of subsets, each consisting of S points.) Then Z_S is:

$$Z_S = \{(Y_1^{(1)}, Y_1^{(2)}, \ldots, Y_1^{(S)}; Y_2^{(1)}, \ldots, Y_2^{(S)}, \ldots$$
$$Y_P^{(S)}, \ldots, Y_P^{(S)}), \tag{23}$$
$$(\hat{X}_{P+1}^{(S)}, \hat{X}_{P+2}^{(S)}, \ldots, \hat{X}_N^{(S)})\}.$$

Such a representation of the vectors united in a group, requires a change in the method of calculating $d(\hat{Z}_S, Z_k)$; that is, the distance between the fuzzy subsets is again calculated by (15). The distance between the simple subsets is calculated as the distance from the point $Y_r^{(k)}$ up to the set $\{Y_r^{(1)}, Y_r^{(R)}, \ldots, Y_r^{(S)}\}$. Then formula (18) is rearranged to

$$d(\hat{Z}_S, Z_k) = (\frac{1}{S} \sum_{n=1}^{P} \sum_{i=1}^{S} \sigma_r(Y_r^{(i)} - Y_r^{(k)})^2$$
$$+ \frac{1}{R} \sum_{n=P+1}^{N} \sum_{t=1}^{R} (\mu_{\hat{X}_n}(S)\ (\ell_n^2)$$
$$- \mu_{X_r}^{(k)}\ (\ell_r^r))^2)^{\frac{1}{2}}. \tag{24}$$

Thus, the algorithm for classifying fuzzy objects with simple non-fuzzy signs present in them, has the same sequence of calculations as in the previous case.

6. APPLICATION

One of the above algorithms was used for determining how the burning regime of a rotary cement kiln influences the output product quality. Two kilns were compared for this purpose. The first one - with a small quality dispersion, and the second - with a large one. The effect of the initial raw material on the quality of clinker was excluded. The vector characterizing the burning regime is as follows:

$$\tilde{Z}_S = \{X_1^{(S)}, X_2^{(S)}, X_3^{(S)}\},$$

where X_1 is the "term-set position of sintering zone", X_2 is "degree of kiln heating", and X_3 is "temperature of waste gases".

X_3 is a result of accurate measurement but X_1, X are fuzzy variables evaluated by a kiln operator.

Each vector Z_S from Z was compared with the quality of clinker (28-days activity). As a result of the experiment the following initial data were obtained:

S:	X_1:	X_2:	X_3:	X_4:
S	medium	weak	240	478
S+1	short	overheated	228	579
S+2	close to medium	medium	250	567

Term forms X_1 and X_2 were obtained as a result of expert evaluations and during calculations were represented as a discrete function. Vectors representing the difference between regimes of kilns 1 and 2 were classified. Classification data that were obtained are shown in Fig. 1. The curves a, B, C correspond to the classification with the weight coefficients σ_r and with X_3 0.01, 0.1 and 0.25 respectively. In Fig. 2 ΔA is the quality difference between output products of the kilns 2 and 1, i.e. $\Delta A = A_1 - A_2$. Thus, zone 1 with a minimal dispersion corresponds to group 1 together with the regimes of both kilns. Zones II and III, with greater dispersion, correspond to the regimes of kiln 2, which are different from the regimes of kiln 1. This in general verifies the process engineer's hypothesis that the burning regime influence the output product quality.

The data obtained verifies the usefulness of the classification algorithm and also the possibility of obtaining a model of the object under investigation and so the algorithms for excercising control over this object.

ACKNOWLEDGEMENTS

Experimental data used in the article were prepared and presented by engineer V.A. Kivenko, to whom the authors address their sincere thanks.

REFERENCES

1. Гусев Л.А., Смирнова И.М. Развитие теории размытых множеств. Измерения, контроль, автоматизация, 1978, вып.3, стр.39-47.
2. Дорофеюк А.А. Алгоритмы обучения машин распознаванию образов без учителя, основанные на методе потенциальных функций. Автоматика и телемеханика, 1966, №10, стр.78-87.

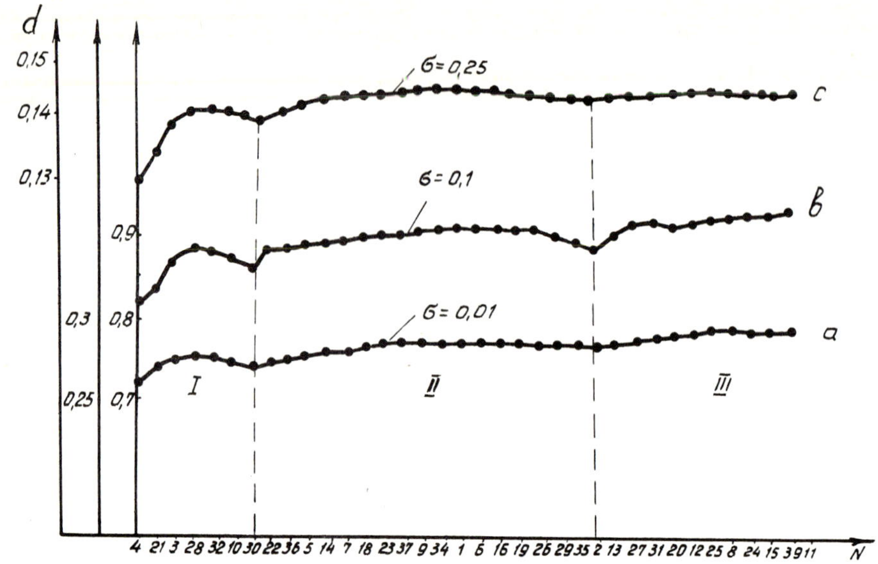

Figure 1.

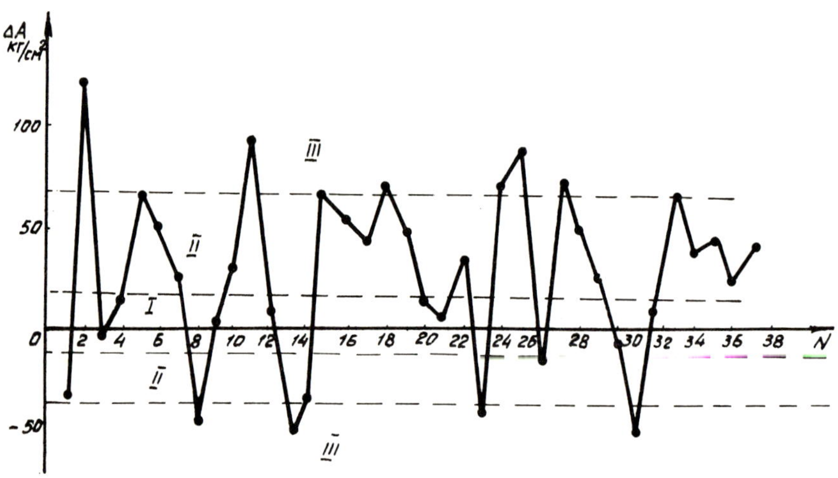

Figure 2.

Approximate Reasoning in Decision Analysis
M.M. Gupta and E. Sanchez (eds.)

ON THE UNCERTAINTY OF FUZZY CLASSIFICATIONS

Jiří Šustal

Technical University of Brno,
Faculty of Electrical Eng., Dept. of Mathematics,
Brno, Czechoslovakia

Properties of the uncertainty are studied which often arises in situations where we are to classify an object into one of n classes.

KEYWORDS. Uncertainty, classification, fuzzy sets.

The fuzzy classification /3/ usually does not provide us with a result which would be a disjoint partition of a set X into n classes. Ruther we obtain n fuzzy sets u_i over X satisfying, for each $x \in X$, $\sum_1^n u_i(x)=1$ where $u_i(x)$ measures the extent to which an element x has been associated with a class C_i, $i \in \overline{1,n}$. If we want to go yet one step further and to determine on the basis of the fuzzy classification a hard partition of the set X, the uncertainty inevitably arises about the executed decision. We prefer to have this uncertainty as low as possible and in this way we can exploit it to discriminate between several concurrent fuzzy partitions. In the paper /4/ one considers in the first place the uncertainty associated with a classification of a particular element $x \in X$, so called local uncertainty. Measures of the overall uncertainty, so called global uncertainty, can then be derived using the concept of the local uncertainty.

In this contribution we shall get to know some properties of the local uncertainty. Consequently this paper is closely related to /4/. The exposition, however, is presented in such a way that the reader needs no previous knowledge of /4/.

First let us specify which kind of uncertainty associated with the classification of an object $x \in X$ into n classes C_i we have in mind. We can distinguish at least three types of such an uncertainty.

1. The uncertainty which class to choose or alternatively, whether the chosen class is the best one.

2. The uncertainty whether the class C_i is better than the class C_j.

3. The uncertainty whether the class C_i is better than some of the other classes.

For the latter two types of uncertainty, the most important case occurs when we choose for C_i such a class or one of such classes which correspond to the highest $u_i(x)$. Let it be the class C_1, which can always be achieved by reenumerating the classes. In this way we arrive at the uncertainty which will be the subject of our study, namely

3′. The uncertainty whether the class C_1 is better than some of the other classes.

This uncertainty is associated with two mutually exclusive hypotheses: H_1, that C_1 is the best class, and H_2, that some of the other classes is the best one.

As far as it is known to the author, only the uncertainty of the type 1 has been studied in connection with the fuzzy classification, e.g. /1/, /2/. On the other hand it seems that the uncertainty of the type 3´, though simpler to analyse, can be used equally well for discriminating between several fuzzy partitions. In this connection let us note that Shannon´s entropy, which is often used to measure the uncertainty of the type 1, arises from the different problem setting of the information generation and transmission, and in the above classification problem no use has been made of the additivity property of Shannon´s entropy.

In order to simplify the notation we shall write x_i instead of $u_i(x)$. The set of all vectors $\bar{x}=(x_1,\dots,x_n)$ is denoted G_x, hence $G_x=\{\bar{x}: 0\leq x_i\leq 1, \sum_1^n x_i=1\}$. With the aim to make the exposition more lucid, it is convenient to work over ordered n-tuples $\bar{x}$ rather than over disordered ones. They are denoted $\bar{y}$, so that $y_1\geq y_2\geq\dots\geq y_n$. G_y stands then for the set of all $\bar{y}$, $G_y=\{\bar{y}: y_1\geq y_2\geq\dots\geq y_n\geq 0, \ \sum_1^n y_i=1\}$. By ordering co-ordinates of an $\bar{x}$ we get the respective $\bar{y}$. We can then write $\bar{y}=\nu(\bar{x})$ where ν is a continuous mapping from G_x onto G_y.

Let us denote a new value of a variable z after a change Δz as z', hence $z'=z+\Delta z$. Further denote

$$u_i=y_1-y_i, \quad v_i=y_{i-1}-y_i, \quad i\in\overline{2,n}. \qquad (1)$$

A measure of the local uncertainty will be a function H_y defined on G_y (or H_x defined on G_x). If we wish to stress a particular n, we shall write H_y^n. It seems that the values u_i determine the uncertainty much more directly than the values y_i. Hence we would like to express the uncertainty also as a function H_u of $\bar{u}=(u_2,\dots,u_n)$ and we may ask what its relation to H_y is. The expression (1) maps G_y on the region $G_u=\{\bar{u}: 0\leq u_2\leq u_3\leq\dots\leq u_n\leq y_1$, where y_1 denotes $(1+\sum_2^n u_i)/n$ and $y_1\in[0,1]\}$. (1) is further a bijection between G_y and G_u and is continuous. Therefore we can see that it is no problem to change from H_u to H_y and reversely and that one function determines the other uniquely. If not otherwise mentioned, the function H will be understood in the sequel as a function of $\bar{y}$ and the subscript y will be omitted.

In /4/ the following properties of the local uncertainty have been introduced and discussed.

P1. H^n, $n\geq 2$, is a function defined and continuous in the region G_y with reals as its values.

(P2. This property is used only for H_x defined on G_x and says that H_x is a symmetric function of its arguments.)

P3. $H^{n+1}(y_1,\dots,y_n,0)=H^n(y_1,\dots,y_n)$.

P4. $H^n(y_1,\dots,y_n)\leq H(1/n,\dots,1/n)$ with its only maximum at $\bar{y}=(1/n,\dots 1/n)$.

P5. $H^n(y_1,\dots,y_n)\geq H^n(1,0,\dots,0)$ with its only minimum at $\bar{y}=(1,0,\dots,0)$.

P6. For each $j\in\overline{2,n}$ the value of H^n decreases (increases) with the increase (decrease) of u_j supposing that the other $u_i, i\neq j$, are constant.

P7. For each $j\in\overline{2,n}$ the value of H^n decreases (increases) with the increase (decrease) of v_j supposing that the other v_i, $i \neq j$, are constant.

P8. Denote I_N the set of integers not less than N. To every $\varepsilon > 0$ there is a natural $N(\varepsilon)$ such that for each $j, n \in I_N$, $j \leqq n$, if we change according to P6 $\bar{y}$ to $\bar{y}'$, it holds $|H^n(\bar{y}') - H^n(\bar{y})| \leqq \varepsilon$.

P9. Denote I_N the set of integers not less than N. To every $\varepsilon > 0$ there is a natural $N(\varepsilon)$ such that for each $j, n \in I_N$, $j \leqq n$, if we change according to P7 $\bar{y}$ to $\bar{y}'$, it holds $|H^n(\bar{y}') - H^n(\bar{y})| \leqq \varepsilon$.

P10. To every $\varepsilon > 0$ there is a natural $N(\varepsilon)$ such that for each $n > N$ if we change u_n holding the other u_i, $i < n$, constant, then $|H^n(\bar{y}') - H^n(\bar{y})| \leqq \varepsilon$.

Property P10 is a mere special case of P8 and of P9 too). Though the human uncertainty is a very subjective category there are sound reasons for the above stated properties except for P9.

In /4/ it has been shown that under a rather weak assumption, namely that P1 holds, property P6 implies P7 but not reversely.

As has been pointed out in /4/, the more distinctive the value y_1 over the others, the lower our uncertainty and reversely. Properties P6 and P7 are mere consequences of this rule. We can also imagine other consequences, some are given below as the following properties:

P11. The value of H^n decreases (increases) with the increase (decrease) of the distance from y_1 to the arithmetical mean of the other y_i, $i \in \overline{2,n}$, i.e., according to the change of

$$y_1 - \left(\sum_2^n y_i/(n-1) \right).$$

More generally

P12. The value of H^n decreases (increases) with the increase (decrease) of the distance from y_1 to a weighted mean of the other y_i, $i \in \overline{2,n}$, i.e. according to the change of

$$y_1 - \sum_2^n w_i y_i, \quad w_i > 0, \quad \sum_2^n w_i = 1.$$

Though these properties are quite suggestible, there may be some objections to their ultimate form, particularly why precisely the weighted mean has been chosen as a reference point and not other value, e.g. the quadratic mean $\sum_2^n y_i^2/(n-1)$. We prove further that under some reasonable assumptions properties P11 and P12 are in contradiction with P3.

Denote the distance from y_1 to the arithmetical or weighted mean of the other y_i, $i \in \overline{2,n}$, as d^n (or simply only by d).

<u>THEOREM 1</u>. Under the supposition that for some n H^n and H^{n+1} can be rewritten as composed functions $h \circ d^n$ and $h \circ d^{n+1}$ P11 contradicts P3.

<u>Proof</u>. Let us have a $\bar{y} = (y_1, \ldots, y_n) \in G_y^n$, $y_1 < 1$, and its corresponding $\bar{y}' = (y_1, \ldots, y_n, 0) \in G_y^{n+1}$ as required in P3. Then

$$d^n(\bar{y}) = y_1 - \frac{\sum_2^n y_i}{n-1} < y_1 - \frac{\sum_2^n y_i}{n} = d^{n+1}(\bar{y}').$$

Property P11 implies that h is a strictly decreasing function on the range of d^n and d^{n+1}. Consequently we have $H^n(\bar{y}) = h(d^n(\bar{y})) > h(d^{n+1}(\bar{y}')) = H^{n+1}(\bar{y}')$ which conflicts with P3. □

<u>THEOREM 2</u>. Let H satisfy property P12 and let the weights w_i in the weighted means be determined in such a way that proceeding from some case n to the next case n+1 we have $w_i^n \geqq w_i^{n+1}$, $i \in \overline{2,n}$, where at least one inequality is sharp and

where w_i^n, w_i^{n+1} denote weights in the first and in the second case, respectively. Further let it be possible to write H^n, H^{n+1} as $H^n=h\circ d^n$, $H^{n+1}=h\circ d^{n+1}$. Then we have a contradiction with P3.

The proof is very similar to that of theorem 1 if we choose an appropriate $\bar{y}$ and write

$$d^n(\bar{y})=y_1-\sum_2^n w_i^n y_i<y_1-\sum_2^n w_i^{n+1} y_i=d^{n+1}(\bar{y}').$$

In the following we give another argument in favour of P6 and P7 by proving that they are a consequence of P11 or P12.

THEOREM 3. It holds that P11⇒P12⇒P6 but not reversely, i.e. P6⇏P12⇏P11.

Proof. The assertions P11⇒P12 and P12 ⇏ P11 are obvious. We shall now prove that P12⇒P6: The distance from y_1 to the weighted mean of the others equals

$$d=y_1-\sum_2^n w_i y_i=\sum_2^n w_i y_1-\sum_2^n w_i y_i=\sum_2^n w_i(y_1-y_i)=\sum_2^n w_i u_i. \quad (2)$$

Let P12 hold. Make the change of $\bar{y}$ to $\bar{y}'$ by increasing u_j and holding the other u_i constant as requested in P6. Owing to (2) d increases and by the virtue of P12 H decreases. Similarly for a decrease of u_j.

P6⇏P12: Choose the expression $-\sum_2^n c_i u_i^2 = -\sum_2^n c_i(y_1-y_i)^2$ as a particular H. It is obvious that H obeys property P6. Let there exist weights $w_2,\dots,w_n$ such that H obeys P12 too. We shall show that this supposition leads to a contradiction. The distance d_n from y_1 to the weighted mean equals $\sum_2^n w_i u_i$ according to (2). Consider a vector $\bar{u}_o$ inside of G_u. For small increments Δu_i we have then $\Delta d=\sum_2^n w_i\Delta u_i$ and approximately also $\Delta H=-\sum_2^n c_i 2u_{io}\Delta u_i$. Let $n>2$. To simplify our notation we denote quantities $w_{n-1}, w_n, c_{n-1}2u_{n-1\,o}, c_n 2u_{no}, \Delta u_{n-1}, \Delta u_n$ as a,b,c,e,x,y respectively. Put $\Delta u_i=0$ for all i, $2\leq i<n-1$. Then the expressions for Δd and ΔH are reduced to $\Delta d=ax+by$ and approximately $-\Delta H=cx+dy$. Since for each $\bar{u}$ it holds $0\leq u_2\leq\dots\leq u_n\leq y_1\leq 1$, we can choose $\bar{u}_o$ so that $0<c<e$ and $\frac{b}{a}<\frac{e}{c}$. We shall distinguish 3 cases: a<b, a=b, a>b.

Let a<b. Choose a number k such that $\frac{b}{a}<k<\frac{e}{c}$ and set $|x|=k|y|$, $x>0$, $y<0$, where $|x|$ and $|y|$ are sufficiently small. Then $\Delta d>0$, $-\Delta H<0$, hence $\Delta H>0$, which is a contradiction with P12.

Let a=b. Choose a number k such that $1<k<\frac{e}{c}$ and set $|x|=k|y|$, $x>0$, $y<0$, where $|x|$ and $|y|$ are sufficiently small. Then $\Delta d>0$, $-\Delta H<0$, consequently $\Delta H>0$, which is a contradiction with P12.

Let a>b. Choose $|x|=|y|$, $x>y$, $y<0$, $|x|$ and $|y|$ sufficiently small. Then $\Delta d>0$, hence $\Delta H>0$, which is again a contradiction with P12. □

If we have two situations of maximal ambiguity, one with n elements, the other with n+1 elements, i.e. $\bar{y}^1=(1/n,\dots,1/n)\in G_y^n$ $\bar{y}^2=(1/(n+1),\dots,1/(n+1))\in G_y^{n+1}$, then the uncertainty with the second one should be greater. This is expressed by the property

P13. $H^n(1/n,\dots,1/n)<H^{n+1}(1/(n+1),\dots,1/(n+1))$.

THEOREM 4. P13 is implied by P3 and P6, or by P3 and P7.

Proof. It suffices to prove that P3 and P7 imply P13 since P7 is a consequence of P6. According to property P3

$H^n(1/n,\dots,1/n)=H^{n+1}(1/n,\dots,1/n,0)$. On the other hand $H^{n+1}(1/n,\dots,1/n,0)<H^{n+1}(1/(n+1),\dots,1/(n+1))$ by property P7 since the vector$(1/(n+1),\dots,1/(n+1))$ can be obtained from the vector $(1/n,\dots,1/n,0)$ through the decrease of v_n by $1/n$ holding the other v_i, $i<n$, constant, i.e. zero. □

In the paper /4/ a measure has been proposed which satisfies properties 1 to 10 and, by theorem 4, also P13.

$$H^n(y_1,\dots,y_n)=-\sum_2^n \lambda_i(y_1-y_i)-y_1\sum_{n+1}^{\infty}\lambda_i=$$
$$=-\sum_2^n \lambda_i u_i-y_1\sum_{n+1}^{\infty}\lambda_i \qquad (3)$$

where $\{\lambda_i\}$, $i=2,3,\dots$ is a sequence of numbers such that $\lambda_i>0$, $\sum_2^{\infty}\lambda_i=1$.

The sequence $\{\lambda_i\}$ has not been so far specified. By theorem 4 the sequence of numbers $Q_n=H^n(1/n,\dots,1/n)$, $n=2,3,\dots$ should increase with growing n. We can use this property and determine $\{\lambda_i\}$ by choosing an appropriate neat $\{Q_n\}$.

By (3) we have

$$Q_n=-\frac{1}{n}\sum_{n+1}^{\infty}\lambda_i \quad , \quad Q_{n+1}=-\frac{1}{n+1}\sum_{n+2}^{\infty}\lambda_i . \qquad (4)$$

We see that $Q_n<0$ and $Q_n\to 0$ as $n\to\infty$. Consequently the difference $(\lim_{n\to\infty} Q_n-Q_2)$ is finite and we cannot use for $\{Q_n\}$ the sequence of logarithms as was done in the case of Shannon's entropy. This case witnesses as well that we cannot use for $\{Q_n\}$ an arbitrarily growing sequence. An example of an appropriate $\{Q_n\}$ will be given below.

In order to determine $\{\lambda_n\}$ from (4), we write

$$-nQ_n=\sum_{n+1}^{\infty}\lambda_i=\lambda_{n+1}+\sum_{n+2}^{\infty}\lambda_i$$

$$-(n+1)Q_{n+1}=\sum_{n+2}^{\infty}\lambda_i$$

hence

$$\lambda_{n+1}=(n+1)Q_{n+1}-nQ_n \quad \text{or} \quad \lambda_{n+1}=n(Q_{n+1}-Q_n)+Q_{n+1}, \qquad (5)$$

$n=2,3,\dots$ E.g. if we choose $Q_n=-\frac{1}{n^2}$, $n=2,3,\dots$, we have $\lambda_{n+1}=-\frac{1}{n+1}+\frac{1}{n}=\frac{1}{n(n+1)}$. λ_2 is determined from the condition that $\sum_2^{\infty}\lambda_i=1$, which gives $\lambda_2=\frac{1}{2}$.

REFERENCES:

[1] Bezdek, J.C., Mathematical models for systematics and taxonomy, in Estabrook, G. (ed.), Proc. 8th Annual Internat. Conf. on Numerical Taxonomy (Freeman Co, San Francisco, 1975).

[2] Capocelli, R.M. and De Luca, A., Fuzzy sets and decision theory, Information and Control 23 (1973) 446-473.

[3] Dunn, J.C., A fuzzy relative of the isodata process and its use in detecting compact, well-separated clusters, Cybernetics 2 (1973).

[4] Šustal, J., On measures of fuzzy classification uncertainty, submitted for publication in Fuzzy Sets and Systems.

Approximate Reasoning in Decision Analysis
M.M. Gupta and E. Sanchez (eds.)

CHARACTER RECOGNITION USING FUZZY SIMILARITY RELATIONS

B. N. Chatterji
Department of Electronics and Electrical Communication Engineering,
Indian Institute of Technology,
Kharagpur, India 721302

Patterns of handwritten characters are found to be fuzzy to a certain extent and hence the theory of fuzzy set provides an approximate and effective means of describing such patterns. In this paper an attempt has been made to use the concept of fuzzy similarity relation as a tool for classification of handwritten english characters. The features used for the method are the distances of the pattern from eight different points of the square frame. Using these features a fuzzy similarity function has been found out. The function is proved to be reflexive, symmetric and transitive. For the recognition of handwritten english characters ideal alphabets are generated using standard features. The fuzzy similarity value between the unknown pattern to be classified and all the 26 standard english alphabets are then determined. The unknown pattern is recognized to be that english alphabet for which the fuzzy similarity value is maximum. The recognition technique has been tested by a simulation procedure

Keywords: linguistic variables, similarity function, feature extraction, character generation, classification, simulation.

1. INTRODUCTION

The concept of fuzzy set was introduced by Zadeh (1965) for the analysis of complex systems and decision processes. This concept is based on the philosophy that the elements of human thinking consists of transitions from membership to nonmembership in a gradual fashion rather than abrupt and hence are considered to be a fuzzy set and not numbers. The human thought processes were considered to be imprecise and ambiguous by the classical mathematics. The fuzzy set theory gave mathematical precesion to such processes. The three main characteristics of fuzzy set theoretic approaches are :

(i) use of 'linguistic variables' instead of or in addition to 'numerical variables'

(ii) use of 'fuzzy conditional statements' for representing simple relations between the variables

(iii) use of 'fuzzy algorithms' for representing complex relations between the variables.

The concept of fuzzy set theory was adopted by scientists of many disciplines for theoretical work as well as for applications in areas likes economics, management science, biology, medicine, psychology, information retrieval, artificial intelligence, linguistics, pattern recognition, social science and control engineering. This is not only due to scientific talent and convincing effort of Zadeh but also the research efforts of scientists like Gupta (1975, 1977). Pattern recognition is an area where the fuzzy set theory got the attention from the very begining of its existence. Here the fuzzy set theory has influenced tremendously in both the decision theoretic and syntactic methods. Fuzzy languages, fuzzy grammar, fuzzy automata theories and fuzzy algorithms were developed for pattern recognition problems. Some of the interesting results reported are those due to Bellman, Kalaba and Zadeh (1966); Chang (1967); Gitman and Levine (1970); Ruspini (1972); Bezdek (1973); Dunn (1974); Saridis (1974); Koczy and Haznel (1975); and Shimura (1975).

One class of pattern recognition problems is character recognition. Most of the early works in character recognition were based on the use of correlation techniques and probabilistic concepts. Here we have a segmentation stage followed by a classification stage. Segmentation stage is based on a priori knowledge of the characters and a minimal set of features which completely characterize the patterns of the characters are determined. The features are determined heuristically and are used during the recognition process. The patterns of handwritten characters have biological origin and hence the variability is more appropriately represented by the concept of uncertainty than by the concept of probability. Hence it was thought that for badly written characters instead of using probability function one should use fuzzy membership function. Some of the work in character recognition using this new fuzzy set theoretic concept are those due to Tamura, Higuchi and Tanaka (1971); Siy and Chen (1974); Shimura (1974); Kickert and Koppelaar (1976); Pal, Datta Majumdar and Chaudhuri (1977) and Gupta, Saridis and Gaines (1977).

The concept of fuzzy similarity relation was given by Zadeh (1971) as an extension of the concept of fuzzy sets. In this paper this concept was used for the recognition of hand-written english characters. As will be seen in the succeeding sections, a fuzzy similarity function is found out for this purpose which satisfies all the required conditions. Both the feature extraction and classification stages of the character recognition are described to incorporate this function. The method needs standard handwritten characters which are found by a heuristic method using fuzzy set theoretic approach. The recognition accuracy was found to be comparable with other existing methods. But the method has some advantages and shortcomings.

2. FUZZY SIMILARITY RELATION

Let X and Y be two sets. The fuzzy relation between them is represented a fuzzy subset of the cartesian product X x Y (Zadeh 1971) given by

$$R = \int_{(x,y) \in X \times Y} [\mu(x,y) \mid (x,y)] \quad \ldots (1)$$

where $\mu(x,y)$ is their membership functions. The relation R said to be similarity relation if it is reflexive, symmetric and has max-min transitivity. In other words

$$\mu(x,x) = 1 \text{ and } \mu(x,y) < 1, \quad y \neq x, \quad \forall x \in X \quad \ldots (2)$$

(Reflexive Property)

$$\mu(x,y) = \mu(y,x), \quad \forall (x,y) \in Y \quad \ldots (3)$$

(Symmetric Property)

$$\mu(x,z) \geq \text{max-min}\,[\mu(x,y), \mu(y,z)], \quad \forall x,y,z \in X, y \in X \quad \ldots (4)$$

(Max-Min Transitivity Property)

3. FEATURE EXTRACTION

Feature extraction is an important step in the character recognition process. The features used for this method are the distances of the pattern from the different points on the frame in the predetermined directions. The frame of the pattern is a (20x20) binary matrix (Fig. 1(a)) in which the character is written. The presence of the character is represented

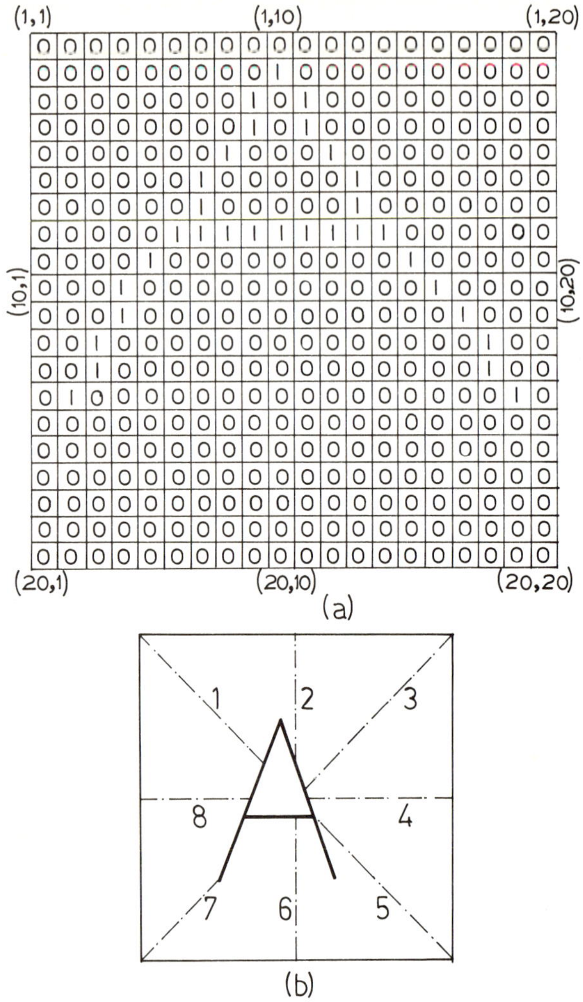

Fig.1. Feature Extraction (a) Pattern Frame (b) Feature Vector.

by the bit '1' and the absence by the bit '0'. The distance of the character is measured from eight different points of the frame along the eight directions (Fig. 1(b)). These are:

(i) (1,1) point of the matrix, i.e., the left hand top corner point of the frame along the direction 1.

(ii) (1,10) point of the matrix, i.e., the top middle point of the frame along the direction 2.

(iii) (1,20) point of the matrix, i.e., the right hand top corner of the frame along the direction 3.

(iv) (10,20) point of the matrix, i.e., the right hand middle point of the frame along the direction 4.

(v) (20,20) point of the matrix, i.e., the right hand bottom corner of the frame along the direction 5.

(vi) (20,10) point of the matrix, i.e., the bottom middle point of the frame along the direction 6.

(vii) (20,1) point of the matrix, i.e., the left hand bottom corner of the frame along the direction 7.

(viii) (10,1) point of the matrix, i.e., the left hand middle corner of the frame along the direction 8.

These eight measured distances form the unnormalized feature vector, i.e.,

$$\text{Feature vector FV} = (d_1,d_2,d_3,d_4,d_5,d_6,d_7,d_8) \quad \ldots (5)$$

These distances may not be same for different samples of identical characters. To avoid this problem, the distances are to be normalized. The normalization technique consists of

(i) Determination of the maximum distance of the pattern from the frame, i.e., the maximum Max (d_i) of the distances $d_1, d_2, \ldots, d_8$.

(ii) Division of the distances d_i, $i=1,2, \ldots, 8$ by Max(d_i) giving

$$a_i = d_i/\text{Max}(d_i),\ i=1,2, \ldots 8 \quad \ldots (6)$$

The normalized feature vector FVN is given by

$$\text{FVN} = (a_1,a_2,a_3,a_4,a_5,a_6,a_7,a_8) \quad \ldots (7)$$

The value of each feature lies within (0,1), i.e.,

$$0 \leq a_1 \leq 1 \quad \ldots (8)$$

4. FUZZY SIMILARITY FUNCTION FOR CLASSIFICATION

The classification of the characters is done with the help of fuzzy similarity function. If the normalized feature vector FVN (eq.7) is represented by X, i.e.,

$$\{X_i\} \in X \text{ or } X_i \in X \text{ for } i = 1,2, \ldots N \quad \ldots (9)$$

where N is the number of characters, then a fuzzy similarity function for the feature is given by

$$\mu_s(X_i,X_j) = 1-\left[\sum_{k=1}^{8}(a_i^k - a_j^k)^2\right]^{\frac{1}{2}} \quad \ldots (10)$$

for $X_i, X_j \in X$

The function must be

(a) Reflexive
(b) Symmetric
and (c) Max-Min Transitive

Since, $\mu_s(X_i,X_i) = 1 - \left[\sum_{k=1}^{8}(a_i^k-a_i^k)^2\right]^{\frac{1}{2}} = 1,$

the function $\mu_s(X_i,X_j)$ is reflexive. Again

$$\mu_s(X_j,X_i) = 1 - \left[\sum_{k=1}^{8}(a_j^k - a_i^k)^2\right]^{\frac{1}{2}} = 1 - \left[\sum_{k=1}^{8}(a_i^k - a_j^k)^2\right]^{\frac{1}{2}} = \mu_s(X_i, X_j)$$

which proves that the function $\mu_s(X_i,X_j)$ is symmetric.

To prove the max-min transitivity property, we have to prove

$$\mu_s(X_i,X_j) \geq \vee\left[\mu_s(X_i,X_1) \wedge \mu_s(X_1,X_j)\right] \ldots (11)$$

where $\vee$ stands for the maximum and $\wedge$ stands for the minimum. Let us define,

$$\mu_{F_{ij}}(X_i,X_j) = \left[\sum_{k=1}^{8}(a_i^k - a_j^k)^2\right]^{\frac{1}{2}} \quad \ldots (12)$$

and the fuzzy sets

$$F_{ij} = (X_i,X_j)/\mu_{F_{ij}}(X_i,X_j) \quad \ldots (13)$$

$$F_{i1} = (X_i,X_1)/\mu_{F_{i1}}(X_i,X_1) \quad \ldots (14)$$

and

$$F_{1j} = (X_1, X_j)/\mu_{F_{1j}}(X_1, X_j) \quad \ldots (15)$$

The inequality (11) modifies to

$$1-\mu_{F_{ij}}(X_i,X_j) \geq \vee\left[(1-\mu_{F_{i1}}(X_i,X_1)) \wedge (1-\mu_{F_{1j}}(X_1,X_j))\right]$$

or $1 - F_{ij} \geq \vee\left[(1-F_{i1}) \wedge (1-F_{1j})\right]$

or $1 - F_{ij} \geq \vee\left[1-(F_{i1} \vee F_{1j})\right]$

or $1 - F_{ij} \geq \left[1 - \wedge(F_{i1} \vee F_{1j})\right]$

or $F_{ij} \leq \Sigma(F_{i1} \vee F_{1j})$

$$\text{or } F_{ij} \leq \Sigma(F_{il} \vee F_{lj})$$

(Ref. Siy and Chen 1972)

$$\text{or } F_{ij} \leq \text{Some } (F_{il} \vee F_{lj}) \qquad \ldots(16)$$

(Ref. Siy and Chen 1972)

In case $\mu_{F_{il}} > \mu_{F_{lj}}$, the inequality (16) becomes

$$F_{ij} \leq \text{Some } F_{il} \qquad \ldots(17)$$

For l = j the inequality (17) becomes an identity and hence is valid. Similarly, for $\mu_{F_{lj}} > \mu_{F_{il}}$,

$$F_{ij} \leq \text{Some } F_{lj} \qquad \ldots(18)$$

Again, for l=i, the inequality (18) is an identity and hence is valid. Thus, the inequality (11) is proved to be valid one and in other words the fuzzy similarity function given by eq. (10) is max-min transitive.

The reflexive, symmetric and max-min transitivity properties of the fuzzy similarity function given by eq. (10) were verified by actual simulation in TDC 316 digital computer. A set of all english handwritten uppercase alphabets were considered. A fuzzy similarity function matrix S was found in which (i,j)th element was the fuzzy similarity function between the ith and jth english alphabets. It was observed that the diagonal elements of the matrix S to be all unity which verifies the reflexive property. The matrix S is symmetric which verifies the symmetric property. For verifying the max-min transitivity property, another matrix SOS was formed where the operation 'O' is defined by the right hand side of the inequality (11). It was found that SOS=S which verifies that the fuzzy similarity function given by eq. (10) is max-min transitive.

5. STANDARD CHARACTER GENERATION

During the classification stage standard (or ideal) english alphabets are needed. The standard alphabets can be obtained from a large handwritten samples by statistical method. Otherwise they are to be generated. Here the second approach is used and the standard alphabets are generated by a pattern recognition technique using the concept of fuzzy set membership function. Eight basic features were used for the generation of uppercase english characters. These are (i) horizontal stroke –, (ii) vertical stroke |, (iii) right slant stroke /, (iv) left slant stroke \, (v) A curve ∩, (vi) u curve U, (vii) c curve C and (viii) D curve ⊃. For each character, node points are defined as those points where two or more of these basic features meet and the different english characters are given different linguistic definitions involving these basic features. For example, the character A is represented as two left slant strokes, two right slant strokes and one horizontal stroke. The linguistic definitions of all the 26 english uppercase alphabets are given in Table-1.

For the generation of a standard english alphabet, the handwritten character is checked whether it follows the definition of any alphabet given in Table-1. For this, the node points of the character is first determined. The strokes between different node points are then determined. Each stroke is identified as one of the eight features with the help of membership function for the different features (Pal, Datta Majumdar and Chaudhury 1977) and using a heuristic approach.

The membership function for the feature to be straight line (Fig.2) is expressed as

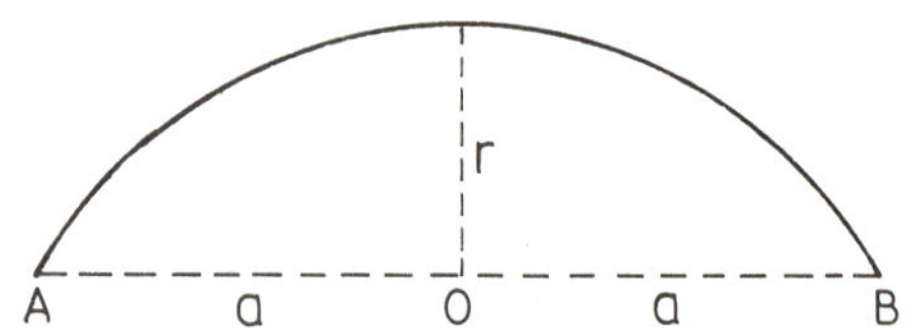

Fig.2. Representation of an arc

$$\mu_{SL} = (1 - \frac{r}{a}) \text{ if } r < a$$
$$= 0 \quad \text{otherwise} \qquad \ldots (19)$$

where 2a is the length of the line AB joining two node point of the arc (stroke between node A and B). The deviation measured from the centre O is r. The membership functions μ_H and μ_V for the feature to be horizontal and vertical strokes are given by

$$\mu_H = 1 - |m_x| \quad \text{for } |m_x| \leq 1$$
$$= 0 \quad \text{for } |m_x| > 1 \qquad \ldots (20)$$

$$\mu_V = 1 - |1/m_x| \quad \text{for } |m_x| \geq 1$$
$$= 0 \quad \text{for } |m_x| < 1 \qquad \ldots (21)$$

where m_x is the slope of the feature.

The membership function for the feature to be oblique (i.e. either left slant or right slant) is expressed as

$$\mu_{ob} = 1 - \left| \frac{\theta - 45}{45} \right| \quad \text{for } 0 \leq |m_x| < \infty \ldots \quad (22)$$

$$\text{where } \theta = \tan^{-1} m_x \qquad \ldots (23)$$

TABLE 1 Linguistic Definitions of uppercase English Alphabets

ENGLISH CHARACTER	LINGUISTIC DEFINITION	CODE
A	Two left slant+two right slant+one horizontal stroke	10220000
B	Two D curve+two vertical stroke	02000002
C	One C curve	00000010
D	One vertical stroke+one D curve	01000001
E	Three horizontal stroke+ two vertical stroke	32000000
F	Two horizontal stroke+two vertical stroke	22000000
G	One C curve+one D curve	00000011
H	One horizontal stroke+four vertical stroke	14000000
I	One vertical stroke	01000000
J	Two horizontal stroke+one vertical stroke+one U curve	21000100
K	Two vertical stroke+one left slant+one right slant	02110000
L	One horizontal stroke+one vertical stroke	11000000
M	Two vertical stroke+one left slant+one right slant	02110000
N	Two vertical stroke+one left slant	02010000
O	One A curve+one U curve	00001100
P	Two vertical stroke+one D curve	02000001
Q	Two left slant+one C curve+one D curve	00020011
R	Two vertical stroke+one left slant+one D curve	02010001
S	One C curve+one D curve	00000011
T	Two horizontal stroke+one vertical stroke	21000000
U	One U curve	00000100
V	One right slant+one left slant	00110000
W	Two right slant+two left slant	00220000
X	Two right slant+two left slant	00220000
Y	One vertical stroke+one left slant+one right slant	01110000
Z	Two horizontal stroke+one right slant	20100000

The sign of m_x determines whether the feature is left slant or right slant. The membership function for the feature to be horizontal curve (i.e., either 'A' curve or 'U' curve) is given by

$$\mu_{HC}=1-\text{MIN}\left[\text{MIN}(|\theta|, |180-\theta|, |360-\theta|)/90,\ 1\right] \quad \ldots(24)$$

where $\theta = \tan^{-1}$ (slope of the straight line joining the end points of the curve) ...(25)

Similarly the membership function for the feature to be vertical curve (i.e., either 'C' curve or 'D' curve) is expressed as

$$\mu_{VC}=1-\text{MIN}\left[\text{MIN}(|90-\theta|, |270-\theta|)/90,\ 1\right] \quad \ldots(26)$$

Here also θ is defined by eq. (25). The identification process consists of the following eight steps :

Step 1 : Determine μ_{SL} from eq. (19). If it is less than 0.4 (which is found out by trial and error method) then go to step 5 through step 8. Otherwise go to step 2 through step 4.

Step 2 : Find the slope m_x of the feature by least square error method, i.e.,

$$m_x = \frac{M \sum_{i=1}^{M} X_i Y_i - \sum_{i=1}^{M} X_i \sum_{i=1}^{M} Y_i}{M \sum_{i=1}^{M} X_i^2 - \left[\sum_{i=1}^{M} X_i\right]^2} \quad \ldots(27)$$

Step 3 : Determine μ_H, μ_V and μ_{ob} using eqns. (20), (21) and (22) respectively.

Step 4 : Find the maximum of μ_H, μ_V and μ_{ob}. If μ_H is maximum, the feature is a horizontal stroke. If μ_V is maximum, the feature is a vertical stroke. If μ_{ob} is maximum, the feature is right slant for positive m_x and is left slant for negative m_x.

Step 5 : Determine μ_{HC} and μ_{VC} using equns. (24) and (26) respectively.

Step 6 : Determine the maximum of μ_{HC} and μ_{VC}.

Step 7 : If μ_{HC} is maximum then the feature is a horizontal curve. To decide whether it is 'A' curve or 'U' curve the following rule is used :

(a) For 'A' curve as shown in Fig. 3(a), the |Y| coordinate of any point on the curve $\leq$ MAX(|Y| coordinate of point A, |Y| coordinate of point B).

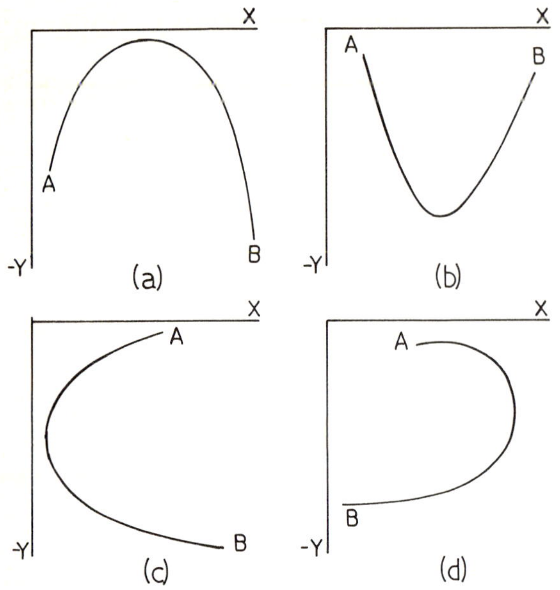

Fig.3. Representation of horizontal and vertical curves (a) A-curve (b) U-curve (c) C-curve (d) D-curve.

(b) For 'U' curve, as shown in Fig. 3(b), the $|Y|$ coordinate of any point on the curve $\geq$ MIN ($|Y|$ coordinate of point A, $|Y|$ coordinate of point B).

Step 8: If μ_{VC} is maximum then the feature is a vertical curve. To decide whether it is 'C' curve or 'D' curve the following rule is used :

(a) For 'C' curve, as shown in Fig. 3(c), the $|X|$ coordinate of any point on the curve $\leq$ MAX($|X|$ coordinate of point A, $|X|$ coordinate of point B).

(b) For 'D' curve, as shown in Fig. 3(d), the $|X|$ coordinate of any point on the curve $\geq$ MIN($|X|$ coordinate of point A, $|X|$ coordinate of point B).

After extracting the features by this method the character is given the linguistic definition in the code form as $(f_1,f_2,f_3,f_4,f_5,f_6,f_7,f_8)$ where f_1 and f_2 are the horizontal and vertical strokes in the character, f_3 and f_4 are the right slant and left slant strokes in the character and f_5,f_6,f_7 and f_8 are the 'A', 'U', 'C' and 'D' curves in the character. The coded definition of the handwritten character is then checked whether it follows the definition given in Table 1. In case it does not follow, the character is written again and the whole process is repeated for checking.

6. CLASSIFICATION

For classification the standard english alphabets are generated for all the 26 characters. For the unknown character, which is to be recognized, the feature vector is first determined. The fuzzy similarity value between the unknown pattern and all the 26 standard english alphabets are then determined using eq. (10). The unknown character is classified to be that english alphabet for which the fuzzy similarity value is maximum.

Let us consider 'β' is an unknown handwritten character to be classified. The feature vector of 'β' is given by

$$F(\beta) = (a_\beta^1, a_\beta^2, a_\beta^3, a_\beta^4, a_\beta^5, a_\beta^6, a_\beta^7, a_\beta^8) \quad ...(28)$$

The fuzzy similarity values are given by

$$\mu_S(\beta, X_i) = 1 - \left[\sum_{k=1}^{8} (a_\beta^k - a_i^k)^2\right]^{\frac{1}{2}} \quad ...(29)$$

where $X_i \in$ set of all standard english alphabets ...(30)

$$\text{and } F(X_i) = (a_i^1, a_i^2, a_i^3, a_i^4, a_i^5, a_i^6, a_i^7, a_i^8) ...(31)$$

The unknown character 'β' is classified as the mth english character if,

$$\mu_S(\beta, X_m) > \mu_S(\beta, X_i) \quad ...(32)$$

$$\text{for all } X_i \text{ but } X_m \neq X_i$$

7. RESULTS AND CONCLUSION

As mentioned in section 3, a 20x20 frame was used for writing the alphabets. From this, a 20x20 binary matrix was obtained and from this matrix the features were extracted. Standard english alphabets were determined for all the 26 characters and their features were found out. For testing the character recognition method, different persons were asked to write the characters in the 20x20 frame. From their handwriting the features were extracted and the characters were recognized by the procedure outlined in the previous section. It has been found that the method gave very good results with recognition accuracy of about 96%. TDC 316 computer was used for the simulation study and the recognition time was found to be less than 1 msec.

This method has the advantage that it requires no threshold value for classification and has less restrictions on the shape of the alphabets. But the method requires standard english alphabets and a large memory capacity to store the feature vectors of the standard characters.

REFERENCES:

1. Bellman, R. E., Kalaba, R. and Zadeh, L. A., Abstraction and Pattern Classification, J. Math. Anal.& Appl. 13 (1966) 1-7.

2. Bezdek, J. C., Fuzzy Mathematics in Pattern Classification, Ph.D. Thesis, Centre for Applied Mathematics, Cornell Univ. (1973).

3. Chang, C. L., Fuzzy Sets and Pattern Recognition, Ph.D. Thesis, University of California (1967).

4. Dunn, J. C., Some Recent Investigations of a New Fuzzy Partitioning Algorithm and Its Application to Pattern Classification Problems, J. Cybernetics 4 (1974) 1-5.

5. Gitman, I., and Levine, M. D., An Algorithm for Detecting Unimodal Fuzzy Sets and Its Application as a Clustering Technique, I.E.E.E. Trans. Comp., 19 (1970) 583-93.

6. Gupta, M. M., Fuzzy Automata and Decision Process: The First Decade, Sixth Triennial World IFAC Congress, Boston, Cambridge (August 24-30, 1975).

7. Gupta, M. M., Saridis, G. N. and Gaines, B. R., Fuzzy Automata and Decision Processes (North Holland, Amsterdam, 1977).

8. Kickert, W. J. M. and Kopelaar, H., Application of Fuzzy Set Theory to Syntactic Pattern Recognition of Handwritten Capitals, I.E.E.E. Trans. Syst. Man Cybernet. 6 (1976) 148-151.

9. Koczy, L. T. and Hajnel, M., A New Fuzzy Calculus and Its Application as a Pattern Recognition Technique, 3rd Internat. Cong. of Cybernetics and Systems, Bucharest, Rumania (August 1975).

10. Pal, S. K., Dutta Majumdar, D. and Chaudhury, B. B., Fuzzy Set in Handwritten Character Recognition, Recent Developments in Pattern Recognition and Digital Techniques, Calcutta (1977)63-71.

11. Ruspini, E. H., Optimization in Sample Descriptions : Data Reduction and Pattern Recognition Using Fuzzy Clustering, I.E.E.E. Trans. Syst. Man Cybernet. 2 (1972) 541.

12. Saridis, G. N., Fuzzy Notions in Nonlinear System Classification, J. Cybernetics 4(1974) 67-82.

13. Shimura, M., An Approach to Pattern Recognition and Associative Memories Using Fuzzy Logic, in Zadeh, L. A., Fu, K. S.,Tanaka, K. and Shimura, M. (eds.), Fuzzy Sets and Their Applications to Cognitive and Decision Processes (Academic Press, New York, 1975, 449-476).

14. Shimura, M., Application of Fuzzy Set Theory to Pattern Recognition, J. JAACE 19 (1975a) 243-248.

15. Siy, P. and Chen, C. S., Minimization of Fuzzy Functions, I.E.E.E. Trans.Comp.21 (1972) 100-102.

16. Siy, P. and Chen, C. S., Fuzzy Logic for Handwritten Numerical Character Recognition, I.E.E.E. Trans. Syst. Man Cybernet. 4(1974) 570-575.

17. Tamura, S., Higuchi, S. and Tanaka, K., Pattern Classification Based on Fuzzy Relations, I.E.E.E. Trans. Syst. Man Cybernet. 1 (1971) 61-66.

18. Zadeh, L. A., Fuzzy Sets, Information and Control 8 (1965) 338-353.

19. Zadeh, L. A., Similarity Relations and Fuzzy Orderings, Information Science 3 (1971) 177-200.

Approximate Reasoning in Decision Analysis
M.M. Gupta and E. Sanchez (eds.)

A FUZZY SCALE INDUCED BY INTRANSITIVE ORDERING

Yajiro Morita and Yuzo Oka

Department of Control Engineering
Tokyo Institute of Technology
Tokyo, Japan

The authors suggest that a scale may be given a property not possessed by real numbers. The basic issue in the paper is that the transitivity of order relationship may not hold in measuring and evaluating objects of the real world. The measured objects may be locally ordered with no fuzziness, but there is no guarantee that the whole set of objects is compatible with one transitive order scale, not to mention a ratio scale. The authors present an analysis of intransitively ordered set. The loop, the main path diagram and the pseudo-interval order are defined and studied.

The paper includes two examples to explain how the authors' analysis of intransitively ordered sets can be applied to a practical problem of evaluation. In connection with the theory of fuzzy set, the ideas developed in the paper seem to reveal a genuine foundation for the use of a membership function, which, sometimes is criticized as being too much presumptive.

KEYWORDS: Measurement, Fuzzy Scale, Intransitive Order, Loop, Pseudo-Interval, Classification

1. INTRODUCTION

"The purpose of measurement is to make things less fuzzy" stated a scholar. This statement sounds alright at first, but a careful listener may brood questions. Aren't there some things inherently fuzzy? What if the measurement makes it clear that the things remain fuzzy after all? Is it not an ill-possessed idea that things ought to be less fuzzy?

The noun "things" and the adjective "fuzzy" must be carefully defined if we are to answer these questions. More important, we ought to have a clear idea about the scale we are using for the measurement. A scale by which we measure our height may tell us something about our weight (a tall man will weigh more than a short man) but nothing about our age. So there is a kind of matching between the measured object and the used scale. Traditionally, the real numbers are the basis of a scale for every observed variable in physics, chemistry and other natural sciences. Are the real numbers good enough to be the basis of a scale to measure human, social, psychological and/or metaphysical variables? This is the question which motivated our investigation.

Many researchers have pointed out the need of a fundamental theory of measurement and written good books[1][2]. Generally, the use of traditional scales is taken for granted. Another practical approach to measure non-physical variables may be the method of multidimensional scaling (MDS). It tells us, for example, how best we may find few traditional linear scales to evaluate a set of data[3]. When the data do not line-up along a straight line, we would say the data contain some untraceable error lying within a tolerance limit of measurement. By saying so, we are just sweeping all unknowns under the rug. The data may possess in themselves a bit more complicated and interesting infrastructure than being described by an MDS. In this paper we point out that data, especially those obtained by subjective judgement, may be described otherwise.

The now-famous membership function in the theory of fuzzy sets is supposed to express a degree of quantities measured or evaluated by human judgement[4]. Whenever human judgement is involved, a special scaling problem seems to appear. It is probably unfair to ask a fuzzy-theorist to probe into the cause of fuzziness expressed by a membership function; for, his main interest is in the development of propositions and operations with the given membership functions. However, the present paper will provide him with two plausible grounds to support his idea of membership: (1) It is unlikely that the man's subjectivity is random; therefore, the fuzziness thereof is not statistical. It is rather a consequence of the complexity of the relations among the elemental factors affecting his judgement. (2) A man may judge local elements quite logically and consistently, but he may not be able to see the whole collection of the elements to be judged compatible with his local criteria.

In the next chapter, we shall discuss some features of a scale and traditional ways of treating the fuzziness of measurement using the scale.

2. SCALE AND FUZZINESS

A scale is generally thought of the transformation, or map, ψ between a set A and the real number R_e. Let us denote the transformation as:

$$\psi: \quad (A, H_A) \rightarrow (X, H_X) \qquad (1)$$

where $A = \{a, b, c, \ldots.\}$ is, for now, a finite set $X \subset R_e$. H_A and H_X denote some topological structures of A and X respectively. A notable example of H_X may be the subsets of Borel set with the usual topology on R_e.

In the mathematical measure theory, the topology of R_e is very strong. However, the pre-image (A, H_A) in any technical measurement represents a set of physical objects. They are given an abstract property (length, weight, etc.) and mapped into R_e. Here comes a subtle interplay between the real physical object, its abstract property and the Borel set of R_e. We assume measurability (with respect to the σ-fields) for ψ: $(A, H_A) \rightarrow R_e$; namely, the set A is measurable if and only if there is an element $\phi^{-1}(x) \in H_A$ for any x belonging to the Borel set of R_e[5]. So when we assign a strong topology H_X on X, A must have also a strong topology. In such a case, we are dealing not with the measurability of the original physical objects but with that of their abstract property. If A is a finite set, H_X is finite also in order that ψ: $(A, H_A) \rightarrow (X, H_X)$ be measurable.

So we have a hint there to change or enlarge our viewpoint. We say the definition of measurability in the mathematical measure theory may be thought to be a formal statement of our common understanding that the pre-image (A, H_A) must possess a structure matching the image (X, H_X). In this paper we borrow the term "measurable" or "measurability" to mean the matching of (A, H_A) and (X, H_X). No formal definition will be given, however, to avoid unnecessary rigorism.

Now the image (X, H_X) is going to be constructed on R_e to measure the pre-image (A, H_A). There are several types of images.

2.1 Additively - measurable ψ from A to a discrete set X

The pre-image A may be a set of lengths, weights, or the like. The image is a set of finite real numbers. This is the case of a ratio scale. Sometimes A is a set of temperatures, densities or the like. Then the scale is called a difference scale. An extensive discussion concerning these scales will be found in the literature[2]. There is no fuzziness in X here. The image X can be either finite or countable.

2.2 Order - measurable ψ from A to a discrete set X

The image X lies on R_e, but ψ preserves an order relationship only. Traditionally, a linear, weak or partial order has been discussed. A property such as hardness is said to be measurable by this scale. A fuzzy measure may have this property[6]. In the following chapters of the present paper, the authors extend the discussion into the case of intransitive order, which, of course, has a completely different topological structure.

In the technical measurement, the image (X, H_X) is supposed to represent a physical standard (a straight edge, a micrometer, a block gauge, etc.). However, people knew that a physical standard could never be ideally represented by a point on R_e. This is really a beginning of ambiguity or fuzziness in the scale. The fuzziness came from practical consideration here and the solution was to make the image X to be a set of intervals.

2.3 Tolerance-type ψ from A to a set X of intervals on R_e

The intervals are on R_e and their mid-points are the nominal image of an element in A. Thus a bar is 100 ± 0.1 mm long for instance (Fig. 1). The modern notion of fuzziness is not yet apparent here. Taking the mid-points, the scale can be treated in much the same way as that of 2.1.

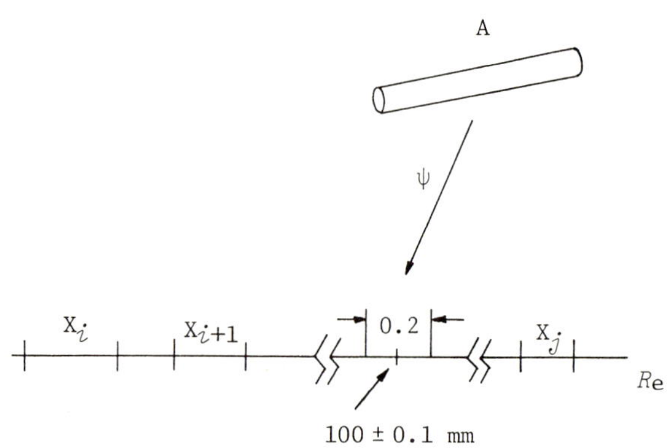

Fig. 1 Tolerance-type ψ from A to a set X of intervals on R_e.

2.4 Statistical-type ψ from A to a set X of probability density function

Morimura discussed the amount of information that can be obtained from a scale, assuming that the image (X, H_X) is a discrete set of normalized probability density functions[7]. Fig. 2, in contrast to Fig. 1, will be self-explanatory of the nature of the problem.

The scholars of mathematical psychology, decision making and elusive measurement have been more concerned about the binary relationships in the pre-image A. Some fuzzy-theoretic ideas may be incorporated in constructing the

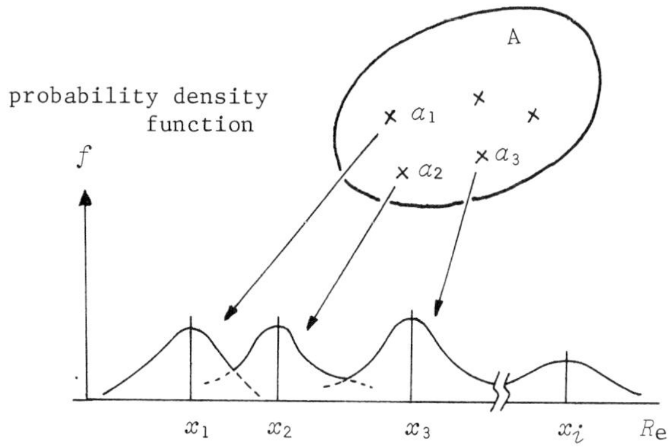

Fig. 2 Statistical-type ψ from A to a set X of probability density functions

scale. Many variations along this line of development are conceivable. Let us take one.

2.5 Fuzzy-type ψ from A to a set of fuzzy intervals on R_e.

Ichikawa et al. published a paper on the representation problem of a set A having fuzzy binary relationships among its members[8]. The pre-image A is mapped into a set of fuzzy intervals on R_e (Fig. 3). In the paper, the fuzzy

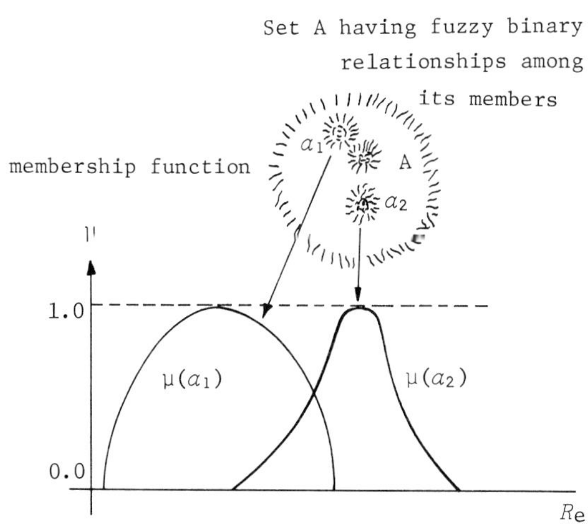

Fig. 3 Fuzzy-type ψ from A to a set of fuzzy intervals on R_e

interval order is defined among the fuzzy intervals, each of which is a bounded convex interval on R_e. The membership given to the fuzzy interval is normalized so that its maximum value is always 1. It is pointed out that the interval order defined by Fishburn[9] for crisp intervals is a special case of the fuzzy interval order.

Reviewing the traditional and current ways of handling the fuzziness in a scaling problem, we note that the various properties of R_e are utilized in varying degrees. As the scale gets fuzzier, less properties of R_e remain. We also note that a weak topology of H_X makes the scale measurable but ignors some known structure of the pre-image (A, H_A). For example, if H_X consists of the empty set and the whole set (or the whole interval) only, they will have corresponding pre-images in A, but the image $\psi(a)$ of a proper subset $a \in$ A will have no clear place in X.

3. INTRANSITIVITY AND A SCALE

Our first ambiguity cited above in 2.3 comes from practical limitations of a gauge's accuracy. We actually do not know where $\psi(a)$ will be within the tolerance. In the next case 2.4 we have a likelihood of $\psi(a)$, but we are still genuinely at a loss as to where $\psi(a)$ is going to be on R_e. Now, the situation becomes a bit different when we have a pre-image (A, H_A) of entities among which the binary relationship stems from human judgement rules.

Let us take an order relationship among the elements of A. The linear, weak or partial order is, by definition, transitive. The transitivity prevails the whole set A and it is measurable with a subset X of R_e because the elements of R_e are transitively ordered. Suppose we drop transitivity and take pair-wise comparability. Assume further that $\forall a, b \in$ A either $a > b$ or $b > a$ (no equivalence relation exists). We can easily propose a plausible example in evaluating commodity, say, a bag, by applying a 2-out-of-3 decision rule. Two bags are compared with respect to three key adjectives, say, handsome, handy and hardy. If $a > b$, bag a wins either 2 or 3 points concerning the above three adjectives against bag b.

Our pre-image A now has a structure which cannot be well measured by a subset X of R_e. Three points, with $a > b$, $b > c$ and $c > a$, are not separable on R_e. The important difference here, in comparison with Fig. 1 or Fig. 2, is that the relationship in A is clear. A man knows the relationship in the pre-image but has no measurable ψ with X on R_e. A statistical ψ such as the one in Fig. 2 is not describing the situation because the man's decision is utterly deterministic. A fuzzy ψ such as the one in Fig. 3 will be closer to the desirable scale because the man's subjectivity works both in deciding the relationship in A and in giving the membership of X on R_e. However, it is the restricted property of R_e which is making our ψ fuzzy here. We shall investigate the intransitively ordered set more in details in the following sections and suggest how A could be made best measurable with X on R_e.

3.1 Definitions and basic properties of an intransitively ordered set

We give fundamental definitions in this and next sections. The proofs of the 13 propositions and one theorem there are not given. They are straightforward and given in the authors' references [10], [11].

Def. 1 X is a finite set consisting of n(>0) elements and → is a binary relation on X. The pair <X, R> is called a graph if → satisfies the following two conditions where $R = \{(x_i, x_j); x_i \to x_j\} \subset X^2$.

(1) If for any $x_i \in X$ and $x_j \in X$ ($i \neq j$, $i, j=1, 2, \cdots, n$) $x_i \to x_j$, then $x_j \to x_i$ never holds.

(2) For any $x_i \in X$ and $x_j \in X$ ($i \neq j$, $i, j=1, 2, \cdots, n$) either $x_i \to x_j$ or $x_j \to x_i$ always holds.

An element $x_i \in X$ is called a point of <X, R> and $r \in R$ an arrow. When $r = (x_i, x_j) \in R$, x_i and x_j are called a starting point and a terminal point of r, respectively. Hereafter <X, R> is abbreviated as <X, →>.

Def. 2 If a set Y ($\neq \phi$: empty set) $\subset$ X in <X, →>, then a graph <X, $R \cap Y^2$> is called a subgraph of <X, →> and abbreviated as <Y, →>.

Def. 3 When $x_i \in X$ ($i=1,2, \cdots, n$) is not coincident with x_j($j=1,2, \cdots, n$, $i \neq j$), a diagram $x_1 \to x_2 \to \cdots \to x_n$ is called a path with length n-1 and each x_i($i=1,2, \cdots, n$) a point on the path.

Def. 4 A set Y ($\subset$ X) consisting of all the points on a path in <X, →> is called path representable and the path is called the representative path.

[Proposition 1] The set X of <X, →> is path representable.

Def. 5 If there exists a path from x_i to x_j ($i \neq j$) in <X, →>, x_i is called to be reachable to x_j.

Def. 6 If x_i ($i=1,2, \cdots, n$) is not coincident with x_j($i \neq j$, $i,j=1,2, \cdots, n$), the path being cyclic is called a cycle of size n (Fig. 4) and each x_i a point of the cycle.

Def. 7 A subset Y ($\subset$ X) consisting of all the points of a cycle in <X, →> is called to be cycle representable and the cycle the representative cycle. (Fig. 4)

Def. 8 A subset Y ($\subset$ X) being cycle representable in <X, →> is called a loop and the number of points constituting the representative cycle is defined as the size of the loop.

Def. 9 When a subset of a loop X is cycle representable, the subset is called a subloop of X.

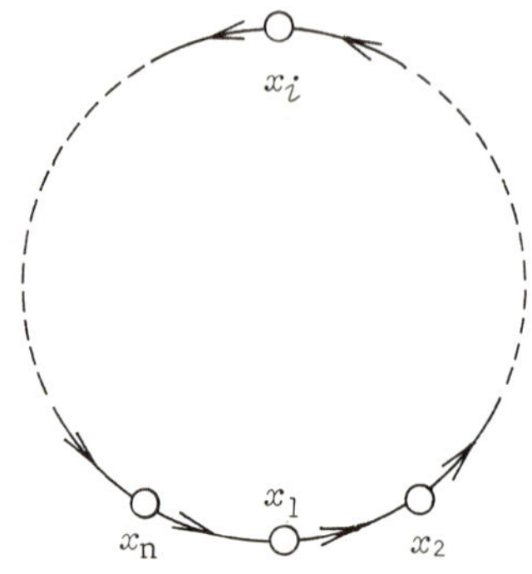

Fig. 4 Representative cycle of X

Def. 10 If a three-points set of X has a representative cycle in <X, →>, then the set is called a circular triple. Otherwise the set is called a transitive triple.

Def. 11 A subset Y ($\subset$ X) is called to generate a loop when loops $L_1, L_2, \cdots, L_n$ satisfy the following three conditions.

(1) $\bigcup_{i=1}^{n} L_i = Y$.

(2) $L_{j+1} \cap \bigcup_{i=1}^{j} L_i = \phi (j=1,2,\cdots, n-1)$ and L_{j+1} and $\bigcup_{i=1}^{j} L_i$ do not include each other.

(3) L_{j+1} does not include L_i ($j \geq i$).

Def. 12 If a loop Y and a circular triple C have two common points in <X, →>, then they are called to intersect each other. If a loop Y and a circular triple C have only one common point in <X, →>, then they are called to be tangent at the point.

The set <X, →> we are investigating here is a graph and the definitions given above parallel those given in the elementary textbooks of graph theory[12]. A subset (X, H_X) of R_e (the real line) is path representable according to Defs. 1 and 4, and the path has a set of uniquely ordered elements. However, (X, H_X) is not cycle representable. Proposition 1 tells us that <X, →> is path representable and therefore, is measurable with (X, H_X) on R_e. Let us see <X, →> superposed on (X', H_X). The non-unique order of elements of <X, →> on R_e is an indication, together with some backward arrows connecting two points apart (we will not allow two adjacent points backwardly connected as will be seen in the following), that <X, →> is a lot more complicated and fuzzier than (X, H_X).

Now we shall proceed onto the formal definition of <X, →> to be laid on R_e, the main path diagram.

Def. 13 The diagram determined by the following two operations in <X, →> is called to be a main path diagram and the representative path of the following operation (1) a main path.

(1) Choose a representative path in <X, →> having arrows towards the right hand side.

(2) Add all the inversely ordered arrows (defined as arcs) against the above mentioned representative path as in Fig. 5.

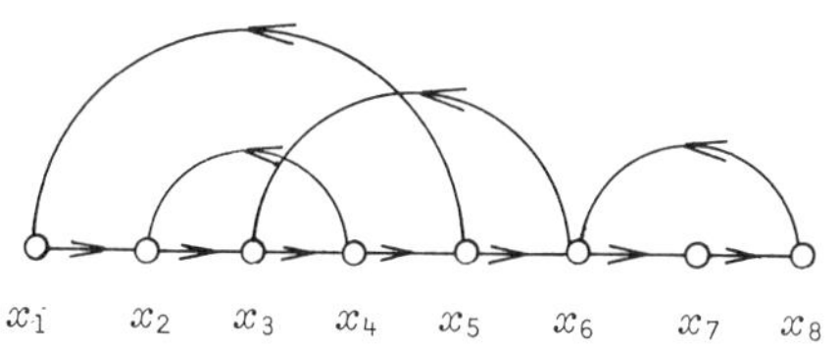

Fig. 5 Example of a main path diagram

Def. 14 Let A ($\neq \phi$) be a set of (ordered) arcs is a main path diagram of <X, →>. Injection Γ: A → 2^X is defined as

$\Gamma(a) = \{y_i;\ i=1,2,\ \cdots,\ n\}$

for any $a \in A$ (Fig. 6).

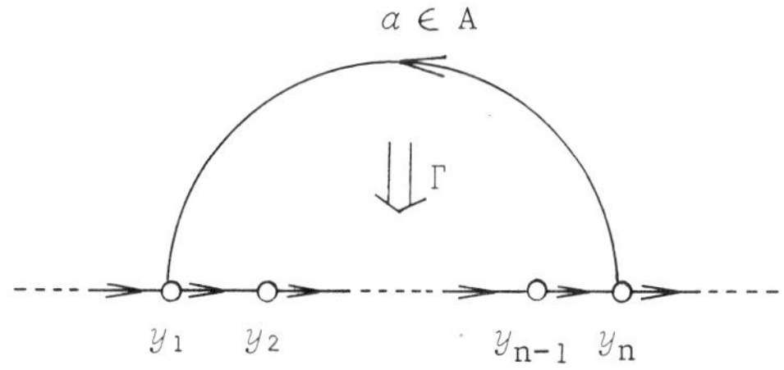

Fig. 6 Injection Γ of a

Def. 15 Let A be a set of ordered arcs in a main path diagram. For any $a_1 \in A$ and $a_2 \in A$:

(1) If $\Gamma(a_1) \cap \Gamma(a_2) = \phi$, then a_1 is called to be disjoint to a_2.

(2) If $\Gamma(a_1) \subset \Gamma(a_2)$, then it is called that a_2 contains a_1.

(3) Let's assume that a_1 is not disjoint to a_2 and does not contain a_2.

(i) If $\Gamma(a_1)$ and $\Gamma(a_2)$ have only one common point x, then it is called that a_1 and a_2 are mutually tangential at the point x.

(ii) If $\Gamma(a_1)$ and $\Gamma(a_2)$ have more than one common point, then it is called that a_1 and a_2 intersect (mutually).

(4) If an arc a_1 contains itself only, then a_1 is called to be maximal. If an arc a_1 is contained by itself only, then a_1 is called to be minimal.

(5) If $x \in \Gamma(a_1)$, then it is called that a_1 contains x. If a point x is neither the starting point of an arc a_1 nor the terminal point, then it is called that a_1 steps over x.

[Proposition 2] If a is defined as an arbitrary arc in a main path diagram, then $\Gamma(a)$ is a loop.

[Proposition 3] If two arcs a_1 and a_2 in a main path diagram intersect each other, then $\Gamma(a_1) \cap \Gamma(a_2)$ is a loop.

[Proposition 4] Let C be a circular triple in a main path diagram of <X, →>. Then there exists an arc such that the starting point and the terminal point of the arc are contained in C.

[proposition 5] Let y be the starting point of a minimal arc C stepping over a given point x and z be the terminal point. Then, x, y and z construct a circular triple.

[Proposition 6] If two arcs in a main path diagram are tangential at point x and at least either of them is maximal, then x and other two extreme points of them construct a circular triple.

Given <X, →>, we are assured by Proposition 1 that there is at least one main path diagram for <X, →>. In the linear path of a main path diagram, any two adjacent points are connected by an arrow toward the right. Any two non-adjacent points are connected either by an arrow toward the right or by an arc toward the left, but the arrow toward the right is not drawn. A loop has at least one main path diagram, but it needs not to be unique. In fact, the variations in describing a loop by the main path diagram motivated our further investigation.

3.2 Representation of a loop

Def. 16 Exclude all the arcs of a main path diagram, the points of the main path diagram lie on a path as if to satisfy the transitive law. The path is called the original transitive path of the main path diagram.

[Proposition 7] A subgraph $\langle Y, \twoheadrightarrow\rangle$ of $\langle X, \twoheadrightarrow\rangle$ constructs a loop if and only if the following two conditions are satisfied.

(1) The size of Y is greater than or equal to three.

(2) Either of the following two conditions holds at the point x of the original transitive path of a main path diagram other than the maximal or minimal point of it.

(i) There exists an arc stepping over x.

(ii) There exist two arcs tangential at x.

Def. 17 Let Y be a loop. Assume that Y does not constitute a loop if an arbitrary selected arc is excluded from the main path diagram. Then the diagram obtained from Y is called a k-th order fundamental pattern if the number of arcs is k.

[Proposition 8] Arcs of a fundamental pattern are not only maximal but also minimal.

Def. 18 If the diagram excluding all the arcs in a main path diagram other than the maximal arcs shows a k-th order fundamental pattern, then the main path diagram is called a k-th order extended fundamental pattern.

[Proposition 9] A k-th order fundamental pattern is also a k-th order extended fundamental pattern.

Def. 19 The following algorithm in a main path diagram is called upper algorithm.

1st step: Denote x_1 as the maximal point of the original transitive path in a main path diagram.

2nd step: Let a_1 be the arc having y_1 as the terminal point and x_1 as the starting point.

i+1st step: Let $\Gamma(a_0) = \{x_1\}$.
(i=1,2, $\cdots$)
If y_1 is not the minimal point of the original transitive path, then choose the arc a_{i+1} whose terminal point is the maximal in $\Gamma(a_i) - \Gamma(a_{i-1})$.

Def. 20 The algorithm derived from changing the words of maximal, terminal, starting and minimal into minimal, starting, terminal and maximal in Def. 19, respectively, is called a lower algorithm.

[Proposition 10] An upper (or a lower) algorithm satisfies the following.

(1) If the size of a loop Y is n, then the algorithm reaches the minimal (or maximal) point of the original transitive path at most by [2/3(n-1)] steps, where $[x]$ denotes the maximum integer not exceeding a positive number x.

(2) Each of the arcs $a_1, a_2, \cdots, a_n$ is maximal.

(3) The diagram obtained by excluding all the arcs other than $a_1, a_2, \cdots, a_n$ shows a fundamental pattern.

Def. 21 The diagram obtained by an upper (or a lower) algorithm is called an upper (or a lower) lowest order fundamental pattern. If the upper lowest order fundamental pattern coincides with the lower lowest order fundamental pattern, the diagram is called the lowest order fundamental pattern. (Fig. 7, Fig. 8)

[Proposition 11] The upper lowest order fundamental pattern derived from a k-th order extended fundamental pattern coincides with the lowest order fundamental pattern.

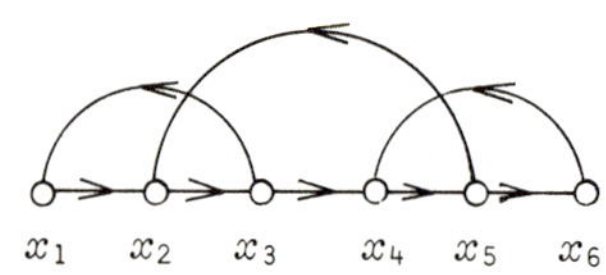

Fig. 7 The lowest order fundamental pattern for a $\langle X, \twoheadrightarrow\rangle$ of size 6

[Proposition 12] If a subset Y ($\subset$ X) is a loop, then the subgraph $\langle Y, \twoheadrightarrow\rangle$ is represented by a 1st order extended pattern.

[Proposition 13] If a loop Y is represented by an n-th (>1) order extended fundamental pattern, then Y can be also represented by an (n-1)th order extended fundamental pattern.

[Theorem 1] If a loop $\langle Y, \twoheadrightarrow\rangle$ is represented by an n-th order lowest fundamental pattern derived from its main path diagram, $\langle Y, \twoheadrightarrow\rangle$ can be represented by a main path diagram having an (n-1)th order lowest fundamental pattern.

In concluding this chapter, we remind our-

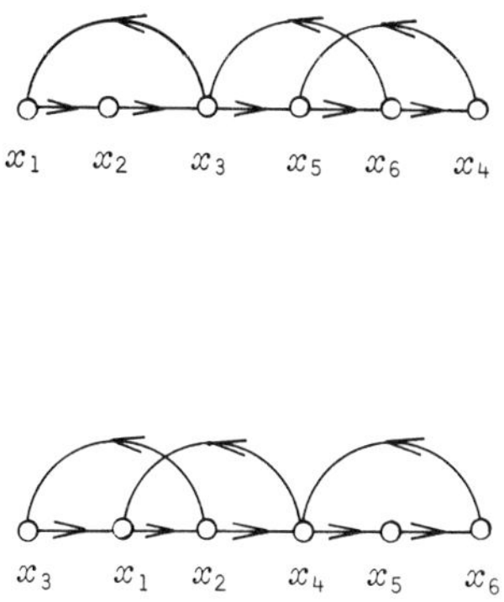

Fig. 8 The other lowest order fundamental patterns of a 3rd order

selves that our original problem of scaling : $(A, H_A) \to (X, H_X)$ is now that of ψ: $\langle X, \twoheadrightarrow \rangle \to (X, H_X)$ with a particular emphasis on loops that may appear in $\langle X, \twoheadrightarrow \rangle$. From the above investigation, we know there can be many main path diagrams of a loop, and there can be better main path diagrams than others in the sense that the measurability of ψ is better. The introduction of the fundamental pattern and its order is a way to evaluate the measurability since the higher the order k is, the more like (X, H_X) $\langle X, \twoheadrightarrow \rangle$ becomes.

4. PSEUDO-INTERVAL ORDER AND THE SCALE TO MEASURE A LOOP

The loop is fundamentally different from a path (Def. 3) on R_e. However, when the loop is drawn as a main path diagram (Def. 13), it has its original transitive path (Def. 16) which can be mapped into R_e. The original transitive path needs not be unique. In fact, there may be quite a few original transitive paths of a loop. This means that we can look at the loop or its cycle representation (Def. 7) in so many different ways. Some of them are better than the others in that we can see the loop's global order structure more clearly.

It is not strange that we should have an order structure of a loop globally as well as locally, since for each pair of points in the loop a definite order exists. There may be points which are the starting points (Def. 1) to most other points. Conversely, there may be points which are the terminal points (Def. 1) to most other points. A loop, in which the points are more or less evenly starting points and terminal points, will have a poor measurability with a subset (X, H_X) of R_e. The circular triple (Def. 10) is the simplest example.

For loops which are better measurable with a subset (X, H_X) of R_e, a pseudo-interval order can be defined as follows. It is characteristic of an intransitively ordered set, but it is parallel to an interval order defined among the subsets of R_e. Let us begin with the definition of the interval order.

Def. 22 Let $\langle x, \twoheadrightarrow \rangle$ be a graph. The subfamily of X i.e., $\{S_i: i=1,2, \ldots, n\}$ satisfying the following two conditions is called to construct an interval order.

(1) For any $x \in S_i$ $(i=1,2, \ldots, n)$ the relation $x \to x$ does not hold.

(2) If the relation $x \to y$ and $z \to w$ are held for any $x, y \in S_i$ and any $z, w \in S_j$ $(i \neq j$ $i, j=1,2, \ldots, n)$, then either $y \to z$ or $w \to x$ holds.

The above definition may represent the simplest form of defining an order among subsets on the real line. This definition is different from an interval order based on the usual order relationship ($<$ or $\leq$) on R_e. Fishburn's definition [9], for instance, will yield a partial overlapping of two compared subsets S_i and S_j on R_e, if our $\to$ is replaced by $<$ and transitivity is imposed on the binary relationship among the elements of S_i and S_j. The idea itself of intervals on R_e is based upon the tacit assumption that the order relationship ($<$ or $\leq$) is transitive on R_e.

The authors' pseudo-intervals to be defined in the following are basically different in this respect. One can map the pre-image $\langle X, \twoheadrightarrow \rangle$ on R_e and the image namely, the main path, is divided into pseudo-intervals. They are not so clearly separated as the usual intervals are on R_e. And yet there are some pseudo-intervals closely together and other pseudo-intervals relatively far apart. We shall now proceed onto the formal definition of pseudo-intervals.

Def. 23 The subfamily of X i.e., $\{S_i: i=1,2, \ldots, n\}$ satisfying the following three conditions is called to construct a pseudo-interval order.

(1) $S_i \cap S_j = \phi$ $(i \neq j, i, j=1,2, \ldots, n)$.

(2) For any $x \in S_i$ and any $y \in S_{i+1}$ $(i=1,2, \ldots n-1)$ either the following (i) or (ii) holds.

(i) If $y \to x$, then there exists a sequence $\{z_i; i=1,2, \ldots, k\}$ such as $x \to z_1 \to z_2 \to \ldots \to z_k \to y$.

(ii) If $x \to y$, then there exists a sequence $\{z'_i;\ i=1,2,\ \ldots,\ k'\}$ such as $y \to z'_1 \to z'_2 \to \ldots \to z'_{k'} \to x$.

(3) For any $x \in S_i$ and any $y \in \bigcup_{j=i+2}^{n} S_j$ $(i=1,2,\ \ldots,\ n-2)$ the relation $y \to x$ always holds.

[Proposition 14] Let maximal arcs constructing the lowest fundamental pattern on a main path diagram be $a_1,\ a_2,\ \ldots,\ a_k$. The terminal point of a_i lies on the right side of other terminal points of a_j $(i < j)$ in the original transitive path. For any $x \in \bigcup_{j=i+2}^{k} \Gamma(a_j) - \Gamma(a_{i+1})$ and any $y \in \Gamma(a_i)$ $(i=1,2,\ \ldots,\ k-2)$ the relation $x \to y$ always holds.

(Proof) There exists z satisfying $y \to z$ by use of the constructing algorithm of the lowest order fundamental pattern if and only if z is contained in one of $\Gamma(a_1),\ \Gamma(a_2),\ \ldots,\ \Gamma(a_{i+2})$. As $x \in \Gamma(a_j)(j=1,2,\ \ldots,\ i+1)$, then $x \to y$ always holds.

Q.E.D.

[corollary 1] Assume $\Gamma(a_0) = \phi$, $S_i = \Gamma(a_i) - \Gamma(a_{i-1})$ $(i=1,2,\ \ldots,\ k)$. For any $x \in \bigcup_{j=i+2}^{k} S_j$ and any $y \in S_i$ $i=1,2,\ \ldots,\ k)$ $x \to y$ always holds.

[Corollary 2] For any $x \in S_i$ and $y \in \bigcup_{j=1}^{\ell-2} S_j (i=1,2,\ \ldots,\ k-2,\ \ell=3,4,\ \ldots,\ k)$ $x \to y$ always holds.

[Proposition 15] For any $x \in \bigcup_{j=i+3}^{k} \Gamma(a_j) - \Gamma(a_{i+2})$ and any $y \in \Gamma(a_i)$ $(i=1,2,\ \ldots,\ k-3)$ the circular triple containing x and y cannot exist in a main path diagram.

(Proof) Consider a point $z \in Y$ other than x and y. If $z \in \bigcup_{j=i+3}^{k} \Gamma(a_j) - \Gamma(a_{i+2})$, either $x \to z$ or $z \to x$ holds. As $z \to y$ is always held, either $x \to z \to y$ or $z \to x \to y$ holds. If $z \in \Gamma(a_{i+2})$, then $x \to z \to y$ is held. If z belongs to one of $\Gamma(a_{i+1})$, $\Gamma(a_i)$ and $\Gamma(a_{i-1})$, then either $x \to z \to y$ or $x \to y \to z$ is derived. If $z \in \bigcup_{j=\ell}^{i-2} \Gamma(a_j)$, then $x \to y \to z$ is derived. In all the cases above mentioned set $\{x,\ y,\ z\}$ constructs a transitive triple.

Q.E.D.

[Corollary 3] For any $x \in \bigcup_{j=i+3}^{k} S_j$ and any $y \in S_i$ $(i=1,2,\ \ldots,\ k-3)$ circular triple containing x and y in Y cannot exist in Y at all.

[Corollary 4] For any $x \in S_i$ and $y \in \bigcup_{j=1}^{i-3} S_j$ $(i=1,2,\ \ldots,\ k)$ circular triple containing x and y in Y cannot exist in Y at all.

[Theorem 2] Let a loop Y have a k-th order fundamental pattern and the maximal arcs be $a_1,\ a_2,\ \ldots,\ a_k$. The terminal point of a_i lies on the right side of other terminal points of $a_j (j > i,\ i=1,2,\ \ldots,\ k)$ in the original transitive path. If $\Gamma(a_0) = \phi$ and $S_i = \Gamma(a_i) - \Gamma(a_{i-1})$ $(i=1,2,\ \ldots,\ k)$, then the family $\{S_i:\ i=1,2,\ \ldots,\ k\}$ constructs a pseudo-interval order.

(Proof) It is clear that $\{S_i:\ i=1,2,\ \ldots,\ k\}$ satisfies (1) of Def. 23 from S_i's definition and the deriving algorithm of the lowest fundamental pattern. It is also clear that $\{S_i:\ i=1,2,\ \ldots,\ k\}$ satisfies (3) or Def. 23 from corollary 1.

Let $\Gamma(a_i) = \{z^i_j:\ i=1,2,\ \ldots,\ \ell\}$ and $\Gamma(a_{i+1}) = \{z^{i+1}_j:\ i=1,2,\ \ldots,\ \ell'\}$. For any $x \in S_i$ and $y \in S_{i+1}$ $(i=1,2,\ \ldots,\ k-1)$ the following three cases can be considered with respect to x and y.

Case 1 $x \to y$;

This case happens when $x \in \Gamma(a_i) \cap \Gamma(a_{i+1})$. Let j^* be the maximum integer of j such as $x \to z^{i+1}_j$ for any $z^{i+1}_j \in S_{i+1}$ and j^{**} be the maximum integer of j such as $z^i_j \to x$ for any $z^i_j \in S_i$. Then the following sequence can be obtained.

$$y \to z^{i+1}_{j^*} \to z^{i+1}_{j^*+1} \to \cdots \to z^{i+1}_{\ell} \to z^i_1 \to z^i_2 \to \cdots \to z^i_{j^{**}} \to x.$$

Case 2 $y \to x$ and $x \in \Gamma(a_i) \cap \Gamma(a_{i+1})$;

Let $z^i_{j^{**}}$ be the starting point of the arc a_{i+1}, j^* be the minimum integer of j such as $x \to z^i_j$ and j'^{**} be the maximum integer of j such as $z^{i+1}_j \to y$. Then the following sequence can be obtained.

$$x \to z^i_{j^*} \to z^i_{j^*+1} \to \cdots \to z^i_{j^{**}} \to z^{i+1}_1 \to z^{i+1}_2 \to \cdots \to z^{i+1}_{j^{**}} \to x.$$

Case 3 $y \to x$ and $x \notin \Gamma(a_i) \cap \Gamma(a_{i+1})$;

Let $z^i_{j^{**}}$ be the starting point of the arc a_{i+1}, j^* the maximum integer of j such as $x \to z^i_j$ and $j^{**'}$ the maximum integer of j such as $z^{i+1}_j \to y$. Then the following sequence can be obtained.

$$x \to z^i_{j^*} \to z^i_{j^*+1} \to \cdots \to z^i_{\ell} \to z^i_1 \to z^i_2 \to \cdots \to z^i_{j^{**}} \to z^{i+1}_1 \to z^{i+1}_2 \to \cdots \to z^{i+1}_{j^{**'}} \to y$$

As there exists at least one point between x and y in all the cases, each sequence above mentioned always exists on the main path. Therefore it is clear that either (i) or (ii) of Def.

23 can be satisfied from the cases 1 to 3.

Q.E.D.

[Theorem 3] If the size of a loop X is n, the order of the lowest fundamental pattern derived from X is at most [2/3(n-1)].

(Proof) It is clear from Propositions 10 and 12.

Q.E.D.

The family of subsets $\{S_i: i=1,2, \ldots, k\}$ satisfying the property of a pseudo-interval order can be arranged on a main path diagram and compared with a subset (X, H_X) on R_e but the arrangement is less clear-cut and more fuzzy than that of subsets satisfying an interval order. For any $x \in S_i$ and any $y \in S_{i+1}$ we cannot always give unique ordering with respect to superiority or inferiority. If two points x and y are chosen from S_i and S_j $(j \geq i+2)$, respectively, the ordering between x and y is uniquely determined.

5. ON EVALUATION AND A FUZZY SCALE

In the foregoing chapters, we discussed how an intransitively ordered set could be mapped into a subset of R_e. The image, which we call a main path diagram, has backward arrows and pseudo-interval orders (Def. 23) due to the intransitivity. Now we have a way to sort out the complex maze of intransitive order and to reach a most reasonable fuzzy (or rough) ordering of the original set. Two questions seem to remain awaiting the authors to answer. What good does the discussion do in practical problems? How do we program to find a most reasonable fuzzy ordering?

The answer to the first question is a bit philosophical. The authors would like to pose a few counter questions. Is it the only way to evaluate people and things that they are mapped into R_e? Granted that dichotomy is the fundamental form of decision making, what is the fundamental form of treating a collection of dichotomy? The authors believe that a transitive order is a mathematical convenience. If there is a way to analyse intransitivity, the mathematical convenience should give way to a practical reality. To answer the second question in the above paragraph, the authors have investigated all the possible types and patterns of loops of size up to 24. It takes a little practice to convert a main path diagram to another to get the lowest order. No program has been written yet to get the lowest order automatically.

Table 1 is an example of a loop of size 9. It may be thought of a league series' outcome. We have the following terminology and related propositions.

Def. 24 The dominance number is defined as the

Table 1 Results of paired-comparison of the given points $x_1, x_2, \ldots, x_9$ and dominance numbers where +1 means that the row element wins a victory over the corresponding column element

	x_1	x_2	x_3	x_4	x_5	x_6	x_7	x_8	x_9	victory vs. defeat	dominant number
x_1	X	+1	+1	-1	+1	+1	+1	+1	+1	7 - 1	+6
x_2	-1	X	+1	+1	+1	+1	+1	+1	+1	7 - 1	+6
x_3	-1	-1	X	+1	+1	+1	-1	+1	+1	5 - 3	+2
x_4	+1	-1	-1	X	+1	+1	+1	+1	+1	6 - 2	+4
x_5	-1	-1	-1	-1	X	+1	+1	+1	+1	4 - 4	0
x_6	-1	-1	-1	-1	-1	X	+1	+1	-1	2 - 6	-4
x_7	-1	-1	+1	-1	-1	-1	X	+1	+1	3 - 5	-2
x_8	-1	-1	-1	-1	-1	-1	-1	X	+1	1 - 7	-6
x_9	-1	-1	-1	-1	-1	+1	-1	-1	X	1 - 7	-6

difference between victories and defeats under paired comparison with respect to superiority or inferiority.

The basic propositions of the dominance number can be easily obtained as follows, but the proofs are not given to save pages.

[Proposition 16] If dominance numbers corresponding to all the given points are all different in the final sum, then loop cannot exist in the set.

[Proposition 17] There exists a loop in a given set if and only if at least two points have the same dominance number.

It can be expected that there is intimate relation between the distribution of the dominance numbers and the arrangement of the points with respect to ordering on the lowest fundamental pattern.

[Proposition 18] The highest order of the lowest fundamental pattern cannot be obtained by the point lying on the left end of the original transitive path, which has the maximum dominance number.

[Proposition 19] If the order of the lowest fundamental pattern has the maximum, the points having positive dominance number tend to lie on the right part of the original transitive path.

Fig. 9 is the main path diagram of Table 1. We have a nice symmetric fuzzy scale and two sets $\{x_1, x_2, x_3, x_4\}$ and $\{x_6, x_7, x_8, x_9\}$ laid in a pseudo-interval order.

Looking at Table 1 without any knowledge

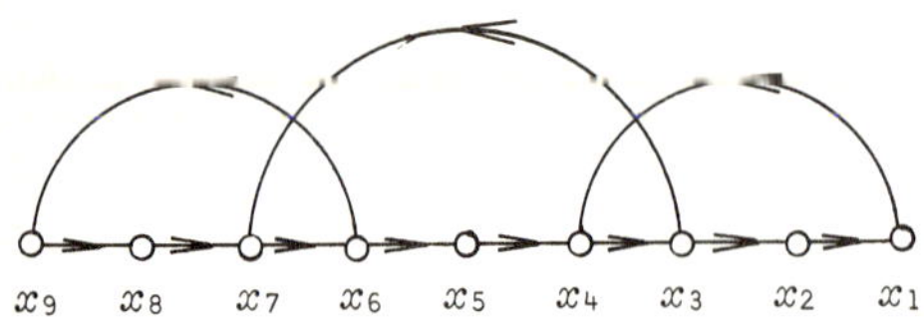

Fig. 9 A main path diagram obtained by Table 1

of the present paper, one may rank the elements solely on the basis of the dominance number. His evaluation then will be something like "x_1 and x_2 share the top place followed by x_4, x_3, x_5, x_7 and x_6 in that order, the lowest place is shared by x_8 and x_9". Now in the authors' Fig. 9, there is a fuzzy distinction between x_1 and x_2 (or x_8 and x_9), there is an exchange of rank between x_4 and x_3 (or x_7 and x_6). The authors are now extending the analysis of the relationship between the dominance number and the main path, to say something more than propositions 16 through 19.

The merit of evaluation by Fig. 9 may be in the following points:

(1) It takes into account all the pertinent relationships among the elements of the set, whereas the dominance number may obscure some of them.

(2) It is useful if we are to distinguish a genuine tie from a slightly uneven tie.

(3) The pseudo-interval order between the two subsets may become effective in classifying the elements.

(4) The membership function given to the elements of subsets classified by the pseudo-interval order will have a very strong ground for its meaning.

6. HEURISTIC ALGORITHM TO CONSTRUCT A PSEUDO-INTERVAL ORDER

Let us review what we have discussed so far about handling an intransitively ordered set. We regard the whole set as a loop, lay it on a real line R_e, draw the main path and all the backward arcs to obtain an extended fundamental pattern. This is our starting line. Our goal is to divide the whole set into subsets satisfying a pseudo-interval order and, if possible, to make the division finer.

As pointed out in the last chapter, it takes a little thought to justify our approach. Does a finer division with respect to the pseudo-interval order give us more information regarding the order, in the usual sense, of the points of the set? The answer seems to depend on the reader's attitude whether or not he accepts the new kind of scale in his mind. The authors should like, however, to point out that an intransitively ordered set are generally regarded as a fuzzy whole and no serious effort has been given to draw some information out of it.

Now, an extended fundamental pattern with a high order will, as shown in the following, give us a fine division. It is important, therefore, to start with a higher-order extended fundamental pattern. No systematic algorithm has yet been found to obtain the highest order extended fundamental pattern. The following four propositions 20 to 23 show the general relationships between an extended fundamental pattern and the dominance numbers of the points of a loop. We use these properties to derive a heuristic algorithm for obtaining the higher-order extended fundamental pattern from the given results of paired-comparison. They are given without proofs to save pages.

[Proposition 20] The sum of the absolute values of the numbers among all the points is greater than or equal to $2[3/2(k+1)]-6$ where k is the order of the extended fundamental pattern.

[Proposition 21] The point with the maximum dominance number is contained in either the maximal arc lying on the right end of the main path or the maximal arc lying next to the right end maximal arc. The point with the minumum dominance number is contained in either the maximal arc lying on the left end of the main path or the maximal arc lying next to the left end maximal arc.

[Proposition 22] Take a maximal arc a and set $\Gamma(a)$ on the main path. Suppose there are two maximal arcs, a_ℓ, a_r intersecting a, one from the left and the other from the right. $\Gamma(a_\ell) \cap \Gamma(a_r) = \phi$ by the definition of a maximal arc. For any two points $x \in \Gamma(a) - (\Gamma(a) \cap \Gamma(a_\ell))$ and $y \in \Gamma(a) - (\Gamma(a) \cap \Gamma(a_r))$, the difference between the dominance numbers of x and y is greater than 6 or equal to 6.

[Proposition 23] The order of an extended fundamental patterns constructed by n points is at most $[2/3(n-1)]$ and all the injections of the arcs of a $[2/3(n-1)]$-th order extended fundamental pattern are cyclic triples.

In order to obtain a pseudo-interval of the studied set, it is necessary to try to obtain a $(k+1)$-th order extended fundamental pattern when a k-th order extended fundamental pattern is given. Through trial and error we now have some operations to make the order of an extended fundamental pattern higher. They prove to be effective with the finite sets studied so far by the authors.

Def. 25 Let us assume that the main path $x_1 \to x_2 \to \ldots \to x_n$ of Fig. 10-(I) is transformed to the main path $x_n \to x_1 \to \ldots \to x_{n-1}$ of Fig. 10-(II). Then the operation transforming Fig. 10-(I) to Fig. 10-(II) is called to be "+1 operation". The operation transforming Fig. 10-(I) to Fig. 10-(III) is called to be "-1 operation".

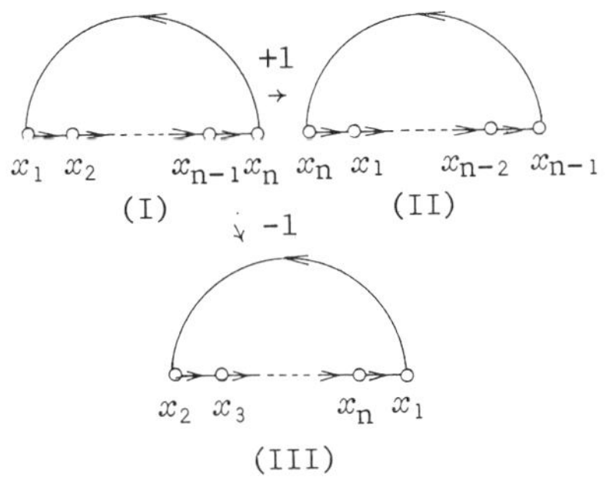

Fig. 10 The +1 and -1 operations

[Proposition 24] If we apply +1 and -1 operations to the 1st order extended fundamental patterns of Fig. 11-(I) and (III), respectively, we obtain the 2nd order extended fundamental patterns of Fig. 11-(II) and (IV).

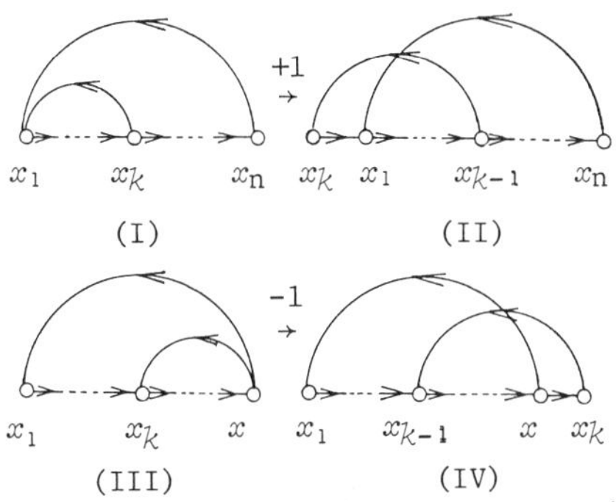

Fig. 11 How to make the order of an extended fundamental pattern higher

We can derive the following heuristic algorithm to obtain a higher order extended fundamental pattern from propositions 19 to 24.

Step 1: Calculate the dominance number of each point from the results of paired-comparison of the given points.

Step 2: Arrange the points in a row in the order of their dominance numbers as done in proposition 19. If there exist more than two points having the same dominance number, they are grouped as a column in the row.

Step 3: Construct a main path. The relation between adjacent two points on the main path does not contradict the results of paired-comparison.

Step 4: Complete the extended fundamental pattern by adding arcs to the two non-adjacent points not contradicting the results of paired-comparison on the main path.

Step 5: Check whether the extended fundamental pattern satisfies proposition 20 to 23 or not. If it seems to be impossible to make the order of the extended fundamental pattern higher, go to step 7.

Step 6: Apply +1 or -1 operations to the extended fundamental pattern and try to make the order higher.

Step 7: Construct the lowest order fundamental pattern obtained by the maximal arcs of the extended fundamental pattern. Let the order be k and the maximal arcs be $a_1, a_2, \ldots, a_k$ from right end on the main path.

Step 8: Now $\Gamma(a_0) \triangleq \phi$, $S_i \triangleq \Gamma(a_i) - \Gamma(a_{i-1})$ $(i=1,2,\ldots,k)$
We obtain a family $\{S_i: i=1,2,\ldots,k\}$ as a division of the given set satisfying pseudo-interval order. (See Theorem 2.)

As an example we consider the case of Table 2 and apply the above-stated heuristic algorithm to the results of paired-comparison of 10 points $x_1, x_2, \ldots, x_{10}$ for obtaining the highest order extended fundamental pattern.

Table 2 Results of paired-comparison of the given points $x_1, x_2, \cdots, x_{10}$ and dominance numbers

	x_1	x_2	x_3	x_4	x_5	x_6	x_7	x_8	x_9	x_{10}	dominance number
x_1	X	-1	-1	+1	-1	-1	-1	-1	-1	-1	-7
x_2	+1	X	-1	-1	-1	-1	-1	-1	-1	-1	-7
x_3	+1	+1	X	-1	-1	+1	-1	-1	-1	-1	-3
x_4	-1	+1	+1	X	-1	-1	-1	-1	-1	-1	-5
x_5	+1	+1	+1	+1	X	-1	-1	+1	-1	-1	+1
x_6	+1	+1	-1	+1	+1	X	-1	-1	-1	-1	-1
x_7	+1	+1	+1	+1	+1	+1	X	-1	-1	+1	+5
x_8	+1	+1	+1	+1	-1	+1	+1	X	-1	-1	+3
x_9	+1	+1	+1	+1	+1	+1	+1	+1	X	-1	+7
x_{10}	+1	+1	+1	+1	+1	+1	-1	+1	+1	X	+7

Step 1: The dominance number of each point is shown in Table 2.

Step 2: $\begin{matrix} x_1 \\ x_2 \end{matrix} \quad x_4 \quad x_3 \quad x_6 \quad x_5 \quad x_8 \quad x_7 \quad \begin{matrix} x_9 \\ x_{10} \end{matrix}$

Step 3: We can obtain a main path as follows,
$x_1 \to x_2 \to x_3 \to x_4 \to x_5 \to x_6 \to x_7 \to x_8 \to x_9 \to x_{10}$.

Step 4: The following extended fundamental pattern (Fig. 12-(I)) is derived from the above main path and the results of paired comparison.

Step 5: (Proposition 20) Substitute $k=4$ into $2[3/2(k+1)]_{k=4}-6 = 8$. As the sum of the absolute values with respect to the maximum and the minimum dominance number of the points is 14, the order of the extended fundamental pattern can be made higher up to six because of $2[3/2(k+1)]_{k=6}-6 = 14$.
(Proposition 21) The extended funda-

mental pattern satisfies this condition. (Proposition 22) The case, in which the difference between the dominance numbers of two points is greater than 6, happens with the following 12 pairs.
(x_1, x_5), (x_1, x_6), (x_2, x_5), (x_2, x_6), (x_4, x_5), (x_4, x_7), (x_4, x_8), (x_5, x_9), (x_6, x_7), (x_6, x_9), (x_6, x_{10})
By looking at the pairs, we see a possibility of having an additional arc among x_4, x_5 and x_6. However we have found no proof concerning the existence or non-existence of the arc.

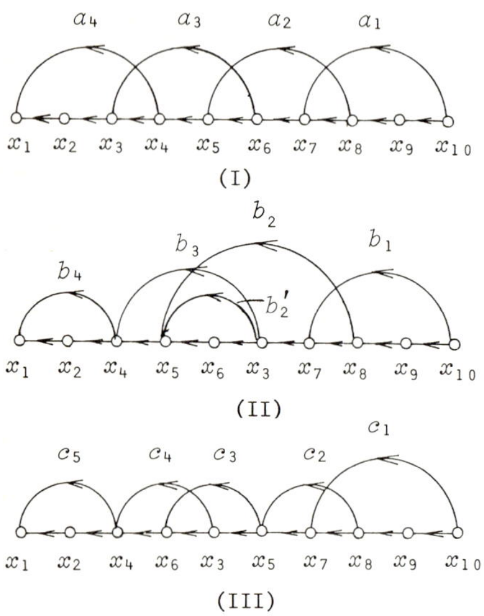

Fig. 12 Extended fundamental patterns represented by Table 1

From proposition 23 $[2/3(n-1]_{n=10} = 6$.

Step 6: Apply -1 operation to the arc a_3 of Fig. 12-(I). Then another 4th order extended fundamental pattern (Fig. 12-(II)) is derived. Apply -1 operation to the arc b_2' of Fig. 12-(II). Then 5th order extended fundamental pattern (Fig. 12-(III)) is derived. No higher-order extended fundamental pattern can be obtained by +1 or -1 operation.

Step 7: Fig. 12-(III) is the lowest order fundamental pattern.

Step 8: We obtain the following family $\{S_i: i = 1, \ldots, 5\}$,
$S_1=\{x_7,x_8,x_9,x_{10}\}$, $S_2=\{x_5\}$, $S_3=\{x_3,x_6\}$, $S_4=\{x_4\}$, $S_5=\{x_1,x_2\}$

7. SUMMARY AND CONCLUSION

7.1 One aspect of fuzzy things is that they often have complex relation among them. This paper takes up intransitive order and proposes a way to measure an intransitively ordered set by means of a scale.

7.2 Some types of scaling are compared with one another and their common ground and different points are shown. It is made clear that fuzziness in measurement not necessarily has a statistical nature.

7.3 When an intransitively ordered set is measured by a scale, the image will have properties not possessed by a subset on R_e, the real numbers.

7.4 The scaling of an intransitively ordered set requires some newly defined representation of the set. By defining the main path diagram and studying its structure, the concept of pseudo-interval order comes out.

7.5 The evaluation and/or classification of an intransitively ordered set may be effectively performed by pseudo-interval order. Two examples explain the authors' proposal that a seemingly untangible maze of intransitive order relationships may be studied to draw meaningful conclusions.

8. REFERENCES

[1] Rosen, R., Fundamentals of measurement and Representation of Natural Systems (North-Holland, New York, 1978).

[2] Krantz, D.H., et al., Foundations of Measurement, Volume I (Academic Press, New York, 1971).

[3] Shepard, R.N., et al., Multidimensional Scaling, Volume I (Seminar Press, New York, 1972).

[4] Zadeh, L.A., Fuzzy sets, information and control, 8 (1965) 338-353.

[5] Ash, R.B., Measure, Integration and Functional Analysis (Academic Press, New York, 1972).

[6] Sugeno, M., Theory of Fuzzy Integrals and Its Application, Doctoral Dissertation, Dpt. of Control Engg., Tokyo Institute of Technology (1974).

[7] Morimura, M., Amount of information obtained by taking readings, SICE Transactions, 1 (1965) 364-371.

[8] Ichikawa, A., et al., Fuzzy interval order and its representation theorem, SICE Transactions, 17 (1981) 150-152.

[9] Fishburn, P.C., Interval representations for interval orders and semiorders, J.Math. Psychology, 10 (1973) 91-105.

[10] Morita, Y., et al., Properties of intransitive ordering in evaluation, SICE Transactions, 17 (1981) 223-230.

[11] Morita, Y., et al., Decomposition of intransitively ordered set and pseudo-interval order appearing in evaluation, SICE Transactions, 17 (1981) 380-395.

[12] Carré, B., Graphs and Networks (Clarendon Press, Oxford, 1979).

Approximate Reasoning in Decision Analysis
M.M. Gupta and E. Sanchez (eds.)
© North-Holland Publishing Company, 1982

VECTORIAL I-FUZZY SETS

László T. Kóczy

Technical University of Budapest, Dept. of Communication Electronics

After a brief introduction of I-fuzzy sets, an overview of the generalization of fuzzy concept for n-dimensional range of the membership function is shown. Then the paper introduces the k-component vector valued fuzzy sets, defining also some basic and a few more special operations on them. Finally, different similarity measures are treated, in order to get a means for classifying fuzzy objects.

Interactive fuzzy operations, nth level fuzzy sets, vector valued membership function, similarity measures

1. INTRODUCTION: I-FUZZY SETS

In this part we sketch the algebraic structure of fuzzy sets or logic in a form deviating from the generally accepted "non-interactive" structure: we shall name it the fuzzy I-structure. For a few years we have considered different aspects of using so named interactive fuzzy operations and corresponding axiomatic systems, instead of the max-min operation type accepted by most authors. At this place, we have no opportunity to go into detail with sketching our experience, we should like to mention only, that we have found more than one fields, where this type of operations could be used for constructing efficient algorithms, while using the non-interactive ones would not have brought any results. This is why we are going to discuss in this chapter only this type of fuzzy structures, although it is clear, that similar generalizations for max-min operations bear no theoretical difficulty.

The I-fuzzy structure itself has not been published yet in the form given on the next pages, however, it is quite similar to the Pre-R-fuzzy structure defined and used in (1,2).

Definition 1

$\mathcal{J} = \langle ⓧ, X, \mathcal{P}, +, *, d, M, \vee, \wedge, \neg \rangle$

is named an I-fuzzy structure if the following axioms are fulfilled:

1. $\mathcal{P}$ is a bounded ordered set containing its minimum /0/ and maximum /1/, it is closed over the binary operations +, $*$ and d so that / $<$ denotes the ordering in $\mathcal{P}$/:
   a. $a + b = b + a$
   b. $/a + b/ + c = a + /b + c/$
   c. $a + 0 = a$
   d. $/a * b/ + /a * c/ \geqq a * /b + c/$ if $/a * b/ + /a * c/ \neq 0$ and $a * /b + c/ \neq 1$
   e. $/a + b/ * /a + c/ \leqq a + /b * c/$ if $/a + b/ * /a + c/ \neq 1$ and $a + /b * c/ \neq 0$
   f. $a + b > a$ if $a \neq 1$ and $b \neq 0$
   g. $a * b < a$ if $a \neq 0$ and $b \neq 1$
   h. $a * 0 = 0$
   i. $d/a, a/ = 0$
   j. $d/a, b/ < d/a, c/$ if $a < b < c$
   k. $d/a, b/ = d/b, a/$
   l. $d/1, 0/ = 1$
   m. $d/1, d/1, a/$
   n. $d/1, a + b/ = d/1, a/ * d/1, b/$
   o. $d/a, b/ = d/d/1, a/, d/1, b//$
   p. equation $a + x = b$ $/a \neq 1/$ has maximally one solution for $x \in \mathcal{P}$
   r. equation $a * x = b/a \neq 0/$ has maximally one solution for $x \in \mathcal{P}$

In the above $a, b, c \in \mathcal{P}$

2. x is a non-empty set /named the universe/.

3. ⓧ is a set having at least two different elements /named the superset of fuzzy sets or statements/, ⓧ is closed over the unary operation $\neg$ and the binary operations $\vee$ and $\wedge$ in the following sense. There is a one-to-one mapping M, so that

$M : ⓧ \longrightarrow \mathcal{F}$

where $\mathcal{F} = \{q \mid q : X \longrightarrow \mathcal{P}\}$ /the functions q are named membership functions/

and

a. $\neg A = M^{-1} /d/M/A/,M/1///$

b. $A \vee B = M^{-1} /M/A/ + M/B//$

c. $A \wedge B = M^{-1} /M/A/ * M/B//$,

where $A, B \in ⓧ$

It is easy to prove, that a very simple representation of the I-fuzzy algebra is as follows. /These operations have been introduced earlier by several authors/:

$\mathcal{P} = [0, 1]$

$a + b = a + b - a . b$

$a * b = a . b$

$d/a,b/ = a - b$

$0 = 0$

$\neg 0 = 1$

/On the right side notations in the ordinary sense./
X is an arbitrary set, ⓧ is the superset of all fuzzy subsets of X.

This representation can be used for different applications in which we are not interested here. There has been also established the most general form of + and * among rational functions in (3), basing on some results in (4). We do not discuss in this paper, why we have chosen this way for defining fuzzy operations; this has been done in (1) and had been supported also by independent experimental results (5) .

2. n-I-FUZZY SETS

There are more than one way for generalizing the above concept. One of the most important is the concept of n-fuzzy sets. This has been approached from different sides as e.g. in (6) and (7). One useful way, consistent with the basic definition of fuzzy sets /not only the I-fuzzy version/ has been sketched in (2), we give here a similar definition:

Definition 2

$\mathcal{J}^n = \langle ⓧ^n, X, \mathcal{P}_1, \dots, \mathcal{P}_n, +, *, d, M^n, \vee, \wedge, \neg \rangle$
is named an n-fuzzy I-structure if the following axioms are fulfilled:

1. $\mathcal{P}_1, \dots, \mathcal{P}_n$ are bounded ordered sets, $\mathcal{P}_n$ having all properties of $\mathcal{P}$ in Def.1,1.

2. X like in Def. 1, 2.

3. $ⓧ^n$ like ⓧ in Def. 1, 3, however instead of M, consider M^n, so that

$$M^n : ⓧ^n \longrightarrow \mathcal{F}_x^n$$

where

$$\mathcal{F}_x^n = \{ q^n \mid q^n : X \longrightarrow \mathcal{F}^{n-1}_{\mathcal{P}_1} \}$$

$$\dots$$

$$\mathcal{F}^i_{\mathcal{P}\, n-i} = \{ q^i \mid q^i : \mathcal{P}_{n-i} \longrightarrow \mathcal{F}^{i-1}_{\mathcal{P}_{n-i+1}} \}$$

$$\dots$$

$$\mathcal{F}^1_{\mathcal{P}\, n-1} = \{ q^1 \mid q^1 : \mathcal{P}_{n-1} \longrightarrow \mathcal{P}_n \}$$

We define now ⓧ as the superset of fuzzy sets over the universe

$$Y = X \times \mathcal{P}_1 \times \mathcal{P}_2 \times \dots \mathcal{P}_{n-1}$$

and mapping M belonging to ⓧ as follows:

$$M/A/ /x, p_1, p_2, \dots, p_{n-1}/ =$$
$$= M^n/A^n/ /x/ /p_1/ /p_2/ \dots /p_{n-1}/, \qquad /1/$$

/shortly we denote /1/ by $M/A/ \quad M^n/A^n//$
where $A \in ⓧ$, $A^n \in ⓧ^n$, $x \in X$, $p_i \in \mathcal{P}_i$
so $ⓧ^n$ is closed over the operations:

a. $\neg A^n = B^n$, where $M^n/B^n/ \sim M/\neg A/$

b. $A^n \vee B^n$, where $M^n/C^n/ \sim M/A \vee B/$

c. $A^n \wedge B^n = C^n$, where $M^n/C^n/ \sim M/A \wedge B/$

In practice, $\mathcal{P}_i = \mathcal{P} = [0, 1]$.

In the above definition, important is the way of generalizing the concept of fuzzy operations. On the basis of /1/ a simple way can be given for defining an arbitrary m-ary operation over n-fuzzy sets /independently from the original structure being I-fuzzy or else/ as follows /here $\langle X, qA \rangle$ stands for A, as it is given by the double of the universe and the membership function $M/A/ = qA; \langle X, qA^n \rangle$ is the n-fuzzy set A^n/:

Let $\circledast$ be an arbitrary m-ary operation over fuzzy sets, such that

$$\circledast /A_1, A_2, \dots, A_m/ = \circledast$$

$$= /\langle X, qA_1 \rangle, \langle X, qA_2 \rangle, \dots, \langle X, qA_m \rangle/ =$$
$$= \langle X, F/qA_1, qA_2, \dots, qA_m/ \rangle,$$

where $F: M^m \longrightarrow M$, $M = \{q\}$

and $F/qA_1, qA_2, \dots, qA_m/ /x/ =$
$$= f/qA_1/x/, \dots, qA_m x//, \qquad /2/$$

where $f : \mathcal{P}^m \longrightarrow \mathcal{P}$

Let now C_x^n be an n-fuzzy set of X such that

$$C_x^n = \langle X, qC^n \rangle,$$

where

$$qC^n/x/ = \langle P_1, qC_x^{n-1} \rangle$$

$$qC_x^{n-1} /P_1/ = \langle P_2, qC^{n-2}_{x,p_1} \rangle, p_1 \in P_1$$

$$qC_{x,p_1,p_2,\dots,p_{n-2}} /p_{n-1}/ =$$
$$= qC/x, p_1, p_2, \dots, p_{n-1}/ ;$$

$$P_1 = P_2 = \dots = P_{n-1} = \mathcal{P}$$

Let C be the fuzzy equivalent of C_X^n /in the sense $M^n/C_X^n/ \sim M/C./$:

$C = \langle X \times \mathcal{P}^{n-1}, qC \rangle = \langle Y, qC \rangle$, and

$Y = \{y\} = \{/x, p_1, \dots, p_m/\}$.

Now, $*$ is to be extended for n-fuzzy sets in the following way:

Let E be a one-to-one mapping from the superset of n-fuzzy sets of X to the set of fuzzy sets of Y such that:

$$E/C_X^n/ = E/C/ \text{ iff } M^n/C_X^n / \sim M/C/$$

Then

$$* /A_{1X}^n, A_{2X}^n, \dots, A_{mX}^n/ =$$

$$= */\langle X, qA_1^n \rangle, \langle X, qA_2^n \rangle, \dots, \langle X, qA_m^n \rangle =$$

$$= \langle X, q \ */A_1, A_2, \dots, A_m/^n \rangle$$

means, that

$$q */A_1, A_2, \dots, A_m/^n \ /y/ =$$

$$= f/qE/A_{1X}^n/ \ /y/, qE/A_{2X}^n/ \ /y/, \dots, qE/A_{mX}^n/ \ /y/.$$

This is equivalent to

$$* /A_{1X}^n, A_{2X}^n, \dots, A_{mX}^n/ = E^{-1}$$

$$= E^{-1}/ * /E/A_{1X}^n/, E/A_{2X}^n/, \dots, E/A_{mX}^n///.$$

Although the above definiton might seem to be quite complicated at first sight, in reality it is very simple: the operations must be computed point by point in n-fuzzy cases.

Do n-fuzzy sets have any connection with practical problems? The answer seems to be yes, especially linguistic problems can be described well by using this concept. In this paper we, however, propose another way for generalizing the original concept for fuzziness: vector valued fuzzy sets. As motivation we refer to (8), as we intend to publish this paper also here, we do not go in to details, only mention, that vvf sets can be used as pattern descriptors.

3. VVF I-SETS

First we give a definition similar to these in the first two sections:

Definition 3

$$\underline{J}_n = \langle \otimes_n, X, \mathcal{P}_1, \dots, \mathcal{P}_n, +_1, \dots, +_n, *_1, \dots *_n, d_1, \dots, d_n, \quad M_n, \vee, \wedge, \neg \rangle$$

is named an n-dimensional vector valued fuzzy I-structure if the following are fulfilled:

1. $\mathcal{P}_1, \dots, \mathcal{P}_n$ are bounded ordered sets, all of them fulfilling separately conditions 1. a-r in Def. 1, $\mathcal{P}_i$ with $+_i$, $*_i$ and d_i.

2. X like in Def. 1,2.

3. $\otimes_n$ like $\otimes$ in Def. 1,3 but $\underline{M}_n$ instead of M, so that:

$$\underline{M}_n : \otimes_n \to \underline{\mathcal{F}}_n ,$$

where

$$\underline{\mathcal{F}} = \{\underline{q} \mid \underline{q} : X \to \prod_{i=1}^{n} \mathcal{P}_i\}$$

and

a. $\neg \underline{A} = \underline{M}_n^{-1} /D/\underline{M}_n/\underline{A}/, /\underline{M}_n/\underline{1}///$

b. $\underline{A} \vee \underline{B} = \underline{M}_n^{-1}/\underline{M}_n /\underline{A}/ \# \underline{M}_n /B//$

c. $\underline{A} \wedge \underline{B} = \underline{M}_n^{-1}/\underline{M}_n /\underline{A}/ \divideontimes \underline{M}_n /\underline{B}//$

where

$$D/\underline{qA}, qB/ = \begin{bmatrix} d_1/q_1\underline{A}, q_1\underline{B}/ \\ d_2/q_2\underline{A}, q_2B/ \\ \dots\dots \\ d_n/q_n\underline{A}, q_n\underline{B}/ \end{bmatrix}$$

$$\underline{q}\ \underline{A} \# \underline{q}\ \underline{B} = \begin{bmatrix} q_1\underline{A} +_1 q_1 \underline{B} \\ q_2\underline{A} +_2 q_2 \underline{B} \\ \dots\dots\dots \\ q_n\underline{A} +_n q_n \underline{B} \end{bmatrix}$$

$$\underline{q}\ \underline{A} \divideontimes \underline{q}\ \underline{B} = \begin{bmatrix} q_1 \underline{A} *_1 q_1 \underline{B} \\ q_2 \underline{A} *_2 q_2 \underline{B} \\ \dots\dots\dots\dots \\ q_n \underline{A} *_n q_n \underline{B} \end{bmatrix}$$

Similarily to Section 2, a general form of an arbitrary m-ary operation over vvf sets can be given /for simplicity,

$\mathcal{P}_i = \mathcal{P}$ and $*_i = *$ /:

Let $*$ be as in /2/, and let $\underline{C}_n$ be a vvf set of X such that

$$\underline{C}_n = \langle X, \underline{q}\ \underline{C}_n \rangle.$$

then

$$*/\underline{A}_{n1}, \underline{A}_{n2},\dots,\underline{A}_{nm}/ =$$
$$= */\langle X, \underline{q}\,\underline{A}_{n1}\rangle ,\dots,\langle X, \underline{q}\,\underline{A}_{nm}\rangle/ =$$
$$= \langle X, \begin{bmatrix} */q_1\underline{A}_{n1}, q_1\underline{A}_{n2},\dots, q_1\underline{A}_{nm}/ \\ */q_2\underline{A}_{n1}, q_2\underline{A}_{n2},\dots,q_2\underline{A}_{nm}/ \\ \dots\dots \\ */q_n\underline{A}_{n1}, q_n\underline{A}_{n2},\dots,q_n\underline{A}_{nm}/ \end{bmatrix} \rangle$$

For illustrating this definition, let us consider the following example:

Example 1. Given two vector valued fuzzy sets /n=3/ over

$X = \{a, b\}$ by

$\underline{q}\,\underline{A}\,/a/ = /0.1, 0.2, 0.1/;$
$\underline{q}\,\underline{A}\,/b/ = /0.2, 0.3, 0.5/;$
$\underline{q}\,\underline{B}\,/a/ = /0.1, 0.3, 0.7/;$
$\underline{q}\,\underline{B}\,/b/ = /0.2, 0.4, 0.6/.$

Then

$\underline{q}\,\underline{C}\,/a/ = /0.01, 0.06, 0.07/$
$\underline{q}\,\underline{C}\,/b/ = /0.04, 0.12, 0.3/$
if $\underline{C} = \underline{A} \wedge \underline{B}$.

For practical applications a special case of vvf sets is presented:

If the dimensionality of $\{x_j\} = X$, i.e. $\# X = c$ is finite, a vvf set over X can be given by a fuzzy matrix of size c x n :

$$\underline{\underline{M}}_{\underline{A}} = [\underline{q}\,\underline{A}\,/x_1/\ q\,\underline{A}\,/x_2/\dots\underline{q}\,\underline{A}\,/x_c/] = \begin{bmatrix} p_{11} & p_{12} & \cdots & p_{1c} \\ p_{21} & p_{22} & \cdots & p_{2c} \\ \cdot & & & \\ \cdot & & & \\ \cdot & & & \\ p_{n1} & p_{n2} & \cdots & p_{nc} \end{bmatrix} = [p_{ij}],$$

where

$$p_{ij} = \underline{q}\,\underline{A}\,i\,/x_j/.$$

Assume, that two vvf sets $\underline{A}$ and $\underline{B}$ are given over X by their matrices $\underline{\underline{M}}_{\underline{A}} = [p_{i,j\underline{A}}]$ and $\underline{\underline{M}}_{\underline{B}} = [p_{i,j\underline{B}}]$, respectively, then the operation $\underline{C} = A * \underline{B}$ over the vvf sets of $\underline{\otimes}_n$ belonging to X is given by

$$\underline{\underline{M}}_{\underline{C}} = [\ f/p_{i,j\underline{A}},\ p_{i,j\underline{B}}\ /]$$

where f is the function corresponding to operation * .

We illustrate it on the data of example 1:

$$\underline{\underline{M}}_{\underline{A}} = \begin{bmatrix} 0.1 & 0.2 \\ 0.2 & 0.3 \\ 0.1 & 0.5 \end{bmatrix} \qquad \underline{\underline{M}}_{\underline{B}} = \begin{bmatrix} 0.1 & 0.2 \\ 0.3 & 0.4 \\ 0.7 & 0.6 \end{bmatrix}$$

and

$$\underline{\underline{M}}_{\underline{C}} = \begin{bmatrix} 0.01 & 0.04 \\ 0.06 & 0.12 \\ 0.07 & 0.30 \end{bmatrix}$$

We introduce now some new operators on vvf sets /if $\mathcal{P}_i = \mathcal{P}$/:

Definition 4

Given $\underline{A}$, a vvf set over X, then the conjunctive compression of $\underline{A}$, i.e. A is an ordinary fuzzy set over $\{x\} = X$, where

$$\tilde{A} = \bigwedge_{i=1}^{n} A_i,$$

where

$$A_i = \langle X, q_{\underline{A}i}\rangle,$$

thus

$$\tilde{q}_A = \prod_{i=1}^{n} q_{\underline{A}i}$$

Definition 5

Similary

$$\bar{A} = \bigvee_{i=1}^{n} A_i$$ is the disjunctive compression of $\underline{A}$.

Definition 6

The universal quantifical $\forall\,\underline{A}$ of a vvf set $\underline{A}$ over X for $\underline{A}$ is

$/0,0,\dots,0/_n^T$ if $\# X = \infty$

and

$/\sum_{j=1}^{o} q_{\underline{A}i}\ /x_j//^T$ if $\# X = c < \infty$

$i = 1,\dots,n$

Definition 7

Similary the existential quantifical $\exists\,\underline{A}$ of $\underline{A}$ is

$/1,1,\dots,1/_n^T$ if $\# X = \infty$

and

$$/\sum_{j=1}^{c} q_{\underline{A}i} /x_j//^T \quad \text{if} \quad X = c$$

$i = 1, \ldots, n$

In the special case, when $n = 1$, i.e. $\underline{A} = A = \langle X, q_A \rangle$ is an ordinary fuzzy set, $\forall\underline{A}$ and $\exists\underline{A}$ are scalar values. We give here some examples:

Example 2. For $\underline{A}$ in Example 1

$$\underline{\underline{M}}_A = \begin{bmatrix} 0.1 & 0.2 \\ 0.2 & 0.3 \\ 0.1 & 0.5 \end{bmatrix}$$

$$q\tilde{A} = \begin{bmatrix} 0.002 & 0.03 \end{bmatrix}$$

$$q\bar{A} = \begin{bmatrix} 0.352 & 0.72 \end{bmatrix}$$

$$\forall\underline{A} = \begin{bmatrix} 0.02 \\ 0.06 \\ 0.05 \end{bmatrix}$$

$$\exists\underline{A} = \begin{bmatrix} 0.28 \\ 0.44 \\ 0.55 \end{bmatrix}$$

Finally

$$\forall\tilde{A} = 0.00006 \text{ etc.}$$

At the end of the paper we give some definitions for characterizing the similarity of vvf sets over the same finite universe:

4. SIMILARITY MEASURES OF VVF SETS

The similarity measure of two vectorvalued fuzzy sets can be given by the similarity set, characterized by the similarity matrix as defined below.

Definition 8

Given $\underline{A}$ and $\underline{B}$, two vvf sets over X, where $\# X < \infty$, then the vvf set $\underline{S}$ /$\underline{A}$, $\underline{B}$/ is the similarity set of $\underline{A}$ and $\underline{B}$, where

$$\underline{\underline{S}}_{AB} = \left[s_{i,j}\right] = \underline{\underline{M}}_A \equiv \underline{B} = \left[p_{i,jA} \equiv p_{i,jB}\right],$$

where

$$A \equiv B = /A \wedge B/ \vee /\bar{A} \wedge \bar{B}/,$$

for $\underline{A} \equiv \underline{B}$ see Definition 3.

Definition 9

By using Definitions 3 and 4 let us define the similarity of two samples $\underline{A}$ and $\underline{B}$ over the set of basic attributes

$\{x_i\}$ by $\tilde{S}$ /$\underline{A}$, $\underline{B}$ /.

Definition 10

Similarily, by Definitions 8 and 6, the similarity of two samples $\underline{A}$ and $\underline{B}$ on the set of their qualitative attributes or grades is given by

$$\forall\underline{S} /\underline{A}, \underline{B}/.$$

Definition 11

The similarity index of two samples $\underline{A}$ and $\underline{B}$ is given by

$$S_{\underline{AB}} = \forall\tilde{S} /\underline{A}, \underline{B}/.$$

By the above three definitions we gained two vectors and one scalar, all three typical for the similarity of two samples.

/Now we consider samples as fuzzy sets over the universe of basic attributes, while $\mathcal{P}_i$ are considered as grades of qualitative attributes, for easier interpretation of the new definitons./

From the practical point of view $S_{\underline{AB}}$ is not easy to handle, as it becomes in most cases a very small number. Instead of it

$$\lg S_{\underline{AB}} \quad \text{or} \quad \sqrt[c]{S_{\underline{AB}}}$$

can used in a concrete examination.

In (8) some examples taken from metallographic practice are given to show, how these concepts can be utilized for classification of textures.

Note, that our similarity measures are in the sense of the interactive fuzzy approach, where the following basic philosophy is accepted. If the data are strongly fuzzy, the result will be very inexact. Let us explain this by a simple example taken from another field. Someone tells that both objects A and B have a colour that can be considered red in a fuzzy degree of 0.8. Can it be then stated that the two objects have exatly the same colour? As a matter of course, not. As we have only very faint knowledge on the colour, the similarity of the colours can be stated only even fainter. So two samples with the same matrix descriptor will have $\forall\tilde{S}$ /$\underline{A}$, $\underline{B}$/ = 1 only then, if all elements in

$$\underline{\underline{M}}_A \quad \text{and} \quad \underline{\underline{M}}_B$$

are equal to either 0 or 1, i.e. if none of the two samples is described in a really fuzzy way.

As a matter of course, section 4 can be interpreted also in another way: using noninteractive fuzzy operations. Our examinations in (8) , however, have proven the usefulness of this approach, as the results were in accardance with subjective and statistical classification.

REFERENCES

[1] Kóczy,L.T. and Hajnal,M., A New Fuzzy Calculus and Its Application as a Pattern Recognition Technique, in Rose,J. and Bilciu,C. /eds./ Modern Trends in Cybernetics and Systems II. /Springer Verlag, Berlin-Heidelberg-New York, 1977/

[2] Kóczy,L.T., Interactive σ-Algebras and Fuzzy Objects of Type N, Journal of Cybernetics 8 /1978/ 273-290

[3] Kóczy,L.T., Fuzzy algebrák és müszaki alkalmazásaik néhány kérdése /Fuzzy algebras and some questions of their technical applications/, Ph.D.Thesis, Dept. of Proc. Contr., Tech.Univ. Budapest /May 1976/

[4] Hamacher,H.,Über logische Verknüpfungen unscharfer Aussagen und deren zugehörige Bewertungsfunktionen, Arbeitsbereicht, Lehrst. für Unternehmensforschung RWTH Aachen /July 1975/

[5] Rödder,W., On "and" and "or" connective in fuzzy set theory, WP Lst. für Unt. forsch. RWTH Aachen /Jan. 1975/

[6] Zadeh, L.A., The concept of liguistic variable and its application to approximate reasoning I, Information Sci. 8 /1975/ 199-249

[7] Mizumoto, M. and Tanaka, K., Some properties of fuzzy sets of type 2, Information and Control 31 /1976/ 312-340

[8] Hajnal,M. and Kóczy,L.T., Texture Analysis by vector valued fuzzy sets, Busefal /1980/ Été, see also this volume.

Approximate Reasoning in Decision Analysis
M.M. Gupta and E. Sanchez (eds.)

CLASSIFICATION OF TEXTURES BY VECTORIAL FUZZY SETS

M. HAJNAL[+], L.T. KÓCZY[++]

Technical University of Budapest
[+]Dept. of Process Control
[++]Dept. of Communication Electronics
Budapest, Muegyetem rkp. 9.
Hungary, 1111

The paper gives an application of the method based on vector valued fuzzy sets. At first a special fuzzy matrix descriptor featuring the texture is defined, next the corresponding similarity measures are introduced. To demonstrate the usefulness of the method the results of an application example taken from the practical metallurgy are given. Finally, a test method based on second order statistics, verifying the results obtained by the fuzzy approach is treated.

Keywords: vector valued fuzzy sets, texture analysis, statistical descriptors, recognition of microstructures

1. INTRODUCTION

In [1] a system deviating from generally accepted fuzzy structure was presented. In this paper we intend to show an application example, taking the technical problem from a field, where exact, non-fuzzy treating is practically impossible. The paper strongly bases on definitions and concepts introduced in the mentioned chapter on vector valued fuzzy sets and [1]. Human visual perception is based on detection of edges and textures. The definition of edge is well known, but very hard to interprete the texture, which is generally the specific appearance form of spatial distribution of brightness in a 2-D picture. This definition is, however, as general, as unusable to understand natural textures. On the other hand, texture can be qualitatively evaluated by subjective adjectives, such as coarse, lineated, granulated, spotted, rippled, etc. Till now very few attempt have been done to map the semantic meaning of these adjectives into exact tonal and spatial distributional properties or descriptors. Nevertheless this mapping could be very important in exact analysis and distinction of textures for classification or segmentation. The usual aproaches, such as statistical and structural [2] are far from the human evaluation so they are not lifelike enough. The aim of this paper is to give an attempt for texture description and analysis which is standing near to human view and, same time, makes comparable textures described on different levels. In other words: the aim is to establish an interactive fuzzy approach based on vector valued fuzzy sets, in order to take out traditional subjective evaluation. The vvf sets defined before describe the textures in two recpects, namely, basic and additional qualitative attributes, gathering them into a fuzzy matrix descriptor. Next the corresponding similarity measures, providing the degrees of textural adjacency in both the basic and the qualitative attributes as well as in general sense, are computed. as already mentioned, the approach is based on the interactive fuzzy similarity measures suggested by the authors [1], [3].

2. CHARACTERIZATION OF TEXTURES

Textures in general can be described by pictorial manifestations. These manifestations appear as features or attributes, which can be viewed in two different dimensions:
(i) Type of texture - basic attributes, describing the general character of the texture, without quantitative meaning.
(ii) Degree of the different properties - qualitative attributes, expressed by some measurable but not numerical locutions.
It is very difficult to establish a full and final set of the properties mentioned above. As many problem types - as many different texture categories. If the problem is the automatic classification of different types of textile material, it is natural that a fine

scale of diverse textile textures must be considered in group (i), while all other types of texture have very little importance. If the problem is more special: e.g. the automatic quality control of a certain textile product, more attention must be paid to group (ii), where such properties as homogeneity, etc. are gathered. Our example will be taken from a field, where a relatively wide range of texture types can appear. So we established group (i) for purposes sufficiently basing on Brodatz' textures [4] and own investigations [5,6] in the following way:

($X=\{x_i\}$ denotes the set of basic attributes.):

x_1 : netted, see Fig.1,
x_2 : celluar, see Fig.2,
x_3 : mosaic, see Fig.3,
x_4 : granular, see Fig.4,
x_5 : dotted, see Fig.5,
x_6 : radiated, see Fig.6,
x_7 : thready, see Fig.7,
x_8 : needled, see Fig.8,
x_9 : banded, see Fig.9,
x_{10}: textile-like, see Fig.10.

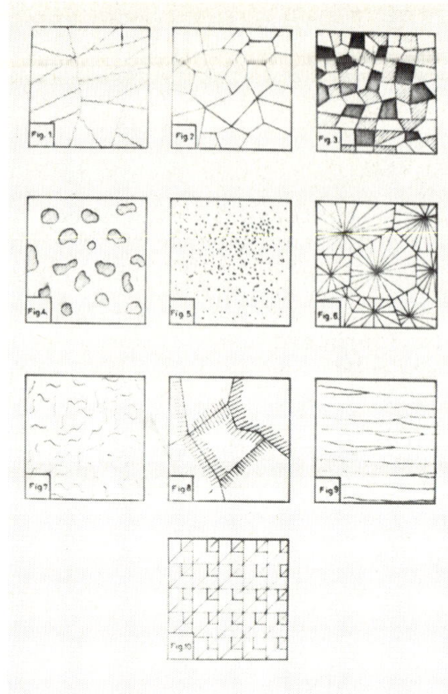

Figs. 1...10

For fuzzy representation X is considered as the universe. For a given sample a membership grade is ordered to each elements x_i - so we gain a simple fuzzy set featuring the sample in question. Similar classification methods are quite common in literature (see e.g. [7]). Now we define also property group (ii):

1 coarseness Figs.11.
2 directionality Figs.12.
3 homogeneity Figs.13.
4 regularity Figs.14.

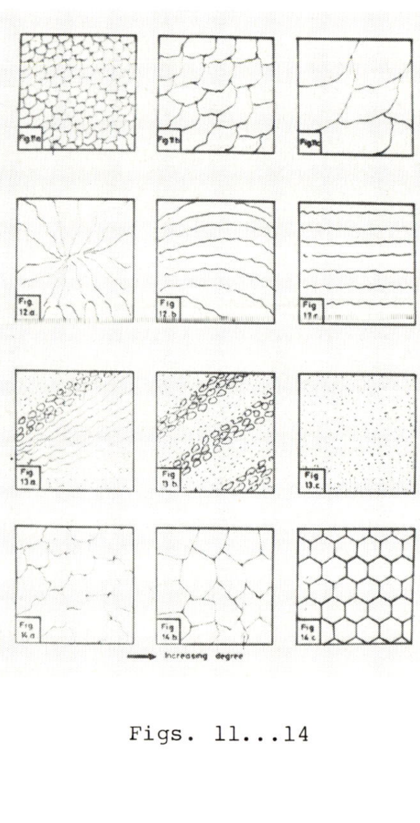

Figs. 11...14

Now, using the notations in [1] and considering a sample as a vvf, this 4 properties - i.e. the degrees ordered to a sample - build the sets P_1, P_2, P_3 and P_4 respectively. Thus any of the particular texture can be described by a vvf set

$$\underline{A} = \langle X, \underline{q}_{\underline{A}} \rangle , \qquad (1)$$

where

$$X = \{x_1, \ldots, x_{10}\} ,$$

$$\underline{q}_{\underline{A}} : X \to [0,1]^4 ,$$

resp. by the matrix $\underline{\underline{M}}_{\underline{A}}$ of size max.10x4. A certain degree $q_{\underline{A}i}(x_j)$ gives the value ordered to sample A belonging to texture type x_j with property P_i. For example:

$$q_{\underline{A}1}(x_3) = 0.8$$

means, that sample A is a coarse mosaic type texture in grade 0.8 (a relatively high grade).

3. THE CLASSIFICATION PROBLEM AND A CONTROL METHOD

Our investigations were aimed at the classification of particular metallographical textures of high speed steels having different carbide morphology on the basis of photomicrographs. Qualification of the distribution of carbides is important because it influences the critical properties of steel. For this reason there exist prescriptions stated in standards for carbide morphology. In practical metallography the qualification of the carbide distribution is performed by subjective visual comparison with standard micrographs.
In our experiments some of the standard pictures from [8] were used, namely A1,A5,A8. On the other hand, we used own-made photomicrographs of annaeled 6-5-2 high speed steel forged to different size, denoted by X1,X2,X3. (The standards are to be seen on Figs. 15, 16 and 17 respectively, the samples to classify on Figs. 18, 19 and 20.)
Before presenting the results gained by using the vvf sets similarity measure method, we show a control procedure. To test our results an own developed statistical texture analysis method was used:
Assume, that the digitized picture of the photomicrograph or any texture can be represented by a homogenous ergodic Markovian random field $\mathcal{Z}$. Let a possible realization of $\mathcal{Z}$ be a matrix

$$\underline{\underline{Z}}_{M,N} = \left[z(k)_{i,j}\right] \quad .$$

Define on the matrix $\underline{\underline{Z}}_{M,N}$ the following discrete valued two dimensional conditional distribution:

$$\underline{\underline{\Phi}}\,(z|\mathcal{K}) = \left\{\text{Prob}(z(i),z(j))|\mathcal{K}\right\} = [\varphi_{i,j}], \quad i.j = 1,2,\ldots,n_G, \qquad (2)$$

where $\mathcal{K}$ is the spatial constraint predicate, n_G is the number of gray-scale levels.
Actually, $\mathcal{K} = \langle \mathcal{A}, D\rangle$, where $D(z_{k,l}, z_{m,n}) = d$ is d-step Manhattan distance,

$$\mathcal{A} = \vartheta_r \pm \beta, \; \vartheta_r \in \Theta, \qquad \Theta = \{0, \pi/4, \pi/2, 3\pi/4\} \;, \qquad (3)$$

thus the matrix falls into four submatrices each belonging to one of the orientations in Θ :

$$\underline{\underline{\Phi}}(z|d, \vartheta_r) = [\text{Prob}(z_{k,l}, z_{m,n})|d, \vartheta_r]. \quad (4)$$

The elements of $\underline{\underline{\Phi}}$ mean the relative frequency of co-occurence of pixels having gray level i and j, (the scale of gray-levels see on Fig.21.) under the constraints given by $\mathcal{K}$. To get a concise description of the texture in question, a set of one-number statistics $\{r_L\}$ is computed from matrices $\underline{\underline{\Phi}}$. The statistics $\{r_L(\vartheta_k)\}$ form a vector $\underline{r}$, describing the statistical properties of the original picture well ($L=1,2,\ldots,n_r$, $k=1,2,3,4$).
In order to get a more concise descriptor we used discriminant analysis for feature selection and formed new concentrated features, e.g.

$$h_1 = r_1(\vartheta_1)/r_1(\vartheta_3), \qquad (5)$$

etc. Using the transformation $\underline{\underline{T}}$ based on the eigenvectors of the scatter matrices on the data set:

$$\underline{u} = \underline{\underline{T}}\,\underline{h} \;, \qquad (6)$$

where

$$\underline{h} = [h_1,\ldots,h_{n_r}]^T \;,$$

we get a new vector $\underline{u}$ with lower dimensionality. Similarly using the transformation

$$\underline{v} = \underline{\underline{E}}\,\underline{h} \;, \qquad (7)$$

where transformation matrix $\underline{\underline{E}}$ was chosen by the rules of the Karhunen-Loeve expansion. From Eq. (7) we get the optimal extracted features of the texture carried by the vector $\underline{v}$.
Finally for the classification we used the Mahalanobis distance derived from the maximum-likelihood criterion:

$$d_k^2 = (\underline{h} - \mu_k)^T \underline{\underline{K}}^{-1} (\underline{h} - \mu_k), \qquad (8)$$

$$h \sim C_i, \text{ if } d_i^2 = \min d_j^2, C_i \in \Omega_C, \quad 1 \leq j \leq n_C$$

where $\mu_k = E(\underline{h}|C_k)$, $\underline{\underline{K}}$ is the covariance matrix of data set $\underline{h}$, E denotes the expected value. The further details of the above method are described in [5].
Using the above method, clustering was done on the digitized pictures of A1,A5, A8 and X1,X2,X3 respectively (taking different segments of the pictures).
In Fig. 22. the results of clustering the standards based on vector $\underline{u}$ derived by Eq. (1) are shown.
Similarly, the results of clustering the samples based on vector $\underline{v}$ derived by Eq. (2) are shown in Fig. 23.

Fig. 15a

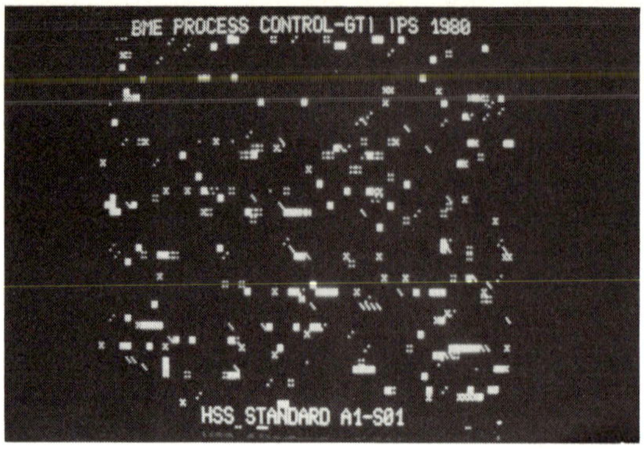

Fig. 15b

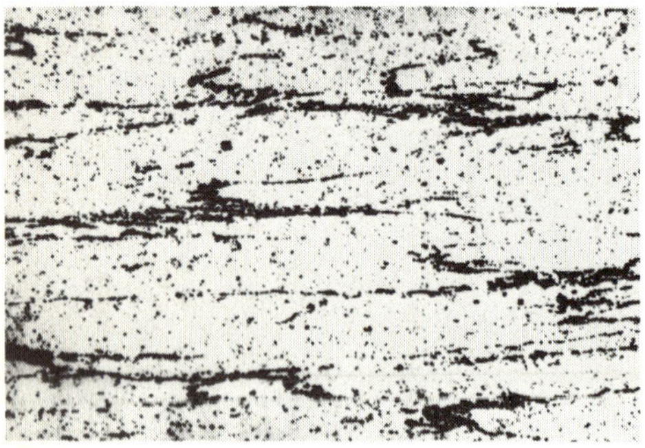

Fig. 16a

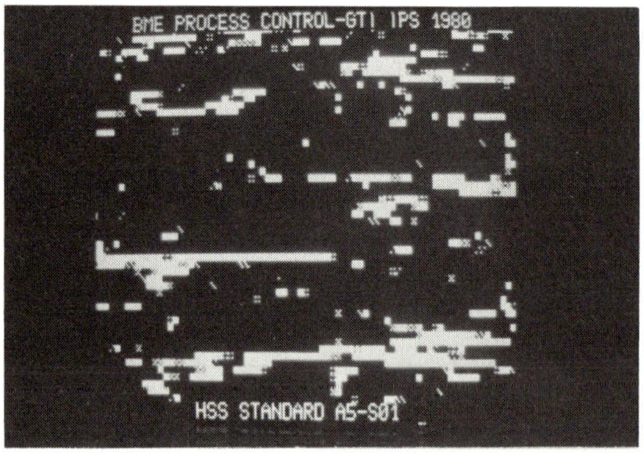

Fig. 16b

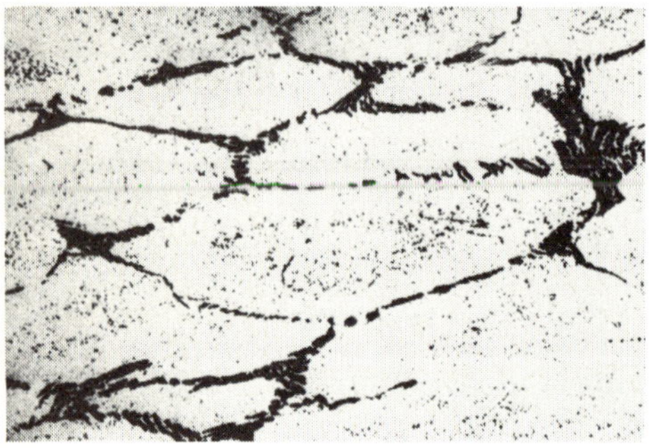

Fig. 17a

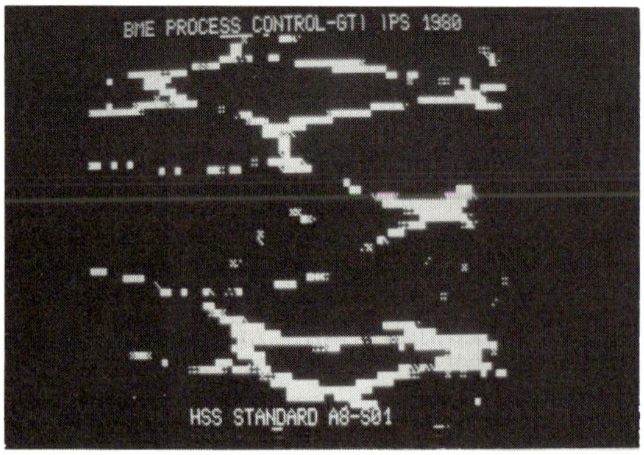

Fig. 17b

a: photomicrograph

b: digitized picture

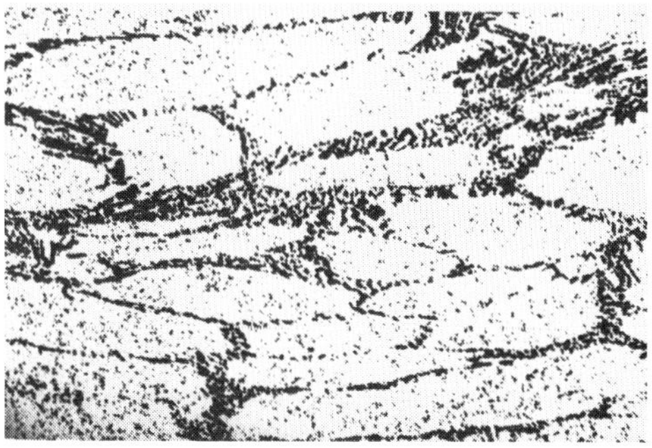

Fig. 18a

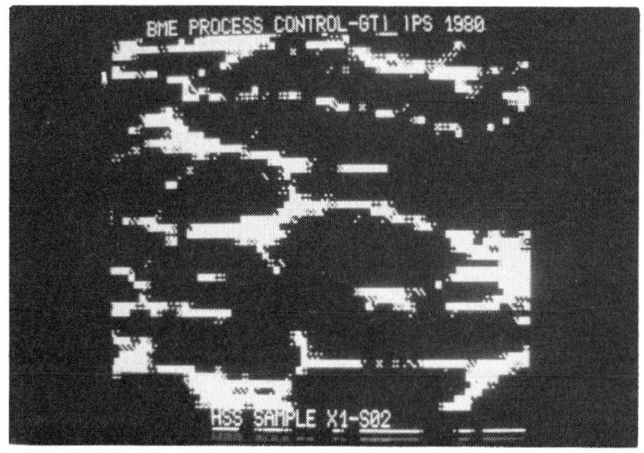

Fig. 18b

Fig. 19a

Fig. 19b

Fig.2oa

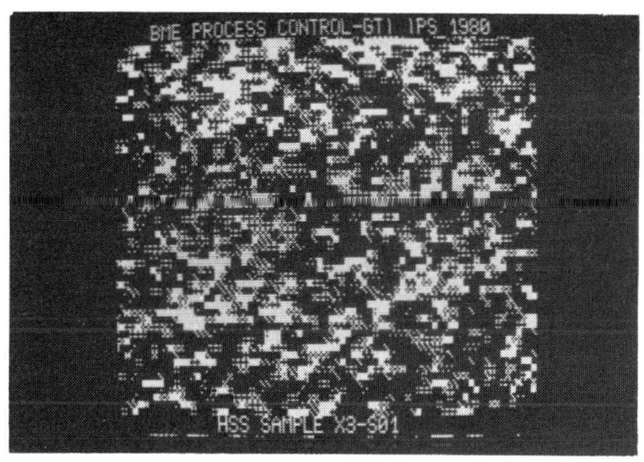

Fig. 2ob

a: photomicrograph

b: digitized picture

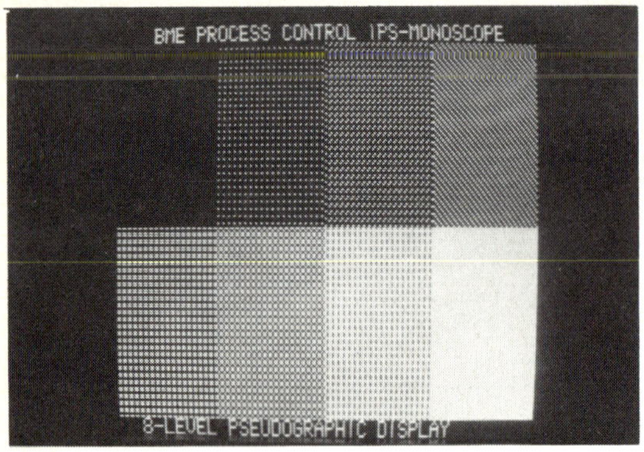

Fig. 21

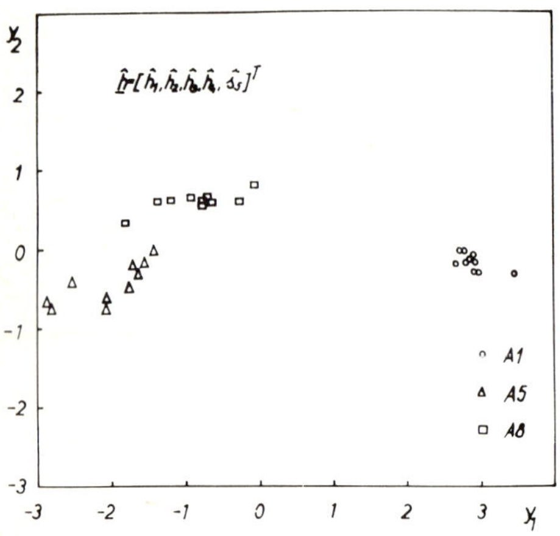

Fig. 22

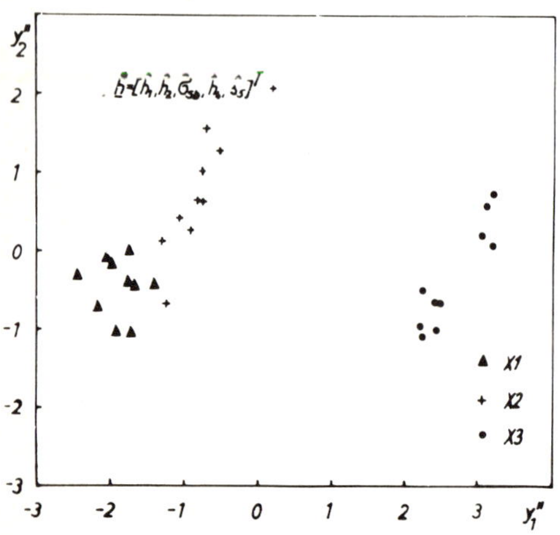

Fig. 23

4. CLASSIFICATION BY VVF SETS SIMILARITY MEASURES

To perform our experiment a set of the 6 photomicrographs (of magnification 100x) were handed over to ten outstanding experts of the metallography for estimation of the elements of matrices $\underline{\underline{M}}$. As our examinations were restricted to a special group of textures, to five among the above established ten types of textures only membership grades of practically equal to 0 were attached. So, in order to handle simpler matrices, we used for classification:

$$X = \{x_1, x_2, x_4, x_5, x_9\},$$

while

$$Y = \{P_1, P_2, P_3, P_4\}$$

remained the set of qualitative properties. The three vvf set matrices, belonging to the standard photomicrographs A1,A5,A8 gained by the mean value of ten estimation membership grades for each element, are as follows:

$$\underline{\underline{M}}_{A1} = \begin{bmatrix} .00 & .00 & .31 & .87 & .05 \\ .00 & .00 & .82 & .73 & .31 \\ .00 & .00 & .63 & .52 & .18 \\ .00 & .00 & .21 & .02 & .10 \end{bmatrix}$$

$$\underline{\underline{M}}_{A5} = \begin{bmatrix} .25 & .12 & .02 & .25 & .91 \\ .30 & .19 & .24 & .30 & .82 \\ .05 & .01 & .05 & .05 & .35 \\ .01 & .02 & .04 & .03 & .27 \end{bmatrix}$$

$$\underline{\underline{M}}_{A8} = \begin{bmatrix} .49 & .96 & .05 & .08 & .23 \\ .23 & .31 & .08 & .14 & .21 \\ .18 & .22 & .00 & .00 & .02 \\ .10 & .13 & .00 & .00 & .00 \end{bmatrix}$$

Similarly, the matrices belonging to the samples to classify: X1,X2,X3:

$$\underline{\underline{M}}_{X1} = \begin{bmatrix} .62 & .90 & .04 & .02 & .20 \\ .41 & .29 & .06 & .00 & .17 \\ .09 & .16 & .00 & .00 & .00 \\ .09 & .06 & .00 & .00 & .00 \end{bmatrix}$$

$$\underline{\underline{M}}_{X2} = \begin{bmatrix} .12 & .08 & .08 & .20 & .96 \\ .16 & .14 & .26 & .24 & .90 \\ .03 & .00 & .05 & .02 & .50 \\ .00 & .00 & .08 & .00 & .30 \end{bmatrix}$$

$$\underline{\underline{M}}_{X3} = \begin{bmatrix} .06 & .03 & .62 & .98 & .05 \\ .00 & .00 & .41 & .28 & .11 \\ .00 & .00 & .75 & .69 & .08 \\ .00 & .00 & .51 & .40 & .00 \end{bmatrix}$$

Then we have computed according to the definitions in [1] all

$$\binom{6+2-1}{2} = 21$$

similarity matrices between the possible pairs, finally all 21 similarity indices. As an example, we give here the similarity matrices between X1 and X1,X2,X3, A1,A5,A8 (Table 1).

Table 1

$$\underline{\underline{S}}_{X1X1} = \begin{bmatrix} .473 & .811 & .921 & 1 & .654 \\ .457 & .545 & .884 & 1 & .697 \\ .829 & .713 & 1 & 1 & 1 \\ .829 & .884 & 1 & 1 & 1 \end{bmatrix}$$

$$\underline{\underline{S}}_{X1X2} = \begin{bmatrix} .383 & .157 & .883 & .8 & .217 \\ .528 & .626 & .7 & .76 & .223 \\ .883 & .84 & .95 & .98 & .5 \\ .91 & .94 & .92 & 1 & .7 \end{bmatrix}$$

$$\underline{\underline{S}}_{X1X3} = \begin{bmatrix} .381. & .121 & .38 & .02 & .762 \\ .59 & .71 & .565 & .72 & .743 \\ .91 & .84 & .25 & .31 & .92 \\ .91 & .94 & .49 & .6 & 1 \end{bmatrix}$$

$$\underline{\underline{S}}_{X1A1} = \begin{bmatrix} .38 & .099 & .666 & .13 & .762 \\ .59 & .71 & .21 & .27 & .595 \\ .91 & .84 & .369 & .479 & .82 \\ .91 & .94 & .79 & .98 & .9 \end{bmatrix}$$

$$\underline{\underline{S}}_{X1A5} = \begin{bmatrix} .395 & .186 & .94 & .75 & .24 \\ .485 & .598 & .718 & .7 & .267 \\ .865 & .831 & .95 & .95 & .65 \\ .9 & .921 & .96 & .97 & .73 \end{bmatrix}$$

$$\underline{\underline{S}}_{X1A8} = \begin{bmatrix} .418 & .235 & .093 & .25 & .626 \\ .442 & .409 & .296 & .3 & .626 \\ .191 & .256 & .05 & .05 & .35 \\ .164 & .125 & .039 & .029 & .27 \end{bmatrix}$$

The similarity indices are given in Table 2. Note, that e.g. $5E\text{-}3 = 5\ 10^{-3}$. (We mentioned in [1] the problems with the very small value of similarity indices in the case of real fuzzy samples. We hope, however, that our results are easy to evaluate even so, especially as we have given them in a normal form.)

Table 2

	A1	A5	A8	X1	X2	X3
A1	5E-3	-	-	-	-	-
A5	1E-5	3E-3	-	-	-	-
A8	5E-16	6E-15	6E-5	-	-	-
X1	2E-7	1E-4	4E-15	2E-2	-	-
X2	1E-5	4E-5	1E-16	7E-5	8E-3	-
X3	1E-3	3E-6	7E-15	5E-7	1E-6	4E-3

To compare the above results with the results of the statistical test experiments treated in Section 3, a table is given containing the respective Mahalanobis distances

$11^{-3}\ h^2$ by eq. (8). (Table 3).

Note, that the Mahalanobis distant function is sensitive for the order of arguments.

Table 3

	A1	A5	A8	X1	X2	X3
A1	0.38	1.76	1.05	-	-	-
A5	26.7	0.16	1.63	-	-	-
A8	11.5	0.77	0.17	-	-	-
X1	32.4	9.65	18.1	0.08	0.24	16.6
X2	28.6	9.10	19.5	0.60	0.09	15.0
X3	7.26	10.3	12.8	1.80	1.29	0.22

5. CONCLUSIONS

Evaluating the similarity indices shown by Table 2, they seem to correspond to the expected relations, as well as to the results of statistical analysis shown by Table 3. Clearly, the main diagonals in both matrices test and verify the methods themself, and the other elements show the psychological and statistical similarity between the different sample sets, respectively. The results confirm that, although the samples X1,X2,X3 to classify were not very typical examples for the three types of steel structures standardized in A1,A5, A8,the relative values refer to the expected classification, except of X1. Thus by the different similarity indices the grade of similarity to the corresponding standard is characterized. The strong difference between e.g. X2 and X8 is indicated by

$$s_{X2A8} = 10^{-16}.$$

Otherwise the absolute values of the similarity indices in Table 2 show only the exactness or fuzzyness in definition of textures.

In sum, the results are encouraging and allow to conclude that an efficient method for mapping the subjective attributes to an exact scale has been found. It is however, suggested, that fuzzy classification should be done beside of other type of methods, as e.g. statistical ones. We present a complex scheme of texture analysis including the fuzzy method, it is intented to brought into being by the authors and collegues in the future (Fig.24).

The method will be based on the system shown in general in Fig. 25 and in detail in Fig. 26. The hardware background of the system has been established already, finding the most efficient auxiliary statistical algorithmus has to be done yet.

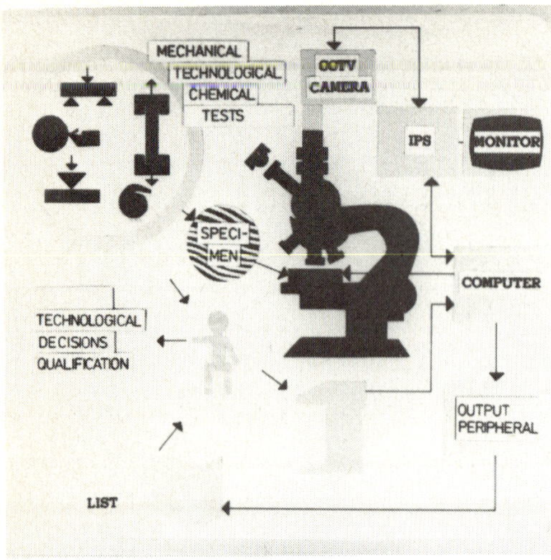

Fig. 25

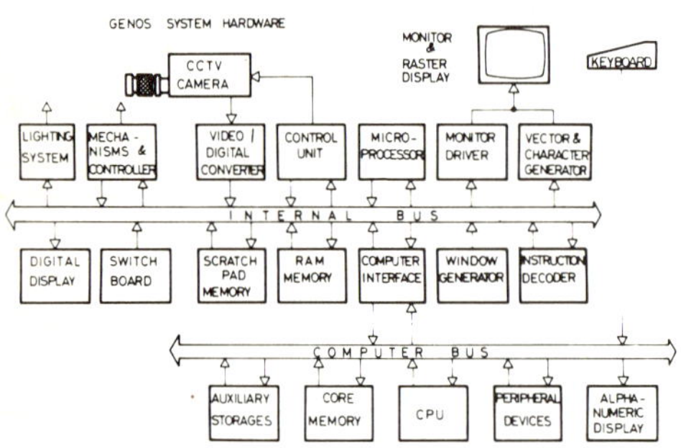

Fig. 26

REFERENCES:

[1] Koczy, L.T.: Vector Valued Fuzzy Sets BUSEFAL, ETE 1980, pp 41-57.

[2] Haralick, Robert: Statistical and Structural Approaches to Texture. Proceeding of the Fourth International Joint conference on Pattern Recognition (nov.7-10, 1978, Kyoto, Japan) p. 45-68.

[3] Koczy, L.T., Hajnal, M.: A New Fuzzy Calculus and Its Application as a Pattern Recognition Technique. In:Modern Trends in Cybernetics and Systems (Eds.: Rose and Bilciu) Vol.II., Springer Verlag, Berlin-Heidelberg-New York, 1977, pp. 103-118.

[4] Brodatz, Ph.: Textures. Dover, New York, 1966.

[5] Hajnal, M., Kőnyves-Toth, M., Reti, T.: Quality Control in Metallurgy by Texture Analysis. Proc. of the 6th IFAC/IFIP Conference on Digital Computer Applications to Process Control (Düsseldorf, Oct. 14-17, 1980) Pergamon Press, Oxford, New York, Toronto, Sydney, Paris, Frankfurt. 1980. p. 291-300.

[6] Hajnal, M., Lovanyi, I., Vajta, L.: Visual Measurement in Industrial Research ACTA IMEKO VIII. Congress. Measurement for Progress in Science and Technology (21-27, May, 1979, Moscow, USSR) Sect.IV. North Holland Publ.Co. Amsterdam, Netherlands, 1980. p. 559-570.

[7] Gaines, B.R., Kohout, L.J.: The Fuzzy Decade: A Bibliography of Fuzzy Systems and Closely Related Topics, Int. I. Man-Machine Studies (1977) 9, pp.1-68, Items Classified by "PAT" and Party by "DEC".

[8] Stahl-Eisen Prüfblatt 1615. Mikroskopische and makroskopische Prüfung von Schnellarbeits-stahlen... DIN, Verlag Stahleisen m.b.H., Düsseldorf, 1975.

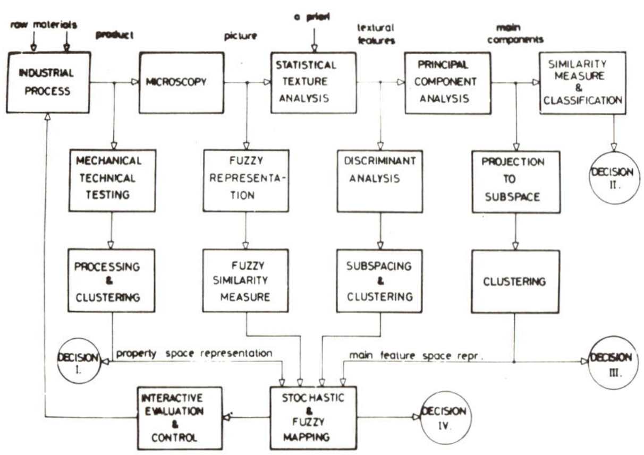

Fig. 24

Approximate Reasoning in Decision Analysis
M.M. Gupta and E. Sanchez (eds.)
© North-Holland Publishing Company, 1982

THE PROCESS OF CLASSIFICATION AND LEARNING THE MEANING OF LINGUISTIC DESCRIPTORS OF CONCEPTS

J. AGUILAR MARTIN* and R. LOPEZ DE MANTARAS*

Laboratoire d'Automatique et d'Analyse des Systemes du CNRS. 7, Av. du Colonel Roche. 31400 Toulouse FRANCE

Facultat d'Informatica.Universitat Politecnica. J. Girona Salgado, 31. BARCELONA - 34. SPAIN

This paper presents a system capable of learning the meaning of linguistic descriptors of concepts, characterizing a set of classes corresponding to higher level concepts.

Each class is represented by a set of possibility distributions [1] modelizing the linguistic descriptors that characterize the class. The learning will consist in the adaptation of these possibility distributions and it is based on a dialog with a human teacher. Therefore we need a Man-Machine interface to translate sentences in natural language into the meaning representation language called PRUF [1]. The translator that we designed is based on an Augmented Transition Network [3] , and a Semantic Network [2].

The initial information consists in a table representing a fuzzy relation between the set of linguistic descriptors to be learned and a set of elements to which these descriptors can be applied. After a self-learning classification process, each class will contain elements that can be characterized by the same descriptors and to approximatively the same degree.

The chacracterization of each class, will appear as a PRUF expression in which each descriptor X is restricted by a fuzzy restriction F. More precisely we would say that the possibility distribution of X is given by the possibility assignment equation [1]: $\Pi_X=F$. At this point, if the human teacher disagrees with the type of fuzzy restriction F in some of (or all) the descriptors, he/she may interact with the system in order to modify the corresponding possibility distributions. After that, a reclassification of the elements will occur and the new resulting classes will be checked again by the human teacher who will continue the teching process until the fuzzy restrictions, on the concepts describing the resulting classes, are correct according to his/her criterion.

In the first part of the paper we discuss the general aspects of recursive learning algorithms and we describe our classification algorithm to build up the classes corresponding to the higher level concepts.

In the second part, we present an example in which the set of concepts consist in 14 descriptors (concepts) of the working conditions of 18 workers (elements to be classified) in a lumber factory. Each resulting class corresponds to a higher level concept. For example the class of "Unqualified workers" could be characterized by the following descriptors in a PRUF expression:

(CLASS-OF-UNQUAL.-WORKER ($\Pi_{\text{Physical Effort}}$=HIGH)
($\Pi_{\text{Responsability}}$=LOW)
($\Pi_{\text{Initiative}}$= LOW)

KEYWORDS:Classification, Learning, Possibility distribution, Fuzzy partition, Estimation, Fuzzy relation.

1. GENERAL ASPECTS OF LEARNING ALGORITHMS.

Multivariate data analysis has become the more popular way to deal with a great amount of data and structurate it by means of discovering clusters and dispersions between items. Such an analysis starts usually with a given set of real objects upon which individual observations are made, some are described by measures, others by qualities. Next, distances must be defined in order that the set becomes a metric space. If only representation and visualisation are aimed, the analysis looks for the directions, called factors, along which the dispersion is bigger and makes a choice of factorial planes in order to visualize the set of data by projection. A further step of sophistication creates clusters and gives a partition of the initial set.

If, instead of a given set to analize, we are given a flow of data coming from a source set, or set of possibilities, it seems more appropiate to attempt to give at every instant an estimation of the partition of the source set. The estimation

* Collaboration made possible by the "Acción Integrada Hispano-Francesa" nº 36 - 1982 from the Spanish-French cooperation program.

must be a measurable function of the past data (the only available information at each instant) taking its values among the possible partitions. Moreover it seems suitable that the estimation procedure should be recursive so that the estimated partition represents the state of the procedure and no past data needs to be stored.

Present data, after being used to class the item from which it comes, gives its information for the eventual modification of the partition. Such a procedure shall be called self-learning classification.

Algorithms based on those principles may sometimes be "forced" to class an item to a given a priori class, when that happens we say that the learning process works with a teacher;it is usually a good way for initialisation. Intermediate behaviours between teacher directed and self learning can be imagined where the teacher may give merely an evaluation of goodness, or assist the algorithm only when no confident decisions can be made.

The learning algorithm can be summarized in the following way:A set of objects $\theta_1 \ldots\ldots \theta_N$ is "perceived" sequentially and yields a sequence of observations $\{x_s\}_{t_o}^{t} = X^t$ to the system.

The learning process consists in the construction of

a) an estimation of the set of objects

b) an inferred relational structure on the set of estimated objects

both based on the past information X^t. That enables the system

a) to "recognize" the source of a new observation x_{t+1}, i.e., to decide from which object 0_i this observation might come. This recognition is obviously subject to eventual error

b) to "produce" estimated objects consistent with the inferred relational structure.

Sequential learning is restricted to the situation where no more than one observation can be processed at the same time, and no storage of observations is available.

The system must start with an a priori guess or after a previous learning period; the next observation gives a new amount of information and it must confirm or contradict the previous concepts memorized.

Two functions appear:

- Classification of the item the observation of which is being perceived (decision)

- Modification of previous memory (estimation)

The closeness of a new observation to an expected observation and its frequence are the working materials from which these two functions can be performed. Learning should then always include a statistic or counting procedure and the essential feature will be the estimation of a probability law, or of a membership function in the framework of fuzzy set theory.

2. CLASSIFICATIONS AND PARTITIONS.

A classifier is a system that, given a set Ω, assigns a class c_i from a Partition $P=\{c_i\}_{i=1}^{N}$ to any element $x \in \Omega$

A Partition P is equivalent to a set of characteristic functions

$$\chi=\{\chi_i(x)\}_{i=1}^{N} \text{ where } \chi_i(x)=\begin{cases}1 & \text{if } x\in C_i\\ 0 & \text{if } x\notin C_i\end{cases}$$

to which we add a decision rule $\mathcal{R}(\cdot|P)$ or classifier. A decision rule is a mapping $\Omega \rightarrow P$ and $\mathcal{R}(x|P)=C_j$ such that $x\in C_j$. The equivalence relation generated by this decision rule is

$$x.Eq.y \Leftrightarrow \mathcal{R}(x|P)=\mathcal{R}(y|P);$$

P is the quotient set $\Omega|\mathcal{R}$

This decision rule can be described as

$$\{C_j=\mathcal{R}(x|P)\,|\,\chi_j(x) = \max_1 \chi_i(x)\}$$

We can then replace the characteristic functions $\{\chi_i\}_{i=1}^{N}$ by a set of membership functions $M=\{\mu_i\}_{i=1}^{N}$ without altering the partition, as far as the decision rule remains unchanged;that is, if

$$\mu_j(x) = \max_i \mu_i(x) \Longleftrightarrow \chi_j(x) = \max_i \chi_i(x) \quad \forall x$$

Figure 1 shows a simple case where this situation holds.

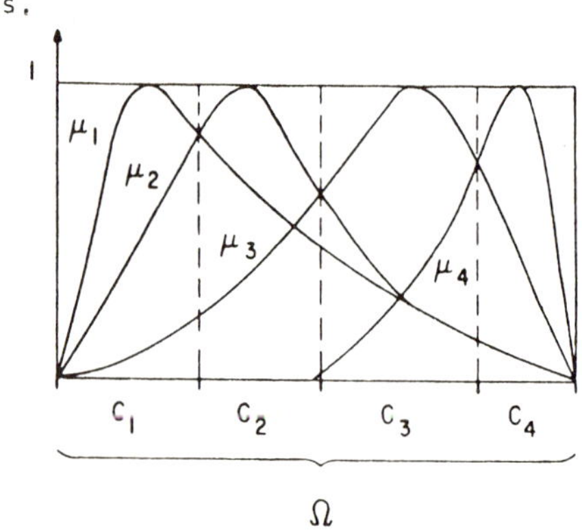

-Figure 1-

In that case we shall write the decision rule as follows:

$$\mathcal{R}(x|P) = \mathcal{R}(x|M)$$

A particularity interesting case is when all functions μ_i belong to the same parametric family such that $\mu_i(x) = f(x,\theta_i)$. Then the set M is completely determined by the set of parameters

$$\theta = \{\theta_i\}_{i=1}^{N}$$

and we may represent the classifier as $\mathcal{R}(x|\theta)$. To determine the partition P is, therefore, the same as to find the set of functions $\mathcal{M}$ or, if parametization is possible, to find the set of parameters θ, and then to reduce to a problem of parameter estimation. To transpose the analysis of parameter estimation to partition estimation is not an easy task because a metric should be defined on partitions and convergence can only be studied in that space.

It has to be noticed that the estimated partition is not necessarily the real partition of the already processed observations, and neither the teacher's partition. This estimated partition is a set of estimated functions $\mathcal{M}_t=\{\mu_i(t)\}_{i=1}^N$ or estimated parameters $\theta_t=\{\theta_i(t)\}_{i=1}^N$ based on past information X^t. They are measurable functions in the σ-algebra induced by X^t.

We shall call "historical partition" the record of the past decision rules applied only to the elements of X^t. As is normal in natural learning, an element can be misclassified in the early stages of the process and, therefore, is likely to change its class as the quality of the estimated partition improves.

The estimated partition can be used to reclassify the set of past observed elements X^t, by re-processing the same data (e.g. externally recorded..) inhibiting the learning process of modification of classes:that will give the "instantaneous classification".

3. RECURSIVE LEARNING ALGORITHMS.

Let us assume that, at time t-1, the estimation of the parameter set is

$$\{\theta_i(t-1)\}_{i=1,\dots,N}$$

At time t a new observation y(t) is to be processed.

3.1. Class assignment (decision)

The estimated parameter set defines a set of membership functions $\{\mu_i(t-1,x)\}_{i=1,\dots,N}$ and the measured element x(t) is assigned to the class C_j such that $\mu_j(t-1,x)$ is the maximum.

3.2. Updating (estimation)

The parameters $\theta_i(t-1)$ according to the general mechanism:

$$\theta_j(t)=\theta_j(t-1)+\alpha(t)\,[f(x(t))-g(\theta_j(t-1))]$$

$$\theta_i(t)=\theta_i(t-1) \quad ; \; i \neq j$$

functions f and g are determined by the nature of measurements and the type of representation of calsses. α(t) is a gain, or weighting, driving the convergence and adaptivity of the estimation.

A particularity simple example is given by the recursive mean where:

$$f(y)=y, \quad g(\theta)=\theta \;, \quad \alpha(t)=\frac{1}{t}$$

Another remarquable case is given by the counting algorithm:

$$\theta(t)=\text{frequency of a given event}:\frac{n(\text{events})}{n(t)}$$

$$f(y)=\begin{cases}1 & \text{when ocurrence is observed}\\ 0 & \text{otherwise}\end{cases}$$

$$g(\theta)=\theta \quad \text{and} \quad \alpha(t)=\frac{1}{n(t)}$$

Justified by this algorithm, that we consider the most elementary learning, we call the general mechanism "generalized counting algorithm".

n(t) corresponds to the actual number of elements assigned to a class.The function α(t) is called "statistical gain".

3.3. Threshold of membership (potential creation of classes).

In self-learning situations,the number of classes is unknown a priori, therefore the estimated partition must provide an "empty class" C_0 such that if the maximum membership of an element x(t) is $\max_{j\neq 0} \mu_j(x(t)) < \mu_0(x(t))$ the empty class C_0 accepts such an element and is therefore modified by it, a new empty class is then needed to maintain this possibility at t+1. So the new class shall be labelled C_{N+1} and C_0 shall remain an empty class.

The membership of any measured element x to C_0 must be independent of the measure x

$$\mu_0(x) = \mu_0$$

So we shall also call this class the "indifferentiate class". And μ_0 is merely a threshold of membership so that no assignation decision shall be made below it. If for practical reasons a maximum number is allowed, no class assignment will be made below the threshold.

3.4. Initialization of classes.

When an element x(t) is assigned to the class C_0 its parameters are modified and become those of C_{N+1}

$$\theta_{N+1}(1) = \theta_0 + \alpha(1)\,[\,f(x(t))-g(\theta_0)]$$

Particular care must be given to this value $\theta_{N+1}(1)$, because it initialises the class C_{N+1}

If the parameter $\theta_{N+1}(1)$ is such that $\mu_{N+1}(y) < \mu_0$ for all $y \neq x(t)$, then it is clear that the number of classes created would be the number of different observed elements.

On the contrary, if $\mu_{N+1}(y) > \mu_{j\neq N+1}(y)$ then the new created class would absorb all other observed elements.

An intermediate situation can be attained by adjusting $\alpha(1)$ properly.

3.5. Structure of a learning process.

Figure 2 shows the different components of a learning process. One can see that the learning mechanism is only active in the estimation, or modification of partition. The estimated partition plays a role of passive memory, and the classifier is merely a decision process.

The possibility of introducing a "teacher" is also represented by the diversion of information arriving to the learning system.

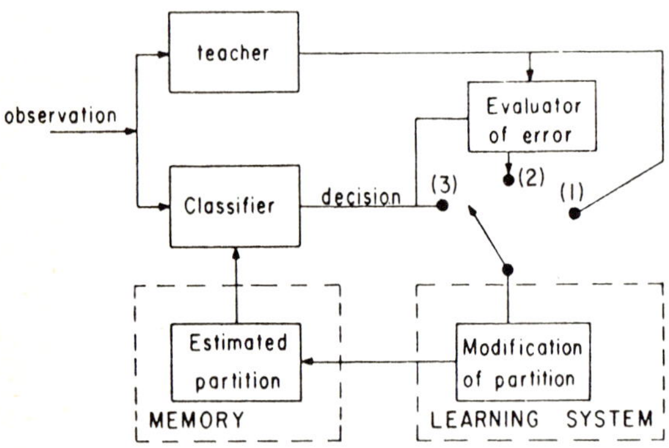

-Figure 2-

4. ESTIMATION OF A PARTITION IN THE UNIT CUBE [4,5].

4.1. Description of the set of data.

Let us consider data given by a sequence of samples of points in the unit cube $U \subset R^n$; that is

$$x(t)=\begin{bmatrix} x_1 \\ \vdots \\ x_n \end{bmatrix} \quad \text{with } 0\leqslant x_i\leqslant 1 \text{ being measurements on an object}$$

To each class C_k corresponds a vector of parameters characterizing the class.

$$\rho_k=\begin{bmatrix} \rho_{1,k} \\ \vdots \\ \rho_{n,k} \end{bmatrix} \quad \text{with} \quad 0<\rho_{i,k}<1$$

The set of parameters characterizing the partitions is

$$R=\{\rho_i\}_{i=1}^{N}$$

and the membership function of an element $x\in U$ to a class C_k is given by the function

$$\mu_k(x)=\prod_{i=1}^{n} \rho_{i,k}^{x_i}\,(1-\rho_{i,k})^{(1-x_i)}$$

the decision rule being the maximum as shown before.

4.2. Particular case of the set of vertexes.

If we assume that $x_i\in\{0,1\}$ then we define.

$$\rho_{i,k}=\text{prob}\,[\,x_i=1\,|\,x\in C_k]$$

and $\mu_k(x)=\text{prob}\,[\,x\,|\,x\in C_k]$.

Therefore $\rho_k(t)$ is the maximum likelihood estimator of that probability since we have:

$$\frac{\partial \mu_k(w)}{\partial \rho_k}=0 \quad \text{for } x=\rho_k$$

And it can be easily proved that for an independent sequence $\{x_s\}_{s=1}^{T}$ we have:

$$\text{prob}[\{x_s\}_{s=1}^{T}|\rho_k]=\prod_{s=1}^{T}\prod_{i=1}^{M}\rho_{i,k}^{x_{i,s}}\,(1-\rho_{i,k})^{1-x_{i,s}}$$

and finally its derivative with respect to ρ_k vanishes for

$$\rho_k=\frac{1}{T}\sum_{s=1}^{T}x_s$$

The figure 3 shows the curves $\mu=f(x|\rho)$ as membership functions of x parametrized by ρ.

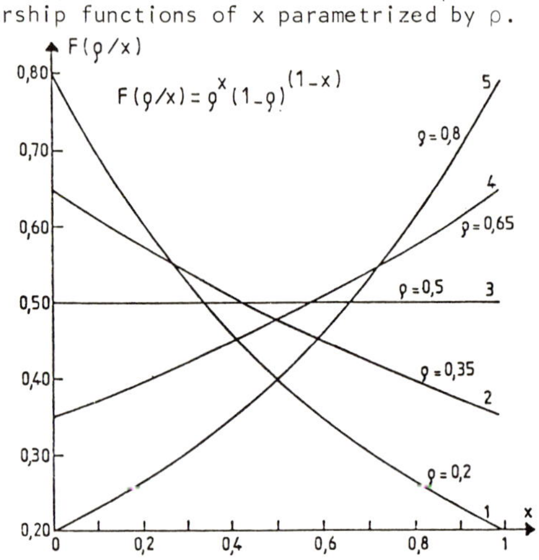

-Figure 3-

4.3. Direct extension to the inside of the cube.

It appears that for $0\leqslant x_i\leqslant 1$, we must replace the membership function by the following probability density.

$$p[x|x\in C_k]=p[x|\rho_k]=\prod_{i=1}^{n}K(\rho_{i,k})\cdot\prod_{i=1}^{n}\rho_{i,k}^{x_i}(1-\rho_{i,k})^{(1-x_i)}$$

The presence of $K(\rho_{i,k})$ is necessary to normalize this functions in order to obtain a probability density. Therefore

$$K(\rho_{i,k})=\frac{\text{Log}\,\dfrac{\rho_{i,k}}{1-\rho_{i,k}}}{2\rho_{i,k}-1}$$

With these considerations, if we adopt a bayesian procedure, we must take in account an a priori distribution for ρ_k so that the decision of assignation of a point to a class is taken according to the value of the posterior probability density for each class.

That is $$p[\rho_k|x] = \frac{p[x|\rho_k].p[\rho_k]}{p[x]}$$

For a given observation, $p[x]$ is fixed and does not take part in the comparison procedure.

The lack of knowledge of the prior density of ρ_k may lead us to chose the equiprobability in (0,1). Nevertheles it appears that by an appropiate choice different of the equiprobability we may be able to recover the initial simplicity of function $\mu_k(x)$. For that reason, we choose

$$p[\rho_k] = \frac{\lambda}{K(\rho_k)}$$

where λ is a normalizing constant. It can be shown that such prior density tends to zero when x tends to zero and when x tends to one, and remains near to one for all the other values of $\bar{x}$.

4.4. Estimation procedure.

As shown in 3.2., if an observed element $x(t)$ is assigned to a class C_k, and if this is the $N_k(t)$ element that has been assigned to that class, the estimator $\hat{\rho}_k(t)$ of its parameter ρ_k, is modified into $\hat{\rho}_k(t+1)$ by the following recursive formulation

$$\hat{\rho}_k(t+1) = \hat{\rho}_k(t) + \frac{1}{N_k(t)+a}(x(t)-\hat{\rho}_k(t))$$

So, if a=1, this estimator is exactly the mean of all the observations assigned to C_k, where "a" is a parameter that represents the fictive initial number of elements in each class.

4.5. Adaptativity.

If the updating equation for the estimator is purely statistical, the algorithm becomes less and less sensible to new data as the number of elements $N_k(t)$ in a class increases. To avoid this lack of sensibility and to introduce adaptativity, $N_k(t)$ can be replaced by a constant N_k^* such that the weight of the past remains constant. This enables the algorithm to follow eventual changes in the generation of data and its practical implementation remains similar. In that case, the gain $\alpha = \frac{1}{N_k^*+1}$ is called "versatility".

4.6. Characterization of the classes.

For a given class C_k the representative set of parameters is the vector $\hat{\rho}_k$. The discrete function

$$h_k(i) = \hat{\rho}_k(i)$$

gives the profile of the class. This can be interpreted as the values of the components of the most representative element belonging to the class C_k.

Direct reading of these profiles gives a good idea of the typology obtained and can be used for comparison and interpretation of the classes.

We shall see next, how a class can be interpreted in terms of possibility distributions.

4.7. Possibility distribution of the estimated partition.

At any time we have an estimated partition determined by the set $\{\rho_k\}_{k=1}^N$ of estimated parameters.

This partition is such that any vector of the unit cube $x \in U^n$ has the following membership function to the class C_k:

$$\mu_k(X) = \prod_{i=1}^{n} \rho_{i,k}^{x_i}(1-\rho_{i,k})^{(1-x_i)}$$

The projection of $\mu_k(x)$ on any coordinate axis (component of x) gives the membership function on that axis:

$$\mu_k^i(x_i) = \rho_{i,k}^{x_i}(1-\rho_{i,k})^{(1-x_i)}$$

The possibility for a descriptor i to take the value x_i for an object of class C_k, depends on the total partition, this possibility is:

$$\Pi_k(x_i) = \frac{\mu_k(x_i)}{\mu_M(x_i)} \cdot \frac{1-\mu_M(x_i)}{1-\mu_k(x_i)}$$

where:

$\mu_k(x_i)$ is the degree of membership of x_i to C_k

$1-\mu_k(x_i)$ is the degree of non membership of x_i to C_k

$\mu_M(x_i) = \max_{j=1..N}[\mu_j(x_i)]$ is the maximum degree of membership of x_i considering all the classes.

$1-\mu_M(x_i)$ is the minimum degree of non-membership.

Since the decision for the assignment of elements to classes is the maximum membership, the possibility distribution $\Pi_k(x_i)$ takes the value 1 if $\mu_k(x_i)=\mu_M(x_i)$.

The set $\{\Pi_k(x_i)\}_{k=1...N}$ of these possibility distributions defines a fuzzy partition on each axis, it is then easy to associate to each possibility distribution a fuzzy restriction related to the representation of this axis in such a way that these possibility distributions modelize the characteristics of the class.

5. LINGUISTIC CHARACTERIZATION OF CLASSES

5.1. Intensity indicators.

The intensity (goodness or frequency) assigned

to each component in the characterization of classes may be chosen among linguistic modifiers like adverbs:"little", "few", "many", "very"...., "seldom", "often"... or adjectives:"low", "poor", "high", "medium".

We have adopted five levels of intensity like, for example:"very little", "little", "medium", "high", "very high".

The semantics of these words are represented by simplified possibility distributions:$r_l(x_i)$,that have a "core" where the possibility value is 1 and two zones called "penumbras" [9] where the possibility value monotonically varies between 0 and 1.

In our application, these possibility distributions are defined by the user by means of the lower and upper cut points. Between these two points the value of the possibility distribution is set to 1 and it decreases linearly to 0 on the left and on the right of these points.

5.2. Matching of the intensities.

A process of matching the possibility distribution $\Pi_k(x_i)$, that represents the value of the descriptor (or component) i in class C_k, with the intensity value $r_l(x_i)$has to be performed to be able to give automatically the linguistic characterization of this descriptor.

This is made using again the same algorithm described previously but excluding the learning possibility.

Intensities $r_l(x_i)$ are discretized for 20 values of x_i as well as $\Pi_k(x_i)$. The $r_l(x_i)$ are taken as Kernels of 5 classes and a recognition process of $\Pi_k(x_i)$ is run. Thus the attribution of an intensity l to the axis i is made with the same type of distance that was used to cluster the elements into classes. Figure 4 shows the actual structure

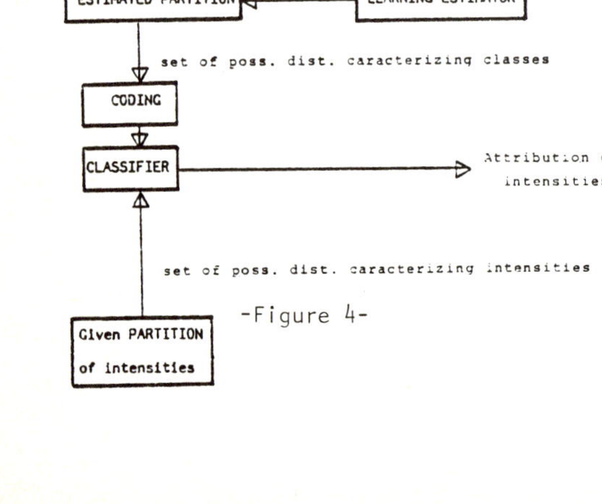

-Figure 4-

Moreover that procedure lets the possibility of introducing a mechanism for learning the meaning of the intensity indicators (as shown in figure 5) by means of a teacher who could adjust the possibility distribution r_l by using a set of tipical patterns [10,11]

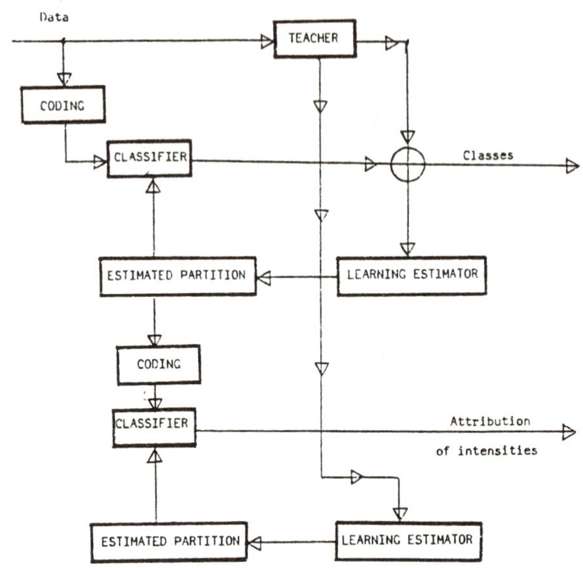

-Figure 5-

6. EXAMPLE

Let us go through an example to illustrate the above ideas.

The following example concerns the analysis of the set of multivariate data obtained by evaluating the characteristics of the working situations in a lumber factory;the 18 x 14 matrix so obtained is a fuzzy relation between workers (lines) and descriptors (columns). By such an analysis it is expected to find a small number of homogeneous groups of workers, and to be able to interpret their properties as well as to give linguistic labels to each one.

a) Descriptors.

The descriptors of the working conditions of each worker are given in the following list:

I- Personal Aptitudes.

1. Professional training.
2. Professional experience.
3. Initiative.
4. Skill.

II- Effort.

5. Physical effort.
6. Intellectual effort.

III- Social Interaction.

7- Incidence in the production process.
8. Control of machinery.
9. Responsability.

10. Public Relations.
11. Supervision of tasks.

IV - Working Environment.

12. Adverse environmental conditions.
13. Adverse climatic conditions.
14. Risk of accidents.

b) Elements to be classified.

The set of elements to be classified is composed of 18 workers whose functional denominations are:

1. Assistant to the team head.
2. Maintenance Machinist (1).
3. Staff organization supervisor.
4. Operator of forest machinery (1).
5. Assistant to the staff manager.
6. Unqualified worker (1).
7. Maintenance Machinist (2).
8. Foreman.
9. Wood cutting specialist (1).
10. Ranger.
11. Wood cutting specialist (2).
12. Operator of forest machinery (2).
13. Unqualified worker (2).
14. Maintenance supervisor.
15. Operator of forest machinery (3).
16. Inventory Controller.
17. Team manager,
18. Supervisor of machinery organization.

c). Set of data.

The following fuzzy relation represent the evaluation of 14 linguistic descriptors of the working conditions of 18 workers in the lumber factory.

$\underset{\sim}{R}$	C1	C2	C3	C4	C5	C6	C7	C8	C9	C10	C11	C12	C13	C14
P 1	0.8	0.6	0.6	0.1	0.1	0.5	0.4	0.1	0.5	0.3	0.4	0.2	0.1	0.1
P 2	0.2	0.4	0.3	0.5	0.1	0.2	0.2	0.1	0.1	0.2	0.	0.3	0.1	0.3
P 3	0.1	0.4	0.3	0.1	0.1	0.3	0.3	0.1	0.1	0.2	0.2	0.2	0.1	0.1
P 4	0.2	0.4	0.1	0.4	0.2	0.3	0.2	0.4	0.1	0.2	0.	0.3	0.1	0.4
P 5	0.3	0.5	0.4	0.1	0.1	0.4	0.6	0.1	0.5	0.3	0.4	0.2	0.1	0.1
P 6	0.1	0.1	0.1	0.3	0.5	0.1	0.1	0.1	0.1	0.1	0.	0.3	0.2	0.4
P 7	0.2	0.5	0.4	0.5	0.4	0.2	0.2	0.1	0.1	0.2	0.	0.2	0.1	0.3
P 8	0.1	0.1	0.3	0.1	0.1	0.2	0.2	0.1	0.1	0.2	0.1	0.2	0.1	0.1
P 9	0.1	0.2	0.1	0.3	0.5	0.2	0.1	0.3	0.1	0.2	0.	0.3	0.2	0.4
P10	0.1	0.2	0.1	0.1	0.1	0.1	0.1	0.1	0.1	0.2	0.	0.1	0.1	0.1
P11	0.1	0.3	0.1	0.4	0.6	0.2	0.2	0.2	0.1	0.1	0.	0.4	0.2	0.4
P12	0.1	0.4	0.1	0.5	0.2	0.3	0.1	0.4	0.1	0.2	0.	0.3	0.2	0.3
P13	0.1	0.1	0.1	0.3	0.5	0.1	0.1	0.1	0.1	0.1	0.	0.3	0.2	0.4
P14	0.6	0.8	0.4	0.2	0.1	0.4	0.4	0.3	0.5	0.3	0.2	0.1	0.1	0.1
P15	0.1	0.4	0.1	0.4	0.2	0.2	0.2	0.4	0.1	0.2	0.	0.3	0.1	0.4
P16	0.2	0.4	0.3	0.1	0.2	0.2	0.4	0.1	0.1	0.2	0.	0.1	0.1	0.1
P17	0.8	0.5	0.5	0.1	0.1	0.5	0.7	0.1	0.5	0.3	0.4	0.2	0.1	0.1
P18	0.2	0.4	0.3	0.1	0.1	0.3	0.4	0.1	0.1	0.2	0.1	0.3	0.1	0.1

d) Classification results.

Two parameter values are asked by the program:

- Adaptativity gain ($0<\alpha<1$)
- Initialization (N_0)

Increasing the adaptativity gain decreases the weight of the first elements assigned to a class, therefore, α=0,5 gives the same weigth to the prior value and to the first element.

Increasing the initial number of elements reduces the probability of the empty class and, thus, tends to reduce then number of new classes.

Results of the run with α=0,5, N_0=5

4 classes appear:

```
<1>  !!  1
<2>  !!     2
<3>  !!     2
<4>  !!     2
<5>  !!  1
<6>  !!        3
<7>  !!     2
<8>  !!           4
<9>  !!        3
<10> !!           4
<11> !!        3
<12> !!     2
<13> !!        3
<14> !!  1
<15> !!     2
<16> !!           4
<17> !!  1
<18> !!           4
```

We can see in the previous figure that:

- Class 1 = {1,5,14,17}

and this corresponds to workers having a relatively high academic standards and having an intellectual activity as well as initiative. This can be seen in its profile (see fig. 6) where the highest components are {1,2,7,9} and the lowest {5,13,14}.

- Class 2 = {2,3,4,7,12,15}

which corresponds to workers without high academic standards whose activities involve skill and experience (workers who operate machines) and their degree of responsability is rather low. This interpretation can be confirmed by the profile, where the highest components are {8,4,12 and 14} and the lowest are {11 and 9}.

- Class 3 = {6,9,11,13}

corresponding to workers developping a high physical effort and exercing very little responsability or initiative. This is clearly seen in the profile where 4 and 14 are the highest components and 3,9,11 the lowest.

- Class 4 = {8,10,16,18}

it corresponds to relatively specialized workers, having intellectual activities but exercing low responsabilities and being probably subordinated to class 1. Its profile, when compared with that of class 1, shows that it is similar, and slightly reduced except for the components 1,9 and 11 that are much lower that those of class 1.

```
COMPONENT 1  !>>>>>>>>>>>>>>>>>>>>>>
COMPONENT 2  !>>>>>>>>>>>>>>>>>>>
COMPONENT 3  !>>>>>>>>>>>>>>>
COMPONENT 4  !>>>>
COMPONENT 5  !>>>
COMPONENT 6  !>>>>>>>>>>>>>>>
COMPONENT 7  !>>>>>>>>>>>>>>>>>>>
COMPONENT 8  !>>>>>
COMPONENT 9  !>>>>>>>>>>>>>>>>
COMPONENT 10 !>>>>>>>>>>
COMPONENT 11 !>>>>>>>>>>>
COMPONENT 12 !>>>>>>
COMPONENT 13 !>>>
COMPONENT 14 !>>>
PROFILE CLASS  1
```

-Figure 6-

The four classes that we have obtained, contain the following elements:

```
----> CLASS  1 <----
ASSISTANT TO THE TEAM HEAD
ASSISTANT TO THE STAFF MANAGER
MAINTENANCE SUPERVISOR
TEAM MANAGER

----> CLASS  2 <----
MAINTENANCE MACHINIST (1)
STAFF ORGANIZATION SUPERVISOR
OPERATOR OF FOREST MACHINERY (1)
MAINTENANCE MACHINIST (2)
OPERATOR OF FOREST MACHINERY (2)
OPERATOR OF FOREST MACHINERY (3)

----> CLASS  3 <----
UNQUALIFIED WORKER (1)
WOOD CUTTING SPECIALIST (1)
WOOD CUTTING SPECIALIST (2)
UNQUALIFIED WORKER (2)

----> CLASS  4 <----
FOREMAN
RANGER
INVENTORY CONTROLLER
SUPERVISOR OF MACHINERY ORGANIZATION
```

7. THE MAN-MACHINE COMMUNICATION SYSTEM.

After the classification process, each class is represented by a set of possibility distributions modelizing its characteristics. For example let's assume that the class of "white collars" is represented by the following set of possibility distributions:

COMPONENT 1

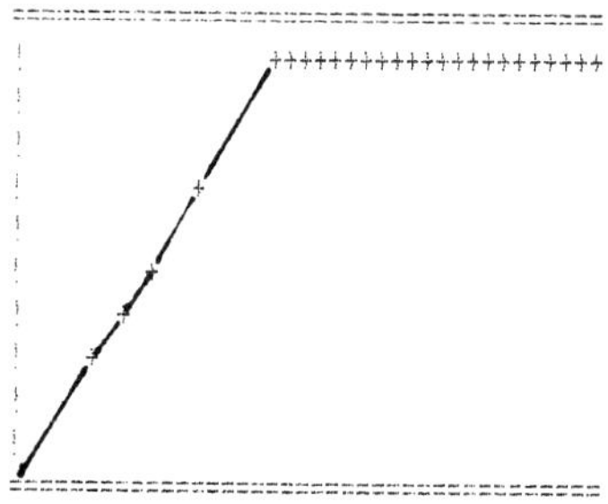

COMPONENT 8

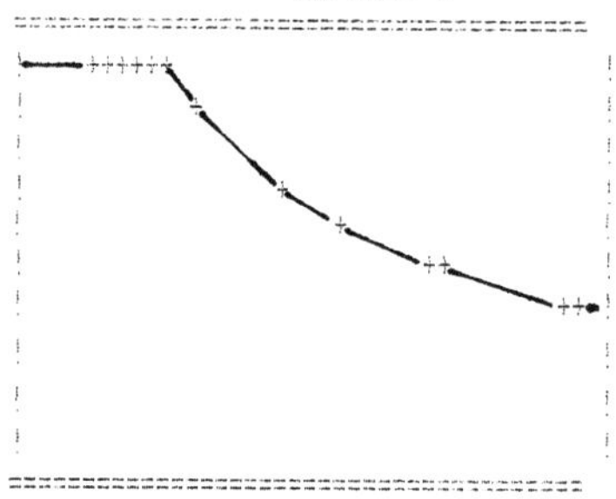

COMPONENT 14

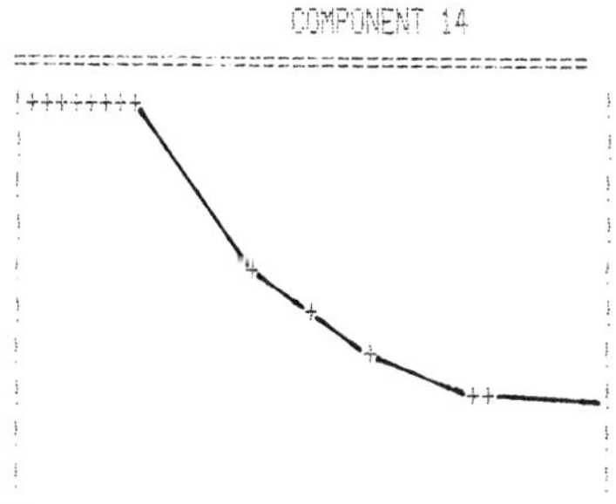

Finally we get a PRUF expression representing the class, matching these possibility distributions (using the "linguistic matching" process described in 5.2) against the set of possibility distributions corresponding to the intensity indicators:VERY-LOW; LOW; MEDIUM; HIGH and VERY-HIGH shown in the following figure:

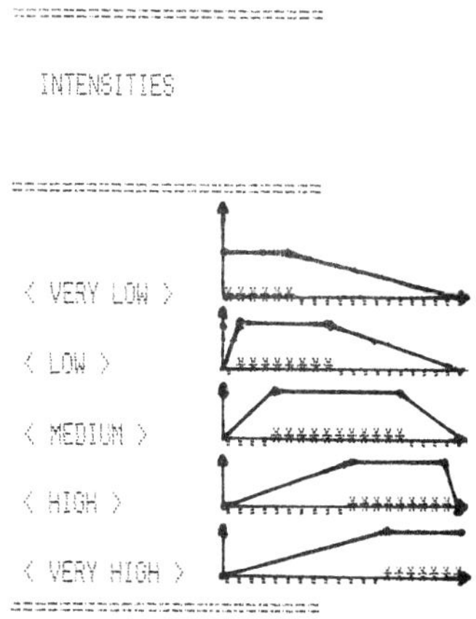

The PRUF-like expressions that we obtained for each class are:

```
++++++++++++++++++++++++
==== CLASSE 1 ====
PROFESSIONAL TRAINING :HIGH
PROFESSIONAL EXPERIENCE :HIGH
INITIATIVE :HIGH
SKILL :VERY LOW
PHYSICAL EFFORT :VERY LOW
INTELLECTUAL EFFORT :HIGH
INCIDENCE IN THE PRODUCTION :HIGH
ENGINE CONTROL :LOW
RESPONSIBILITY :HIGH
PUBLIC RELATIONS :MEDIUM
SUPERVISION OF TASKS :MEDIUM
ADVERSE ENVIRONMENTAL CONDITIONS :VERY LOW
ADVERSE CLIMATIC CONDITIONS :VERY LOW
RISK OF ACCIDENTS :VERY LOW
++++++++++++++++++++++++
==== CLASSE 2 ====
PROFESSIONAL TRAINING :VERY LOW
PROFESSIONAL EXPERIENCE :MEDIUM
INITIATIVE :VERY LOW
SKILL :HIGH
PHYSICAL EFFORT :LOW
INTELLECTUAL EFFORT :LOW
INCIDENCE IN THE PRODUCTION :LOW
ENGINE CONTROL :MEDIUM
RESPONSIBILITY :VERY LOW
PUBLIC RELATIONS :LOW
SUPERVISION OF TASKS :VERY LOW
ADVERSE ENVIRONMENTAL CONDITIONS :MEDIUM
ADVERSE CLIMATIC CONDITIONS :VERY LOW
RISK OF ACCIDENTS :MEDIUM
```

```
==== CLASSE 3 ====
PROFESSIONAL TRAINING :VERY LOW
PROFESSIONAL EXPERIENCE :VERY LOW
INITIATIVE :VERY LOW
SKILL :MEDIUM
PHYSICAL EFFORT :HIGH
INTELLECTUAL EFFORT :VERY LOW
INCIDENCE IN THE PRODUCTION :VERY LOW
ENGINE CONTROL :LOW
RESPONSIBILITY :VERY LOW
PUBLIC RELATIONS :VERY LOW
SUPERVISION OF TASKS :VERY LOW
ADVERSE ENVIRONMENTAL CONDITIONS :MEDIUM
ADVERSE CLIMATIC CONDITIONS :MEDIUM
RISK OF ACCIDENTS :HIGH
++++++++++++++++++++++++++
==== CLASSE 4 ====
PROFESSIONAL TRAINING :LOW
PROFESSIONAL EXPERIENCE :LOW
INITIATIVE :LOW
SKILL :VERY LOW
PHYSICAL EFFORT :VERY LOW
INTELLECTUAL EFFORT :LOW
INCIDENCE IN THE PRODUCTION :LOW
ENGINE CONTROL :VERY LOW
RESPONSIBILITY :VERY LOW
PUBLIC RELATIONS :LOW
SUPERVISION OF TASKS :VERY LOW
ADVERSE ENVIRONMENTAL CONDITIONS :LOW
ADVERSE CLIMATIC CONDITIONS :VERY LOW
RISK OF ACCIDENTS :VERY LOW
```

8. LEARNING BY CONVERSATIONAL ADAPTATION OF SEMANTICS [11]

At this point, if the professor who is interacting with the system does not agree with one or many of the fuzzy restrictions:HIGH, VERY-HIGH, etc... in the characteristics, for example if he/she thinks that the experience should be higher then he/she says "The experience should be higher" and the parameter ρ corresponding to the characteristic "experience" in this class is increased and a reclassification takes place. If the professor had said "The experience should be lower", then the corresponding parameter ρ would be decreased.

Then the system gives again the PRUF expressions describing the new classes. At this point the professor checks again the characteristics in each class and he/she eventually continues the teaching process. This situation would also fit in the schema represented by figure 5.

8.1. The need of automatic translation.

Since the human teacher interacts using a subset of natural language with the system, it is necessary to provide an automatic translation into PRUF of the information given by the teacher.

In our case we only consider propositions which have the following canonical form:N is F;where N will be the name of a descriptor or characteristic of the class, and F a Fuzzy set of a universe of discours U. Then N is F translates into the possibility assignment equation $\Pi(X) = F$, where X is a variable taking values in U:

For example, the proposition:"The experience should be higher";translates into

$$\Pi(\text{experience}) = \text{HIGHER-THAN } \Pi(\text{experience})$$

Where HIGHER-THAN is a fuzzy operator that modifies the previous fuzzy restriction in the possible values of the characteristic "Experience".

8.2. The translator (2).

L.A. Zadeh (1) defines four types of translation rules for propositions in natural language: Type I- pertaining to modification;Type II- pertaining to composition;Type III- pertaining to quantification;Type IV- pertaining to qualification. In the automatic translation problem, we have focused our attention on rules of types I,II and III, leaving the translation of propositions involving truth qualification for future work.

The translator is based on an ATN parser (3) together with a network that contains semantic information about the entries of a lexicon. The syntactic information is given by the lexicon.

A fundamental action in our ATN, will be to trigger a search through the semantic network in order to retrieve the necessary information of a word.

9. CONCLUDING REMARKS

The translator and the classification algorithm have been successfully implemented, as well as the implementation of the linguistic matching process that leads to the PRUF expression representing the class.

Now we are working on the implementation of the procedure for learning the meaning of the intensity indicators using the L-FUZZY language [7].

The main features of our approach are:

- The intended meaning of the descriptors depends of the context and of the subjective criterion of the teacher.

- The imprecision in the descriptors is modelized by possibility distributions.

- The meaning of the descriptors is adapted by means of a learning process.

- There are two levels of learning, an inner level, used in the classification process, in which the parameters ρ characterizing each class are adapted by self-learning. And an outer level where the system learns the shape of the possibility distributions, modelizing the meaning of the descriptors, by means of increasing or decreasing the value of the corresponding parameters ρ depending on the information given by the teacher.

- The initial information consists in a fuzzy relation between the descriptors and a set of elements or objects to which they can be applied. This leads to a classification which is the starting point of the outer level learning in which the teacher adapts the meaning of the linguistic descriptions of the resulting classes.

REFERENCES

[1] Zadeh,L.A., PRUF-A Meaning Representation Language for Natural Languages, Int. J.Of Man-Machine Studies, 10, (1978), 395-460.

[2] López de mantaras, R., Translation of Natural Language Descriptions of Simple Objects into PRUF, Symposium of Artificial Intelligence and Cognitive Processes, XXII International Congress of Psychology, Leipzig (GDR), (1980).

[3] Woods, W.A., Transition Network Grammars for Natural Language Analysis, Computational Linguistics, 13, (1970), 591-606.

[4] Aguilar Martin,J.;Balssa,M.;López de Mantaras, R., Estimation Recursive d'une Partition. Exemples d'Apprentissage et Auto-apprentissage dans R^n et I^n, Collection Seminaires INRIA sur Classification Automatique et Perception par Ordinateur, Edited by INRIA, Paris, (1980).

[5] Balssa,M., Analyse et Conception de Processus d'Auto-apprentissage Application a la Classification de Données Muntidimensionelles, Doctoral Thesis, University Paul Sabatier, Toulouse, (1980).

[6] Lopez de Mantaras, R., Learning the Meaning of Imprecise Concepts by Adaptation of their Possibility Distributions, Round Table on Recent Developments of the Theory of Fuzzy Sets, Lyon (France), (1980).

[7] Freksa,C., L-FUZZY, An AI Language with Linguistic Modification of Patterns. Memorandum UCB/ERL M80/10, University of California, Berkeley, (1980).

[8] Freksa,C., Communication about Visual Patterns by means of Fuzzy Characterizations, Symposium of Artificial Intelligence and Cognitive Processes, XXII International Congress of Psichology, Leipzig (GDR), (1980).

[9] Freksa,C., Linguistic Pattern Characterization and Analysis, PhD dissertation, University of California, Berkeley, (1981).

[10] Lopez de Mantaras,R.;Freksa, C.;Aguilar Martin,J.;Algorisme d'Adaptació Recursiva de Funcions de Possibilitat per a l'Aprenentatge de la Significació de Conceptes Imprecisos, Convenció d'Informatica Llatina, Barcelona,Spain (1981).

[11] Freksa,C.,;Lopez de Mantaras,R.;An Adaptive Computer System for Linguistic Characterization of Soft Observations in Expert Systems and in the Social Sciences, Second World Conference on Mathematics of the Service of Man, Canary Islands (Spain), (1982).

Approximate Reasoning in Decision Analysis
M.M. Gupta and E. Sanchez (eds.)

USE OF FUZZY RULES IN A SPEECH UNDERSTANDING SYSTEM

Renato De Mori[+] Piero Laface[++] Lorenza Saitta[+]

[+]Istituto di Scienza dell'Informazione (Università di Torino)
Corso Massimo D'Azeglio 42
10125 - TORINO (Italy)

[++]Istituto di Elettrotecnica Generale (Politecnico di Torino)
Corso Duca degli Abruzzi 24
10129 - TORINO (Italy)

The complexity of the processes required for interpreting continuous speech hinders from efficiently applying standard pattern recognition methods. This is mainly due to the great amount of knowledge needed to interpret an uttered sentence; this knowledge refers to all the various aspects (acoustics, phonetics, syntax, semantics, etc.) which contribute to assign a "meaning" to a speech waveform. The overall recognition process may be then viewed as a set of activities, performed by different Knowledge Sources cooperating in analyzing the input data. The structural knowledge, embedded in each Knowledge Source, is mostly made of fuzzy rules. The fuzziness reflects the imprecision and vagueness affecting the knowledge we have about speech decoding. Because of the imprecision of the rules and the fuzziness and ambiguity of pattern descriptions, alternative hypotheses are allowed, each one of which is associated a score. The, each Knowledge Scource uses fuzzy hypotheses for generating fuzzy hypotheses of another kind. The structure of the rules for mapping descriptions of acoustic cues into phonetic and phonemic hypotheses are discussed in detail. Decision criteria are evaluated and experimental results are provided for phoneme hypothesization in continuously spoken sentences, of an unrestricted text, from many speakers.

Keywords: Fuzzy rules, Automatic learning, Speech processing, Phoneme classification

1. INTRODUCTION

Considerable efforts have been made in the last few years to develop systems capable of understanding connected speech. Reviews of the problems involved in designing such systems may be found in [1-5].

The purpose of this paper is to describe a method for interpreting speech patterns and to give some experimental results of its application.

The method is based on an active model of speech understanding. This model has, as main task, the interpretation of speech patterns, obtained by numerical transformations of the speech signal, using all the available knowledge gained in many related fields and allowing interactions between different levels.

Two types of mathematical background are of general interest for the proposed model, i.e. the mathematical theory of languages, that is widely used for representing structural knowledge, and the algebra of ill-defined sets, which is believed to be the proper tool for representing the imprecision of the knowledge incorporated in the model.

The interpretation of speech patterns is mostly a complex set of non-numerical operations, consisting in the generation and verification of hypotheses about the linguistic message carried by the speech signal. This message is non-numerical in nature. The speech pattern is usually a three-dimensional representation of energy-frequency-time obtained by short-term spectral analysis of a spoken sentence; time is represented along an horizontal axis, frequency along a vertical one and the energy by gray levels. The short-term spectra are obtained by Fast Fourier Transformation and they show that acoustic patterns are not sequences of steady-state configurations; rather, they display continuously varying elements. Furthermore, there is no immediate evidence of beginning and end of each word in a sentence and complex interactions among adjacent sound units (phonemes) and across word boundaries are also present.

It is then impractical to store prototypes for every sentence; thus, some segmentation has to be performed on the sentence in order to reduce the dimensions of the interpretation problem.

A simple approach to segmentation could be that of splitting the entire sentence into segments of equal duration. Such an approach is not the

best, because we speak at different speeds. Very short segments have little significance if their context is ignored, because their spectra may be strongly affected by coarticulation. Large segments of fixed duration may have a large and unpredictable variety of contents; their interpretation may become practically impossible if it is not known a priori whether their content is a phoneme, a syllable or a word.
Because of these difficulties, an asynchronous segmentation is more suitable. Segments partially overlap each other and allow one to generate interpretation hypotheses based only on data which are inside the segment. These segments have been called Pseudo-Syllable-Segments (PSS). Before starting the interpretation of a PSS, their bounds have to be established.
Segmentation of continuous speech into pseudo-syllabic nuclei can be performed after some general phonetic features have been detected in the acoustic pattern. The detection of these features must be made by algorithms which do not require any knowledge about the context. These general phonetic features will be indicated in the following as "context-independent-features".
Some portions of the spectrogram exhibits, in the 0÷3 kHz band, lines of high gray level; these lines represent the time evolution of the main resonances of the vocal tract and correspond to a phonetic feature which will be called "sonorant". All the vowels, the nasal consonants, the semi-vowels and the glides have the feature "sonorant". Other portions of the spectrogram exhibit silences of "buzz-bar" traces at very low frequencies, frication or aspiration noise traces, for which the areas of high gray levels are not concentrated into lines but are diffused over large frequency intervals. All these acoustic features are correlates of the phonetic feature "nonsonorant" which belongs to the continuant, affricate and plosive sounds. The distinction between sonorant and nonsonorant phonemes is not specific of a particular language; rather it is a general feature for characterizing the speech sounds in every language.
Using information about the time evolution of broad-band energies, which can be extracted from spectrograms, some other context-independent features useful for segmentation can be extracted. One of these features is "vocalic"; it belongs only to vowels and diphtongs. Another feature is "nonsonorant-interrupted-lax" which belongs only to the plosive consonants /b/, /d/,/g/. When these sounds are pronounced in vowel-consonant-vowel (VCV) utterances, the consonant has coarticulation effects on both vowels. The same extension of the coarticulation effects is often observed when sonorant consonants are pronounced in VCV utterances.
The detection of the "context-independent-features" is a sort of "precategorical classification" of the elements of the speech signal. This detection will be indicated by this name in the following.
A "categorical classification" will refine the precategorical one by applying algorithms which may be context-dependent. The context-independent-features may be used for setting context constraints.
The acoustic features of a spectrogram are mainly qualitative and, even when they are numerical, their extraction requires some measurements to be performed on shapes which have to be previously detected. This implies that a description of the speech pattern has to precede its interpretation.
First of all, the signal has to be pre-processed and the pre-processing contains:

- sampling and quantizing,
- detection of the start and end point of a sentence,
- evaluation of the pitch contour, when it exists,
- calculation of speech spectra.

Once the pre-processing has been completed, a bottom-up precategorical classification is performed.
As previously mentioned, pattern description requires a pattern grammar to be known and a syntactic procedure to be used for analyzing a pattern and for making hypotheses about its structure. The proper background for this is the mathematical theory of languages.
Hypothesizing the structure of a pattern is a difficult task, because any vagueness may affect the features extracted from the acoustic data and there is a degree of imprecision in the relations between acoustic features and their phonetic or phonemic interpretation. For example, a sonorant intervocalic consonant may be characterized by some shapes in the gross spectral features, such as marked dip in the time evolution of the signal energy in the 3÷5 kHz frequency band; furthermore, for such consonants, the low frequency energy (roughly below 1 kHz) is much higher than the high frequency energy (above 5 kHz). Given a specific acoustic pattern of an intervocalic consonant with its adjacent vowels, a speech understanding system trying to interpret the pattern may consider the possibility that the consonant is sonorant.
This possibility can be evaluated numerically, following the Possibility Theory proposed by Zadeh [6]. To evaluate this possibility, the vagueness inherent in the terms "marked dip" and "much higher energy" have to be numerically represented by degrees of compatibility between

these statements and the acoustic pattern. The algorithms used to evaluate the possibility of a hypothesis will be referred to as fuzzy algorithms. The approach proposed in this paper is an algebraic one, attempting to formalize the intuitive logic used by a phonetician. The advantages of such an approach lie in its flexibility for modelling ill-defined non-numerical information. Fuzzy relations and possibility distributions can be established to represent, as closely as possible, the knowledge attained in research on phonetics and to optimize the recognition performances.

Fuzzy algorithms are used whenever a hypothesis is generated. Each hypothesis is evaluated and a degree of worthiness is assigned to it in such a way that it can be further processed for generating and coherently evaluating hypotheses about higher level items (e.g. words or syntactic structures).

The reasons for using possibilities instead of probabilities or purely heuristic methods for scoring hypotheses can be summarized as follows. The theory of possibility, in contrast with heuristic approaches, offers algorithms for composing hypothesis evaluations which are consistent with axioms in a well-developed theory; the theory of possibility, rather than the theory of probability, relates to the perception of evidence instead of likehood or frequency. The aim of the approach proposed in this paper is to express the evidence of a hypothesis concerning a speech pattern with the possibility of having high evidence measurements for clearly interpretable patterns even if the patterns and the features considered are scarcely probable.

The use of phonetic and phonemic features as syntactic categories of a fuzzy grammar is a new idea allowing one to incorporate in a knowledge source the vagueness with which the relations between acoustic and phonetic or phonemic features are known.

Using such rules, degrees of evidence of speech interpretations can be obtained and a change of a single rule may have the same effect of updating a large number of prototypes in a more conventional parametric approach.

In a previous paper [7], a method for obtaining acoustic patterns was proposed, together with a language for their description and syntax-directed procedures for the recognition of the vowel positions and for the segmentation of continuous speech into pseudo-syllable-segments. In this paper a method based on possibility distributions is described for relating acoustic features with phonetic and phonemic interpretations.

The results are limited to one type of PSS, namely vowel-consonant-vowel (VCV) pseudo-syllables, but they refer to every possible coarticulation of such syllables in the Italian language; the syllables were extracted from continuous speech without any limitation and the results were obtained by applying the same rules for different (male and female) speakers.

2. ALGORITHMS FOR PRECATEGORICAL CLASSIFICATION

Precategorical classification consists primarily of the assignment of phonetic features to non--vocalic segments. The main purpose of such a classification is to segment continuous speech into pseudo-syllable segments and to drive a context-dependent extraction of more detailed features.

The spectra are then processed in order to obtain the following "gross spectral features":

- S : total energy of a spectrum,
- B : energy in the 200÷900 Hz band,
- F : energy in the 5÷10 kHz band,
- A : energy in the 3÷5 kHz band,
- R_v : ratio between B and F.

The gross features are described by a language presented in [7] and the description in terms of these features (denoted DGF) is used for precategorical classification (denoted PC in the following). PC is then used for segmenting continuous speech into pseudo-syllabic units by a syntactic recognition algorithm.

The results of PC are used for driving the extraction of detailed spectral features such as formants evolution, characteristics of frication noise, burst, etc.. Such features are then described by a language and a linguistic description of the acoustic patterns may be obtained. PC has also been postulated in human perception [8]. The tree of Fig. 1 summarizes a scheme for PC that has been implemented giving satisfactory results with few ambiguities. A node represents a feature that can be hypothesized only if the feature corresponding to the father has been previously hypothesized. Thus, for example, the feature "affricate" can be hypothesized only for nonsonorant consonants. Let us call such features Precategorical-Classification-Features (PCF).

The phonetic features shown in the tree of Fig.1 are syntactic categories related to the lowerlevel description DGF of acoustic features by a "branching questionnaire" of the type proposed by Zadeh [9]. Thus PCF's are assigned to speech segments after answering composite classificational questions Q_i ($1 \le i \le K$), where the bodies of the component questions Q_{ij} ($1 \le j \le N_i$) are fuzzy sets $B_1, B_2, \dots, B_n$ defined over the range of acoustic measurements that phoneticians have found useful for characterizing distinctive features.

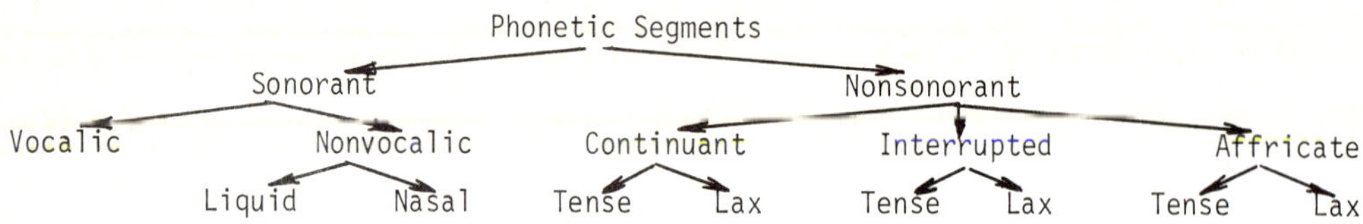

Fig. 1 - Tree of the features detectable at the level of precategorical classification using context-independent algorithms.

$B_1, B_2, \ldots, B_n$ represent linguistic variables.
Let Q_i ($1 \le i \le K$) be the composite question related to the i-th PCF to be hypothesized. The answers to component questions Q_{ij} of the composite question Q_i are fuzzy linguistic variables (e.g. high, medium, low, more or less high, etc.) whose membership functions are computed from diagrams stored in the phonetic source of knowledge of the SUS and are defined over the universe of an acoustic measurement.
The answers to the composite question Q_i are related by syntactic rules to the answers to the component questions Q_{ij}; thus, each answer to Q_i can be associated with a membership function whose value is computed under the control of semantic rules from the values of the membership functions associated with each answer to the component questions.
This use of fuzzy algorithms models, to some extent, the fact that most of the acoustic-phonetic properties of speech sounds are only known with a degree of vagueness, e.g. the signal energy is high for vowels, nonsonorant consonants have high frequency components, in unvoiced stops there is an interval of silence followed by some noise.
A linguistic variable, representing a judgement that can be expressed after the inspection of some acoustic parameter, is a symbol X with associated a fuzzy set R(X) over the values u of the acoustic parameter X. Thus, a possibility distribution:

$$\Pi_X = R(X)$$

is induced, such that the possibility that X is u is $\mu_{R(X)}$.
For the sake of simplicity, the membership functions will be labelled by abbreviations of adjectives of phonetic features. Fig. 2 shows the possibility distribution of the fuzzy variable:

X = <high consonant duration>

over the universe of the possible values of u, which represents time in this example.
The possibility distribution function associated with each linguistic variable was established subjectively, after inspection of the distribution of acoustic measurements made on a large number of sound samples.
Let Σ be the alphabet of the linguistic variables that may be answered to the component questions of the questionnaire used for characterizing the phonetic feature FF. Let p be an acoustic pattern represented by its description in terms of acoustic features. We are interested in the following possibility: Poss{FF is in p}.

Let $H \in \mathcal{H} \subset 2^{\Sigma}$ be a string of linguistic variables. The string H identifies a composite possibility distribution defined on some of the acoustic attributes of p. The KS invoked for generating or verifying the hypothesis that FF is in p is a fuzzy naming relation.
Fuzzy naming relations have been introduced by Zadeh[11] and are represented, in the approach proposed in this paper, by simple fuzzy grammars. Fuzzy grammars, also introduced by Zadeh [11] are similar to stochastic grammars [12]; their rewriting rules are associated with a degree of plausibility. In our case this degree of plausibility represents the imprecision of knowledge.
The possibility that a feature FF is present in a pattern p can be obtained as follows:

$$\text{Poss\{FF is in p\}} = \sup_{H \in \mathcal{H} \subset 2^{\Sigma}} \{ \mu_p(H) \wedge \mu(FF,H) \} \quad (1)$$

where $\wedge$ is the "min" operator, $\mu_p(H)$ is the compatibility of the string H with the pattern p and $\mu(FF,H)$ is the compatibility of the name FF with the string H.
The use of linguistic variables and fuzzy algorithms in an attempt to represent acoustic-phonetic knowledge, which is mostly expressed in a non-numerical form, by a formalism suitable for computer system. Acoustic-phonetic features are then processed in a logical, non-linear, hierarchical system. Such a system is more suitable, for application in SUS, than the crude mathematical approach of measuring distances in an N-dimensional space. Furthermore, the degrees of consistency of a hypothesis do not need to be known with great accuracy and should reflect a subjective, heuristic evaluation of the help the hypothesis can offer in grasping the meaning of the spoken sentence.
The hypothesis assignment consists basically of

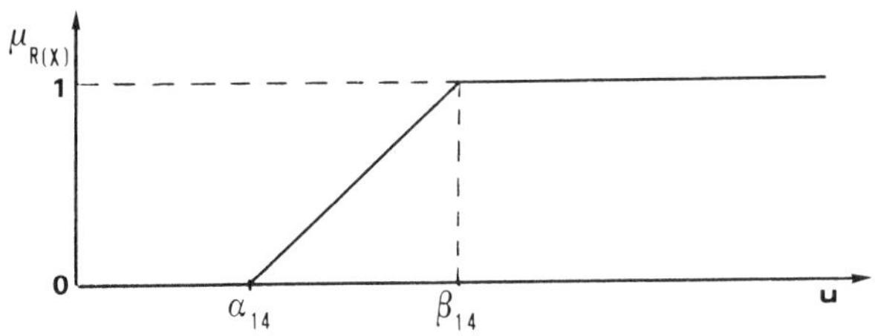

Fig. 2 - Possibility distribution function of Π_X, where X - <high consonant duration>

table look-up and the evaluation of min-max functions, making the program execution rapid; this aspect, toghether with flexibility in modifying the strategy as well as the sources of knowledge, adds motivations for using the proposed method in SUS design.

2.1. Sonorant-Nonsonorant Classification

The classification of a consonant as sonorant or nonsonorant is performed after the detection of vocalic intervals [7] and is obtained as an answer to a composite question:

Q_1 = Is the interval corresponding to the acoustic pattern p nonsonorant?

The question Q_i has six component questions:

- Q_{11} = How high is R_v ?
- Q_{12} = How low is the minimum dip in R_v with respect to the values of R_V in the preceding and following vowels ?
- Q_{13} = What is the minimum value of S with respect to the value assumed by S on the silence ?
- Q_{14} = What is the duration of the signal dip ?
- Q_{15} = What is the minimum dip in the signal ?
- Q_{16} = What is the maximum dip in R_v ?

Each question admits two possible answers: "low" or "high". These answers will be indicated as $\ell_{1,j}$ and $h_{1,j}$, where the subscript j ($1 \le j \le 6$) refers to the answer of the j-th question; it is assumed that:

$$h_{1,j} = \neg \ell_{1,j}$$

The answer to such questions are fuzzy linguistic variables, defined over the ranges in which the parameters they refer to may vary. Such parameters are defined as follows:

- $u_{11} = R_v$
- $u_{12} = \min(R_{vp} - R_{vc}, R_{vf} - R_{vc})$
- $u_{13} = \min_{S \in dip} (S - S_{sil})$
- u_{14} = consonant duration
- $u_{15} = \min (S_p - S_c, S_f - S_c)$
- $u_{16} = \max (R_{vp} - R_{vc}, R_{vf} - R_{vc})$

where the subscript p refers to the detected vowel preceding the interval in which a nonsonorant feature is being sought; the subscript f refers to the detected vowel following the interval, the subscript c refers to the consonant interval and S_{sil} is the level of the signal energy in the silence. The membership functions of $h_{1,j}$ and $\ell_{1,j}$ were defined after considering the range of the above parameters for each consonant in every context, assigning to $\mu_{h_{1,j}}$ and $\mu_{\ell_{1,j}}$ ($1 \le j \le 6$) values different from 1 and 0 only in the range where sonorant and nonsonorant sounds may coexist. Notice that $\mu_{h_{1,j}}$ is for $\mu_{high}(u_{1,j})$; furthermore:

$$\mu_{h_{1,j}} = 1 - \mu_{\ell_{1,j}} \tag{2}$$

The possibility distribution functions obtained from the experiments and corresponding to the linguistic values "high" show the behaviour represented in Fig. 2; the break-points, indicated as α_{14} and β_{14} in Fig. 2, are the bounds of the interval where the memberships are neither 0 nor 1. In general, the break-points for the variable h_{1j} will be indicated as α_{1j} and β_{1j}; these parameters assume different values depending on the questions Q_{1j}, as listed in Table 1.

Table 1 - Values of the break-points in the definition of the fuzzy linguistic variable "high" as answer to the question Q_{1j} ($1 \le j \le 6$)

Variable	α_{1j}	β_{1j}	Dimensions
u_{11}	- 15	7	dB
u_{12}	- 3	21	dB
u_{13}	2	20	dB
u_{14}	50	130	msec
u_{15}	6	23	dB
u_{16}	0	24	dB

The answers to atomic questions are related to the values of hypotheses about phonetic features by fuzzy rewriting rules. These rules are the usual syntactic rules involved in the definition of phrase grammars. Furthermore, a degree of "grammaticality" and a semantic rule are associated with each syntactic rule. The grammaticality is an a-priori evaluation of the plausibility of the syntactic rule. The semantic rule associated with a syntactic one is used to compute the value of the hypothesis expressed by the left-hand-side member of the syntactic rule as a function of the membership functions of the right-hand-side components.

A set of fuzzy rules has been inferred for defining the syntactic categories Sonorant and Nonsonorant that correspond to the answer to Q_1. The inference method is described in [13]. The inferred rules are given by the following:

$$\langle \text{nonsonorant} \rangle \overset{1}{::=} \langle \text{dip in } S \rangle$$
$$\langle \text{nonsonorant} \rangle \overset{1}{::=} \langle \text{dip in } R_v \rangle$$
$$\langle \text{dip in } S \rangle \overset{0.85}{::=} \ell_{13} p_S$$
$$\langle \text{dip in } S \rangle \overset{0.90}{::=} h_{14} p_S$$
$$\langle \text{dip in } S \rangle \overset{1}{::=} h_{15} p_S$$
$$\langle \text{dip in } S \rangle \overset{1}{::=} h_{14} \ell_{13} p_S$$
$$\langle \text{dip in } R_v \rangle \overset{0.60}{::=} \ell_{11}$$
$$\langle \text{dip in } R_v \rangle \overset{0.90}{::=} h_{12}$$
$$\langle \text{dip in } R_v \rangle \overset{0.90}{::=} h_{16}$$
$$\langle \text{dip in } R_v \rangle \overset{1}{::=} \ell_{11} h_{12}$$
$$\langle \text{dip in } R_v \rangle \overset{1}{::=} \ell_{11} h_{16}$$
$$\langle \text{dip in } R_v \rangle \overset{1}{::=} h_{12} h_{16}$$

The notation $\langle \text{dip in } S \rangle \overset{0.85}{::=} \ell_{13}$ means that ℓ_{13} (a low difference between the minimum of S and the silence level) allows us to generate the hypothesis that there is a dip in S with 0.85 plausibility.

The semantic rule associated with the syntactic definition of ⟨dip in S⟩ is derived from (1) as follows:

$$\mu_{\langle \text{dip in } S \rangle} = p_S \wedge \{(0.85 \wedge \mu_{\ell_{13}}) \vee (0.90 \wedge \mu_{h_{14}}) \vee \mu_{h_{15}} \vee (\mu_{\ell_{13}} \wedge \mu_{h_{14}})\}$$

In the preceding formulae p_S is defined as follows:

$$p_S = \begin{cases} 1 & \text{if } (S - S_{sil}) \le 8 \text{ dB} \\ 0 & \text{if } (S - S_{sil}) > 8 \text{ dB} \end{cases}$$

The semantic rule associated with the definition of ⟨dip in R_v⟩ is defined in an analogous way.

The symbols $\vee$ and $\wedge$ represent the "max" and "min" operators, respectively.

The definition of the syntactic category ⟨sonorant⟩ could be simply established as $\neg$⟨nonsonorant⟩. Neverthless, it has been found that this phonetic feature is better characterized in terms of fuzzy rules involving the answers to component questions that chiefly characterize the sonorant consonants. These elements are the complements of the elements appearing in the definition of nonsonorant:

$$\langle \text{sonorant} \rangle \overset{0.90}{::=} \langle \text{SRV} \rangle$$
$$\langle \text{sonorant} \rangle \overset{0.90}{::=} \langle \text{SS} \rangle$$
$$\langle \text{sonorant} \rangle \overset{1}{::=} \langle \text{SRV} \rangle \langle \text{SS} \rangle$$
$$\langle \text{SRV} \rangle \overset{0.85}{::=} h_{11}$$
$$\langle \text{SRV} \rangle \overset{0.85}{::=} \ell_{12}$$
$$\langle \text{SRV} \rangle \overset{1}{::=} \ell_{16}$$
$$\langle \text{SRV} \rangle \overset{1}{::=} h_{12} \ell_{12}$$
$$\langle \text{SS} \rangle \overset{1}{::=} \ell_{14}$$
$$\langle \text{SS} \rangle \overset{1}{::=} \ell_{15} p_S$$

The semantic rule associated with the definition of ⟨SRV⟩ and ⟨SS⟩ are given as follows:

$$\mu_{\langle \text{SRV} \rangle} = (0.85 \wedge \mu_{h_{11}}) \vee (0.85 \wedge \mu_{\ell_{12}}) \vee \mu_{\ell_{16}} \vee (\mu_{\ell_{12}} \wedge \mu_{h_{12}})$$

$$\mu_{\langle \text{SS} \rangle} = \mu_{\ell_{14}} \vee (p_S \wedge \mu_{\ell_{15}})$$

The measure of the hypotheses ⟨sonorant⟩ and ⟨nonsonorant⟩ are computed using (1), considering ⟨dip in S⟩, ⟨dip in R_v⟩, ⟨SRV⟩, ⟨SS⟩ as descriptions of the acoustic pattern p and the grammaticalities of the rules as memberships of the fuzzy relations between the left-hand-side and the right-hand-side phrases. One gets:

$$\text{Poss}[\langle \text{nonsonorant} \rangle \text{ is in } p] = \mu_{\langle \text{dip in } S \rangle} \vee \mu_{\langle \text{dip in } R_v \rangle}$$

$$\text{Poss}[\langle \text{sonorant} \rangle \text{ is in } p] = (\mu_{\langle \text{SRV} \rangle} \wedge 0.90) \vee (\mu_{\langle \text{SS} \rangle} \wedge 0.90) \vee (\mu_{\langle \text{SRV} \rangle} \wedge \mu_{\langle \text{SS} \rangle})$$

2.2 Classification of "Continuant", "Interrupted" and "Affricate"

The features "Continuant", "Interrupted" and "Affricate" are further hypothesized for nonsonorant consonants. The motivations for this selection come from the evidence obtained by spectrogram reading experiments and from the possibility of deriving fast, simple and efficient algorithms for their hypothesization.

For the same reasons, the possibility of hypothesizing other two features, namely "Tense" and "Lax" for nonsonorant consonants has been introduced. The acoustic parameters utilized are defined as follows:

- $(S_{dip} - S_{sil})$: The level of the total energy in the dip with respect to the level of noise in the silences (conventional units).
- R_{min} : The minimum of the ratio R in the dip (conventional units)

- SR : Ratio between the minimum level of the total energy S in the dip plus a constant α and the minimum value of R_V in its dip plus a constant β (conventional units)
- $(t_{R_{V_{dip}}} - t_{S_{dip}})$: Delay in the dip in the total energy S with respect to the dip in R_V, (msec).
- CDUR : Consonant duration, (msec).
- $R_{vdip}{}^{DUR}$: Duration of the dip in R_V, (msec).
- BBE : Buzz-bar energy, (conventional units).

The rules are given in the following using an algebraic notation:

<nonsonorant interrupted> =

$$= \mathrm{DDTE}\ (\mathrm{VVLTE \cdot NHR2} + \mathrm{NHTE \cdot DSPDRV \cdot LR2}) + \mathrm{HFE}\ (\mathrm{RTHR1} + \mathrm{NVLR1 \cdot RTLTE \cdot DSPDRV \cdot RTLDC}) + \mathrm{DRFDS}\ (\ell_6 \cdot \mathrm{DSNPDR}) + 0.6\ \mathrm{DDTE \cdot NHR2 \cdot NHTE}$$

<nonsonorant affricate> =

$$= \mathrm{DDTE}\ (\mathrm{VVLTE \cdot HR2 \cdot DSPDRV} + 0.6 \cdot \mathrm{HR2 \cdot RTLTE}) + \mathrm{DRFLS}\ (\mathrm{NAT}_a + \mathrm{NAL}_a) + \mathrm{HFE}\ (\mathrm{ADRDS})\ \ell_1$$

<nonsonorant continuant> =

$$= 0.6\ \mathrm{DDTE}\ (h_1 + \ell_4 + a_4\, b_6 + \mathrm{LDURC} \cdot b_4) + \mathrm{HFE}\ (h_4 + \mathrm{DRPDS})$$

The non-terminal symbols of the rules just introduced are defined below. A comment is added for explaining their intuitive meaning; The symbols DDTE (deep dip in total energy), HFE (high frequency energy) and DRFDS (dip of R follows dip of S) are non fuzzy variables describing primitive forms. These forms are defined on the pattern of gross spectral features. The definition of non-terminal symbols is given in the following:

$\mathrm{NAT}_a = \mathrm{DRFDS}\ (h_4 + \ell_1 + h_5 + h_6)$

$\mathrm{NAL}_a = \mathrm{DRFDS}\ (\mathrm{ADRDS}\ (\mathrm{LTE} + \ell_6))$

$\mathrm{VLTE} = \ell_1 + a_1 + b_1$; very low total energy

$\mathrm{LTE} = \mathrm{VLTE} + c_1$; low total energy

$\mathrm{RTLTE} = \mathrm{LTE} + d_1 + \ell_1$; rather low total energy

$\mathrm{VVLTE} = \ell_1 + a_1$; very very low total energy

$\mathrm{LR2} = \ell_2 + a_2 + b_2 + c_2$; low ratio

$\mathrm{HR2} = k_2 + h_2$; high ratio

$\mathrm{RTHR1} = d_3 + \ell_3 + f_3 + h_3$; rather high R_V minimum

$\mathrm{DSPDRV} = \ell_4 + h_4$; dip in total energy S precedes dip in R_V very much

$\mathrm{ADRDS} = d_4 + \ell_4$; average delay between dip in R_V and dip in S

$\mathrm{DRPDS} = \ell_4 + a_4 + b_4$; dip in R_V precedes dip in S

$\mathrm{LDURC} = \mathrm{VLDURC} + b_5$; low consonant duration

$\mathrm{VLDURC} = \ell_5 + a_5$; very low consonant duration

$\mathrm{RTLDC} = \mathrm{LDURC} + c_5 + d_5$; rather low consonant duration

A set of rules for relating interrupted tense and interrupted lax with acoustic features has been inferred, using the algorithm described in [13]. The results are described in the following. First of all, two sets ET and EL of empirical features were identified respectively for the tense and lax interrupted:

$\mathrm{ET} = \{\overline{\mathrm{ULB}}, \mathrm{LTG}, \mathrm{AVTG}, \overline{\mathrm{LDURC}}, \mathrm{HLFE}, \mathrm{RLLFE}, \mathrm{HTG}, \mathrm{HDURC}\}$

$\mathrm{EL} = \{\mathrm{VLDURC}, \overline{\mathrm{RLTG}}, \mathrm{ULB}, \overline{\mathrm{LTG}}, \overline{\mathrm{AVTG}}, \mathrm{LDURC}, \mathrm{HLFE}, \overline{\mathrm{RLLFE}}\}$

The components of ET and EL are defined in the following toghether with other components describing significant acoustic features.

$\mathrm{RLLFE} = d_1\, a_7 + \ell_1\, a_7 + \mathrm{HTE} \cdot a_7$; composite rather low buzz energy

$\mathrm{ULB} = \mathrm{VLTE}\ b_7 + b_7 + c_1\, b_7 + d_1\, b_7$; composite burst

$\mathrm{LTG} = \mathrm{RLR2} \cdot c_3$; composite low ratio

$\mathrm{AVTG} = \mathrm{AVR2} \cdot c_3$; composite average ratio

$\mathrm{HLFE} = \mathrm{HLF} \cdot \ell_1 + \mathrm{HLF} \cdot c_1 + \mathrm{RTHTE \cdot HLF}$; composite high buzz

$\mathrm{HTG} = \mathrm{RHR2} \cdot c_3$; composite high ratio

$\mathrm{HDURC} = d_5 + e_5 + b_5$; high consonant duration

$\mathrm{RLTG} = \mathrm{RLR2} \cdot c_3$; composite rather low ratio

The inferred rules for ET and EL are the following:

<ET> = $0.914\ \overline{\mathrm{ULB}} + 0.816\ \mathrm{LTG} + 0.931\ \mathrm{AVTG} + 0.866\ \overline{\mathrm{HLFE}} + 0.911\ \mathrm{HDURC} + 0.935\ \overline{\mathrm{HLFE}}\ \mathrm{RLLFE} + 0.939\ \overline{\mathrm{ULB}}\ \mathrm{HTG\ HDURC} + 0.939\ \mathrm{LTG\ AVTG}\ \overline{\mathrm{HLFE}}\ \mathrm{RLLFE} + 0.939\ \mathrm{AVTG}\ \overline{\mathrm{LDURC}}\ \overline{\mathrm{HLFE}}\ \mathrm{RLLFE\ HTG\ HDURC}$

<EL> = $0.788\ \mathrm{ULB} + 0.746\ \mathrm{LDURC} + 0.244\ \overline{\mathrm{RLLFE}} + 0.950\ \mathrm{VLDURC}\ \overline{\mathrm{RLTG}} + 0.964\ \mathrm{VLDURC\ ULB} + 0.948\ \overline{\mathrm{RLTG}}\ \mathrm{ULB} + 0.716\ \mathrm{HLFE}\ \overline{\mathrm{RLLFE}} + 0.867\ \overline{\mathrm{RLTG}}\ \overline{\mathrm{LTG}}\ \overline{\mathrm{AVTG}}\ \mathrm{LDURC\ HLFE}\ \overline{\mathrm{RLLFE}}$

Significant acoustic features and their corresponding fuzzy linguistic variables for the hypotheses "tense" and "lax" are listed in Table 2. The inferred rules are the following:

<tense> = $0.643\ \mathrm{B5} + 0.604\ \overline{\mathrm{C1}} + 0.640\ \mathrm{ET} + 0.659\ \mathrm{ET}\ \overline{\mathrm{C1}} + 0.957\ \mathrm{ET}\ \overline{\mathrm{C1}}\ \mathrm{B5} + 0.910\ \mathrm{NBZ\ ET\ B5}$

<lax>= $0.657\ \mathrm{CBZ} + 0.443\ \mathrm{BRL} + 0.155\ \mathrm{RTHTE} +$

+ 0.852 EL + 0.899 LBZ BRL + 0.801 CBZ RTHTE+
+ 0.898 BRL RTHTE

Table 2 - Acoustic features and corresponding linguistic variables for the hypothesization of <tense> and <lax>.

Acoustic Feature	F.l.v. for tense	F.l.v. for lax
Burst	BRT	BRL
Buzz bar energy	NBZ	CBZ
Total energy	$\overline{C1}$	RTHTE
Delay of dip of R	B5	-
Empirical feature	ET	EL
Duration	LDURC	VLDURC
	HDURC	LDURC

3. PHONEME CLASSIFICATION

Phoneme classification is a context-dependent operation, except for non-reduced vowels that can be recognized with no knowledge of the context. Vowels belong to sonorant segments, for which formants are tracked. Emission of hypotheses about vowels is primarily based on the analysis of the plot of F2 (the second formant frequency) versus F1 (the first formant frequency) for the sonorant portion of the PSS. The graph drawn in the F1-F2 plane by the pronounciation of a syllable is described by a language whose detailed definition is given in [7].
Formant tracking [14] is performed on a pseudo--syllable segment by looking for formant arcs made by concatenation of spectral peaks having high energy. Particular care has to be taken in order to guarantee as much as possible agreement between FFT and LPC spectra and to control formant tracking by transition rules.
The primitives of the language are basically stable zones (SZ) and lines (LN) [15]. Stable zones correspond to the stationary portions of the speech waveform. It is assumed that non-reduced vowels are always represented by stable zones, with duration of more than 40 msec.
Vowel classification is based on the detection of stable zones in speech intervals that have been previously hypothesized as vocalic segments. Some SZs in segments that have not been previously classified as "vocalic" may also cause this assignment if some conditions, involving relations with gross spectral features, are satisfied. This assignment is controlled by rules that are omitted here for the sake of brevity.
The vocalic SZs are then labelled by one or more vowel symbols, and a possibility value is assigned to each label. This operation uses a definition of vowel loci as fuzzy sets in the F1-F2 plane. Each SZ has the coordinates of its center of gravity as attributes. The coordinates identify a point in the F1-F2 plane that may belong to one or more vowel loci with certain possibility values.
A vocalic hypothesis v_i is defined by the following rule:

$$v_i \ ::= <vocalic><SZ_v> v_i \ (F_1,F_2) \qquad (3)$$

where <vocalic> is a phonetic feature attached during precategorical classification, $<SZ_v>$ represents the fact that a vocalic stable zone has been found inside the vocalic segment and $v_i(F_1,F_2)$ represents the fact that the center of gravity of SZ_v is in the locus of the vowel v_i.
A semantic rule is associated to rule (3), to evaluate the vocalic hypothesis v_i:

$$\mu_i = \mu_{<vocalic>} \wedge \mu_{<SZ_v>} \wedge \mu_{v_i(F_1,F_2)}$$

where $\mu_{<vocalic>}$ is a result of the precategorical classification, $\mu_{v_i(F_1,F_2)}$ is the degree of membership of the center of gravity of SZ_v in the fuzzy set which is the locus of v_i in the F1-F2 plane, and $\mu_{<SZ_v>}$ is a measure, defined by heuristic rules, of the "stationarity" of the spectra of the vocalic segment.
After experiments on liquid and nasal intervocalic consonants it has been found that, if the algorithm used for vowels finds consistent paths with no discontinuities joining the formant lines of the two vowels, it generally tracks the right formants. This result, together with the constraint that the first formant is allowed to have only a downward shift in its frequency interval, made it possible to track correctly the formants for all liquid and for some of the nasal consonants. Such a correctness was confirmed in many cases by synthesis experiments.
For some nasal consonants, particularly in the context of two front vowels, formant tracking appears to be very difficult (especially for the second formant of /m/) even if FFT and up to 16 pole LPC spectra are used together. This is due to the complex interaction of the anti-resonances of the vocal tract and the resonances of the pharingal and nasal tract.
Such difficulties have been successfully avoided by controlling formant tracking with rules for those cases for which there is not a single, consistent path in the consonantal region that joins, with no discontinuities, the formant lines of the vowels.

3.1. Liquid/Nasal classification

The liquid/nasal classification is a process of

generation of hypotheses about the consonant sounds classified as sonorant in the precategorical classification.

Once time bounds of a hypothesis for a single sonorant consonant have been set, the algorithm for hypothesizing the phonetic features "liquid" and "nasal" is applied. The relation between these phonetic features and acoustic cues are the following:

<liquid> ::= (<deep <u>and</u> short> <u>or</u> <not deep <u>and</u> long>) <dip of S>

<nasal> ::= <deep <u>and</u> long><dip of S>

The adjectives "short", "high","deep" and "low" are labels for fuzzy sets defined over acoustic parameters.

3.2. Classification of liquids

The classification of liquids mainly concerns /ℓ/ and /r/, because the liquid /gl/ (like in the spanish word Sevilla) is easily distinguished by a syntax controlled procedure that recognizes typical evolutions in the F1-F2 graph.

The generation of the hypotheses about the liquid consonants is based on the following rules:

/r/ ::= <high FFD1> <u>and</u> <high FFD2>

/ℓ/ ::= <low FFD1> <u>and</u> <low FFD2>

where FFD1 is the minimum value and FFD2 is the maximum value of the time derivative of the first formant amplitude.

The recognition rules for classification of nasals were inferred subjectively with the goal of avoiding a wrong answer with degree of worthiness equal to one and trying to minimize the number of times the wrong answer assumes a degree of worthiness higher than the right answer.

The vocalic contexts are represented by places of articulation, determined on the basis of the values assumed by the second formant on the stationary portion of the vocalic segment, according to the following definition:

$F_2 \geqslant 1900$ Hz front (f)

$1300 \text{ Hz} < F_2 < 1900$ Hz central (c)

$F_2 \leqslant 1300$ Hz back (b)

An analytic representation of the inferred rules is the following:

$$
\begin{aligned}
/m/ = {} & [ff](\ell_{N1} + \ell_{N2}) + [fc](\ell_{N3} + \ell_{N4} + \ell_{N5}) + \\
& + [fb](\ell_{N6} + \ell_{N7} + \ell_{N8}) + [cf](\ell_{N9} + \ell_{N10}) + \\
& + [cc](\ell_{N11} + \ell_{N12}) + [cb](\ell_{N13} + \ell_{N14}) + \\
& + [bf](\ell_{N15} + \ell_{N16} + \ell_{N17}) + \\
& + [bc](\ell_{N18} + \ell_{N19} + \ell_{N20}) + [bb](\ell_{N21} + \ell_{N22})
\end{aligned} \qquad (4)
$$

$$
\begin{aligned}
/n/ = {} & [ff](h_{N1} + h_{N2}) + [fc](h_{N3} + h_{N4} + h_{N5}) + \\
& + [fb](h_{N6} + h_{N7} + h_{N8}) + [cf](h_{N9} + h_{N10}) + \\
& + [cc](h_{N11} + h_{N12}) + [cb](h_{N13} + h_{N14}) + \\
& + [bf](h_{N15} + h_{N16} + h_{N17}) + [bc](h_{N18} + h_{N19} + h_{N20}) + \\
& + [bb](h_{N21} + h_{N22})
\end{aligned} \qquad (5)
$$

In rules (4) and (5) [i,j] (i,j=f,b,c) represents the context.

3.3. Classification of stop sounds

For the recognition of plosive consonants two types of acoustic features have been considered, namely formant transitions (FOR) and burst spectra (SP).

For each plosive sound and for each of the two features just introduced, a non-terminal symbol has been introduced. These symbols are defined in the following:

BFOR : Formant transitions for /b/
DFOR : " " " /d/
GFOR : " " " /g/
PFOR : " " " /p/
TFOR : " " " /t/
KFOR : " " " /k/

BSP : Burst spectrum for /b/
DSP : " " " /d/
GSP : " " " /g/
PSP : " " " /p/
TSP : " " " /t/
KSP : " " " /k/

Let X denote a generic plosive sound; XFOR and XSP are expressed as function of some components which are represented by other variables. The rules and the symbols used depend on the type of syllabic nucleus in which the stop sound appears. Syllabic nuclei of the type VCV for lax plosive and CV for tense plosive are considered in this paper. It is believed that most of the rules presented here can be generalized and applied to plosives in other types of syllabic nuclei.

The syntactic category XFOR is expressed in terms of the following features:

XFL : formant pseudo-loci
XFS : formant slopes
XBZ : buzz-bar characteristics at the onset of the first formant toward the vowel following the plosive.

XBZ appears only in the rules of XFOR with X lax. When X is lax, XFL and XFS are expressed in terms of two other nonterminals, namely XFLP, XFLF,XFSP and XFSF, where the last letter makes references to the vowel preceding (P) the plosive or following (F) it.

The general rule for rewriting the phonemic hypothesis is:

$$X \xrightarrow{\alpha_X} XFOR$$
$$X \xrightarrow{\beta_X} XSP$$
$$X \xrightarrow{\gamma_X} XFOR\ XSP$$

where α_X, β_X, $\gamma_X \in [0,1]$ represent the"grammaticalities" of the corresponding syntactic rules. The following semantic rule is used for obtaining the possibility value of the hypothesis X:

$$\text{Poss}\{X \text{ is in } p\} = [\alpha_X \wedge \text{Poss}\{XFOR \text{ is in } p\}] \vee$$
$$\vee[\beta_X \wedge \text{Poss}\{XSP \text{ is in } p\}] \vee$$
$$\vee[\gamma_X \wedge \text{Poss}\{XFOR \text{ is in } p\} \wedge \text{Poss}\{XSP \text{ is in } p\}]$$

For the sake of simplicity the syntactic rules defining X are expressed as follows:

$$X = \alpha_X\ XFOR + \beta_X\ XSP + \gamma_X\ XFOR\ XSP$$

The pseudo-loci are the values of the formant frequencies taken when the formant amplitude has an abrupt decay (before the plosive) or a large increase at the transition toward the vowel following the plosive. These values are indicated as FiY, where i (i=1,2,3) indicates the i-th formant and Y is P or F depending on whether the pseudo-loci are taken at the beginning or at the end of the plosive, respectively.
To collect large statistics of the pseudo-loci would have been impractical, because of the great number of different possible configurations. Rather, the designer has used some observations and his knowledge in defining the fields of existence of the pseudo-loci and has moreover introduced fuzzy restrictions (softy bounded intervals) instead of binary restrictions (sharply bounded intervals). To each fuzzy restriction a linguistic variable is associated.
The whole set of linguistic variables defined over an acoustic measurement (like a pseudo-locus) can be characterized by a vector of break-points:

$$V(x) = [x_1, x_2, \dots, x_n]$$

Let V(x) be the vector of the break-points of the linguistic variables defined over the acoustic parameter F_j taking values x. Let the linguistic variable covering the lowest part of the interval over the x-axis be ℓ_j (j being the subfix of the acoustic feature F_j). The membership of ℓ_j takes value 1 for $x \le x_2$ and decreases linearly, taking the value 0 on x_3. The linguistic variable immediately following ℓ_j is a_j; its membership is 1 for $x_2 \le x \le x_3$ and decreases linearly to 0 from x_2 to x_1 and from x_3 to x_4.

Going from left to right along the x-axis, the linguistic variables are b_j, c_j and so on, in alphabetic order excluding ℓ_j and h_j. The linguistic variable whose membership function takes value 1 for the highest values of x ($x \ge x_{n-1}$) is named h_j; its membership decreases linearly from x_{n-1} and reaches value 0 on x_{n-2}. Fig. 3 shows an example where j = 9, x = F3P and n = 5.

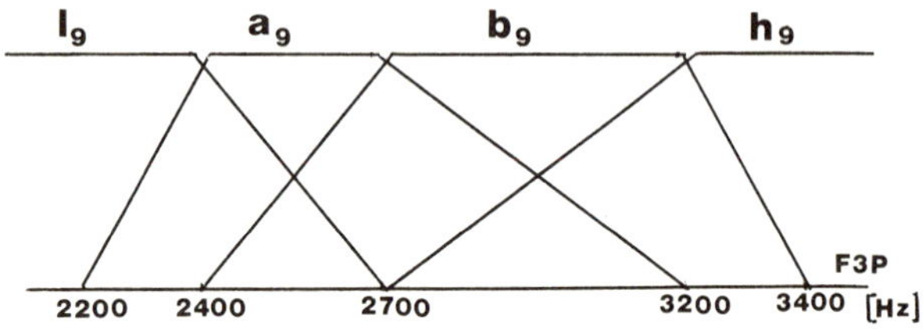

Fig.3 - Definition of fuzzy linguistic variables for F3P

The formant slope XSFS is defined as the difference between the value of the second formant frequency when the formant amplitude reaches the absolute maximum on a vowel and the frequency of the pseudo-locus; the opposite of such a difference defines XSFP.
The linguistic variables corresponding to the formant slopes are named A (ascendent), H (horizontal), D (descendent).
The feature XBZ is the maximum increase of the derivative of the first formant amplitude measured in conventional units.
XSP describes the spectral characteristics of the burst for plosive X. The burst is detected by looking for a short peak in the total energy with low ratio between low and high frequency energy, before the beginning of the successive vowel.
The acoustic parameters of the burst spectra are defined in the following:

- F_{14} = Ratio R between low (200÷900 Hz) and high (5÷10 kHz) frequency energies (conventional units),
- F_{13} = Center of gravity B in the (1÷10 kHz) interval,
- F_{11} = Center of gravity BL in the (1÷5 kHz) interval,
- F_{12} = Center of gravity BH in the (5÷10 kHz) interval.

Finally, a set of linguistic variables is defined on consonant duration DURC (= F_5).
Some rules are given in the following, as an example.

$$BFLP = [f,*]\ (\ell_9+a_9)\ h_{10} + [f,f\ ](\ell_9 + a_9)(f_{10} + d_{10}) + [f,c]\ (\ell_9 + a_9)\ c_{10} + [c,f]\ \ell_9\ c_{10} + [f,b]\ a_9\ c_{10} + [b,f{+}c]\ (\ell_9 + b_9)\ b_{10} + [c,*]\ \ell_9\ b_{10} + [f,b]\ a_9\ b_{10} + [b,f{+}b]\ (\ell_9{+}b_9)\ a_{10} + [b,b]\ (\ell_9 + b_9)\ \ell_{10}$$

$$GFLP = [f,*]\ (a_9 + b_9 + h_9)\ (h_{10} + f_{10}) + [c,*]\ \ell_9\ (d_{10} + c_{10}) + [b,*](\ell_9 + h_9)\ h_{10}$$

$$BFLF = [c,f]\ a_9\ f_{10} + ([f,f]\ (b_9 + h_9) + [*,f]\ a_9)\ f_{10} + [f,f]\ d_{10} + [c{+}b,f]\ c_{10} + ([*,b{+}c] + [b,f])\ (a_{10} + b_{10}) + [*,b]\ \ell_{10}$$

$$DFLF = [*,f]\ f_{10}\ (a_9 + b_9 + h_9) + [c{+}f,f]\ d_{10} + [b,b]\ c_{10} + [*,b]\ (a_{10} + b_{10}) + [b,b]\ \ell_{10}$$

$$GFLF = [*,f]\ (h_{10} + a_9\ f_{10}) + [f,c]\ d_{10} + [b,c]\ c_{10} + ([b,*] + [f{+}c,b])\ (a_{10}{+}b_{10}) + [b,*]\ \ell_{10}$$

$$TFL = [f]\ f_{10}\ (a_9 + b_9 + h_9) + [f]\ (\ell_9{+}a_9)\ d_{10} + [c]\ (b_9 + h_9)\ d_{10} + [f{+}c]\ c_{10} + [b]\ (a_{10} + b_{10} + \ell_{10})$$

$$KFL = [f]\ (h_{10} + (d_{10} + f_{10})(b_9 + h_9)) + [b{+}c]\ (\ell_9 + z_9)\ d_{10} + [b]\ (a_{10} + b_{10})$$

$$BBZ = [*,f]\ (a_8 + b_8 + c_8 + h_8)(z_5 + a_5) + [*,c]\ a_5\ (b_8 + r_8) + [*,b]\ (a_8 + b_8)(z_5 + a_5)$$

$$GBZ = [*,f{+}c]\ (\ell_8 + a_8) + [*,b]\ (\ell_8 + a_8)$$

$$BFSP = [f{+}c,\ ]\ D + [b,*]\ (H{+}D)$$

$$BFSF = [f{+}c]\ A + [*,b]\ (A + H)$$

$$DFSP = [b,*]\ (A{+}H) + [c,*]\ H + [f,*]\ (D{+}H)$$

$$DFSF = [*,b]\ D + [*,c]\ H + [*,f]\ (A{+}H)$$

$$GFSP = [f,*]\ A + [b,*]\ (H{+}D) + [c,f{+}c]\ A + [c,b]\ (H{+}D)$$

$$GFSF = [*,f]\ (H{+}D) + [*,c]\ D + [*,b]\ (D{+}H)$$

A single rule is very seldom useful for hypothesis generation if used alone. Rather, rules have to be combined in order to let the evidence of the right hypothesis emerge over the competing ones.

An algebraic representation of the rules is given in the following. The string weights have been learned from a sample:

BFOR = 0.605 BFLF + 0.028 BFSP BFLF + 0.505 BFLP BFLF + 0.628 BFSP BFSF BFLF + 0.908 BFSP BFLP BFLF + 0.944 BFSF BFLP BFLF + 0.955 BFSP BFSF BFLP BFLF

DFOR = 0.655 DFLF + 0.825 DFLP DFLF + 0.832 DFSP DFSF DFLF + 0.955 DFSF DFLP DFLF

GFOR = 0.055 GFSF + 0.655 GFLF + 0.720 GFSP GFLF + 0.955 GFLP GFLF

BBB = 0.600 BBZ + 0.502 BSP + BBZ BSP

DBB = DBZ + 0.700 DSP

GBB = 0.800 GBZ + 0.200 GSP

/b/ = 0.800 BFOR + 0.927 BBB

/d/ = 0.628 DFOR + 0.908 DBB + 0.944 DFOR DBB

/g/ = 0.900 GFOR + 0.980 GBB + GFOR GBB

An analogous set of rules has been inferred for the plosive tense, which are reported in the following:

PFOR = 0.800 PFL + 0.850 PFS + PFL PFS

TFOR = 0.970 TFL + 0.950 TFS + TFL TFS

KFOR = 0.730 KFL + 0.880 KFS + KFL KFS

/p/ = 0.950 PFOR + 0.900 PSP + PFOR PSP

/t/ = 0.780 TFOR + 0.850 TSP + TFOR TSP

/k/ = 0.820 KFOR + 0.920 KSP + KFOR KSP

4. EXAMPLE AND EXPERIMENTAL RESULTS

Fig. 4 shows the formants of the syllable /adu/ extracted from continuous speech. The following results have been obtained by applying the algorithms described in the preceding sections:

$\mu_{<sonorant>} = 0.70$ $\mu_{<nonsonorant>} = 0.85$

$\mu_{<nonsonorant\ interrupted>} = 0.62$ $\mu_{<nonsonorant\ continuant>} = 0.00$

$\mu_{<nonsonorant\ affricate>} = 0.00$

$\mu_{<tense>} = 0.40$ $\mu_{<lax>} = 0.80$

Thus, the fuzzy algorithm for the hypothesization of nonsonorant-interrupted-lax is applied first. The formants are tracked and the pseudo-loci (marked by circles in Fig. 4) are extracted. The following values (all in Hz) are obtained:

F2P = 1430 F3P = 2430 F2F = 1110 F3F = 2350

The context "central,back" is recognized with full evidence. The linguistic variables which have obtained possibility 1 are: a_9 and c_{10}; then, only DFLP has compatibility 1 with F2P and F3P. But GFLP and BFLP receive both a possibility value of 0.9. For F2F and F3F, the variables ℓ_9 and b_{10} obtain possibility 1; then,

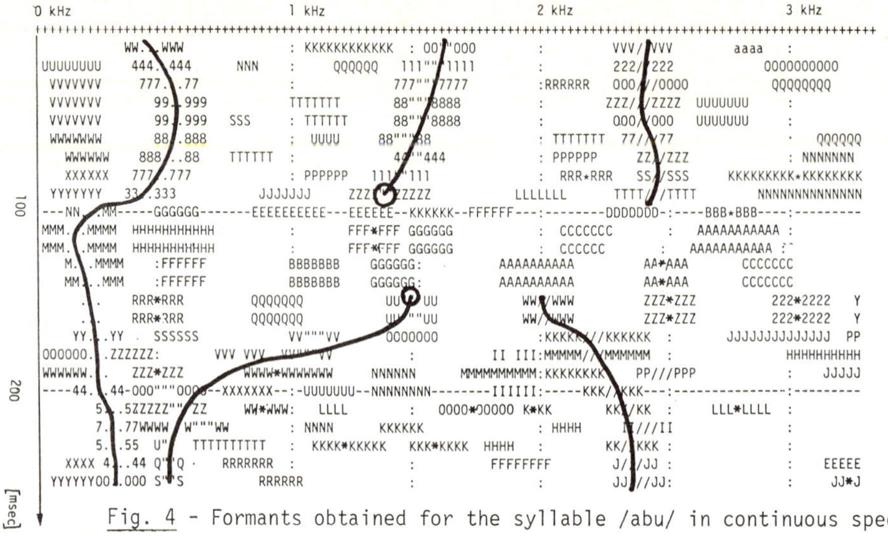

Fig. 4 - Formants obtained for the syllable /abu/ in continuous speech

BFLF, DFLF and GFLF have all possibility 1.
Going to the general features of the pseudo-loci, only DFL has possibility 1.
For the sake of brevity, the details of formant slopes analysis are omitted; the results are that BFS receives a possibility value of zero, while GFS and DFS receive both a possibility value of 0.7. For the buzz-bar energy, BBZ obtaines a possibility value of zero, whereas GBZ and DBZ receive both a possibility value of 1.
Thus :

$$\mu_{DFOR} = 0.70 \qquad \mu_{GFOR} = 0.70 \qquad \mu_{BFOR} = 0.95$$

For the burst analysis, the following data are measured:

$$R = -2.3 \qquad B = 5.2 \text{ kHz}$$
$$BH = 7;12 \text{ kHz} \qquad BL = 3.02 \text{ kHz}$$

The variables obtaining possibility 1 from these data are:

$$b_{13} \qquad d_{14} \qquad a_{11} \qquad a_{12}$$

thus obtaining:

$$\mu_{BBB} = 0.50 \qquad \mu_{DBB} = 1.00 \qquad \mu_{GBB} = 0.80$$

From these data we get:

$$\mu_{/b/} = 0.70 \qquad \mu_{/d/} = 0.90 \qquad \mu_{/g/} = 0.85$$

The hypothesis accepted is /d/.
Experiments on several hundreds of syllables uttered in continuous speech by four male and one female speakers gave the right interpretation with the highest evidence value in more than 90 % of the cases.
Table 3 summarizes some experimental results obtained in the bottom-up generation of hypotheses about the feature "sonorant" and "nonsonorant". These results show an average error rate of 5%. The results refer to syllables extracted from continuously spoken sentences of various and unconstrained syntactic structure. A hundred syllables were analyzed for each talker.

Table 3 - Summary of experimental results for four speakers.

Feature	Error Rate
Sonorant/Nonsonorant	5 %
Continuant/Interrupted/Affricate	7 %
Tense/Lax	6 %
Nasals	6 %
Plosives	10 %
Vowels	3 %

REFERENCES

[1] D.R. Reddy: Speech Recognition by Machine, A Review, Proc. IEEE 64 (1976) 501-531.

[2] F. Jelinek: Continuous Speech Recognition by Statistical Methods, Proc. IEEE 64 (1976) 532-556.

[3] T.B. Martin: Practical Applications of voice input to Machines, Proc. IEEE 64 (1976) 487-501.

[4] D.H. Klatt: Review of the ARPA Speech Understanding Project, J. Acoust. Soc. America 62 (1977) 1345-1366.

[5] R. De Mori: Recent Advances in Speech Recognition, Invited paper to 4-th International Joint Conference on Pattern Recognition (Kyoto, 1978) 106-124.

[6] L.A. Zadeh: Fuzzy Sets as a Basis for a Theory of Possibility, Fuzzy Sets and Systems 1 (1978) 3-28.

[7] R. De Mori, P. Laface, E. Piccolo: Automatic Detection and Description of Syllabic Features in Continuous Speech, IEEE Trans. on Acoustic, Speech and Signal Processing, ASSP-24 (1976) 365-379.

[8] K.N. Stevens: Potential Role of Property Detectors in the Perception of Consonants, MIT-RLE Quarterly Progress Report N. 110 (1973) 155-168.
[9] L.A. Zadeh: A Fuzzy Algorithmic Approach to the Definition of Complex or Imprecise Concepts, Int. J. Man-Machine Studies 8 (1976) 249-291.
[10] L.A. Zadeh: The Concept of a Linguistic Variable and its Application to Approximate Reasoning, II, Information Sciences 8 (1975) 301-357.
[11] L.A. Zadeh: Fuzzy Languages and their Relation to Human and Machine Intelligence, Proc. Int. Conf. on Man and Computer (Bordeaux, France, 1972) 130-165.
[12] K.S. Fu: Syntactic Methods in Pattern Recognition, Academic Press, 1974.
[13] R. De Mori, L. Saitta: Automatic Learning of Fuzzy Naming Relations over Finite Languages, Information Sciences 21 (1980) 93-136.
[14] P. Laface: Ambiguities in Feature Extraction from Continuous Speech, Proc. 4-th Int. Joint Conf. on Pattern Recognition (Kyoto, 1978)
[15] R. De Mori: A Descriptive Technique for Automatic Speech Recognition, IEEE Trans. Audio and Electroacoustics, AU-21 (1973) 89-100.
[16] R. De Mori, P. Laface: Use of Fuzzy Algorithms for Phonetic and Phonemic Labelling of Continuous Speech, IEEE Trans. on Pattern Analysis and Machine Intelligence, PAMI-2 (1980) 136-148.
[17] R. De Mori: Computer Models of Speech Using Fuzzy Algorithms, Plenum Press (1982)

Approximate Reasoning in Decision Analysis
M.M. Gupta and E. Sanchez (eds.)

TOWARD A THEORETICAL AND EXPERIMENTAL APPROACH OF FUZZY LEARNING

A. F. Rocha

Dep. Physiology and Biophysics, Institute of Biology
UNICAMP 13.100 Campinas, Brasil

The animal's behavior is considered to be dependent on how messages spread in his brain (NS). Neural connectivities, in turn, is modifiable by both external and internal histories and it is evaluated as a fuzzy relation between (input) pre and (output) postsynaptic entropies. The neural graph for message distribution is obtained by a max-min operation over neural connectivities and the message interpretation depends on the language defined upon such graphs. Because of this acceptability and refutability of learned models are evaluated by automata having their set of states as sets of neural connectivities. Some experimental data were presented to support such propositions.

Key words: Neural systems, Deductive process, Fuzzy reasoning, Learning Conditioning.

1. INTRODUCTION

We may consider to learn as to model the observed world in order to get the understanding of the whole universe. Models generating superstition, religion and/or scientific knowledge. Scientific knowledge involving not only formal scientific theories, but also any coherent set of relations between observed data whenever the truth is not imposed by coercitive systems or it does not have a divine origin.

A model is a set M of relations R between evidences (E) or observed data

$$M = \{R \subset M \;/\; R \subset E^n\} \qquad (1);$$

the relations being furnished by inductive (external) and/or deductive (self-refeared) processes of learning. A model is also a process to represent reality in order to get comprehension and to provide communication and predictability.

That learning is performed by brains was one of the main achievements of science during the last century and how brain realizes it is one of the most exciting endeavour in contemporary research. The general rules governing learning must be deductible from properties of neurons. Indeed, Rocha, 1981 has shown that some important learning properties may be theoretically deduced from the actual knowledge about neural systems, mainly those rules governing synaptic relations.

The main questions arising in such line of reasoning are how learned models are realized over the neural substrates; how they are guided by the basic neural properties and what are their qualities induced by the neural contexts? The answers to these questions require us to learn how to model the learning mechanisms for modeling, but the time is ripe to begin this kind of formalization using the man's knowledge about his own brain. This paper intends to be an attempt in such a direction.

2. LEARNING: A FORMAL CONCEPTUALIZATION

Learning may be considered as

a process	to abstract features (F) from and related to a proposed question
in order	to develop a model about these features
which can	predict (comprehension) and may be used to transmit (communication) the future behavior of the system posing the question.
	Thus, the model M_j
must have	high predictability and
must present	low rates of disagreement and error.

Representation of the observable world W in the neural systems (NS) is a process founded over the recognition and interpretation of messages channeled by sensory systems. Reality is, therefore, a model of W expressing the relations (as provided by associative circuits AS) between NS and evidences E furnished by the sensory systems SS. Utilizing its effector systems ES, NS manipulates the universe U according to R to generate its own actual world R_W (perhaps real, perhaps imaginary). This Neural Pattern Recognition (NPR) process is formalized as

$$NPR: W \times SS \to E \quad (2a)$$
$$NPR: E \times AS \to R \quad (2b)$$
$$NPR: R \times ES \to R_W \subset U \quad (2c)$$

and it is partially closed because

$$R_W \cap W \neq \emptyset \quad (2d)$$

This means that part of the evidences are generated by NS itself (from R_W) and part of them come from the actual external world ($\mathcal{C}_U R_W$).

Being self-observable, NS may have its attention programed by R (Hernandez-Pêon et al., 1956; Rocha, 1980) in order to channel over it the desired evidences E to any inherited and/or learned model M_i:

$$NPR(M_i): M_i \subset R \times ES \to R_{W_i} \subset W \quad (2e)$$
$$NPR(M_i): R_{W_i} \times SS \to E_i \quad (2f)$$
$$NPR(M_i): E_i \times AS \to F_i \cap M_i \neq \emptyset \quad (2g)$$

Here, $NPR(M_i)$ represents NPR if focused by a model M_i.

This attentional process permits

1) the evaluation of the pertinence of an evidence to the domain of M_i, that is

$$NPR(M_i): W \times SS \to E \quad (3a)$$
$$NPR(M_i): E \times AS \to F\ ?\ M_j \quad (3b)$$

Once neural processing is fuzzy, this pertinence becomes

$$\mu(E, M_i) : F \times M_i \to [0, 1] \quad (3b')$$

2) to determine whether or not a new M_j can be generate from M_i

$$NPR(M_i): W \times SS \to E \quad (3c)$$
$$NPR(M_i): E \times AS \to F \subset M_i \text{ or } \mathcal{C}_R M_i \quad (3d)$$
$$NPR(M_i): F \times ES \to M_j\ ?\ R_W \quad (3e)$$

Because NPR is partially closed, this new M_j may be incorporated into R whenever it shows a better predictability and/or generates less disagreement and error

$$NPR(M_j): R_W \times SS \to E \quad (4a)$$
$$NPR(M_j): E \times AS \to M_j \subset R \quad (4b)$$

Also, if two neural systems NS_i, NS_j share a non-empty world intersection

$$R_{W_i} \cap R_{W_j} \neq \emptyset \quad (5a)$$

one of them (say N_i) may insert any of its M_i into this intersection

$$NPR_i(M_i): R \times ES \to M_i \subset R_W \cap R_{W_j} \quad (5b)$$

in order to transport M_i into the other system (say NS_j)

$$NPR_j: W_j \times SS_j \to E_j \quad (5c)$$
$$NPR_j: E_j \times AS_j \to M_i \subset R_j \quad (5d)$$

This characterizes an educational process between NS_i, NS_j.

Summing up, learned models must have or be (Definition M-0)

i) plasticity: M_j must provide the necessary conditions (as in 3c, d and e) to the development of new models M_k;

ii) autonomy or self-reproduction: M_j must have the capacity to be maintained or recriated in NS (as in 4a, b) in order to provide the substrate for comprehension, and

iii) mobility or exogenous-reproduction: M_j must have the capacity to be recriated into another NS (as in 5a, b, c and d) in order to provide the substratum for communication.

iv) generative: M_j, must provide the necessary interpretation about U, including expectancies and predictions about $\mathcal{C}_U W$, thus

$$R_W \cap U \neq R_W \cap W \quad (6)$$

NPR being partially closed determines

$$NPR(M_j): R_W \times NS \to R \quad (7a)$$

but being partially opened it may induce

$$NPR(M_j): W \times NS \to R' \quad (7b)$$

Because $\mathcal{C}_{NS}R$ must contain those interpretations NS can provide to E other than M_j, then

$$\mu(R', R): R' \times R \to [0, 1] \quad (7c)$$
$$\mu(R', \mathcal{C}_{NS}R): R' \times \mathcal{C}_{NS}R \to [0, 1] \quad (7d)$$

measure, respectively, the membership between R' and R or $\mathcal{C}_{NS}R$, such that

$$\mu(R', R) = 1 \to R' \subsetneq R \quad (7e)$$
$$\mu(R', \mathcal{C}_{NS}R) = 1 \to R' \subsetneq \mathcal{C}_{NS}R \quad (7f)$$

Definition M-1: The predictability ($p(M_j)$) of M_j is its capacity to generate correct interpretations about U, that is, to furnish a stable reality R despite the pertubations in U. Thus

$$p(M_j) = \mu(R', R) \quad (8a)$$

traduces the NS's certainty about U regarding its previons learning $M_i \subset R$ and also it measures the pertinence of the evidences E to the domain of M_j.

Definition M-2: The disagreement ($d(M_j)$) and the error ($e(M_j)$) of M_j are the discrepancies between the predictions of M_j and, respectively, the new evidences from U and the reobserved data from W. Both $d(M_j)$ and $e(M_j)$ measure the instability of R concerning U. Thus

$$d(M_j) + e(M_j) = \mu(R', \mathcal{C}_{NS}R) \quad (8b)$$

traduces the uncertainty of NS about U regarding its previous learned model $M_j \subset R$ and measures also the pertinence of the evidences E to the domain of $\mathcal{C}_R M_j$.

3. THE ORGANIZATION OF NEURAL SYSTEMS

Despite holistic or localizacionist proposals, the main assumption in contemporary neurophysiology considers any brain processing as dependent upon the distributions messages may have over its neurons and upon the activity triggered in these neurons by the incoming stimulus (e.g. Rocha et al., 1980, Rocha, 1981, John, 1972). Such ideas were formalized using fuzzy graph theory to represent the message spread and fuzzy languages to describe the productions in these neural networks (Rocha et al., 1980, Rocha, 1980 and 1981).

Briefly, any neuron N_j in NS is assumed to be a fuzzy automaton (Rocha et al, 1980, Rocha, 1981 a,b)

$$N_j = (S,\ SC,\ Q,\ \P,\ \beta) \qquad (9a)$$

where 1) S is the set of inputs or stimuli; 2) SC is the set of outputs or classes of neural responses; 3) Q is the set of states; 4) β is the output function:

$$\beta:\ S \times Q \times SC \to [0,\ 1] \qquad (9b)$$

5) $\P$ is the family of state membership ($\mu(q,\ q')$) matrices, such that

$$\mu(q,\ q'):\ Q \times Q \times S \to [0,\ 1] \qquad (9c)$$

$$\mu(q,q') = \mu(\zeta,t).f(r).\mu(s,s').\mu(sc,sc') \qquad (9d)$$

depends on:

5a) the instant the stimulus is applied in respect to the neuron recovery time describing its memory ($\mu(\zeta,\ t)$);

5b) the grade of stimulus uniformity $f(r)$;

5c) the stimulus membership $\mu(s,\ s')$ and

5d) the neural control $\mu(sc,\ sc')$ exercized by structures other than N_j.

Two neuron N_a, N_j are functionally coupled if the output of one of them (say N_a) is the input to the other N_j (Rocha et al., 1980), that is

$$N_j = (SC_a,\ SC_j,\ Q_j,\ \P_j,\ \beta_j) \qquad (10a)$$

This coupling describes the synaptic behavior and its strength must be assumed as the capacity of N_a to elicit different responses of N_j. The synaptic strength $\mu(N_a,\ N_j)$ is, therefore, defined as

$$\mu(N_a,\ N_j):\ SC_a \times SC_j \to [0,\ 1] \qquad (11b)$$

$$\mu(N_a,\ N_j) = h(SC^{a,j})/h(SC_j) \qquad (11c)$$

$$SC^{a,j} = \beta_j(q,\ SC_a) \qquad (11d)$$

that is to say $\mu(N_a,\ N_j)$ is evaluated as a relation between the transmitted ($h(SC^{a,j})$) and N_j's ($h(SC_j)$) entropies.

The traffic of messages ($\mu_t(N_a,\ N_j)$) between any pair of neurons N_a, N_j is dependent upon the balance between inhibition (I) and excitation (E), thus

$$\mu_t(N_a,N_j):\ \{SC_e\}_E \times \{SC_i\}_I \to [-1,1] \qquad (12a)$$

$$\mu_t(N_a,N_j) = \mu(E,\ N_j) - \mu(I,\ N_j) \qquad (12b)$$

The fuzzy graphs to be defined over NS become

$$FG = (\{SC_j\}_{NS},\ \{\mu(N_a,\ N_j)\}_{NS}) \qquad (13a)$$

$$OG = (\{SC_j\}_{NS},\ \{\mu_t(N_a,\ N_j)\}_{NS}) \qquad (13b)$$

where FG and OG describe, respectively, the functional and operational message distributins.

Because neurons may be disposed in series (s) or parallel (p), message distribution over FG, OG can be evaluated by means of the coupling power (cp) in these circuits

$$cp(FG) = \bigvee_p \bigwedge^s \mu(N_a,\ N_j)$$

$$\text{or } cp(OG) = \bigvee_p \bigwedge^s \mu_t(N_a,\ N_j) \qquad (13c)$$

The fuzzy grammars realized over such graphs are fuzzy relational grammars (Negoita and Ralescu, 1975, Rocha et al. 1980), the productions being of the type

$$SC_a \xrightarrow{\psi(\rho)} SC_j \qquad (14a)$$

where $\psi(\rho)$ expresses the dependence on the neural context

$$\psi(\rho) = \mu(SC^{a-1,\ a},\ SC^{a,j})$$

$$\text{or } \psi(\rho) = \mu_t(SC^{a-1,\ a}\ \ SC^{a,j}) \qquad (14b)$$

The fuzzy language L(NG) (NG denoting FG or OG) defined by such a grammar will be composed by productions

$$L(NG)\ (\theta) = \vee[(p_1) \wedge (p_2) \wedge \ldots \wedge (p_{m+1})] \qquad (14d)$$

the supremum being taken over all derivation chains from the point basis to the node θ (Negoita and Ralescu, 1975, Rocha et al., 1980).

4. NEURAL ORGANIZATION OF LEARNED MODELS M_j

Any neural model M_j becomes fully characterized if its structural description is provided by the neural graph NG_j underlying it and if its interpretation is furnished by the neural language $L(NG_j)$ defined over this NG_j. Thus

$$NPR(M_j):\ W \times NG_j \to R_W \subset L(NG_j) \qquad (15a)$$

Also, because message spread over NG_j is evaluated by means of $cp(NG_j)$, then

$$\mu(R', R) = p(M_j) = cp(NG_j) \qquad (8a')$$

$$\mu(R', \mathcal{C}_{NS}R) = e(M_j) + d(M_j) = cp(\mathcal{C}_{NS}NG_j)$$
(8b')

Theorem M-1: Whenever

$$d(M_j) + e(M_j) \to .5$$

a question will be raised in NS about the choice of the NG to represent the evidences generated by W.

Proof: In such a condition

$$cp(\mathcal{C}_N NG_j) \to .5 \qquad (T1 - 1)$$

which implies

$$\mu(E, \mathcal{C}_{NS}M_j) \to .5 \qquad (T1 - 2)$$

despite the fact that

$$\mu(E, M_j) \neq 0 \qquad (T1 - 3)$$

because $p(M_j) \neq 0$ (T1 - 4)

Since, NS is self-observable and the degree of attention provided by a model M depends on the coupling power cp(NG) of its substrate NG (Rocha, 1979), conditions 1 - 1 to 1 - 4 will generate a question about the pertinence of E, because messages may not be precisely channeled according with M_j or $\mathcal{C}_{NS}M_j$.

Theorem M-2: Whenever

$$d(M_j) + e(M_j) \to .5$$

there exists a procedure to evaluate the possibility of a new model M_k to be developed from a previous M_j or from its complementar reality $\mathcal{C}_{NS}M_j$.

Proof: Theorem M-1 guarantees that the above condition implies

$$NPR(M_j): W \times NS \to F?\ M_j$$

and at least operationally

$$\mu_t(E, M_j) \to 0 \qquad (T2 - 1)$$

Thus, to determine if a new M_k may be developed from M_j is to evaluate if

$$\mu_t(E, M_j) > \mu_t(E, \mathcal{C}_{NS}M_j) \qquad (T2 - 2)$$

This may be accomplished looking for expanded $e \sim M_j$ or reduced $\rho \sim M_j$ models of M_j.

Let $\rho \sim M_j$ to be considered a reduced model of M_j if furnished by the following ρ ~ cut level graph of NG_j (Negoita and Ralescu, 1975; Rocha et al., 1980)

$$\rho \sim NG_j = (\{SC\}_{NG_j}, \{\rho \sim \mu(N_a, N_j)\})$$
(T2 - 3)

$$\rho \sim M_j \subset L(\rho \sim NG_j) \qquad (T2 - 4)$$

$$\rho \sim \mu(N_a, N_j) = \begin{cases} 0 \text{ if } \mu(N_a, N_j) \leqslant \rho \\ \mu(N_a, N_j) \text{ otherwise} \end{cases}$$

If

$$\lim_{\rho \to 0}(e(\rho \sim FG_j) + d(\rho \sim FG_j)) < .5 \qquad (T2-6)$$

then $cp(\mathcal{C}_{NS}\rho \sim NG_j) < .5$ (T2 - 7)

which means that there exists an operational $\rho \sim OG_j$ to which

$$cp(\rho \sim OG_j) > 0 \qquad (T2 - 8)$$

because $\mu_t(N_a, N_j) = \mu(E, N_j) - \mu(I, N_j)$

$$E \subset \rho \sim NG_j \text{ and } I \subset \mathcal{C}_{NS}\rho \sim NG_j$$

Condition T2 - 8 guarantees at least one association between $\rho \sim NG_j$ and another neural chain NG_c in NS as preferential regarding the association between NG_c and $\mathcal{C}_{NS}\rho \sim NG_j$. In such a condition, it is possible to search for a new M_k:

$$M_k \subset L(NG_k) \qquad (T2 - 9)$$

$$NG_k = \rho \sim NG_j \cup NG_c \qquad (T2 - 10)$$

such that

$$\mu(E, M_k) = \rho(M_k) \to 1 \qquad (T2 - 11)$$

$$\mu(E, \mathcal{C}_{NS}M_k) = d(M_k) + e(M_k) \to 0 \qquad (T2-12)$$

If such M_k exists, $\rho \sim M_j$ will be the germ for its development. How this development may take place will be discussed latter.

By a similar reasoning, if

$$\lim_{\rho \to 0}(e(\rho \sim M_j) + d(\rho \sim M_j)) > .5 \qquad (T2 - 6')$$

then $cp(\mathcal{C}_{NS}\rho \sim M_j) > .5$ (T2 - 7')

and the above M_k may be tried as provided by

$$NG_k = \mathcal{C}_{NS}\rho \sim NG_j \cup NG_c \qquad (T2 - 10')$$

Finally, if

$$\lim_{\rho \to 0}(e(\rho \sim M_j) + d(\rho \sim M_j)) = .5 \qquad (T2- 6'')$$

then

$$cp(\rho \sim OG_j) = cp(\mathcal{C}_{NS}\rho \sim OG_j) = 0 \qquad (T2 - 7'')$$

and no preferential association may be intended between NG_c and $\rho \sim NG_j$ or $\mathcal{C}_{NS}\rho \sim NG_j$. In such a context, no prediction may be made in relation to the development of M_k.

The expanded model $e \sim M_j$ is an working hypothesis equivalent to take into accouting reduced models in $\mathcal{C}_{NS}NG_j$.

Proposition M-2: Neural models M_j developed in neural basins BS have strong autonomy or high plasticity.

Proof: Let be given

$$M_j \subset L(NG_j) \qquad (P2 - 1)$$

It follows from T2 - 3, T2 - 4 and T2- 5 that

$$NG_j = \rho \sim NG_j \cup NG_c \qquad (P2 - 2)$$

Since NG_j is a neural basin BS, then (Rocha, 1981)

$$cp(NG_j) \to 1 \quad cp(\mathcal{C}_{NS} NG_j) \to 0 \text{ or } -1 \quad (P2 - 3)$$

Therefore

$$\lim_{\rho\to 0} cp(\rho \sim NG_j) \to 1 \qquad (P2 - 4)$$

$$\lim_{\rho\to 0} cp(\mathcal{C}_{NS} \rho \sim NG_j) \to 0 \qquad (P2 - 5)$$

In such a condition, any new model M_k to be learned must be developed as (Theorem M-2)

$$M_k \subset L(NG_k) \qquad (P2 - 6)$$

$$NG_k = \rho \sim NG_j \cup NG'_c \qquad (P2 - 7)$$

If NG_c in P2 - 2 presents $cp(NG_c) \to 1$

then $NG_k = \rho \sim NG_j \cup NG_c = NG_j \quad (P2 - 8)$

According with Definition M-0, this implies a strong autonomy to M_j. On the contrary, if $cp(NG_c) \to 0$

then $NG_k \neq NG_j \qquad (P2 - 8')$

because NG_c tends to be different from NG_c'. This means a high plasticity to NG_j.

The results in theorem M-2 are tigthly dependent on the assumed limit of ρ determining the actual workable $\rho \sim NG$. Precision and rigor increases as $\rho \to 0$. Relaxing this limit, NS may favour the autonomy of a considered model M_j, because if may, favour conclusions of the type

$$NPR(M_j): W \times SS \to E' \; ? \; E \qquad (16a)$$

and/or $NPR(M_j): R \times ES \to R'_w \; ? \; R_w \qquad (16b)$

instead of $NPR(M_j): E' x\, AS \to F' ? \; M_j \quad (16c)$

Assumptions 16a and/or 16b mean that observation and conclusion are questioned whereas no doubt is raised about the pertinence of the evidences to the domain of the model M_j (16c).

Strong autonomy may favour 16a, b as a consequence from P2 - 8, whereas plasticity implies the opposite. In such a context, the concepts of acceptability ($a(M_j)$) and refutability ($R(M_j)$) of a model M_j (Popper, 1967) turn to be much more useful than of predictability, disagreement and error.

5. ACCEPTABILITY AND REFUTABILITY

Let be given the following automaton

$$NA = \{E, Z, S, F^n(Z), \P, \beta_a, \beta_r\} \qquad (17a)$$

with 1) the set of input as a set E of evidences; 2) the set Z of states as the set of graphs NG in NS; 3) ¶ as the family of transition matrices of connectivities in NS

$$cp(NG) = \bigvee_{\rho}\bigwedge^{S} \mu(\Gamma,t).f(r).\mu(e,e').\mu(sc,sc')$$
(17b)

4) G as the set of initial states or germs in NS

$$G = \{\rho \sim NG\}_{NS} \qquad (17c)$$

5) the set of final states $F^n(Z)$ as a ρ-level set

$$F^o(Z) = Z \qquad (17d)$$

$$F^1(Z) = \{f_1 \mid f_1 . Z \to Z' \subset Z, cp\, \mathcal{C}_{NS} NG > cp\, \mathcal{C}_{NS} NG'\}$$
(17e)

and so recursively

$$F^n(Z) = F^n(F^{n-1}(Z)); \; \lim_{n\to\delta} cp(\mathcal{C}_{NS} NG) \to 0$$
(17f)

$$6)\ \beta_a: Z \times F^n(Z) \to [0, 1] \qquad (17g)$$

as a family of relations measuring the pertinence of the actual state $z \in Z$ to the actual set $F^n(Z)$ of final states:

$$\mu_a(z, F^n(Z)) \to \begin{cases} 1 & \text{if } z \in Z \text{ tends to belong to } F^n(Z) \\ 0 & \text{otherwise} \end{cases} \qquad (17h)$$

$$7)\ \beta_r: Z \times F^n(Z) \to [0, 1]$$

as a family of relations between Z and the actual $F^n(Z)$, such that

$$\mu_r(Z, F^n(Z)) \to \begin{cases} 1 & \text{if } n \to 0 \text{ and } F^n(Z) \to Z \\ 0 & \text{otherwise} \end{cases}$$

In such a context, a set of evidences E is assumed to belong to the domain of a model M_j (Gaines and Kohout, 1976; Hopcroft and Ullman, 1969; Negoita and Ralescu, 1975) if

$$z = \P(z', E), \; z' = \rho \sim NG_j \in G$$

and $\mu_a(z, F^n(Z)) \to 1 \qquad (18a)$

In other words, E is accepted by M_j if it promotes a state transition from an initial state $\rho \sim NG_i$ or $\rho \sim NG_j \in G$ to a final state $NG_j \in Z$ belonging to the defined set of final states $F^n(Z)$. Thus the acceptability of E as set of evidences for NG is measured by $\mu_a(z, F^n(Z))$, such that:

18b) as $\mu_a(z, F^n(Z)) \to 1$ greater is the acceptability of E.

Because final states

$$NG_j = \rho \sim NG_j \cup NG_c, \; \mu(NG_c, \mathcal{C}_{NS} \rho \sim NG_j) \to 1$$
(18c)

tend to be included in $F^n(Z)$ as $n \to 0$, the relation $\mu_r(Z, F^n(Z))$ measures the refutability of the hypothesis in 18a, that is

18d) as $\mu_r(Z, F^n(Z)) \to 1$ greater is the

refutability of E.

Proposition M-3: Let δ_t at the instant t be a monotonic function of $a_{t-1}(M_j)$ at the instant t-1, then

$\delta_t = f(1/a_{t-1}(M_j))$ for cooperative actions (19a)

$\delta_t = f(a_{t-1}(M_j))$ for competitive actions (19b)

and coercion is favoured for 19a and avoided for 19b.

Also, the dependence of δ on $a(M_j)$ may be established in two different but not mutually exclusive modes. δ is dependent on $a(M_j)$ evaluated by the same automaton using it to calculate $F^n(Z)$ if the homotopic mode is considered, whereas it is dependent on $a(M_j)$ calculated by an automaton NA_i other NA_j accepting NG_j if the heterotopic mode is concerned. In this latter condition

$$\delta_j = f(a_i(M_j)) \text{ or } f(1/a_i(M_j))$$

δ_j being a parameter for NA_j and $a_i(M_j)$ being furnished by $NA_i \subset \mathcal{C}_{NS} NA_j$

The homotopic mode describes the mechanisms of neural facilitation ($\delta = f(1/a(M_j))$) and depression ($\delta = f(a(M_j))$) following the activation of a given pathway, as observed in the case of postetanic facilitation or inhibition (Magleby, 1973; Magleby and Zengel, 1975; Model et al, 1975; Segundo et al, 1969). The heterotopic mode is related to those phenomena of heterosynaptic facilitation and competion, by means of which cooperative systems facilitate each other and antagonistic ones compete for the dominion of a given synapsis (Hamory, 1973, Sidman and Ravick, 1973).

Theorem M-3: The models M_k preconized by theorem M-2 as developed from $\rho \sim M_j$ or $\mathcal{C}_{NS}\rho \sim M_j$ are those accepted by NA_j with refutabilities < .5 and > .5, respectively.

Proof: Theorem M-2 preconizes that any

$$M_k \subset L(NG_k)$$

is performed over

$NG_k = (cp(\rho \sim NG_j) \vee cp(\rho \sim \mathcal{C}_{NS} NG_j) \vee cp(NG_c))$ (T3 - 1)

if $d(M_j) + e(M_j) \neq .5$ (T3 - 2)

However $cp(NG) = \underset{\Gamma}{\overset{s}{\vee\wedge}} \mu(N_a, N_j)$ or $\mu_t(N_a, N_j)$ (T3 - 3)

and from eqs 9d, 11b, c and d and 12a, b, c and d

$cp(NG) = \underset{\Gamma}{\overset{s}{\vee\wedge}} \mu(\Gamma,t).f(r).\mu(e,e').\mu(sc,sc')$ (T3 - 4)

Also, NSP is a partially closed process permitting the following transformations

$NPR(\rho \sim M_j): M_k \times ES \rightarrow R_w$ (T3 - 5)

$: R_w \times SS \rightarrow E$ (T3 - 6)

$: E \times AS \rightarrow M_k \text{ ? } R$ (T3 - 7)

which guarantee that M_k can be inserted into E in 17a. Thus the acceptability of M_k in the context R may now be evaluated by NA_j

The acceptability of M_k by NA_j may be made to approach 1 by adjusting $\lim_{n\to\delta} F^n(Z)$.

This implies $\mu_a(Z, F^n(Z)) \rightarrow 1$ as $n \rightarrow 0$ (T3 - 8)

If $\mu_r(Z, F^n(Z)) < .5$ (T3 - 9)

then from 18c $\mu(NG_c, \mathcal{C}_{NS}\rho \sim NG_j) < .5$ (T3 - 10)

and we may conclude that

$cp(\rho \sim NG_j) > cp\, \mathcal{C}_{NS}\rho \sim NG_j$ (T3 - 11)

and that NG_k in T4 - 1 tends to become

$NG_k = \rho \sim NG_j \cup NG_c$ (T3 - 12)

On the contrary, if

$\mu_r(Z, F^n(Z)) > .5$ (T3 - 13)

their NG_k must tend to be

$NG_k = \mathcal{C}_{NS}\rho \sim NG_j \cup NG_c$

Here, an important remark is the fact that both relations $\mu_a(Z, F^n(Z))$ and $\mu_r(Z, F^n(Z))$ may have a subjective evaluation because they depend on self-observation. Because of this, the results in theorem M-4 become very dependent on the ratio between $\mu_a(z, F^n(Z))$ and $\mu_r(Z, F^n(Z))$, which measures the relative importance given to acceptability or refutability in the case of the fuzzy decisions preconized in theorems 3 and 4. In such line of reasoning, we can define the degree of coercion in a given NS as

$$c(NS) = \mu_a(z, F^n(Z))/\mu_r(Z, F^n(Z)) \quad (20)$$

keeping in mind that this measurement is both environmental and genetically dependent.

6. INDUCTIVE AND DEDUCTIVE PROCESSES

Let be given two automata NA_d, NA_i

$NA_x = \{E, Z_x, F^n(Z_x), \P_x, \beta_a^x, \beta_r^x\}$ (21a)

such that 1) in NA_d

$cp(NG) = \mu(\Gamma,t).f(r).\underset{\Gamma}{\overset{s}{\vee\wedge}} \mu(e,e').\mu(sc,sc')$ (21b)

2) in NA_i

$$cp(NG) = \mu(sc,sc').\bigvee_{\Gamma}\bigwedge^{s} \mu(\Gamma,t).f(r).\mu(e,e') \quad (21c)$$

3) E, Z_x, $F^n(Z_x)$, β^x_a and β^x_r

are defined in a similar way to that used in the case of NA in 17.

Also let be: $Z_x = Z$ (21d)

$F^{n_i}(Z_i) = F^{n_d}(Z_d) = F^n(Z)$ if $n_i = n_d = n$ (21e)

and let no restriction to be imposed to

β^d_a, β^j_a and β_a or β^d_r, β^i_r and β_r (21f)

Besides the above, NA_i and NA_d will be coupled in a heterotopic mode, that is

$\delta_x = f(a_y(M))$, $\delta_y = f(a_x(M))$ (21g)

or $\delta_x = f(1/a_y(M))$, $\delta_y = f(1/a_x(M))$ (21h)

with $x = i$ or d and $y = d$ or i.

Theorem M-4: There exists an algorithm to approach the acceptability of a model M_j as evaluated by NA_i or NA_d to that calculated for the same model in NA.

Proof:- Let be considered that at the instant t

$cp_x(M_j) > cp_y(M_j)$ $F^{n_x}(Z_x) = F^{n_y}(Z_y)$

$a_x(M_j) > a_y(M_j)$ (T4 - 1)

Now, in the case of competitive systems and at the instant t

$\delta_x = f(a_y(M))$, $\delta_y = f(a_x(M))$ (T4 - 2)

such that $\delta_y > \delta_x$, $n_y > n_x$

$F^{n_y}(Z_y) \supset F^{n_x}(Z_x)$ (T4 - 3)

In such a conditions

$a_y(M_j)$, $r_y(M_j) \to 0$ and $a_x(M)$, $r_x(M) \to 1$ as $t \to \infty$ (T4 - 4)

In the case of cooperative systems and at the instant t

$\delta_x = f(1/a_y(M_j))$, $\delta_y = f(1/a_x(M_j))$ (T4 - 5)

such that

$\delta_y < \delta_x$, $n_y < n_x$, $F^{n_y}(Z_y) \subset F^{n_x}(Z_x)$ (T4-6)

In such a conditions

$r_x(M)/r_y(M) \to 0$ and $a_x(M)/a_y(M) \to 1$ (T4 - 7)

If, initially

a) $a(M_j) > a_x(M_j) > a_y(M_j)$ (T4 - 8)

then $a_x(M_j)$ may be approached to $a(M_j)$ in a competitive system by means of a max operation of acceptabilities, because from T4 - 4

$a_x(M_j) \vee a_y(M_j) = a_x(M_j) \to a(M_j)$ as $t \to \infty$ (T4 - 9)

b) $a_x(M_j) > a_y(M_j) > a(M_j)$ (T4 - 10)

then $a_y(M_j)$ may be approached to $a(M_j)$ in a competitive NA_i, NA_d system by means of a min operation of acceptabilities, because from T4 - 4

$a_x(M_j) \wedge a_y(M_j) = a_y(M_j) \to a(M_j)$ as $t \to \infty$ (T4 - 11)

c) $a_y(M_j) < a(M_j) < a_x(M_j)$

then $a_x(M_j)$ or $a_y(M_j)$ may be approached to $a(M_j)$ in a cooperative system NA_i, NA_d by means of max or min operations of acceptabilities, because from T4 - 7

$a_x(M_j) \vee a_y(M_j)$ or $a_x(M_j) \wedge a_y(M_j) \to a(M_k)$ as $t \to \infty$ (T4 - 12)

Because the refutabilities $r_x(M_j)$ and/or $r_y(M_y)$ may be made equal to $r(M_j)$ depending on the degrees of coercion in NS

$c(NS) = f(\beta_a/\beta_r)$, $c_d(NS) = f(\beta^d_a/\beta^d_r)$ and $c_i(NS) = f(\beta^i_a/\beta^i_r)$

we may propose

Theorem M-5: Theorem M-4 is a procedure in order to obtain an equivalence between NA and the system NA_i, NA_j.

Definition M-4: Inductive learning is characterized as an external refeared process as described by the automaton NA_j.

Definition M-5: Deductive learning is characterized as a self-refeared process as described by the automaton NA_d.

Conditioning (including operant conditioning) is the best studied paradigm of inductive learning, which has in turn been succesfully formalized (Rocha, 1981). In contrast, deductive processes has been worked by neurophysiology if not by all neurosciences with less impetus. The difficulties to both the theoretical and laboratorial approaches of the human reasoning are the justification for such discrepancy concerning the attention experimentally paid to these two processes. However, the recent development of the fuzzy theory, at one hand, and the increasing use of electroencephalographic techniques to study normal human brains (see, e.g., John, 1978, Rocha and Françozo, 1980), at the other hand, render now deductive learning a reachable subject to electrophysiological research.

7. CONCLUSION OR THE DEDUCTIVE PROCESS NEUROPHYSIOLOGICALLY APPROACHED

Let $M_j \vdash M_k$ (22a)

to denote that M_k may be deductible from M_j in the context R, also let be given the truth set

$$V = \{\text{true, false}\} \qquad (22b)$$

then from the previons section and from Gaines and Kohout, 1976:

$$a(M_k):\ (M_j \vdash M_k) \times V \times R \to [0,\ 1] \qquad (22c)$$

$$r(M_k):\ (\mathcal{C}_{NS} M_j \vdash M_k) \times V \times R \to [0,\ 1] \qquad (22d)$$

This implies that if M_k is deductible from M_j in the context R with the acceptability a (M_k)

$$M_j \underset{R}{\overset{a(M_k)}{\vdash}} M_k \qquad (22e)$$

then M_k may also be derived from $_{NS}M_j$ with the acceptability $\bar{a}(M_k) = r(M_k)$

$$\mathcal{C}_{NS} M_j \underset{R}{\overset{\bar{a}(M_k)}{\vdash}} M_k \qquad (22f)$$

Also, M_k and M_j are inconsistent in the context R if (Rocha, 1980)

$$c_p(NG_j \cap NG_k) = 0,\quad c_p(NG_k \cap NG_j) = 0 \qquad (22g)$$

because this implies

$$NG_j \cap NG_k = \emptyset \qquad (22h)$$

Now, we may propose the following modification of definition 1 in Loefgreen, 1976:

Definition M-6: Let E be a description of an observation and $H = \rho \sim M \cup L(NG)$ be a description of an hypothesis with respect to a priori knowledge R, thus $\rho \sim M \subset R$, such that E and H are consistent with respect to R and H is genuinely hypothetical ($H \cap \mathcal{C}_w R_w = \emptyset$).

Then

i) E verifies H in R with the acceptability a(H) if

$$E \underset{R}{\overset{a(H)}{\vdash}} H$$

ii) E supports H in R with the acceptability a(H) if

$$H \underset{R}{\overset{a(H)}{\vdash}} E \quad \text{and} \quad \underset{R}{\not\vdash} E$$

that is to say E is not self-deductible in the context R

iii) E falsifies H in R with a degree r(H) if

$$E \underset{R}{\overset{r(H)}{\vdash}} \mathcal{C}_{NS} H$$

iv) E is neutral for H in R if R(H, E) inconsistent, that is to say H and E are inconsistent in the context R but not to the context R.

1) E confirms H in R with acceptability a(H) if i or ii

2) E has a relevance for H in R if 1 or iii,

3) E is irrelevant for H in R if iv.

Theorem M-6: The following statements are equivalent

E falsifies H in R with a degree r(H)

E verifies $\mathcal{C}_{NS} H$ in R with a degree r(H)

$\mathcal{C}_U E$ supports H in R with a degree a(H)

the ratio a(H)/r(H) depending on the degree of coercion in NS.

Proof:- A consequence from 22c, d, i and iii above and 20.

Sensory stimulus may elicit well characterized electrical waves in the electroencephalogram (EEG) which are called evoked potentials (EP). John et al, 1975 demonstrated that such EPs may be splited into early components related with the physical aspects of the stimulus and latter waves well correlated with both the psychological and/or the behavioral response of the subject. The early components may, therefore, be assumed as reflecting the neural work extracting the sensory evidences E used latter by learned models M_j, as indicated by the following waves.

Sutton et al, 1965 have shown that EPs to different sensory modalities are dependent on both the guess and the uncertainty of the subject about the stimulus modality, confirming the partial closure of NPR. Begleiter et al., 1973 recorded EPs correlated with expected strong or week stimuli if, instead of them, mediuns ones were presented, thus supporting the idea of a NPR modulated by an attentional process.

Sutton et al., 1967 have demonstrated that when subjected predicted a stimulus pattern distribution, EPs signalized both the agreements as well as the errors. Furthermore, for these latters, EPs appeared both in respect to the moment of the expected as well as the actual incoming stimuli. These results may be interpreted as EPs signalized both the acceptability and refutability of the old hypothesis.

Rocha and Françozo, 1978 and 1980 a, b studying the EPs to the intonational emphasis carrying the linguistic contrast

GIVEN x NEW in sentences, observed that

1) the evoked activity became earlier as the repetition of the same emphasis in the same sentence increased the acceptability of a pattern or model;

2) a new EP appeared besides the old one(s) whenever the intonational emphasis changed in the same sentence, signalizing both the error as well as the acceptability of the new hypothesis;

3) this was further confirmed, because repetition of the new pattern reprised the same behavior in 1 and resulted also in the reduction of the EP related with the previons emphatic position, and

4) evoked activity was correlated to the perceived better than to the actual physical emphasis, showing that coercion may vanish refutability.

In verbal communication, theme is the subject of this communication and rheme is what is said about it (Rocha and Françozo, 1980). Speech (S) may be organized into two different ways concerning the theme/rheme relation. In a divergent approach, theme T is given first followed by the set of evidences supporting its rheme $\mathcal{R}$

$$T\mathcal{R} \mathrel{\mathop{\vdash}\limits^{\rho_1}_{C}} \mathcal{R} \mathrel{\mathop{\vdash}\limits^{\rho_2}_{C}} E_i \dots \mathrel{\mathop{\vdash}\limits^{\rho n}_{C}} E_j \qquad (23a)$$

whereas the opposite is true in the case of a convergent strategy

$$E_j \mathrel{\mathop{\vdash}\limits^{\rho_1}_{C}} \dots \mathrel{\mathop{\vdash}\limits^{\rho_k}_{C}} E_i \mathrel{\mathop{\vdash}\limits^{\rho_{k+1}}_{C}} T \mathrel{\mathop{\vdash}\limits^{\rho_{k+2}}_{C}} T\mathcal{R}$$

(23b)

The mode in 23a implies $T\mathcal{R}$ supported in the context C by a set of evidences $E_i \dots E_j$ ordered by their degree of acceptability ρ_i. The approach in 23b means that a set of evidences $E_j \dots E_i$, ordered by ρ_i in the context C, verifies a rheme $\mathcal{R}$ about the theme T.

Because $T\mathcal{R}$ must be contained in C

$$\begin{aligned} NPR(C): & \; S \times SS \to E & (24a)\\ : & \; E \times AS \to T\mathcal{R} \subset C & (24b)\end{aligned}$$

different decodings may be expected in different NSs enjoying different realities or contexts. Also, acceptabilities and refutabilities are dependent on C (see 17c, d and e and 18b and d), therefore different evaluations of ρ are expected even for those NS decoding the same $T\mathcal{R}$.

We have played a divergent text to subjects while recording their EEG and latter asked them to recall in writen the perceived $T\mathcal{R}$ and the evidences supporting it (Rocha and Françozo, 1980 a, b). The text deals with the country's problems in the field of science, technology and energy.

Briefly, we have observed that subjects selected fewer evidences either to support $T\mathcal{R}$ in 23a (80% of the subjects) or to verify it in a convergent decoding (20% of the subjects). In many instances, subject chose only part of a sentence as relevant to the decoded $T\mathcal{R}$ or even have joined parts of different sentences into new evidences. The choice of $T\mathcal{R}$s other than the original one in either strategy, beared a strong relation with environmental (social, cultural, etc) context of the subject or with incidental variations of context in news media related with the used text.

Paralleling such findings, we discovered a coherent variability of the recorded EEG. First of all, only those sentences or part of them judged relevant to the decoding, elicited an augmented EEG activity. The contrast was greatly evidenced in those instances when just a few words in a sentence was picked up, because only these words triggered clear EPs in the corresponding EEG epoch. Besides this, the results seems to point to a correlation between the degree of acceptability of an evidence and the amount of elicited EEG activity, because both the amplitude and standart deviation of averaged EPs to repeated thematic words (the relevant words for both T and $\mathcal{R}$) beared a correlation with the subject performance, evaluated both by the number of recalled sentences and the degree of concatenation between them. As much as the recalled text structure turned lousy, greater was the standart deviation and less averaged the EPs.

Summing up, all the above experimental results supports the idea that EEG may disclose the neural activity undergoing complex human behaviors as fuzzy reasoning during speech processing. This opens the pathway for a joint approach by formal fuzzy theories and experimental electrophysiology in the attempt to learn how to learn. The necessary condition for this exciting endeavour is a close development between fuzzy systems and neurosciences.

REFERENCES:

(1) Begleiter, H., Porjfesz, B., Yerre, C. and Kissin, B. Evoked potential correlates of expected stimulus intensity. Science, 179(1973) 814-816.

(2) Gaines, B.R. and Kohout, L.J. The logic of automata. Int. J. Gen. Systems, 2(1976) 191-208.

(3) Hamori, J. The inductive role of presynaptic axons in the development of postsynaptic spines. Brain Res. 62(1973) 337-344.

(4) Hernandez-Péon, R., Scherrer, H. and Jouvet, M. Modification of electric activity in Cochlear Nucleus during "attention" in unanesthetized cats. Science, 123(1956) 331-332.

(5) Hopecroft, J. E. and Ullmaw, J.D. Formal languages and their relation to automata (Addison Wesley, 1969).

(6) John, E.R. Switchboard versus statistical theories of learning and memory. Science, 177(1972) 850-864.

(7) John, E.R., Barlet, F., Shimokochi, M. and Kleinman, D. Electrophysiological signs of the readout memory I: Raw data observations. J. Behav. Biol. 14(1975) 247-282.

(8) John, E.R. and Schwartz, E.L. The neurophysiology of information processing and cognition. An. Rev. Psychol. 29(1978) 1-29.

(9) Kleinman, D. and John, E.R. Contradiction of auditory and visual information by brain stimulation. Science, 187(1975) 271-273.

(10) Loefgren. Descriptive and interpretative complexities. Int. J. Gen. Systems 3(1976) 26-39.

(11) Magleby, K.L. The effect of repetitive stimulation on facilitation of transmitter release at the frog neuromuscular junction. J. Physiol. (Lond.) 234(1973) 327-352.

(12) Magleby, K.L. and Zengel, J.E. A dual effect of repetitive stimulation on post-tetanic potentiation of transmitter release at the frog neuromuscular junction. J. Physiol. (Lond.) 245(1975) 163-182.

(13) Model, P.G., Highstein, S.M. and Bennet, M.V.L. Depletion of vesicles and fatigue transmission at vertebrate central synapse. Brain Res. 98(1975) 209-218.

(14) Negoita, C.V. and Ralescu, D.A. Applications of fuzzy sets to systems analysis. (Birkhause Verlag, 1975).

(15) Popper, K.R. El desarrollo del conocimiento científico. Conjeturas y refutaciones (Paidós, Buenos Aires, 1967).

(16) Rocha, A.F. Brain's entropy partitions. An. Acad. Brasil. Cienc. 51 (1979) 591-595.

(17) Rocha, A.F. Temporal influences of reticular formation on sensory processing, in J.A. Hobson and M.A.B. Brazier (eds.), The Reticular Formation Revisited, (Raven Press, 1980)

(18) Rocha, A.F. Basic properties of neural circuits. Fuzzy Sets and Systems (in press) 1981.

(19) Rocha, A.F. and Françozo, E. Linguistic performance in the context of neurophysiology. Society for Neurosciences 4(1978) 155.

(20) Rocha, A.F. and Françozo, E. EEG correlates of thematic structure in Portuguese XXVIII Int. Cong.Physiol. Scie., Budapest (1980a), pp 665.

(21) Rocha, A.F. and Françozo, E. EEG activity during the speech perception. Rev. Phon. Appl. 55-56(1980 b) 307-311.

(22) Rocha, A.F., Françozo, E., Hadler, M.I., Balduino, M.A. Neural Languages. Fuzzy Sets and Systems 3 (1980) 11-35.

(23) Segundo, J.P. Takenaka, T. and Encapo, H. Electrophysiology of bulbar reticular formation. J. Neurophys. 30(1969) 1194-1220.

(24) Sidman, R.L. and Ravick, P. Neuronal migration, with special reference to developing human brain: a review. Brain Res. 63(1973) 1-36.

(25) Sutton, S., Braren, M., Zubin, J. and John, E.R. Evoked potential correlates of stimulus uncertainty. Science, 150(1965) 1187-1188.

(26) Sutton, S., Tueting, P., Zubin, J. and John, E.R. Information delivery and the sensory evoked potential. Science, 155(1967) 1436-1439.

ACKNOWLEDGMENT

I am grateful to Miss Mildred A. Heinzl for typing the text.

PART FIVE

EXPERT SYSTEMS AND MEDICAL DIAGNOSIS

Approximate Reasoning in Decision Analysis
M.M. Gupta and E. Sanchez (eds.)

A SURVEY ON MEDICAL DIAGNOSIS AND FUZZY SUBSETS

KLAUS-PETER ADLASSNIG

Department of Medical Computer Sciences
(Director: Prof.Dr. G. Grabner)
University of Vienna
A-1090 Vienna, Garnisongasse 13, Austria

Fuzzy set theory with its capability of defining inexact medical entities as fuzzy subsets, with its linguistic approach providing an excellent approximation to medical texts as well as its power of approximate reasoning seems to be perfectly appropriate for designing and developing computer-assisted diagnostic, prognostic and treatment recommendation systems. The detailed survey of fuzzy approaches to medical decision making shows the wide and deep interest of researchers all over the world to find a solid fuzzy theoretical basis for the representation of medical knowledge as well as for the diagnostic process and to use it in practical applications.

Keywords: fuzzy set theory, medical diagnosis, survey.

1. INTRODUCTION

Since the very beginning of developing computer-assisted diagnostic methods and medical decision aids in the years 1958 /1/ and 1959 /2/, a great number of medical diagnostic models applied in different medical fields with varying results (bibliographies in computer-assisted diagnosis can be found in /3-5/) have been proposed and a certain number of them has been tested.

The first logical approach to medical decision making (as opposed to numerical models [1] based on Bayes' Theorem, likelihood ratio, linear and nonlinear discriminant analysis, clustering methods, factor and principal component analysis, decision analysis, adaptive threshold logic unit, perceptron algorithm, etc.) has been suggested by LEDLEY and LUSTED in 1959 /2/ (see also LEDLEY /6/).

Since that year, several systems using Boolean logic to express functional and etiological relationships between symptoms and diseases have been proposed /7/ and established /8-16/. In 1969 GANGL, et al. /11/ proved the usefulness of such approaches. The described batch system considered 82 liver diseases and 323 symptoms (history, physical examination, laboratory tests, X-ray findings, special tests). In each of the 20 test cases the clinically confirmed diagnosis was put out as diagnostic hypothesis (among 3-6 others). These results were very encouraging.

Later then, as a logical consequence, the symptoms and diagnoses were not only considered to be present or absent as in two-valued systems but the truth-values "present", "absent", or "not examined" were assigned to symptoms and "present" (confirmed), "absent" (excluded), and "possible" (hypothesis) to diagnoses. Thus tri-valued logic was introduced as a means for the representation of medical knowledge /17-20/.

In the report about the computer-assisted medical diagnostic consultation system CADIAG-1 /19/, the tri-valued logical system of KLEENE /21/ seems to be adequate to formalize medical judgement in an abstract and computable way, understandable by and acceptable to the medical community. This system has now been established for 308 diseases from internal medicine (rheumatology, hepatology, coagulation defects and pancreatic diseases) and takes about 2.500 symptoms into account.

The possibility of expressing medical knowledge in terms of predicate logic was also mentioned in /19/.

In the last ten years, some very powerful computer-based medical decision and consultation systems have been developed by researchers working in the field of artificial intelligence. SHORTLIFFE, et al. give in /22/, among others, an excellent introduction to these symbolic reasoning approaches.

The MYCIN system (see /22,23/) has been designed to assist physicians in the detection of the cause of infectious diseases and to recommend therapies. The medical knowledge about the diseases considered is represented in IF-THEN production rules associated with certainty factors.

CASNET /22,24,25/ offers associational links between Boolean combinations of tests and single pathophysiological causal states that carry confidence factors. Furthermore, state network rules associated with a given likelihood for the effect S_j to follow from the occurrence of the cause S_i are used in CASNET. Finally, classification rules that are Boolean combinations of confirmed or denied states implying diagnostic statements are incorporated in order to represent medical knowledge. CASNET was created for glaucoma consultation.

The EXPERT system /26-28/ permits the definition of rules with confidence levels and hierarchical concepts to convert medical knowledge into a computable form. It has been applied in rheumatology, endocrinology and ophtalmology /29/.

A further system applicable in the field of internal medicine is called INTERNIST /22,30,31/. Symptom-disease (frequency of occurrence) as well as disease-symptom relationships (evoking strength) are stored on the basis of an ad hoc scoring method.

MYCIN, CASNET and EXPERT are logical in the sense that relationships between all kinds of observations on the patient form the basis for IF-THEN inferences (modus ponens in classical logic, implication in terms of logical operations) but the inferences do not necessarily have a definite character. They are associated with certainty factors, confidence factors, likelihoods, or confidence levels that express the fuzziness, the non-definiteness of the relationships. The "evoking strength" of the INTERNIST system also belongs into this category.

Other authors who use IF-THEN statements

but without any elements of uncertainty are BUTTON /32/ and GIESZL /33/.

Fuzzy set theory with its capability of defining inexact medical entities as fuzzy subsets, with its linguistic approach providing an excellent approximation to medical texts as well as its power of approximate reasoning, seems to be perfectly appropriate for designing and developing computer-assisted diagnostic, prognostic and treatment recommendation systems. A detailed review of fuzzy approaches to medical diagnosis published until now follows in the next paragraphs.

In order to conclude this section it should be mentioned that disease descriptions using the theory of formal languages /34/ or automata /35,36/ as well as methods using decision table techniques /37/ also belong into the category of logical diagnostic systems.

2. REVIEW OF PUBLISHED METHODS

2.1. Symptoms, signs, and test results and fuzzy subsets

ALBIN /38/, PEREZ-OJEDA /39/, MOON, et al. /40/, and ESOGBUE and ELDER /41/ propose the application of fuzzy subsets to determine *normal* or *pathological* ranges as well as the boundaries for *low*, *normal*, *high* or *normal*, *slightly decreased*, *decreased*, etc. for clinical or diagnostic tests. The membership functions of these fuzzy subsets define the affiliation strength of a numerical test result in the fuzzy subsets under consideration. In this way, ALBIN /38/ presents appropriate membership functions for *normal* and *long IVY bleeding time*, for decreased, *slightly decreased*, and *normal platelet count*, for *normal*, *slightly long*, and *long thrombin time*, etc. In /41/, for example, a suitable linear function for the fuzzy subset Ω_t of *abnormal cholesterol* levels, expressed in milligrams per 100 milliliters of serum, is given by

$$\mu_{\Omega_t}(r_t)=\begin{cases} 0 & \text{for } r_t<260 \\ \dfrac{r_t}{340}-\dfrac{26}{34} & \text{for } 260\leq r_t\geq 600 \\ 1 & \text{for } r_t>600. \end{cases} \qquad (1)$$

where $r_t\in\Omega_t$ is any possible numerical result of the cholesterol test t and Ω_t expresses the set including all possible test results. Thus, the degree of abnormality of the cholesterol test result is reflected by the membership function $\mu_{\Omega_t}(r_t)\in[0,1]$. Performing the cholesterol test on a patient and getting a result of $r_t<260$ mg/100 ml means that the patient shows a *normal cholesterol* level. When a test result $r_t>600$ mg/100 ml is obtained, the patient under consideration reveals an *abnormal cholesterol* level. Furthermore, a test result between 260 and 430 mg/100 ml ($r_t=430$ mg/100 ml is the value where $\mu_{\Omega_t}(r_t)$ becomes 0.5) seems to be "more normal" than a test result between 430 and 600 mg/100 ml.

ESOGBUE and ELDER /41/ propose the use of fuzzy subsets to characterize the severity levels of nonbinary symptoms such as *headache* or *cyanosis*. The membership functions would reflect the painfulness or blueness of these symptoms. But compared to the laboratory test descriptions using fuzzy subsets, the definition of the reference sets for symptom fuzzy subsets is less natural and clear. A subjective (patient or physician) assignment of the observed symptom value (patient's pain, or blue discoloration) in the fuzzy subset is needed.

PEREZ-OJEDA /39/ and MOON, et al. /40/ use linguistic modifiers (also termed hedges /42-44/) to calculate the degree of membership of a test result in the fuzzy subset S_2 out of the degree of membership in S_1. Linguistic modifiers are for example very, more or less, not, etc. By using them, MOON, et al. /40/ compute the degree of membership of the result x of the urine sodium concentration test in the fuzzy subset very high urine sodium concentration $\mu_{S_2}(x)$ out of high urine sodium concentration $\mu_{S_1}(x)$ by performing

$$\mu_{S_2}(x)=\mu_{\underline{very}\ S_1}(x)=[\mu_{S_1}(x)]^2. \qquad (2)$$

In /41/, ESOGBUE and ELDER introduce fuzzy subsets to determine diseases or disorders in the patient's past history which might be missed or remain undiagnosed. The presence or absence of such diseases might then be decided on from past undiagnosed symptoms, but the physician only considers the "prominent" symptoms of past diseases. The fuzzy subset Σ_j, containing the prominent symptoms of past disease j is defined as

$$\Sigma_j=\{(x_{ij},\mu_{\Sigma_j}(x_{ij}))/x_{ij}\in\beta_j,\mu_{\Sigma_j}(x_{ij})\geq\alpha\} \qquad (3)$$

where $\mu_{\Sigma_j}(x_{ij})\in[0,1]$ and $0\leq\alpha\leq1$.

The set of possible symptoms for past undiagnosed disease j is β_j, where $1\leq j\leq p$ and p is the number of undiagnosed diseases in the patient's past history. Wherever the physician designates the membership function $\mu_{\Sigma_j}(x_{ij})$ of symptom x_{ij} for disease j over a specified level α, the symptom of β_j becomes a "prominent" symptom.

2.2. Diseases/diagnoses and fuzzy subsets

SMETS, et al. /45/ mention the fuzziness of diagnostic terms like arteriosclerosis or angina pectoris. Mostly, diseases are not clearly defined entities. It is often impossible to determine precisely the symptoms related to a disease. Diagnoses are defined to be fuzzy subsets with symptoms as elements. The symptoms are combined with a degree of membership which characterizes the intensity of belonging to the fuzzy subset that represents the disease under consideration.

ALBIN /38/ considers patients suffering from a certain disease as points in the n-dimensional symptom space S, where n is the number of symptoms taken into account. Now, every given patient with disease D_j exhibiting symptoms $(S_1,...,S_n)\in S$ is combined with a degree of membership $\mu_{D_i}(S_1,...,S_n)\in[0,1]$ that shows the affiliation of the patient in D_i. Because $\mu_{D_i}(S_1,...,S_n)$ is not necessarily 1 for i=j and 0 for i≠j, patients suffering from the same disease do not form clusters with sharp boundaries.

2.3. Fuzzy relations between symptoms and diseases

In /39/, PEREZ-OJEDA proposes a network presentation of medical knowledge (associative memory, semantic network) in which the facts, symptoms, diseases, etc., are linked by relations. Six types of nodes are considered: disease-complex nodes, disease nodes, symptom-complex nodes, symptom nodes, statement nodes (relations) and test nodes. PEREZ-OJEDA translates medical statements like

"Acute pyelonephritis usually presents bladder irritation and infection." and "Acute pyelonephritis presents occasionally fever, or chills, and malaise." into

OR (usually (acute pyelonephritis, AND (bladder irritation, infection)), occasionally (acute pyelonephritis, AND (OR (fever, chills), malaise)).

The relations used in this information structure (usually, occasionally, always, almost always, etc.) are frequency or probabilistic modifiers. They are represented as fuzzy subsets, e.g.

always=0.1/0.7+0.3/0.8+0.6/0.9+1.0/1.0,

of the universe of discourse

U= 0+0.1+0.2+0.3+0.4+0.5+0.6+0.7+0.8+0.9+1.0.

A network in the fashion described above has been built which consists of 23 disease-complex and disease nodes, 101 symptom nodes and 227 statements.

SANCHEZ /46,47/ starts by considering the introduction of a fuzzy relation $R \subset S \times D$ between symptoms S and diseases D. SANCHEZ calls this "medical knowledge" expressing associations between symptoms and diseases. Let, further, A be a fuzzy subset of S related to the patient, then the computation of the max-min [2] composition $B=A \circ R$ [3] is assumed to describe the state of the patient in terms of diagnoses as a fuzzy subset B of D, characterized by its membership function

$$\mu_B(d)=\max_{s \in S} \min\{\mu_A(s);\mu_R(s,d)\},\quad d \in D. \tag{4}$$

If we consider several patients belonging to a set P and define a relation $Q \subset P \times S$, equation (4) becomes

$$\mu_T(p,d)=\max_{s \in S} \min\{\mu_Q(p,s);\mu_R(s,d)\}, \tag{5}$$

where $p \in P$ and T is a fuzzy relation on $P \times D$. The composition is written as

$$T=Q \circ R. \tag{6}$$

In fuzzy logic, (6) is called a compositional rule of inference (ZADEH /44/, BELLMANN and ZADEH /42/ or a fuzzy meta-implication (KAUFMANN /48/).

Moreover, the composition $B=A \circ R$ of a fuzzy subset A with a fuzzy relation R corresponds to the concept of the fuzzy conditional statement: IF A THEN B BY R (see /42,44,52,53/).

Applied in the field of medical diagnosis, the conditional statement allows to infer medical diagnoses B out of patient's symptoms A by means of the "medical knowledge" [4] which is presented in a relation matrix R established by medical specialists.

If the relationships between symptoms and diseases are considered to be either 0 (no relationships) or 1 (strong relationship), e.g. $\mu_R(s,d) \in \{0,1\}$, and patient's symptoms can be evaluated as 0 (absent) or 1 (present), e.g. $\mu_A(s) \in \{0,1\}$, then the max-min composition (4) or (5), respectively, is reduced to a Boolean sum-product composition (see also /46-48/).

JOLY, et al. /54/ report an application of the max-min composition in the field of cardiopathies. Cardiologists have determined a fuzzy relation R in order to reflect the degrees of association between five cardiological symptoms and the diagnoses normal [5], left ventricular hypertrophy and valvular cardiopathy. Five symptoms have been partitioned into classes (7 binary and 16 quantitative symptoms). The results obtained by the diagnostic procedure carried out for 21 patients with disparate cardiopathies were used "to confirm the classical concepts about cardiac function."

Another problem treated by SANCHEZ is related to equation (6). Knowing R and Q in (6), it is easy to find T. However, it is often as interesting to find R from given T and Q. In medicine, the problem frequently arises to determine degrees of association between symptoms and diseases from real patient data in Q and known diagnoses in T that have been established by medical specialists.

SANCHEZ presents in /46,47/ a solution of the problem by obtaining the greatest R for T=Q∘R (see also DUBOIS and PRADE /43/). But because of getting the greatest solution for R from the solution set, which also can be void, R may contain degrees of association between symptoms and diseases that are stronger than in reality. Thus it depends on the control structure of the computer-based diagnostic system that uses the computed R in which way results are interpreted: "diagnostic hypotheses or confirmed diagnoses".

The problem to find Q from given T and R can be considered in analogy to the problem mentioned above. This task presents itself when studying different fuzzy subsets of S, i.e. patient's symptom evaluations contained in Q that keep the composition T=Q∘R without changing T and R. The corresponding medical question would be: "How far can patients' data vary until other diagnoses have to be made?".

Obtaining the greatest Q of possible Q's is demonstrated by SANCHEZ in /46, 47/. In /46,47,55/ the converse problems of (6) treated in the last two sections are also investigated by SANCHEZ in terms of Brouwerian logic.

An application of a converse problem of (6) to the differential diagnosis of icterus is given by SOULA, et al./56/. In this example four diseases and ten symptoms are taken into acount.

Furthermore, in /57/, SANCHEZ has investigated the applicability of inverses of fuzzy relations in medical diagnosis.

SANCHEZ and SAMBUC /53/ and SAMBUC, et al. /58/ propose an interesting application of Φ-fuzzy sets [6] to the medical diagnostic problem. Φ-fuzzy sets take their values in the set of intervals of the form $[a_1,a_2]$ that are included in the real interval [0,1]. To illustrate how symptoms are represented in this way, we will quote an example from /58/ for the sign "pain on palpation" in patient p

$\mu(p)=[0,0]$	absence of pain on palpation
$\mu(p)=[0.8,0.8]$	marked pain
$\mu(p)=[0,1]$	totally indeterminate value
$\mu(p)=[0.2,0.6]$	there is hesitation between mild and relatively marked pain.

After defining suitable connectives for Φ-fuzzy variables, Φ-fuzzy functions of the form hyperthyreoidism = (tachycardia OR weight loss) AND (thermophobia OR increased thirst) AND (increased seric T4 values OR increased seric T3 values) are evaluated. The following possible results are noted in /58/:

hyperthyroidism=[0,1]: Impossible to determine from the available signs whether or not the patient is hyperthyroid.
hyperthyroidism=[0.7,0.8]: The patient suffers from frank hyperthyroidism.
hyperthyroidism=[0.35,0.45]: The patient presents a tableau of borderline hyperthyroidism.

ADLASSNIG proposes in /59/ an approach to computer-assisted medical diagnosis using fuzzy subsets that is based on two different relationships between symptoms S_i and diseases D_j:

1) S_iD_j-occurrence relationships and
2) S_iD_j-confirmability relationships.

Occurrence and confirmability are considered to be linguistic variables with always, almost always, very very often, very often, rather often, often, more or less often, unknown, more or less seldom, seldom, rather seldom, very seldom, very very seldom, almost never, never as elements (see BELLMAN and ZADEH /42/). Single S_iD_j-indications can be deduced from the S_iD_j-occurrence and S_iD_j-confirmability relationships. Examples for fuzzy subsets used to determine single S_iD_j-indications are strong and weak. Finally, one obtains total indications of the patient's symptom pattern to disease D_j by consolidating the single S_iD_j-indications.

TUSCH /60,61/ uses this model /59/ in a slightly modified form for the cranial computer tomography. The application considers five tumor diagnoses: malignomata, semimalignomata, metastases, malformation tumors and benignomata. 25 symptoms gathered by seven different examinations describe every case: number of foci, structure of foci (native), edemata, localisation of edemata, form and position of ventricles, sulci and cisterns. The symptoms are dichotomous, with "symptom present" and "symptom absent/not investigated" as the two distinct values. TUSCH examines different algorithms in order to calculate total indications of the patient's symptom pattern to diseases D_j. The efficiency of the procedures lies between 55 and 76% compared to physicians' diagnoses. 802 tumor cases were used to perform this calculation. The S_iD_j-occurrence and S_iD_j-confirmability relationships have been documented linguistically by a neuroradiologist.

2.4. Symptom combinations and fuzzy subsets

ALBIN /38/ proposes a fuzzy linguistic approach to medical diagnosis. In /38/, it is said that physicians normally try to fit patients to certain prototypes of diseases. As a first approximation to such an approach, disease prototypes can be defined as shown in Table 1.

The definition of fuzzy membership functions for long S_1, decreased S_2, normal S_2, etc., then allows the calculation of degrees of membership in the fuzzy subset long S_1, decreased S_2, normal S_2, etc. given symptom values measured on the patient. Fuzzy disease membership values of patients can now be computed by using the MAX definition

Table 1: Disease prototype definitions for two hemorrhagic disorders (from /38/, p. 128).

Disorder	S_1 IVY Bleeding Time	S_2 Platelet Count	S_3 QUICK Time	S_4 Partial Thromboplastin Time	S_5 Thrombin Time
D_1 <u>Thrombocytopenia</u>	<u>Long</u>	<u>Decreased</u>	<u>Normal</u>	<u>Normal</u>	<u>Normal</u>
D_2 <u>Von Willebrand's Disease</u>	<u>Long</u>	<u>Normal</u>	<u>Normal</u>	<u>Normal</u> or <u>Long</u>	<u>Normal</u>

for fuzzy set union and MIN definition for fuzzy set intersection, for example:

$$\begin{aligned}\mu_{D_1}(p) = {} & \mu_{\underline{\text{long}}\ S_1}(12 \text{ min.}) \\ & \wedge \mu_{\underline{\text{decreased}}\ S_2}(60\,000/\text{mm}^3) \\ & \wedge \mu_{\underline{\text{normal}}\ S_3}(12 \text{ sec.}) \\ & \wedge \mu_{\underline{\text{normal}}\ S_4}(37 \text{ sec.}) \\ & \wedge \mu_{\underline{\text{normal}}\ S_5}(18 \text{ sec.}) \\ = {} & 0.95\end{aligned}$$

Patient p, in our example, fits the prototype definition of D_1 almost exactly and if additionally computed fuzzy disease membership values $\mu_{D_i}(p)$, where $i \neq 1$, are much smaller than $\mu_{D_1}(p)$, diagnosis D_1=<u>thrombocytopenia</u> is presumably the correct diagnosis for patient p.

In /62/, SANCHEZ, et al. propose a similar linguistic approach to the classification of hyperlipoproteinemias. But in the diagnostic procedure described, predetermined bandwidths of the symptoms depending on the measuring accuracy of the laboratory performing the tests are additionally taken into account. The application involves five lipoprotein tests determined by electrophoretic methods. The degrees of membership in three types of <u>dyslipoproteinemia</u> were calculated for five test cases.

MOON, et al. /40/ present symptom combinations as AND and OR functions. The calculation of the symptom combinations is performed using the fuzzy intersection for AND and the algebraic sum for OR. A different way of presenting the OR function is mentioned: MOON, et al. use the convex combination

$$\mu_D(S_1,\ldots,S_k) = \frac{\sum_{i=1}^{k} w_i \mu_{S_i}}{\sum_{i=1}^{k} w_i \lceil \mu_{S_i} \rceil} \qquad (7)$$

where $\lceil \mu_{S_i} \rceil$ is the ceiling function of μ_{S_i} and the weights w_i are set equal to the posterior probabilities $p(D/S_i)$ calculated for the single symptom S_i.

CERUTTI and PIERI /63/ also use linguistic variables as an alternative to numerical variables in order to characterize complex relationships between symptoms and diseases. Primary linguistic terms (<u>small</u>, <u>medium</u>, <u>large</u>)

that express intervals on the numerical symptom scale compounded with linguistic hedges (very, slightly, more or less) are connected by AND and OR to compose fuzzy logical combinations. By evaluating the fuzzy logical combination, a membership function is obtained that calculates non-fuzzy values (for details see /63/).

2.5. Medical diagnosis using procedural fuzzy concepts

In /64/, WECHSLER proposes a procedural knowledge base system using fuzzy concepts. Instead of using fuzzy membership degrees, classes of functions f_i^p are established whose task is to define implicitly fuzzy sets. A class is related to a concept and it contains one or more functions f_i^p where p stands for the property to be checked and i relates to some context, e.g. to the observer i. For example:

f_i^{age} (teenage)=(age 12,age 18)

f_i^{age} (young) =(age 17,age 30)

Subsequently, two kinds of order-decisions that determine whether or not a given object has the property in question are presented:

1) Middle order: The closer the value of the property of a given object is to the middle of the interval defined by f_i^p the better it fits the property to be checked. For example: Age 18 fits "teenage" better than "young".

2) LB order: The first member of the interval defined in f_i^p is the best.

Then the medical knowledge is embedded in procedures and a possible program checking for ulcers may look like [7]:

```
(LAMBDA(←D ULCERS)
     (PROGRAM ()
(EXISTS Patient pain-location slightly
                below the top of
                xiphoid process f_u^p1)
 (EXISTS Patient time of pain breakfast f_u^p2))).
```

2.6. Fuzzy cluster analysis in medical diagnosis

In /38/, ALBIN has developed a fuzzy clustering approach using an elliptic metric to define distance in the symptom space $S_1 x \ldots x S_n = S \in R^n$. The proposed fuzzy clustering method is compared with a Bayesian approach on the basis of some test patients.

FORDON /65/, and FORDON and BEZDEK /66/ present a very interesting application of fuzzy clustering techniques to the diagnosis of hypertensive patients. Different distance measurements are used. In one example, a fuzzy k-means algorithm diagnosed 218 essential and renovascular hypertensive cases described by four continuous parameters. The overall efficiency of the algorithm was 80.7%.

In /67/, BEZDEK applied the fuzzy ISODATA clustering algorithm to feature selection of medical data. In the numeric example, 11 binary symptoms of 107 stomach disease patients who had either hiatal hernia or gallstones were considered.

A further paper proposing the use of fuzzy clustering methods in medical diagnosis is the one by ESOGBUE and ELDER /68/. That paper gives an instructive example of applying a criterion function that is a modified form of the minimum MINKOWSKI metric to rheumatic valvular heart diseases.

2.7. Fuzzy decision analysis in medical diagnosis

Imprecision in decision analysis is modeled using fuzzy set theory in NOMURA, et al. /69/ and MISHIMA, et al. /70/. These reports propose an interesting model that represents probability or utility by a membership function. The model selects an optimal treatment by comparing among degrees of truth of some propositions on expected utilities. This method is applied to managing patients with panceratic diseases centered around primary cancer. The decision process starts from a point at which a patient is very likely to be suffering from any one of four pancreatic diseases taken into account. In clinical practice the procedure helps to decide whether or not a radical operative invasion against the supposed disease should be performed.

2.8. Bayesian approach and fuzzy subsets

In /38/, ALBIN argued that it is entirely reasonable to assign

$$\mu_{D_i}(S_1,\ldots,S_n)=P(D_i/S_1,\ldots,S_n) \qquad (8)$$

under the condition that good Bayesian values can be obtained for the probability indices $P(D_i/S_1,\ldots,S_n)$.

"Calling $P(D_i/S_1,\ldots,S_n)$ the value of the membership function μ_{D_i} at $(S_1,\ldots,S_n)$ in R^n is much more reasonable than calling it a probability, since the manner of estimating $P(D_i/S_1,\ldots,S_n)$ is very inexact. Physicians' estimates based on their own medical knowledge have also been used in computing $P(D_i/S_1,\ldots,S_n)$ from $P(S_1,\ldots,S_n/D_i)$ and $P(D_i)$, so these estimates should be used with equal validity for $\mu_{D_i}(S_1,\ldots,S_n)$."

quoted from /38/, p. 84

2.9. Miscellaneous

CHENG and McINNIS describe in /71/ an algorithm for multiple attribute (symptoms), multiple alternative (diagnoses) decision problems (see also KICKERT /72/). The relative importance of a symptom j denoted by μ_{w_j}, and the rating $\mu_{r_{ij}}$ that indicates the importance of the symptom j with respect to disease i have been established for 12 blood chemistry tests considering 78 diseases. On this basis the computer program calculates possible diseases which are ranked and arranged in descending order.

In FOX /73/, some critical remarks concerning WECHSLER's paper /64/ are put forward. FOX emphasizes that clinical and professional acceptability of computer-based medical consultation systems is of primary importance. Technology should be planned with this in mind.

OHSATO, et al. /74/ established a fuzzy relation in a preoperative nursing care system. The relation between preoperative patient's state and postoperative state is determined by using patient's attributes before and after the operation estimated by a nurse, e.g. degree of seriousness of preoperative and postoperative patient's states.

3. FINAL REMARKS

The detailed survey of fuzzy approaches to medical decision making shows the wide and deep interest of researchers all over the world to find a solid fuzzy theoretical basis for the representation of medical knowledge as well as for the diagnostic process and to use it in practical applications.

The survey was made with the intention of studying fuzzy approaches in medicine in order to use the knowledge for developing the general fuzzy computer-assisted diagnostic system CADIAG-2. CADIAG-2 is described in a companion paper in the same edition /75/. A first theoretical approach to CADIAG-2 was made in /76/.

FOOTNOTES

1) Such categorization is a little bit arbitrary. It shall only emphasize the difference between methods mainly based on numerical calculations in order to find out diseases shown by the patient and methods using logical inference for the most part to obtain patient's diagnoses.

2) Instead of the max-min composition the more general term sup-min composition is often used (see for example DUBOIS and PRADE /43/).

3) SANCHEZ /46,47/ and KAUFMANN /48-51/ write $B=R \circ A$, which is equivalent to the notation used above.

4) At this juncture it becomes necessary to mention that the "medical knowledge" matrix R reflects only a very small part of the entire (diagnostic) medical knowledge.

   By establishing the matrix R a physician would ask: "What does the degree of association between a symptom S_i and a disease D_j really mean? Is it the frequency of occurrence of S_i at disease D_j? Is it a certainty factor of "confirmed by"? Is it an evoking strength /30,31/ of S_i for D_j or what else?"

   Furthermore a symptom, sign, test result, or finding often gains in importance with respect to a certain disease if it occurs with other symptoms or signs. For example, the symptom sacroileitis may occur in several diseases, as ankylosing spondylitis, juvenile arthritis, psoriatic arthropathy, Reiter's syndrome, Crohn's disease, and others. In combination with other nonspecific symptoms, e.g. concomitant mouth ulcer and conjunctivitis the diagnosis "Reiter's syndrome" can be established.

   Next, the "degree of association" expressed as real number on [0,1] does not remain constant with respect to time, place and individuum. It changes with sex, age, season. For instance, in spring and autumn influenza is more probable as well as in times of a flu epidemic.

   Finally, concepts used in medicine, such as hierarchy of symptoms and diseases, co-occurrence of diseases at the same patient and at the same time, evidence of symptoms depending on their time of duration, handling of unexplained symptoms at the end of the diagnostic process, etc. cannot be taken into account by only one "medical knowledge" matrix.

5) In classification theory, the normal, healthy, typical, unchanged pattern or class representative from which the abnormal, ill, untypical pattern is to be separated is always regarded as one class.

6) DUBOIS and PRADE /43/ term them interval-valued fuzzy sets.

7) The example is expressed in notation of QA4 (see /64/), a question-answering language implemented in LISP. Furthermore, it shall be mentioned that in order to diagnose ulcer the procedure is incomplete with regard tothe medical point of view.

REFERENCES

/1/ LIPKIN, M., J.D.HARDY: Mechanical Correlation of Data in Differential Diagnosis of Hematological Diseases. J.Am.Med.Ass. 166 (1958) 113-125.

/2/ LEDLEY, R.S., L.B.LUSTED: Reasoning Foundations of Medical Diagnosis. Science 130 (1959) 9-21.

/3/ ROGERS, W., B.RYACK, G.MOELLER: Computer-Aided Medical Diagnosis: Literature review. Int.J. Bio-Medical Computing 10 (1979) 267-289.

/4/ WAGNER, G., P.TAUTU, U.WOLBER: Problems of Medical Diagnosis: A Bibliography. Meth.Inform.Med. 17 (1978) 55-74.

/5/ WARDLE, A., L.WARDLE: Computer-Aided Diagnosis: A Review of Research. Meth.Inform.Med. 17 (1978) 15-28.

/6/ LEDLEY, R.S.: Use of Computers in Biology and Medicine. McGraw-Hill Book Company New York, 1965.

/7/ GREMY, F., M.GOLDBERG: Decision Making Methods in Medicine. Springer Verlag Berlin-Heidelberg-New York, 1977, 419-459.

/8/ ADLASSNIG, K.-P., T.GERGELY, H.GRABNER, G.GRABNER: A Computer-Assisted System for Diagnostic Decision Making-Online Usage of the Database of the Medical Information System WAMIS. In SHIRES, D.B., H.WOLF (Eds.): MEDINFO 77. North-Holland Publishing Company Amsterdam-New York-Oxford, 1977, 213-218.

/9/ BAUER, P., A.GANGL, G.GRABNER: Ein Computer-Verfahren zur Zuordnung eines Krankheitsbildes zu einer Diagnoses-Gruppe. Wien Z. Inn. Med. 11 (1970) 407-509.

/10/ BAUER, P., A.GANGL, G.GRABNER, O.JAHN: Ein Computer-Verfahren zur Unterstützung des Arztes bei der Erstellung von Differential-Diagnosen. Impuls 10 (1968) 705-712.

/11/ GANGL, A., G.GRABNER, P.BAUER: Erste Erfahrungen mit einem Computerprogramm zur Differentialdiagnose der Lebererkrankungen. Wien.Z.inn.Med. 50 (1969) 553-586.

/12/ SPINDELBERGER, W., G.GRABNER: Ein Computerverfahren zur diagnostischen Hilfestellung. In FELLINGER, K. (Hrsg.): Computer in der Medizin - Probleme, Erfahrungen, Projekte. Verlag Brüder Hollinek Wien, 1968, 189-221.

/13/ FIESCHI, M., M.JOUBERT, D.FIESCHI, M.ROUX: Medical Diagnostic Aid: Application of the Method of Refutation of DAVIS and PUTNAM. In LINDBERG, D.A.B., S.KAIHARA (Eds.): MEDINFO 80. North-Holland Publishing Company Amsterdam-New York-Oxford, 1980, 764-768.

/14/ PIRTKIEN, R.: Computereinsatz in der Medizin. Georg Thieme Verlag Stuttgart, 1971.

/15/ SCHILD, W., B.GAVISH, B.LUNENFELD: Computer-Assisted Medical Diagnosis with an Application to Endocrinology. IBM Israel Scientific Center, Technical Report 014, 1974.

/16/ SPECHTMEYER, H., H.E.WICHMANN, R.GROSS: Kliniknahe computerunterstützte Diagnostik am Beispiel der Hämatologie. Dt.med.Wschr. 103 (1978) 545-549.

/17/ ADLASSNIG, K.-P., G.GRABNER: Approaches to Computer-Assisted Diagnosis in Gastroenterology. EDV in Medizin und Biologie 11 (1980) 74-80.

/18/ ADLASSNIG, K.-P., G.GRABNER: The Viennese Computer-Assisted Diagnostic System. Its Principles and Values. AUTOMEDICA 3 (1980) 141-150.

/19/ ADLASSNIG, K.-P., G.KOLARZ, F.LIPOMERSKY, I.GRÖGER, G.GRABNER: CADIAG-1: A Computer-Assisted Diagnostic System on the Basis of Symbolic Logic and its Application in Internal Medicine. In O'MOORE, R.R., B.BARBER, P.L.REICHERTZ, F.ROGER (Eds.): Medical Informatics Europe 82. Springer-Verlag Berlin-Heidelberg-New York, 1982, 495-505.

/20/ SALAMON, R., M.BERNADET, F.GREMY: Ternary Algebra: Theoretical Aspects and Possible Applications. In DOMBAL, F.T. de, F.GREMY (Eds.): Decision Making and Medical Care: Can Information Science Help? North-Holland Publishing Company Amsterdam-New York-Oxford, 1976, 505-513.

/21/ RESCHER, N.: Many-valued logic. McGraw-Hill Book Company New York, 1969.

/22/ SHORTLIFFE, E.H., B.G.BUCHANAN, E.A.FEIGENBAUM: Knowledge Engineering for Medical Decision Making: A Review of Computer-Based Clinical Decision Aids. Proceedings of the IEEE 67 (1979) 1207-1224.

/23/ SHORTLIFFE, E.H.: Computer-Based Medical Consultations: MYCIN. Elsevier New York-Oxford-Amsterdam, 1976.

/24/ WEISS, S., C.A.KULIKOWSKI, A.SAFIR: Glaucoma Consultation by Computer. Comput.Biol.Med. 8 (1978) 25-40.

/25/ WEISS, S.M., C.A.KULIKOWSKI, S.AMAREL, A.SAFIR: A Model-Based Method for Computer-Aided Medical Decision-Making. Artificial Intelligence 11 (1978) 145-172.

/26/ LINDBERG, D.A.B., G.C.SHARP, L.C.KINGSLAND, III, S.M.WEISS, S.P.HAYES, H.UENO, S.E.HAZELWOOD: Computer Based Rheumatology Consultant. In LINDBERG, D.A.B., S.KAIHARA (Eds.): MEDINFO 80. North-Holland Publishing Company Amsterdam-New York-Oxford, 1980, 1311-1315.

/27/ UENO, H., D.A.B.LINDBERG, L.C.KINGSLAND, III, J.H.ESTHER: Design of a Criteria-Based Rheumatology Consulting System for a Microcomputer. In LINDBERG, D.A.B., S.KAIHARA (Eds.): MEDINFO 80. North-Holland Publishing Company Amsterdam-New York-Oxford, 1980, 1316-1320.

/28/ WEISS, S.M., C.A.KULIKOWSKI: EXPERT: A System for Developing Consultation Models. Proceedings of the 6th International Joint Conference on Artificial Intelligence Tokyo, 1979, 942-947.

/29/ WEISS, S.M., C.A.KULIKOWSKI: Data Base Analysis Aids for Designing Consultation Systems. In LINDBERG, D.A.B., S.KAIHARA(Eds.): MEDINFO 80. North-Holland Publishing Company Amsterdam-New York-Oxford, 1980, 794-797.

/30/ POPLE, H.E., J.D.MYERA, R.A.MILLER: DIALOG: A Model of Diagnostic Logic for Internal Medicine. Proceedings of the 4th International Joint Conference on Artificial Intelligence Tbilisi, 1975, 848-855.

/31/ POPLE, H.E.: The Formation of Composite Hypotheses in Diagnostic Problem Solving - An Exercise in Synthetic Reasoning. Proceedings of the 5th International Joint Conference on Artificial Intelligence Cambridge, 1977, 1030-1037.

/32/ BUTTON, K.F.: Laboratory Diagnosis by Computer. Comput.Biol.Med. 3 (1973) 131-136.

/33/ GIESZL, L.R.: An Interactive Intelligence System for Medical Decision Aids. In LINDBERG, D.A.B., S.KAIHARA (Eds.): MEDINFO 80. North-Holland Publishing Company Amsterdam-New York-Oxford, 1980, 809-814.

/34/ LEDLEY, R.S.: Syntax-Directed Concept Analysis in the Reasoning Foundations of Medical Diagnosis. In JACQUEZ, J.A. (Ed.): Computer Diagnosis and Diagnostic Methods. Charles C.Thomas Springfield, 1972, 152-168.

/35/ BARTHEL, D.: Automatische Diagnosestellung. Wissenschaftliche Zeitschrift der Karl-Marx-Universität Leipzig 17 (1968) 515-528.

/36/ BARTHEL, D.: Prinzipien der automatischen Diagnosestellung. VEB Georg Thieme Leipzig, 1970.

/37/ KAMSTIESS, R., H.G.DINKLOH, M.MÜLLER: Entscheidungstabellentechnik als Mittel der Verständigung zwischen Medizinern und Systemanalytikern. Informatik-Spektrum 2 (1980) 79-85.

/38/ ALBIN, M.A.: Fuzzy Sets and Their Application to Medical Diagnosis and Pattern Recognition. PhD diss. University of California, Berkeley, 1975.

/39/ PEREZ-OJEDA, A.: Medical Knowledge Network: A Database for Computer-Aided Diagnosis. Thesis. University of Toronto, Toronto, 1976.

/40/ MOON, R.E., S.JORDANOV, A.PEREZ, I.B.TURKSEN: Medical Diagnostic System with Human-Like Reasoning Capability. In SHIRES, D.B., H.WOLF (Eds.): MEDINFO 77. North-Holland Publishing Company Amsterdam-New York-Oxford, 1977, 115-119.

/41/ ESOGBUE, A.O., R.C.ELDER: Fuzzy Sets and the Modelling of Physician Decision Processes, Part I: The Initial Interview-Information Gathering Session. Fuzzy Sets and Systems 2 (1979) 279-291.

/42/ BELLMAN, R.E., L.A.ZADEH: Local and Fuzzy Logics: Memorandum NO.ERL-M584, Electronics Research Laboratory, College of Engineering, University of California, Berkeley 94720, 11 May 1976.

/43/ DUBOIS, D., H.PRADE: Fuzzy Sets and Systems: Theory and Applications. Academic Press New York-London, 1980.

/44/ ZADEH, L.A.: Outline of a New Approach to the Analysis of Complex Systems and Decision Processes. IEEE Transactions on Systems, Man, and Cybernetics, Vol.SMC-3, No.1, January 1973, 28-44.

/45/ SMETS, PH., H.VAINSEL, R.BERNARD, F.KORNREICH: Bayesian Probability of Fuzzy Diagnosis. In SHIRES, D.B., H.WOLF (Eds.): MEDINFO 77. North-Holland Publishing Company Amsterdam-New York-Oxford, 1977, 213-218.

/46/ SANCHEZ, E.: Medical Diagnosis and Composite Fuzzy Relations. In GUPTA, M.M., R.K.RAGADE, R.R.YAGER (Eds.): Advances in Fuzzy Set Theory and Applications. North-Holland Publishing Company Amsterdam-New York-Oxford, 1979, 437-444.

/47/ SANCHEZ, E.: Compositions of Fuzzy Relations. In GUPTA, M.M., R.K. RAGADE, R.R.YAGER (Eds.): Advances in Fuzzy Set Theory and Applications. North-Holland Publishing Company Amsterdam-New York-Oxford, 1979, 421-433.

/48/ KAUFMANN, A.: Introduction to the Theory of Fuzzy Subsets. Volume I. Fundamental Theoretical Elements. Academic Press New York-San Francisco-London, 1975.

/49/ KAUFMANN, A.: Introduction à la Théorie des Sous-Ensembles Flous. Tome II. Application à la Linguistique et à la Sémantique. Masson Paris, 1975.

/50/ KAUFMANN, A.: Introduction à la Théorie des Sous-Ensembles Flous. Tome III. Applications à la Classification et à la Reconnaissance des Formes aux Automates et aux Systèmes, au Choix des Critères. Masson Paris, 1975.

/51/ KAUFMANN, A.: Introduction à la Théorie des Sous-Ensembles Flous. Tome IV. Compléments et Nouvelles Application. Masson Paris, 1977.

/52/ SANCHEZ, E.: Resolution of Eigen Fuzzy Sets Equations. Fuzzy Sets and Systems 1 (1978) 69-74.

/53/ SANCHEZ, E., R.SAMBUC: Relations floues. Fonction Φ-floues. Application à l'aide au diagnostic en pathologie thyroidienne. In LAUDET, M., J.ANDERSON, F.BEGON (Eds.): Medical Data Processing. Taylor and Francis Ltd. London, 1976, 513-524.

/54/ JOLY, H., E.SANCHEZ, J.GOUVERNET, J.VALTY: Applications of Fuzzy Set Theory to the Evaluation of Cardiac Function. In LINDBERG, D.A.B., S.KAIHARA (Eds.): MEDINFO 80. North-Holland Publishing Company Amsterdam-New York-Oxford, 1980, 91-95.

/55/ SANCHEZ, E.: Solutions in Composite Fuzzy Relation Equations: Application to Medical Diagnosis in Brouwerian Logic. In GUPTA, M.M., G.N.SARIDIS, B.R.GAINES (Eds.): Fuzzy Automata and Decision Processes. Elsevier North-Holland New York, 1977, 221-234.

/56/ SOULA, G., J.GOUVERNET, A.BARRE, J.L.SAN MARCO: Application of Fuzzy Relations to Medical Decision Making. In LINDBERG, D.A.B., S.KAIHARA (Eds.): MEDINFO 80. North-Holland Publishing Company Amsterdam-New York-Oxford, 1980, 844-848.

/57/ SANCHEZ, E.: Inverses of Fuzzy Relations. Application to Possibility Distributions and Medical Diagnosis. Fuzzy Sets and Systems 2 (1979) 75-86.

/58/ SAMBUC, R., E.SANCHEZ, J.GOUVERNET, J.L.SAN MARCO: Φ-Fuzzy Functions. Application to Mecial Diagnosis. In LINDBERG, D.A.B., S.KAIHARA (Eds.): MEDINFO 80. North-Holland Publishing Company Amsterdam-New York-Oxford, 1980, 784-788.

/59/ ADLASSNIG, K.-P.: Ein einfaches Modell zur medizinischen Diagnostik mit fuzzy Teilmengen. EDV in Medizin und Biologie 13 (1982) in press.

/60/ TUSCH, G.: Fuzzy Mengen und Anwendungen. Diplomarbeit. Universität Hannover, Hannover, 1980.

/61/ TUSCH, G.: Ein fuzzy Algorithmus zur diagnostischen Klassifizierung in der cranialen Computertomographie (CCT). In BRAUER, W. (Ed.): GI-11. Jahrestagung. Springer-Verlag Berlin-Heidelberg-New York, 1981, 598-605.

/62/ SANCHEZ, E., J.GOUVERNET, R.BARTOLIN, L.VOVAN: Linguistic Approach in Fuzzy Logic of the WHO Classification of Dyslipoproteinemias. International Congress on Applied Systems Research and Cybernetics, Acapulco, 1980.

/63/ CERUTTI, S., C.T.PIERI: A Method for the Quantification of the Decision-Making Process in a Computer-Oriented

Medical Record. Int.J.Bio-Medical Computing 12 (1981) 29-57.

/64/ WECHSLER, H.: A Fuzzy Approach to Medical Diagnosis. Int.J.Bio-Medical Computing 7 (1976) 191-203.

/65/ FORDON, W.A.: Computer-Aided Differential Diagnosis of Hypertension. PhD diss. Purdue University, Purdue, 1976.

/66/ FORDON, W.A., J.C.BEZDEK: The Application of Fuzzy Set Theory to Medical Diagnosis: In GUPTA, M.M., R.K. RAGADE, R.R.YAGER (Eds.): Advances in Fuzzy Set Theory and Applications. North-Holland Publishing Company Amsterdam-New York-Oxford, 1979, 445-461.

/67/ BEZDEK, J.C.: Feature Selection for Binary Data-Medical Diagnosis with Fuzzy Sets. National Computer Conference, AFIPS Press, 1976, 1057-1068.

/68/ ESOGBUE, A.O., R.C.ELDER: Fuzzy Sets and the Modelling of Physician Decision Processes. Part II: Fuzzy Diagnosis Decision Models. Fuzzy Sets and Systems 3 (1980) 1-9.

/69/ NOMURA, Y., M.NAKAMURA, H.MISHIMA, N.KATO: An Application of Fuzzy Decision Analysis to the Management of Pancreatic Cancer. Automedica 3 (1980) 131-139.

/70/ MISHIMA, H., N.KATOH, T.HATTORI, Y. NOMURA, M.NAKAMURA: A Fuzzy Decision Analysis for the Management of Pancreatic Cancer. In LINDBERG, D. A.B., S.KAIHARA (Eds.): MEDINFO 80. North-Holland Publishing Company Amsterdam-New York-Oxford, 1980, 830-834.

/71/ CHENG, Y.-Y.M., B.McINNIS: An Algorithm for Multiple Attribute, Multiple Alternative Decision Problems Based on Fuzzy Sets with Application to Medical Diagnosis. IEEE Transactions on Systems, Man, and Cybernetics, SMC-10 (1980) 645-650.

/72/ KICKERT, W.J.M.: Fuzzy Theories on Decision-Making. Martinus Nijhoff Social Sciences Division Leiden-Boston-London, 1978.

/73/ FOX, J.: Some Observations on Fuzzy Diagnosis and Medical Computing. Int.J.Bio-Medical Computing 8 (1977) 269-275.

/74/ OHSATO, A., T.SEKIGUCHI, T.NAKAI, K.YAMAZAKI: Information Processing for Nursing by Fuzzy Relation. In LINDBERG, D.A.B., S.KAIHARA (Eds.): MEDINFO 80. North-Holland Publishing Company Amsterdam-New York-Oxford, 1980, 62-66.

/75/ ADLASSNIG, K.-P., G.KOLARZ: CADIAG-2: Computer-Assisted Medical Diagnosis Using Fuzzy Subsets. In GUPTA, M.M., E.SANCHEZ (Eds.): Fuzzy Information and Decision Processes. North-Holland Publishing Company Amsterdam-New York-Oxford. In press.

/76/ ADLASSNIG, K.-P.: A Fuzzy Logical Model of Computer-Assisted Medical Diagnosis. Meth.Inform.Med. 19 (1980), 141-148.

Approximate Reasoning in Decision Analysis
M.M. Gupta and E. Sanchez (eds.)

CADIAG-2: COMPUTER-ASSISTED MEDICAL DIAGNOSIS USING FUZZY SUBSETS

KLAUS-PETER ADLASSNIG, GERNOT KOLARZ

Department of Medical Computer Sciences
(Director: Prof.Dr. G. Grabner)
University of Vienna
A-1090 Vienna, Garnisongasse 13, Austria
and
Ludwig Boltzmann Institute for Rheumatology and Focal Diseases
(Directors: Prof.Dr. F. Endler and Prof.Dr. N. Thumb)
A-2500 Baden, Kaiser-Franz-Ring 8, Austria

A model of a computer-assisted medical diagnostic system using fuzzy subsets has been developed and implemented. Two aspects of symptom-disease relationships - occurrence and confirmability - are documented linguistically by medical experts or on the basis of medical database evaluations. Symptom combinations and their relationships to diseases are part of the stored medical knowledge.

Given patients' symptom patterns, the diagnostic process provides confirmed and excluded diagnoses as well as diagnostic hypotheses. Detailed explanations for the diagnostic results are given and proposals for further examinations on the patients are made.

An extended application in rheumatology with 1.000 cases including about 2.000 symptoms, signs and test results and 186 diseases is at present being tested.

Keywords: Computer-assisted diagnosis, medical consultation, fuzzy subsets, fuzzy logic, fuzzy relationships, acquisition of medical knowledge, confirmed diagnoses, excluded diagnoses, diagnostic hypotheses, rheumatology, hepatology, coagulation defects, pancreatic diseases.

1. INTRODUCTION

In medical science it is seldom possible to work with exact definitions, descriptions or assertions. In medical diagnosis there is very rarely a sharp boundary between diseases and the appearance of more than one disease in the patient at the same time destroys the expected symptom patterns of disease hypotheses, which makes the diagnostic and therapeutic decision more difficult. The assignment of laboratory test results to the ranges normal or pathological is arbitrary in borderline cases, the intensity of pain can only be described verbally and depends on the subjective estimation of the patient, and precise relationships between symptoms, signs, test results, findings, i.e. any observation on the patient (short: symptoms) and diagnoses can very seldom be found in descriptions of diseases.

Thus you might read in /1/ the following statements about acute pancreatitis:

- Acute pancreatitis is almost always connected with sickness and vomiting (p. 678).
- Typically, acute pancreatitis begins with sudden aches in the abdomen (p. 677).
- The case history frequently reports about ulcus ventriculi and duodeni (p. 676).

In /2/ one can find similar medical descriptions, e.g. for the general differential diagnosis of icterus:

- Bilirubinurie excludes the hemolytic icterus but bilirubin is detectable with hepatocellular or cholestatic icterus (p. 561).

In the field of rheumatology, ZÖLLNER /3/ writes about the attack of gout:

- The typical attack of gout occurs almost always in men after the 25th year of life (p. 677).
- It is characterized by sudden start out of full health, by restriction to one joint, by strong aches, by the intensive inflammation with rubor, swelling and heat and by the almost always good therapeutic success with colchicin (p.677).
- But the attack of gout does not always proceed in the above-mentioned course (p. 677).

In /4,5/ one can read similarly weak assertions and descriptions of diseases.

Firm relationships between symptoms or combinations of them and diagnoses sometimes appear and it is necessary to use them, but they are rare. So , KOLARZ gives in /6/, partly according to the American Rheumatism Association, clearly defined criteria for the rheumatology diseases rheumatic fever, rheumatoid arthritis, Sjögren's disease, psoriatic arthritis, Reiter's disease, Behcet's disease, Bechterew's disease, systematic lupus erythematosus, sclerodermia and gout. Certain combinations of symptoms prove these diagnoses if excluding symptoms are missing.

In the computer-assisted diagnostic system CADIAG-1 based on tri-valued logic /7-16/ the firm relationships proving, excluding and obligatory (as well as the weak relationships facultative and not proving) between symptoms and diseases are used in the diagnostic process.

The theory of fuzzy subsets developed by L.A.ZADEH /17/ (general literature see /18-28/, fuzzy bibliographies see /29-31/) is an attempt at a mathematical theory of vagueness and imprecision. This theory seems very useful in the development of computer-assisted medical diagnostic models because of its power to formalize soft and complex concepts.

Such a model is able to handle weak and firm medical assertions like

- symptom S_i is often present and seldom proving for diagnosis D_j or

- strongly increased symptom S_i is almost always present and always proving for diagnosis D_j.

On this basis, the computer-assisted diagnostic system CADIAG-2 establishes fuzzy logical relationships between the patient's symptom pattern and diagnoses in order to deduce medical diagnoses logically and to reason them. In the case of an insufficient diagnostic output, proposals for further examinations on the patient are established by the system. Co-occurrence of diseases which is very common in internal medicine is treated by restarting the diagnostic procedure at the end of a diagnostic iteration with unexplained patient's symptoms.

A survey on medical diagnosis and fuzzy sets is given in a companion paper in the same edition /32/.

2. INTENDED AIMS

The following requirements are imposed on the computer-aided medical consultation system CADIAG-2:

1) Medical diagnostic knowledge shall be stored in form of logical relationships between symptoms and diseases, between symptoms, between diseases and between symptom combinations and diseases. The system shall be capable of gathering and formalizing empirical and judgemental as well as statistical knowledge.

Relationships between single symptoms and single diseases shall express the degree of certainty to infer from one symptom to a specific diagnosis. Relationships between symptoms and between diseases shall be introduced in order to obtain hierarchical dependencies, i.e. super- and sub-relations among symptoms and among diseases. Relationships between symptom combinations and diseases shall incorporate the kind of medical knowledge that considers clinically found combinations of symptoms having a high evidence for diagnoses, or combinations of symptoms proposed as internal guideline principles by medical associations for the confirmation or exclusion of diagnoses.

2) The logical relationships may be fuzzy. They do not necessarily correspond to Boolean or tri-valued logic /7-16/.

3) Frequent as well as rare diagnoses shall be offered after analyzing the patient's medical data. The only criterion for offering diagnoses shall be that they match patient's symptom pattern.

4) The diagnostic process shall be performed iteratively. In this way it will be possible to confirm or exclude diagnostic hypotheses step by step. Furthermore, it shall be possible to put in confirmed diagnoses at the beginning of an iteration. The diagnostic procedure shall then erase symptoms explained by confirmed diagnoses and continue with the unexplained symptoms. Such a procedure shall help to solve the problem of co-occurrence of diseases in a patient that is very common in internal medicine /8,13,33,34/.

5) Explanations for every diagnostic output during the consultation session of CADIAG-2 shall be given by the system. This central requirement is imposed to insure that

- CADIAG-2 is accepted by the medical community and that
- CADIAG-2 is used for educational pur-

poses in medical students' and professional training.

6) Meaningful proposals for patient's further examination shall be provided, with consideration of the financial costs of the examination and its risk for the patient.

7) Retrospective applications for scientific studies as well as prospective use in clinical practice shall be possible.

3. CADIAG-2 SYSTEM: THEORETICAL ASPECTS [1)]

3.1. General considerations

Let $\Sigma=\{S_1,S_2,...,S_m\}$ be the set of symptoms, $\Delta=\{D_1,D_2,...,D_n\}$ the set of diseases or diagnoses [2)] resp. and $\Pi=\{P_1,P_2,...,P_q\}$ the set of patients under consideration. The cardinality of Σ,Δ and Π is given by m, n and q. Σ,Δ and Π are non-fuzzy sets.

REMARK 1:
Every $S_i \in \Sigma$, $1 \leq i \leq m$, is a fuzzy subset of a reference set [3)] $\Omega=\{x_1,x_2,...\}$ characterized by a membership function $\mu_{S_i}(x)$. Set Ω contains all possible values x which can be assumed by S_i. The membership function $\mu_{S_i}(x)$ defines the strength of affiliation of $x \in \Omega$ in S_i.

Example:
Let S_i be potassium, increased in mmol/liter then $\Omega=\{1.0...15.0\}$ (more than 15.0 mmol and less than 1.0 mmol liter are outside the possible range) defines the reference set. Assuming a normal range of measured potassium from about 3.5 mmol/liter to about 5.2 mmol/liter yields

$\mu_{\text{potassium,increased}}(5.2)=0.5$ or
$\mu_{\text{potassium,increased}}(6)=1.$

REMARK 2:
Every $D_i \in \Delta$, $1 \leq i \leq n$, is a fuzzy subset of a reference set $\Pi=\{P_1,P_2,...P_q\}$ characterized by a membership function $\mu_{D_i}(p)$. The function $\mu_{D_i}(p)$ assigns to every patient P_j a degree of membership of $P_j \in \Pi$ in D_i (Figure 1).

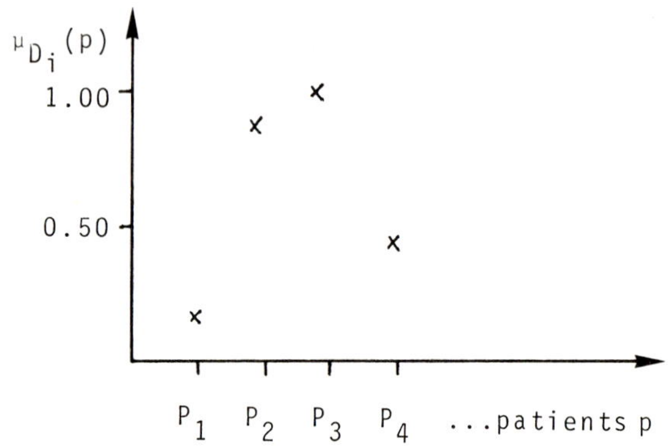

Fig. 1: Diagnosis D_i as a fuzzy subset of the reference set Π that contains all patients p under consideration.

The following definition is equivalent to the above-mentioned:

Every $P_j \in \Pi$, $1 \leq j \leq q$, is a fuzzy subset of a refernce set $\Delta=\{D_1,D_2,...,D_n\}$ characterized by a membership function $\mu_{P_j}(d)$. The function $\mu_{P_j}(d)$ assigns to every diagnosis D_i a degree of membership of $D_i \in \Delta$ in P_j (Figure 2).

It will be noticed that for $d=D_i$ and $p=P_j$

$$\mu_{D_i}(P_j)=\mu_{P_j}(D_i). \tag{1}$$

Example:
Given three patients P_1,P_2 and P_3 and let D_1 be gout, then, for example, $\mu_{\text{gout}}(P_1)=1$, i.e. patient P_1 suffers from

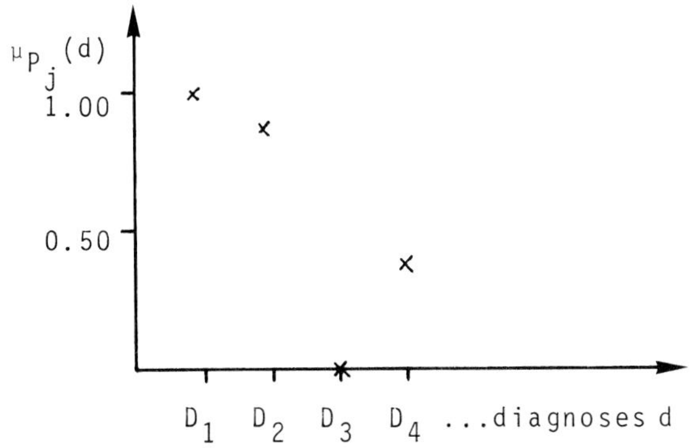

Fig. 2: Patient P_j as a fuzzy subset of the reference set Δ that contains all diagnoses d under consideration.

gout, $\mu_{gout}(P_2)=0.7$, i.e. patient P_2 shows signs of gout, and $\mu_{gout}(P_3)=0$, i.e. patient P_3 does not suffer from gout. It is obvious that $\mu_{gout}(P_1)=\mu_{P_1}(gout)$, etc.

REMARK 3:
From a geometrical point of view (see ALBIN /38/), patients p are considered as points in a m-dimensional space which is set by symptoms $S_i \in \Sigma$, $1 \le i \le m$. Every patient p exhibiting symptom values $x_i \in \Omega_i$ is associated to degrees of membership $\mu_{D_j}(p) \subset [0,1]$, where $D_j \in \Delta$, $1 \le j \le n$. The membership values $\mu_{D_j}(p)$ show the affiliation of patient p to diagnoses D_j. In other notation, patient p is always represented by a symptom value pattern, thus

$$\mu_{D_j}(p)=\mu_{D_j}(x_1,x_2,\ldots,x_m) \qquad (2)$$

where $D_j \in \Delta$, $1 \le j \le n$, and $x_1 \in \Omega_1$, $x_2 \in \Omega_2$, ..., $x_m \in \Omega_m$. Patients suffering from the same disease show a similar [4)] symptom value pattern. They form clusters in the space. Every cluster represents a disease but because $\mu_{D_j}(p)$ is not necessarily 0 or 1 the disease clusters do not show sharp boundaries. To illustrate this see Figure 3.

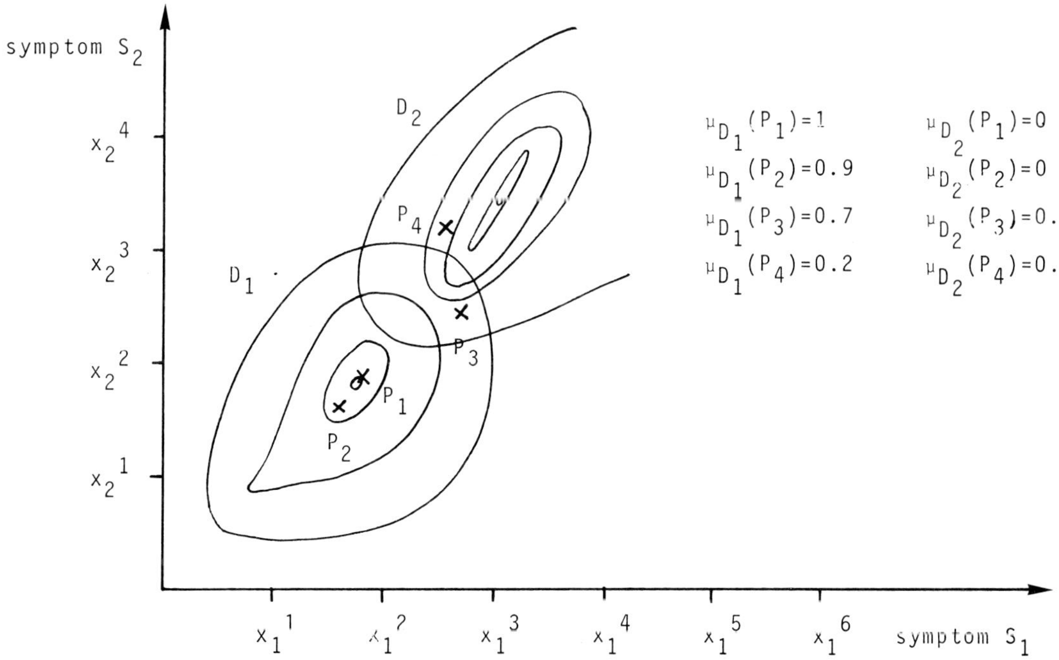

Fig. 3: Patients P_i suffering from the same disease D_j form clusters without sharp boundaries.

3.2. Representation and acquisition of medical knowledge

3.2.1. Symptom-disease fuzzy relationships

Two aspects of a symptom S_i are of essential value in order to find out its relation to a disease D_j:

1) occurrence of S_i in case of D_j and
2) confirmability of S_i for D_j.

Occurrence provides knowledge about the presence of symptom S_i with a patient p when he suffers from disease D_j. From a statistical point of view occurrence is the frequency of S_j with D_j.

Confirmability describes the power of symptom S_i to confirm a certain diagnosis D_j if it occurs in patient p.
Example:
Symptom dyspnoe often occurs in patients suffering from scleroderma but dyspnoe has such a small discriminating value in differential diagnosis of rheumatic diseases that its confirmability for scleroderma is low. In contrast, symptom chorea minor occurs very seldom at patients suffering from rheumatic fever but if it occurs it confirms rheumatic fever.

In terms of fuzzy set theory occurrence of S_i at D_j is defined as a fuzzy subset O of the reference set $\Phi_O(x)=\{0,1,2,\ldots,100\}$, where x means the frequency of S_i in x of one hundred cases of D_j. Similarly, confirmability of S_i for D_j is determined as a fuzzy subset C of the reference set $\Phi_C(x)=\{0,1,2,\ldots,100\}$, i.e. S_i has been confirmed D_j in x of one hundred cases.

It must be stated that the above-defined reference sets Φ_O and Φ_C are based on relative values of frequencies. They have been defined relative to 100. Also, the frequencies do not have to be statistically determined. They can be directly defined, estimated subjectively or based on judgemental knowledge (see paragraph 3.2.2.)

The membership functions of O and C are very simple. They are:

$$\mu_O(x)=f_1(x;1,50,99) \quad ,x\in\Phi_O \tag{3}$$
$$\mu_C(x)=f_1(x;1,50,99) \quad ,x\in\Phi_C \tag{4}$$

where $f_1(x;\alpha,\beta,\gamma)$ is the following standardized function (see ZADEH /39/):

$$f_1(x;\alpha,\beta,\gamma)=\begin{cases} 0 & \text{for } x\leq\alpha \\ 2\left(\frac{x-\alpha}{\gamma-\alpha}\right)^2 & \text{for } \alpha<x\leq\beta \\ 1-2\left(\frac{x-\gamma}{\gamma-\alpha}\right)^2 & \text{for } \beta<x\leq\gamma \\ 1 & \text{for } x>\gamma. \end{cases} \tag{5}$$

The membership functions $\mu_O(x)$ and $\mu_C(x)$ are shown in Figure 4.

It is also possible to use another monotonously increasing function to define O and C, e.g. $\mu_O(x)=\mu_C(x)=\frac{x}{100}$.

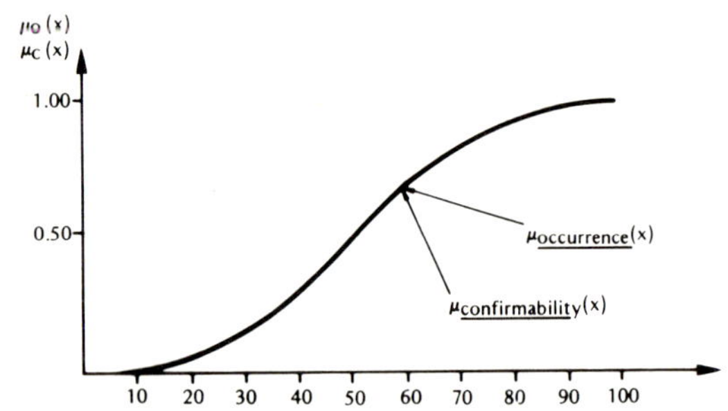

Fig. 4: Membership functions $\mu_O(x)$ for occurrence of S_i with D_j and $\mu_C(x)$ for confirmability of S_i for D_j.

3.2.2. Acquisition of symptom-disease fuzzy relationships

There are two different ways (and a combination of the two) to determine the occurrence and confirmability relationships between symptoms and diseases:

1) Linguistic documentation by medical experts and
2) Medical database evaluation by statistical means.

3.2.2.1. Linguistic documentation

Symptom-disease relationships can be documented by predefined terms that express the interconnections between the considered medical entities. A medical expert or, in order to advance the acceptance of the documented knowledge by the medical community, a team of diagnostic experts document S_iD_j occurrence relationships as well as S_iD_j confirmability relationships by answering the following questions:

1) Occurrence: "How often does S_i occur with D_j?"
2) Confirmability: "How strongly does S_i confirm D_j?"

In this way judgemental medical knowledge founded either directly on medical textbooks (examples have been given in paragraph 1.) or on a clinician's experience can be incorporated. No statistical or computational assumptions (availability of patients data to estimate probabilities of symptoms or diseases in a population or to estimate conditional probabilities of symptoms that appear in case of a disease, availability of sample cases with or without fixed assignments to diseases in order to adapt discriminant equations or to compute disease clusters, etc.) have to be fulfilled to determine S_iD_j relationships.

The possible set of physician's answers to specify occurrence and confirmability may be the fuzzy subsets O_i and C_i, $1 \leq i \leq 9$, and the answer "unknown" (Table 1).

Table 1: Fuzzy subsets for occurrence and confirmability for physician's linguistic documentation of symptom-disease relationships.

i	occurrence O_i	confirmability C_i
1	always [5]	always [6]
2	almost always	almost always
3	very often	very often
4	often	often
5	unspecific	unspecific
6	seldom	seldom
7	very seldom	very seldom
8	almost never	almost never
9	never [7]	never
	unknown	unknown

The fuzzy subsets O_i and C_i have the same reference sets Φ_{O_i} and Φ_{C_i} as the reference sets of O and C, i.e.

$$\Phi_{O_i} = \Phi_O \quad \text{and} \quad \Phi_{C_i} = \Phi_C \;, \quad 1 \leq i \leq 9. \tag{6}$$

The fuzzy subsets $O_1, O_2, O_4, O_5, O_6, O_8$ and O_9 are defined by the following membership functions [8]:

$$\begin{aligned} \mu_{\text{always}}(x) &= f_1(x;97,98,99) \\ \mu_{\text{almost always}}(x) &= f_1(x;80,85,90) \\ \mu_{\text{often}}(x) &= f_1(x;40,60,80) \\ \mu_{\text{unspecific}}(x) &= f_2(x;20,50) \\ \mu_{\text{seldom}}(x) &= 1-f_1(x;20,40,60) \end{aligned} \tag{7}$$

$$\mu_{\underline{\text{almost never}}}(x)=1-f_1(x;10,15,20)$$
$$\mu_{\underline{\text{never}}}(x)=1-f_1(x;1,2,3)$$

where $f_2(x;\alpha,\beta)$ is also a standardized function (see /39/)

$$f_2(x;\alpha,\beta)=\begin{cases} f_1(x;\beta-\alpha,\beta-\frac{\alpha}{2},\beta) & \text{for } x\leq\beta \\ 1-f_1(x;\beta,\beta+\frac{\alpha}{2},\beta+\alpha) & \text{for } x>\beta. \end{cases} \quad (8)$$

By using the modified form of the following operation on fuzzy subsets (see /25/), also called linguistic hedge /19,40/ or linguistic modifier /39/,

$$\text{concentration:}\ \mu_{\underline{\text{very}}\ A}(x)=[\mu_A(x)]^2 \quad (9)$$

the determination of O_3 and O_7 leads to

$$\mu_{\underline{\text{very often}}}(x)=[\mu_{\underline{\text{often}}}(x)]^4$$
$$\mu_{\underline{\text{very seldom}}}(x)=[\mu_{\underline{\text{seldom}}}(x)]^4. \quad (10)$$

The definition of $C_1,C_2,\ldots,C_9$ will be performed in analogy to the operation for $O_1,O_2,\ldots,O_9$. The membership functions for O_i and C_i are shown in Figure 5.

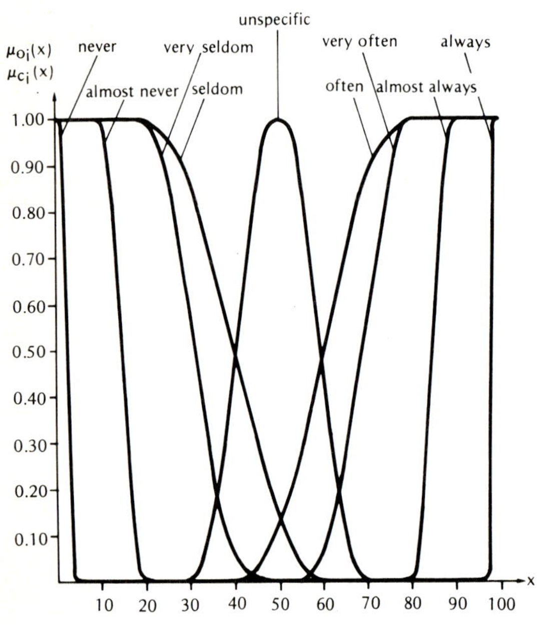

Fig. 5: Fuzzy membership functions of O_i and C_i.

Having defined the fuzzy subsets O_i and C_i, the following question arises:

What numerical degree of affiliation of symptom S_i to disease D_j shall be selected when the medical expert who documents the S_iD_j relationships chooses a linguistic representation O_i or C_i for characterizing the symptom-disease relationships?

The answer is given in the following manner:

It seems understandable that, at the moment of documenting a certain S_iD_j relation, the physician imagines "fuzzy" ranges for describing occurrence and confirmability. If, for example, the physician claims that S_i very often appears with D_j, then he selects a "fuzzy" range from about 70 to 80 occurrences of S_i with D_j in his mind (relative to 100) and terms this "fuzzy" range very often. The same is valid for confirmability. If, for example, the physician chooses always in order to describe confirmability of S_i for D_j then he considers a "fuzzy" range of about 99 to 100, i.e. medical studies have produced the result that in 99 or 100 cases S_i confirms D_j.

In order to get suitable ranges for all linguistic terms O_i and C_i that are labels of fuzzy subsets it seems rational to consider those ranges of the reference sets Φ_O and Φ_C where the membership functions $\mu_{O_i}(x)\geq 0.5$ and $\mu_{C_i}\geq(x)$ 0.5 resp. Because of

$$O_1\subset O_2\subset O_3\subset O_4 \quad \text{and} \quad O_9\subset O_8\subset O_7\subset O_6, \quad (11)$$

with $\subset$ as the inclusion [10)] of fuzzy subsets which is defined (see /17/) as

$$A\subset B \text{ if } \mu_A(x)\leq\mu_B(x),\ x\in X,$$

where A and B are fuzzy subsets of the reference set X, the ranges are overlapping. Assuming ranges r_{O_i} given by O_i we exclude

r_{O_1} from r_{O_2}, r_{O_2} from r_{O_3}, r_{O_3} from r_{O_4}

and

r_{O_9} from r_{O_8}, r_{O_8} from r_{O_7}, r_{O_7} from r_{O_6}

to overcome this problem.

To give an example, consider O_2=almost always that defines r_{O_2}=85-100. But because O_1=always occupies the range 98-100 we calculate r_{O_2}=85-98. The analoguous way is valid for the computation of ranges r_{C_i} for C_i.

Subsequently, we calculate the means x_{O_i} and x_{C_i} from the determined r_{O_i} and r_{C_i}. We now consider the means to be the numerical representatives of the linguistic terms O_i and C_i [11]. By obtaining the means x_{O_i} and x_{C_i} which are elements of the reference sets $\Phi_O(x)$ and $\Phi_C(x)$ we are able to determine $\mu_O(x_{O_i})$ and $\mu_C(x_{C_i})$ for every i, $1 \leq i \leq 9$.

Figure 6 shows the considered ranges r_{O_i} and r_{C_i} and the calculated means x_{O_i} and x_{C_i}.

Table 2 presents a survey of the determined $\mu_{occurrence}(x)$ and $\mu_{confirmabilty}(x)$ based on the linguistic possibilities to document O_i and C_i.

3.2.2.2. Medical database evaluation

In Hospital Information Systems /14,15, 41,42/ medical databases are applied to store both patients personal and medical data. On the one hand patients medical data are the basis for daily routine in hospital (test result tables, drug tables, statistics of available beds, etc.).

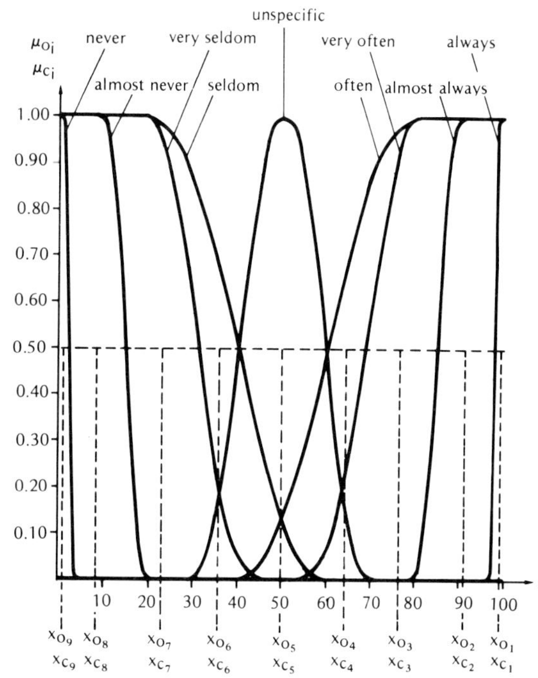

Fig. 6: Ranges r_{O_i} and r_{C_i} and the calculated means x_{O_i} and x_{C_i} for the fuzzy subsets O_i and C_i.

On the other hand patients' medical data are utilized to carry out medical research (analysis of symptom patterns that characterize diseases, course of patient recovery from diseases after administration of certain drugs, etc.).

If a medical database contains a big amount of medical records of patients including all relevant symptoms as well as final diagnoses established by clinicians at discharge of patients from hospital or after the treatment period of outpatients, it can be used to calculate S_iD_j relationships. With respect to the two aspects of a S_iD_j relationship

Table 2: Determination of $\mu_{occurrence}(x)$ and $\mu_{confirmability}(x)$ from the linguistic possibilities to document O_i and C_i.

Fuzzy Subsets O_i or C_i	Ranges r_{O_i} or r_{C_i}	Means x_{O_i} or x_{C_i}	Degrees of Membership $\mu_O(x_{O_i})$ or $\mu_C(x_{C_i})$
always	98 to 100	99	1.00
almost always	85 to 98	91.5	∿0.99
very often	∿69 to 85	∿77	∿0.90
often	60 to ∿69	∿64.5	∿0.75
unspecific	40 to 60	50	0.50
seldom	∿31 to 40	∿35.5	∿0.25
very seldom	15 to ∿31	∿23	∿0.10
almost never	2 to 15	8.5	∿0.01
never	0 to 2	1	0.00

the following considerations are made:

Consideration 1:

Occurrence of a symptom S_i in case of a disease D_j is defined by the relative frequency of occurrence of S_i with D_j.

Assuming x_2 cases of D_j and counting a frequency of x_1 for S_i, we calculate a relative frequency x_O by

$$x_O=\frac{x_1}{x_2}\cdot 100. \tag{12}$$

We are now able to compute a degree of membership of x_O in the fuzzy subset occurrence by applying (3)

$$\mu_O(x_O)=f_1(x_O;1,50,99). \tag{13}$$

Example:
Let us assume 67 patients suffering from gout. In 13 cases we found tophi at the patients. We calculate

$$x_O=\frac{13}{67}\cdot 100\approx 19.4\ .$$

This yields

$$\mu_O(x_O)=f_1(19.4;1,50,99)\approx 0.07\ ^{12)}.$$

Consideration 2:

Confirmability of a symptom S_i for a disease D_j is defined by the relative frequency of occurrence of D_j with S_i. Assuming x_4 cases of S_i and counting a frequency of x_3 for D_j we calculate a relative frequency x_C by

$$x_C=\frac{x_3}{x_4}\cdot 100. \tag{14}$$

In analogy to the above we are able to compute a degree of membership of x_C in the fuzzy subset confirmability by applying (4)

$$\mu_C(x_C)=f_1(x_C;1,50,99). \tag{15}$$

Example:
Let us assume 13 cases of tophi. We found in all these cases the diagnosis gout. We calculate

$$x_C=\frac{13}{13}.100=100$$

and obtain

$$\mu_C(x_C)=f_1(100;1,50,99)=1.00$$ [13].

3.2.2.3. Problems and conclusions

A lot of problems appear in practical attempts at determining symptom-disease relationships:

1) Linguistic documentation

Problem 1:

S_iD_j relationships can be documented linguistically but only after the symptom-disease relationships have been analysed in medical studies. But because not all S_iD_j relationships will have been investigated, $\mu_O(x)$ or $\mu_C(x)$ are often impossible to define [14].

Problem 2:

Medical studies have often yielded different results considering the same symptom-disease relationship where the percentage of occurrence covers two or more linguistic terms. In /1/ (p. 676), for example, we read that "...C...could find abusus of alcohol in 70% and K... and H...in 40% of the cases of acute pancreatitis."

2) Medical database evaluation

Problem 1:

Patients go to a hospital several times suffering from several diseases. The first problem to get statistical material is to consider patients' data only from one stay in hospital or from one series of visits in an outpatient department. In patient's records such a period is characterized by the dates of admission, discharge and the final diagnoses established by the responsible medical person /14,15/.

Problem 2:

A medical history, a general status, X-ray, ECG, EEG, histological, ultrasonic, and rheumatological findings, etc. are made during one stay in hospital. Additionally, several laboratory tests are performed. For the most part, examinations are two, three and more times in the course of one illness period. Now the question arises which examination results should be considered with respect to the final diagnoses. In CADIAG-2, this problem is solved by taking the first values of these examinations that are performed twice or more times during one stay in hospital, to avoid effects of therapy.

Due to these considerations the results are well-established patients' symptom patterns connected to final diagnoses (Table 3).

Problem 3:

In order to count frequencies S_i with D_j and D_j with S_i, symptom patterns with only one final diagnosis were necessary. In general, such data are not available in internal medicine. The process of studying and solving this problem has not been completed yet. So far, the frequencies of S_i with D_j are calculated by taking every symptom S_i in patients' symptom patterns into account considering a certain disease D_j (vice versa for calculating the frequencies of D_j with S_i).

Table 3: Patients' pattern in a medical database which are the starting point for statistical evaluations.

patients	patients symptom pattern with final diagnoses
Patient 1	$D_1\ D_2\ D_3\ D_4 \,\|\, S_1\ S_2\ S_3\ S_7 \ldots$
Patient 1[15]	$D_3\ D_5\ D_6 \,\|\, S_2\ S_{10}\ S_{20}\ S_{30} \ldots$
Patient 2	$D_7 \,\|\, S_{100}\ S_{101}\ S_{102} \ldots$
Patient 3	$D_4\ D_6\ D_7\ D_8\ D_9\ D_{10} \,\|\, S_3\ S_{10} \cdot$
Patient 4	$D_{11}\ D_{12} \,\|\, S_{100}\ S_{101}\ S_{102} \ldots$
.	.
.	.
.	.

Example (from Table 3):

Occurrence:

S_1 with D_1: 1 of 1 → $x_O=100$ $\mu_O(x_O)=1$
S_2 with D_1: 1 of 1 → $x_O=100$ $\mu_O(x_O)=1$
.
.
.
S_1 with D_3: 1 of 2 → $x_O=50$ $\mu_O(x_O)=0.5$
.
.
.
S_7 with D_6: 0 of 2 → $x_O=0$ $\mu_O(x_O)=0$

Confirmability:

D_1 with S_1: 1 of 1 → $x_C=100$ $\mu_C(x_C)=1$
D_1 with S_2: 1 of 2 → $x_C=50$ $\mu_C(x_C)=0.5$
.
.
.
D_3 with S_1: 1 of 1 → $x_C=100$ $\mu_C(x_C)=1$
.
.
.
D_6 with S_7: 0 of 1 → $x_C=0$ $\mu_C(x_C)=0$

But it is obvious that with the use of this method, errors can and will appear.

Example:
Hypertension is a very common disease not directly related to any rheumatic disease. Elevated blood pressure is the obligatory symptom in hypertension, retinal disorders may occur. In a given patient gonarthrosis, a degenerative knee joint disease, and hypertension due to constriction of blood vessels may be found. If the patient's symptom pattern is used for the described evaluation, high blood pressure and eye disturbances are linked not only to hypertension but also to gonarthrosis, a disease which certainly has nothing to do with eye troubles.

3.2.3. Symptom-symptom fuzzy relationships

Apart from the knowledge about symptom-disease relationships, medical knowledge also includes judgement about relations among symptoms. Symptoms very often exclude the presence of other symptoms. On the other hand, symptoms often imply the presence of symptoms or have to be necessarily present with other symptoms. CADIAG-2 takes this into account by means of always and never occurrence and always and never confirmability relationships among symptoms.

Always occurring and always confirming relationships express hierarchical dependencies between symptoms. The sub-term confirms the super-term. It follows that the super-term is obligatory, i.e. it is always occurring in respect of each of its sub-terms. If the super-symptom is set to be "not present" then every sub-symptom has to be set to "not present".

Table 4: Symptom-symptom and disease-disease relationships considered in CADIAG-2 with their degrees of membership in occurrence and confirmability.

S_iS_j- and D_iD_j-relationships			
occurrence	confirmability	$\mu_O(x)$	$\mu_C(x)$
always	always	1	1
(obligatory and proving)			
unknown	always	-	1
(facultative and proving)			
always	unknown	1	-
(obligatory and not proving)			
never	never	0	0
(excluding)			
unknown	unknown	-	-

Examples:
Symptom GOT, normal excludes GOT, increased, GOT, highly increased, GOT, decreased. Further, diffuse swelling, right hand as well as diffuse swelling, left hand confirm diffuse swelling, hand or recurrent high fever confirms high fever. But if the diffuse swelling, hand is denied, it can be concluded that neither a diffuse swelling of the right hand nor of the left hand is present.

CADIAG-2 only considers strong symptom-symptom relationships. The relationships taken into account and the attached degrees of membership in the fuzzy subsets occurrence of S_i for S_j and confirmability of S_i for S_j are shown in Table 4. The fuzzy subsets occurrence and confirmability are defined in the same manner as described in paragraph 3.2.1.

During the diagnostic consultation, CADIAG-2 uses S_iS_j relationships in a symptom-symptom inference module. The input of the module consists of patients' symptom patterns established from the patients' medical database /14,15/ or from physician's input. The output that is the starting point for the inner diagnostic process [16)] consists of an enlarged symptom pattern including the original and the inferred symptoms attached with their cause.

3.2.4. Disease-disease fuzzy relationships

Medical knowledge about diseases to a great extent includes hierarchical concepts. In order to incorporate hierarchical disease dependencies into CADIAG-2, disease-disease relationships have been established.

Examples:
A bacterial arthritis can be caused by gonococci, meningococci, salmonelli or others. Therefore, sub-terms of bacterial arthritis are bacterial arthritis by gonococci, - by meningococci, - by salmonelli etc. On the other hand, an acute arthritis by fungi or viruses excludes a bacterial arthritis (see Figure 7).

In analogy to the definition of relationships among symptoms, only strong disease-disease relationships are taken into

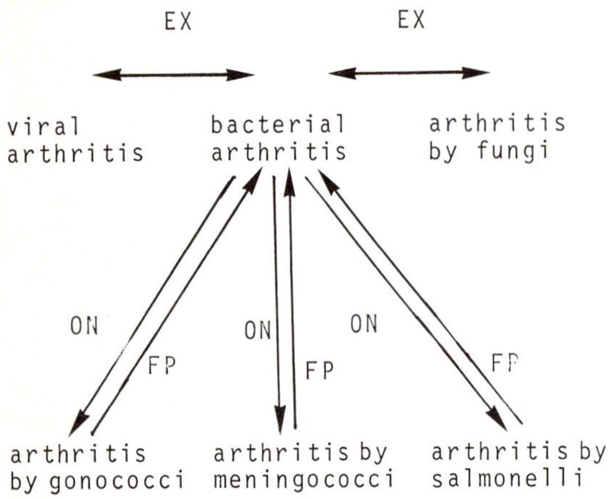

EX: excluding ($\mu_O(x)=0; \mu_C(x)=0$)

FP: facultative and proving($\mu_C(x)=1$)

ON: obligatory and not proving($\mu_O(x)=1$)

Fig. 7: Section of disease-disease relationships in CADIAG-2.

account [17] (see Table 4).

Disease-disease relationships are used in CADIAG-2, in a similar way as symptom-symptom relationships, in a disease-disease inference module. The module is activated in two different parts of CADIAG-2. Firstly, the input of the module consists of a patient's known diseases (patient's past history or result of a previous iteration of CADIAG-2) or secondly, of the diagnostic output of the inner diagnostic process. In the first case, the patients known disease pattern will be enlarged. In the second case it will be ascertained if confirmed diagnoses imply other diagnoses or if excluded diagnoses are compulsory for diagnoses not yet excluded.

3.2.5. Symptom combination-disease fuzzy relationships

A physician often attributes a low value to a single symptom but if it appears together with other symptoms, this combination can be a strong indication for a specific diagnosis. Computer-assisted diagnostic systems have to incorporate this kind of medical knowledge.

Most clinically found symptom combinations give only a slight evidence for diseases (see MYCIN /43/). Furthermore, established clinical symptom combinations are often not accepted in the entire medical community to be a definite criterion to prove or exclude a disease. Different medical schools insist on their own medical concepts.

Therefore the possibility to establish "soft" or "fuzzy" relationships between symptom combinations and diseases should be given. Strong, proving combinations of symptoms for diseases with consideration of excluding criteria have been established and were published as international guiding principles (see, for example, the diagnostic criteria of the American Rheumatism Association for rheumatoid arthritis /44/ or of the American Heart Association for rheumatic fever /45/), but they are rare.

In CADIAG-2, symptom combinations are considered to be fuzzy logical combinations (LC) [18] with symptoms and diseases as fuzzy variables connected by the fuzzy logical operations "conjunction", "disjunction", "negation", "minimal" and "maximal" (see below). Moreover, combinations have fuzzy relationships to diseases.

1. Example:

The symptom combination low back pain, limitation of motion of the lumbar spine, and diminished chest expansion in a man between 20 and 40 years is highly characteristical for ankylosing spondylitis. But in various rare diseases, e.g. psoriatic spondylitis, Reiter's syndrome, enteropathic arthritis, the same symptom combination may occur.

2. Example (from American Heart Association publication /45/):

In order to diagnose rheumatic fever the following criteria have to be considered:

Major criteria:

1. Carditis (SCP1)
2. Polyarthritis (SCP2)
3. Synderham's chorea (SCP3)
4. Erythema marginatum (SCP4)
5. Subcutaneous nodules (SCP5)

Minor criteria:

6. Fever (SCP6)
7. Arthralgia (SCP7)
8. History of previous rheumatic fever or rheumatic cardiopathia (SCP8)
9. Elevated ESR (SCP9)
10. Positive C-reactive protein or leucocytosis (SCP10)
11. Prolonged PR-interval (SCP11)

The diagnosis rheumatic fever is established if two major criteria or one major criterion and two minor criteria are fulfilled and if, additionally, a preceding streptococcal infection (SCP12) (elevated antistreptolysin titer or streptococci in throat swab or precedent scarlatina) can be detected. The absence of the latter should make the diagnosis questionable, except in situations where rheumatic fever is only discovered after a long latent period from the antecedent infection (e.g., Synderham's chorea or low grade-carditis).

Because of the fact that symptoms considered to be diagnostic criteria are often "higher level" symptoms that express a pathophysiological state or similar concepts [19] a two level definition of symptom combinations has been realized in CADIAG-2.

In the first step the "higher level" symptoms are established from directly observed symptoms $S_i \in \Sigma$ and given diseases $D_j \in \Delta$ of the patient. "Higher level" symptoms are called symptom combinations primary (SCP) in CADIAG-2. In this way the establishing of the "higher level" symptom

"joint aches in at least one joint when subjected to passive motion or pressure" yields "pain on passive motion or tenderness in one MCP $\vee$ in one PIP $\vee$ in one DIP $\vee$ in one wrist $\vee$ in one elbow $\vee$ in one shoulder $\vee$ in one acromioclavicular $\vee$ in one sternoclavicular $\vee$ in one jaw $\vee$ in one hip $\vee$ in one knee $\vee$ in one ankle $\vee$ in one toe joint."

This has been defined as a major criterion for rheumatoid arthritis by the American Rheumatism Association /44/. In practical use the sets Σ and Δ are given by using hierarchical thesauri that form the basis for the documentation of symptom-disease relationships. Beside this, every "higher level" symptom is named and included in a thesaurus of SCP. The decision as to whether or not a medical term is considered to be a symptom or a SCP is made by the documenting physician. So, for

Table 5: Rules of the contextfree language that defines the syntactical structure of symptom combination primary and secondary.

<table>
<tr><th colspan="3">rules</th></tr>
<tr><td colspan="3"><symptom combination secondary>::=<identifier secondary>=<expression secondary>;</td></tr>
<tr><td><identifier secondary></td><td>::=SCS<integer></td><td rowspan="2">⇐ mapping in a thesaurus of symptom combinations secondary</td></tr>
<tr><td><expression secondary></td><td>::=<factor secondary>{∧<factor secondary>|∨<factor secondary>}*</td></tr>
<tr><td><factor secondary></td><td>::=[~]<variable secondary></td><td></td></tr>
<tr><td><variable secondary></td><td>::=<identifier primary>|(<expression secondary>)|
<mima-term secondary></td><td></td></tr>
<tr><td><mima-term secondary></td><td>::={↑|↓}*<integer>/<integer>:<variable list secondary></td><td rowspan="2">⇐ "left"integer≤"right" integer=number of expressions secondary in variable list secondary</td></tr>
<tr><td><variable list secondary></td><td>::=<expression secondary>;{<variable list secondary>}*</td></tr>
<tr><td><symptom combination primary></td><td>::=<identifier primary>=<expression primary>;</td><td></td></tr>
<tr><td><identifier primary></td><td>::=SCP<integer></td><td rowspan="2">⇐ mapping in a thesaurus of symptom combinations primary</td></tr>
<tr><td><expression primary></td><td>::=<factor primary>{∧<factor primary>|∨<factor primary>}*</td></tr>
<tr><td><factor primary></td><td>::=[~]<variable primary></td><td></td></tr>
<tr><td><variable primary></td><td>::=<symptom>|<disease>|(<expression primary>)|
<mima-term primary></td><td></td></tr>
<tr><td><symptom></td><td>::=S<integer></td><td>⇐ mapping in a symptom thesaurus</td></tr>
<tr><td><disease></td><td>::=D<integer></td><td>⇐ mapping in a diagnosis thesaurus</td></tr>
<tr><td><mima-term primary></td><td>::={↑|↓}*<integer>/<integer>:<variable list primary></td><td rowspan="2">⇐ "left"integer≤"right" integer=number of expressions primary in variable list primary</td></tr>
<tr><td><variable list primary></td><td>::=<expression primary>;{<variable list primary>}*</td></tr>
<tr><td><integer></td><td>::=<digit>[<integer>]</td><td></td></tr>
<tr><td><digit></td><td>::=0|1|2|3|4|5|6|7|8|9</td><td></td></tr>
</table>

instance, we included carditis in the thesaurus of SCP because it is determined by "pancarditis ∨ endocarditis ∨ pericarditis" which are all defined as symptoms in Σ.

Table 5 presents the rules of a context-free language that defines the syntactical structure of SCP. The definition of the language has been carried out in extended BACKUS-NAUR form (see /49/). The syntax can be analyzed by a recursive descent parser /49-51/.

Examples:

SCP1=S1vS2vS3;
(carditis=pancarditis ∨ endocarditis ∨ pericarditis)

SCP2=D96vD97;
(clinical pattern of an acute infectious arthritis=acute arthritis, pyogenic microorganism ∨ acute arthritis, non-pyogenic microorganism)

Symptom and diagnoses are considered to be fuzzy variables taking their values in [0,1]. Let $x_1, x_2, \ldots$ be fuzzy variables, in general the following operations are defined:

$$\begin{aligned}&\text{conjunction}(\vee): x_1 \wedge x_2 = \text{MIN}(x_1, x_2)\\ &\text{disjunction}(\vee): x_1 \wedge x_2 = \text{MAX}(x_1, x_2)\\ &\text{negation}\ (\sim):\ \sim x_1 = 1 - x_1\end{aligned} \tag{16}$$

and

$$\text{minimal } (\uparrow): \uparrow N_1/N_2: x_1; x_2; \ldots; x_{N_2};$$
$$\text{maximal } (\downarrow): \downarrow N_1/N_2: x_1; x_2; \ldots; x_{N_2}; \quad (17)$$

where N_1 and N_2 are natural numbers with $N_1 \leq N_2$.

Connectives (16) are well-known (see DUBOIS and PRADE /19/), the "minimal" and "maximal" connectives (17) [20] have to be explained:

In Boolean logical sense $\uparrow N_1/N_2: x_1; \ldots; x_{N_2};$ means that at least N_1 of the N_2 logical variables $x_1; x_2; \ldots; x_{N_2}$ have to be true to make the result true /9/. Another notation would be (example):

$$\uparrow 2/3: x_1; x_2; x_3; \equiv (x_1 \wedge x_2) \vee (x_1 \wedge x_3) \vee (x_2 \wedge x_3).$$

In fuzzy logic, this latter notation is rational and yields

$$\uparrow N_1/N_2: x_1; x_2; \ldots; x_{N_2}; \equiv \text{MIN}(N_1 \text{ greatest values of } x_1; x_2; \ldots x_{N_2};). \quad (18)$$

As a pendant the "maximal" operation was introduced. In Boolean logic $\downarrow N_1/N_2: x_1; x_2; \ldots; x_{N_2};$ means that at the most N_1 of the N_2 logical variables are or can yet be true to make the result true /9/. In equivalent notation (example):

$$\downarrow 2/4: x_1; x_2; x_3; x_4; \equiv \sim\{(x_1 \wedge x_2 \wedge x_3) \vee (x_1 \wedge x_2 \wedge x_4) \vee (x_1 \wedge x_3 \wedge x_4) \vee (x_2 \wedge x_3 \wedge x_4)\}$$

This makes obvious that the maximal operator is expressable in fuzzy logic by

$$\downarrow N_1/N_2: \quad x_1; x_2; \ldots; x_{N_2}; \equiv 1-\text{MIN}(N_1+1 \text{ greatest values of } x_1; x_2; \ldots; x_{N_2};). \quad (19)$$

Let us summarize the first step in establishing symptom combinations. Symptom S_i and diseases D_j are connected by the logical operations "conjunction", "disjunction", "negation", "minimal" and "maximal" to symptom combinations primary $SCP_k \in \Lambda_1 = \{SCP_1, SCP_2, \ldots, SCP_s\}$, where Λ_1 is the non-fuzzy set of SCP taken into account and s its cardinality. Given fuzzy values $x_i = \mu_{S_i}(x)$ for S_i and $x_j - \mu_{D_j}(x)$ for D_j a degree of affiliation

$$\mu_{SCP_k}(x_1, x_2, \ldots, x_n)$$

is calculated with $x_i, x_j \in x_1, x_2, \ldots, x_n$ and n as the number of S_i and D_j taken into account to establish SCP_k. The SCP rules are of the form:

$$LC(S_i, D_j) \xrightarrow{\mu_{SCP_k}(x_i\ )} SCP_k \quad (20)$$

In the second step of the two level definition of symptom combinations, fuzzy logical combinations of "higher level" symptoms are established that have fuzzy relationships to diseases. These combinations are called symptom combinations secondary (SCS) [21].

$SCS_l \in \Lambda_2 = \{SCS_1, SCS_2, \ldots, SCS_t\}$ where Λ_2 defines the non-fuzzy set of the SCS taken into account, and t its cardinality. Table 5 gives the rules to define the syntactical structure of SCS.The syntax can be analyzed by a recursive descent parcer.

Example (see 2nd example stated above): Considering the major and minor criteria of <u>rheumatic fever</u> as SCP, the SCS is given by

$$SCS1=((\uparrow 2/5:SCP1;SCP2;SCP3;SCP4;SCP5; \vee (\uparrow 1/5\ :SCP1;SCP2;SCP3;SCP4;SCP5; \wedge \uparrow 2/6:SCP6;SCP7;SCP8;SCP9;SCP10;SCP11;)) \wedge SCP12) \vee (SCP3 \wedge SCP8);$$

Let us summarize the second step in establishing symptom combinations. SCP_k

are connected by the logical operations "conjunction", "disjunction", "negation", "minimal" and "maximal" to $SCS_1 \in \Lambda_2$. Given fuzzy values $x_i = \mu_{SCP_k}(x)$ for SCP_k, a degree of affiliation

$\mu_{SCS_1}(x_1, x_2, \ldots, x_n)$

is calculated with $x_i \in x_1, x_2, \ldots, x_n$ and n as the number of SCP_k taken into account to establish SCS_1. The SCS rules are of the form:

$$LC(SCP_k) \xrightarrow{\mu_{SCP_k}(x_i)} SCS_1. \qquad (21)$$

Now, in analogy to symptom-disease fuzzy relationships, two aspects are of high value to find out relationships between SCS and diseases:

1) Occurrence of SCS_1 in case of D_j and
2) Confirmability of SCS_1 for D_j.

These two aspects can be defined in the same way as for symptom-disease relationships. The membership functions for occurrence and confirmability are analogous to Figure 4. The fuzzy relationships between SCS_1 and D_j are defined linguistically by medical experts. The possible set is analogous to Table 1.

Examples (see 1st and 2nd examples above):

1. Example:
The SCS for ankylosing spondylitis often occurs in ankylosing spondylitis, but as mentioned above this symptom combination does not confirm the diagnosis ankylosing spondylitis.

2.Example:
The SCS for rheumatic fever often occurs with rheumatic fever, but if it occurs, it always confirms rheumatic fever.

3.3. Symptoms as fuzzy subsets

All observable properties of a patient are used in medical diagnosis. These can be symptoms, signs, laboratory test results and complaints related to the patient (also information about his family and his living circumstances) at any observation time. Let us term every property as a symptom.

As stated above, every symptom $S_i \in \Sigma$, $1 \leq i \leq m$, is a fuzzy subset of a reference set $\Omega = \{x_1, x_2, \ldots\}$ characterized by a membership function $\mu_{S_i}(x)$.

Let us now distinguish two different kinds of reference sets Ω.

1. $\Omega = \{x_1, x_2, \ldots\}$ contains continuous values, e.g. as Ω for S= increased alcaline phosphatase.

2. $\Omega = \{0,1\}$, i.e. the symptom S_i is a binary symptom, which can be absent (0) or present (1) (see also /52,53/), e.g. as Ω for S= drug history, medicine against rheumatism (see Figure 8).

Most of the laboratory test results and some of the signs observed during physical examination (e.g. SCHOBER distance, normal ≥ 4 cm, pathological < 4 cm) provide continuous values as a result of the investigation, and most of symptoms of patient's history, complaints, evidence or infection, X-ray findings, etc. are binary symptoms. Some of the binary symptoms are real ones, e.g. drug history, medicine against rheumatism, others are not, e.g. headache. But we do not want to establish fuzzy subsets to define the severity level of symptoms, because so far it does not seem practical to calculate numerical values for, e.g. severe headache.

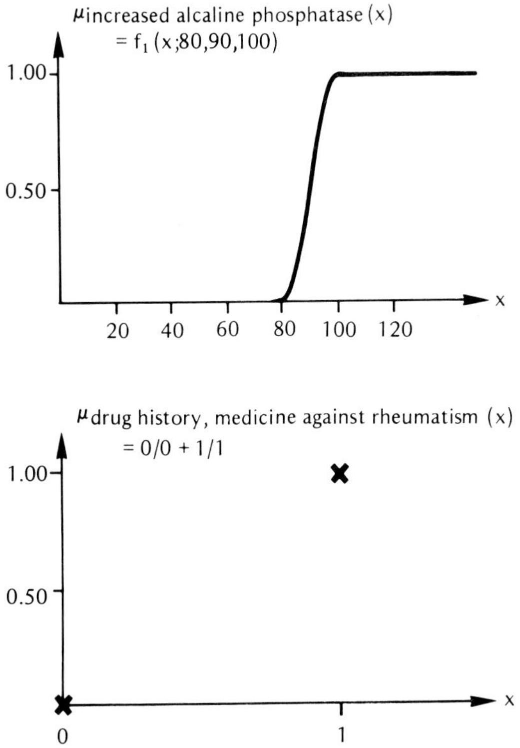

Fig. 8: Symptom membership functions.

All symptoms taken into account may now be defined to have one of the two kinds of reference sets. Uninvestigated symptoms are not considered.

3.4. Diagnostic fuzzy indications

Given a patient's symptom pattern both the

- symptom-disease relationships and the
- symptom combination-disease relationships and the
- diseases-disease relationships

yield fuzzy diagnostic indications that are the basis for establishing confirmed and excluded diagnosis as well as diagnostic hypotheses.

3.4.1. Indications from symptom-disease relationships

Let us introduce a binary fuzzy relation R_0 which is a fuzzy subset of $\Sigma x \Delta$ and characterized by the two parameter membership function $\mu_{R_0}(S_i,D_j)$ in the interval [0,1]. The $\mu_{R_0}(S_i,D_j)$ are identical to $\mu_0(x)$ which has been documented for S_i with regard to D_j as <u>occurrence</u> relationship.

The <u>confirmability</u> relationships form the elements of the binary fuzzy relation $R_C \subset \Sigma x \Delta$. Thus, R_C is defined by $\mu_{R_C}(S_i,D_j)$ which is equal to $\mu_C(x)$ considering the symptom S_i and diagnosis D_j.

Furthermore, we introduce the binary fuzzy relation $R_S \subset \Pi x \Sigma$. The sets Π and Σ are given when the symptom patterns of the patients under consideration are available. Symptoms which have not been investigated but are considered in the documentation work of the physician have to be dropped from the relation matrices R_P and R_C. Now, the functions $\mu_{R_S}(p,S_i)$ which characterize the fuzzy relation R_S are identical with $\mu_{S_i}(x)$ calculated for the patient p and corresponding to the defined fuzzy subset S_i.

Finally, four different fuzzy indications are calculated by means of fuzzy relation compositions:

1. S_iD_j occurrence indication $R_1 = R_S \circ R_0$
$$\mu_{R_1}(p,D_j) = \underset{S_i}{\text{MAX}}\ \text{MIN}\ \{\mu_{R_S}(p,S_i);\mu_{R_0}(S_i,D_j)\} \quad (22)$$

2. S_iD_j confirmability indication $R_2 = R_S \circ R_C$
$$\mu_{R_2}(p,D_j) = \underset{S_i}{\text{MAX}}\ \text{MIN}\ \{\mu_{R_S}(p,S_i);\mu_{R_C}(S_i,D_j)\} \quad (23)$$

3. S_iD_j non-occurrence indication $R_3 = R_S \circ (1-R_0)$
$$\mu_{R_3}(p,D_j) = \underset{S_i}{\text{MAX}}\ \text{MIN}\ \{\mu_{R_S}(p,S_i);1-\mu_{R_0}(S_i,D_j)\} \quad (24)$$

4. S_iD_j non-symptom indication $R_4=(1-R_S)\mathrm{o}R_0$

$$\mu_{R_4}(p,D_j)=\underset{S_i}{\mathrm{MAX}}\ \mathrm{MIN}\ \{1-\mu_{R_S}(p,S_i);\mu_{R_0}(S_i,D_j)\} \quad (25)$$

where $p\in\Pi, S_i\in\Sigma, 1\leq i\leq m$ and $D_j\in\Delta, 1\leq j\leq n$.

3.4.2. Indications from symptom combination-disease relationships

The binary fuzzy relation $\overline{R}_0$ which is a fuzzy subset of $\Lambda_2\times\Delta$ is characterized by the membership function $\mu_{\overline{R}_0}(SCS_1,D_j)$. The $\mu_{\overline{R}_0}(SCS_1,D_j)$ express the SCS_1D_j occurrence relationships documented by a medical expert.

A further $\overline{R}_C\subset\Lambda_2\times\Delta$ is introduced. The characteristic function $\mu_{\overline{R}_C}(SCS_1,D_j)$ expresses the SCS_1D_j confirmability relationship for SCS_1 and a disease D_j. Moreover, it is necessary to introduce a binary fuzzy relation $\overline{R}_{SCS}\subset\Pi\times\Lambda_2$. Given patients p with their symptoms S_i and known diseases D_j, the $\mu_{\overline{R}_{SCS}}(p,SCS_1)$ can be calculated as illustrated in Figure 9.

In analogy to (22), (23), (24), and (25), relations between patients p and disease D_j can be determined by

1. SCS_1D_j occurrence indication $R_5=R_{SCS}\mathrm{o}\overline{R}_0$

$$\mu_{R_5}(p,D_j)=\underset{SCS_1}{\mathrm{MAX}}\ \mathrm{MIN}\{\mu_{R_{SCS}}(p,SCS_1);\mu_{\overline{R}_0}(SCS_1,D_j)\} \quad (26)$$

2. SCS_1D_j confirmability indication $R_6=R_{SCS}\mathrm{o}\overline{R}_C$

$$\mu_{R_6}(p,D_j)=\underset{SCS_1}{\mathrm{MAX}}\ \mathrm{MIN}\{\mu_{R_{SCS}}(p,SCS_1);\mu_{\overline{R}_C}(SCS_1,D_j)\} \quad (27)$$

3. SCS_1D_j non-occurrence indication $R_7=R_{SCS}\mathrm{o}(1-\overline{R}_0)$

$$\mu_{R_7}(p,D_j)=\underset{SCS_1}{\mathrm{MAX}}\ \mathrm{MIN}\{\mu_{R_{SCS}}(p,SCS_1);1-\mu_{\overline{R}_0}(SCS_1,D_j)\} \quad (28)$$

4. SCS_1D_j non-SCS indication $R_8=(1-R_{SCS})\mathrm{o}\overline{R}_0$

$$\mu_{R_8}(p,D_j)=\underset{SCS_1}{\mathrm{MAX}}\ \mathrm{MIN}\{1-\mu_{R_{SCS}}(p,SCS_1);\ \mu_{\overline{R}_0}(SCS_1,D_j)\} \quad (29)$$

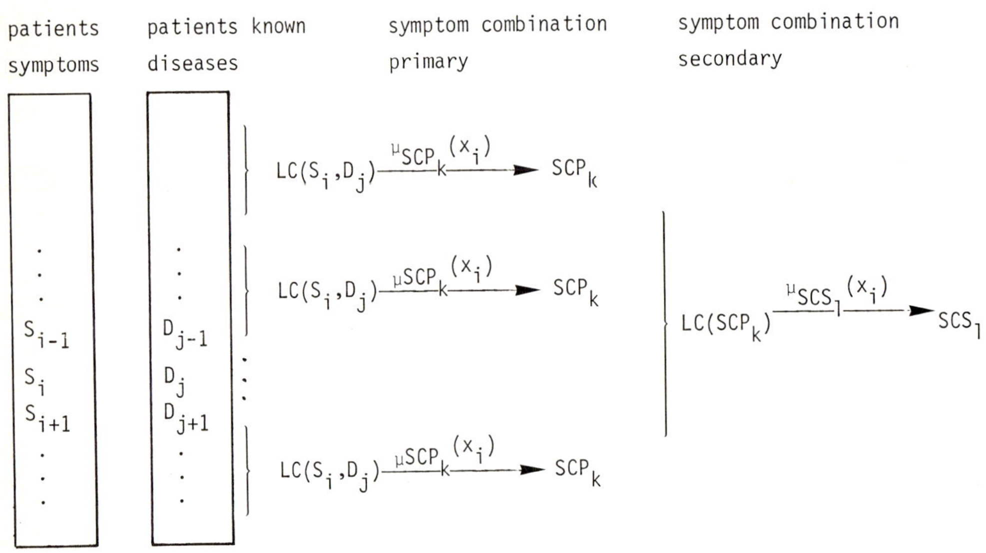

Fig. 9: Process of calculating the membership functions $\mu_{SCS_1}(x)$ for SCS_1.

where $p \in \Pi$, $SCS_l \in \Lambda_2$, $1 \leq l \leq s$ and $D_j \in \Delta$, $1 \leq l \leq n$.

3.4.3. Indications from disease-disease relationships

A stated in paragraph 3.2.4. disease-disease fuzzy relationships are established in CADIAG-2 and can be used to infer diagnoses from confirmed or excluded diagnoses provided by the last diagnostic iteration. The representation of this consideration by means of compositions of fuzzy relations yields the following:

1. D_iD_j occurrence indication $R_9 = R_D \circ R_O^*$

$$\mu_{R_9}(p,D_j) = \max_{D_i} \min\{\mu_{R_D}(p,D_i); \mu_{R_O^*}(D_i,D_j)\} \quad (30)$$

2. D_iD_j confirmability indication $R_{10} = R_D \circ R_C^*$

$$\mu_{R_{10}}(p,D_j) = \max_{D_i} \min\{\mu_{R_{D_i}}(p,D_i); \mu_{R_C^*}(D_i,D_j)\} \quad (31)$$

3. D_iD_j non-occurrence indication $R_{11} = R_D \circ (1-R_O^*)$

$$\mu_{R_{11}}(p,D_j) = \max_{D_i} \min\{\mu_{R_D}(p,D_i); 1-\mu_{R_O^*}(D_i,D_j)\} \quad (32)$$

4. D_iD_j non-disease indication $R_{12} = (1-R_D) \circ R_O^*$

$$\mu_{R_{12}}(p,D_j) = \max_{D_i} \min\{1-\mu_{R_D}(p,D_i); \mu_{R_O^*}(D_i,D_j)\} \quad (33)$$

3.5. Diagnostic results

By using the above-defined relations $R_1, R_2, \ldots, R_{12}$, only three categories of diagnostic results are distinguished:

1) Confirmed diagnoses
   All D_j are put out as confirmed diagnoses if either

$$\mu_{R_2}(p,D_j) = 1.00 \quad (34)$$

or

$$\mu_{R_6}(p,D_j) = 1.00 \quad \text{or} \quad (35)$$

by considering $\mu_{R_2}(p,D_j)$ or $\mu_{R_6}(p,D_j)$ as $\mu_{R_D}(p,D_i)$ in (31),

$$\mu_{R_{10}}(p,D_j) = 1.00. \quad (36)$$

2) Excluded diagnoses
   All D_j are displayed as excluded diagnoses if either

$$\mu_{R_3}(p,D_j) = 1.00 \quad (37)$$
$$\mu_{R_4}(p,D_j) = 1.00 \quad \text{or} \quad (38)$$
$$\mu_{R_7}(p,D_j) = 1.00 \quad (39)$$
$$\mu_{R_8}(p,D_j) = 1.00. \quad (40)$$

or, by considering $\mu_{R_2}(p,D_j)$, $\mu_{R_6}(p,D_j)$ or $\mu_{R_{10}}(p,D_j)$ as $\mu_{R_D}(p,D_i)$ in (32),

$$\mu_{R_{11}}(p,D_j) = 1.00 \quad (41)$$

or, by considering $\mu_{R_3}(p,D_j)$, $\mu_{R_4}(p,D_j)$, $\mu_{R_7}(p,D_j)$, $\mu_{R_8}(p,D_j)$ and $\mu_{R_{11}}(p,D_j)$ as $\mu_{R_D}(p,D_i)$ in (33),

$$\mu_{R_{12}}(p,D_j) = 1.00. \quad (42)$$

3) Diagnostic hypotheses
   All diagnoses D_j where a degree of membership $\mu_H(p,D_j)$ of either

$$0.50 < \mu_H(p,D_j) = \max\{\mu_{R_1}(p,D_j); \mu_{R_2}(p,D_j)\} \quad (43)$$

or

$$0.50 < \mu_H(p,D_j) = \max\{\mu_{R_5}(p,D_j), \mu_{R_6}(p,D_j)\} \quad (44)$$

or

$$0.50 < \mu_H(p,D_j) = \max\{\mu_{R_9}(p,D_j); \mu_{R_{10}}(p,D_j)\}. \quad (45)$$

is calculated are considered to be diagnostic hypotheses.

3.6. Reasonings for diagnostic results

The acceptance of a computer-assisted medical consultation system is highly dependent on the ability of the system

Table 6: Reasonings for confirmed diagnoses.

a) D_j proved by a symptom $S_i(R_2)$				
Name of S_i	Numerical value incl. units of S_i	$\mu_{R_S}(p,S_i)$ and the function that calculated the degree of membership	$\mu_{R_O}(S_i,D_j)$ and its linguistic correspondence	$\mu_{R_C}(S_i,D_j)$ and its linguistic correspondence
b) D_j proved by a symptom combination secondary $SCS_l(R_6)$				
Name of SCS_l		$\mu_{R_{SCS}}(p,SCS_l)$ and the logical combination of SCS_l	$\mu_{\overline{R}_O}(SCS_l,D_j)$ and its linguistic correspondence	$\mu_{\overline{R}_C}(SCS_l,D_j)$ and its linguistic correspondence
Names of SCP_k		$\mu_{R_{SCP}}(p,SCP_k)$ and the logical combinations of SCP_k		
Names of S_i	Numerical value incl. units of S_i	$\mu_{R_S}(p,S_i)$ and the function that calculated the degree of membership		
Names of D_j		$\mu_{R_D}(p,D_j)$ and its cause		
c) D_j proved by a diagnosis $D_i(R_{10})$				
Name of D_i		$\mu_{R_D}(p,D_i)$	$\mu_{R^*_O}(D_i,D_j)$ and its linguistic correspondence	$\mu_{R^*_C}(D_i,D_j)$ and its linguistic correspondence

to explain its diagnostic output. In CADIAG-2, reasonings for diagnoses displayed as confirmed or excluded diagnoses or as diagnostic hypotheses are given on request.

The following kinds of reasonings for confirmed diagnoses are possible (see Table 6).

The reasoning process for excluded diagnoses and diagnostic hypotheses are performed similarly.

3.7. Proposals for patient's further examination

To give the physician proposals for further examinations of the patient after the first diagnostic consultation of CADIAG-2 is one of the main objectives in establishing computer-aided medical decision aids. In rheumatology, for example, the first diagnostic consultation starts with symptoms and signs from patient's rheumatological history. If no confirmed diagnoses can be found or if some symptoms in the patient's symptom pattern remain unexplained by the established confirmed and excluded diagnoses and diagnostic hypotheses, CADIAG-2 proposes further examinations. In the first step CADIAG-2 proposes class-1 symptoms, e.g. symptoms that can be routinely checked. In the second step it proposes class-2 symptoms, e.g. simple lab tests, and class-3 symptoms, e.g. tests that are expensive to carry out or invasive procedures. Thus the tests to be performed can be optimized with respect to their financial costs and their risk for the patient.

3.8. Explanation of patient's symptoms by diagnostic results

The aim of the diagnostic iterations is to obtain diagnostic results which together explain patient's symptom pattern, i.e. no symptoms, signs, or test results that the patient shows must remain unexplained. If symptoms remain unexplained then the physician consulting CADIAG-2 has to decide if an unimportant symptom is in question or not. For example, if headache remains unexplained then the physician has to decide if it originates in, e.g. "too much liquor last night", or if a brain tumor is possible and the diagnostic process has to be continued. Table 7 shows the different kinds of explaining patient's symptoms.

Table 7: Explanation of patient's symptoms by diagnostic results.

diagnostic results	explain
confirmed diagnoses and diagnostic hypotheses D_j	present symptoms S_i with S_iD_j relationships $\mu_O(S_i,D_j)>0.50$ or $\mu_C(S_i,D_j)>0.50$.
excluded diagnoses	present symptoms S_i with S_iD_j relationships $\mu_O(S_i,D_j)<0.50$.
——	absent symptoms have not to be explained.

4. ILLUSTRATIVE EXAMPLE

Let us consider a patient with the following symptom pattern:

Table 8: Section of patients' symptom pattern.

symptoms	measured or present	fuzzy value $\mu(p,S_i)$
S_1	37.5 °C	1.00
S_2		0.60
S_3	Yes	1.00
S_4	Yes	1.00
S_5	Yes	1.00
S_6	Yes	1.00
S_7	Yes	1.00
S_8	?	?
S_9	Yes	1.00

Table 9: Section of symptom-disease relationships.

Symptom S_i \ Disease D_j	D_1 rheumatic fever $\mu_O(S_i,D_1)$	$\mu_C(S_i,D_1)$	D_2 infectious arthritis by staphylococci $\mu_O(S_i,D_2)$	$\mu_C(S_i,D_2)$
S_1 fever	often		very often	
S_2 elevated fever	often		very often	
S_3 hydrops of the knee	seldom		seldom	
S_4 carditis	very often	often	almost never	
S_5 joint pain	almost always		almost always	
S_6 erythema	often		very seldom	
S_7 previous tonsillitis	very often		very seldom	
S_8 synovial fluid examination staphylococci	never	never	always	always
S_9 AST elevated	almost always		seldom	

We now imagine the following documented symptoms of rheumatic fever and infectious arthritis by staphylococci (see Table 9).

In the first diagnostic iteration the following diagnostic results are calculated:

Table 10: Results of the medical diagnostic process.

Diagnostic results	Reasonings for diagnostic results	Proposals for further examinations
Diagnostic hypotheses:		
D_1	S_5=1.00 O=almost always; S_4=1.00 C=often	S_8 O=never C=never
D_2	S_5=1.00 O=almost always	S_8 O=always C=always

Performing the synovial fluid examination on patient P and finding S_8= staphylococci would prove D_2=infectious arthritis by staphylococci as the correct diagnosis of P .

5. DISCUSSION AND CRITISM

So far the CADIAG-2 system has been designed and implemented but not yet tested with a representative number of hospital patients. Design considerations and the presentation of the control structure of CADIAG-2 are not included in this paper.

Nevertheless, some main points that give an impression of the scope of CADIAG-2 and of the way of establishing it in clinical practice shall be mentioned.

The frame and rule based medical knowledge system of CADIAG-2 consists of about 2.500 symptoms and 308 diseases from the fields of rheumatology (186), hepatology (74), coagulation defects (34) and pancreatic diseases (10). The documentation of strong relationships between symptoms and diseases (occurrence: always or never and/or confirmability: always or never) as well as among symptoms and among diseases has been finished. SCS that can confirm rheumatic fever, rheumatoid arthritis, Sjögren's disease, psoriatic arthritis, Reiter's disease, Behcet's disease, Bechterew's disease, systematic lupus erythematosus, sclerodermia or gout have been implemented.

Patients' records from a rheumatological hospital are gathered and stored by means of a hospital information system /14,15/. Patients' data consists of

1) Physical examination
(513 binary positions in documentary system
⇓
282 binary symptoms in CADIAG-2)

2) Rheumatological history
(372 binary positions in documentary system
⇓
158 binary symptoms in CADIAG-2)

3) Rheumatological examination
(1227 binary positions in documentary system
⇓
453 binary symptoms in CADIAG-2)

4) Laboratory tests
(80 lab tests
⇓
305 binary symptoms in CADIAG-2)

5) X-ray findings

(78 binary symptoms in CADIAG-2)

6) Histological findings

(75 binary symptoms in CADIAG-2)

and the final rheumatological diagnoses confirmed by the rheumatologist. By means of the final diagnosis, the diagnostic results provided by CADIAG-2 can be com-

Table 11: Status of the medical knowledge system of CADIAG-2.

relationships	occurrence	confirmability	rheumatology	hepatology	coagulation defects	pancreatic diseases
S_iD_j	always	always	18	1	2	0
	always	-	189	113	67	0
	-	always	34	13	4	2
	never	never	536	54	558	0
S_iS_j	always	always	0	0	0	0
	always	-	419	4	0	0
	-	always	419	4	0	0
	never	never	2.395	143	786	34
D_iD_j	always	always	0	-	0	-
	always	-	54	-	6	-
	-	always	54	-	6	-
	never	never	1.370	-	0	-
SCS_lD_j	-	always	10	-	-	
	always	-	1	-	-	-

pared and the accuracy of the method can be calculated. The connection of CADIAG-2 to the medical database of the hospital information system has been realized. The CADIAG-2 database interface includes the calculation of degrees of membership in fuzzy symptom subsets given numerical lab test results (about 300 appropriate membership functions were defined) and the evaluation of logical combinations (similar to SCP_k and SCS_l) for the simplest documentary data.

CADIAG-2 is planned to be used

1) in retrospective mode to evaluate and improve the medical knowledge system (about 1.000 patients' records are available) and

2) in prospective mode to optimize the number of necessary lab tests, X-ray, puncture findings, etc.

Moreover, CADIAG-2 provides a deep insight in a physician's mental diagnostic process because of its explanation and reasoning capabilities and is highly suitable in medical diagnostic training.

FOOTNOTES

1) A first theoretical approach to CADIAG-2 was made by ADLASSNIG /35/.

2) In the context of this paper the only difference between the terms "disease" and "diagnosis" will be the following (see /36,37/:

- "Diseases" are described by nosograms that have been established in the field of nosology. For example: "Acute pancreatitis is characterized by sudden aches of the abdomen, sickness, vomiting, etc.". "Syndrome" is considered to be a synonym to "disease".

- The term "diagnosis" always appears in conjunction with patients. "Diagnosis" is an idiogram about an individuum. For example: "Smith suffers from acute pancreatitis".

3) The term "reference set" is used in KAUFMANN /21-24/. ZADEH /17,28/ calls it "universe of discourse". DUBOIS and PRADE /19/ name it "field of reference" or "universe" for short.

4) On the basis of a defined metric and distance in a space, similarity between P_i and P_j means a small distance $d(P_i,P_j)$ between P_i and P_j (see DUBOIS and PRADE /19/, KAUFMANN /21/).

5) In terms of CADIAG-1 /7-16/, "Symptom S_i always occurs in case of disease D_j." means that the presence of S_i is obligatory if D_j shall be confirmed.

6) "Symptom S_i always confirms disease D_j." means if S_i occurs then S_i proves the presence of D_j.

7) "Symptom S_i never occurs with D_j." means if S_i occurs then D_j has to be excluded.

8) The parameters of the membership functions have not been proved in clinical practice yet. If appropriate the parameters can be changed.

9) $[\mu_A(x)]^4$ for $\mu_{\text{very } A}(x)$ seems to fit physicians' experience better.

10) ZADEH /17/, DUBOIS and PRADE /19/ and KAUFMANN /21/ call it "inclusion". RICKERT /25/ terms it "containment".

11) To consider the means to be the numerical representatives of the linguistic terms is arbitrary. But the x_{O_i} and x_{C_i} are suitable values because they increase with the linguistically expressed strength of S_iD_j relationships in an ordered manner. They are helpful for numerical computation and never appear on screen during the medical diagnostic consultation.

12) Comparing with the linguistic approach $x_O \approx 19.40$ is in the range of very seldom.

13) In linguistic terms, tophi are always confirming gout (tophi are proving gout).

14) In the similar tri-valued logical approach of CADIAG-1 /10/, about 40% of the symptom-disease relationships have been found unknown.

15) Patient 1 stayed in hospital two different times.

16) Inner diagnostic process terms the part of the consultation system that indicates confirmed and excluded diagnoses as well as diagnostic hypotheses given a certain symptom pattern.

17) Certainly, soft relationships like almost always, often, seldom, etc. (see paragraph 3.2.1.) can also be used to express symptom-symptom and disease-disease relationships. In that case well-formed and extensive statistical material about relations among symptom and among diseases have to be available.

18) KAUFMANN /21/ terms such combinations "functions of fuzzy variables". DUBOIS and PRADE /19/ name it "fuzzy expressions".

19) WEISS, et al. /46,47/ call it "pathophysiological state" and the relationships between observations (history, symptoms, signs and laboratory tests) and states are associational. LINDBERG, et al. /48/ denote these combinations "intermediate hypotheses".

20) In a first consideration, ↑ and ↓ were introduced to handle major and minor criteria in rheumatology. But these simple operations have been found to be a useful and practical aid for the definition of symptom combinations in general.

21) In WEISS, et al. /46,47/ a similar concept is used. "Classification table rules" are established that are Boolean combinations of confirmed or denied states.

REFERENCES

/1/ KASPER, H., H.SOMMER. Klinik der akuten Pankreatitis. In SCHWIEGK, H. (Hrsg.): Handbuch der Inneren Medizin, 3.Band: Verdauungsorgane, Teil 6. Springer-Verlag Berlin-Heidelberg-New York, 1976.

/2/ AMMANN, R.: Ikterus. In SIEGENTHALER, W. (Hrsg.): Differentialdiagnose innerer Krankheiten. Georg Thieme Verlag Stuttgart, 1975.

/3/ ZÖLLNER, N.: Gicht. In GROSS, R., P.SCHÖLMERICH (Hrsg.): Lehrbuch der Inneren Medizin. F.K.Schattauer Verlag Stuttgart-New York, 1977.

/4/ OVERZIER, C.: Systematik der Inneren Medizin: Daten, Fakten, Übersichten. Georg Thieme Verlag Stuttgart, 1975.

/5/ SCHALDACH, H. (Hrsg.): Wörterbuch der Medizin. VEB Verlag Volk und Gesundheit Berlin, 1974.

/6/ KOLARZ, G.: Diagnosekriterien entzündlich rheumatischer Erkrankungen. In SINGER, F. (Hrsg.): Entzündlich-rheumatische Erkrankungen - ihre Bedeutung für den praktizierenden Arzt. Pensionsversicherungsanstalt der Arbeiter und Fa.Merck Sharp & Dohme Wien, 1977, 39-42.

/7/ ADLASSNIG, K.-P., T.GERGELY, H. GRABNER, G.GRABNER: A Computer-Assisted System for Diagnostic Decision Making-Online Usage of the Database of the Medical Information System WAMIS. In SHIRES, D.B., H.WOLF (Eds.): MEDINFO 77. North-Holland Publishing Company Amsterdam-New York-Oxford, 1977, 213-218.

/8/ ADLASSNIG, K.-P., G.GRABNER: Approaches to Computer-Assisted Diagnosis in Gastroenterology. EDV in Medizin und Biologie 11 (1980) 74-80.

/9/ ADLASSNIG, K.-P., G.GRABNER: The Viennese Computer-Assisted Diagnostic System. Its Principles and Values. AUTOMEDICA 3 (1980) 141-150.

/10/ ADLASSNIG, K.-P., G.KOLARZ, F. LIPOMERSKY, I.GRÖGER, G.GRABNER: CADIAG-1: A Computer-Assisted Diagnostic System on the Basis of Symbolic Logic and its Application in Internal Medicine. In O'MOORE, R.R., B.BARBER, P.L.REICHERTZ, F.ROGER (Eds.): Medical Informatics Europe 82. Springer Verlag Berlin-Heidelberg-New York, 1982, 495-505.

/11/ BAUER, P., A.GANGL, G.GRABNER: Ein Computer-Verfahren zur Zuordnung eines Krankheitsbildes zu einer Diagnose-Gruppe. Wien.Z.inn.Med. 51 (1970) 497-509.

/12/ BAUER, P., A.GANGL, G.GRABNER, O.JAHN: Ein Computer-Verfahren zur Unterstützung des Arztes bei der Erstellung von Differentialdiagnosen. Impuls 10 (1968) 705-712.

/13/ GANGL, A., G.GRABNER, P.BAUER: Erste Erfahrungen mit einem Computerprogramm zur Differentialdiagnose der Lebererkrankungen. Wien.Z.inn.Med. 50 (1969) 553-586.

/14/ GRABNER, G., H.GRABNER: The Viennese General Medical Information System. Proceedings of MEDIS'75 TOKYO, Kansai Institute of Information Systems, 1975, 156-163.

/15/ GRABNER, H., G.GRABNER: Aims and Structure of the Vienna General Medical Information System WAMIS. In ANDERSON, J., J.M.FORSYTHE (Eds.): MEDINFO 74. North-Holland Publishing Company Amsterdam-New York-Oxford, 1974, 375-379.

/16/ SPINDELBERGER, W., G.GRABNER: Ein Computerverfahren zur diagnostischen Hilfestellung. In FELLINGER, K. (Hrsg.): Computer in der Medizin - Probleme, Erfahrungen, Projekte. Verlag Brüder Hollinek Wien, 1968, 189-221.

/17/ ZADEH, L.A.: Fuzzy Sets. Information and Control 8 (1965) 338-353.

/18/ BELLMAN, R.E., L.A.ZADEH: Local and Fuzzy Logics: Memorandum NO. ERL-M584, Electronics Research Laboratory, College of Engineering, University of California, Berkeley 94720, 11 May 1976.

/19/ DUBOIS, D., H.PRADE: Fuzzy Sets and Systems: Theory and Applications. Academic Press New York-London, 1980.

/20/ GUPTA, M.M., R.K.RAGADE, R.R.YAGER (Eds.): Advances in Fuzzy Set Theory and Applications. North-Holland Publishing Company Amsterdam-New York-Oxford, 1979.

/21/ KAUFMANN, A.: Introduction to the Theory of Fuzzy Subsets. Volume I. Fundamental Theoretical Elements. Academic Press New York-San Francisco-London, 1975.

/22/ KAUFMANN, A.: Introduction à la Théorie des Sous-Ensembles Flous. Tome II. Application à la Linguistique et à la Sémantique. Masson Paris, 1975.

/23/ KAUFMANN, A.: Introduction à la Théorie des Sous-Ensembles Flous. Tome III. Applications à la Classification et à la Reconnaissance des Formes aux Automates et aux Systèmes, au Choix des Critères. Masson Paris, 1975.

/24/ KAUFMANN, A.: Introduction a là Théorie des Sous-Ensembles Flous. Tome IV. Compléments et Nouvelles Application. Masson Paris, 1977.

/25/ KICKERT, W.J.M.: Fuzzy Theories on Decision-Making. Martinus Nijhoff Social Sciences Division Leiden-Boston-London, 1978.

/26/ NEGOITA, C.V., D.A.RALESCU: Applications of Fuzzy Sets to System Analysis. Birkhäuser Verlag Basel-Stuttgart, 1975.

/27/ WECHLER, W.: The Concept of Fuzziness in Automata and Language Theory. Academie-Verlag Berlin, 1978.

/28/ ZADEH, L.A.: Outline of a New Approach to the Analysis of Complex Systems and Decision Processes. IEEE Transactions on Systems, Man, and Cybernetics, Vol.SMC-3, No.1, January 1973, 28-44.

/29/ GAINES, B.R., KOHOUT, L.J.: The Fuzzy Decade: A Bibliography of Fuzzy Systems and Closely Related Topics. Int.J.Man-Machine Studies 9 (1977) 1-68.

/30/ KANDEL, A., R.R.YAGER: A 1979 Bibliography on Fuzzy Sets, Their Applications, and Related Topics. In GUPTA, M.M., R.K.RAGADE, R.R. YAGER (Eds.): Advances in Fuzzy Set Theory and Applications. North-Holland Publishing Company Amsterdam-New York-Oxford, 1979, 621-744.

/31/ TOTH, H.: Fuzzy Bibliography (Stand vom 20.02.1982). Versuch einer Weiterführung von KANDEL/YAGER: A 1979 Bibliography on Fuzzy Sets, Their Application and Related Topics. Personal Communication.

/32/ ADLASSNIG, K.-P.: A Survey on Medical Diagnosis and Fuzzy Subsets. In GUPTA, M.M., E.SANCHEZ (Eds.): Fuzzy Information and Decision Processes. North-Holland Publishing

Company Amsterdam-New York-Oxford. In press.

/33/ POPLE, H.E., J.D.MYERA, R.A.MILLER: DIALOG: A Model of Diagnostic Logic for Internal Medicine. Proceedings of the 4th International Joint Conference on Artificial Intelligence Tbilisi, 1975, 848-855.

/34/ POPLE, H.E.: The Formation of Composite Hypotheses in Diagnostic Problem Solving - An Exercise in Synthetic Reasoning. Proceedings of the 5th International Joint Conference on Artificial Intelligence Cambridge, 1977, 1030-1037.

/35/ ADLASSNIG, K.-P.: A Fuzzy Logical Model of Computer-Assisted Medical Diagnosis. Meth.Inform.Med. 19 (1980), 141-148.

/36/ SADEGH-ZADEH, K.: Krankheitsbegriffe und nosologische Systeme. METAMED 1 (1977), 4-41.

/37/ SADEGH-ZADEH, K.: Grundlagenprobleme einer Theorie der klinischen Praxis, Teil 1: Explikation des medizinischen Diagnosebegriffs. METAMED 1 (1977), 76-102.

/38/ ALBIN, M.A.: Fuzzy Sets and Their Application to Medical Diagnosis and Pattern Recognition. PhD diss. University of California, Berkeley, 1975.

/39/ ZADEH, L.A.: A Fuzzy-Algorithm Approach to the Definition of Complex or Imprecise Concepts. In BOSSEL, H., S.KLACZKO, N.MÜLLER (Eds.): System Theory in the Social Sciences. Birkhäuser Verlag Basel-Stuttgart, 1976, 202-282.

/40/ ZADEH, L.A.: A Fuzzy Set-Theoretic Interpretation of Linguistic Hedges. J.Cybern. 2 (1972), 4-34.

/41/ GRAMS, R.R.: Medical Information Systems: The Laboratory Module. The Humana Press Clifton-New Jersey, 1979.

/42/ SHANNON, R.H.(Ed.): Hospital Information Systems. North Holland Publishing Company Amsterdam-New York-Oxford, 1979.

/43/ SHORTLIFFE, E.H.: Computer-Based Medical Consultations: MYCIN. Elsevier New York-Oxford-Amsterdam, 1976.

/44/ ROPES, M.W., G.A.BENNETT, S.COBB, R.JACOX, R.A.JESSAR: 1958 Revision of Diagnostic Criteria for Rheumatoid Arthritis. Arthr.Rheum. 2 (1959) 16-20.

/45/ American Heart Association, Rheumatic Fever Committee of the Council on Rheumatic Fever and Congenital Heart Disease. Circulation 43 (1971), 983-988.

/46/ WEISS, S., C.A.KULIKOWSKI, A.SAFIR: Glaucoma Consultation by Computer. Comput.Biol.Med. 8 (1978) 25-40.

/47/ WEISS, S.M., C.A.KULIKOWSKI, S.AMAREL, A.SAFIR: A Model-Based Method for Computer-Aided Medical Decision-Making. Artificial Intelligence 11 (1978) 145-172.

/48/ LINDBERG, D.A.B., G.C.SHARP, L.C.KINGSLAND, III, S.M.WEISS, S.P.HAYES, H.UENO, S.E.HAZELWOOD: Computer Based Rheumatology Consultant. In LINDBERG, D.A.B., S.KAIHARA (Eds.): MEDINFO 80. North-Holland Publishing Company Amsterdam-New York-Oxford, 1980, 1311-1315.

/49/ WIRTH, N.: Compilerbau. B.G. Teubner Stuttgart, 1977.

/50/ AHO, A.V., J.D.ULLMAN: Principles of Compiler Design. Addison-Wesley Publishing Company, 1978.

/51/ GRIES, D.: Computer Construction for Digital Computers. John Wiley and Sons, Inc., 1971.

/52/ ESOGBUE, A.O., R.C.ELDER: Fuzzy Sets and the Modelling of Physician Decision Processes, Part I: The Initial Interview-Information Gathering Session. Fuzzy Sets and Systems 2 (1979) 279-291.

/53/ TAUTU, P., G.WAGNER: The Process of Medical Diagnosis: Routes and Mathematical Investigations. Meth. Inform.Med. 1 (1978), 1-10.

Approximate Reasoning in Decision Analysis
M.M. Gupta and E. Sanchez (eds.)

LEARNING OF FUZZY PRODUCTION RULES FOR MEDICAL DIAGNOSIS

Leonardo Lesmo, Lorenza Saitta and Pietro Torasso

Istituto di Scienze dell'Informazione
Università di Torino, Turin, Italy

The methods used so far to develop systems for medical consultation relied either on classical probabilistic and pattern recognition schemata or on techniques developed in the field of Artificial Intelligence. The statistical approach guarantees the availability of efficient learning algorithms, but the structure of the decision rules is too far from the methods used by the physicians, thus preventing the designer from inserting good explanation facilities into the system. On the other hand, artificial intelligence systems generally require a noticeable effort to encode the expert's knowledge in a form suitable to perform inferences on the available data.

The system described in this paper tries to combine the respective advantages of the mentioned approaches, by using fuzzy production rules as the basic deductive mechanism. The paper outlines an algorithm for the automatic learning of the fuzzy production rules and shows its application to the domain of liver pathology. The effectiveness of the learning algorithm is shown by reporting a set of experimental results which allow to compare the outcome of the learned production rules with the classification available from the experts.

0. KEYWORDS
Expert systems, Production rules, Automatic learning, Possibility theory, Medical diagnosis

1. INTRODUCTION

The evolution of Expert Systems in the last ten years has pointed out a set of features that such systems must exhibit in order to increase their acceptability in the environment where they will operate [1,2]. Among these features the explicative power, the modularity and the existence of an interface in (quasi) natural language increase the ease of interaction between the system and the human user. In particular, the presence of explanation facilities allows the user to understand what is going on in the system during the reasoning process, the subdivision of the whole knowledge in a set of chunks independent of each other (rules) makes easy the process of revision and update of the sytem and finally a natural language interface avoids the effort of learning new languages (and reduces the number of errors that a user not acquainted with artificial languages may make).

On the other hand, the Expert Systems which have been developed using Artificial Intelligence (AI) techniques required, in most cases, a big effort in encoding the knowledge available from the human expert in the domain (see [3-7] among others). Even if this effort may be reduced by means of efficient dialogue techniques [8] (i.e. by means of automated procedures which inquire about the expert's knowledge), the decision of acquiring all knowledge from a human expert implies that the user is always forced to translate his experience in terms understandable by the system, a task which may be difficult and may introduce inconsistencies [9].

Aim of the research described in this paper is to develop a system devoted to the diagnosis of liver diseases and to the evaluation of the hepatic functionality [10]. Because one of the main goals of the authors was to structure the system in a way suitable to perform automatic acquisition of the rules constituting the knowledge of the domain, the current version of the system operates at a somewhat lower level than the AI systems devoted to automating the diagnostic process [3-7]; in fact, the knowledge is limited in that it does not include information regarding the pathophysiological mechanisms and the treatment which has to be recommended in a particular case and it does not take into account the data about the evolution of the illness.

As stated above, the goals of the system are to screen the patients as regards liver diseases, to determine the diagnostic class to which the illness of the patient belongs and to evaluate the functional assessment of the liver. The knowledge required to accomplish these tasks is concerned with the relationships existing between findings (symptoms, signs, biochemical test results, etc.), diagnostic classes and impairment degrees in the functional assessment.

The goals introduced above could suggest to model the behavior of the system as a multi-stage classification process, thus adopting the paradigm of statistical pattern recognition, which offers the further advantage of putting at disposal some well known, sound and efficient algorithms for the automatic learning of the classification rules [11]. However, a set of well known problems is associated with this approach:

- a large amount of data is required for estimating the parameters which appear in the discrimination rules, mainly because of the large number of features which are used normally to characterize an individual;
- the presence of non-continuous features (in our case most of the symptoms and signs) introduces a dishomogeneity in the classification method;
- not always the statistical hypotheses underlining these methods (e.g. independence of the variables, type of distribution, etc.) are satisfied by the data in the domain.

Moreover, it is not clear how to avoid the black box situation inherent in the statistical approach, in the sense that there is no way of paraphrasing the operations of the system (which reduce to the application of a single rule or a set of them in sequence in the multi-stage approach) in terms easily comprehensible to the user [1].

In order to preserve both the possibility of automatic acquisition of knowledge and the capability of explanation, a different approach has been chosen. It is based on fuzzy production rules structured as condition- decision pairs: the condition part of each rule is a logical expression involving linguistic variables, each of which is defined as a fuzzy restriction [13] on the values of a particular finding and the decision part consists in the emission of a hypothesis about a diagnostic class (or a particular kind of impairment of the hepatic functionality); futhermore, also the strength of implication is approximated by a linguistic variable.

The use of fuzzy production rules has been suggested by different considerations. First of all the production rules [14] have become the most popular tool to deal with the problem of simulating the behavior of human experts; they have been applied to very different fields of expertise and their appeal stands on their ability to provide simple solutions to the problem of inserting into the system the explanation facilities mentioned at the beginning of this introduction. As regards the adoption of an approach based on fuzzy set theory, it has been suggested by the ability of fuzzy linguistic variables to characterize both the condition part of the production rules and the strength with which the decision may be inferred. As for the condition part, it should be noticed that in the medical practice a given finding is usually characterized by means of a restricted set of adjectives, even when it may assume continuous values. The fuzzy linguistic variables seem to be the formal tool which deals in the most appropriate way with the adjectives used by the physicians; in fact it is possible to define the set of linguistic variables which have to be used to qualify a particular finding on the basis of the set of adjectives which a physician uses to qualify that finding. Moreover, the fuzzy linguistic variables are not exclusive, in the sense that a particular value of a finding may be described by more than one variable; this enables the system to model the vagueness characterizing the association of a particular adjective with a definite range of values of the finding. Finally the use of linguistic variables for describing the strength of implication reflects the vagueness with which a conclusion may be inferred from the match between the condition part of the rule and the data relative to the patient under investigation.

Section 2 contains a brief description of the overall organization of the system, whereas Section 3 is devoted to describe the actual structure of the fuzzy production rules and the algorithm used to learn them; finally, some experiments carried out to test the performance of the system are reported and discussed in Section 4.

2. OVERVIEW OF THE SYSTEM

The basic assumption underlying the design of the system are the following ones:

- the clinical data (history, symptoms, signs elicited during the physical examination) play an essential role as a starting point for the diagnostic process;
- the different kinds of information characterizing the status of a patient may be more or less easy to obtain; in fact the clinical history and the symptoms may be collected simply by making the patient fill an appropriate questionnaire, whereas the physical examination requires the activity of (at least) a general practitioner; still worse, the laboratory tests are not only quite expensive (in general), but many of them should be avoided when possible, since they are based on invasive techniques.

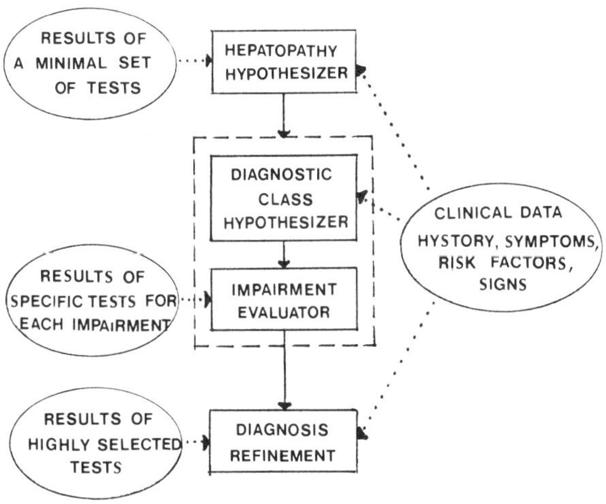

Fig.1 - Interconnections among data and modules composing the consultant system.

These considerations suggested to decompose the system into different modules and to use the clinical data for emitting hypotheses and the results of suitable laboratory tests for verifying them. The modules composing the system and the interconnections among them are shown in Fig. 1 .

The control flow is driven by means of categorical meta-rules, which select the module to which the control must be transferrred at a given stage of the diagnostic process. The meta-rules operate on the basis of the current status of the process and issue, as a side effect, the request to the human user for inputting that subset of data which is needed by the selected module and is not available to the system. These meta-rules do not operate only to guide the activation of the different modules, but also to control the flow of operations performed within the modules as will be explained during the description of the modules composing the system.

2.1 Hepatopathy Hypothesizer

The task of the Hepatopathy Hypothesizer is to screen the patients in order to detect the presence of a liver disease. This task is accomplished by means of three different sets of rules:

HH1) the rules belonging to this first set operate only on clinical data to state whether these data allow to determine the presence of a liver disease with a sufficiently high degree of evidence (the hepatopathy is considered "likely" on the sole basis of clinical data);

HH2) these rules are similar to the ones of the first set, but the strength of the hypothesis of presence of a disease is somewhat smaller, in the sense that the degree of evidence is lower (the hepatopathy may be considered "possible"); also in this case no result of laboratory tests is involved in the hypothesis formation;

HH3) this last set contains rules which support the hypothesis about the presence of a liver disease on the basis of a small set of laboratory test results.

Table 1 - Example of rules used in the Hepatopathy Hypothesizer.

SET	EXAMPLE OF RULES
HH1	IF at least two "major clinical features" are present (even with <u>low</u> intensity) THEN the hepatopathy is <u>likely</u>
HH2	IF there is a chronic alcohol intake and at least one "minor symptom" is present with <u>high</u> intensity THEN the hepatopathy is <u>possible</u>
HH3	IF serum albumin is <u>altered</u> THEN the hepatopathy is <u>likely</u>

where: "major clinical features" are jaundice, hepatomegaly, hepatosplenomegaly, ascites; "minor symptoms" are anorexia, nausea, vomiting, weight loss, etc.

The activation of a particular set of rules is determined by the meta-rules introduced above. In particular, the start of the process implies the activation of the rules of HH1 and the request of inputting the clinical data relative to the patient under investigation. If the condition part of none of the rules belonging to HH1 is satisfied, then the set HH2 is activated (without any further request of data). In case the rules of the set HH2 fail, then there is no evidence at all of the presence of an hepatic disease and the system considers the patient as healthy (at least as regards the liver); in the opposite case (the hepatopathy is considered "possible") the evidence of the hypothesis is still too low, so that the rules of the set HH3 are invoked (and the suitable labtests are requested) to confirm the hypothesis of illness.

The rules composing the three sets of the Hepatopathy Hypothesizer have been obtained essentially by encoding the physician's knowledge. For this reason these rules are not further discussed and three examples of them (one for each set) are reported in Table 1 (it is worth noticing that the underlined adjectives are fuzzy linguistic variables).

2.2 Diagnostic Class Hypothesizer and Impairment Evaluator

When the presence of a hepatopathy is considered likely by the first module of the system, the control is transferred to the Diagnostic Class Hypothesizer. The task of this second module is to select one or more gross diagnostic classes which are considered as hypotheses for a more detailed classification of the actual liver disease of the patient. A hypothesis regarding a particular diagnostic class is emitted when the evidence gathered from the findings is above a given threshold; the evidence degree is evaluated by means of a set of rules which relate clinical data (history, symptoms, physical examination) to the diagnostic class.

At the present stage of development, the final result of the system which is being described is an evaluation of the hepatic functionality. The functionality of the liver is described in terms of different aspects (presently four: Cholestasis, Biosynthesis, Cytolysis, Reactivity), each of which would require, for the correct determination of its impairment degree, a particular set of laboratory tests. The system takes advantage of the diagnostic classes hypothesized in the previous step in order to focus its attention. In fact, appropriate meta-rules contain the knowledge regarding the relationships between the diagnostic classes and the aspects of the hepatic functionality. This knowledge is useful since, in general, a given disease does not alter all the aspects of the functionality of the liver.

After the completion of the operations of the diagnostic class hypothesizer, these meta-rules suggest, on the basis of the diagnostic classes which have been hypothesized, what aspects of the functionality of the liver are more likely to be altered(i.e. they focus the attention of the system on those aspects).

The second sub-module, i.e. the Impairment Evaluator, is composed by rules which relate the results of the selected biochemical tests with the severity of the specific impairments, so that the evaluation of the hepatic functionality is achieved by using these rules to assign a severity degree to each one of the aspects. The severity degrees are represented by means of linguistic variables which range from "absent" to "very severe". These rules, as well as the ones composing the Diagnostic Class Hypothesizer, have been automatically learned according to the methodology described in the following section of the present paper, whereas the meta-rules have been built following the suggestions of expert physicians.

2.3 Diagnosis refinement

The third module of the system is devoted to the refinement of the diagnosis: its task is to select the final diagnosis by constraining the subset of diagnostic classes to a single class and by discriminating among the diagnoses belonging to that class. This result is achieved by taking into account the liver functional assessment, by considering again the history, the symptoms and the signs elicited during the physical examination and, possibly, by requesting more laboratory tests specific to a particular diagnostic class.

The structure of this module, as well as the knowledge which is required and the best way to represent it, is still under investigation; the preliminary studies, however, seem to suggest that the knowledge which may be represented in a simple fuzzy production rules approach is not powerful enough to deal with the problem of differential diagnosis. By "simple fuzzy production rules approach" we mean that all the conclusions are inferred in a bottom-up fashion, i.e. by using the findings (and the laboratory tests) to hypothesize diagnostic classes and evaluate the impairment degrees. One of the most important inadequacies of that approach is the lack of a mechanism for representing horizontal (i.e. contextual) inferences, which should be driven by the knowledge regarding the relationships between different hypotheses (e.g. causality, mutual exclusion, etc.).

Our future efforts will be towards the design of such a mechanism, in order to allow the system to cope with differential diagnosis in an efficient and accurate way.

3. FUZZY PRODUCTION RULES

This section is devoted to the description of the actual structure of the production rules and of the algorithm which has been used to learn them from a training set.

A fuzzy production rule has the following structure:

$$((V_1 \text{ is } \lambda_{1,k_1}) \text{ and } (V_2 \text{ is } \lambda_{2,k_2}) \text{ and } \ldots \text{ and } (V_m \text{ is } \lambda_{m,k_m})) \xrightarrow{w} H \qquad (1)$$

where the left-hand side of (1) is the condition part of the rule and:

- V_j $(1 \leq j \leq m)$ is a linguistic variable,
- λ_{j,k_j} is a linguistic term, qualifying V_j, belonging to an alphabet Λ_j,
- H is the decision part of the rule and represents a hypothesis, whose emission depends on

the evaluation of the condition part,
- w is the strength of the implication between the condition and the decision part.

It should be noticed that two alphabets Λ_i and Λ_j (i≠j) may be disjoint or may contain some common terms; even in the latter case the interpretations of a common term are different, because they depend on the physical characteristics related to the linguistic variables V_i and V_j.

The possibility value $\Pi(H)$ of the hypothesis H, for a given patient is computed according to Zadeh's Possibility Theory [15]. In particular, $\Pi(H)$ is the maximum of the possibility values $\Pi_r(H)$ relative to different rules, where r ranges over all the rules which have H as right-hand side. The existence of different rules referring to the same hypothesis H is motivated by the fact that the same conclusion may be drawn from different sets of findings. The values $\Pi_r(H)$ are computed according to:

$$\Pi_r(H) = \min\left[w_r, \min(\mu_{1,k_1}, \ldots, \mu_{m,k_m})\right] \tag{2}$$

where each μ_{j,k_j} is a possibility value representing the degree of compatibility between the term (V_j is λ_{j,k_j}) and the actual findings related to the linguistic variable V_j, reported for the patient under examination.

It must be noticed that, in order to allow the learning algorithm to handle the large number of clinical data characterizing the status of a patient, intermediate levels of hypothesis formation have been introduced. In this way a hierarchical organization is defined, since a hypothesis emitted at a given level of the process (which therefore appears in the right-hand side of some rule) may occurr in the condition part of other rules operating at a higher level.

3.1 Definition of Linguistic Variables

Each linguistic variable V_j occurring in the condition part of the production rules relating clinical data to diagnostic classes tries to capture a particular but significant aspect of the clinical status of the patient. For this reason, in some cases a linguistic variable is associated with a single symptom or sign (e.g. jaundice, ascites, abdominal pain, etc.); in other cases a linguistic variable summarizes a status represented, in the record of a given patient, by more than one measurement (e.g. haemorragic phenomena, chronic alcohol intake, etc.). In the first case the base variable for V_j is the datum stored in the patient record which represents the symptom or sign. In the latter the measurement involved in V_j must be combined by a function (defined in a heuristic way) to get a global value x_j; the range of x_j is assumed to be the range of a variable ξ_j, acting as base variable for V_j. For example, in the case of the linguistic variable Chronic Alcohol Intake two measurements are involved: the average amount q_i of strong drink D_i intaken per die by a given patient (D_i = wine, beer, spirit, etc.) and the number of years t_i during which D_i has been intaken. These measurements are combined to get a single value x, which is the value assumed by the base variable ξ for the patient under examination (x may range in the interval [0,1]).

As regards the definition of the alphabets Λ_j, we have chosen to take into account the medical knowledge, in the sense that each linguistic term tries to approximate a qualification used in medical practice. Let us consider as an example the linguistic variable Serum Albumin; over the interval [0,10] four possibility distribution have been introduced (see Fig.2), each of which corresponds to a linguistic term in the set Λ:

Λ = {Normal, Slightly Altered, Altered, Very Altered}

It is worth noticing that, for example, the term Normal is defined on an interval of values which most physicians agree to consider normal.

3.2 Learning of Fuzzy Production Rules

Given a hypothesis H and the set of associated findings $F = \{f_1, \ldots, f_m\}$, we can define, as previously described, the corresponding linguistic variables V_j ($1 \le j \le m$) and the linguistic terms $\lambda_{j,k_j} \in \Lambda_j$ ($1 \le j \le m$). If no a-priori knowledge is available, all the possible conditions on findings should be considered in order to fire the hypothesis H, i.e. all possible production rules of the form:

$$(V_{r_1} \text{ is } \lambda_{r_1,k_1}) \text{ and } \ldots \ldots \text{ and } (V_{r_n} \text{ is } \lambda_{r_n,k_n}) \xrightarrow{w} H \tag{3}$$

have potentially to be taken into account; if m_j indicates the cardinality of Λ_j, the number of different terms (V_{r_i} is λ_{r_i,k_i}) which may occurr in the left-hand side of (3) is:

$$M = \sum_{j=1}^{m} m_j$$

In each rule only n ($1 \le n \le M$) terms occur and the number of possible rules is thus $2^M - 1$. It is intuitive that not all these rules are equally relevant to the hypothesization of H; the relevance of a particular rule is expressed by

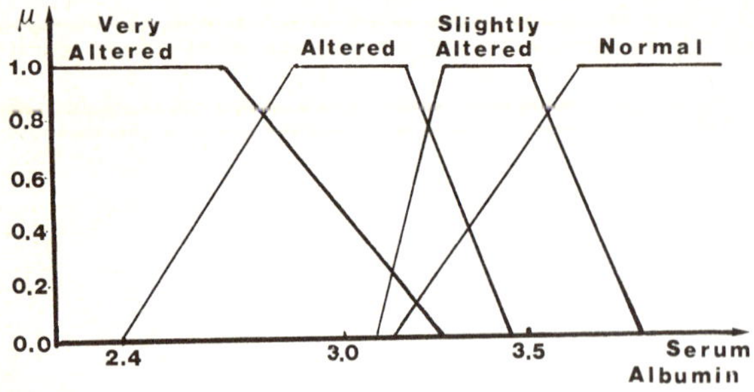

Fig.2 - Definition of the linguistic terms characterizing the linguistic variable Serum Albumin

its strength w. The algorithm described in [16, 17] has been applied to automatically infer these strengths from a training set.

In order to make this work self-consistent, a brief outline of the algorithm is given in the following. Let L_r denote a generic logical expression appearing in the left-hand side of (3). Let moreover be:

$$L_r^{(t)} \xrightarrow{w_r^{(t)}} H_t \qquad (1 \leq r \leq R_t) \qquad (4)$$

where H_t $(1 \leq t \leq T)$ belongs to a set of alternative hypotheses.

Let $Z = \{z_1, \ldots, z_N\}$ be the set of subjects used as training set. For each subject $z_k \in Z$ the possibility values of the left-hand side of (4), i.e. $\mu_r^{(t)}(z_k)$, may be computed for each value of $r \in [1, R_t]$ and for each t $[1,T]$. According to the possibility theory [15], the global possibility value of each hypothesis H_t will result, for a given subject z_k:

$$\Pi_t(z_k) = \max_{1 \leq r \leq R_t} \min(\mu_r^{(t)}(z_k), w_r^{(t)}) \quad (1 \leq t \leq T) \quad (5)$$

The strengths $w_r^{(t)}$ $(1 \leq r \leq R_t,\ 1 \leq t \leq T)$ are determined in such a way that the misclassification probability (i.e. the probability that the correct hypothesis obtains a possibility value not greater than that of a wrong one) is minimized. In order to avoid the combinatorial explosion of the number of rules (4), a pre-selection of the rules is performed. This is accomplished by taking into account that the evaluation of the right-hand side of (5) reduces to the evaluation of a number of terms linear with respect to the number m of involved linguistic variables [16]. It turns out that many of the logical expressions $L_r^{(t)}$ never (or very seldom) intervene in the decision process: for this reason the strengths of the production rules containing these logical expressions may be set equal to zero. Then the error rate may be expressed in terms of the survived rule strengths [16] and it is minimized using standard methods. At this stage a further selection of rules is (possibly) performed, by eliminating all those rules whose strength is under a given threshold; this may be accomplished, in general, without a significant increase in the error rate [17]. As a final step, possibility distributions, corresponding to linguistic approximations of evidence degrees, may be defined over the range of the strength values, i.e. the interval [0,1].

A more detailed description of the learning methodology of fuzzy production rules is reported in [18], with particular emphasis on the conversion of the strength of the rules into linguistic form.

The described learning procedure has been applied to infer two sets of rules. As previously mentioned, the rules of the first set are used in the Diagnostic Class Hypothesizer and those of the second set are used in the Impairment Evaluator to emit hypotheses about the presence of a particular impairment in the functional assessment of the liver. In the following are reported some examples of rules of the two sets.

Let us consider firstly the process of hypothesizing a dignostic class and, in particular, the Cirrhosis diagnostic class. Two rules are given as an example:

(CIRRHOSIS-RISK-FACTORS is Very Relevant) and (CIRRHOSIS-SYMPTOMS is Very Significant) $\xrightarrow{\text{Evident}}$ CIRRHOSIS (R1)

(CIRRHOSIS-RISK-FACTORS is Slightly Relevant) and (CIRRHOSIS-SYMPTOMS is Significant) and (CYRRHOSIS-SIGNS is Very Significant) $\xrightarrow{\text{Very Evident}}$ CIRRHOSIS (R2)

The linguistic variables occurring in the condition part of R1 and R2 appear also in the decision part of other rules, like the following ones:

(ALCOHOL-INTAKE is Very High) $\xrightarrow{\text{Relevant}}$ CIRRHOSIS-RISK-FACTORS (R3)

(NEUROLOGICAL-ABNORMALITY is Very Severe) and (ASCITES is Severe) and (COLLATERAL-PORTAL-CIRCULATION is Present) $\xrightarrow{\text{Very Significant}}$ CIRRHOSIS-SIGNS (R4)

As regards the impairment degrees of the liver

functionality, let us consider, as an example, the biosynthetic impairment, which is normally present in patients suffering from cirrhosis. The biosynthetic impairment is hypothesized on the basis of three laboratory tests : Serum Albumin (ALB), Serum Cholin Esterase (CHE), Protrombin Time (PT); each of them corresponds to a linguistic variable, assuming values belonging to the following term set:

{Normal, Slightly Altered, Altered, Very Altered}

The choice of ALB, CHE and PT has been made on the basis of their discriminant power, as indicated by a previous work [19].

As described in Section 2, for each impairment four levels of severity have been defined, namely: Absent, Low, Severe, Very Severe. Some rules referring to the biosynthetic impairment are reported in the following:

(ALB is Normal) and (CHE is Normal) and
(PT is Normal) $\xrightarrow{\text{Very very Evident}}$
BIOSYNTHETIC-IMPAIRMENT-ABSENT (R5)

(ALB is Normal) and (CHE is Normal) and
(PT is Altered) $\xrightarrow{\text{Very Evident}}$
BIOSYNTHETIC-IMPAIRMENT-LOW (R6)

(ALB is Very Altered) and (CHE is Altered) and
(PT is Slightly Altered) $\xrightarrow{\text{Evident}}$
BIOSYNTHETIC-IMPAIRMENT-SEVERE (R7)

(ALB is Very Altered) and (CHE is Very Altered)
and (PT is Very Altered) $\xrightarrow{\text{Very Very Evident}}$
BIOSYNTHETIC-IMPAIRMENT-VERY-SEVERE (R8)

(CHE is Very Altered) $\xrightarrow{\text{Very Evident}}$
BIOSYNTHETIC-IMPAIRMENT-VERY-SEVERE (R9)

4. EXPERIMENTAL RESULTS

The acceptability of a consultant system depends on a number of factors (consider for example its explanation facilities), but the most important of them is obviously its ability to reach conclusions which agree with the ones of an expert in the field. In our case a preliminary evaluation of the performances of the system may be obtained by comparing the diagnostic class proposed by the system with the one suggested by the physician and the impairment degrees determined by the system for the different aspects of the hepatic functionality with the evaluation of the functional assessment as given by the physician on the basis of the available findings. Because the interpretation of the results of such a comparison is affected by the characteristics of the data used to perform the learning phase and by the way the reference classification has been obtained, a brief description of them is required.

As regards the training set used to learn the rules (both of the Diagnostic Class Hypothesizer and of the Impairment Evaluator), it was composed of 179 subjects selected from an initial set of 288 individuals. The initial set contained subjects actually suffering from liver diseases and healthy subjects acting as a control group. For each subject the diagnosis and the functional assessment evaluation was determined by six different medical equipes on the basis of an accurate historical data collection and physical examination and of a very detailed laboratory investigation including more than 120 data from biochemical, immunological and special tests. The criteria used to select the training set from the initial set were based on the actual diagnosis and functional assessment of the subjects and on the availability of the necessary data. First of all, the subjects were grouped according to gross diagnostic classes and those groups were ruled out which contained too few subjects or which were less interesting from a pathological point of view (e.g. that one containing dispeptic subjects with no evidence of liver diseases). Then, among the remaining patients, that ones were selected for whom all relevant data (symptoms, signs and laboratory test results) were available. The 179 subjects composing the training set were subdivided into five groups, according to the known diagnosis; four groups referred to pathological classes, whereas the last one contained healthy subjects. The size of the five groups is:

- Acute Hepatitis: 44 subjects
- Chronic Hepatitis: 28 "
- Liver Cirrhosis: 69 "
- Obstructive Jaundice: 8 "
- Normal: 30 "

(so that the total number of pathological subjects is 149).

As stated above, an evaluation of the system must refer to its ability to classify the subjects in a way consistent with the reference classification. This means that, whereas the learning phase is concerned only with the second and third module of the present system, such an evaluation must take into account also the behavior of the first module. As regards the first module (the Hepatopathy Hypothesizer), whose rules have been obtained by encoding the medical knowledge, what is needed is an estimation of the misclassification error obtained by

Table 2 - Classification of the 179 subjects of the test set after the application of the rules of the sets HH1 and HH2

		Reference Classification	
		NORMAL	PATHOLOGICAL
Automatic Classification	ABSENT	17	0
	POSSIBLE	13	14
	LIKELY	0	135

Table 3 - Classification of the 179 subjects of the test set as obtained by the Hepatopathy Hypothesizer

		Reference Classification	
		NORMAL	PATHOLOGICAL
Automatic Classification	ABSENT	27	1
	LIKELY	3	148

applying those rules to a test set. Our choice has been to use as test set the previously described training set of 179 subjects. On the sole basis of history, symptoms and signs, i.e. after the application of the set of rules HH1 and HH2, the subjects in the test set where classified as shown in Table 2. For 27 of them the hepatopathy was considered "possible" by the system. The "possibility" of hepatopathy was furtherly verified by means of the rules of the set HH3; in order to apply these rules, the system requested the results of a minimal set of laboratory tests (actually three: Serum Albumin (ALB), Gamma-Glutamyl-Transpeptidase (GGT) and Transferrase-GP (GPT)); the final outcome of the Hepatopathy Hypothesizer is reported in Table 3. Notice that the misclassification error is 2.2%, but the only error which can not be recovered by the subsequent diagnostic investigation concerns the pathological subject (suffering from a chronic persistent hepatitis) for whom the hepatopathy is considered absent. This patient, however, did not present any significant alteration of the hepatic functionality.

As regards the Diagnostic Class Hypothesizer, it is apparent that its behavior depends on the choice of the threshold, i.e. of the minimum evidence degree necessary for a hypothesis to be fired. It should be noticed that this second module assumes that the subjects which are submitted to it are actually ill, so that it only takes into account the four pathological classes (acute hepatitis, chronic hepatitis, liver cirrhosis, obstructive jaundice). For this reason the Diagnostic Class Hypothesizer has been tested on the subjects for which the hepatopathy was considered "likely" by the first module (151 subjects; see Table 3). Notice, however, that three of them are actually healthy, but for all of them the Diagnostic Class Hypothesizer did not emit any hypothesis, even when the threshold was set to the lowest significant value (0.75 in Table 4).

Table 4 illustrates the behavior of the Diagnostic Class Hypothesizer with different thresholds for the 148 remaining subjects. Each row of Table 4 refers to a particular threshold value; the first column contains in the first subcolumn the number of subjects for whom at least one hypothesis gathered an evidence degree greater than the threshold value, whereas the first subcolumn of the following four columns tells how many times exactly n hypotheses ($1 \leq n \leq 4$) were above the threshold. The second and third subcolumns of each column indicate respectively how many times the correct diagnostic class appeared among the emitted hypotheses and how many times the correct diagnostic class was ranked first (these values are given in percents with respect to the first subcolumn).

The last set of rules which has to be discussed is the one used by the Impairment Evaluator. The rules of this last module operate on the sole basis of laboratory test results, without any further reference to symptoms, history or signs.

For each aspect of the hepatic functionality the rules involve only three laboratory tests; the selection of the most significant tests has been performed by analyzing both with fuzzy and with statistical techniques the discrimination capability of different sets of tests [19]. After the evaluation of that capability (which showed an impressive agreement between fuzzy and statistical techniques) a second selection

Table 4 - Results of the Diagnostic Class Hypothesizer (explanations given in the text)

THRESHOLD VALUE	AT LEAST ONE HYPOTHESIS EMITTED			EXACTLY ONE HYPOTHESIS EMITTED			EXACTLY TWO HYPOTHESIS EMITTED			EXACTLY THREE HYPOTHESIS EMITTED			EXACTLY FOUR HYPOTHESIS EMITTED		
0.75	148	100%	93%	80	100%	100%	40	100%	90%	22	100%	82%	6	100%	67%
0.80	109	94%	89%	83	97%	97%	20	80%	60%	6	100%	67%	0	-	-
0.87	94	93%	91%	89	93%	93%	4	75%	50%	1	100%	0%	0	-	-

step was applied in order to rule out those sets containing laboratory tests based on invasive techniques (e.g. Brom-Sulphaleine) even if the system would have performed better by taking into account those results.

Tables 5a, 5b, 5c and 5d report the results of the automatic evaluation of the functional assessment of the liver with respect to the four functional aspects introduced above (Cytolysis, Cholestasis, Biosynthesis, Reactivity). These results refer to the test set of 148 individuals for whom the Diagnostic Class Hypothesizer gathered sufficient evidence (threshold = 0.75) to fire at least one hypothesis.

The last experiment which has been performed has the purpose of ascertaining that the Impairment Evaluator performs well also on a set of subjects larger than the training set used to learn the rules (179 subjects). The test set in this experiment consists of 276 subjects selected from the initial set of 288 subjects by ruling out that ones for whom not all the required laboratory test results were available. Notice that, contrary to the assumption made by the Diagnostic Class Hypothesizer (all the submitted subjects are ill), it is not assumed by the Impairment Evaluator that all subjects show an alteration of the hepatic functionality, so that it makes sense to test it also against subjects with a normal functionality. Tables 6a, 6b, 6c and 6d report the comparison between the impairment degree hypothesized by the Impairment Evaluator and the one assigned to the subject by the physicians.

5. CONCLUDING REMARKS

The problem of automatic knowledge acquisition received an increasing attention by Artificial Intelligence researchers. Most of the systems devoted to automatic learning purported to extract from a variety of examples a sort of generalization accounting for the characteristic features common to the examined set of examples (see, for instance, [20]). However, most of the methods which have been developed are difficult to apply to problems related to medical decision making; one of the main difficulties resides in the large number of features needed to characterize an individual; moreover, it is very rare that a feature ia associated in a categorical way to a class (i.e. it is pathognomonic, in medical terms), so that it is always necessary to weight the amount of evidence carried by a particular feature in support of a hypothesis about the assignment of an individual to a class. The most remarkable examples of rule learning for diagnostic applications are [21], where only the weight of the rules is learned automatically, and [9].

Our approach, based on fuzzy set theory, offers the main advantage of representing in an uniform way, that is by means of linguistic variables, all kinds of findings (binary, discrete, continuous, etc.) as well as the strength of implication (i.e. the weights associated with the condition-decision rules). This representation not only increases to a large extent the readibility of the rules, but also makes them more robust, by reducing their sensitivity to small variations of the parameters, which are approximated by means of fuzzy linguistic variables.

The learning algorithm produces a set of rules by determining both their condition parts and their weights. The condition parts of the rules referring to the same hypothesis contain only a small subset of the findings taken into account and the effectiveness of the algorithm is shown by the small number of rules needed to characterize the different hypotheses (less than ten rules for each hypothesis).

The experiments reported in the fourth section showed how the adopted methodology deals well with the complex deductive processes associated with medical decision making; moreover, they demonstrated the effectiveness of the learning algorithm for inferring a set of rules which allow the system to accurately classify the subjects. However, good classification results does not necessarily imply that the rules are acceptable from a medical point of view. In fact the small size of the training set, expecially as regards some particular diagnostic classes, does not guarantee the completeness of the set of rules (in the sense that some particular clinical aspects could not occurr in the sample); moreover the definition of the diagnostic classes used by the current system should be refined in order to make the system more sound from the medical point of view. However, the main reason which could make a physician judge the rules as inadequate stands on the exceedingly simple control structure, which, as mentioned above, does not allow the insertion of rules referring to causal relationships among diseases and to the knowledge regarding the evolution of the diseases. Nevertheless, the latter remark concerns mainly the reasoning involved in the diagnostic process; the difficulties arising when the complex mechanisms of inference and deduction have to be modeled in an accurate and deep way are not so apparent when classification problems must be handled. For this kind of problems the de-

Table 5 - Final classification results of the Impairment Evaluator for the test set of 148 subjects

	ABSENT	LOW	SEVERE	VERY SEVERE	
ABSENT	28 (96.6%)	1 (3.4%)	0 –	0 –	29
LOW	2 (4.0%)	42 (84.0%)	6 (12.0%)	0 –	50
SEVERE	0 –	2 (4.4%)	39 (86.7%)	4 (8.9%)	45
VERY SEVERE	0 –	0 –	1 (4.2%)	23 (95.8%)	24

a) Cytolysis (Mean misclassific. error = 9.2%)

	ABSENT	LOW	SEVERE	VERY SEVERE	
ABSENT	12 (80.0%)	3 (20.0%)	0 –	0 –	15
LOW	7 (13.7%)	38 (74.5%)	6 (11.8%)	0 –	51
SEVERE	0 –	13 (25.0%)	37 (71.2%)	2 (3.8%)	52
VERY SEVERE	0 –	0 –	0 –	30 (100.%)	30

b) Cholestasis (Mean misclass. error = 18.6%)

	ABSENT	LOW	SEVERE	VERY SEVERE	
ABSENT	29 (93.5%)	2 (6.5%)	0 –	0 –	31
LOW	9 (17.0%)	35 (66.0%)	9 (17.0%)	0 –	53
SEVERE	0 –	9 (20.5%)	28 (63.6%)	7 (15.9%)	44
VERY SEVERE	0 –	0 –	1 (5.0%)	19 (95.0%)	20

c) Biosynthesis (Mean misclass. error = 20.5%)

	ABSENT	LOW	SEVERE	VERY SEVERE	
ABSENT	18 (85.7%)	3 (14.3%)	0 –	0 –	21
LOW	6 (14.6%)	29 (70.8%)	6 (14.6%)	0 –	41
SEVERE	0 –	13 (22.0%)	44 (74.6%)	2 (3.4%)	59
VERY SEVERE	0 –	0 –	4 (14.8%)	23 (85.2%)	27

d) Reactivity (Mean misclass. error = 20.9%)

Table 6 - Final classification results of the Impairment Evaluator for the test set of 276 subjects

	ABSENT	LOW	SEVERE	VERY SEVERE	
ABSENT	125 (92.6%)	10 (7.4%)	0 –	0 –	135
LOW	3 (4.8%)	53 (85.5%)	6 (9.7%)	0 –	62
SEVERE	0 –	3 (5.4%)	48 (87.3%)	4 (7.3%)	55
VERY SEVERE	0 –	0 –	1 (4.2%)	23 (95.8%)	24

a) Cytolysis (Mean misclassific. error = 9.7%)

	ABSENT	LOW	SEVERE	VERY SEVERE	
ABSENT	94 (87.0%)	9 (8.3%)	5 (4.7%)	0 –	108
LOW	11 (14.5%)	57 (75.0%)	8 (10.5%)	0 –	76
SEVERE	0 –	13 (22.4%)	43 (74.2%)	2 (3.4%)	58
VERY SEVERE	0 –	0 –	0 –	34 (100.%)	34

b) Cholestasis (Mean misclass. error = 16.0%)

	ABSENT	LOW	SEVERE	VERY SEVERE	
ABSENT	130 (92.2%)	11 (7.8%)	0 –	0 –	141
LOW	11 (16.7%)	44 (66.6%)	11 (16.7%)	0 –	66
SEVERE	0 –	9 (18.4%)	32 (65.3%)	8 (16.3%)	49
VERY SEVERE	0 –	0 –	1 (5.0%)	19 (95.0%)	20

c) Biosynthesis (Mean misclass. error = 20.2%)

	ABSENT	LOW	SEVERE	VERY SEVERE	
ABSENT	106 (93.8%)	6 (5.3%)	1 (0.9%)	0 –	113
LOW	6 (9.5%)	48 (76.2%)	9 (14.3%)	0 –	63
SEVERE	0 –	13 (18.0%)	49 (68.1%)	10 (13.9%)	72
VERY SEVERE	0 –	0 –	4 (14.3%)	24 (85.7%)	28

d) Reactivity (Mean miclass. error = 19.1%)

scribed methodology is particularly well suited, as it has been shown by means of the experiments involving the module named "Impairment Evaluator".

ACKNOWLEDGEMENTS

This work is part of a research project supported by the Regione Piemonte and carried out in co-operation with the Second Medical Clinic of the University of Turin and with the Institute of Electrical Engineering of the Politechnic of Turin.

The authors are indebited in particular with Prof. G. Molino and Dr. C. Cravetto of the Second Medical Clinic for many useful discussions and suggestions, and for providing the data used in the experiments.

REFERENCES

[1] Kulikowski, C.A.: Artificial Intelligence methods and systems for medical consultations, IEEE Trans. on Pattern Analysis and Machine Intelligence, PAMI-2 (1980) 464-476.

[2] Gomez, F. and Chandrasekaran, B.: Knowledge organization and distribution for medical diagnosis, IEEE Trans. on Systems, Man and Cybernetics, SMC-11 (1981) 34-42.

[3] Davis, R., Buchanan, B. and Shortliffe, E.: Production rules as a representation for a knowledge-based consultation program, Artificial Intelligence 8 (1977) 15-45 .

[4] Pople, H.: The formation of composite hypotheses in diagnostic problem solving, Proc. 5th Int. Joint Conf. on Artificial Intelligence (Cambridge MA, 1977) 1030-1037.

[5] Weiss, S., Kulikowski, C.A., Amarel,S. and Safir, A.: A model based method for computer aided medical decision making, Artificial Intelligence 11 (1978) 145-172.

[6] Patil, R.S., Szolovits, P. and Schwartz, W.: Causal understanding of patient illness in medical diagnosis, Proc. 7th Int. Joint Conf. on Artificial Intelligence (Vancouver B.C., 1981) 893-899.

[7] Chandrasekaran, B., Gomez, F., Mittal, S. and Smith, J.: An approach to medical diagnosis based on conceptual structures, Proc. 6th Int. Joint Conf. on Artificial Intelligence (Tokyo, 1979) 134-142.

[8] Davis, R.: Interactive transfer of expertise: acquisition of new inference rules, Artificial Intelligence 12 (1979) 121-158 .

[9] Michalski, R.S. and Chilausky, R.L.: Knowledge acquisition by encoding expert rules versus computer induction from examples: a case study involving soybean pathology, Int. Journal of Man-Machine Studies 12 (1980) 63-87 .

[10] Lesmo, L., Saitta, L. and Torasso, P.: Computer aided evaluation of liver fuctional assessment, Proc. 4th Annual Symp. on Computer Applications in Medical Care (Washington D.C., 1980) 181-189 .

[11] Tou, J.T and Gonzalez, R.C.: Pattern Recognition principles (Addison Wesley, Reading, 1974).

[12] Szolovitz, P. and Pauker, S.G.: Categorical and probabilistic reasoning in medical diagnosis, Artificial Intelligence 11 (1978), 115-144.

[13] Zadeh, L.A.: The concept of a linguistic variable and its application to approximate reasoning, Information Sciences 8 (1975), 199-250 .

[14] Waterman, D.A. and Hayes-Roth, F. (eds.): Pattern-directed inference systems (Academic Press, New York, 1978).

[15] Zadeh, L.A.: Fuzzy Sets as a basis for a theory of possibility, Fuzzy Sets and Systems 1 (1978) 3-28 .

[16] De Mori, R. and Saitta, L.: Automatic learning of fuzzy naming relations over finite languages, Information Sciences 21 (1980) 93-139 .

[17] Saitta, L. and Torasso, P.:Fuzzy characterization of coronary disease, Fuzzy Sets and Systems 5 (1981) 245-258 .

[18] Lesmo, L., Saitta, L. and Torasso, P.: Fuzzy production rules: a learning methodology, in Wang, P.P.: Advances in Fuzzy Sets Theory and Applications (Plenum Press, in press)

[19] Milanese, M., Molino, G., Belforte, G., Cravetto, C., Frediani, S., Bona, B. and Saitta, L.: Qualitative and quantitative, evaluation of liver disease, Proc. 4th Annual Symp. on Computer Applications in Medical Care (Washington D.C., 1980) 555-563 .

[20] Dietterich, T.G. and Michalski, R.S.: Inductive learning of structural descriptions evaluation criteria and comparative review of selected methods, Artificial Intelligence 16 (1981) 257-294 .

[21] Weiss, S.M., Kulikowski, C.A. and Nudel, B.: Learning production rules for consultation systems, Proc. 6th Int. Joint Conf. on Artificial Intelligence (Tokyo, 1979) 948-950 .

[22] Lesmo, L., Magnani, D. and Torasso, P.: A deterministic analyzer for the interpretation of natural language commands, Proc. 7th Int. Joint Conf. on Artificial Intelligence (Vancouver B.C., 1981) 440-442 .

Approximate Reasoning in Decision Analysis
M.M. Gupta and E. Sanchez (eds.)

A RULE-BASED INFERENCE WITH FUZZY SET FOR STRUCTURAL DAMAGE ASSESSMENT†

MITSURU ISHIZUKA[1], K. S. FU[2] AND JAMES T. P. YAO[3]

[1]School of Electrical Engineering, Purdue University.
Since Nov. 1981, Institute of Industrial Science,
University of Tokyo, 7-22-1, Roppongi, Minato-ku, Tokyo, 106, JAPAN

[2]School of Electrical Engineering, Purdue University
West Lafayette, IN 47907, U.S.A.

[3]School of Civil Engineering, Purdue University
West Lafayette, IN 47907, U.S.A.

ABSTRACT

The state-of-the-art of damage assessment in civil engineering profession is that only a few experienced engineers are well qualified to practice it. In this paper, to develop a computer-based damage assessment system of existing structures particularly subjected to earthquake excitation, a rational rule-based inference procedure is presented under the framework of expert system. Because it is difficult to express the relevant knowledge in a precise manner, the inference procedure should deal with the rules including uncertainty and fuzzy restrictions. The Dempster and Shafer's probability which seems to be superior to the Bayesian probability in expressing subjective uncertainty is employed as a certainty measure. With the inference procedure, the certainty measure can propagate through a hierarchical inference network. Eventually, we can obtain the degree of the certainty of the hypotheses in the final gaol, which will provide a reasonable answer for decision-making purposes.

KEY WORDS: expert system, inference, uncertainty, fuzzy set, Dempster & Shafer's theory, damage assessment.

1. INTRODUCTION

The efficient utilization of the knowledge of human experts is a major topic in knowledge engineering [9], in which artificial intelligence techniques are applied to solve complex problems in the real world. Because a system which is designed on the basis of knowledge engineering is intended to work as a human expert, it is often called an expert system. The important parts of such a system consist of a knowledge base and an inference machine as shown in Fig. 1.

A knowledge base refers to a storage in a computer, in which useful knowledge is stored in a stylized form suitable for the inference. An inference machine is a control process which can be used to deduce an answer from a given problem situation by using the knowledge stored in the knowledge base. In the inference process, questions are initiated to obtain additional information in case of need. For example, consider the medical diagnosis [20,26], in which a physician draws a conclusion by synthesizing many observed symptoms and his/her knowledge. A schematic diagram of the expert system is shown in Fig. 1.

In a complex problem, it is an efficient way to express relevant knowledge as a collection of many small pieces of knowledge. The problem reduction approach [21,22] can be used to decompose a problem into simpler sub-problems with the relations of AND and OR. Those sub-problems are further decomposed into even simpler sub-problems. Hence the whole problem can be described hierarchically, and it has its own final goal to be achieved. Likewise each sub-problem has its own sub-goal to be achieved from available information. For the decomposition of a problem including uncertainty, a "combination" relation which is denoted by COMB [17] is becoming important in addition to AND/OR relations. The relation "combination" refers to the situation that the goal is supported separately from more than two different

†This work was supported by NSF under Grant No. PFR79-06296.

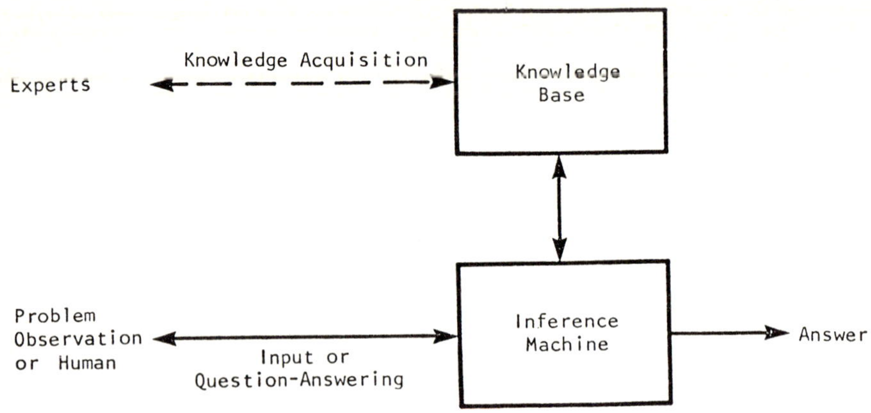

Fig. 1 Expert system.

evidences. For example, this type of problem decomposition is used in a medical consultation system MYCIN [24,25].

The production system approach [4,29] provides a convenient way to express a piece of knowledge. When the knowledge is expressed with uncertainty, it can be written as a production rule with a certainty measure C, which may have a value between 0 and 1, in the following basic form:

Rule IF: X ,
THEN: H with C ,

where IF and THEN clauses are called premise (condition) and action (conclusion), respectively. Moreover, if the restrictions as implied by the premise and action clauses are not precise, they may be expressed in terms of fuzzy subsets.

In this paper, the inference procedure for the decomposed problem with the combination relation is presented. Such a procedure can be used to synthesize a certainty measure of the hypothesis in a goal state from its evidential states and available rules. To-date, several intuitive functions have been employed in the inference procedure [24,27] to realize the synthesizing effect. Although those intuitive functions have been reported to work well in particular domains, their performances in other application domains are unpredictable.

It is desirable to develop a rational inference procedure which always yields a rational solution as long as the expressed pieces of knowledge are correct. Duda, Hart and Nilsson [8] have shown one of those procedures for subjective probability. This paper presents a rational inference procedure using the Dempster and Shafer's probability [5,23] which is preferable to the Bayesian probability in quantifying subjective uncertainty. After the inference procedure for the rules with uncertainty and non-fuzzy restrictions is described in section 3 , its extension to include the rules with fuzzy restrictions is presented in section 4.

Once the inference procedure is described, the certainty measure can propagate through the hierarchical inference network. Eventually we can obtain the degree of certainty of the hypotheses in the final goal, which will provide a reasonable answer for decision-making purposes.

2. MOTIVATION

The applications of fuzzy set theory in civil engineering problems are reviewed and summarized elsewhere [1,2,13,33,34]. The inference mechanism based on the rules including uncertainty and fuzzy restrictions was motivated by the need to develop a damage assessment system of existing structures [16,17]. The role and the state-of-the-art of the damage assessment in civil engineering profession was described by Yao [32]. Frequently, the safety and reliability of a particular or a number of existing structures need to be evaluated either as a part of a periodic inspection program or immediately following a given hazardous event [3,31]. Because only a few experienced engineers can practice it well to-date, it is planned to establish a systematic way for the damage assessment of existing structures.

SPERIL [16,17] is a computerized damage assessment system as designed by the authors particularly for building structures subjected to earthquake excitation. Fu and Yao [11] suggested at first that the problem of damage assessment can be considered in terms of the theory of pattern recognition. Recently, to deal with a large variety of the conditions of structures and to achieve the highly effective utilization of experts' knowledge, the rule-based inference method is employed for the system.

Useful information for the damage assessment comes mainly from the following two sources; (i) the visual inspection at various portions of the structure and (ii) the analysis of accelerometer records during the earthquake. The

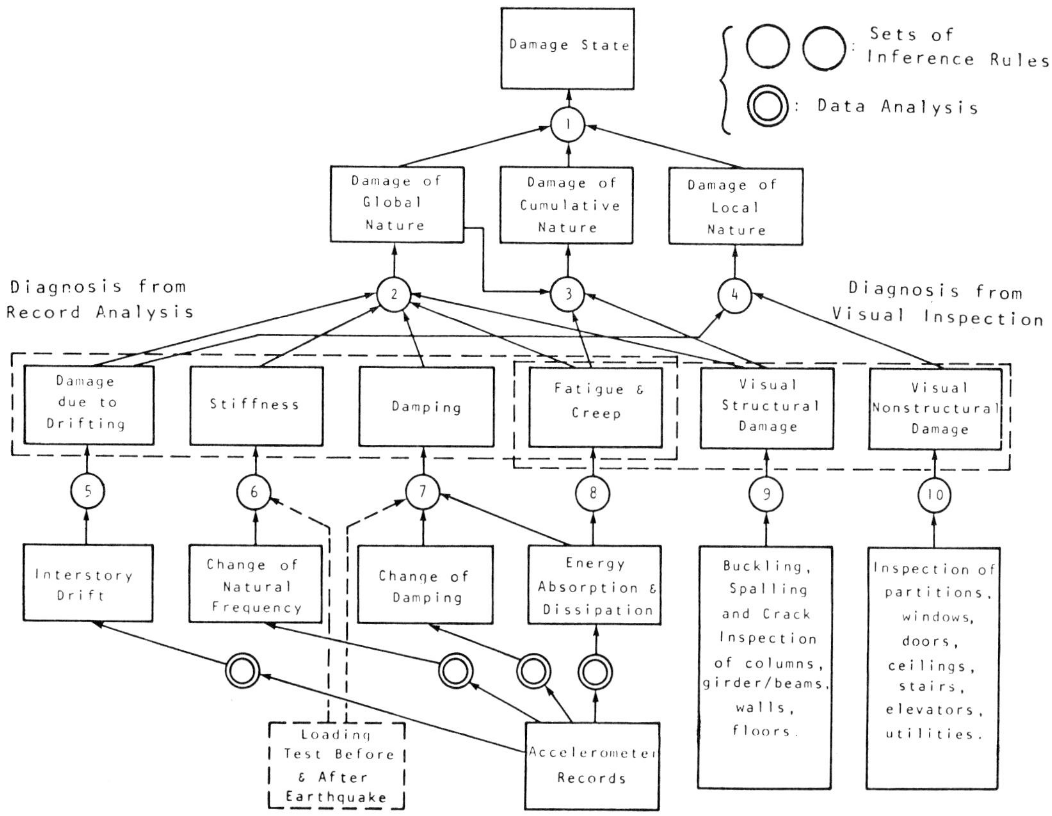

Fig. 2 Inference network for damage assessment of existing structures.

interpretation of these data is influenced to large extent by the particular kind of structure under study [6,15,30]. At present, the useful pieces of knowledge have been collected under the framework of Fig. 2, in which several intermediate diagnostic states are introduced. Although the numerical grades between 0 and 10 as shown in Fig. 3 are used to evaluate the diagnostic states, it is difficult and perhaps even impractical to express the inferential knowledge in a precise manner. Therefore, the rules are written basically with fuzzy subsets [35], such as no damage, slight damage, modelate damage, severe damage and destructive damage with uncertainty. These fuzzy subsets can be characterized by membership functions such as,

$$\mu_{no}(d) = 1/0 + 0.5/1 \ , \tag{2-1}$$

$$\mu_{slight}(d) = 0.5/1 + 1/2 + 0.5/3 \ , \tag{2-2}$$

$$\mu_{modelate}(d) = 0.5/3 + 1/4 + 0.7/5 + 0.3/6 \ , \tag{2-3}$$

$$\mu_{severe}(d) = 0.3/5 + 0.7/6 + 1/7 + 0.7/8 + 0.3/9 \ , \tag{2-4}$$

$$\mu_{destructive}(d) = 0.3/8 + 0.7/9 + 1/10 \ , \tag{2-5}$$

where d is a numerical damage grade as shown in Fig. 3. For example, one rule associated with node 2 of Fig. 2 is written as,

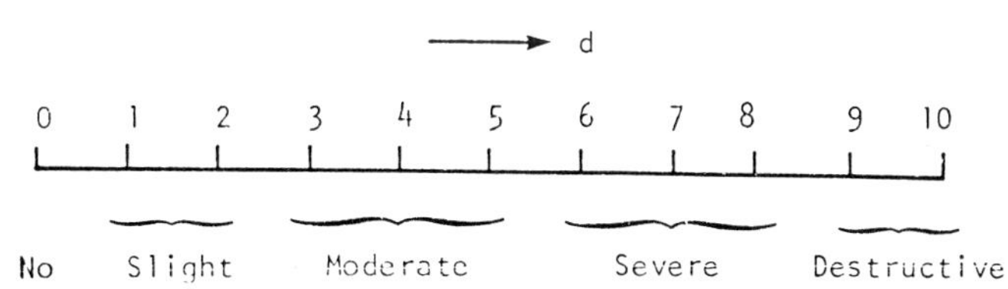

Fig. 3 Grades of damage states and its verbal expressions.

```
Rule 201         IF:  MAT is reinforced concrete,
           THEN IF:  STI is no,
              THEN:  GLO is no with 0.6,
           ELSE IF:  STI is slight,
              THEN:  GLO is slight with 0.6,
           ELSE IF:  STI is moderate,
              THEN:  GLO is moderate with 0.6,
           ELSE IF:  STI is severe,
              THEN:  GLO is severe with 0.6,
           ELSE IF:  STI is destructive,
              THEN:  GLO is destructive with 0.6,
              ELSE:  GLO is unknown with 1,
```

where MAT = structural material,
GLO = damage of global nature,
STI = diagnosis of stiffness,
"unknown" stands for the universe set of damage grade.

To obtain a correct answer by using such knowledge, a rational inference mechanism is required to process the rules expressed with fuzzy subsets along with uncertainty in an effective manner.

3. INFERENCE USING DEMPSTER & SHAFER'S PROBABILITY

The Bayesian probability is one of the most popular measures in statistics. A rule-based inference procedure using the Bayesian probability is considered theoretically in [18]. However, there exist criticisms to express subjective uncertainty with the use of the Bayesian probability. The main criticism is that it cannot be used to deal with ignorance in an effective manner. In other words, the Bayesian theory cannot be use to distinguish between the lack of belief and disbelief, because it requires the additive relation of $P(A) + P(\bar{A}) = 1$, where $P(\bar{A})$ is the probability of the complement subset of A.

In 1967, Dempster [5] proposed a useful concept of lower and upper probabilities to deal with the subjective uncertainty. Shafer [23] refined Dempster's theory and use the terminologies of belief function and plausibility instead of the original lower and upper probabilities, respectively. The lower and upper probabilities are defined following Demspter and Shafer's (DS's) basic probability. The Dempster's theory provides a way to combine more than two DS's basic probabilities which are obtained with respect to the same hypothetical goal state from separate bodies of evidences.

At first, we will consider the application of the Dempster and Shafer's theory to the rule-based inference with uncertainty and crisp restrictions.† Then, in the following section, we will extend the result to include the rules with fuzzy restrictions.

According to Shafer [23], the DS's basic probability $m(A_i)$ (i=0,1,2...) can be visualized as a semi-mobile probability mass which is confined to subset A_i but can move freely to every point of A_i. Let A_0 be a finite universe set and A_i (i=1,2...) denote crisp subsets of A_0. Then, the DS's basic probability can be defined formally as a function $m: 2^{A_0} \rightarrow [0,1]$ which satisfies,

$$\begin{cases} m(\phi) = 0, \quad (\phi\text{: empty set}) \\ \sum_{A_i \subseteq A_0} m(A_i) = 1. \end{cases} \tag{3-1}$$

The degree of ignorance is represented by $m(A_0)$. A_i is called a focal element if $m(A_i) > 0$. The lower probability is defined by using this DS's basic probability as,

$$P_*(A_i) = \sum_{A_j \subseteq A_i} m(A_j) , \tag{3-2}$$

that is, the sum of the DS's basic probabilities confined within the subset A_i. The upper probability is defined by

$$\begin{aligned} P^*(A_i) &= 1 - P_*(\bar{A}_i) \\ &= 1 - \sum_{A_j \subseteq \bar{A}_i} m(A_j) , \end{aligned} \tag{3-3}$$

where $\bar{A}_i$ is the complement set of A_i. It can be understood that the lower and upper probabilities represent respectively the conservative and optimistic amount of probability. If m_1 and m_2 are the DS's basic probabilities inferred from independent evidences and A_{1i} and A_{2j} (i,j=0,1,2,...) are their respective focal

---

†The authors recognized independently the usefulness of Dempster and Shafer's theory under the framework of the rule-based inference. Nevertheless, we have found that the following three papers appeared at the 7th Int'l Joint Conf. on Artificial Intelligence, Vancouver, Aug. 24-28, 1981:
Barnett, J. A., "Computational Methods for A Mathematical Theory of Evidence,"
Friedman, L., "Extended Plausible Inference,"
Garvey, T. D., Lowrance, J. D. and Fischler, M. A., "An Inference Technique for Integrating Knowledge From Disparate Sources."
It is to be noted that the fuzzy sets are not considered in these papers.

elements, then a new DS's basic probability can be obtained by combining m_1 and m_2 as,

$$m(A_k) = \frac{\sum_{A_{1i} \cap A_{2j} = A_k} m_1(A_{1i}) m_2(A_{2j})}{1 - \sum_{A_{1i} \cap A_{2j} = \phi} m_1(A_{1i}) m_2(A_{2j})} \quad (A_k \neq \phi) \qquad (3\text{-}4)$$

The combination of more than two DS's basic probabilities are given, if they are inferred from independent evidences, by the sequential calculation of (3-4). The combination of the lower and upper probabilities can be obtained based on the combined DS's basic probability.

To formulate the inference problem in general, consider a basic case as shown in Fig. 4 where a goal state H is supported by two independent evidential states X and Y and their associated rules. Let the universe sets of X, Y and H be $X_0 = \{x_i\}$ $(i=1,\ldots,I)$, $Y_0 = \{y_j\}$ $(j=1,\ldots,J)$ and $H_0 = \{h_k\}$ $(k=1,\ldots,K)$, respectively. Those elements x_i, y_j and h_k are assumed to be mutually exclusive and exhaustive with respect to X_0, Y_0 and H_0, respectively. In the damage assessment of existing structures, x_i, y_j and h_k are the numerical damage grades. Suppose that the evidential states of X and Y are expressed in terms of conditional DS's basic probabilities $m(X_i|\cdot)$ $(i=0,\ldots,2^I-1)$, $m(Y_j|\cdot)$ $(j=0,\ldots,2^J-1)$, where X_i and Y_j are crisp subsets of universe sets X_0 and Y_0, respectively. The objective in this section is to infer the hypothetical goal state H represented by the DS's basic probability $m(H_k|\cdot)$ $(k=0,\ldots,2^K-1)$

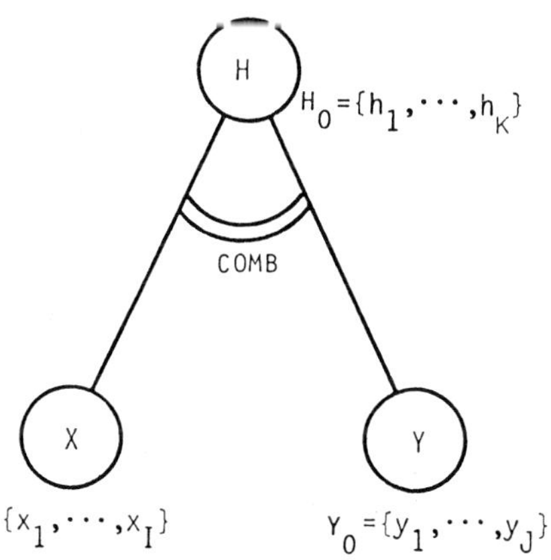

Fig. 4 Inference from the combination of two different evidences.

and thereby the lower and upper probabilities $P_*(H_k|\cdot)$ and $P^*(H_k|\cdot)$ where H_k is a certain subset of universe set H_0.

Rules are written in the following form;

Rule 1 IF: X is X_1,
THEN: H is H_{X1} with $m(H_{X1}|X_1)$,
ELSE IF: X is X_2,
THEN: H is H_{X2} with $m(H_{X2}|X_2)$,
.
.
ELSE: H is H_0 with 1

Rule 2 IF: Y is Y_1,
THEN: H is H_{Y1} with $m(H_{Y1}|Y_1)$,
ELSE IF: Y is Y_2,
THEN: H is H_{Y2} with $m(H_{Y2}|Y_2)$,
.
.
ELSE: H is H_0 with 1.

The function of the first IF-THEN pair of Rule 1, for example, is to assign the DS's basic probability, the amount of which is $m(H_{X1}|X_1)$ at most, to subset H_{X1} according to the degree of satisfaction of the premise clause. The action of assigning the probability to the universe set H_0 implies the degree of ignorance.

Define the degree of satisfaction of the premise clause with the following lower probability as,

$$P_*(X_\ell|\cdot) = \sum_{X_i \subseteq X_\ell} m(X_i|\cdot) \qquad (3\text{-}5)$$

where $\ell = 1,2,\ldots$ and X_i denotes the subset included in X_ℓ. Then the expectation of the DS's basic probability assignment to the subset of H_0 can be deduced from evidential state X and Rule 1 as,

$$m_*(H_{X\ell}|X) = m(H_{X\ell}|X_\ell)\, P_*(X_\ell|\cdot) , \qquad (3\text{-}6)$$

$$m_*(H_0|X) = 1 - \sum_{X_\ell} m(H_{X\ell}|X_\ell)\, P_*(X_\ell|\cdot) . \qquad (3\text{-}7)$$

Let $m_*(H_{X0}|X)$ stand for $m_*(H_0|X)$ hereinafter. Because the deduced amount is associated with the lower probability of X, we shall call it lower basic probability and denote it by m_*.

Similarly, from Rule 2 and the evidential state of Y, the expectation of the basic probability assignment $m_*(H_{Y\ell}|Y)$ $\{\ell = 0,1,2\ldots$ and $m_*(H_{Y0}|Y) = m_*(H_0|Y)\}$ can be deduced.

According to Dempster's rule of combination of (3-4), if two evidences X and Y are independent each other regarding the support of H, $m_*(H_{X\ell}|X)$ and $m_*(H_{Y\ell}|Y)$ ($\ell = 0,1,\ldots$) can be combined to generate a new lower basic probability for the subset H_k of H_0 as follows,

$$m_*(H_k|X,Y) = \frac{\sum_{H_{Xi} \cap H_{Yj} = H_k} m_*(H_{Xi}|X) m_*(H_{Yj}|Y)}{1 - \sum_{H_{Xi} \cap H_{Yj} = \phi} m_*(H_{Xi}|X) m_*(H_{Yj}|Y)}$$

$$(i,j,k = 0,1,2\ldots) \qquad (3\text{-}8)$$

With these $m_*(H_k|X,Y)$, the lower and upper probabilities of the subset H_ℓ ($\ell = 0,1,\ldots 2^{K-1}$) can be obtained in case of need, respectively, as follows,

$$P_*(H_\ell|X,Y) = \sum_{H_k \subseteq H_\ell} m_*(H_k|X,Y) , \qquad (3\text{-}9)$$

$$P^*(H_\ell|X,Y) = 1 - P_*(\overline{H_\ell}|X,Y) = 1 - \sum_{H_k \subseteq \overline{H_\ell}} m_*(H_k|X,Y) . \qquad (3\text{-}10)$$

At the final goal, the decision will be made based on the lower and upper probabilities. If the decision maker is cautious, he or she tends to rely on the lower probability measure rather than the upper probability; if optimistic, he or she takes the upper probability for his/her decision.

4. RULES WITH FUZZY SETS

In addition to uncertainty, if it is difficult or impractical to express the knowledge as the rules with crisp restrictions as in the damage assessment problem of section II, the rules can be written with fuzzy subsets. Suppose that X_ℓ, $H_{X\ell}$, Y_ℓ, $H_{Y\ell}$ (ℓ=1,2,...) of Rule 1 and 2 in section III are fuzzy subsets. To obtain a rational inference procedure in this environment, this paper extends the Dempster and Shafer's theory to include fuzzy sets without loosing its essence. The extension of the results of section III requires the definitions of fuzzily confined basic probability, the degree of inclusion and intersection between two fuzzy subsets.

First, define the DS's basic probability m(A), of which A is a fuzzy subset characterized by $\mu_A(a)$ of an universe set A_0, as the probability which can be considered as a loosely confined semi-mobile probability mass in the sense of Shafer [23]. The more precise interpretation will become clear by the subsequent equations (4-4), (4-7) and (4-9).

Second, we shall define the degree that a subset A_1 is included in another subset A_2 of the same universe set A_0 as,

$$\begin{aligned} I(A_1 \subseteq A_2) &= \min_a\{\mu_{\overline{A_1|-|A_2}}(a)\} / \max_a\{\mu_{A_1}(a)\} \\ &= \min_a\{1 - \mu_{A_1|-|A_2}(a)\} / \max_a\{\mu_{A_1}(a)\} \\ &= \min_a\{1 - \max(0, \mu_{A_1}(a) - \mu_{A_2}(a))\} / \max_a\{\mu_{A_1}(a)\} \\ &= \min_a\{1, 1 - \mu_{A_1}(a) + \mu_{A_2}(a))\} / \max_a\{\mu_{A_1}(a)\}, \end{aligned} \qquad (4\text{-}1)$$

where |-| is called bounded difference in the fuzzy set theory and the denominator is called the height of fuzzy subset. Eq. (4-1) become 1 if A_1 is completely included in A_2 and 0 if $\mu_{A_2}(a) = 0$ at a, at which $\mu_{A_1}(a)$ takes its peak value. Other definitions of the degree of inclusion are available elsewhere [7].

Third, define the degree of intersection of two fuzzy subsets A_1 and A_2 as,

$$J(A_1,A_2) = \frac{\max_a\{\mu_{A_1 \cap A_2}(a)\}}{\min\{\max_a(\mu_{A_1}(a)), \max_a(\mu_{A_2}(a))\}} , \qquad (4\text{-}2)$$

where the intersection $A_1 \cap A_2$ is defined in the fuzzy set theory by

$$\mu_{A_1 \cap A_2}(a) = \min\{\mu_{A_1}(a), \mu_{A_2}(a)\} . \qquad (4\text{-}3)$$

The denominator of (4-2) is 1 if fuzzy subsets A_1 and A_2 are normalized. With $J(A_1,A_2)$ of (4-2), define the degree that the intersection of A_1 and A_2 is ϕ (empty) as $1 - J(A_1,A_2)$.

With the degree of the inclusion of (4-1) and the evidential state $m(X_i|\cdot)$, the degree of satisfaction of the premise clause of Rule 1 can be determined as,

$$P_*(X_\ell|\cdot) = \sum_{X_i} I(X_i \subseteq X_\ell) m(X_i|\cdot), \qquad (4\text{-}4)$$

which corresponds to (3-5).

Then, corresponding to (3-6) (3-7), the expectation of the basic probability assignment to fuzzy subset can be deduced from the evidential state X and Rule 1 as follows;

$$m_*(H_{X\ell}|X) = m(H_{X\ell}|X_\ell) P_*(X_\ell|\cdot) , \qquad (4\text{-}5)$$

$$m_*(H_{X0}|X) = m_*(H_0|X)$$
$$= 1 - \sum_{X_\ell} P_*(X_\ell|\cdot) \quad , \qquad (4\text{-}6)$$

where H_0 is the universe set, thus, is not fuzzy. m_* of (4-5), (4-6) can be called the lower (fuzzy) basic probability. Similarly, from Y and Rule 2, $m_*(H_{Yn}|Y)$ {n=0,1,2..., and $m_*(H_{Y0}|Y) = m_*(H_0|Y)$} can be deduced.

When applying Dempster's rule of combination for two independent evidences X and Y, the expectation to the intersection of the fuzzy subsets is determined according to (4-2). That is, corresponding to (3-8), $m_*(H_{X\ell}|X)$ and $m_*(H_{Yn}|Y)$ are combined to generate a lower basic probability,

$$m_*(H_{X\ell} \cap H_{Yn}|X,Y)$$
$$= \frac{J(H_{X\ell},H_{Yn})m_*(H_{X\ell}|X)m_*(H_{Yn}|Y)}{\sum_{Xi,Yj}\{1 - J(H_{Xi},H_{Yj})\}m_*(H_{Xi}|X)m_*(H_{Yj}|Y)} \quad ,$$

$$(\ell,n,i,j=0,1,2...) \qquad (4\text{-}7)$$

where the intersection subset is defined by

$$\mu_{H_{X\ell} \cap H_{Yn}}(h) = \min_h \{\mu_{H_{X\ell}}(h), \mu_{H_{Yn}}(h)\} \; . \; (4\text{-}8)$$

Eq. (4-7) becomes 0, of course, when $H_{X\ell} \cap H_{Yn} = \phi$. The denominator of (4-7) which is the sum of the commitment to the portion of empty set normalizes the combined lower basic probabilities. When there are more than two independent evidences, their supports can be combined by the sequential calculations of the basic two evidences case.

With these $m_*(H_k|X,Y)$, the lower and upper probabilities of a fuzzy subset H_ℓ can be obtained in case of need, respectively, as follows,

$$P_*(H_\ell|X,Y) = \sum_{H_k} I(H_k \subseteq H_\ell)m_*(H_k|X,Y) \quad , \; (4\text{-}9)$$

$$P^*(H_\ell|X,Y) = 1 - P(\overline{H_\ell}|X,Y)$$
$$= 1 - \sum_{H_k} I(H_k \subseteq \overline{H_\ell})m_*(H_k|X,Y) \; .$$

$$(4\text{-}10)$$

With the inference procedure described above, the certainty measure which is the DS's probability in this case can propagate through the inference network under the environment of the imprecise knowledge.

5. CONCLUDING REMARKS

To develop a system for the damage assessment of existing structures, a rational rule-based inference procedure with uncertainty and fuzzy restrictions has been presented. The Dempster and Shafer's probability which seems to be superior to the Bayesian probability in expressing subjective uncertainty is employed as a certainty measure. The present method could also be useful in many other decision-making problems.

While in the problem reduction with the combination relation, the evidences are assumed to be mutually independent with respect to the support of the hypothesis, such independency is a critical problem in the real world. As an alternative when the independency of the evidences is doubtful, an inference procedure [17,18] utilizing fuzzy reasoning [36] may be effective. For the rule-based inference system as presented in this paper, a systematic knowledge acquisition and an efficient goal search algorithm remain to be further studied. Although the rule-based inference with uncertainty has been described in the light of artificial intelligence, it can be also viewed as a recent syntactic pattern recognition approach [10,12,14] with semantic attributes [28]. A relation between pattern recognition and some artificial intelligence approaches is discussed by Kanal [19].

REFERENCES

[1] Blockely, D. I., "The Role of Fuzzy Sets in Civil Engineering," Fuzzy Sets and System, Vol. 2, pp. 267-278, 1979.

[2] Brown, C. B., "A Fuzzy Safety Measure," Jour. of Eng. Mech. Div., ASCE, Vol. 105, pp. 855-872, Oct. 1979.

[3] Culver, C. G., Lew, H. S., Hart, G. C. and Pinkham, C. W., "Natural Hazards Evaluation of Existing Buildings," NBS Building Science Series 61, Jan. 1975.

[4] Davis, R., Buchanan, B. and Shortliffe, E., "Production Rules as a Representation for a Knowledge-Based Consultation Program," in Artificial Intelligence 8, North-Holland Pub. Co., 1977.

[5] Dempster, A. P., "Upper and Lower Probabilities Induced by a Multivalued Mapping," Annals of Mathematical Statistics, Vol. 38, pp. 325-339, 1967.

[6] Dowrick, D. J., Earthquake Resistent Design, John Wiley & Sons, 1977.

[7] Dubois, D. and Prade, H., Fuzzy Sets and Systems: Theory and Applications, Academic Press, 1980.

[8] Duda, R. O., Hart, P. and Nilsson, N. J., "Subjective Bayesian Methods for Rule-based Inference Systems," Nat. Computer Conf., 1976.

[9] Feigenbaum, E. A., "The Art of Artificial Intelligence: Themes and Case Studies of Knowledge Engineering," 5th Int'l. Joint Conf. on Artificial Intelligence, 1977.

[10] Fu, K. S., Syntactic Methods in Patterns Recognition, Academic Press, 1974.

[11] Fu, K. S. and Yao, J. T. P., "Pattern Recognition and Damage Assessment," The ASCE EMD Specialty Conference at Austin, Texas, Sept. 1979.

[12] Fu, K. S., "Recent Developments in Pattern Recognition," IEEE Trans. Computer, Vol. C-29, pp. 845-854, Oct. 1980.

[13] Fu, K. S., Ishizuka, M. and Yao, J. T. P., "Application of Fuzzy Sets in Earthquake Engineering," in Recent Developments in Fuzzy Set and Possibility Theory, ed. by R. R. Yager, Pergamon Press, 1981.

[14] Fu, K. S., "Recent Advances in Syntactic Pattern Recognition," Report of the Workshop on Structural and Syntactic Pattern Recognition, June 1981.

[15] Hisada, T., ed., Earthquake and Building (in Japanese), Kajima Publ. Co., 1974.

[16] Ishizuka, M., Fu, K. S. and Yao, J. T. P., "Inexact Inference for Rule-Based Damage Assessment of Existing Structures," 7th Int. Joint Conf. on Artificial Intelligence, Aug. 1981.

[17] Ishizuka, M., Fu, K. S. and Yao, J. T. P., "A Rule-Inference Method for Damage Assessment," ASCE Convention at St. Louis, Oct. 1981; Also, Structural Eng. Report, Purdue Univ., CE-STR-81-27, Sept. 1981.

[18] Ishizuka, M., Fu, K. S. and Yao, J. T. P., "Inference Procedure with Uncertainty for Problem Reduction Method," Structural Eng. Report, Purdue Univ., CE-STR-81-24, Aug. 1981.

[19] Kanal, L. N., "Problem-Solving Models and Search Strategies for Pattern Recognition," IEEE Trans. Patt. Analysis and Mach. Intell., Vol. PAMI-1, pp. 193-201, April 1979.

[20] Kulikowski, C. A., "Artificial Intelligence Methods and Systems for Medical Consultation," IEEE Trans. Patt. Analysis and Mach. Intell., Vol. PAMI-2, pp. 464-476, Sept. 1980.

[21] Nilsson, N. J., Problem-Solving Method in Artificial Intelligence, McGraw-Hill, 1971.

[22] Nilsson, N. J., Principles of Artificial Intelligence, Tioga Publ. Co., Palo Alto, 1980.

[23] Shafer, G., A Mathematical Theory of Evidence, Princeton Univ. Press, 1976.

[24] Shortliffe, E. H. and Buchanan, B. G., "A Model of Inexact Reasoning in Medicine," Mathematical Bioscience, Vol. 23, pp. 351-379, 1975.

[25] Shortliffe, E. H., Computer-Based Medical Consultations: MYCIN, American Elsevier, 1976.

[26] Shortliffe, E. H., Buchanan, B. G. and Feigenbaum, E. A., "Knowledge Engineering for Medical Decision Making: A Review of Computer-Based Clinical Decision Aids," Proc. IEEE, Vol. 67, pp. 1207-1224, Sept. 1979.

[27] Szolovits, P. and Pauker, S. G., "Categorical and Probabilistic Reasoning in Medical Diagnosis," Artificial Intelligence, Vol. 11, pp. 115-144, Aug. 1978.

[28] Tsai, W. H. and Fu, K. S., "Attributed Grammars -- A Tool for Combining Syntactic and Statistical Approaches to Pattern Recognition," IEEE Trans. Syst. Man and Cyb., Vol. SMC-10, pp. 873-885, 1980.

[29] Waterman, D. A. and Hayes-Roth, F., "An Overview of Pattern-Directed Inference Systems," in the same authors ed., Pattern-Directed Inference Systems, Academic Press, 1978.

[30] Wiegel, R. L., ed., Earthquake Engineering, Prentice Hall, 1970.

[31] Wright, R., Kramer, S. and Culver, C., ed., "Building Practice for Disaster Mitigation," NBS Building Science Series 46, 1972.

[32] Yao, J. T. P., "Damage Assessment and Reliability Evaluation of Existing Structures," Jour. of Engineering Structures, Vol. 1, pp. 245-251, Oct. 1979.

[33] Yao, J. T. P., "Damage Assessment of Existing Structures," Jour. of Eng. Mech. Div., ASCE, Vol. 96, pp. 785-799, Aug. 1980.

[34] Yao, J. T. P., Fu., K. S. and Ishizuka, M., "Fuzzy Statistics and Its Potential Application in Civil Engineering," ASCE Convention at St. Louis, Oct. 1981; Also, Structural Eng. Report, Purdue University, CE-STR-81-26, September 1981.

[35] Zadeh, L. A., "Outline of a New Approach to the Analysis of Complex Systems and Decision Processes," IEEE Trans. Systems Man & Cyb., Vol. SMC-3, pp. 28-44, Jan. 1973.

[36] Zadeh, L. A., "Fuzzy Logic and Approximate Reasoning," Syntheses, Vol. 30, pp. 407-428, 1975.

Approximate Reasoning in Decision Analysis
M.M. Gupta and E. Sanchez (eds.)

SPHINX : AN INTERACTIVE SYSTEM FOR MEDICAL DIAGNOSIS AIDS

M. FIESCHI, M. JOUBERT, D. FIESCHI, G. SOULA, M. ROUX

Service Universitaire de Biomathématiques, Statistiques
Médicales et Epidémiologiques, Informatique
Faculté de Médecine
Marseille, France

This paper presents a system called SPHINX for medical computer-aided diagnosis that combines the advantages of both fuzzy and logical inferences. The system uses a data-driven approach to problem solving. It is based on methods of inference and pattern-matching used in Artificial Intelligence and on various heuristic features : fuzzy heuristics in relation with the suggestion power of the signs and heuristics based on the costs of complementary investigations. The fuzzy heuristic functions are of great interest since they operate like a physician who only knows a small number of symptoms for a given patient. So the system has an approach to diagnosis search that is understandable by physicians. The first experiments where made in the diagnosis of epigastric pain. Its results are presented and discussed in the paper.

KEY WORDS : Computer aided diagnosis, pattern matching, inference systems, medical decision, epigastric pain, fuzzy heuristics.

1. INTRODUCTION

In a recent paper, Fox and al. [4] explore the problem of medical decision making and explain that the mathematical justification of such methods is hard to assimilate and that the algorithms remain opaque for the physician. In conclusion, Fox suggests that the approach to aided-diagnosis methods should match human reasoning more closely. We agree entirely with this opinion and feel that it is therefore useful to develop other methods and in particular, whenever systems are interactive, the computed system should correspond to the user's reasoning. It is therefore necessary to analyse the logic of the diagnosis process, to define its general rules and to explain the mechanisms which determine the use of such rules in aided-diagnosis.

A number of authors have been working along these lines for the last 8 to 10 years. They have studied the structure of medical knowledge and the processes through which it is manipulated. Several systems have been designed, among which we would like to mention the best known : MYCIN [7], CASNET [10] INTERNIST [6], HELP [12].

The basic components of these systems are signs, symptoms, paraclinical results, diagnoses. These basic components and the knowledge which permits their use - together forming the "expert knowledge" of the system - are dissociated from the programs. The programs are in fact the interpreters of the expert knowledge and perform the matching with the patient's condition.

Two of these systems, MYCIN and INTERNIST, are of great interest because they operate "inexact ressoning" in their diagnosis searches and so, are closer to human behaviour than the other programs. The SPHINX system uses fuzzy heuristics that drives the diagnosis search into the best way as regards the signs known for a patient, just as physicians act with a little of the patient's information [3].

2. BACKGROUND

For some years now, we have been considering the problem of aided-diagnosis [1], [2] and this research has enabled us to design the SPHINX system. However, unlike MYCIN or CASNET, which apply to already fairly narrow domains, our own system deals with the relatively unbounded problem of diagnosis in internal medicine, and in this respect, we come closer to the INTERNIST system.
A general outline of the system is given in Fig. 1.
The first application of this system is in the diagnosis of epigastric pain.

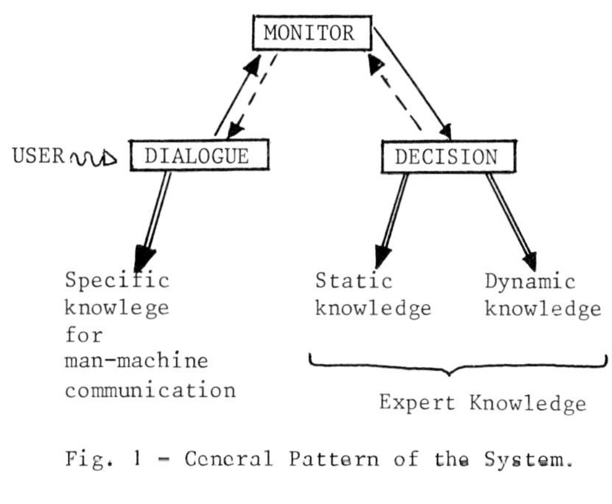

Fig. 1 - General Pattern of the System.

The user is connected with a module called DIALOGUE provided with a specified knowledge in order to solve all the problems relevant to the coherence of the discourse of the user and to set up the information needed in the module of decision making. Neither this module, nor its associated knowledge are described here [5].

The connection between the DIALOGUE module and the DECISION module is activated via the monitor by selecting DIALOGUE or DECISION according to the state of the system.

We wanted to create a system with reactions similar to those of a physician. This system receives information in two ways :
- data provided by the patient about its complaint ;
- data resquested by the system itself. The context of what has already been recorded allows it to go further with the interrogation, to establish hypotheses which will then be confirmed or not by requested examinations.

The DECISION module has two components to solve its problem :
- First is a static component : a set of rules, each one representing a part of clinical medical knowledge (expert knowledge). Each rule can only be applied in well defined contexts. The latter constitute the basis of the diagnosis reasoning and are tree-structured.
- Second is a dynamic component : the control structure which activates and selects the rules.

The rules and the set of signs are determined in relation to predicate calculus which allows a finer analysis of the signs. For instance, if a patient complains of epigastric pain, it is important to determine some attributes of this pain such as : irradiation, intensity, type, periodicity, which constitute the parameters of a predicate name : pain.

The attribute-value of a sign is in relation to an associated knowledge of it. For instance, an arterial pressure of 11 will be appreciated differently according to the age of the patient.

The system behaves in the same way the physician, whose attitude varies during his pre-diagnosis research. First, he remains inactive, listening to the patient who describes the signs. During this period, we think that the physician refers to an orientation knowledge which we call the "suggestion power" of the signs.

At this step, the system processes an approximate reasoning, based on fuzzy sets theory [8], but this process has only a heuristic power likely to suggest a number of diagnostic orientations. The other steps operate the identification of these suggested orientations with the patients data in a first order predicate calculus. The diagnosis will be made after a series of complementary tests required to identify the pathology.

3. SPHINX : A TOOL FOR DECISION MAKING ASSISTANCE

3.1. Basic concepts

Our system is a member of the class of "Pattern Directed Inference Systems" [9] which are conceived from a very rich but simple basic notion : a data-driven program strategy that makes the program react to each change in its environment.

In our system, patterns are organized as tree structures. In our experiment, each one of the trees corresponds to one of the twelve basic syndromes likely to be noted in the clinical data of epigastric pain : syndrome of intoxication, angina, infectious syndrome, cholostatic syndrome... the rules attached to each node include complemetary signs and data that must be or can be required for the accuracy of a diagnosis. Data changes are plain statements : the set of rules connected to each node is true or false.

The control is explicitly carried out by means of several heuristics. They serve to minimize and order the number of ways of research (hypotheses) in a universe of exponential growth.

3.2. The structure of knowledge

3.2.1. Patterns : trees and attached rules

A part of medical knowledge is given in a tree-structured mode in which subtrees correspond to pathological units or to different clinical conditions of diseases. The lower nodes (not necessarily the leaves) are labelled as diagnosis nodes while intermediate nodes between the roots and the diagnosis nodes correspond to clinical states characterized by syndromes of clinical and paraclinical symtomatologies ; these two levels of investigation justify the hierarchy introduced in the tree structure.

The higher nodes (E_2 and E_3 in the diagram) represent the syndromes characterized by signs noted during the interrogation and/or clinical examination. The lowest nodes (E_4, E_9 in the diagram) represent diagnoses confirmed by complementary tests.

Terminal nodes can stand for etiologic diagnoses and intermediate nodes can represent class diagnoses. So the diagnosis is more accurate if it reaches a terminal node. The diagnostic procedure involves, firstly choosing a tree-structure according to what is suggested by the information already known. It continues by systematically following the branches from the root to the leaves of the chosen tree-structure. To each node is attached one or more sets of rules which, when applied, direct a search for signs and request complementary tests.

The rules attached to a node express the conditions necessary to recognise the pathological state that the node represents. They are given in formulae of first-order logic and interpreted in terms of truth values by matching with the patient's data.

For instance :

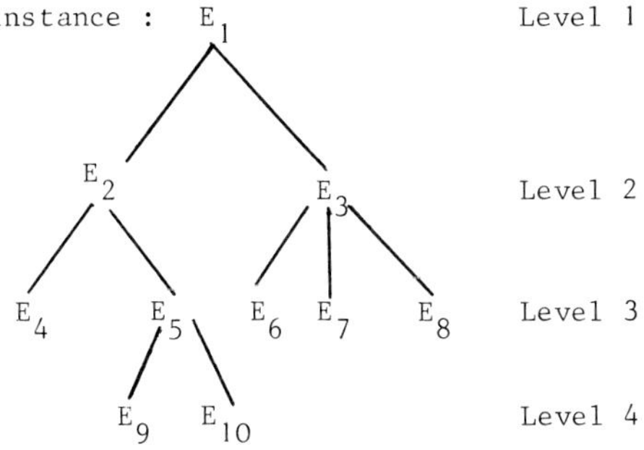

$E_1 \leftarrow \$_{1,1} \vee \$_{1,2} \cdots$

$E_i \leftarrow \$_{i,1} \vee \$_{i,2} \cdots$

$\$_{i,j}$: conjunction of signs associated to E_i

3.2.2. Suggestion power - Rejection power

For a better choice of the branching (that is the set of rules) likely to yield a solution to the problem of diagnosis, the system has heuristic features to evaluate the clinical context of the patient's data and to choose a direction in the diagnostic search. The patient's context is basically an imprecise concept not explicitly calculated. It is taken into account by fuzzy heuristics.

Fuzzy heuristic features are used to determine the range of diagnostic orientations, eventually to reduce the search space, and consequently, to request the tests or signs that a physician would ask for in such clinical cases. The latter is possible by means of the "suggestion power" of clinical signs, which are numerical values lying between 0 and 1.

Thus, depending on its attribute-values (location, irradiation, intensity, circumstances, type of pain), a pain will determine a suggestion power which is different for trees connected with diagnosis of myocardial infarction, benign gastroduodenal ulcer, acute pancreatitis, volvulus of stomach, etc...

In the same way, the absence of some signs can allow the temporary omission of certain diagnostic lines. This is called the "rejection power" of clinical signs and is also given values between 0 and 1. For instance, the absence of signs characterizing a state of shock is a strong element of rejection towards a diagnostic search of some clinical conditions of myocardial infarction or perforated ulcer.

The possible values of an attribute have a tree structure. The different branches reflect the realisations of the attribute, which are exclusive.

Example : The sign APPETITE has an attributed structured as follows :

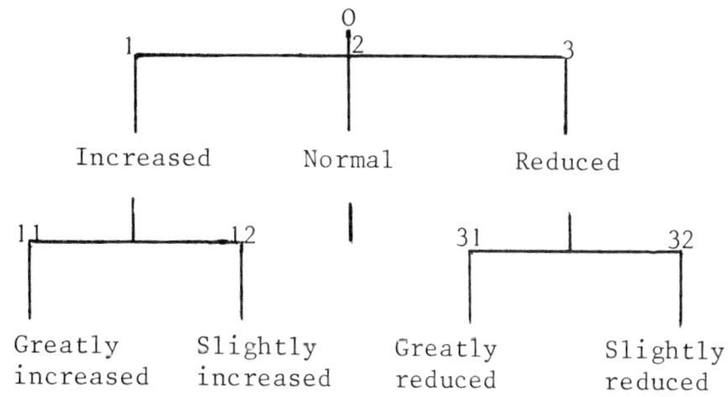

The setting of rejection and suggestion values of clinical signs is an application of extended Modus Ponens and extended Modus Tollens used in fuzzy logic [8]. These notions are somewhat different from the probabilistic notions of sensitivity and specificity.

For all signs, the deduction mechanism used is devided into 2 successive phases :

- Comparison of the sign presented by the patient with the sign noted in the medical knowledge : the result of the comparison is a number "t", between 0 and 1, which indicates that the patient's sign is more or less the same as that of the medical knowledge which leads to the diagnostic line D. Thus, for example, the sign APPETITE (great-reduced) has a suggestion power of 0.6 for the diagnostic line : deterioration of general condition. This constitutes the knowledge given a priori to the system. The problem is to know to what extent a patient presenting the sign APPETITE (reduced) suggests the diagnostic line considered above. This means that the "proximity" of greatly reduced and reduced must be evaluated. We have, therefore, established a similarity index based on the tree structure of the attributes. This index is calculated, in general terms, as follows :

$t = 1$ if the 2 values of the attribute are equal

$t = 1 - \frac{1}{(n+1)^2}$ if the values of the attribute are different

n represents the level in the tree structure of the attribute of the common predecess or these two values.

Example :

- For APPETITE (greatly reduced) and APPETITE (slightly reduced) we obtain :

$$n = 1 \qquad t = 1 - \frac{1}{(2)^2} = .75$$

- For APPETITE (reduced) and APPETITE (normal) we obtain :

$$n = 0 \qquad t = 1 - 1 = 0$$

If the sign is described by several attributes, they are taken into account with a weight fixed when the system is first put into operation.

This weight expresses the importance of each attribute in the evaluation of "t".

- Combination of "t" with the suggestion "e" and rejection "r" of sign for the diagnostic line D. This combination leads to 2 values α and β, defined as follows :

$$\alpha = \text{Max}[(t+e-1),0] \qquad \alpha > 0$$

$$\beta = \text{Min}[(t+1-r),1] \qquad \beta < 1$$

Taking these two results into account simultaneously leads, for all sign S and all diagnostic lines D, to an interval $[\alpha,\beta]$ where the range and values of α and β direct us more or less to the diagnosis D, when we know S.

Example :

Knowledge :
APPETITE (greatly reduced)
suggests (.6) deterioration of general condition
APPETITE (greatly reduced)
rejects (.1) deterioration of general condition

Patient's data :
APPETITE (reduced)

Calculation fo the interval $[\alpha,\beta]$:

$$\alpha = \text{Max}[(t+e-1),0] = \text{Max}[(.75+.6-1),1] = .35$$
$$\beta = \text{Min}[(t+1-r),1] = \text{Min}[(.75+1-.1),1] = 1$$

This means that the sign APPETITE (reduced) presented by the patient produces the interval [.35,1] in favour of the deterioration of the general condition syndrome. By its range, this segment reveals a fairly important indetermination althought elements favour this syndrome since the lower limit is raised to .35.

Limit 1 reflects the rejection power of the sign. That is to say, nothing permits us to affirm that there is not a deterioration of the general condition syndrome.

If several signs S_i direct us towards D, the intervals $[\alpha,\beta]_i$ obtained by applying the deduction rules, are grouped by the operators Max and Min to obtain the final interval [a,b] associated with D.

$$a = \underset{i}{\text{Max}}(\alpha_i) \qquad b = \underset{i}{\text{Min}}(\beta_i)$$

The choice of the diagnostic line is then reduced to the choice of an interval [a,b]. Indeed, an interval $[a_i,b_i]$ is associated to the most suggested, least rejected one. We have chosen the following criterion :

the interval corresponding to $\underset{i}{\text{Max}} \dfrac{a_i + b_i}{2}$

is chosen where several intervals have the same middle, and among these, we choose the one which has the highest lower limit.

Examples of the results of this heuristic feature are given below :

Example 1 :
The following data is given to the system :
- Male
- Age : 55
- Severe Epigastric pain extending toward the neck

Heuristic results :

Diagnoses lines		[: Suggestion power	] : Rejection power
angina	syndrome	.9	1.
ulcerous	syndrome	.9	1.
intoxication	syndrome	.23	1.
icteric	syndrome	.4	1.
acute abdominal	syndrome	.57	1.
abdominal pain	syndrome	.32	1.
deterioration of general condition		.4	1.
shock		.3	1.
externalised hoemorrhage		0.	1.
functional	syndrome	.3	1.
infectious	syndrome	0.	1.

Example 2 :
- Age : 11
- Severe epigastric pain
- No abdominal contraction
- No abdominal meteorism
- No anxiety
- Pulse rate : 76

Heuristic results :

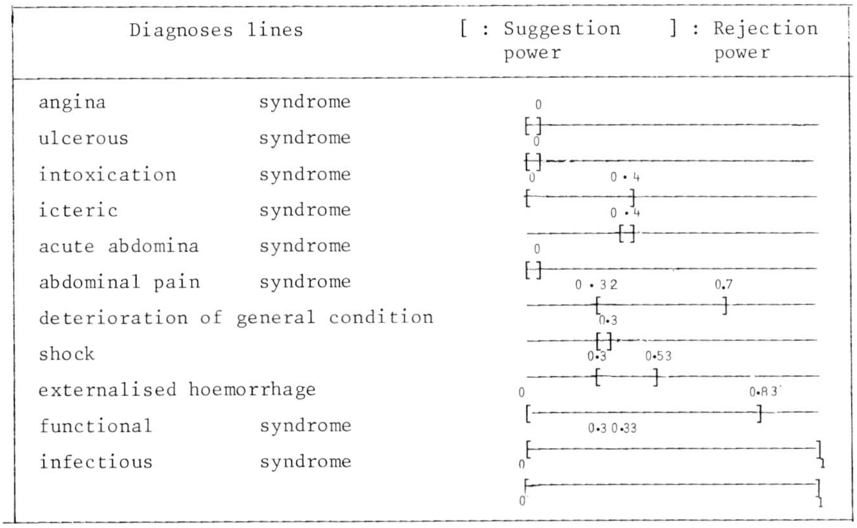

3.2.3. Other heuristic feature :
Examination costs - Successful branching rate

For the diagnoses search two further heuristic features are taken into account :
- costs of examinations ;
- successful branching rate.

These elements are examined by heuristics activated at the farther levels of the branches.
To each examination stored in the SPHINX system corresponds a cost, which is a given value on a scale of 0 to 100 to the financial cost, the pretium doloris and the period of time necessary to obtain the results.

Whenever a success is reached through a node, this success is taken into account. So that the system maintains an heuristic feature based on the frequency of diagnoses. These elements produce a heuristic method dealing with the more frequently identified states and with the costs of complementary examinations necessary for this identification (diagnosis).

3.3. Control structure

The control is explicitly performed according to the system condition. In the initial step, the heuristic application of suggestion power and rejection power is systematically activated to "evaluate" the context.

During the other step, the control structures activate a cost success heuristic an use a depth-first or breadth-first strategy according to the context. For example, to assert the etiology of pericarditis, the control selects a cost-success heuristic, while in case of emergency, the patient's situation will be processed by a breadth-first search. Our system does not mention any hypothesis on diagnoses and does not impose that diagnoses are exclusive. The diagnostic search is carried out within the orientations determined by suggestion power and rejection power higher or equal to a given arbitrary threshold.

4. DISCUSSION AND RESULTS

Having described our "present-illness" system, we now turn to other artificial intelligence programs that deal with medical diagnosis.

The MYCIN system is a rule-based system which tracks along antecedent-consequent links to establish diagnoses and recommand therapies. It deals with problems in a narrow domain and thus has little difficulty in limiting its search space. The nature of the problems tackled by MYCIN allows it to express knowledge in a non-structured way. Our approach is necessarily different because of the nature of the diagnostic problems we deal with. It is thus similar to that of context formation of PAUKER and SZOLOVITS [11]. In the same way as we have defined the suggestion power of a sign these authors define the concept of triggering. The INTERNIST system uses a similar technic, the evoking strength, to direct its diagnostic search in a tree-structured knowledge. Those systems are most like our own in that they are always data-driven. However, the rejection power that we have define introduces a further heuristic knowledge through the possibilities it offers of eliminating some hypotheses. Two "reasonings" are carried out simultaneously - one by suggestion powers, the other by rejection powers - the decision being the synthesis of their results.

This paper reports the results obtained through the processing of an evaluation made with a SPHINX prototype [3].

The evaluation of such a system can be based on various scales of interest and utility : the reliability of the advice expressed by the system, its teaching function and its use by the physicians. It is too soon to assess the teaching that it was one of our purposes in the conception and organization of SPHINX. Moreover, it is difficult to discuss this aspect since the system has not yet been validated and it is not yet available for students.

On the contrary, all the discussion we had with experts in our attempt to give a definition of medical knowledge, showed that they were interested in this research and that they have certainly modified their attitude as regard to the problem of diagnosis. (It is possible to evaluate the reliability of the system before the achievement of the program and this is the first step in our study).

We have made a preliminary study in order to measure the performance of the system namely, the degree of accuracy of the diagnostic classification proposed by the system.

The description and taking into account of the patient's signs being quite different from those used by other systems, it was hardly possible to use already published case reports.

This preliminary study was effected with the use of medical reports on patients in the Departments of Cardiology and Gastroenterology at the Hospital of St Joseph in Marseilles. For each of them the diagnosis was controlled and confirmed by surgery, biopsy or specific paraclinical examination. The results obtained for 50 cases taken at random from the confirmed cases, are resumed in Fig. 2.

Diagnosis of SPHINX / True Diagnosis	1	2	3	4	5	6	7	8	9	10	11	12	13	14	15	?
1 : cancer of lever	3															1
2 : cholecystitis		2														
3 : cancer of biliary tracts			1													1
4 : biliary lithiasis				5												
5 : chronic pancreatitis					2											1
6 : cancer of stomach						6										
7 : cancer of oesophagus							1									
8 : hiatal hernia								1								
9 : gastro duodenal ulcer									7							
10 : perforedulcer										3						
11 : occlusion											2					
12 : infectious hepatitis												1				
13 : angor													3			
14 : myocardial infarction														6		
15 : very complex diagnoses															1	2

Fig. 2 - Results of 50 cases

This table shows 14 out of the 28 diagnoses known by the SPHINX system up to now. Number 15 represents the particulary complex cases concerning a large intricacy of possible diagnoses. These cases presented an accident of pulmonary embolism associated with cholecystitis, a case of chronic pancratitis associated with cholecystitis, and a case of liver cyrrhosis associated with a cancer of liver. Only the last case was correctly diagnosed by SHPINX, the two others were classified in the "?" column, indicating the absence of diagnosis.

At present, SPHINX allows a diagnosis in 80 to 85 per cent of the cases. It must be noted that this evaluation was carried out with in-patient only, that is, in an often complex context both from the point of view of difficulty of diagnosis and of the intricacy of the pathologies which imposed hospital treatment. Taking into account out-patients' records would undoubtedly improve the result. The addition of supplementary knowledge rules - being effected at present - will further increase the possibilities.

AKNOWLEDGMENTS

We are grateful to Prof. J.L. San Marco and Dr G. Botti, Dr D. Moncharmont for their helpful comments.

REFERENCES

[1] Fieschi M, Joubert M., Application d'une méthode logique à l'aide à la décision en médecine. La méthode de Davis et Putnam en logique propositionnelle, IIème Congrès AFCET-IRIA, Reconnaissance des formes et Intelligence Artificielle, Toulouse - France - (Sept 1979).

[2] Fieschi M, Joubert M., Roux M., Sur un modèle de représentation de la connaissance médicale en logique symbolique en vue de l'aide à la décision en médecine, Journées d'Informatique Médicale de Toulouse - France - (Mai 1980).

[3] Fieschi M., Aide à la décision en médecine : le système SPHINX, Application au diagnostic d'une douleur épigastrique, Thèse de Médecine, Laboratoire d'Informatique, Faculté de Médecine de Marseille (Sept 1981).

[4] Fox J., Barber D., Bardhan K.D., Alternative to Bayes ? A quantitative comparison with rule-based diagnostic inference, Meth. Inform. Med., 19 (1980), pp 210-215.

[5] Joubert M., Etude et réalisation d'un programme de dialogue homme-machine d'aide à la décision en médecine, Thèse de Doctorat d'Etat en Biologie Humaine, Laboratoire d'Informatique, Faculté de Médecine de Marseille, (Novembre 1981).

[6] Pople H.E. Jr., Myers J.D., Miller R.A. DIALOG : a model of diagnostic logic for internal medicine, Proc. 4th IJCAI, Tbilissi - USSR -, pp 848-855, (1975).

[7] Shortliffe E.H., Computer based medical consultation MYCIN, Amercian Elservier, New York, (1976).

[8] Soula G., Aide à la décision en logique floue. Application en médecine. Thèse de Doctorat d'Etat en Biologie Humaine, Laboratoire d'Informatique, Faculté de Médecine de Marseille, (1981).

[9] Waterman D.A., Hayes-Roth F., Pattern directed inference systems, Academic Press, New York, (1978).

[10] Weiss S. Kulikowski C.A., Safir A., Glaucoma consultation by computer, Comput. Biol. Med. 8 pp 25-40 (1978).

[11] Pauker S.G., Szolovits P., Analyzing and simulating. Taking the history of the present illness : Context formation, Comput. Linguistics in Medecine, Schneider, Sagvall-Hein eds, North-Holland (1977).

[12] Warner H.R., Olmsted C.M., Rutherford B.D., HELP. A program for medical decision-making, Comput. Biomed. Res. 5, 65-74 (1972).

Approximate Reasoning in Decision Analysis
M.M. Gupta and E. Sanchez (eds.)

THE USE OF FUZZY SET THEORY IN ELECTROCARDIOLOGICAL DIAGNOSTICS

Etienne E. KERRE

Seminar for Mathematical Analysis
State University of Gent
Gent, Belgium.

It is well-known that during the last decenniads the quantitative techniques in electrocardiological diagnostics have reached a very high level of accuracy. The physicians obtain a large number of accurate measurements of the physiological parameters important for the knowledge of the cardiovascular system.
However, in spite of this progress, Kalmanson ([2]) observed that the present day cardiovascular research leads to a deadlock as far as the practical applications are concerned; he was the first to indicate fuzzy set theory as a possible way out.
In practice the physician translates the quantitative results obtained into qualitative linguistic terms. However recent investigations ([10]) have shown that there exists a wide variation in the interpretation of terms such as : expected, probable, sometimes ... in order to indicate the probability that some disease is present. In order to eliminate misinterpretations of such linguistic terms one needs a theory that permits some tolerances.
There is a second reason for consideration and investigation of the applicability of fuzzy set theory, notably the problem of determining limits in order to specify obtained results as normal or not. However R. Zenner ([1]) remarked that for left ventricular hypertrophy for example, the distributions obtained for a normal ECG or VCG are dependent on several parameters such as : age, sexe, weight, height, chest configuration ... . We believe that this distinction can be eliminated by considering the normal specimen as a fuzzy set.
A first important attempt to introduce fuzzy sets in automatic electrocardiography is made by Bressan and others ([4]). These authors use the fuzzy set formalism which is originated by Jain ([5]) in order to create a decision-making-model in the presence of fuzzy variables. The exploration of this model needs an extension principle. Dubois and Prade ([7]) pointed out that Jain's method leads to inexact results. In this paper we want firstly to give the necessary framework of fuzzy set theory and secondly to improve the results of Bressan and others using the well-known extension principle of Gaines.

Keywords : automatic ECG classification, fuzzy linguistics, fuzzy utilities, fuzzy real algebra, extension principle.

1. INTRODUCTION

It is an undeniable fact that nowadays cardiological diseases take a very great part in the mortality causes in our industrial countries. This fact justifies the importance of all efforts to establish cardiological diseases and of course to cure them. The most important means to do this consists in deriving an electro-(ECG) or a vectocardiogram (VCG). An ECG measures in several ways the electrical activity of the myocard. Every contraction of the myocard follows up an electrical activity in the cells of the myocard. One assumes that the electrical activity of the myocard is the resultant of the activity of the different cells composing the myocard. A cell in a position of rest possesses a polarized state. The potential on the surface of the cell is about 100 mV larger then this in the bulk of the cell. Due to some internal and external stimuli some depolarization occurs : the potential of the bulk of the cell is about 25 mV higher then this of the cell surface. By a repolarization the equilibrium state of rest is built up again. This electrical activity takes place in a well-defined order in different cells of the myocard. The first stimulus arose in the Keith-Flack node which lies in the upper part of the right atrium. The graphical reflection of this depolarization is registered as the P-wave.
He is most clearly perceptible in the DII and V_2 derivation. The stimulus propagates with a very low velocity in the atrio-ventricular node : no electrical activity is registered, the A-V node canalizes the stimulus in a ventricular conducting system : the bundle of His, interventricular septum and the network of Purkinje. The depolarization of this part of the myocard is registered as the important QRS-complex. The repolarization of the myocard takes longer time and is known as the T-wave.
The functional disturbances and the anatomical damages of the different conduction parts of the myocard are for a great part responsable for occurring heart diseases.

A normal ECG considers 12 derivations. First of all we have 3 bipolar standard derivations due to Einthoven : they measure the potential difference between left arm and right arm (derivation I), between left leg and right arm (derivation II) and between left leg and left arm (derivation III). Secondly one has the unipolar derivations introduced by Goldberger denoted by aV_R, aV_L and aV_F : they measure the potential difference between left arm, right arm, left leg and a zero electrode. Thirdly one considers six unipolar precordial derivations introduced by Wilson denoted by $V_1, V_2, \ldots$ $\ldots, V_6$.
By means of a VCG one obtains a spatial picture of the electrical activity of the heart. However the clinical information obtained from a VCG is equivalent to that derived from a ECG.
From the ECG graphs one can derive the standard parameters which characterize the cardiological state : P amplitude, P duration, Q amplitude, QRS duration, intrinsic deflection (i.e. the distance between the beginning of the QRS complex and the R top), S-T segment, T duration ....
As the number of registered ECG's increases somewhat exponentially (for the moment about 100 miljon ECG's a year in the USA alone), the need for automatic computer-analysis became inevitable. In the following paragraph we summarize the existing computer programs and their limitations.

2. AUTOMATIC ECG INTERPRETATION

The simplest method for automatic ECG interpretation, the so-called decision-tree method, consists of comparing a set of relevant parameter values against a set of thresholds. This model considers the state of the system exactly known as well as the different pathologies. Another approach of automatic ECG classification is more probabilistic. It considers statistically defined classes and computes the probability of occurrence of a given pathology. The process is modelled through a frequency based interpretation of probability from a training data base. However good validation data basis are rarely available. The cardiologist R. Zenner proves the abscence of good validation basis ([1]). In order to set up "normal" values with respect to the diagnosis of left ventricular hypertrophy, he analyzed a population selected from nurse students, medical students and well-trained athletes. The distributions obtained for the relevant parameters - the voltage of the QRS spatial maximal vector and the ratio Q/R_Z-show remarkable deviations from the widely used Pipberger values which were obtained on a much older population about 50% of the black race. Zenner asked for the ideal data base describing the normal ECG and VCG : "Should we go on characterizing merely "men" (white and black, obese or not, etc) and when using their limits for diagnosing, only "be aware of" or "take into account" the fact that often those limits are influenced by several constitutional variables, the number of which can be arbitrarily chosen as e.g. six, i.e. age, race, weight, height, deviation from ideal weight according to height , chest configuration. Or should we rather establish a book with e.g. 2x2x5x5x5x5 pages where page one would give the limits for a man, white, 20-29y, 50-60 kg, 170-180 cm, chest configuration 70-80 cm, and at each page change a class indicating race (W,B), sex (M,F), age (20-29,30-39, ...) and so on with five possible classes for the last four variables.
Another pessimistic comment on the existing computer programs for automatic ECG diagnostics can be found in Kalmanson ([2]). He too claims that the very sophisticated but merely quantitative approach of the cardiovascular problems leads to a deadlock as far as everyday applications are considered. He was the first to point out the theory of fuzzy sets as a possible way out. In his paper he gives a possible linguistic description of the diastolic return in order to detect aortic insuffiences.

3. THE USE OF FUZZY SET THEORY IN ECG INTERPRETATION

The first remarkable attempt to use the fuzzy set formalism in order to interpret ECG's was carried out by Degani, Pacini e.a. ([3], [4]). Their method relies on papers of R. Jain ([5],[6]), concerning decision-making in the presence of fuzzy variables. However this method used a special type of extension principle. Dubois and Prade ([7]) commented that this extension principle mostly leads to wrong results. They propose to replace Jain's extension principle by the more realistic and widely applied Gaines' extension principle. In this paragraph we will describe the role of fuzzy set theory in order to give a more qualitative interpretation of the state reflected by the ECG waves.
In automatic ECG interpretation on has the following goals :

i. to describe the state of the cardiovascular system in linguistic terms;
ii. to assign utilities which connect the possible states with the alternative pathologies;
iii. to connect the state obtained with the utilities in order to rank the possible alternatives.

We examine these goals separately.

3.1. Description of the cardiovascular state using linguistic fuzzy terms

From the ECG graphs one can detect all relevant

parameters to classify the state of the system. We split up this information into simple and composite measurements. The simple measurements are those which can directly be measured on the signal : QRS duration, Q amplitude, T duration ... . Composite measurements are those which are deduced from two or more simple ones by application of a finite number of algebraic operations e.g. the ratio Q amplitude versus R amplitude. The determination of the simple measurements runs as follows. On a given signal one obtains several results for a same parameter e.g. Q duration measured on the same aV_F derivation may give : 82 ms, 85 ms, 83 ms ... . Which number representing the Q duration will be taken? Classically one takes the arithmetic mean of these values. However in order to take into account all these results, Degani and Pacini propose to consider the parameter e.g. Q duration as a fuzzy set in the universe of the measurements obtained. So they put

$$\text{Q duration} = \{(Q_1,\mu_1),(Q_2,\mu_2),\dots,(Q_p,\mu_p)\} \text{ with}$$

$$\mu_1 = [1+h(Q_1-\frac{Q_1+Q_2+\dots+Q_p}{p})^2]^{-1},$$

h being a constant dependent on the number of measurements and their dispersion about the mean value. The grade of membership of a value Q_1=80 msec is indicated by μ_1 e.g. equal to 0.8. To determine the fuzzy set representing a composite parameter one proceeds as follows. Let the simple measurements Q amplitude and R amplitude be given by the fuzzy sets :

$$\text{Q amplitude} = \{(Q_1,\mu_1),(Q_2,\mu_2),\dots,(Q_p,\mu_p)\}$$

$$\text{R amplitude} = (R_1,\nu_1),(R_2,\nu_2),\dots,(R_q,\nu_q)\}.$$

The fuzzy set Q amplitude versus R amplitude is defined as :

$$\text{Q ampl/R ampl}=\{(\frac{Q_1}{R_1},\min(\mu_1,\nu_1)),(\frac{Q_1}{R_2},\min(\mu_1,\nu_2)), \dots, (\frac{Q_p}{R_q},\min(\mu_p,\nu_q))\}.$$

The cardinality of this set is pq. In order to diminish this large number of elements there exist several reduction methods with conservation of the representativity ([6]). About the occurence of the same element $\frac{Q_i}{R_j}$ with different grades of membership e.g. μ and ν, Degani a.o. follow Jain and propose as final membership grade the probabilistic sum of μ and ν i.e. $\mu+\nu-\mu\nu$. We believe (see [7]) that $\max(\mu,\nu)$ will be a better representation for the final grade of membership. Further reduction of the cardinality may be performed by partitioning the set Q ampl./R ampl. into several disjoint subsets and replacing these by an element having the highest grade of membership (for details see [3]).

The complete state of the system is composed from the simple and composite measurements $M_1,\dots,M_k$, each of them being described as a fuzzy set in suitable universes $U_1,\dots,U_k$. The state M itself can be considered as a fuzzy set in the universe $U_1 x \dots x U_k$ (x denotes classical cartesian multiplication); the grade of membership of an arbitrary set $(m_1,\dots,m_k)$ of parameter values in M is defined by : $M(m_1,\dots,m_k)=\min(M_1(m_1),\dots,M_k(m_k))$ where M_i (m_i) denotes the grade of membership of the element m_i in the fuzzy set M_i.

The following step in the process consists in giving a linguistic description of the fuzzy state of the system. In everyday dialogue between clinicians one uses specific linguistic terms such as : high, large, medium, possible ... in order to characterize relevant parameters such as QRS duration, Q amplitude ... . With respect to this fact we have to mention the results of a recent examination concerning the meaning of such terms in the mind of theirs users and which appeared in the New England Journal of Medicine ([10]). This study reveals a very great variation in the meaning of such linguistic terms. However in spite of this lack of sharp boundaries no serious communication troubles happen. These results form a new argument to introduce fuzzy sets in order to treat the fuzziness inherent to this linguistic communication.

Linguistic variables may be considered as fuzzy sets in the universe of the corresponding measuring values. So we get for the item low (denoted L) with respect to the QRS duration the following membership grades :

L(80)=0.3, L(82)=0.4, L(83)=0.7, L(90)=1.

In order to understand the way to obtain a linguistic description of the full state, we give the following example from Degani and Pacini. Let the state of the system being described by two parameters M_1=QRS duration and M_2=Q amplitude, which are represented by the fuzzy sets :

$$M_1=\{(80,0.7),(82,0.9),(83,0.8)\}$$

$$M_2=\{(300,0.4),(270,0.7),(280,0.8)\}.$$

The linguistic termsets are given by :

$$T(M_1)=\{L,Me\}$$

$$T(M_2)=\{h,l\}$$

with L=large, Me=medium, h=high, l=low.

Let us suppose the following grades of membership for the occuring measurements in the fuzzy sets L, Me, h and l :

L(80)=0.3	L(82)=0.4	L(83)=0.7
Me(80)=0.9	Me(82)=0.8	Me(83)=0.6
h(300)=0.9	h(270)=0.6	h(280)=0.8
l(300)=0.1	l(270)=0.2	l(280)=0.15.

The grade of membership of the composite measurement (80,300) in the fuzzy set $M=(M_1,M_2)$ is defined as $\min(M_1(80),M_2(300))$. So we obtain the fuzzy set M

M={((80,300),0.4),((80,270),0.7),((80,280),0.7),
((82,300),0.4),((82,270),0.7),((82,280),0.8),
((83,300),0.4),((83,270),0.7),((83,280),0.8)}.

With the termsets of M_1 and M_2 corresponds a termset for M, using the cartesian multiplication :

$T(M)=\{X_1,X_2,X_3,X_4\}$

with X_1=(L,h), X_2=(L,l), X_3=(Me,h), X_4=(Me,l).

The membership of a measurement (80,270) in the fuzzy set (L,h) is given by min(L(80),h(270)).

So we obtain for the linguistic terms describing M :

$X_1=\{((80,300),0.3),((80,270),0.3),((80,280),0.3),$
$((82,300),0.4),((82,270),0.4),((82,280),0.4),$
$((83,300),0.7),((83,270),0.6),((83,280),0.7)\}$

$X_2=\{((80,300),0.1),((80,270),0.2),((80,280),0.15),$
$((82,300),0.1),((82,270),0.2),((82,280),0.15),$
$((83,300),0.1),((83,270),0.2),((83,280),0.15)\}$

$X_3=\{((80,300),0.9),((80,270),0.6),((80,280),0.8)$
$((82,300),0.8),((82,270),0.6),((82,280),0.8)$
$((83,300),0.6),((83,270),0.6),((83,280),0.6)\}$

$X_4=\{((80,300),0.1),((80,270),0.2),((80,280),0.15)$
$((82,300),0.1),((82,270),0.2),((82,280),0.15)$
$((83,300),0.1),((83,270),0.2),((83,280),0.15)\}$.

Since the state of the system is not exactly given by e.g. (QRS duration is 80 ms, Q amplitude is 0.3 mV) but these numbers have only a grade of membership equal to 0.4, we have adjust the grade of membership of the measurement (80,300) in e.g. the fuzzy set (QRS duration large, Q amplitude high). We achieve this by taking the minimum of the two grades of membership i.e. by taking the intersection $X_1 \cap M$. We obtain :

$X_1\cap M=\{((80,300),0.3),((80,270),0.3),((80,280),0.3),$
$((82,300),0.4),((82,270),0.4),((82,280),0.4),$
$((83,300),0.4),((83,270),0.6),((83,280),0.7)\}$

and similar results for $X_2\cap M$, $X_3\cap M$ and $X_4\cap M$.
Now it's quite easy to obtain a linguistic description of the state. One defines the membership of a couple (QRS duration large, Q amplitude high) as the maximum of the membership grades appearing in $X_1\cap M$. This grade of membership may be interpreted as a truth-value for the proposition. "QRS duration is large and Q amplitude is high" with respect to the state under consideration. The given example leads easily to the following linguistic description of the state :

$M=\{((L,h),0.7),((L,l),0.2)),(Me,h),0.8),((Me,l),0.2)\}$.

3.2 Description of the fuzzy utilities of the relevant pathologies with respect to a fuzzy linguistic state.

Suppose the state of the system has been obtained in linguistic terms as indicated in the preceding paragraph :

$$M=\{(X_1,\xi_1),(X_2,\xi_2),\ldots,(X_n,\zeta_n)\}.$$

X_i being a linguistic term, ξ_i its grade of membership in the fuzzy state M.
On the other hand there is a set of possible alternatives $A=\{a_1,\ldots,a_m\}$, e.g. A={consistent with LVH, consider LVH, normal with respect to LVH,...} or equivalently A={LVH yes, LVH probable, LVH no,...}.
These two sets M and A are connected using utilities U_{ij} i.e. the utility or the gain of choosing alternative a_i given the state X_j. These utilities are normally specified in linguistic terms such as high, low, very high ... ; these utilities may be of the form :

very low ≡ the option (e.g. LVH no) is out of question
low ≡ the option is unsuitable
medium ≡ the option is possible
high ≡ the option is rather reliable
very high ≡ the option is sure.

In the framework of fuzzy set theory these terms may be described as fuzzy sets in a discrete universe {0,1,...,10}, i.e.

$$U_{ij}=\{(0,\zeta_0^{ij}),(1,\zeta_1^{ij}),\ldots,(10,\zeta_{10}^{ij})\}$$

with for example :

low = {(1,1),(2,1),(3,0.5),(4,0.2)}.

However, since the state of the system is not exactly given by X_j but only for some percentage indicated by ξ_j, we have to settle this in the utilities. The global utility of a choice a_i given the fuzzy state M is given by :

$$U_i=\{(U_{i1},\xi_1),(U_{i2},\xi_2),\ldots,(U_{in},\xi_n)\}.$$

So the elements of the universe of U_i are fuzzy sets too. An element of the universe {0,1,...,10} e.g. 1 has a grade of membership ζ_1^{ij} in the utility U_{ij} and this U_{ij} in turn has a grade of membership ξ_j in U_i; the composition using the minimum operator of these two grades of membership leads to a grade of membership of 1 in U_i for every $j\in\{1,\ldots,n\}$. So we obtain :

$$(1,\min(\zeta_1^{i1},\xi_1)),(1,\min(\zeta_1^{i2},\xi_2)),\ldots,(1,\min(\zeta_1^{in},\xi_n)).$$

As final grade of membership of the element 1 in the utility U_i of the alternative a_i given the state M, Degani and Pacini follow Jain again and take the probabilistic sum of the different grades of membership. As already claimed we prefer the maximum of the different grades of membership as the final value, since a fuzzy model does not take into account the number of occurrences of an event but just the fact this occurrence may happen; this informal postulate is exactly expressed by Gaines fuzzification principle ([11]). In this way we obtain the fuzzy utilities U_i as fuzzy sets in the universe {0,1,...,10}, determining the gain of choosing the pathology a_i in case the state of the system is described by M.

3.3 The problem of ranking the alternatives

The ranking of the alternatives or equivalently the determination of the final diagnosis is not easy to perform since there exists no total order between fuzzy quantities.
In order to determine the optimal alternative, given a linguistic description of a cardiovascular state, Degani and Pacini used the method outlined by Jain ([5]). This method relies on the concept of the maximizing set of a (fuzzy) set, as introduced by L. Zadeh ([12]). The maximizing fuzzy set of the set {0,1,2,....,10} e.g. is given by

$M=\{(0,0),(1,\frac{1}{10}),(2,\frac{2}{10}),\ldots,(10,1)\}$; the grade of membership of the element 2 for example measures is some way the degree to which 2 approximates the maximum 10 of the given set. Further, they consider the intersections $U_{iM} = U_i \cap M$: these can be interpreted as representative for the grades of membership of each utility resulting when alternative a_i is selected. Then the grade of membership of alternative a_i in the fuzzy set A_{opt}, representing the fuzzy optimal alternative, is obtained as the maximum of the grades of membership occurring in $U_i \cap M$. So one obtains the fuzzy set :

$$A_{opt}=\{(a_1,\alpha_1),(a_2,\alpha_2)\dots,(a_m,\alpha_m)\},$$

it gives an idea about the relative utility of each alternative. Finally this alternative is selected whose grade of membership in A_{opt} is equal to $\max\{\alpha_1,\alpha_2,\dots,\alpha_m\}$.
Dubois and Prade gave some relevant comments on the above method ([7]).
Firstly, they noted that the maximizing set of a set is highly influenced by the distance function which is used and accordingly the final ranking will be changed. Moreover, in considering only the highest grade of membership in U_{iM} for the ranking, the fuzziness of the utilities vanishes and with it, a possible intrinsic undecidability of the problem. In order to set up a more realistic method they go back to the crisp decision case : the best alternative is this which has maximal gain i.e. a classification is made using the maximum operation. Due to Gaines extension principle it is possible to fuzzify every arithmetical operation. So, let A and B be two fuzzy numbers, i.e. fuzzy sets on the real line R : the fuzzy maximum of A and B, denoted $\widetilde{\max}(A,B)$, is defined as the fuzzy number :

$$\widetilde{\max}(A,B): R\to[0,1]$$
$$z \mapsto \max\{u \mid u=A(x) \text{ or } u=B(y) \text{ and } \max(x,y)=z\},\ \forall z\in R.$$

In ([13]) Dubois and Prade have shown that this definition of fuzzy maximum can easily be handled for calculation without any sampling of the membership functions.
Moreover this operation possesses several interesting algebraic properties such as the associativity, the commutativity and the absorption laws. In the next paragraph we used this fuzzy algebra in order to treat the numerical example given by Degani and Pacini.

3.4. Example

Suppose the state of the system is given as in 3.1.

$M=\{((L,h),0.7),((L,l),0.2),(Me,h),0.8),((Me,l),0.2)\}$.

Let the set of possible alternatives be given by

$$A=\{a_1,a_2,a_3\}.$$

The linguistic variables U_1,U_2,U_3, representing the sets of the given linguistic utilities are given by :

$$U_1=\{U_{11},U_{12},U_{13},U_{14}\}$$
$$U_2=\{U_{21},U_{22},U_{23},U_{24}\}$$
$$U_3=\{U_{31},U_{32},U_{33},U_{34}\}$$

with

$U_{13}=U_{14}=U_{21}=U_{33}=\text{low}=\{(1,1),(2,1)(3,0.5)\}$

$U_{22}=\text{very low}=(\text{low})^2=\{(1,1),(2,1)(3,0.25)\}$

$U_{32}=U_{34}=\text{medium}=\{(3,0.4),(4,0.7),(5,1),(6,0.7),(7,0.4)\}$

$U_{12}=U_{23}=U_{31}=\text{high}=\{(7,0.5),(8,1),(9,1),(10,1)\}$

$U_{11}=U_{24}=\text{very high}=\{(7,0.25),(8.1),(9,1),(10.1)\}$.

The fuzzy set U_{ij} represents the gain of choosing alternative a_i in case the state of the system is given by X_j. However since the state is not exactly given by one of the X_j's we have to fit the utilities as outlined in the foregoing paragraph. So we obtain :

$U_1=\{(U_{11},0.7),(U_{12},0.2),(U_{13},0.8),(U_{14},0.2)\}$

$U_2=\{(U_{21},0.7),(U_{22},0.2),(U_{23},0.8),(U_{24},0.2)\}$

$U_3=\{(U_{31},0.7),(U_{32},0.2),(U_{33},0.8),(U_{34},0.2)\}$.

Using the minimum operator we may express U_1,U_2 and U_3 as fuzzy sets in the universe $\{0,1,\dots,10\}$. In order to obtain the grade of membership of 1 e.g. in U_1, one proceeds as follows :

i. consider the grade of membership of U_{11} in U_1 i.e. 0.7;
ii. consider the grade of membership of 1 in U_{11}, i.e. 0;
iii. take the minimum of the numbers obtained in i. and ii., i.e. 0;
iv. repeat this process for U_{12} in U_1 and 1 in U_{12} (obtaining 0), for U_{13} in U_1 and 1 in U_{13} (obtaining 0.8), for U_{14} in U_1 and 1 in U_{14} (obtaining 0.2);
v. consider these four grades of membership of 1; the maximum of these grades is taken as the final grade of membership of 1 in U_1 i.e. 0.8;
vi. repeat the above process for all other elements of the universe $\{0,1,\dots,10\}$.

Carrying out this algorithm one obtains U_1, U_2 and U_3 as fuzzy sets in $\{0,1,\dots,10\}$:

$U_1=\{(1,0.8),(2,0.8),(3,0.5),(7,0.25),(8,0.7),(9,0.7),(10,0.7)\}$

$U_2=\{(1,0.7),(2,0.7),(3,0.5),(7,0.5),(8,0.8),(9,0.8),(10,0.8)\}$

$U_3=\{(1,0.8),(2,0.8),(3,0.5),(4,0.2),(5,0.2),(6,0.2),(7,0.5),(8,0.7),(9,0.7),(10,0.7)\}$.

To obtain the optimal alternative i.e. the

alternative with maximal gain, we calculate the fuzzy maximum of the utilities, U_1,U_2,U_3 : $\underset{\sim}{max}(\underset{\sim}{max}(U_1,U_2),U_3)$ or, due to the associativity of the $\underset{\sim}{max}$ operator $\underset{\sim}{max}(U_1,\underset{\sim}{max}(U_2,U_3))$. From the definition we know that $\underset{\sim}{max}(U_1,U_2)$ is a fuzzy set in the same universe of U_1 and U_2, i.e. $\{0,1,\ldots,10\}$. The grade of membership of an element 1 e.g. is defined by :

$$\underset{\sim}{max}(U_1,U_2)(1)=\max_{\substack{max(x,y)=1\\ x\in\{0,1,\ldots,10\}\\ y\in\{0,1,\ldots,10\}}} \min(U_1(x),U_2(y)),$$

There are three choices for (x,y) such that max(x,y)=1 namely (1,0),(0,1) and (1,1). We easily obtain :

$$\underset{\sim}{max}(U_1,U_2)(1)=0.7.$$

A similar calculation gives the other grades of membership. Finally this leads to

$$\underset{\sim}{max}(U_1,U_2)=\{(1,0.7),(2,0.7),(3,0.5),(4,0.2),(7,0.5),(8,0.7),(9,0.8),(10,0.7)\}.$$

In the same way one obtains the fuzzy set

$\underset{\sim}{max}(\underset{\sim}{max}(U_1,U_2),U_3)$ or , by definition,

$$\underset{\sim}{max}(U_1,U_2,U_3)=\{(1,0.7),(2,0.7)(3,0.5),(4,0.2),(5,0.2),(6,0.2),(7,0.5),(8,0.7),(9,0.8),(10,0.7)\}.$$

Note that in contrast with the crisp case, the fuzzy maximum of U_1,U_2 and U_3 is not equal to one of the U_i's.
A possible way to determine the optimal alternative consists in selecting this alternative for which the corresponding fuzzy utility has minimal Hamming distance from the maximum of all utilities. These distances are easily obtained as :

$$d_H(U_1,\underset{\sim}{max}(U_1,U_2,U_3))=1.15$$

$$d_H(U_2,\underset{\sim}{max}(U_1,U_2,U_3))=0.9$$

$$d_H(U_3,\underset{\sim}{max}(U_1,U_2,U_3))=0.3.$$

As final conclusion for the example we can state that alternative a_3 has maximal utility, which reveals some deviation from the result of Degani and Pacini for the same example.

CONCLUSION.

In this paper we have revised the first serious attempt of Degani and Pacini in order to use the framework of fuzzy set theory with respect to electrocardiological diagnostics. The basic idea of this revolutionary approach consists in following the current interpretation method used by the physicians, namely the use of linguistic terms, in order to describe the state and the utilities of the alternative pathologies. The problem of the final ranking of the alternatives has been solved using the fuzzy maximum operation constructed in accordance with Gaines' extension principle. Using this ranking method we obtained results which deviate from the original ones of Degani and Pacini. Finally we note that nowadays serious attempts are taken to construct membership functions for linguistic values of variables and hedges; in this way the problem of the subjective choice of such membership functions will be soon eliminated ([14]).

REFERENCES :

[1] Zenner, R., Which electrocardiological limits should we use? Private communication (1980).
[2] Kalmanson, D., Recherche cardiovasculaire et théorie des ensembles flous, La Nouvelle Press médicale 41 (1973) 2757-2760.
[3] Degani, R. and Pacini, G., Linguistic pattern recognition algorithms for computer analysis of ECG, Proceedings Biosigma 1 (1978) 18-26.
[4] Bressan, M., Volta, S.D., Degani, R. and Pacini, G., Fuzzy diagnostics in automatic electrocardiography, Proceedings electrocardiological congress (Glasgow, 1978) 242-249.
[5] Jain, R., Decisionmaking in the presence of fuzzy variables, IEEE Transactions, Systems, Man and Cybernetics 6 (1976) 698-702.
[6] Jain, R.,Outline of an approach for the analysis of fuzzy systems, Int.J. Control 23 (1976) 627-640.
[7] Dubois, D. and Prade, H., Comment on "Tolerance analysis using fuzzy sets" and "A procedure for multiple aspect decision-making", Int.J. Systems Sci. 9 (1978) 357-360.
[8] Jain, R., A procedure for multiple aspect decisionmaking using fuzzy sets, Int. J. Systems Sci. 8 (1977) 1-7.
[9] Jain, R., Tolerance analysis using fuzzy sets , Int.J. Systems Sci. 7 (1976) 1393-1401.
[10] Bryant, G.D. and Norman, G.R., Expressions of probability : words and numbers, The New England Journal of Medecine 302 (1980) 411.
[11] Gaines, B.R., Foundations of fuzzy reasoning, Int. J. Man-Machines Studies 8 (1976) 263.
[12] Zadeh, L.A., On fuzzy algorithms, E.R.L. Memo M325, University of California, Berkeley (Febr. 1972).
[13] Dubois, D. and Prade, H., Operations on fuzzy numbers, Int.J.Systems Sci. 9 (1978) 613-626.
[14] Kuz'min, V.B., A parametric approach to description of linguistic values of variables and hedges, Fuzzy Sets and Systems 6 (1981) 27-41.

Approximate Reasoning in Decision Analysis
M.M. Gupta and E. Sanchez (eds.)

Fuzzy Set Model For Computerized Diagnosis System In Traditional Chinese Medicine

Guo Rongjian Xie Min Ma Binrong Chen Wuling

(Institute of Automation , Chinese Academia Sinica)

This paper describes some technical aspects of Chinese medical computer diagnosis , mainly, the mathemathical modelof traditional Chinese medicine. It also expounds the necessity of applying Fuzzy Set theory as a mathematical tool to the model building, the formulation of membership function, the adoption of flowting threshold method in the course of diagnosis etc., with examples of the application of the system and its effects given at the end of the paper.

Keywords: Computer Diagnosis, Traditional Chinese Medicine, Fuzzy Set, membership function, Floating Treshold.

1. The Fuzzy Set Model

Computer technology used in medical work began in the early sixties, gained fast development in the last two decades and becomes an important part of computer science nowadays. Computer diagnosis system in traditional Chinese medicine is an expertise system. The experience of veteran Chinese physicians have put in the computer memory system. In a sense, it is a technical equipment system which is not only a new method to record and preserve the medical knowledge of experienced Chinese physicians, but also a conveninet way to make the experts' experience serve more people. This system , be it equioped anywhere, can give the patient the most correct diagnosis and prescription even if it is operated by an ordinary or a junior medical personnel. At present, China is lacking in traditional Chinese physicians. Therefore, the development of such a system has special importance.

The characteristics of computer diagnosis in traditional Chinese medicine may be classified into two aspects. First, terminologies of symptoms and diagnosis are fuzzier than that of the western medicine. This should be considered in building the mathematical model. Second, the diagnosis of traditional Chinese medicine is more dialectic and the number of symptoms to be used as original data, larger in comparison with western medicine. These factors complicate the structure of the computer programming. Besides, we have to adopt the method of simulating to realize the computer diagnosing process.

There are large number of ill defind objects which need mathematical description in the work of medical diagnosis. Both probability theory and fuzzy set theory can be used as mathematical tools to solve these problems. But they are suitable to different objects. The former is suitable to describe events with definit meaning but uncertain occurrence, while the latter is suitable for those with indefinite meaning but their occurrence can be judged with certainty. Up to the present, Bayes formula and maximum likelihood estimation are used mostly in medical science for qualitative and computer diagnosis. The substance of these formulas is to take a priori probability as basis in calculating the posterior probability. In the diagnostic problem of traditional Chinese medicine, symptoms such as anorexia, fatigue, abdominal distension, slippery pulse, thin and white coat of tongue ect., have more fuzziness. The diagnostic terms such as "persistent hepatitis, PI-XU type" made on the basis of the symdrome composed of above symptoms have much more fuzziness. Besides some special sumptoms have very low frequency in the statistics of the medical records but have great value for the diagnosis. In such cases, it is insufficient to depend only on statistics for better diagnosis.

Thus, fuzzy set theory becomes an ideal tool for studying model building in traditional Chinese medical diagnosis. The building process of our mathematical model is described as follow:

Let $a \times b$ symptoms be the object of consideration and it is put on an $a \times b$ network, each square corresponds to a symptom. In the most simple condition, black square denotes the presence and white square denotes the absence of a certain symptom. Thus the problem of medical diagnosis under our consideration becomes a problem of pattern recognizing.

Take the n-dimensional orthogonal bases for the base of a n-dimensional Euclidean space, upon which a coordinate system is constructed. Each coordinating axis of this system corresponds to a symptom. The coorresponding coordinate equals to 1 when certain symptom present, and to 0 when absent. So, each symdrome (i.e. each network picture) corresponds to a point in the N-dimensional space. In the condition of N symptoms, the set of a total 2^n points will be universe of discourse. Let X represents the collective whole of the set, i.e.:

$$X = \{x_1, x_2, \ldots\ldots, x_{2^n}\} \qquad (1)$$

As different types of diseases are translated into different fuzzy subsets, the problem of medical diagnosis is now to determine to what extent a certain element x_i (i.e. a given syndrome) belongs to which fuzzy subset, where $i \in \{1, 2, \ldots\ldots 2^n\}$

Suppose we delimite M fuzzy subsets on $X, \underset{\sim}{A}_1, \underset{\sim}{A}_2, \ldots\ldots, \underset{\sim}{A}_m$, Evidently,

$$\underset{\sim}{A}_j \subseteq X \qquad j \in \{1, 2, \ldots\ldots, m\} \qquad (2)$$

And $\underset{\sim}{A}_j$ is bounded, because in Euclidean space R^n, there exists

$$0 \leqslant \|x\| \leqslant \sqrt{n} \qquad (3)$$

Now, let $\mu_{\underset{\sim}{A}_j}(x_i)$ represent a membership function, where x_i is implied to $\underset{\sim}{A}_j$. We can select a $\mu_{\underset{\sim}{A}_j}(x_i)$ with strong convexity, hence, take the kernel of the fuzzy subset $\underset{\sim}{A}_j$ as x_0^j. We hold that symptoms in x_0^j represent a typical syndrome of $\underset{\sim}{A}_j$ type disease. Since x_0^j is the kernel of $\underset{\sim}{A}_j$, it is obvious that

$$\mu_{\underset{\sim}{A}_j}(x_0^j) = \operatorname{Sup} \mu_{\underset{\sim}{A}_j}(x_i) \qquad i \in \{1, 2, \ldots, 2^n\}; \quad j \in \{1, 2, \ldots, m\} \qquad (4)$$

The following is a discussion on the formulation of $\mu_{\underset{\sim}{A}_j}(x_i)$.

First of all, corresponding weighting coefficients are given to all the symptoms possessed by x_0^j. Their magnitude can be determined by theory of medical diagnosis combining with statistical method or by method of synthetic estimation of fuzzy set theory, and can also be obtained by artifical intelligence through machine learning. These coefficients, once determined, must adjust repeatedly through experiments.

The following is the summation formula:

$$P^0_{\underset{\sim}{A}_j} = \sum_{k=1}^{p} \alpha_k a_k \qquad (5)$$

Where $a_1, a_2, \ldots\ldots, a_p$ is the syndrome possessed by x_0^j, they take the value $1^{1)}$ in (5), while $\alpha_1, \alpha_2, \ldots\ldots, \alpha_p$ are corresponding weighting coefficients. After, any random x_i can also make the following summations :

$$P^{i}_{\underset{\sim}{A}_j} = \sum_{k=1}^{q} \alpha'_k a'_k \qquad (6)$$

Where $a'_1, a'_2, \ldots\ldots, a'_q$ are syndrome possessed by x_i, they take the value $1^{2)}$ in (6), and $\alpha'_1, \alpha'_2, \ldots\ldots, \alpha'_q$ are weighting coefficients of corresponding symptoms.

When the symptom represented by a'_k finds a symptom in x_o^j, with the meaning similar to that of a_k, then α'_k takes the value of α_k. On the contrary, when symptom s possessed by x_i do not exist in x_o^j, then α'_k takes 0 or negative. For some specific differential symptoms which have negative effects, α'_k may take large negative value.

On the basis of (5), and (6), we can now determine the following membership function :

$$\mu_{\underset{\sim}{A}_j}(x_i) \triangleq \begin{cases} 0 & (P_{\underset{\sim}{A}j} < 0) \\ P_{\underset{\sim}{A}j}/P^o_{\underset{\sim}{A}j} & (P_{\underset{\sim}{A}j} \geqslant 0) \end{cases} \quad (7)$$

It is clear that, $\mu_{\underset{\sim}{A}j}(x_i)$ takes the value from $[0, 1]$, and $\mu_{\underset{\sim}{A}j}(x_o^j) = \text{Sup}\, \mu_{\underset{\sim}{A}j}(x_i) = 1$.

The process of medical diagnosis in our model may be regarded as a transformation from a fuzzy set to an ordinary set. The most intuitive way to do this is to give every diagnosis of $\underset{\sim}{A}_j$, $j \in \{1,2,\ldots,m\}$ its corresponding threshold $S_j (0 \leqslant S_j \leqslant 1)$. We may say x_i is implied to an ordinary sub set A_j when $\mu_{\underset{\sim}{A}j}(x_i) \geqslant S_j$ i.e.,

$$A_j \triangleq \{ x \mid x \in X, \mu_{\underset{\sim}{A}j}(x) \geqslant S_j \} \quad (8)$$
$$j = \{1, 2, \ldots\ldots, m\}$$

Evidently A_j is actually a S_j sectional set of $\underset{\sim}{A}_j$.

But in practice, the difficulty we usually encounter is the selecting of the threshold value S_j: when it is relatively large, for a certain x_i, $\mu_{\underset{\sim}{A}j}(x_i) \geqslant S_j$ is unsatisfied with all the j, therefore, x_i does not belong to any one of A_j, conversely, if S_j takes comparative small value, $\mu_{\underset{\sim}{A}j}(x_i) \geqslant S_j$ then is satisfied with several values of j, in which case, X_i may belong to several different A_j. There two methods to overcome the above difficulty.

(Method 1) By adopting floating threshold value. Set S_j in (8) floating between certain selected upper limit $\bar{S}_j$ and lower limit $\underline{S}_j$. In this way, A_j is in fact an sectional set with floating boundary on $\underset{\sim}{A}_j$. For different j, there may have different $\bar{S}_j$ and $\underline{S}_j$ and different floating speed. In the course of floating from the upper limite to the lower limite, we may rearrange the order of A_j according to the necessity of the problem at hand and successively test which one of j first satisfies $\mu_{\underset{\sim}{A}j}(x_i) \geqslant S_j$.

(Method 2) By formulating a new menbership function

$$\mu'_{\underset{\sim}{A}j}(x_i) = \frac{\beta_i\, \mu_{\underset{\sim}{A}j}(x_i)}{\sum_{j=1}^{m} \beta_j\, \mu_{\underset{\sim}{A}j}(x_i)} \quad (9)$$

β_i in the formula is also weighting coefficient which may be determined by the importance of a certain tupe of disease which needs priority consideration. While $\beta_j = 1$, $j \in \{1, 2, \ldots, m\}$, $\mu_{\underset{\sim}{A}j}(x_i)$ representing the extent of x_i " likes " that of x_o^j , The different weights β_j takes indicate the inclusion of a definite type of disease which has the priority consideration.

$\mu'_{\underset{\sim}{A}j}(x_i)$ still takes value in $[0,1]$ at the same time, they have orthogonal characteristics, i.e.

$$\sum_{j=1}^{m} \mu'_{\underset{\sim}{A}j}(x_i) = 1 \quad (10)$$

Due to this characteristics, the entropy of X may be defined as

$$G = -\sum_{j=1}^{m} \mu_{\underset{\sim}{A}_j}(x_i) \ln \mu'_{\underset{\sim}{A}_j}(x_i) \tag{11}$$

It is a measure of the discriminative level of the element x_i in X, i.e., a measure of the level being diagnosed of certain patient. The larger the entropy the lower the diagnositic level.

On the basis of (9), we may say that x_i belongs to A_j if $\mu'_{\underset{\sim}{A}_j}(x_i)$ is the largest among membership functions, i.e.,

$$A_j \triangleq \{x \mid x \in X, \mu'_{\underset{\sim}{A}_j}(x_i) = \max(\mu_{\underset{\sim}{A}_l}(x_i))\}, \quad l \in \{1, 2, \ldots, m\} \tag{12}$$

(8) and (12) are two mathematical models we have obtained.

2. Example and Effects

Based upon the clinical experiences of Prof.Zhao Bingnan, Prof. Guan Youpo, and Prof. Fong Zhixuan, famous physicians of traditional Chinese medicine, we have edited ten copies of software of Chinese medical diagnosis. All of them run well on some small or micro machines like TQ-16, DJS-130, T-1600, TRS-80, Z-80 etc., and can get output in Chinese with Wang 2200-VP. The consistency of the diagnostic results between programmes and physicians has a percentage above 95.0, so the programmes can be regared as attaining the practicallevel.

Beijing Hospital of Chinese Medicine has formally been applying software to serve patients since January 1979.

The following illustrates the software which simulates Prof. Guan Youpo's experience on hepatities. Based on the view point of Chinese medicine and the experience of Prof. Guan, this software classified hepatitis into 8 main types and 36 subtypes, whereby the prescription can be made more precise by adding, reducing and transforming the prescription according to the conditions of different patients and the principle of Chinese medicine. The computer can provide 19 hundred million different prescription calculated with permutstion and combination, so it has enough flesibility to suit changing situations of patients. This software can also give proper treatment to patients of hepatitis with dysfunction of carbohydrate metabolism and proteinuria. For patient insuccessive consultations, the software can rewrite the prescription and change some drugs in accordance with variations of the desease. In the actual work of diagnosing, according to Prof.Guan's experience, there are preparational drugs to be served in the second and third lines for some particular desease. Over two hundred items of symptoms and test indices are adopted by the software. A simplified block diagramme of the structure of diagnosis system is shown in figure 1.

In retrospective test conducted on 266 case-histories, the consistency between computer diagnosis and medical records is 97.7%, in 59 double blined tests, the consistency is 88% and in 100 cases of practical diagnosis, the consistency is 96%.

In addition, preliminary statistical analysis of the curative effects shows that the cure rate of the computer is identical with that of Prof. Guan.

Figure 2 is a medical record edited by the machine, figure 3 is a computer prescription and figure 4 is a medical certificate written by the computer. (See diagrammes next pages)

REFERENCE

Guo Rongjiang etc.: The computer programming for the diagnosis and treatment of liver diseases based on the principle of dialectial treat, emt desogmed.
Chinese Medical Journal 59:654, 1979.

1) In consideration of symptoms of different extents have influence over diagnosis, these symdromes may.

2) Take different values accordingly
2) same as 1)

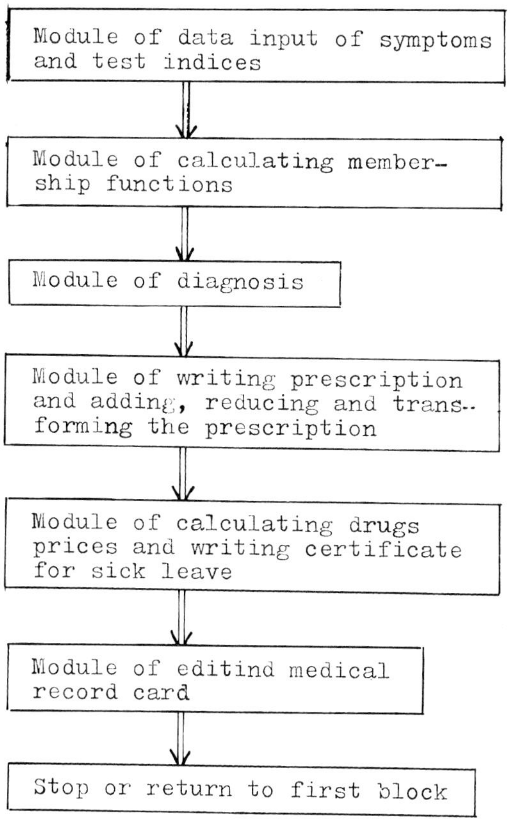

Fig. 1. A simplified block diagram of the structure of the diagnosis system.

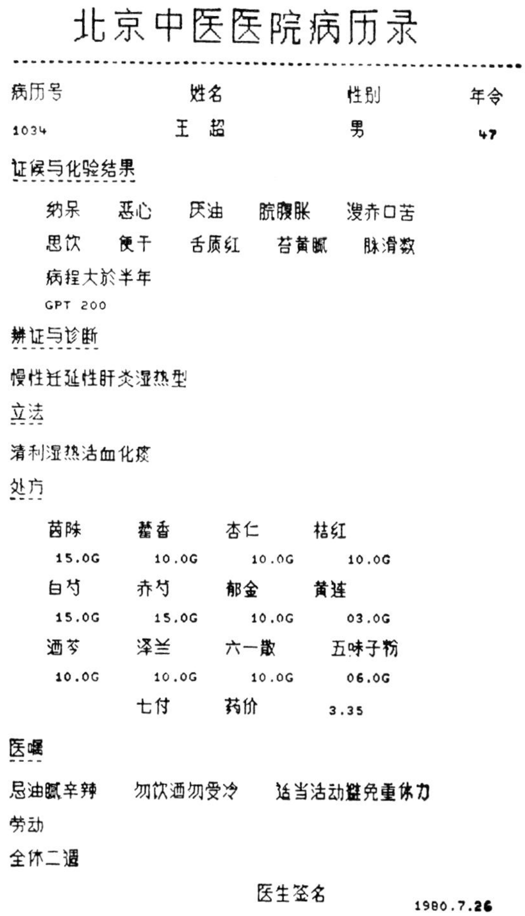

北京中医医院病历录

病历号 姓名 性别 年令
1034 王 超 男 47

证候与化验结果

纳呆 恶心 厌油 脘腹胀 溲赤口苦
思饮 便干 舌质红 苔黄腻 脉滑数
病程大於半年
GPT 200

辨证与诊断

慢性迁延性肝炎湿热型

立法

清利湿热活血化瘀

处方

茵陈 15.0G 藿香 10.0G 杏仁 10.0G 桔红 10.0G
白芍 15.0G 赤芍 15.0G 郁金 10.0G 黄连 03.0G
酒芩 10.0G 泽兰 10.0G 六一散 10.0G 五味子粉 06.0G
七付 药价 3.35

医嘱

忌油腻辛辣 勿饮酒勿受冷 适当活动避免重体力
劳动
全休二週

医生签名 1980.7.26

Fig. 2. A medical record card edited by the computer.

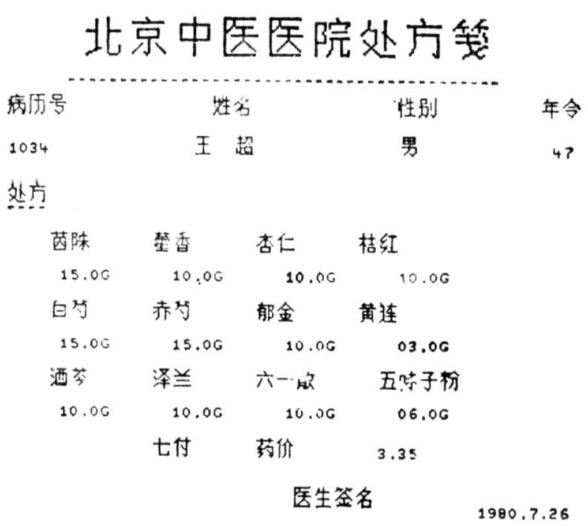

北京中医医院处方笺

病历号 姓名 性别 年令
1034 王 超 男 47

处方

茵陈 15.0G 藿香 10.0G 杏仁 10.0G 桔红 10.0G
白芍 15.0G 赤芍 15.0G 郁金 10.0G 黄连 03.0G
酒芩 10.0G 泽兰 10.0G 六一散 10.0G 五味子粉 06.0G
七付 药价 3.35

医生签名 1980.7.26

Fig. 3. A computer prescription.

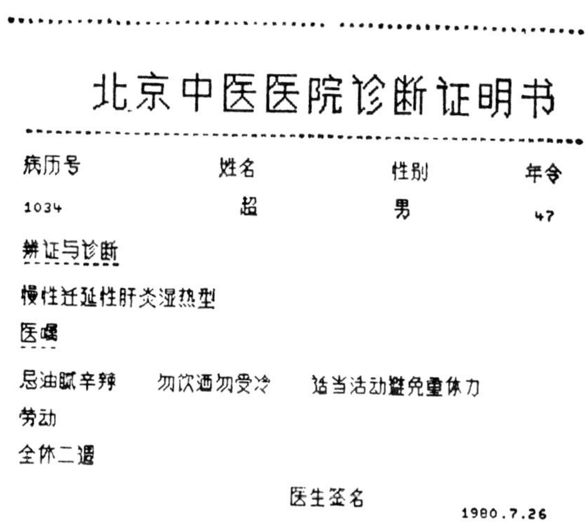

北京中医医院诊断证明书

病历号 姓名 性别 年令
1034 超 男 47

辨证与诊断

慢性迁延性肝炎湿热型

医嘱

忌油腻辛辣 勿饮酒勿受冷 适当活动避免重体力
劳动
全休二週

医生签名 1980.7.26

Fig. 4. A medical certificate written by the computer.

PART SIX

PSYCHOLOGICAL MEASUREMENTS AND HUMAN BEHAVIOR

Approximate Reasoning in Decision Analysis
M.M. Gupta and E. Sanchez (eds.)

TOWARDS FUZZY ALGORITHMS IN BEHAVIOUR MODIFICATION

V. B. Cervin,
Department of Psychology,
University of Windsor,
Windsor, Ontario,
Canada N9B 3P4

and

Ramesh Jain,
Department of Computer Science,
Wayne State University,
Detroit, Michigan, 48202,
USA

In behavior modification (contingency management) procedures, one encounters fuzzy terms. This paper specifies behavior modification procedures which include operations of classification, comparison and choice. Imprecise terms are represented by fuzzy variables and comparisons by fuzzy relations. Empirical studies, which are summarized, show experimental determination of the meaning of the fuzzy variables entering into the algorithms and the dependence of communication on compatibility functions. We hope that precisely specified fuzzy procedures will be more effective than those used at present.

KEYWORDS: behavior algorithms, behavior modification, fuzzy algorithms.

1. INTRODUCTION

Many psychological difficulties that people experience are now considered as psychological problems to solve rather than as illnesses to cure. As a consequence applied psychologists more and more frequently offer help in solving clients' behavioral problems, e.g. behavior therapy, managerial behavior modification, self-management, rather than suggest treatment for mental diseases. Psychologists now actively participate in their clients' problem-solving behavior rather than just listen to their difficulties.

Psychological interventions are based on the principles of scientific psychology, especially behavioral and cognitive psychology. They take the form of arranging, for clients, ordered sequences of events and behavior and instructing them about observation of their own behavior, setting behavioral goals, etc. In this, the psychologist himself follows sequences of rules he has learned to achieve changes in behavior. Since in laboratories we have a very small rate of failures with certain techniques of behavior modification, when failures occur in real environments we think it is not the principles used that are at fault (which have been tested many, many times in the laboratory), but the design of interventions under real life conditions. If so, then by tightening the structure of interventions, explicating the meaning of instructions used, communicating more effectively and formalizing the principles of behavior modification, we can contribute to the improvement of psychological interventions. This can be done by making the algorithmic and fuzzy nature of psychological interventions explicit.

An algorithm is an ordered sequence of rules that leads to a goal or a solution of a problem. Fuzzy algorithms contain imprecise classifications, fuzzy assertions, approximate evaluations and non-categorical imperatives. Imprecise instructions are successfully carried out by people because they, unlike computing machines, can tolerate and cope with vagueness compensating for the missing precision by their own skills and experience. However, errors do occur because of sometimes inappropriate compensations, misinterpretation of the meaning of instructions and faulty communication between the algorithm designer and its user. Such errors could be eliminated by making algorithms mathematically precise (Santos, 1970) but, as Zadeh (1973) has pointed out, mathematical precision and practical applicability of formal structures are inversely related. Therefore we turned to fuzzy algorithms which allow us to preserve sufficient rigour of formalizations and incorporate all the necessary vagueness required in psychological applications.

The purpose of this paper is to formulate the principles of two behavioral problem solving procedures in terms of fuzzy algorithms and to obtain empirical functions for the meanings of the main components of these algorithms, viz., fuzzy functions of assertions, composition of attributes, comparison of expected and actual behavior, comparison of fuzzy instructions and their execution and choice among fuzzy alternative actions (Jain, 1970). The fuzzy meaning functions can be obtained for the user and the algorithm designer and compared. The effectiveness of their communication can then be evaluated objectively in terms of the difference between the parameters of their respective functions. Formalizations of the principles of behavior modification procedures in terms of fuzzy algorithms and the explication of the meaning functions of assertions and instructions involved may clarify relevant psychological princples and improve the effectiveness of behavioral interventions.

2. FUZZY ALGORITHMS

A fuzzy algorithm may be defined as an ordered set of fuzzy instructions which upon execution yield an approximate solution to a specified problem (Zadeh, 1968). The concept of fuzzy algorithm is appealing to researachers from many different fields. In many branches of the soft sciences and in some hard fields such as artificial intelligence and control theory, fuzzy algorithms may allow one to solve complex as yet unsolved problems. Early research in fuzzy set theory and fuzzy algorithms resulted in some activity in different fields; however, the goal of solving real problems using fuzzy algorithms so far met with only limited success. Our study is a contribution to the formulation and experimental test of fuzzy algorithms in applied psychology.

The general formulation of fuzzy algorithms (and fuzzy programs) by researchers has been influenced by automata theory. Let us consider the definiton as given by Chang (1972):

A finite state machine is a system

$$M = (K, X, F, x_0, T)$$

where

- K is a finite nonempty set of machine instructions
- X is a finite nonempty set of internal states
- x_0 is the initial state, an element of X
- T are final states, a subset of X
- F is the transition function from $X*K \rightarrow X$.

A fuzzy machine is a system

$$M = (S, M, f, L)$$

where

- S is a finite nonempty set of fuzzy instructions
- M is the machine defined above
- f is the feasibility function from X*S*K into $\{0,1\}$
- L is the performance function from X*f*K into $[0,1]$

The feasibility function, f, represents the constraints for the execution of fuzzy instructions from set S. If a fuzzy instruction, s_i, can be implemented on machine, M, when it is in state, x, using a nonfuzzy machine instruction, k, then $f(x,s_i,k) = 1$. The performance function, on the other hand, gives a subjective performance evaluation for the machine to execute a machine instruction in a particular situation. Thus, if

$$L(x,f,K1) = 0.95$$
$$L(x,f,K2) = 0.75$$
$$\text{and} \quad L(x,f,K3) = 0.40,$$

then K1 is the best machine instruction in the given situation.

Note that the fuzzy machine is defined in terms of a non- fuzzy machine such that for a fuzzy instruction, there may be more than one feasible nonfuzzy instruction. The best instruction according to some evaluative function is selected at every instant. The above general formalism is strongly motivated by the desire to develop machines capable of executing imprecise instructions (Zadeh, 1971, Chang, 1972). The main concern has been to develop algorithms using ill-defined variables and to study the selection of the best rule which can be executed on the machine in the given situation. The connectives used with fuzzy terms and the operators used to achieve the result are well defined and create no problem for the machine.

Our main concern is to develop algorithms which will be useful in the task of behavior modification. The algorithms in this application are also fuzzy. A major difference in the formalism, however, is required because these algorithms are not to be implemented on a deterministic but on a fuzzy "machine". The fuzzy algorithm is executed by a person who interprets a fuzzy instruction according to his understanding of the meaning of the fuzzy terms used in the specified algorithm, then takes action. The action is usually nonfuzzy.

The person using fuzzy algorithms has to interpret the connections and the operations in a way not very different from that of the algorithm designer. This task can be achieved by (a) using connectives and operators similar to those used by most people, and (b) training the person using the algorithm. The difference in the interpretation by the user and the algorithm designer is a fuzzy variable. Another problem is that in the machines discussed above, the state of the machine is nonfuzzy. In behavior modification, the practitioner has to observe and classify the state of the patient. Two kinds of states are to be observed: the state of behavior readiness (learned, reflexive) and the state of motivation to act (to satisfy a need). These states are observed fuzzily.

In behavior modification we also see interaction between a psychologist (practitioner) and his client (patient) which results in the introduction of fuzzy states, fuzzy observation functions, and the interpretation function. Since a practitioner can only approximately classify the real states of the patient, an observation function must allow the transformation of the client's state into the observer's fuzzy observation. The fuzzy instructions selected by the practitioner are interpreted by the client in a fuzzy manner and implemented by nonfuzzy actions. All these terms, functions, and instructions are summarized in the following fuzzy system and algorithms.

The practitioner and his client are conceived as a fuzzy behavior system $\underline{P}$ consisting of two interacting individuals where the client $\underline{C}$ is a subsystem. In the above and in what follows the underlining indicates fuzziness.

$$\underline{P} = (\underline{D}, \underline{A}, \underline{a}_o, \underline{a}_t, \underline{K}, E, \underline{C}, F, G, L)$$

where

$\underline{D}$ = fuzzy subset of D (client's set of motives)

$\underline{A}$ = fuzzy subset of A (client's responses to stimuli)

$\underline{a}_o$ = fuzzy value of client's initial responding as observed by psychologist

$\underline{a}_t$ = fuzzy value defining client's desired responding

$\underline{K}$ = set of fuzzy instructions to client by practitioner

E = set of prompts, rewards and punishments used by practitioner

F = $A*E \rightarrow A$ transition functions (behavior changes observed by P)

G = observation functions from C to P

L = $A*K*K \rightarrow [0,1]$ set of feasibility and client's interpretation functions

and

$$\underline{C} = (D, A, a_o, a_t, \underline{K})$$

where

D,A = as defined above

a_o, a_t = non-fuzzy subset of client's initial and final responses

$\underline{\underline{K}}$ = subset of $\underline{K}$ (interpretation of instructions by client)

The client's behavioral subsystem C can be visualized as a function of responses A being energized by his motivation D to produce particular patterns of behavior one of which a_o is slated to be changed to give the patterns a_t under the influence of instructions $\underline{K}$ and reinforcement/punishment or prompt E arranged by the psychologist. If the client is a self-managing subsystem, he administers his own prompts/reinforcements/ punishments according to his understanding of instructions, e.g., a client drinks $\underline{a}_o$ = 15 cups of coffee a day which is to be changed (F) to say $\underline{a}_t$ = 5 cups a day. A change in behavior can be achieved in different ways. We are considering here a reduction in the amount of coffee drunk per day by other means than change in his environment, such as his job, viz., by providing acceptable reinforcements other than coffee.

The psychologist's job is to assess (function G) his client's observed behavior $\underline{A}$ (fuzzy subset of A) and his observed motivation $\underline{D}$ (fuzzy subset of D) to determine if indeed his behavior constitutes problem behavior $\underline{a}_o$ which is a fuzzy subset of patient's actual behavior at a particular time when the observation is made. A goal for changing client's behavior into $\underline{a}_t$ is a value to reach by behavior modification approximately. The change of the client's behavior to be achieved by the psychologist is a function F. L is a function of communication between the psychologist and his client and has to be evaluated empirically (see experimental part of this paper).

The change in behavior of subsystem C is to be achieved by applying the principles of behavioral and cognitive psychology according to an ordered sequence of rules represented in the form of algorithms. Basically these algorithms will implement function F mapping previous behavior into new behavior through the influence of reinforcements/punishments or prompts according to two well-known paradigms of training/learning. Algorithms of behavior modification (BM) are based on these two principles and use the following terms:

S = set of stimuli, with the subset $\underline{s}$ in S defining a particular situation

A = set of client's responses, with the subset a in A being client's behavior in that situation

E = set of actions by the practitioner or his client, with the subset e in E used as prompts, rewards or punishments for client's responses in that situation

$\underline{a}_t$ = fuzzy subset of A (desired behaviors)

$\underline{a}_o$ = fuzzy subset of A (problem behavior)

e_d = subset of reinforcements, punishments or prompts appropriate to client's motivation, with complement e' of inappropriate actions

W = subset of practitioner's actions, e.g., waiting for correct behavior

Z = subset of practitioner's actions, e.g, stopping, changing BM

T = set of actions testing client's behavior

Algorithm $BM_1(s, e, a)$, given $\underline{a}_o$ and $\underline{s}$, changes $\underline{a}_o$ into $\underline{a}_t$, $\underline{s}$ remaining constant:

"IF e_d THEN (IF $\underline{a}_t$ THEN T, ELSE Z), ELSE BM"

$$= e_d * \underline{a}_t * T \;\cup\; e_d * \underline{a}_o * Z \;\cup\; e' * BM$$

Algorithm BM_1 defines the so-called prompting procedure (analog of classical conditioning, Cervin et al., 1970).

Algorithm BM_2 (s, a, e), given $\underline{a}_o$ and $\underline{s}$, changes $\underline{a}_o$ into $\underline{a}_t$, $\underline{s}$ remaining constant:

$$\text{"IF } \underline{a}_t \text{ THEN (IF } e_d \text{ THEN T, ELSE Z), ELSE W"}$$

$$= \underline{a}_t * e_d * T \ \cup \ \underline{a}_t * e'_t * Z \ \cup \ \underline{a}_o * W$$

Algorithm BM_2 defines the reinforcement/punishment procedure (analog of operant conditioning, Cervin et al., 1970).

After BM follows test T

$$T = \underline{s} * \underline{a}_t * Z \ \cup \ \underline{s} * \underline{a}_o * BM$$

in which we determine whether or not modified behavior $\underline{a}_t$ has been reached.

The core of either BM algorithm is the particular sequencing of three events: environmental conditions, response, and reinforcement/punishment/prompt (Cervin, Ladd & Scheich, 1970). In actual behavior modification procedures with humans one would mostly rely on secondary (e.g., social) rewards and prompts, but the primary ones are not to be totally excluded (emetics are administered to alcoholics) if the client consents. Combinations of the two basic procedures are of course possible. Particular flow charts are available but are not given here because the purpose of this paper is not to give particular prescriptions but to analyze the algorithms.

3. EXPERIMENTAL STUDIES OF ALGORITHM COMPONENTS

The components of a behavioral algorithm are: events used as prompts/rewards/punishments, and statements of assertion, evaluation, composition of attributes, choice. The first set of events may be verbal or non-verbal, statements are verbal and numerical. Since at least two people are involved in behavior modification (even if self-administered) the question of meaning to be attributed to these events and statements is basic. The meaning of non-verbal events may be described by the aphorism "the proof of the pudding is in the eating". The meaning of verbal statements can be determined with the help of fuzzy set theory.

Following Zadeh (1971) the meaning of statements can be defined as a fuzzy subset of a reference set. For example, if somebody smokes thirty cigarettes a day, the psychological meaning of this fact for our purposes is that he smokes too much. If the number of cigarettes that can be smoked is the reference set we can determine the membership function of the number smoked in the subset "too many cigarettes" smoked which gives us the required meaning for the purpose of behavior modification. Such functions can be empirically determined for both the client and the psychologist. If the two functions agree then they agree that there is a problem. They could similarly agree on the functions for subsets "not too many". This would be the basis for agreeing on the goal of behavior modification. If the membership functions are very different, then the psychologist first has to work on modifying the client's functions so that they would agree with his meaning functions and only then can behavior modification be worked out. Similar considerations apply to other kinds of statements used in BM algorithms mentioned above. The determination of meaning functions is therefore of great practical importance and will serve as a basis of the understanding of the problem, evaluation of the progress, choice of alternatives and statement of the goal. The experimental study (Cervin et al., 1981) was concerned with the question of how meanings can be empirically determined so that they can be used for practical purposes in BM. It is summarized in this section.

The following five functions have been examined:

a) Observation of behavior on both the quantitative and verbal levels, e.g, "the racquet is 'light' (i.e., belongs to the subset Y of light racquets) if it weighs about x grams" (x in X set of weights). The two levels of these statements are connected by a compatibility function $\mu_Y(x) \rightarrow [0,1]$.

b) Comparison of observed and expected behavior and estimation of the compatibility function of a statement, such as "John is cured", i.e. belongs to the subset of well people U, with the measurements of his behavior, b, e.g, if the goal is fuzzy, then $\mu_U(b) = 0.9$ is acceptable.

c) Composition of the compatibility values of observed constituents of an attribute n-tuple to obtain an estimate of the value of the composite attribute from those of the constituent attributes, e.g., the racquet (r) belongs to the subset of "racquets acceptable to me" (V) if it is light (Y) and has a small grip (S), i.e., if the racquet is both light and has a small grip, it is "right":

$$\mu_V(r) = \min(\mu_Y(r), \mu_S(r))$$

d) Choice based on a comparison of objects each characterized by a different degree of the same composite n-tuple of attributes (e.g., Yager, 1980).

e) Measurement of the overall effectiveness of algorithmic communications. This skill was tested by the psychologist's ability to correctly execute an algorithm and achieve a stated goal and was expressed as compatibility of the subset of satisfactory algorithms and all the algorithms requiring changes.

The purpose of the experimental part of this study was to obtain the empirical functions outlined in (a) to (e) above, including compatibility of a fuzzy algorithm and psychologists' behavior in helping a "client" to solve a behavioral problem in a simulated behavior modification. Subjects were selected from "friends" of the experimenters and differed in age, sex, and other characteristics according to the requirements of the particular study (Cervin et al, 1981).

STUDY I. The fuzzy meanings of simple assertions (one grammatical subject and one predicate) concerning observations were determined in terms of the degree of compatibility of verbal descriptions with the numbers x in the corresponding reference set U, x in U, such as "X drinks a lot of coffee" with the number x of cups of coffee drunk by him per day. Amounts each subject drank himself were also obtained.

Thus, the experimenter asked his subject to rate the behavior of several of his (the subject's) real or hypothetical "friends", X's, for compatibility of each X's behavior, x, with the verbal statement "X drinks a lot of coffee" if X indeed drank x cups a day. Other ratings of a similar type were obtained by other experimenters' subjects for statements "X sleeps a lot", "X is young", and "X is usually late for a date". Each of these statements was rated by each experimenter's subjects for compatibility with the number x describing X's actual behavior. There were 28 subjects altogether.

Most curves obtained are obviously straight lines between minima and maxima (cf. MacVicar-Whelan, 1978). Therefore, straight lines were fitted to data. Since the data are discrete and the number of points small, no fancier curves would have been justified. Coefficients R^2 ranged from 0.87 to 0.98, indicating a good fit with the straight lines.

STUDY II. Each experimenter ran a learning experiment. Subjects had to learn a list of words compiled by the experimenter, repeating as many of them as they could remember after each presentation of the list. Subjects rated the degrees of compatibility of the statement "Goal is reached" with the number of errors recorded in the course of learning.

The compatibility functions were again straight lines with slopes ranging from 0.033 to 0.117. The difference between fuzzy and crisp goal functions lay at the points where the asymptote is reached.

STUDY III. Experimenters gave subjects four pairs of constituent attributes with corresponding μ-values, ostensibly describing four people. They were asked to combine each pair into one composite attribute, each with a value derived from the μ-values of the constituents in any way they wished. We wanted to know what intelligent subjects would do if there were no restrictions on their choice of a composition function. There were 22 subjects in this experiment.

Results indicated that for all four problems averaging was the preferred (48%) function, minima second (35%). Maxima were used in 15% of cases, multiplication once.

STUDY IV. Nine subjects were given a problem concerning a choice between two candidates for a job, taken from Yager (1980) and simplified to two candidates.

Eight of nine subjects made the choice consistent with the maximin composition of the decision functions. One subject ignored the information given and flipped a coin. Post-experimental interviews failed to reliably uncover any awareness of the maximin composition rule. Choice behavior with fuzzy data needs more experimental study.

STUDY V. Each of three experimenters ran a training-learning experiment according to written instructions. Instructions to experimenters stated how to conduct the experiment and what instructions to give to subjects. His/her subjects had to learn eight paired-associate items consisting of a given light and an associated button displayed on a panel. This was a simulated behavior modification: initial random button-pressing was modified into correct-button-pressing with few or no errors.

After completion of the experiments which showed that subjects had learned the task to a fuzzy criterion, experimenters evaluated the instructions relative to their own execution of the experiments. Compatibility values were obtained for the statement "Instructions are satisfactory", i.e., belonging to subset H of good instructions, with the number (w) of instructions that did not need changes $\mu_H(w) \rightarrow [0,1]$ One experimenter's subjects should have been told to press the buttons harder in order to avoid errors due to faulty closing of the switches rather than to errors in button selection. This test gave a compatibility value of 0.95. This value indicates satisfactory understanding and execution of the algorithm and satisfactory structure of the algorithm itself.

The experimental procedures were somewhat involved. In practical situations we will have only two persons: a practitioner (psychologist) and a client (patient). The algorithms will be used by the practitioner and communicated in part to the client. In part, the practitioner will use physical stimuli to influence the client's behavior.

4. CONCLUSION

In this paper we discussed some aspects of algorithms for behavior modification. The mathematical formulation indicates the direction to be followed.

We summarized some experiments on how people interpret empirical variables in a fuzzy manner. These are mainly meaning functions representing fuzzy subsets of reference sets. Empirical determination of functions is demonstrated and their relation to communication between the user and the algorithm designer is discussed. The mathematical representation and empirical use of the proposed algorithms demonstrated in this paper should contribute to their effectiveness.

REFERENCES:

[1] Cervin, V.B., Ladd, W.H. and Scheich, S., Comparison of associative learning under three methods and three directional forms of presentation, Psychological Reports, 26 (1970) 603-614.

[2] Cervin, V.B., Gallwey, J., MacFadden, G., Martin, H., Outinen, B., Plourde, L. and Tignanelli, L., Representation of meaning in a fuzzy set framework, unpublished paper, (University of Windsor, 1981).

[3] Chang, S.K., On the execution of fuzzy programs using finite state machines, IEEE Trans. Computers, 2, 3 (1972) 241-253.

[4] Hersh, H.M. and Caramazza, A., A fuzzy set approach to modifiers and vagueness in natural language, Journal of Experimental Psychology: General, 105, 3 (1976) 254-276.

[5] Jain, R., Decision making in the presence of fuzzy variables, IEEE Trans. on Systems, Man, and Cybernetics, Oct. (1976) 698-702.

[6] Lakoff, G., Hedges: A study in meaning criteria and the logic of fuzzy concepts, Journal of Philosophical Logic, 2 (1973) 458-508.

[7] MacVicar-Whelan, P.J., Fuzzy sets, the concept of height, and the hedge very, IEEE Transactions on Systems, Man and Cybernetics, SMC-8 6 (1978) 507-511.

[8] Martin, R.C. and Caramazza, A., A classification in well- defined ill-defined categories: evidence for common processing strategies, Journal of Experimental Psychology: General, 109 (1980) 320-353

[9] Oden, G.C., Fuzziness in semantic memory: choosing exemplars of subjective categories, Mem. Cognit. 5, 2 (1977) 198-204.

[10] Oden, G.C., Integration of fuzzy logical information, Journal of Experimental Psychology: Hum. Percept. Perform. 3, 4 (1977) 565-575.

[11] Santos, E.S., Fuzzy algorithms, Information and Control, 17 (1970) 326-339.

[12] Yager, B., Satisfaction and fuzzy decision functions, in Wang, P.P. and Chang, S.K. (eds.), Fuzzy Sets, (New York: Plenum, 1980)

[13] Zadeh, L.A., Calculus of fuzzy restrictions, in Zadeh, L.A., Fu, K.S., Tanaka, K. and Shimura, M. (eds.), Fuzzy Sets and their Applications to Cognitive and Decision Processes (New York, Academic Press, 1975).

[14] Zadeh, L.A., Fuzzy algorithms, Information and Control 12, (1968) 94-102.

[15] Zadeh, L.A., Towards fuzziness in computer systems -- fuzzy algorithms and languages, in Boulaye, G. (ed.) Architecture and Design of Digital Computers (Paris: Dunod, 1971).

[16] Zadeh, L.A., Outline of a new approach to the analysis of complex systems and decision processes, IEEE Trans. on SMC, 3, No. 1 (1973) 28-44.

ACKNOWLEDGEMENT

The authors are particularly indebted to Mr. L. C. Patil, P.Eng., and to Joan C. Cervin for crucial help in the preparation of this paper. Our warmest thanks.

Approximate Reasoning in Decision Analysis
M.M. Gupta and E. Sanchez (eds.)

LINGUISTIC DESCRIPTION OF HUMAN JUDGMENTS IN EXPERT SYSTEMS AND IN THE 'SOFT' SCIENCES

Christian Freksa
Department of Biostatistics
Max Planck Institute for Psychiatry
Munich, West Germany

A fuzzy-linguistic tool for the representation and analysis of human judgments in expert systems and in the 'soft' sciences is presented. The approach is motivated by fundamental differences between measurements as they are performed in the 'hard' sciences and judgments which form the basis for decisions in the 'soft' sciences. These differences suggest a representation for human judgments which preserves their fuzziness instead of a representation in terms of the "measurement and error" paradigm used in the hard sciences. The paper explains why such a representation not only is more natural to use but also yields more reliable results. Finally, the interactive construction of semantic representations of linguistic descriptors from examples is discussed.

KEYWORDS: linguistic descriptors, soft data representation, possibility distributions, cognitive modelling, information granularity

1. INTRODUCTION

Research and expert areas like psychology, medicine, jurisdiction, etc. deal with 'soft' data [COLLINS et al., 1975; SKALA, 1978; ZADEH, 1979b]. These data result from a different type of interpretation process than 'hard' data in classical physics, chemistry, or engineering. Nevertheless, the same research methodology is being used to process data of both types. The reason for this must be an implicit assumption that both kinds of data are of the same nature, i.e., have the same conceptual framework, and therefore should be analyzed by the same methods.

This paper compares the concepts 'data-driven measurement' and 'goal-driven judgment' [NORMAN & RUMELHART, 1975; NILSSON, 1980] by investigating their underlying processes. Occasionally, these notions will be abbreviated in the following by 'measurement' and 'judgment', respectively. The paper argues that observation data may have fundamentally different semantics depending on the structure of their interpretation processes and should be represented and interpreted accordingly. While data-driven processes yield point data which are to be interpreted with certain error tolerances, goal-driven interpretation processes yield possibility distributions [ZADEH, 1978] which can be constructed such that they are free of errors. It may not be meaningful to think of an error of a soft judgment the same way as of an error of a hard measurement.

By developing adequate representations of observations or judgments we may be able to take advantage of their inherent properties, specifically imprecision, fuzziness, and variable feature resolution [1]. These properties appear disadvantageous in the "measurement and error" paradigm which is conventionally used for the interpretation of observations [e.g. GULLIKSEN & MESSICK, 1960]. A fuzzy-linguistic representation in terms of simplified possibility distributions [FREKSA, 1981] is proposed. This representation is suited for the type of operations that observations are suited for in natural cognition systems: communication, comparison, and judgment.

We will point to empirical results which suggest that more natural (specifically: linguistic) representations of cognitive observations yield more informative and reliable interpretations than traditional arithmomorphic representations. We will demonstrate how semantic representations of linguistic descriptors [2] for cognitive observations can be constructed interactively from examples.

2. DATA-DRIVEN AND GOAL-DRIVEN OBSERVATIONS

We will contrast two extreme examples of a purely data-driven and of a purely goal-driven observation process for our analysis. In these examples, we consider some phenomenon that is to be observed by some device. In the first case, this device is a measuring instrument, in the second case, it is a human observer.

2.1 Examples

EXAMPLE 1: Measurement process in the hard sciences.

Consider the function of a voltmeter. The physical dimension "voltage" may be interpreted in terms of electrical current that flows in a given conductor. The current causes a magnetic field which results in a physical force which displaces the needle of a voltmeter.

The displacement of the needle is an indication of the voltage at the instrument. The instrument yields a point value, i.e., the needle points at one particular position for a given voltage. A physical model relates each needle position to an input voltage at the meter. The position value of the needle therefore can be interpreted as an indication of the voltage. It must be considered an approximation of the actual voltage since certain factors influencing the correspondence between voltage and needle displacement have been ignored in the model (e.g. mechanical friction in the instrument, influence of magnetic field of the earth, etc.). The effect of these factors, however, can be estimated and the error range of the approximation can be determined.

EXAMPLE 2: Judgment process in the soft sciences.

Now consider psychological rating of a continuous quantity, say the degree of well-being of a person. This quantity is not functionally determined in terms of well-defined parameters as in the case of the voltmeter. Nevertheless, no one would argue that we have a definite perception of degree of well-being both for ourselves and for other beings. In certain situations we may be able to distinguish minute differences in well-being reliably, in other situations we can make only coarse distinctions. The outcome of an observation may be a linguistic description like "today she feels better than yesterday", "this feels good", "this is slightly worse", etc.

The description of the observation is an indication of the degree of well-being of the observed person. The resolution (or relative precision [1]) of the observation depends not only on the observer (the instrument) but also on the information on which his judgment is based. The observation process yields a restricted range of possible states of well-being in form of a linguistic description. A heuristic model relates each description to a range of possible states. Although certain indicators for the state of well-being could not be taken into account the description may be a correct indication of the person's state of well-being; additional information could have refined the answer and thus could have further restricted the range of possible states of well-being.

We may view human judgments as cognitive processes which depend on limited data and resources -- input information, processing power, memory -- and thus may operate with fluctuating resolution [NORMAN & BOBROW, 1975].

2.2 Analysis

The two examples exhibit two different processes for feature evaluation. Physical measuring devices like voltmeters generate measurement values by physical analogy or simulation and yield point values corresponding to the single values they simulate. The measurement is a purely data-driven process [LINDSAY & NORMAN, 1977].

Resource-limited cognitive observation processes are goal-driven interpretation processes and do not generate values by functional simulation; they interpret sensory data by collecting evidence for a judgment. The more evidence they collect the finer (preciser) their judgment. In case of determining the state of well-being, a cognitive observation process initially (without any evidence) would judge "I don't know" which means all states of well-being are considered possible. The more information the observer gathers during the observation process, the more he may be able to refine his answer by restricting the range of possibilities down to a level at which no helpful information can be gathered which would modify or refine the judgment [3].

The difference in the type of outcome is a result of the different direction of information processing: the data-driven process synthesizes a result from basic entities; the goal-driven process decomposes an undifferentiated whole into more specific, but still coarse components. In a sense, the final outcome of the observation process is atomic, i.e., it cannot be refined -- at least not by this particular observer in the particular situation. The precision of this observation should not determine the resolution of the representing scale, however, since other observers and/or other situations may allow for a finer judgment. The observation may be said to correspond to a 'granule' rather than to a point on a fine scale [ZADEH, 1979a].

Since the interpretation process does not yield a single point value but a range of possible values, it is not meaningful to speak of a judgment error in the sense of a measurement error because of the incompleteness of the utilized information. Data-driven measurements per se may be precise but erroneous while goal-driven judgments may be correct despite (or: due to) their inherent imprecision. They only become incorrect if the observed feature value is outside the scope of values represented by the descriptor.

To round off the comparison with a data-driven measuring process, the cognitive judgment process outlined above would correspond to a change of shape of the needle of the measuring device: initially the needle would cover the entire range of the scale of the meter ("don't know the voltage"). During the observation process, the needle would become narrower, restricting the possibilities of the actual voltage at the meter. This cannot happen in analogue simulation processes since certain information is required to give a meaningful reading and additional information is not helpful for refining the measurement. The effect achieved by narrowing the needle can be achieved by widening the scale, of course. In practice, voltage measuring processes are frequently supervised by a cognitive process which selects the scale: if we do not know the order of magnitude of the voltage to be measured, we will first select the largest meter range to obtain an approximate reading. Then we will restrict the range and expand the scale to obtain a more precise reading.

2.3 Summary

In summary, a physical measurement obtained by an analogue simulation process yields a point value which may be interpreted as an approximation to some actual value, while a goal-driven cognitive interpretation process yields a range of possible point values. The precision of this interpretation is limited by the resources available to the judgment process. In view of this fact it seems absurd to force imprecise observations into precise representations and in doing so, adding errors to the results. It appears desirable to represent observations at the level of precision that has been obtained by the underlying observation process and to represent them error-free.

3. COGNITIVE ASPECTS OF OBSERVATIONS

If we want to represent observations of human observers, we should consider the cognitive process which leads from the perception to the description by which the observation is communicated. We can view the process of observing, describing, and interpreting a phenomenon as a chain of transformations on cognitive representations of the observed phenomenon.

3.1 Chain of cognitive transformations

```
          object
             |
             v
          percept
             |
             v
   mental representation
             |
             v
    verbal description
             |
             v
   formal representation
             |
             v
       interpretation
```

Fig. 1

We call the observable phenomenon the "object". The object is an entity whose feature values (e.g. color, size, shape) can be viewed as being precise. In other words, there is no imprecision in the objects themselves [RUSSELL, 1923]. Imprecision and fuzziness enters when the object is perceived or represented.

If we assume a goal-driven (interpretative) rather than a data-driven (generative) feature transformation process, computational effort grows with the number of possible outcomes. If the possible outcomes were densly distributed point values, the effort would be enormous. To be able to represent an object with reasonable effort using limited resources, the information must be reduced. It will not be possible to recover the features completely from their description alone. However, if the description serves to select an object from a given context (i.e., the possible outcomes are not densly distributed), 'good' feature descriptors need not represent the object features as precisely as possible, they only need to be able to discriminate between feature values that exist in the given context. The context then provides the additional information for object identification.

3.2 Consequences for the representation

The first transformation occurs in the perception process: due to limited resolution of any perception system only a limited number of feature values can be distinguished. Thus, a perceived object feature cannot be adequately represented by a point on a high-resolution feature scale but rather by an interval which takes into account the granularity of the observation [ZADEH, 1979a].

Limited resolution also implies that the "observation granules", i.e. the intervals which represent the observations, cannot have sharp boundaries. Therefore, the observation granules should be represented by fuzzy rather than by crisp intervals. To simplify the specification of such intervals, we may define fuzzy categories for the classification of the observations.

As a consequence of the granularity -- which is inherent in any observation of phenomena in continuous feature spaces -- it is impossible to reliably classify arbitrary observations into single categories, whether the categories are crisp or fuzzy. Observation granules may overlap the boundary of a category. For this reason, their representation must allow for simultaneous assignment of several neighboring categories if all object feature values which are consistent with the observation are to be accounted for.

If we use crisp categories, the feature resolution cannot exceed half the resolution of the category itself (compare sampling theorem). If we use fuzzy categories, however, we can regain precision by a more differentiated assignment of categories. For example, we may be able to indicate whether a given category is

1. definitely applicable,

2. definitely not applicable, or

3. neither definitely applicable nor definitely inapplicable.

In this way, the position of the observation granule on the feature scale can be recovered more fully. Fig. 2 depicts the classification of an observation granule into crisp and into fuzzy categories.

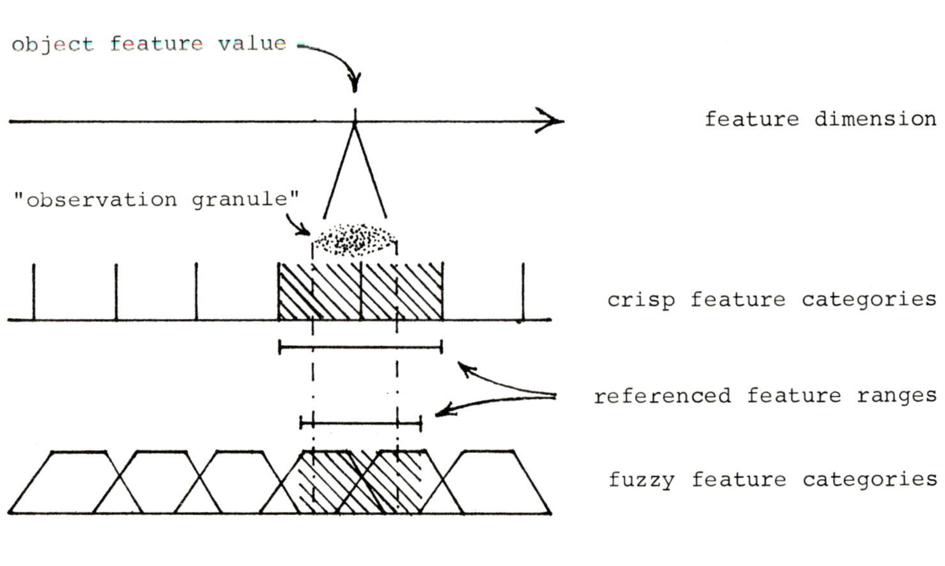

Fig. 2

3.3 Transformations in natural systems

We return to Fig.1 which shows the description generation process as a chain of transformations on information about object features. The first transformation shown (from "object" to "percept") corresponds to the segmentation of input information for the perception system, e.g. into visual or auditory channels. This transformation has been studied anatomically and neurophysiologically for various senses in various animals and a great deal is known about its properties [e.g. LETTVIN et al., 1959].

The second transformation (from "percept" to "mental description") corresponds to the mental organization of this information in memory. Presently, this transformation is the subject of much speculation [e.g. MINSKY, 1980], but very little is actually known.

The third transformation (from "mental description" to "verbal description") is of particular interest in this paper. Since we do not know the structure of the mental description, we cannot evaluate this transformation directly. However, we can study some of its properties by analyzing the correspondence between different descriptions of features of the observed object. In particular, we can examine the consistency between various verbal descriptions of the same features. The degree of inconsistency between those descriptions gives us an indication of the distortion introduced into the information during the cognitive perception process. The verbalizations which introduce the least amount of distortion are suited best to recover the observed object feature.

4. COMPARISON OF THREE REPRESENTATION SCHEMES

4.1 Goal

To illustrate different degrees of distortions which we may get by different representation schemes, we describe a simple empirical experiment which will be reported in detail elsewhere. In this experiment we compared three cognitively processed description types with feature measurements, namely of the height of persons [4]. The experiment consisted of three independent parts. 23 medical students were asked to judge the height of their colleagues by various methods. The "objects" of observation were asked in non-systematic order to present themselves in front of the observers (the remaining 22 students). The observers noted their judgment of the height on a prepared sheet containing the names of the "objects".

4.2 Experiment

PART 1: The observers were asked to estimate the height of the objects in centimeters.

PART 2: The observers were asked to indicate four values (in centimeters) to express their judgment:

1. the minimum height value which they considered possible as an estimate of the actual value;

2. a pair of two height values to specify a range in which they expected the actual height value to be;

3. the maximum height value which they considered possible as an estimate of the actual value.

PART 3: The observers were asked to select from an ordered vocabulary of seven terms (very small, small, rather small, medium, rather tall, tall, very tall), all those terms which described appropriately the actual height of the "objects". In case they selected several terms they could indicate preferences of some terms over others.

After completion of these judgments, the height of the objects was measured (in centimeters) conventionally.

4.3 Results

In part 1 of the experiment, the maximum mis-judgments of the observers ranged between 8 and 13 centimeters. The mis-judgments were non-systematic, i.e., all observers sometimes overestimated and sometimes underestimated the actual height in a given vicinity of height values.

Part 2 of the experiment did not yield better results. Most observers apparently did not have a good feeling for the accuracy and precision of their own centimeter judgments. Frequently, the observers overestimated their ability by indicating too narrow possibility ranges for the height value. In many instances, the measured height value fell into the ranges which were considered entirely impossible by the observers.

Part 3 of the experiment avoided the problem of erroneous label assignment by letting the labels denote just what the observer used it for. But surprisingly, the ranges of referenced height values rarely became larger than for the centimeter labels and frequently the specificity was even higher. In addition, by multiple assignment of labels with overlapping reference ranges the specificity of a description could be further increased.

The foregoing experiment shows that human judgment ability may be better than it appears from numerically expressed judgments. If we allow observations to be expressed in a more appropriate language, higher precision may be obtained. At first glance, this may appear contradictory, since a centimeter scale suggests higher resolution than a set of seven linguistic labels for a range of about 40 centimeters. However, by permitting simultaneous assignment of several labels we increase rather than decrease the potential of resolution. In addition, if these labels are applied in a more consistent manner than the centimeter values, they may resolve specific height values particularly well.

For interpretation of these results it may be helpful to consider again the information transformation model depicted in Fig. 1. The distortion of information introduced in the third transformation (mental description to verbal description) appears to depend on the type of verbalization that is used. Numerical verbalization seems to let rather precise observations appear imprecise, in many observers, while linguistic verbalizations seem to preserve more information from these observers.

We can explain this phenomenon by 'cognitive distance'. A linguistic representation of an observation may require a less complicated transformation than a numerical representation, and therefore less distortion may be introduced in the former than in the latter [PALMER, 1981]. We could say that the linguistic representation is "cognitively closer" to the mental description than the numerical representation. This theory is supported by the impression that the observers can make linguistic judgments more spontaneously than numerical judgments.

5. REPRESENTATION OF SOFT OBSERVATIONS

5.1 Desiderata

On the basis of the arguments brought forward in the foregoing sections we develop a representation system for "soft observations" which should have the following properties:

1. the resolution of the representation should be flexible to account for varying precision of individual observations;
2. the boundaries of the representing objects should not necessarily be sharp and should be allowed to overlap with other representing objects;
3. comparison between different levels of resolution of representation should be possible;
4. comparison between subjective observations of different observers should be possible;
5. the representation should have a small 'cognitive distance' to the observation;
6. it should be possible to construct representing objects empirically rather than from theoretical considerations.

5.2 Simplified possibility distributions

Feature descriptors contain, for the most part, possibilistic information [GAINES & KOHOUT, 1975; ZADEH, 1978]. Thus, a low-resolution descriptor allows for many possible interpretations while a high-resolution descriptor restricts the range of possible interpretations. Imprecise observations correspond to a wide range of possibilities while precise observations correspond to a comparatively narrow range of possibilities. To allow for unsharp boundaries, we express the observations by quadruples representing simplified fuzzy possibility distributions [FREKSA, 1981]. These possibility distributions are semantic representations of linguistic descriptors and can be graphically depicted as shown in Fig. 3:

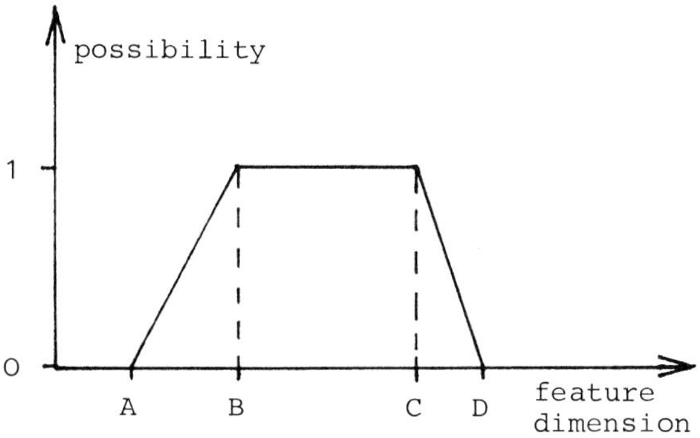

Fig. 3

The interpretation of the quadruple (A,B,C,D) is: it is entirely possible that the actual feature value observed is in the range [B,C]; it may be possible that the actual value is in the ranges [A,B] or [C,D], but more easily closer to [B,C] than further away; an actual value outside of [A,D] is incompatible with the observation. [B,C] is called "core", [A,B] and [C,D] are called "penumbra" of the possibility distribution.

5.3 Construction of semantic representations

Our demand for a 'cognitively close' representation of descriptors requires that the human observer determines the applicability of a descriptor according to his intuition-guided judgment. This is in contrast to the possibility of defining the meaning of descriptors by external criteria as is usually done in applications of fuzzy sets [ZADEH, 1970].

A consequence of this demand is that semantic representation of descriptors will be subjective; each observer may choose his own ranges of applicability of a descriptor. At first glance, this may appear disadvantageous. However, as the experiment above suggests, an external definition would only serve to introduce errors into the observation. Therefore the apparent simplifications for comparing observations would be paid for by loss in informativity. For this reason we prefer subjective semantic representations which necessitate semantic translations for inter-observer comparisons. Such translations are not very difficult to perform with the representation scheme we have chosen.

The construction of a repertoire of semantic representations for linguistic descriptors is done in the following way:

1. the observer selects a set of linguistic labels which allows for referencing all possible values of the feature dimension to be described;

2. the repertoire of linguistic labels is arranged linearily or hierarchically in accordance with their relative meaning in the given feature dimensions;

3. a set of examples containing a representative variety of feature values in the given feature dimension is presented to the observer. The observer marks all linguistic labels which definitely apply to the example feature value with "yes" and the labels which definitely do not apply with "no". The labels which have not been marked may be applicable, but to a lesser extent than the ones marked "yes";

4. from the data thus obtained we construct simplified possibility distributions by arranging the example objects according to their feature values (using the same criterion to which the linguistic labels had been arranged). These values form the domain for the assignment of possibility values;

5. finally, we assign to a given label the possibility value "yes" to the range of examples in which the given label was marked "yes" for all examples and the possibility value "yes" to the ranges in which the given label was marked "no" for all examples. The break-off points between the regions with possibility value "no" and "yes" are connected by some continuous, strongly monotonic function to indicate that the possibility of label assignment increases the closer one gets to the region with possibility assignment "yes".

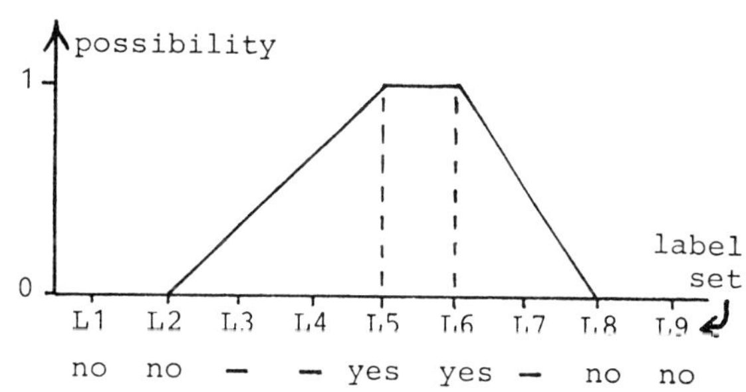

Fig. 4

6. CONCLUSIONS

We have described some characteristics of human judgments, investigated their causes, and proposed a method for representing judgments such that we can take advantage of these characteristics. In this last section we will discuss applications of the system and extensions being planned. Finally we will make a short comparison with related approaches.

6.1 Applications

The meaning representation system described appears useful for a variety of applications. First, it is a method for representing qualitative information and may aid in developing a semantic theory of descriptors as well as a theory of acquisition of imprecise concepts. Second, it is a tool for representing complex data which can be characterized best by humans.

At present, we use the approach for representing psychological judgments in clinical diagnosis. The method is suitable for semantic interpretation of subjective judgments both by graphical methods and by an interactive computer program. The semantic interpretation leads to an objectivization of descriptions and may be useful for person - machine communication as well as for person - person communication.

6.2 Interactive meaning adaptation

In an associated project [AGUILAR-MARTIN & LOPEZ DE MANTARAS, 1982; FREKSA & LOPEZ DE MANTARAS, 1982] learning algorithms for interactive meaning adaptation of linguistic descriptors by means of examples are being developed. In conjunction with a classification program, these algorithms will be helpful for custom tailoring individual descriptor languages for specific context situations. With the aid of these algorithms it will be no longer necessary that different observers use the same vocabulary for their descriptions. The denotation of the different descriptor labels is determined by the algorithms during a learning phase.

6.3 Comparison with other approaches

The representation scheme presented combines advantageous features of a variety of scaling and representation methods [LINDSAY & NORMAN, 1977]:

- ease of label association of a nominal scale;
- ease of comparison of an ordinal scale;
- meaning consistency of absolute scale;
- non-numerical scaling of direct scale;
- intuitiveness of cross-modality matching;
- naturalness of natural language approach.

From a methodological point of view, fuzzy classification of perceptually processed information is preferable over crisp classification. Conventional fuzzy set approaches use a priori definitions of fuzzy sets which apply universally for all observers. The advantage of our approach is increased consistency due to subjectiveness and small cognitive distance of the representation.

ACKNOWLEDGMENT

This research is supported by a fellowship of the Fritz Thyssen Foundation. I wish to thank Susana Berestovoy, Andy Clarke, Heiner Ellgring, Erwin Hansert, and Hartmut Schulz for reading the manuscript and offering helpful criticism. I also wish to acknowledge stimulating discussions with Gerhard Dirlich and Ramon Lopez de Mantaras on the issues discussed in this paper.

NOTES

[1] We use the term 'precision' as a measure of relative specificity: a descriptor is called '<u>precise</u>' if it has only one denotation in the given context, and '<u>imprecise</u>' if it allows for a variety of interpretations.

A descriptor is called '<u>fuzzy</u>' if its applicability varies gradually with respect to a variation of the reference feature and '<u>crisp</u>' if it is either fully applicable or fully inapplicable.

'<u>Variable feature resolution</u>' refers to flexibility in the reference range of a feature descriptor: depending on the particular situation context, the same linguistic descriptor may be taken to refer to a more specific range of feature values.

For more details, see FREKSA (1981).

[2] We use the term '<u>descriptor</u>' if we refer to a single feature dimension and the term '<u>description</u>' if we refer to a general feature space.

[3] This is an idealized judgment process in which no premature conclusion is drawn.

[4] Height was chosen 1) since it can easily be measured, 2) since most people have some experience in judging height, and 3) since height has served as standard example in fuzzy set theory [e.g. ZADEH, 1978; BALDWIN, 1979] and has been used in other psychological studies [e.g. HERSH & CARAMAZZA, 1976].

REFERENCES

AGUILAR-MARTIN, J., LOPEZ DE MANTARAS, R., 1982. The process of classification and learning the meaning of linguistic descriptors of concepts. This volume.

BALDWIN, J.F., 1979. A new approach to approximate reasoning using a fuzzy logic. Fuzzy Sets and Systems 2, 309-325.

COLLINS, A., WARNOCK, E.H., AIELLO, N., MILLER, M.L., 1975. Reasoning from incomplete knowledge. In: Bobrow, D.G. & Collins, A., Representation and understanding, Academic Press, New York.

FREKSA, C., 1981. Linguistic pattern characterization and analysis. Ph.D. thesis, University of California, Berkeley.

FREKSA, C., LOPEZ DE MANTARAS, R., 1982. An adaptive computer system for linguistic categorization of "soft" observations in expert systems and in the social sciences. 2nd World Conf. on Math. at the Service of Man, Las Palmas.

GAINES, B.R., KOHOUT, L.J., 1975. Possible automata. Proc. Int. Symp. Multiple-Valued Logic, 183-196.

GULLIKSEN, H., MESSICK, S., 1960. Psychological scaling. Wiley, New York.

HERSH, H.M., CARAMAZZA, A., 1976. A fuzzy set approach to modifiers and vagueness in natural language. J. Exp. Psych. Gen. 105, 3, 254-276.

LETTVIN, P.H., MATURANA, H.R., MC CULLOCH, W.S., PITTS, W.H., 1959. What the frog's eye tells the frog's brain. Proc. IRE, Nov., 1940-1951.

LINDSAY, P.H., NORMAN, D.A., 1977. Human information processing. Academic Press, New York.

LOPEZ DE MANTARAS, R., 1980. Learning the meaning of imprecise concepts by adaptation of their possibility distributions. Actes de table ronde du CNRS, Lyon.

MINSKY, M., 1980. K-Lines: a theory of memory. Cogn. Science 4, 117-133.

NILSSON, N.J., 1980. Principles of artificial intelligence. Tioga, Palo Alto.

NORMAN, D.A., RUMELHART, D.E., 1975. Explorations in cognition. Freeman, San Francisco.

NORMAN, D.A., BOBROW, D.G., 1975. On data-limited and resource-limited processes. Cogn. Psychology 7, 44-64.

PALMER, S.E., 1981. Transformational structure and perceptual organization. Proc. Third Annual Cognitive Science Conf. 41-49, Berkeley.

RUSSELL, B., 1923. Vagueness. Australasian J. Psych. & Phil. 1, 1, 84-92.

SKALA, H.J., 1978. On many-valued logics, fuzzy sets, fuzzy logics and their applications. Fuzzy Sets and Systems 1, 129-149.

ZADEH, L.A., 1970. Fuzzy languages and their relation to human and machine intelligence. Man and Computer Proc. int. Conf., 130-165, Bordeaux.

ZADEH, L.A., 1978. Fuzzy sets as a basis for a theory of possibility, Fuzzy Sets and Systems 1, 3-28.

ZADEH, L.A., 1979a. Fuzzy sets and information granularity. In: Gupta, M.M. et al., Advances in fuzzy set theory and applications. North-Holland.

ZADEH, L.A., 1979b. Possibility theory and soft data analysis. Memo No. UCB/ERL M79/66, University of California, Berkeley.

Approximate Reasoning in Decision Analysis
M.M. Gupta and E. Sanchez (eds.)

THE MULTISTAGE EVALUATION METHOD IN PSYCHOLOGICAL MEASUREMENT:

AN APPLICATION OF FUZZY SETS THEORY TO PSYCHOLOGY

Ma Mou-chao
Institute of Psychology
Academia Sinica
Beijing
People's Republic of China

Cao Zhi-qiang
Institute of Automation
Academia Sinica
Beijing
People's Republic of China

ABSTRACT

The paper presents a new method of psychological measurement, which is a development of classical rating scales, called the multistage evaluation method.

The method based on fuzzy sets provides a successful means for subject's preference and so on. Using the method the results of measurement, which are some fuzzy sets, provide more information and more perfectly represent psychological conditions than using classical methods e.g. rating cales. For rank-ordering the method not only obtains the same results as using classical methods, but also may obtain other ones when there are several criteria of judgement of rank-ordering.

I. INTRODUCTION

The development of modern psychology reveals more and more that it is a strict, systematic, quantitative science (4). Therefore, how to measure human mind and behavior scientifically is a fundamental important problem.

Up to the present, psychological measurement has already constructed several kinds of scaling. Rating scale is a frequently used one. Its essential is to give several ranks or categories permuted in order; the experimentor asks the subject to choose one of the ranks adequately according to his own view or attitude. In mathematical terms, giving a finite total order set e.g. very satisfactory (A), satisfactory (B), medium (C), unsatisfactory(D), very unsatisfactory (E), people need to give a certain element in these sets, in correspondence with the object measured to express their own degrees of satisfaction. The theoretical design of this method is established on the basis of 2-values logic. For example, a function

$$P(\lambda)=\begin{matrix}1 & \lambda=B \\ 0 & \lambda=A.\ C.\ D.\ E.\end{matrix}$$

expresses that the object P belongs to the rank of "satisfactory" evaluated by the subject. In mathematics $P(\lambda)$ is the characteristic function of the subset (B) of the set (A. B. C. D. E.).

However, when the subject evaluates, he doesn't express his preference very confidently and certainly, he may prefer to say: "inclined to medium or may also evaluate as satisfactory". That is to say, a characteristic function based on multi-value logic should be taken instead of the corresponding function based on (2-values) logic.

In 1965, L. A. Zadeh for the first time established the theory of fuzzy sets (7) affording effective mathematic means for quantitative description of all kinds of fuzzy phenomena. Therefore, new explosion of psychological measurement and psychological research may be inspired from it.

How to determine membership function of fuzzy sets? This is one of the most fundamental problems of fuzzy mathematics. M. Kochen asserted that frequency of reactions used as membership function may be adopted (5). One of the authors of this study has also made similar attempts (1) (2). However, may a more direct method for acquiring membership function be found? If it may be found, then, what advantages will be taken from it. The aim of our study is to solve these problems.

II. MULTISTAGE EVALUATION FUZZY SETS METHOD

Give some categories or evaluated ranks of psychological measurement, e.g. in terms of preference, they may be appointedas strong preference, preference, medium, no preference, strong no preference. Appropriate confidence is used to express degrees of reaction. This method requires the subject to evaluate the object with respect to the whole ranks, not only to indicate which is the derived rank.

Steps of multistage evaluation

First, select from the whole ranks given, in order to determine which is the rank mostly inclined to be evaluated, at the same time give score (0 to 10) of appropriate high confidence. Second, make paired evaluations at 2 ranks of adjacent peak values and give confidence scores. Last, evaluate residual ranks. For example:

Assume that the reaction of some subject to the object given belongs to the medium rank relatively confidently. Next, it seems somewhat preferred with reference to preference and not preference relatively (needless to say, actually, there is only slight difference between the selection of strong preference and strong no preference, the subject often does not make any report with certainty).

For this kind of psychological evaluation, the following scores may be given generally for demonstration:

rank of prefer.	strong prefer.	prefer.	medium	no prefer.	strong no prefer.
scores of confi.	4	6	8	3	1

Divide scores of confidence by constant 10, it will be transformed to a membership function of closed interval.

This method has the following natures or rules that must be noted:

1. When it is most certain that the object is ascribed to some rank, the score of confidence of this rank is the highest. The score of perfect ascription is 10. The score of ascription without any confidence (or completely not belong to) is 0. The scores of confidence between these two extremes are taken between 0 and 10.

2. The more the departure from the rank of the highest confidence, the lower the score. When the score 10 is obtained, the score 0 must appear at the same time.

3. When the preferences are certain, the differences among the scores of different ranks should be relatively large; for the same reason, when it is difficult to appraise the degree of preference, the differences among the ranks should be very small. When it is very difficult to ascribe to any rank, the score of all ranks is 5 (i. e. half certain, half uncertain).

4. The appearance of double peaks is not admitted, that is, the function is of single peak (that the adjacent ranks have the same peak value, is an exception).

Therefore, in order to rank effectively, it is possible that evaluation is divided into two steps: first to make qualitative judgment, that is, to select one from several categories, such as that of rating scale. Then the category obtained is appointed some score from the following: complete disagreement corresponding to score 0; strong disagreement--1 to 2; disagreement--3 to 4; neither disagreement nor agreement--5; agreement--6 to 7; strong agreement--8 to 9; complete agreement--10.

III. THE APPLICATION OF MULTISTAGE EVALUATION METHOD

The application of this method has already obtained the capability of deeply describing human multidimensional decision process. Here, another application is stated.

In order to characterize the psychological change of elevating price of goods on people, this study selected 3 cups of different quantities specially, elevated the prices according to the same ratio, investigated degree of satisfaction as the basis of the function of elevation of prices. This experiment asked subjects to determine themselves first, what are the fairest prices of the 3 cups. Then, in elevating 10%, 20%, 30%, and 40% price conditions, evaluate the 5 ranks of satisfaction by multistage method. 57 adults of both sexes participated. The cultural level of most of them was that of college students and above. The results revealed the average fair prices of the 3 cups were 0.44$, 0.82$ and 1.20$ individually. Let's name them as more expensive; moderate price and cheaper.

Experimental data were treated with fuzzy sets statistics and probability statistics respectively. Fuzzy statistics are based on fuzzy subsets obtained from the result of each subject by multistage evaluation.

Therefore, the statistical result of the whole sample must be a fuzzy subset. It consists of the average confidence of different ranks of the total samples. To speak concretely, it is a function from sets (A', B', C', D', E')* to sets (0, 1, 2, ..., 10). But probability statistics collect only the peak value of confidence for fuzzy subsets of each subject (corresponds to the positive value of 2 values logic). As a result, the statistical data could only be the probability distribution of the peak value on different ranks. There, the largest probability rank is taken as characteristic value.

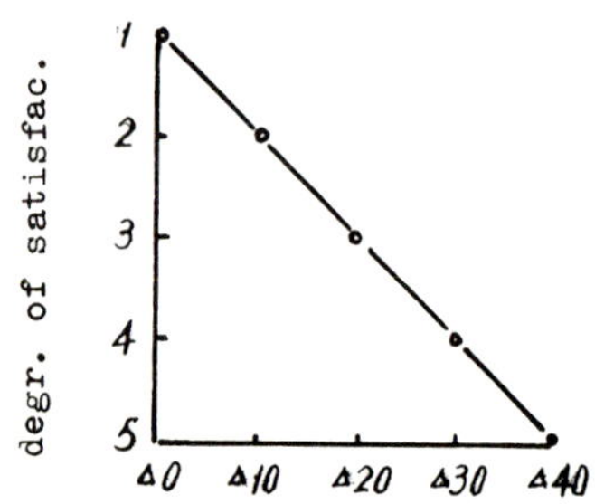

Fig. 1 Degree of satisfaction as a function of elevation of price (probability statistics)

Fig. 1 is the result of the probability statistics. In the fig. "0" represents corresponding peak value of 3 cups. It clearly indicated that human mind changed from very satisfied to very unsatisfied gradually with the elevation of price.

Fig. 2 describes a function from sets (A', B', C', D', E') to sets (0, 1,..., 10). It is the fuzzy statistics results.

It indicated that psychological process with elevation of price may be divided into stages as follows:

Linearly reduced on satisfactory-unsatisfactory scales⟶tilted to the section of satisfactory⟶normal⟶tilted to the section of unsatisfactory⟶linearly increased.

Fig. 3 minutely described the difference of psychological changes elicited by more expensive, moderate price and cheaper, with the elevation of price. These differences may

* (A', B', C', D', E') represents the sets of different degrees of satisfaction.

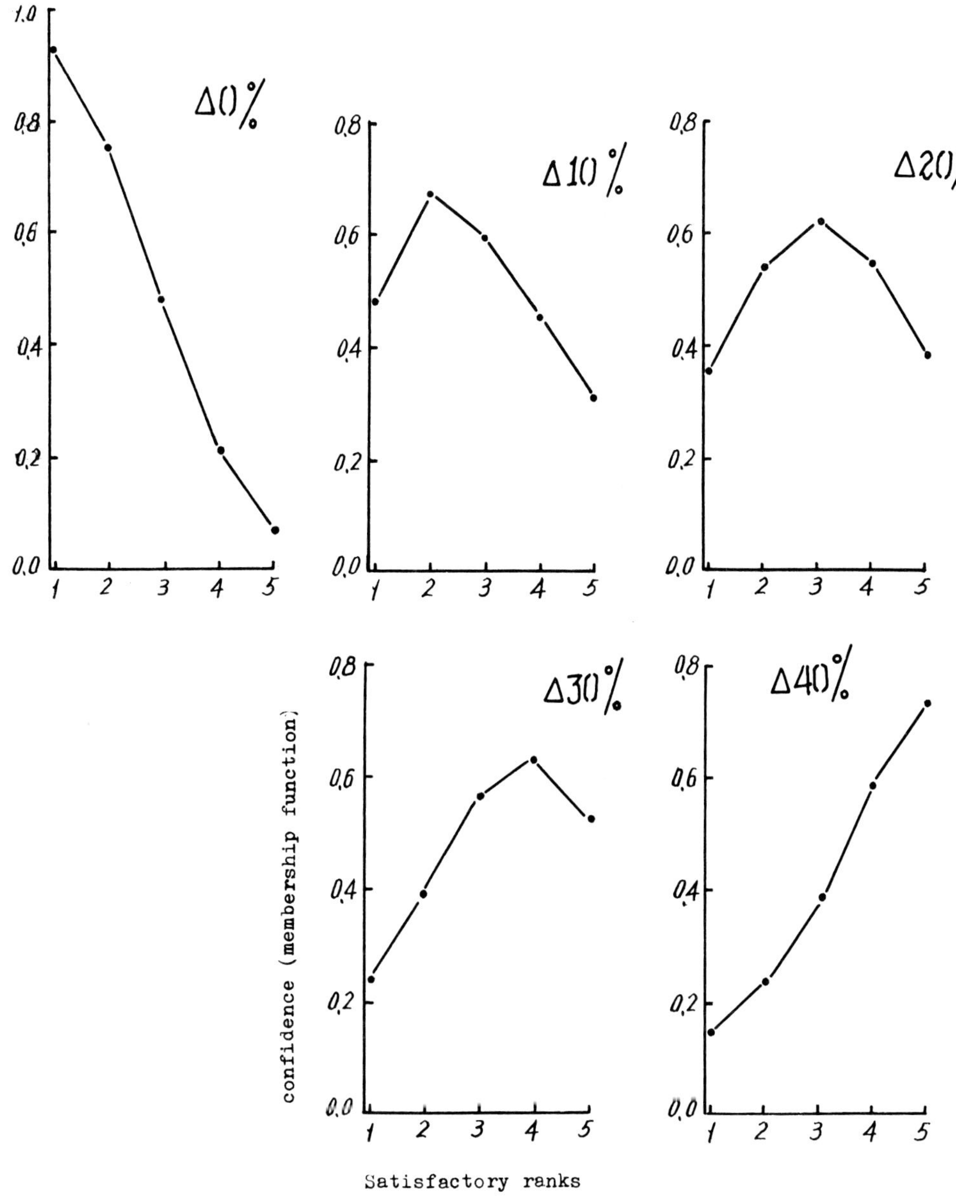

Fig. 2 Psychological changes on various elevating levels of price

be generalized as : within the ranks of "very satisfactory" and "satisfactory", the confidence level of cup of cheaper was higher than that of cup of more expensive; whereas within the ranks of "unsatisfactory" and "strong unsatisfactory" confidence level of more expensive was higher than that of cheaper.

To sum up, fuzzy statistics is (obviously) better than probability statistics. Depending upon the total information obtained, it can minutely reflect the total aspects of psychological changes. On the other hand, probability statistics can obtain only the peak values, excluding much other information, as a result, the description is rather coarse.

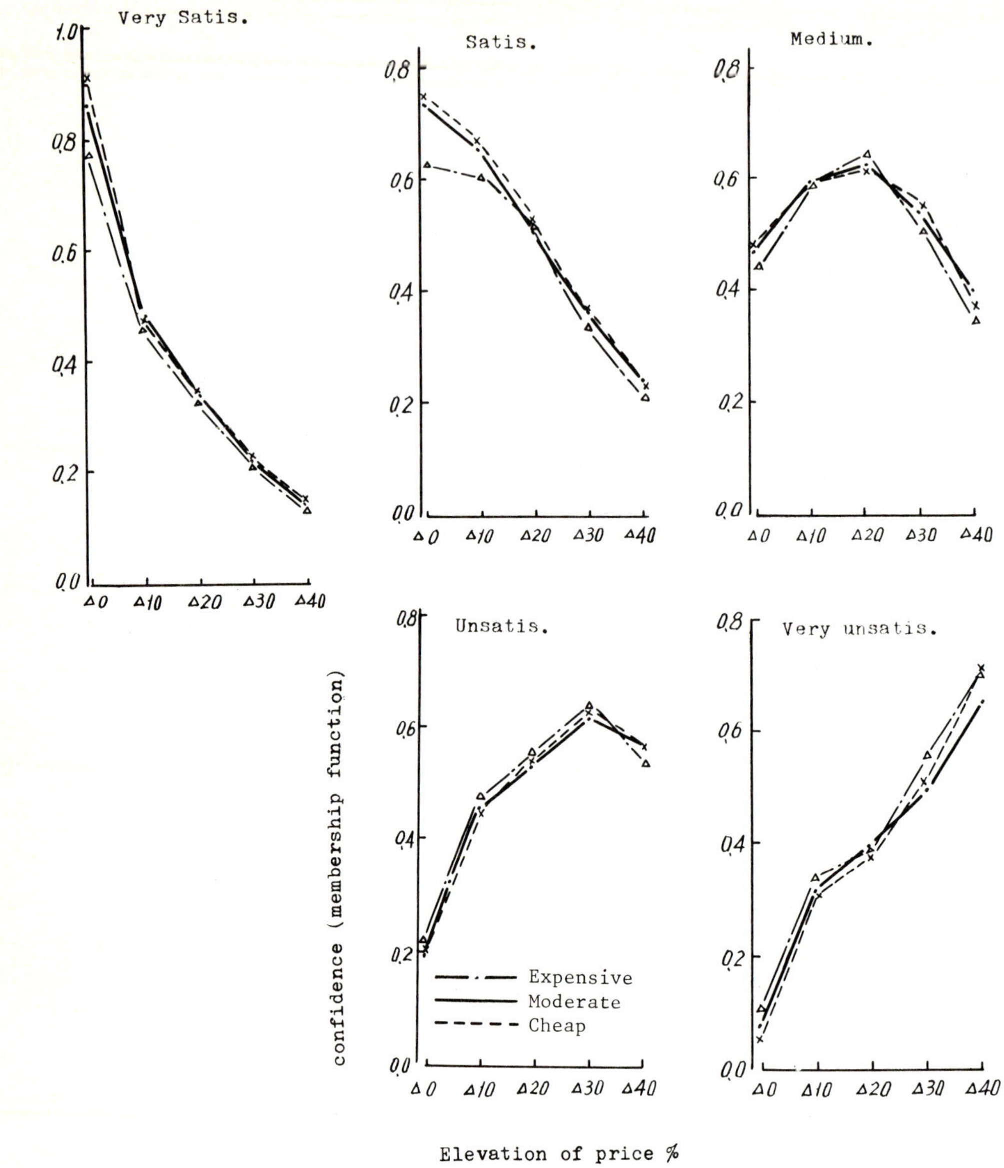

Fig. 3 3 cups corresponding functions for different satisfactory ranks

IV. RANKING ORDER BY MULTISTAGE EVALUATION METHOD

In psychological measurement of preferences, the subject is asked to rank objects from the highest to the lowest in preference. Now, let's introduce how to make rank order in a set of objects on the basis of their repective fuzzy sets.

First, the cut sets concept of fuzzy subsets is necessarily introduced. Let $\underset{\sim}{P}(u)$ represent a fuzzy sets.

P_λ represents the λ-cut sets of $\underset{\sim}{P}(u)$.

$$P_\lambda = \{u : u \in U,\ \underset{\sim}{P}(u) \geq \lambda\}$$

It is classical set, reflecting all elements in these fuzzy sets, which are greater in grades of membership than λ. Therefore, cut sets of various levels, P_λ are usually used to compare the difference of 2 fuzzy sets.

For the need of ranking, this study selected 5 playing balls as experimental objects. Using multistage evaluation method stated before, measurement of preferences of them were carried out respectively. Subjects were 78 4th grade middle school students. 5 curves illustratein Fig. 4, the fuzzy sets of pre-

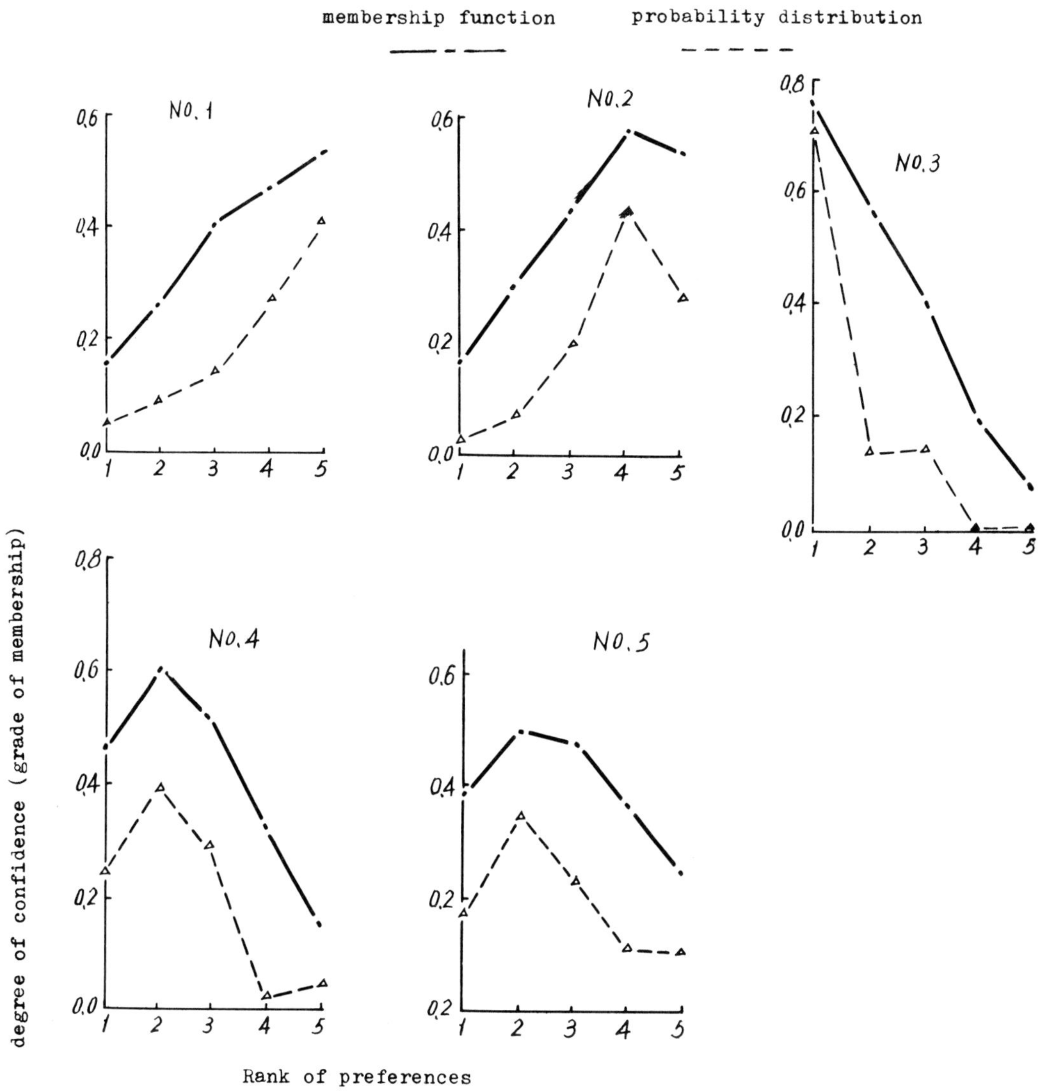

Fig. 4 Fuzzy sets of preferences of 5 different balls evaluated

ference of balls obtained from this experiment. Taking cut sets -λ as peak values of various curves, obviously the ranking order of balls No. 1, 2, 3 was easy (the order was 5, 4, 1). But balls NO. 4 and 5, can not be ranked by this kind of cutting peak value, requiring to cut more values further. For example, from the highest grade of membership of the two sets, get a value every subtraction of 0.10, up to 0.10. Thus, each fuzzy set has a string of classical sets. From the comparson of various strings of classical sets, it is not difficult to make clear the differences among various fuzzy sets.

According to what we did above, fuzzy sets of preference of the balls No. 4 and No. 5 were cut time after time, the result is shown in table 1.

The number of ranks in the table were the ranks of preference involved in the curve at the level of particular λ-cut sets. The scores were calculated as follows: Compare 2 cut sets of the same level, if there is an element included only in one cut sets but not in the other and it preceded the identical element, its score is positive 1; otherwise the score is written as negative 1. If there are many different elements, then their scores should be written separately. Thereafter, add all such elements together, then it is the respective score on this level. Last, sum up the scores of different λ-cut sets, the larger the score, the prior the rank.

In order to compare with the traditional rank order, this study also made an experiment on paired comparison and constructed a

Table 1 Order relation based on cut sets conception

λ =	0.6		0.5		0.4		0.3		0.2		0.1		Σ	order
	Pλ	score	Pλ	score	Pλ	score	Pλ	score	Pλ	score	Pλ	score		
No. ball.4	2	+1	2,3	−1	1,2,3	+1	1,2,3	+1	1,2,3,4	+1	1,2,3,4,5	0	+3	former
No. ball.5		−1	2	+1	2.3	−1	1,2,3,4	−1	1,2,3,4,5	−1	1,2,3,4,5	0	−3	latter

ratio scale by using the same subjects.

The paired comparison method adopted by this study is different from the traditional one. Subjects did not simply indicate which one of the pair is more preferred, but gave appropriate score of preference (0 to 10) to them respectively. Treatment of scores were made according to two ways: one of them, set forth by M. Shimura, solved relative function of multi-parameter on the basis of fuzzy sets.

$$f(x_j/T) = \left\{\min \frac{fx_1(x_j)}{fx_j(x_1)} \cdots \frac{fx_n(x_j)}{fx_j(x_n)}\right\}$$

$$T = [x_i] \in X \quad i = 1, 2, \ldots n$$

The order relation of the objects was ranked according to the least value.

Then obtain average probability of vaious balls, the larger the probability, the former the order. This is the traditional approach.

It is obvious that the order relations ranked by both approaches are rather similar.

Table 2. Order relation based on paired comparison

		ball No.1	No. 2	No.3	No.4	No.5
multiparamets relative function	min	1	0.82	0.40	0.64	0.63
	order	5	4	1	3	2
average probability	P	0.27	0.39	0.79	0.59	0.52
	order	5	4	1	2	3

The construction of ratio scales of this study, in fact, adopted the magnitude estimation method. The data directly obtained were the difference among given objects and referent objects in psychological quantity. Based on these differences, the order relations among objects were also easily acquired.

Table 3. Order relation based on ratio scales*

	No. ball	No.1	No.2	No.3	No.4	No.5
magnitude estimation	scores*	0.18	0.23	1.00	0.51	0.46
	order	5	4	1	2	3
probability	P(i/4)**	0.12	0.10	0.87	0.50	0.37
	order	4	5	1	2	3

The above tables clearly indicate that the order relations among objects obtained by the method of this study and the traditional method are similar. According to the calculation bu Spearman's correlation coefficients, the scores are above +0.9.

V. CONCLUSION

This study sets forth a multistage evaluation method in psychological measurement. It may establish membership function directly and is most suitable for psychological measurement of preference. When the order relation among objects needs to be made, taking appropriate cut sets (their peak values-cut sets, or several values-cut sets when it is necessary) only fuzzy sets can be changed to classical sets, then the order relation among objects can be also obtained as other traditional methods do.

We are greatly indebted to the following for their help: Pan-su, Zou Xian-geng, li Jia-zhi, He Bao-yuan, Cheng Su-you, Wang Pei-zhuang, Ye-xuan.

REFERENCES

1. 馬谋超、汪培庄“青年学生识别汉字的特征——同构异字的识别规则初探”心理学报 1981 第3期.
2. 馬谋超“心理模糊性的测量”心理学报 1981 第1期.
3. Ma Mou-chao, Cao Zhi-qiang "A kind of multi-dimensional decision making and its mathematical model", 1981, in Symposium of "Systems Methodology", Vol. 1, part three, section B, p.1036.
4. 居继宁“心理学及其应用”科技导报 No.2.1980 PP 72-73.
5. Kochen M. "Applications of fuzzy sets in psychology", in "Fuzzy sets and their applications to cognitive and decision processes", 1975, p.395-407.
6. Shimura M. "Fuzzy sets concept in rank-ordering objects", J. Mathe. anal. and appli., 43, 717-733, 1973.
7. Zadeh L. A. "Fuzzy sets", Information and Control, 8, 338-353, 1965.

* evaluation scores were mid-value normalized.

** The probability P(i/4) represents the ratio of the amount of persons who consider the 1st ball better than the 4th ball to total amount.

Approximate Reasoning in Decision Analysis
M.M. Gupta and E. Sanchez (eds.)

FUZZY SIMULATION MODEL OF CIVIL EVACUATION FROM LARGE-SCALE EARTHQUAKE-GENERATED FIRES

Fumio Hara

Department of Mechanical Engineering
Tokyo University of Science
1-3 Kagurazaka, Shinjuku-ku, Tokyo 162, Japan

This paper deals with a mathematical model of the evacuation flow dynamics of people fleeing from large-scale fires, using, principally, the continuity law of evacuating people and an empirical relation between walking velocity and the concentration of people. The most essential part of this model includes psychological effects described in a fuzzy mathematical manner for determining the evacuation flow direction. This paper illustrates the model's validity by comparing the location of people unsuccessful in fleeing in computer simulation with that of casualities cited in documents from the Kanto earthquake. The application of the model to a large, 4 km x 5 km area of Tokyo is also shown.

KEYWORDS: Fuzzy Simulation Model, Civil Evacuation, Fires, Earthquake, Network Flow, Psychological Potential, Model Validity, Application

1. Introduction

Large Japanese cities now, as ever, face such serious, earthquake-caused problems as large-scale devastation by fire and severe damage to buildings, houses, and other urban facilities like those generated by the great Kanto earthquake in Tokyo and its environs September 1, 1923. Japan's national and local governments worry about the impact of an earthquake of a magnitude of 8 or more on urban facilities, civilian life, and economic conditions. In the Kanto quake disaster, over half of residential Tokyo was devastated and about 130,000 people died in earthquake-caused fires. Recent developments in the scientific prediction of large-scale earthquakes have fueled research in assessing earthquake-generated damage to urban facilities and civilian life, and have also forced the Tokyo government to begin framing and implementing anti-disaster policies.

A paragraph translated from a report [1] on the great Kanto quake illustrates how destructive earthquake-caused fires can be:

> The great Kanto earthquake (magnitude 7.9) occurred at 11:58 am, September 1, 1923, causing severe destruction to buildings, houses, and other urban facilities. Some 79 large fires broke out simultaneously in Tokyo, lasting over two and a half days and devastating half of the city. Reports of the time describe the horrors which fleeing people faced.
>
> A fire breaking out in Higashi-daiku-cho moved north, then devastated Tomikawa-cho. About 3:30 pm, the fire surrounded the Sixth Fire Brigade station, closing in fire brigade members. Although suffering beyond description from fire-caused tornados, the firefighters forced themselves to resist the destructive flames. At 5:00 pm, the station was completely overwhelmed, hydrolant systems ceasing to work and cutting fire prevention power. Firefighters strove desperately to protect fleeing people, who ran terrified and screaming in the light of the huge, scarlet flames, and guided them toward safety in the direction of Takehashi and Mannenbashi bridges....

Large-scale fires may thus simultaneously occur during a large earthquake, surrounding fleeing people and forcing them to a point where they cannot be evacuated.

Since over 50 fires--all fortunately small--break out daily in Tokyo, it would be unrealistic to assume no fires would occur during a large earthquake. Large fires would presumably occur during any such earthquake, severely damaging urban facilities and endangering civilian life. Civil evacuation is thus one of the most important matters to be considered in avoiding such a disaster as the foregoing.

Two factors must be considered with regard to safe evacuation from large-scale fires. The first is an evacuationprogram providing suitable evacuation routes and evacuation goals, and the second is actual evacuation guidance of people to safe areas. The former requires much financing and time to provide sufficiently safe evacuation routes and goals. The latter requires careful consideration of the psychological condition of people fleeing in extremely chaotic situations, and of the establishment of evacuation guidelines.

One way to construct such guidelines is to derive essential information from documents about earthquake disasters. Another is to use computer simulation. If a reasonable mathematical model of civil evacuation from large-scale fires could be constructed, computer simulation could be a very powerful tool in deriving safe evacuation guidelines, since no experimental methodology exists at present for this problem.

This paper deals with a mathematical model of the evacuation flow dynamics of people fleeing from large-scale fires, using, principally, the continuity law of evacuating people and an empirical relation between walking velocity and the concentration of people. The most essential part of this model includes psychological effects for determining the evacuation flow direction at each edge of the route network. This paper illustrates the model's validity by comparing the location of people unsuccessful in fleeing in computer simulation with that of those described in documents from the Kanto earthquake. The application of the model to a large, 4 km x 5 km area of Tokyo is also shown.

2. Mathematical Formulation of the Flow of Evacuating People

2.1 Single Route Formulation

From the daily observation of people walking along urban streets, it can be assumed that the movement of evacuating people can be macroscopically treated as a "flow." When the continuity law of evacuating people is applied, the following equation is derived for a unidirectional flow,

$$b\frac{\partial \rho}{\partial t} + \frac{\partial (b\rho U)}{\partial x} = r \qquad (1)$$

where X : space coordinate
ρ : concentration of people
U : walking velocity
b : road width
r : inflow rate

Integrating eq. (1) with respect to X from X = i to X = 1 + i, the equation can be rewritten as

$$\frac{dX(i)}{dt} = b_i Y(i) - b_{i+1}Y(i+1) + Y_r(i) \qquad (2)$$

$$X(i) = (b_i + b_{i+1})\, l\, \rho_i/2$$

where X(i) is the number of people in route unit i, and Y(i) and Y(i + 1) are flow rates at interfaces i and i + 1. Yr(i) is the inflow rate at both sides of a route unit. Again, integrating eq. (2) with respect to time, the equation becomes

$$X(i,t+\Delta t) = X(i,t) + \{b_i Y(i,t) - b_{i+1}Y(i+1,t) + Y_r(i,t)\}\Delta t \qquad (3)$$

$$Y(i,t) = \rho_i(t)U(i,t)$$

In eq. (3), variables X(i) and $U(i)$ are unknown, and a clearer relation is needed. This is empirically determined from the actual flow of walking people. Fujita [2] presented an empirical formula,

$$U = 1.64 - 0.3\rho$$
$$\rho \leq \rho_{max} = 3.85 \qquad (4)$$

When this relation is applied to eq. (3), the flow velocity at interface i may be determined by the concentration of people in route unit i. Thus, a new parameter is introduced to describe flow retardation phenomena,

$$K_i(t) = \frac{b_{i+1}Y(i+1,t) + l\,(b_i + b_{i+1})(\rho_{max} - \rho_i(t))/2\Delta t}{b_i\tilde{Y}(i,t) + \tilde{Y}_r(i,t)} \qquad (5)$$

where $\sim$ is the number of people attempting to flee per unit time, based on Fujita's formulation [2]. The retardation coefficient takes a 1.0 value for the non-retarded flow; if it is less than 1.0, it can be assumed that walking velocity is reduced to Ki x U(i), where U(i) is evaluated from eq. (4). Equations (3), (4), and (5) are simultaneously solved from the route origin to the evacuation goal.

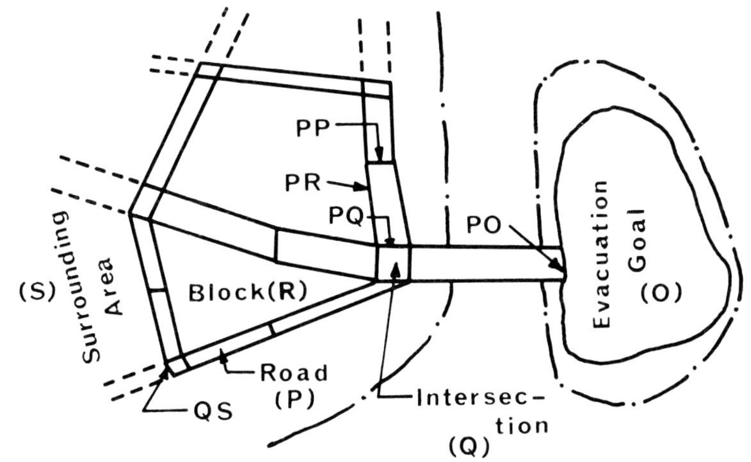

Fig. 1 Five urban elements for representing the evacuation flow network

2.2 Urban Network Formulation

2.2.1 Network Structure Description

The following five elements were considered (Fig. 1) for a mathematical description of the evacuation flow on an urban road network.

road (P)
intersection (Q)
residential block (R)
evacuation goal (O)
surrounding area (S)

Letting the number of people in each element be denoted by $X_k(i)$, k corresponds to P, Q, R, O, or S, and i to time. The following vector expresses the distribution of evacuating people on an urban road network.

$$X(i) = \begin{bmatrix} X_p \\ X_q \\ X_r \\ X_o \\ X_s \end{bmatrix} \qquad (6)$$

where subvector X_p means the numeric distribution of evacuating people at road units, subvector X_q at intersections, subvector X_r at residential blocks X_o at evacuation goals, and X_s at surrounding area units. The dynamic evacuation process can be described by vector X(i), which changes with time.

Referring to eq. (1) in Sec. 2.1, the inflow and outflow of people evacuating to or from an urban element occur at an interface between elements. Thus, the following interfaces should be taken into account--

road to road (P - P)
road to intersection (P - Q)
road to residential block (P - R)
intersection to sur. area (Q - S)

Letting the inflow or outflow rate at each interface be expressed by Yk(i), where k denotes the interface in question, and i time, the following vector describes the flow rate distribution on network interfaces as

$$Y(i) = \begin{bmatrix} Y_{pp} \\ Y_{pq} \\ Y_{pr} \\ Y_{po} \\ Y_{qs} \end{bmatrix} \qquad (7)$$

where subvector Y_{pp} is the flow rate vector at road-to-road interfaces, Y_{pq} at road-to-intersection interfaces, Y_{pr} at road-to-residential blocks, Y_{po} at road-to-evacuation goals, and Y_{qs} at intersection-to-surrounding-area interfaces.

Since the inflow or outflow of people occurs

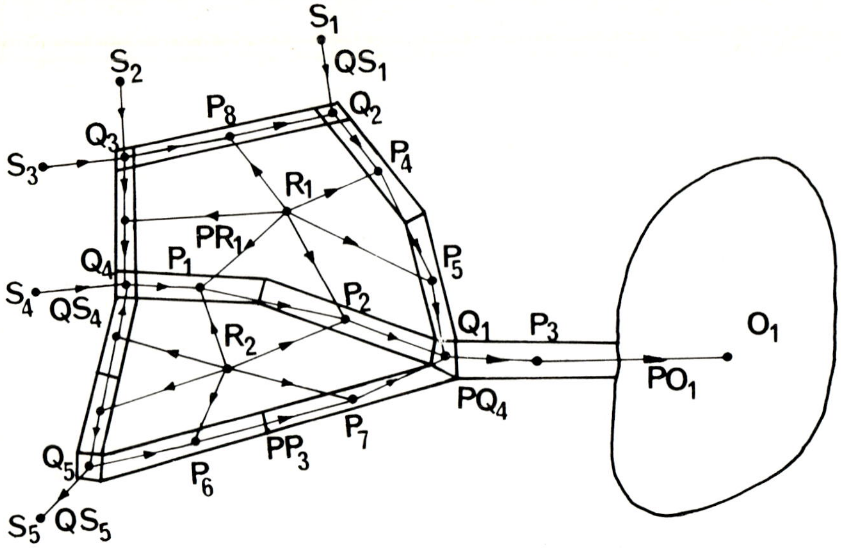

Fig. 2 An example of a directed graph showing evacuation flow directions

at urban element interfaces, a connection for the five kinds of urban elements above is needed to formulate evacuation flow dynamics in the urban network. To describe the connection, including flow direction, a directed graph is adopted, defining urban elements as vertex, and interfaces as edge, including flow direction. Figure 2 shows an example of the directed graph corresponding to Fig. 1. When the following is introduced,

$$\phi_{\nu/\mu} = \begin{cases} 1: & \text{inflow to vertex } \mu \text{ with edge } \nu \\ 0: & \text{no flow or connection} \\ -1: & \text{outflow from vertex } \mu \text{ with edge } \nu \text{ ,} \end{cases} \quad (8)$$

the evacuation flow structure can be expressed by a matrix whose elements are specified by function $\phi_{\nu/\mu}(i)$, where i corresponds to time.

$$\Phi(i) = \begin{bmatrix} \Phi_{pp/p} & \Phi_{pq/p} & \Phi_{pr/p} & \Phi_{po/p} & 0 \\ 0 & \Phi_{pq/q} & 0 & 0 & \Phi_{qs/q} \\ 0 & 0 & \Phi_{pr/r} & 0 & 0 \\ 0 & 0 & 0 & \Phi_{po/o} & 0 \\ 0 & 0 & 0 & 0 & \Phi_{qs/s} \end{bmatrix} \quad (9)$$

Figure 3 shows a concrete example of matrix Φ corresponding to Fig. 2. Here, open areas are where $\phi_{\nu/\mu} = 0$.

For the unit time interval, $\Phi(i)Y(i)$ expresses an incrementation of evacuating people in each urban network element; thus, at time i + 1, the vector $X(i + 1)$ becomes

$$X(i+1) = X(i) + \Phi(i)Y(i) \quad (10)$$

To expand eq. (3) to the urban network, matrix $\Phi(i)$ is divided into two, i.e., an inflow matrix and an outflow matrix,

$$\Phi(i) = \Phi^{(+)}(i) - \Phi^{(-)}(i) \quad (11)$$

where

$$\Phi^{(+)} = [\phi^{(+)}_{\nu/\mu}], \quad \Phi^{(-)} = [\phi^{(-)}_{\nu/\mu}]$$

$$\phi^{(+)}_{\nu/\mu} = \phi_{\nu/\mu}(1 + \phi_{\nu/\mu})/2 \quad (12)$$

$$\phi^{(-)}_{\nu/\mu} = \phi_{\nu/\mu}(1 + \phi_{\nu/\mu})/2$$

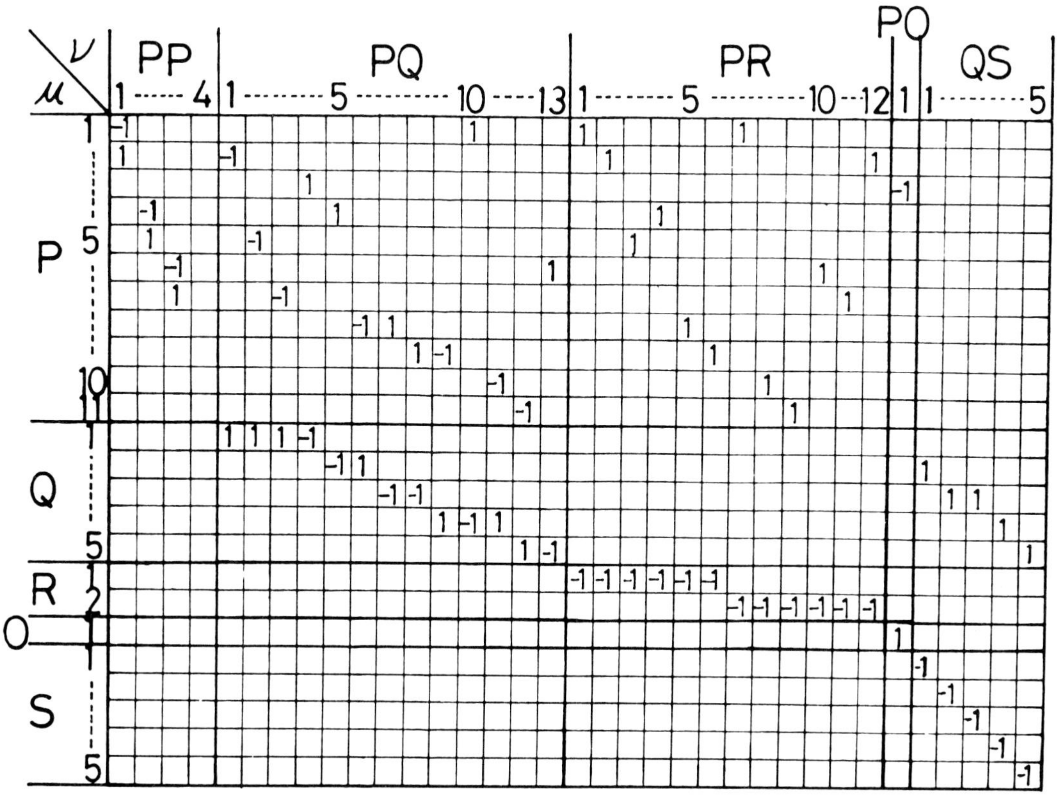

Fig. 3 Matrix expression of the directed graph in Fig. 2

The outflow matrix needs flow rate distribution ratio $\psi_{\nu\lambda(\mu)}$ where urban element μ is connected to several elements; the ratio will be determined in the following section. The outflow matrix is again redefined as

$$\Psi^{(-)} = [\ \psi_{\nu/\mu}\ ], \qquad (12)$$

where

$$\psi_{\nu/\mu} = \psi_{\nu}\, \Phi^{(-)}_{\nu/\mu}$$

$$\psi_{\nu} \in \{\ \psi_{\nu 1},\ \psi_{\nu 2},\ \cdots\ \psi_{\nu\lambda(\mu)}\ \}$$

For retardation phenomena in the evacuation flow, retardation coefficient matrix K, developed from eq. (5), is employed as

$$K = \begin{bmatrix} K_p & & & & \\ & K_q & & 0 & \\ & & K_r & & \\ & 0 & & K_o & \\ & & & & K_s \end{bmatrix} \qquad (13)$$

Effective element width matrix B is further introduced for describing the reduction of urban element width due to earthquake-generated damage or obstacles. The matrix is expressed as

$$B = \begin{bmatrix} B_{PP} & & & & \\ & B_{Pq} & & 0 & \\ & & B_{Pr} & & \\ & 0 & & B_{Po} & \\ & & & & B_{qs} \end{bmatrix} \quad (14)$$

$$\chi_{Po/o} = \mathcal{D}[\Phi^{(+)T}_{Po/o} K_o \Phi^{(+)}_{Po/o}]$$
$$\chi_{qs/s} = \mathcal{D}[\Phi^{(+)T}_{qs/s} K_s \Phi^{(+)}_{qs/s}]$$
$$\chi_{qs/q} = \mathcal{D}[\Phi^{(+)T}_{qs/q} K_q \Phi^{(+)}_{qs/q}]$$

According to Fujita's formulation, vector $Y(i)$ can be written as

$$Y(i) = \begin{bmatrix} B_{PP}\chi_{PP/P}\Psi^{(-)}_{PP/P}, & 0 & 0 & 0 \\ B_{Pq}\chi_{Pq/q}\Psi^{(-)}_{Pq/P}, & B_{Pq}\chi_{Pq/P}\Psi^{(-)}_{Pq/q}, & 0 & 0 \\ B_{Pr}\Psi^{(-)}_{Pr/P}, & 0 & B_{Pr}\chi_{Pr/P}\Psi^{(-)}_{Pr/r}, & 0 \\ B_{Po}\chi_{Po/o}\Psi^{(-)}_{Po/P}, & 0 & 0 & 0 \\ 0 & B_{qs}\chi_{qs/s}\Psi^{(-)}_{qs/q} & 0 & B_{qs}\chi_{qs/q}\Psi^{(-)}_{qs/s} \end{bmatrix} \quad (15)$$

$$\times \begin{bmatrix} U_P A_P^{-1} & 0 & 0 & 0 & 0 \\ 0 & U_q A_q^{-1} & 0 & 0 & 0 \\ 0 & 0 & U_r A_r^{-1} & 0 & 0 \\ 0 & 0 & 0 & 0 & U_s A_s^{-1} \end{bmatrix} \begin{bmatrix} X_P \\ X_q \\ X_r \\ X_o \\ X_s \end{bmatrix}$$

using vector $X(i)$. An operator can then be defined to make off-diagonal elements to be zero as $\mathcal{D}$, and thus $\chi_{PP/P}, \ldots\ldots\ldots$, are described as follows--

$$\chi_{PP/P} = \mathcal{D}[\Phi^{(+)T}_{PP/P} K_P \Phi^{(+)}_{PP/P}]$$
$$\chi_{Pq/q} = \mathcal{D}[\Phi^{(+)T}_{Pq/q} K_q \Phi^{(+)}_{Pq/q}]$$
$$\chi_{Pq/P} = \mathcal{D}[\Phi^{(+)T}_{Pq/P} K_P \Phi^{(+)}_{Pq/P}]$$
$$\chi_{Pr/P} = \mathcal{D}[\Phi^{(+)T}_{Pr/P} K_r \Phi^{(+)}_{Pr/P}]$$

$U.$ is a diagonal matrix composed of the evacuation flow velocity at each urban element corresponding to P, Q, R, or S. $A_.^{-1}$ is a diagonal matrix corresponding to the effective areas of each urban element. Note here that each element value in the matrix is determined by eq. (4), where the density of people is evaluated as $A_.^{-1}X.$ for each urban element.

2.2.2 Network Dissolution

Large-scale fires spreading in an urban area become a tremendous obstacle to evacuation. Thus, this situation is described as a means of dissolving the network connection at each edge a fire would have reached. Mathematically, this is the expression

$$\phi_{\nu/\mu}(j) = 0, \quad \text{if } (\nu, \mu) \in \mathcal{F} \quad (16)$$

where $\mathcal{F}$ means the burned area at time i.

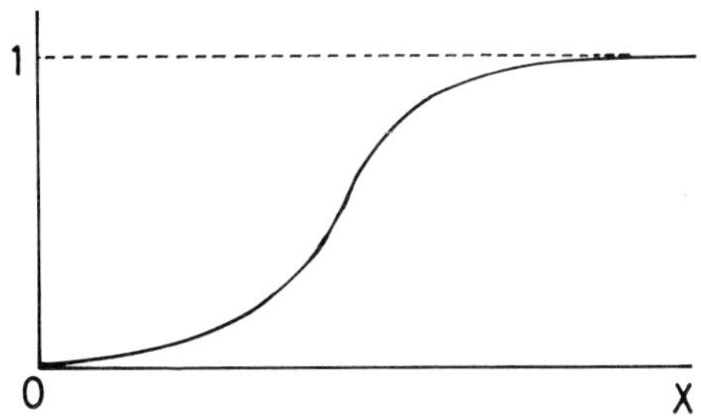

Fig. 4 Membership function expressing the degree of "distantness" from a fire front

Table 1 Fuzzy value of psychological potential determined by distances from fire and evacuation goal

y \ x	VC	C	M	F	VF
VC	M	M	S	S	VS
C	L	M	S	S	VS
M	VL	L	M	M	S
F	VL	VL	L	M	S
VF	VL	VL	VL	L	M

3. A Fuzzy Model for Determining Evacuation Flow Direction

3.1 Fuzzy Psychological Potential

In eq. 15, evacuation flow direction at each interface is assumed apriori without referring to the manner of determining flow direction. The flow direction might, it was assumed, be determined by psychological factors related to large-scale fires and evacuation goals, that is, fear of large-scale fires and desire to reach evacuation goals. These factors are necessarily fuzzy since they are completely related to or generated by the human visual sense or feeling with relation to distance. When two variables for expressing distances from a certain urban element to one for the closest and to the evacuation goal are introduced as x and y, the human feeling of being close to a fire or far from a goal is expressed by the membership function shown in Fig. 4. To represent the degree of psychological tension evacuation people would have at an urban element, only these two variables employed. If fuzzy values VC (very close), C (close), M (medium, F (far), or VF (very far) are assigned to x or y, psychological tension f. might be expressed by fuzzy values as in Table 1, where VL = very large, L = large, M = medium, S = small, and VS = very small.

For fuzzy values VL, L, M, S, or VS, an ordering was introduced as VL>L>M>S>VS. Thus, the evacuation flow direction can be determined at each interface as follows--

$$\phi_{\nu/\mu} = \begin{cases} 1 & : f_\mu < f_{j(\nu)} \\ 0 & : f_\mu = f_{j(\nu)} \\ -1 & : f_\mu > f_{j(\nu)} \end{cases} \qquad (17)$$

where $j(\nu)$ is an urban element connected with by edge ν .

3.2 Numerical Representation of Fuzzy Psychological Potential

Fuzzy psychological potential defined above can be represented by the mathematical formula

$$f_\mu(i) = \frac{x_\mu + C_1}{y_\mu + C_2} \qquad (18)$$

where C1 and C2 are constants. Figure 5 illustrates the function, where VL, L, M, S, VS correspond as in Table 1. Equation (18) means the evacuation flow direction is determined for the potential to decrease; thus $\phi_{\nu/\mu}$ is consistently defined as follows--

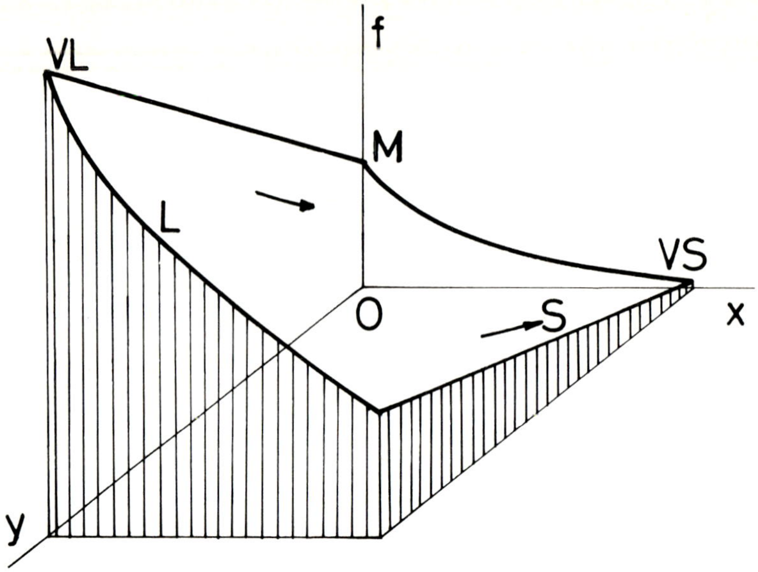

Fig. 5 Illustration of the psychological tension described by Eq. (18)

$$\phi_{\nu/\mu} = \begin{cases} 1 & : f_\mu - f_{j(\nu)} < 0 \\ 0 & : f_\mu - f_{j(\nu)} = 0 \\ -1 & : f_\mu - f_{j(\nu)} > 0 \end{cases} \tag{19}$$

which is a classical numerical expression corresponding to eq. (17). This psychological potential function is also used to determine outflow ratio ψ_ν in eq. (12) so that

$$\psi_\nu = \frac{f_{k(\nu)}}{\sum_{j=1}^{\nu_{\lambda(\mu)}} f_j} \tag{20}$$

$$k(\nu) = 1, 2, \cdots, \nu_{\lambda(\mu)}$$

where $k(\nu)$ is an element connected to μ, and ν_λ is the number of edges routed at element μ.

Evacuation in each residential block is initiated in the model by parameter l_f, i.e., people who are in a band area with width l_f from the fire front must flee to evacuation roads.

4. Computation Structure

4.1 Ordering of Computation

There is a certain computational ordering in eq. (1) since, in a general sense, downstream retardation coefficients are needed to obtain the number of people at each urban element. This is illustrative when concretely describing an equation for the case of Fig. 1--

$$\begin{aligned} X_{P1}(i+1) &= X_{P1}(i) + \\ &\{ -b_{PP1} K_{P2} U_{P1} \rho_{P1} \\ &+ b_{Pq10} K_{P1} U_{q4} \rho_{q4} + \\ &K_{P1}(Y_{r1} + Y_{r2})/6 \} \end{aligned} \tag{21}$$

where Kpl and Kp2 are the retardation coefficients of road #1 and Road #2. Road #2's coefficient, which is the downstream element to #1, is needed for Xpl (i + 1) calculation. Solid arrows in Fig. 6 show computational ordering in retardation coefficient calculation and empty arrows show evacuation flow direction.

4.2 Computation Process

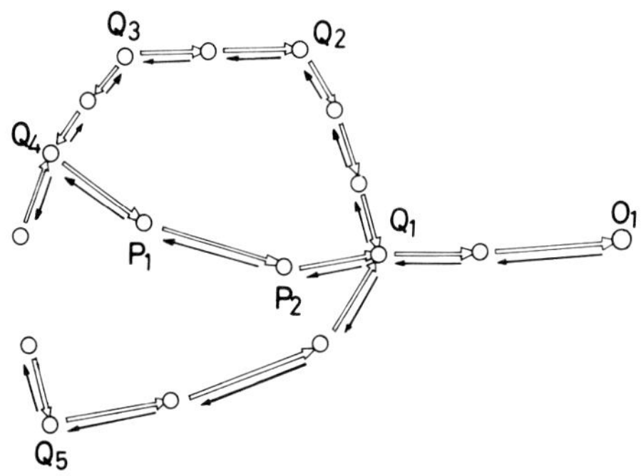

Fig. 6 Computational ordering in the retardation coefficient calculation for the network in Fig. 2

Figure 7 shows the generation computation scheme, which contains ten major subroutines for simulating the civil evacuation process. The function of each subroutine is, briefly, as follows.

NETSTR: Construct the urban network using input data with respect to road, intersection, residential block, surrounding area, and evacuation goal.

DISTAN: Calculate the distance between evacuation goals and other network elements and burnout time of each element.

FIRE: Calculate the area burned out by the time in question.

DILOAD: Select the shortest road from the representative point in the residential block.

DIRECT: Determine the flow direction at each control surface.

RUNAWY: Calculate the number of people to be evacuated and the human flow ratio at each control surface.

RATIO: Calculate the fire danger index and flow ratio at each control surface.

ORDER: Determine the calculation order of eq. (3).

FLRATE: Calculate the human flow rate at each control surface.

CALLAT: Calculate the number of people in evacuation goals, residential blocks, and retardation coefficients

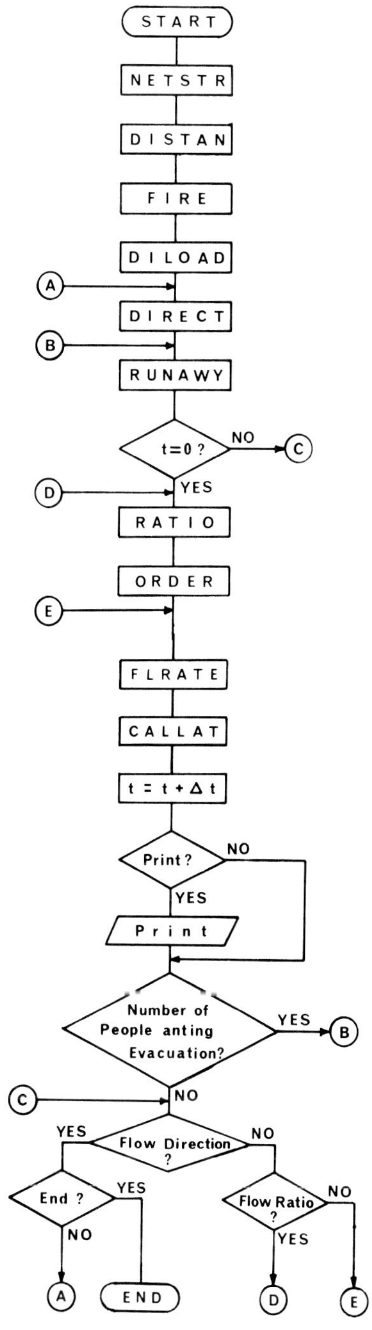

Fig. 7 Computation scheme

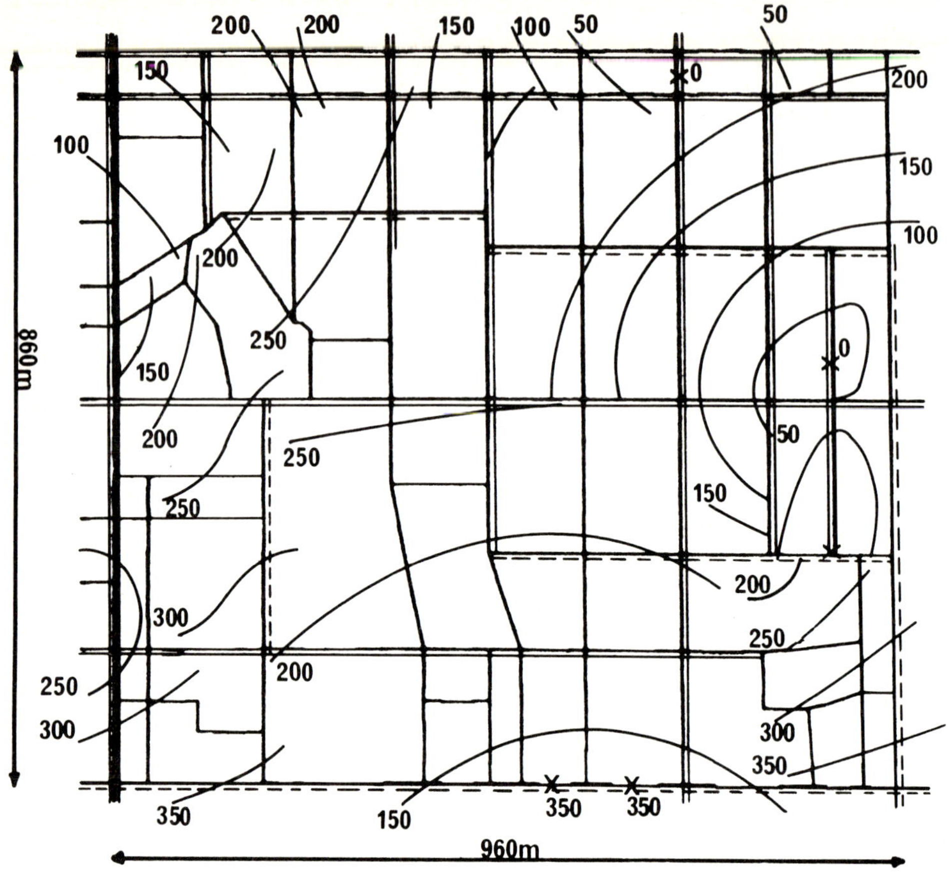

Fig. 8 Road network and equi-time contours (in minutes) of fire fronts in the 1 km x 1 km area used to examine model validity (═══ 25 m, ═══ 15 m ------- 8 m, ____ 5 m)

As a part of the documentation on the great Kanto earthquake disaster in 1923 was introduced in a previous section, it is illustrative to do a computer simulation for a fire-caused evacuation process in the same area as that of the Kanto quake case. The area adopted here, about 1 km square, was in Koto Ward, Tokyo. Some 42,858 people were in the area, but only half were accounted for in the simulation, since the Kanto quake occurred almost at noon. Table 2 shows the number of network elements. Figure 8 shows topological information about area and equi-time contours of fire propagation, in which the symbol x means the location of fire initiation.

Figure 9 shows two road segments protected from fires for the computer simulation, be-

Table 2 Urban element number used in computer simulation for examining the validity of the model

P	307	PP	244
Q	100	PQ	323
R	61	PR	537
O	1	PO	1
S	16	QS	16

cause it was concluded from documentation at the time of the Kanto quake that these would be used for evacuation to a goal or to surrounding areas.

Figure 10 indicates the evacuation flow direction for the first 10 minutes in simulation and for stages two, four, and six hours after fire initiation. In this figure, the absence of arrows indicates a place burned out by the time indicated in the figure, showing people fleeing to and fro have been forced into the dreadful situation of being surrounded by fire.

The following figure shows computer simulation results for the percentage distribution of people unable to flee, where the percentage is based on the total number of such people.

Figure 11 shows computer simulation results for a 0.8 initial evacuation ratio, meaning that 80% of all people in the simulation area evacuated to roads at fire initiation. This figure indicates the most dangerous urban section in the evacuation network; actually, for the simulation, a quarter area in the northwest section and a corner in the southwest section are the most dangerous.

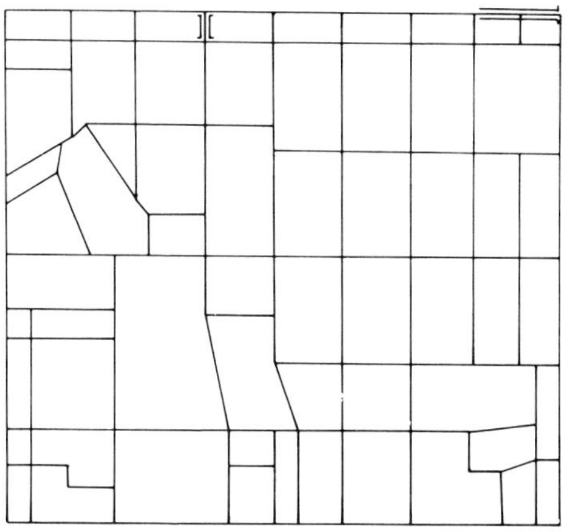

Fig. 9 Road sections protected from fires, indicated by the symbol

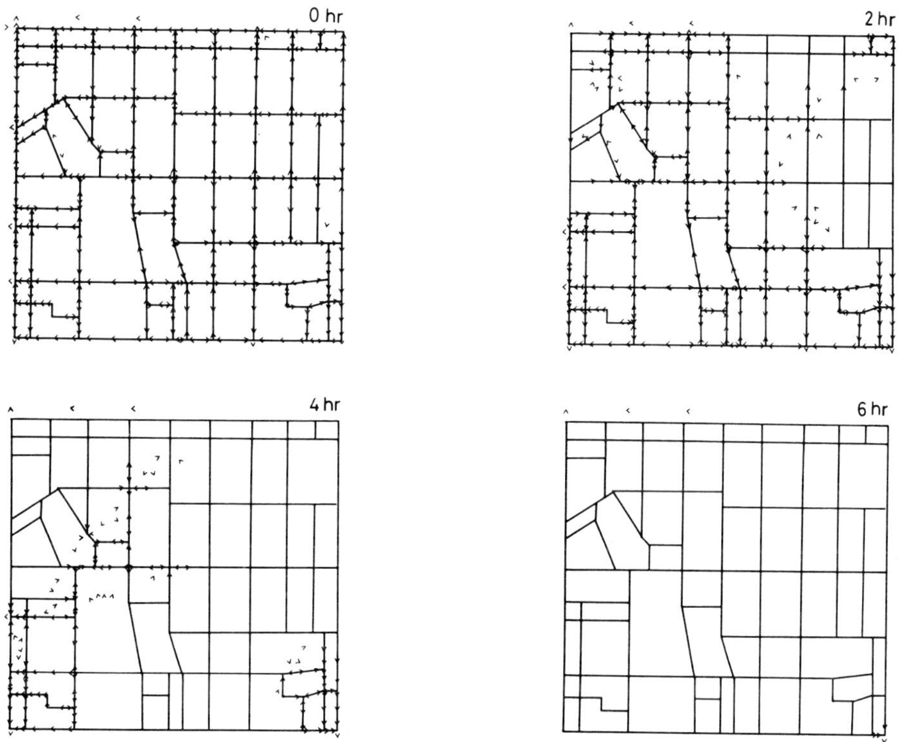

Fig. 10 Evacuation flow directions determined in simulation by eq. (19)

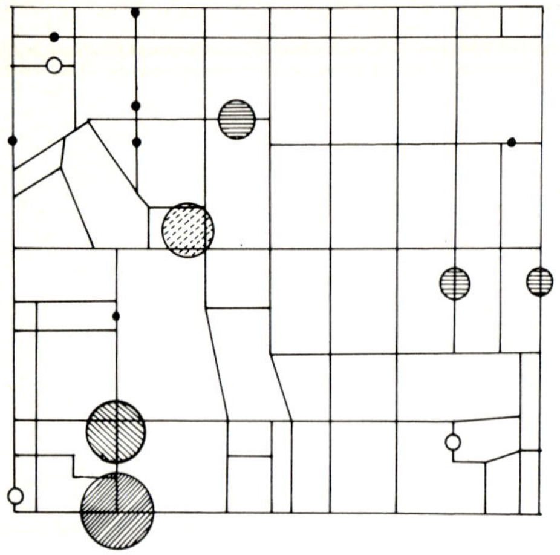

Fig. 11 Location and relative number of people unable to escape (in simulation)
(25% 21% 14% 10% ○ 2% ● 1%)

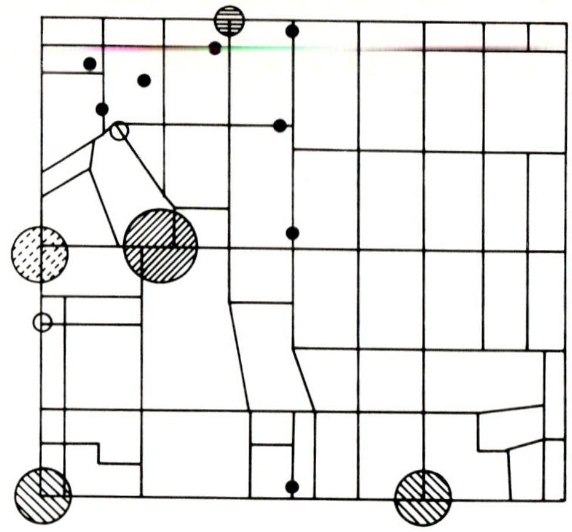

Fig. 12 Location and relative number of people killed in the great Kanto earthquake
(25% 20% 18% 9% ○ 2% ● 1%)

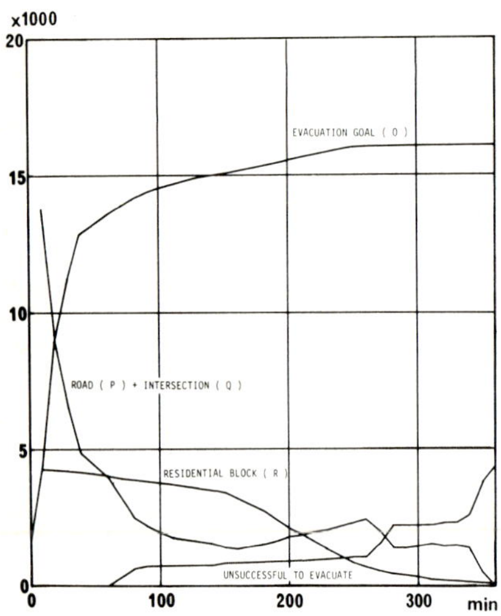

Fig. 13 Time-wise change in number of people in evacuation goal (O), road (P), and intersection (Q), residential block (R) and of those people unable to escape

Figure 12 shows a percentage distribution of people dying mostly from fires during the great Kanto quake for the same area as that of the computer simulation. Comparing Fig. 11 and 12, the computer simulation model indicates rather well the dangerous section in fire-caused evacuation.

Figure 13 shows the time history of the number of people in road + intersection, residential block, evacuation goal, and people unable to flee for the case of initial evacuation ratio 0.8. The total number of people unable to escape was about 4,000 which is almost the same number of dead in that area accounted for during the Kanto disaster.

6. Application

To test the applicability of this fuzzy simulation model to civil evacuation from large-scale fires, a 4 km x 5 km area in Koto Ward, Tokyo, was employed, in which eight fires were assumed to have started and devastated about 66% of the area over a 12-hour period. The evacuation road network and fictitious fire propagation process is shown in Fig. 14, where the symbol ● shows the spot of fire origin and ⯑ indicates the place of fire onset through discontinuous propagation. Contours show the fire front at each point (hour) fires devastated the area. Table 3 shows the number of urban elements used in the simulation; the population in the area in question was 170,000.

Table 4 shows other parameters used in the simulation for specifying evacuation scheme, conditions in surrounding areas, evacuation route specification, conditions for evacuation onset, initial evacuation ratio, effective road width, C1, and C2. The time step was one

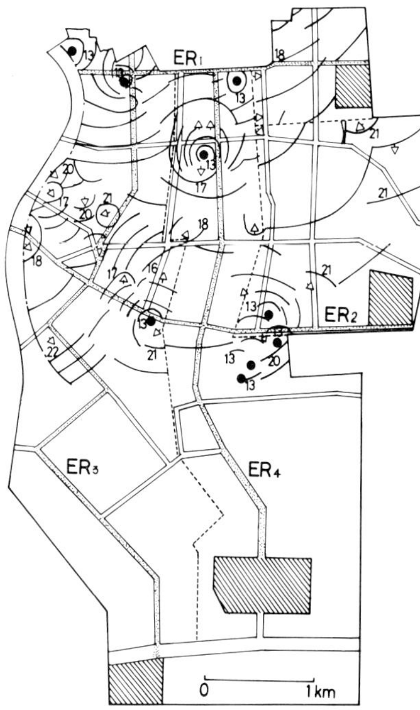

Fig. 14 Road network and equi-time contours of fires (in hours) in the 4 km x 5 km area examined (● : location of fire outbreak; ♤ : location of discontinuous fire propagation; ▨ : evacuation goals; -----: prescribed evacuation sectors)

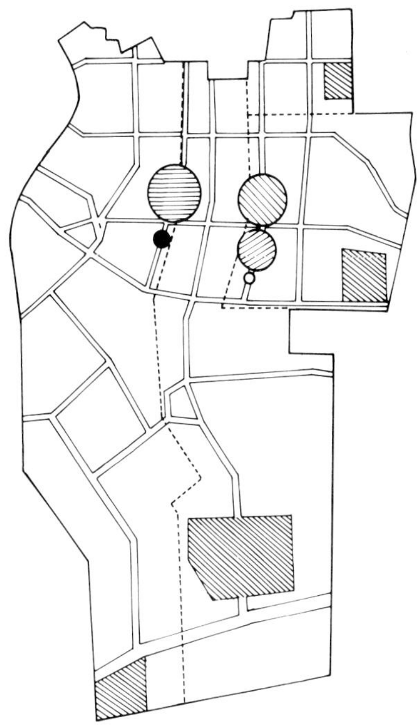

Fig. 15 Location and relative number of people unable to escape (in simulation) (⊜38% ⊘ 34% ⊘ 21% ● 5% ○ 2%)

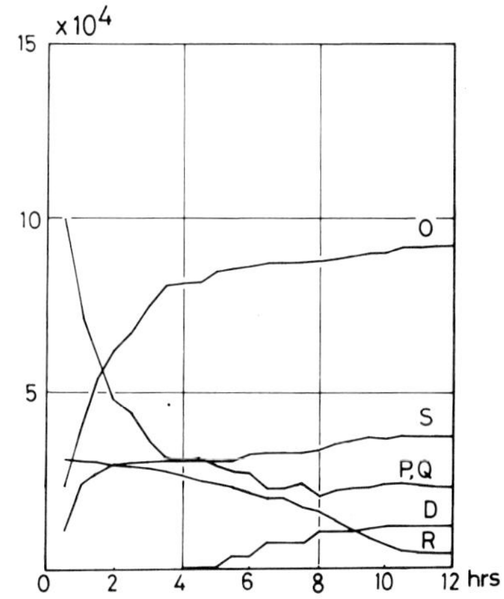

Fig. 16 Time-wise change in number of people in each urban element and of those unable to escape

Table 3 Urban element number used in large area 4 km x 5 km evacuation simulation

P	120	PP	54
Q	47	PQ	128
R	46	PR	230
O	4	PO	4
S	18	QS	18

minute, and at each ten-minute interval the evacuation flow direction at each interface was determined by eq. (19).

Figure 15 shows a relative distribution map of

Table 4 Other parameters used in computer simulation for evacuation of a large, 4 km x 5 km area

Evacuation scheme:	Prescribed sector method
Surrounding area:	Burned
Evacuation route:	ER_1, ER_2, ER_3, ER_4
Evacuation onset:	10 minutes before fire devastation
Initial evacuation:	80% of total number of residents
Effective road width:	70% of original width
C_1 and C_2:	0

people unable to flee (in percentage), indicatting the most dangerous places -- i.e., those surrounded by fires. Figure 16 shows a timewise variation of people in each urban element. In this figure, D is the number of people unable to flee, which increases after five hours from fire initiation, and it corresponded to 15% of the devastated area. This simulation result is very illustrative for deriving evacuation guidelines, i.e., earthquake-generated fires should be controlled and put out while fire-devastated areas are within about 10% of the area in each evacuation district.

7. Conclusion

This paper presented a mathematical model for the flow of people evacuating over a large-scale urban network from earthquake-caused fires. The model was basically constructed from two laws-- the continuity law of evacuating people and the empirical relation of the walking velocity of the human concentration involved. The essential part of the model was to determine the evacuation flow direction through decrementation of a fuzzy psychological potential between two consecutive urban elements.

The validity of the model was examined through comparison of computer simulation results with documentation of the great Kanto earthquake disaster for a 1 km x 1 km area in Koto Ward, Tokyo, showing that the model offered good agreement in the distribution of people killed by fire. An application of this model to a large-scale area 4 km x 5 km was made to show the feasibility of computer simulation with regard to the evacuation problem.

In conclusion, the mathematical model offers, through computer simulation, a reasonable prediction of the human evacuation process from large-scale earthquake-generated fires.

Acknowledgments

The author wishes to express his gratitude to Prof. T. Fujita, University of Tokyo, for his kind permission to use his computer program for developing a fuzzy simulation model of civilian evacuation flow over a road network. He also wishes to thank the Toyota Foundation for the financial aid to this research in 1979.

References

[1] Reports on the Great Kanto Earthquake Disaster (Iwanami-shoten Pub. Co., 1925), p. 290.

[2] Fujita, T., A Study on Computer Simulation of Earthquake Disaster, Ph.D. Dissertation, Dept. of Mech. Eng., Tokyo Univ. (1973), p. 313.

PART SEVEN

APPROXIMATE REASONING AND DECISION ANALYSIS

Approximate Reasoning in Decision Analysis
M.M. Gupta and E. Sanchez (eds.)

A FUZZY SETS BASED LINGUISTIC APPROACH: THEORY AND APPLICATIONS

Piero P. Bonissone

General Electric Company
Corporate Research and Development
Building 37-579
1 River Road
Schenectady, NY 12345

Fuzzy sets theory and fuzzy logic constitute the basis for the linguistic approach. Under this approach, variables can assume linguistic values. Each linguistic value is characterized by a label and a meaning. The label is a sentence of a language. The meaning is a fuzzy subset of a universe of discourse. Models, based on this approach, can be constructed to simulate approximate reasoning. The implementation of these models presents two major problems, namely, how to associate a label to an unlabelled fuzzy set on the basis of semantic similarity (linguistic approximation) and how to perform arithmetic operations with fuzzy numbers. For each problem a solution is proposed. Two illustrative applications to decision analysis and natural language processing are discussed.

0. KEYWORDS

Fuzzy Sets, Linguistic Approach, Linguistic Approximation, Fuzzy Numbers, Decision Making, Natural Language Processing

1. INTRODUCTION

There are situations where it is more natural to handle uncertainty by fuzzy set theory [31] than by probability theory.[1] Such is the case when dealing with the inherent imprecision of concepts involved in human reasoning and natural language [10-12],[17],[34-35]. The theory of fuzzy sets has been the basis for the development of the linguistic approach [34] and its corresponding fuzzy logic [3].

In this approach any variable is treated as a linguistic variable, i.e., it can assume linguistic values. A linguistic value is composed of its syntactic value or label, a sentence belonging to a term set, and its semantic value, the membership distribution of a fuzzy set defined on a universe of discourse. Fuzzy logic is a logic whose truth-values are linguistic. More precisely, fuzzy logic is a fuzzification of Lukasiewicz infinite - valued logic or $L_{aleph-1}$ [23],[28].

An important feature of fuzzy logic is its ability to deal with approximate causal inference. Given a conditional fuzzy rule "if P then C", where P and C are fuzzy propositions representing the premise and the conclusion of the rule, it is possible from a proposition P´, which approximately matches P, to deduce C´, which is similar to C, by means of a logical interpolation referred to as "generalized modus ponens". Thus, a decision table can be constructed by taking the union of several conditional fuzzy rules "IF P_i THEN C_i". When a fuzzy proposition P´ is given, the decision table will produce an inference <u>without the need of an exact pattern-matching</u> between P´ and the premise P_i of each rule [35].

This type of inference, which is impossible in ordinary logic systems, enables us to build a model to simulate approximate reasoning. This model can accept a set of sentences as input and, based on the information contained in them, can upon request derive conclusions or answer questions.

Fuzzy logic provides the logical operators ($\cup, \cap, \neg, \rightarrow$) used to build the model. The extension principle [34] provides the mathematical tool to perform any arithmetic function on fuzzy sets required by the model. Models of this type have been tested in fields such as process control [13-14],[16],[20-21],[32], decision analysis [1-2],[15],[26-27],[33],[36], artificial intelligence [5-6], etc.

2. THE LINGUISTIC APPROACH: THEORY

For any given problem context, a data base, composed of a term set, is generated. The term set is a set of sentences belonging to a language ℓ. This language can be generated by a context free grammar G as proposed by Zadeh [32] or by a regular grammar. Since the generative grammar G is a 4-tuple (V_N, V_T, S, P) where V_N is the set of non-terminals, V_T is the set of terminals, S is the starting symbol and P the productions, then our choice of these will determine the size and form of the term set. Obviously, this will be problem dependent, but in general ℓ should be large enough such that any possible situation of the problem context can be described.

However, in most practical cases, ℓ does not have to be infinite, since only an approximate description of each particular situation is required. Moreover, ℓ must be easily understandable. Thus, complex syntactic structures, such as the illimited recursive use of the same production rule by means of a cyclic non-terminal (which yields to an infinite language) should be avoided.

The syntactic representation is given by a set of labels. Its semantic characterization is provided by a set of membership distributions. A distribution is associated with each label. Therefore, a language can be seen as a fuzzy relation ℓ from a set of terms S to a universe of discourse U, which assigns to pair (s, u), element of SxU, a grade of membership $\mu_\ell(s,u)$.

If we fix s, the membership function $\mu_\ell\,(s,u)$ determines a fuzzy subset A(s) of U whose membership function is:

$$\mu_{A(s)}(u) = \mu_\ell\,(s,u) \qquad u \in U,\ s \in S$$

The fuzzy subset A(s) of U is taken as the meaning of s.

The term s is the label of A(s).

Among the terminals of G we find primary terms (e.g., young, middle-aged, old), hedges (e.g., not, much, very, rather, more or less), relations (e.g., younger than, older than), conjunctions (e.g., and, but), and disjunctions (e.g., or). While the primary terms are labels of primary fuzzy sets, the rest can be seen as labels of different kinds of operators which act on the primary fuzzy sets, modifying their original membership distributions [12],[17],[34]. Thus, any sentence s of language ℓ, regardless of its syntactic complexity, is associated with a fuzzy set A(s), characterized by its membership function $\mu_{A(s)}(u)$ or, for simplicity of notation, $\mu_s(u)$.

3. COMPUTATIONAL PROBLEMS

Various models, based on this approach, have been implemented on the computer [4-6],[9],[21],[26],[29]. In most of them, a context free grammar generated the language.[2] The membership distribution representing the meaning of each sentence, was obtained by proper modification of primary fuzzy sets. It was sampled and stored as a vector associated with the sentence. APL was the high level language used to construct the models.

However, the computational burden of the implementation of these models has been considerable. The flexibility introduced by the linguistic approach is a valuable tool only if it becomes efficient. In order to achieve this efficiency, two computational problems must be solved.

The first problem arises when the output produced by the model is required to have the same nature as the input, i.e., to be linguistic. The model, by operating on the fuzzy sets associated with the input, generates as output another fuzzy set. The problem, also referred to as linguistic approximation [4-5],[9],[21], consists of finding a label, generally a sentence in a language, whose meaning is the same or the closest to the meaning of the unlabelled fuzzy set generated by the model. Because of the inefficiency of performing pairwise comparisons for all the sentences of the language, the solution to this problem is based on pattern recognition techniques [4-5].

The second computational problem is related to the implementation of the extension principle. This principle enables any non-fuzzy function to accept fuzzy sets as arguments. The resulting function value is also a fuzzy set with a uniquely defined membership distribution. This principle is invoked every time that an arithmetic operation is required by the model.

However, the use of the extension principle with sampled membership distributions generates a considerable increase in the finite discrete support of the result. Furthermore, the membership distribution of the result is no longer sampled at regular intervals and only some of its membership values are actually correct [26].

The solution to this problem consists of using a parameter-based representation for fuzzy sets. The arithmetic operations are defined as function of these parameters. Sampling is performed on the output set. Existing studies on this problem [7-8] are expanded in this paper and a table of formulae of basic arithmetic operations is provided.

4. SOLUTION TO THE FIRST PROBLEM (LINGUISTIC APPROXIMATION)

As briefly mentioned in section 3, the problem of linguistic approximation consists of associating a label with a membership distribution on the basis of semantic similarity. This can be seen as a mapping from the crisp set of all fuzzy subsets of the universe of discourse U into the language ℓ. The proposed solution to this problem relies on feature extraction and other pattern recognition techniques.

It is based on the assumption that the cardinality of the term set is finite, i.e., $|\ell| < M < \infty$. This assumption was heuristically justified by the requirements imposed on the language ℓ in section 2.

The following is a more detailed explanation of this solution. The semantic part of the term set is mapped from the space of membership distributions into a feature space, by evaluating four weekly correlated features for each distribution. Assume that the universe of discourse, U, on which the fuzzy sets are defined, is finite and discrete and that $|U| = D$. Then we define a function F such that

$$F:\ [0,1]^D \to R^N,\ N << D$$

which maps each fuzzy set L_i onto the N-dimensional space $\mathbb{P}$. Each element in $\mathbb{P}$ is a point (denoted by the vector $\underline{P}_i$) corresponding to the values of the characteristic features of L_i. Thus

$$F(\mu_{L_i}(x)) = \underline{P}_i \stackrel{\Delta}{=} (p_i^1, p_i^2, \ldots, p_i^N)$$

This is a crucial step, since the correct selection of features determines the success or failure of almost any pattern recognition process. In choosing these, we try to have the minimum number consistent with a good representation of the original data. Four features have proved themselves to be efficient in practice [4-5].

The first feature is the power of the fuzzy set. That is

$$p_i^1 = \sum_{k=1}^{D} \mu_{L_i}(x_k)$$

The second feature is a measure of the fuzziness of the set. Using a definition proposed by Loo [18]:

$$p_i^2 = \left[\sum_{k=1}^{D} H^2(\mu_{L_i}(x_k)) \right]^{0.5}$$

where $H(h) = h$, $0 \leq h \leq 0.5$, and $H(h) = 1 - h$, $0.5 \leq h \leq 1$.

The third and fourth features are the first moment of the membership distribution of the fuzzy set and its skewness. They are, respectively, a measure of the center of gravity and of the asymmetry.

Then, each sentence in the language is represented by a pattern of characteristic features. The proposed method proceeds in two main steps. The first step consists of evaluating the four features of the unlabelled fuzzy set generated by the model. In our notation this fuzzy set will be referred to as Z. A quadratic weighted distance in the feature space is used as a metric to evaluate similarity between two fuzzy sets. That is

$$d_1(P_1, P_2) = \{ \sum_{i=1}^{N} W_i^2 (p_1^i - p_2^i)^2 \}^{1/2}$$

The weights W_i play an important role since they allow different features to be emphasized. They are defined as $W_i = I/R_i$, where R_i is the length of the range of values that feature p^1 takes over all the points in the data set, and I_i is the relative importance of parameter p^1 in evaluating semantic similarity. Clearly, I_i depends on the user's subjective perception of similarity, for the given problem context. It is suggested to obtain the value of I_i from the user by means of pairwise comparison tests, using the concept of cardinal ratio scale to establish a preference cardinal ordering [5],[24-25].

A search in this low order pattern space is performed. The result of this pre-screening process of the language is a small crisp subset of sentences, LA(Z), all of them close in meaning to the unlabelled fuzzy set Z (according to some tolerance parameter).

In the second step, the final assignment of the label is obtained when the membership distributions of these preselected sentences are compared with the distribution of the unlabelled fuzzy set. For this purpose, a measure to evaluate the semantic similarity of two fuzzy sets is proposed. The metric we use is a modified form of Bhattacharya distance that is defined by

$$d_2(L_i, Z) = [1 - R(L_i, Z)]^{1/2}, \quad L_i \in LA(Z)$$

where R is called the Bhattacharya coefficient. In the discrete case this is given by

$$R(L_i Z) = \sum_{k=1}^{D} \left[\frac{\mu_{L_i}(x_k)\mu_Z(x_k)}{\text{power}(L_i)\,\text{power}(Z)} \right]^{1/2}$$

5. SOLUTION TO THE SECOND PROBLEM (ARITHMETIC OPERATIONS)

Before we use the proposed parameter-based representation for fuzzy sets, let us introduce the definition of fuzzy number. A fuzzy number is simply a fuzzy subset of the real line and is completely defined by its membership function such that

$$\mu: \mathbb{R} \to (0,1)$$

For our purposes, we further restrict this definition to those fuzzy numbers which are both normal and convex. Thus, in addition to the above constraint, we have

$$\text{normality: } \bigvee_{x} \mu(x) = 1.0 \quad x \in \mathbb{R}$$

$$\text{convexity: } \mu(\lambda x_1 + (1-\lambda)x_2) \geq \mu(x_1) \wedge \mu(x_2)$$

$$\forall x_1, x_2 \in \mathbb{R}, \quad \forall \lambda \in [0,1]$$

where $\vee$ and $\wedge$ indicate supremum and minimum, respectively.

With the requirement of convexity, a piecewise continuity in the membership distribution is assured. This requirement also implies that the points of the real line, with the highest membership values, are clustered around a given real interval (or point). This fact allows us to easily understand the semantics of a fuzzy number by looking at its distribution and to associate it with a properly descriptive syntactic label (e.g., "approximately 100").

The requirement of normality implies that, among the points of the real line with the highest membership value, there exists at least one which is completely compatible with the predicate associated with the fuzzy number. In other words, it is totally possible for the fuzzy number to take that (or those) particular value(s) on the real axis.

It should be noted that fuzzy numbers do not form a ring, since they lack the inverse element for the operations of "+"(sum) and "x"(multiplication). Moreover, only positive convex fuzzy numbers form a commutative semi-ring [7-8],[19]. In fact, negative fuzzy numbers are not closed under "x". Any other type of fuzzy numbers do not satisfy the distributive law.

Any normal convex fuzzy number may be characterized by a 4-tuple (a,b,α,β) where $[a,b]$ is the closed interval on which the membership function is equal to 1.0, α is the "left bandwidth" and β is the "right bandwidth".[3] Figure 1 illustrates this characterization.

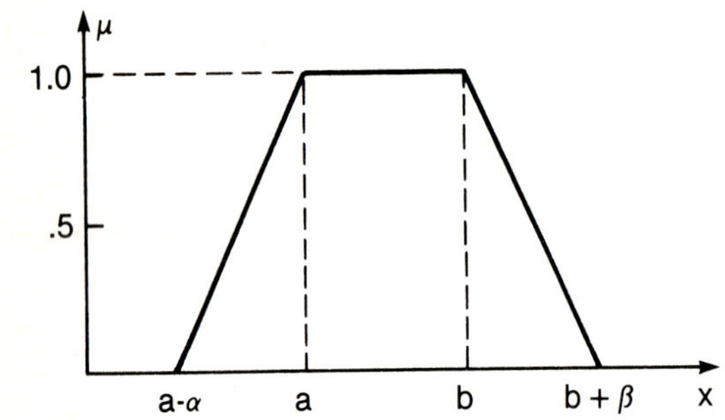

Fig. I Characterization of Fuzzy Number $A=(a,b,\alpha,\beta)$

Notice that crisp numbers can be represented in this form by $(a,a,0,0)$ and that interval numbers may be written as $(a,b,0,0)$. Thus, this characterization allows for the use of "mixed" arithmetics, where fuzzy numbers can be easily combined with interval numbers or crisp numbers in the cases where more precise information is available.

If we now limit the shape of the left and right slopes of the membership function to be an even function, $S(*)$, such that $S(-x) = S(x)$ and $S(0) = 1$, then, if $S(*)$ is also monotonically decreasing on $(0,+\infty)$, the simple algebraic operations can be written as formulae involving the parameters in the 4-tuple.

So, if $\tilde{m} \triangleq (a,b,\alpha,\beta)$ and $\tilde{n} \triangleq (c,d,\gamma,\delta)$ with the understanding that the left slopes are given by $S(a-x/\alpha)$ and $S(c-x/\gamma)$, and the right slopes by $S(x-b/\beta)$ and $S(x-d/\delta)$, then Table 1 gives the formulae for inverse, logarithm, addition, subtraction, multiplication, division and power.

Note that only formulae (1), (4) and (5) are exact. The remaining formulae are only approximate in that the left and right bandwidths of the result are not exact. However, they introduce very little error and in practice have proved themselves to be of great value [26].

It is interesting to note that the above formulae are consistent and the following identities are preserved:

Identities	Formulae Numbers
$\tilde{m} + \tilde{n} = \tilde{m} + (-\tilde{n})$	(1), (5)
$\tilde{m} \div \tilde{n} = \tilde{m} \times \frac{1}{\tilde{n}}$	(2),(7),(8),(9),(10) (11),(12),(13),(14)
$\tilde{m}^{-1} = \frac{1}{\tilde{m}}$	(2), (16), (18)
$e^{\log \tilde{m}} = \tilde{m}$	(3), (4)
$\tilde{m}^2 = \tilde{m} \times \tilde{m}$	(15), (17), (7)
$\left(\tilde{m}^{\tilde{n}_1}\right) \times \left(\tilde{m}^{\tilde{n}_2}\right) = \tilde{m}^{\tilde{n}_1+\tilde{n}_2}$	(15),(16),(17),(18),(5)
$\left(\tilde{m}^{\tilde{n}_1}\right)^{n_2} = \tilde{m}^{\tilde{n}_1 \times \tilde{n}_2}$	(15),(16),(17),(18),(7), (8),(9),(10)

However, since the inverse elements for sum and multiplication are missing, the following two identities, valid for crisp numbers, are no longer valid for fuzzy numbers:

$$m + (-m) = 0 \qquad \text{I1}$$

$$m \times \frac{1}{m} = 1 \qquad \text{I2}$$

Nevertheless, formulae (4) and (1), for I1, and (6), (9), and (2), for I2, provide the corresponding approximation, e.g.:

$$\tilde{m} + (-\tilde{m}) = (a-b,\ b-a,\ \alpha+\beta,\ \alpha+\beta)$$

$$\tilde{m} + \left(\frac{1}{\tilde{m}}\right) = \left(\frac{a}{b},\ \frac{b}{a},\ \frac{a\beta+b\alpha}{b(b+\beta)},\ \frac{a\beta+b\alpha}{a(a-\alpha)}\right) \text{for } \tilde{m} > 0$$

$$= \left(\frac{b}{a},\ \frac{a}{b},\ \frac{-a\beta-b}{a(a-\alpha)},\ \frac{-a\beta-b}{b(b+\beta)}\right) \text{for } \tilde{m} < 0$$

We now have a compact way of representing the kind of fuzzy sets in which we are interested. Furthermore, because we can perform algebraic operations with these representations, we do not need to use the extension principle but we can compute the output set induced by a mapping in a direct way. Sampling needs only then to be performed on the output set, at which stage we can fix the number of sample points in accordance with our requirements.

Table 1

Operation	Result	Conditions	Formula No.
$-\tilde{n}$	$(-d, -c, \delta, \gamma)$	all $\tilde{n}$	(1)
$\frac{1}{\tilde{n}}$	$\left(\frac{1}{d}, \frac{1}{c}, \frac{\delta}{d(d+\delta)}, \frac{\gamma}{c(c-\gamma)}\right)$	$\tilde{n} > 0, \tilde{n} < 0$	(2)
$e^{\tilde{n}}$	$(e^c, e^d, e^c(1-e^{-\gamma}), e^d(e^{\delta}-1))$	$\tilde{n} > 0$	(3)
$\log \tilde{n}$	$\left(\log c, \log d, \log \frac{c}{(c-\gamma)}, \log \frac{(d+\delta)}{d}\right)$	$\tilde{n} > 0$	(4)
$\tilde{m} + \tilde{n}$	$(a+c, b+d, \alpha+\gamma, \beta+\delta)$	all $\tilde{m}, \tilde{n}$	(5)
$\tilde{m} - \tilde{n}$	$(a-d, b-c, \alpha+\delta, \beta+\gamma)$	all $\tilde{m}, \tilde{n}$	(6)
$\tilde{m} \times \tilde{n}$	$(ac, bd, a\gamma+c\alpha-\alpha\gamma, b\delta+d\beta+\beta\delta)$	$\tilde{m} > 0, \tilde{n} > 0$	(7)
	$(ad, bc, d\alpha-a\delta+\alpha\delta, -b\gamma+c\beta-\beta\gamma)$	$\tilde{m} < 0, \tilde{n} > 0$	(8)
	$(bc, ad, b\gamma-c\beta+\beta\gamma, -d\alpha+a\delta-\alpha\delta)$	$\tilde{m} > 0, \tilde{n} < 0$	(9)
	$(bd, ac, -b\delta-d\beta-\beta\delta, -a\gamma-c\alpha+\alpha\gamma)$	$\tilde{m} < 0, \tilde{n} < 0$	(10)
$\tilde{m} \div \tilde{n}$	$\left(\frac{a}{d}, \frac{b}{c}, \frac{a\delta+d\alpha}{d(d+\delta)}, \frac{b\gamma+c\beta}{c(c-\gamma)}\right)$	$\tilde{m} > 0, \tilde{n} > 0$	(11)
	$\left(\frac{a}{c}, \frac{b}{d}, \frac{c\alpha-a\gamma}{c(c-\gamma)}, \frac{d\beta-b\delta}{d(d+\delta)}\right)$	$\tilde{m} < 0, \tilde{n} > 0$	(12)
	$\left(\frac{b}{d}, \frac{a}{c}, \frac{b\delta-d\beta}{d(d+\delta)}, \frac{a\gamma-c\alpha}{c(c-\gamma)}\right)$	$\tilde{m} > 0, \tilde{n} < 0$	(13)
	$\left(\frac{b}{c}, \frac{a}{d}, \frac{-b\gamma-c\beta}{c(c-\gamma)}, \frac{-a\delta-d\alpha}{d(d+\delta)}\right)$	$\tilde{m} < 0, \tilde{n} < 0$	(14)
$\tilde{m}^{\tilde{n}}$	$\left(a^c, b^d, a^c-(a-\alpha)^{c-\gamma}, (b+\beta)^{d+\delta}-b^d\right)$	$\tilde{m} \in [1,\infty)$ $\tilde{n} > 0$	(15)
	$\left(b^c, a^d, b^c-(b+\beta)^{c-\gamma}, (a-\alpha)^{d+\delta}-a^d\right)$	$\tilde{m} \in [1,\infty)$ $\tilde{n} < 0$	(16)
	$\left(a^d, b^c, a^d-(a-\alpha)^{d+\delta}, (b+\beta)^{c-\gamma}-b^c\right)$	$\tilde{m} \in [0,1]$ $\tilde{n} > 0$	(17)
	$\left(b^d, a^c, b^d-(b+\beta)^{d+\delta}, (a-\alpha)^{c-\gamma}-a^c\right)$	$\tilde{m} \in [0,1]$ $\tilde{n} < 0$	(18)

where $\tilde{m} \triangleq (a, b, \alpha, \beta)$ and $\tilde{n} \triangleq (c, d, \gamma, \delta)$

6. APPLICATION OF THE SOLUTIONS

6.1 Example 1: An Application in Decision Analysis

The validity of the proposed solutions to the above problems is illustrated by a short example. The example summarizes the author's recent work in decision analysis [26-27], where the two solutions were extensively used.

A one-stage multi-choice multi-criteria decision problem, simulated by a computer implemented system, describes the following investment situation.

A private citizen has a moderately large amount of capital which he wishes to invest to his best advantage. He has selected five possible investment areas $\{a_1, a_2, a_3, a_4, a_5\}$ and has four criteria $\{c_1, c_2. c_3, c_4\}$ by which to judge them. These are

a_1 - the commodity market

a_2 - the stock market

a_3 - gold and/or diamonds

a_4 - real estate

a_5 - long term bonds

and

c_1 - the risk of losing the capital sum

c_2 - the vulnerability of the capital sum to modification by inflation

c_3 - the amount of interest received

c_4 - the cash realizability of the capital sum.

His rating of the alternatives with respect to the criteria $\{r_{ij}: i=1,\ldots,5, j=1,\ldots,4\}$ is expressed linguistically as shown in Table 2. His problem is to select one of the a_i with the additional constraint that he does not consider the criteria to be equally important but gives them linguistic weights $\{\alpha_1,\alpha_2,\alpha_3,\alpha_4\}$ as shown in Table 3.

Table 2

	c_1	c_2	c_3	c_4
a_1	high	more or less high	very high	fair
a_2	fair	fair	fair	more or less good
a_3	low	from fair to more or less low	fair	good
a_4	low	very low	more or less high	bad
a_5	very low	high	more or less low	very good

Table 3

α_1	α_2	α_3	α_4
moderately important	more or less important	very important	more or less unimportant

In both cases, describing the weights and the ratings, the system provides the user with a term set of linguistic values. These linguistic values are fuzzy numbers defined on the closed interval [0.1] of the real line. Furthermore, S(*) is linear, giving a particularly simple form. Only seven basic set shapes are used to represent the range of linguistic values (see Figure II). This means that each set has several interpretations. Table 4 illustrates the definitions and interpretations of the linguistic values.

The first step in solving this problem is to compute a suitability set for each of the alternatives. Since the linguistic ratings and weights are appropriately defined fuzzy numbers, we just use a fuzzy weighted sum to give.

$$S_i = \sum_{j=1}^{4} \alpha_j r_{ij}$$

These operations are executed by means of the formulae of Table 1. The results are as shown in Figure III.

Applying the concept of dominance relation[4] to the suitability sets, we obtain the overall degree to which each of the alternatives dominates the others [26-27]. A fuzzy set Z equal to the difference between the best alternative and a weighted average of the remaining ones constitute the "degree of preferability" of the chosen alternative. The weights used in this average are the degree of dominance of the selected alternative.[5]

The obtained fuzzy set Z represents the amount by which the chosen solution is preferable to the other ones. By using the linguistic approximation technique, this is interpreted and labelled.

In the case of this example, alternative 4 (real estate) was selected, since S_4 dominates the other suitability sets. The preferability of the solution was labelled "from indifferent with to marginally better than the other alternatives". This weak statement about the strength of the decision was due to the proximity of S_3 (gold/diamonds) to the chosen S_4 (real estate).

Table 4

		Interpretation when used with				
Shape	Fuzzy Numbers	c_1	c_2	c_3	c_4	Weights
1	(0,0,0,.2)	Very high	Very high	Very low	Very bad	Very unimportant
2	(0,.1,0,.2)	High	High	Low	Bad	Unimportant
3	(.2,.2,.2,.2)	More or less high	More or less high	More or less low	More or less bad	More or less unimportant
4	(.5,.5,.2,.2)	Fair	Fair	Fair	Fair	Indifferent
5	(.8,.8,.2,.2)	More or less low	More or less low	More or less high	More or less good	More or less important
6	(.9,1,.2,0)	Low	Low	High	Good	Important
7	(1,1,.2,0)	Very low	Very low	Very high	Very good	Very important

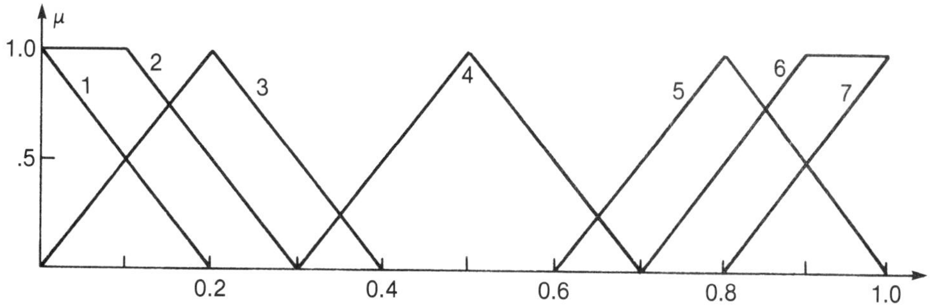

Fig. II Linguistic Ratings and Weights

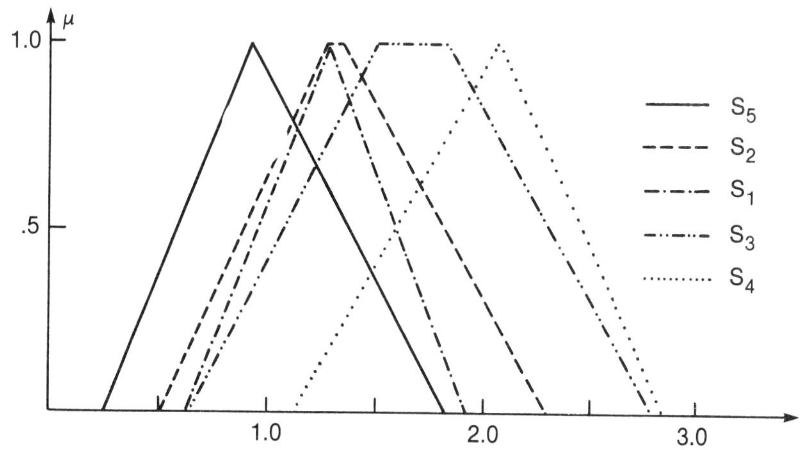

Fig. III Suitability Sets

6.2 Example 2: An Application in Artificial Intelligence

The simple example, used in this section, deals with a typical problem of Artificial Intelligence, namely, natural language understanding and approximate reasoning.

In this problem, the input is a sequence of sentences belonging to a subset of English, limited by a lexicon of 96 words. An Augmented Finite State Transition Network parser [30], implemented in APL, analyzes each sentence, verifies its syntactic correctness and interprets its associated meaning. The meaning, as mentioned in Section 2, is represented by a fuzzy set.

For example, the sentence "Ann is very tall and Nancy is much shorter than Ann" is transformed into:

Height (Ann) = very tall
Height (Nancy) = much shorter than very tall

where "Tall" is a primitive fuzzy subset of a universe of discourse U representing values of height. "Very tall" is a fuzzy set obtained by applying the modifier "very" to the fuzzy set "tall" [17],[33]. This is illustrated in Fig. IV. In this example the linguistic value assigned to Height (person) has the same meaning for both males and females.

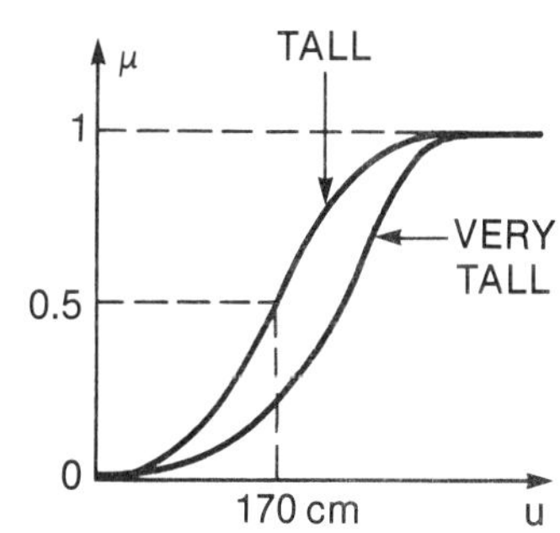

Fig. IV Representation of "Tall" and "Very tall"

We could consider the entire procedure as the assignment of a linguistic value, e.g., very tall, to a linguistic variable, e.g., Height (Ann). Each time a sentence is parsed, the linguistic variables, present or identifiable in the sentence, are assigned their corresponding values. After parsing the sentences, the system is ready to answer questions related to the data. The answer to these questions can be viewed as finding the final value of a particular linguistic variable.

To clarify this presentation, we list the sentences used as input to the parser. Given that:

Ann is very short,
Nancy is much taller than Ann,
Gail is indeed very tall,
Nancy is not much shorter than Gail,
Paola is medium-height,
Mary is taller than Ann,
Mary is taller than Paola is false,
John is very tall is rather false,
John is taller than Paola,
Dennis is shorter than John,
Dennis is taller than Mary,
Piero is shorter than Nancy,
Piero is taller than Paola,

we may want to ask "What is the height of Dennis" or "What is the height of John". The answers are obtained by taking the intersection, e.g., AND, of the assignments (clauses) associated with the linguistic variables Height (Dennis) or Height (John).

This is a purely syntactic procedure. Therefore some answers could be lengthy and incomprehensible as the answer Height (Dennis) = ((SHORTER THAN (((VERY TALL) IS RATHER FALSE)) AND (TALLER THAN MEDIUM-HEIGHT))) AND ((TALLER THAN ((TALLER THAN VERY SHORT)) AND ((TALLER THAN MEDIUM-HEIGHT) IS FALSE))) which would be obtained by following the described syntactic procedure.

At this point, the linguistic approximation technique is used to simplify the answer. The meaning of each answer is determined, by obtaining the corresponding membership distribution, and a more understandable label is associated with it. In our example, we queried the system about the height of Nancy, Mary, Piero, John and Dennis, with the following results:

Height (Nancy) = Very tall
Height (Mary) = From sort of short to medium-height
Height (Piero) = Between medium-height and rather tall
Height (John) = Sort of tall
Height (Dennis) = Between medium-height and sort of tall

Details of the computer implementation of this example can be found in [5].

It is important to note that the obtained answers are not precise in meaning, since they do not specify a given height in units such as meters or feet. On the contrary, they reflect the fuzziness of the input data. Nevertheless, the answers are perfectly consistent with the ones provided by a human on the basis of his/her intuitive understanding of the data and approximate reasoning capabilities.

7. CONCLUSIONS

We have described the linguistic approach, analyzed its problems, and suggested two solutions to efficiently implement linguistic approximations and operations with fuzzy numbers.

Applications to decision making and artificial intelligence have been used to evaluate and verify the proposed solutions. These new techniques will reduce the computational burden associated with the implementation of conceptual models based on the linguistic approach.

8. ACKNOWLEDGEMENTS

I would like to thank Lotfi A. Zadeh and Richard M. Tong for the helpful discussions on this paper and related topics.

9. FOOTNOTES

1- Probability related to randomness, deals with the uncertainty of whether a given element belongs or does not belong to a well defined set. On the other hand, fuzzy set theory and its associated possibility theory [37] are related to fuzziness. They deal with the uncertainty derived by the partial membership of a given element to a set whose boundaries are not sharply defined.

2- The language used in these implementations was a finite one, since no cyclic non-terminals were allowed in the grammar. Thus, a regular grammar could have been used to generate the same language.

3- Given a convex normal fuzzy number A = (a,b,α,β), we define its left and right bandwidth by:

$$\text{Left Bandwidth }(A) = L_A = [(a-\alpha),a]$$

$$\text{Right Bandwidth}(A) = R_A = [b,(b+\beta)]$$

where:

$$(a-\alpha) = \min\{r \in \mathbb{R} \mid \mu_A(r) > 0\}$$

$$a = \min\{r \in \mathbb{R} \mid \mu_A(r) = 1\}$$

$$b = \max\{r \in \mathbb{R} \mid \mu_A(r) = 1\}$$

$$(b+\beta) = \max\{r \in \mathbb{R} \mid \mu_A(r) > 0\}$$

4- Given two convex fuzzy sets A and B, we define the degree of dominance of A over B by:

$$\delta(A,B) = \bigvee_x (\mu_{\leq A}(x) \wedge \mu_B(x))$$

where $\leq A$ is the fuzzy set "less than or equal to A" formed from A by setting

$$\mu_{\leq A}(x) = 1.0, \qquad x < x^*$$

$$= \mu_A(x), \qquad x \geq x^*$$

with x^* being the left-most (i.e., lowest) value of x for which $\mu_A(x) = 1.0$.

The dominance relation is the matrix $R_\delta = [R_\delta(i,j)]$ where $R_\delta(i,j) = \delta(S_i,S_j)$.

5- The weights are defined by:

$$W(i) = \bigwedge_j R_\delta(i,j)$$

W(i) represents the overall degree to which alternative "i" dominates the other ones. The fuzzy set Z_k is defined by:

$$\mu_{Z_k}(u) = \bigvee_{\substack{(x_1,\ldots,x_m) \\ s.t. g_k(.) = u}} \left| \bigwedge_{i=1}^{m} \mu_{S_i}(x_i) \right|$$

where:

m is the number of independent alternatives (in this case m = 5)

$g_k(.)$ is the weighted difference function defined by

$$g_k(x_1,\ldots,x_m) = x_k - \frac{\sum_{i=1, i\neq k}^{m} W(i)\cdot x_i}{\sum_{i=1, i\neq k}^{m} W(i)}$$

where the index k corresponds to a position in W for which W(k) = 1. We can then compute the fuzzy preference set Z_k, induced by $g_k(\cdot)$ when x_i is replaced by S_i. The actual computation of Z_k was obtained using the formulae defined in Table 1. For further details, refer to [26-27].

REFERENCES

[1] Baas S.J., Kwakernaak H., Rating and ranking of multiple-aspect alternatives using fuzzy sets, Automatica, vol 13, pp. 47-58, (1977).

[2] Bellman R.E., Zadeh L.A., Decision making in a fuzzy environment, Management Science, vol. 17, No.4, pp.141-164, (1970).

[3] Bellman R.E., Zadeh L.A., Local and fuzzy logic, Memorandum No. ERL-M584, University of California, Berkeley, (1976). Also in Modern Uses of Multiple-Valued Logic, pp. 103-165, J.M. Dunn and G. Epstein eds., D. Reidel Publishing Co., Dordretch, Holland, (1977).

[4] Bonissone P.P., A pattern recognition approach to the problem of linguistic approximation in system analysis, Memorandum No. UCB/ERL M78/57, University of California, Berkeley, (1978). Also in the Proceedings of the IEEE 1979 International Conference on Cybernetics and Society, pp. 793-798, Denver, Colorado, (October 1979).

[5] Bonissone P.P., The problem of linguistic approximation in system analysis, PH.D. Dissertation, Department of Electrical Engineering and Computer Sciences, University of California, Berkeley, (November 1979). Also in University Microfilms International Publications #80-14,618, Ann Arbor, Michigan.

[6] Bonissone P.P., A fuzzy set based linguistic approach: theory and applications, Proceedings of the 1980 Winter Simulation Conference, pp. 99-111, Orlando, Florida, (December 3-5, 1980).

[7] Dubois D., Prade H., Operations on fuzzy algebra, International Journal of Systems Science, pp. 613-626, (1978).

[8] Dubois D., Prade H., Fuzzy real algebra, Fuzzy Sets and Systems, vol 2, No. 4, pp. 327-348, (1979).

[9] Esragh F., Mamdani E.H., A general approach to linguistic approximation, Internal Report, Department of Electrical and, Electronic Engineering, Queen Mary College, London, England, (1978). Also in International Journal of Man-machine Studies, vol. 11, number 4, pp. 501-519, (July 1979).

[10] Gaines B.R., Foundations of fuzzy reasoning, International J. Man-Machine Studies, vol 6, pp. 623-668, (1976).

[11] Gupta M.M., Saridis G.N. eds., Fuzzy automata and decision processes , North-Holland Publishing Company, New York, NY, (1977).

[12] Hersch H.M. Caramazza A., A fuzzy set approach to modifiers and vagueness in natural language, Journal Experimental Psychology, vol 105, No. 3, pp. 254-276, (1975).

[13] Kickert W.J.M., Van Nauta Lemle H.R., Application of a fuzzy controller in a warm water plant, Automatica, vol. 12, pp. 301-308, (1976).

[14] Kickert W.J.M., Mamdani E.H., Analysis of a fuzzy controller, Fuzzy Sets and Systems, vol 1, pp. 29-44, (1978).

[15] Kickert W.J.M., Fuzzy theories on decision-making , Martinus Nijhoff Social Sciences Division Leiden, The Netherlands, (1978).

[16] King P.J., Mamdani E.H., The application of fuzzy control system to industrial processes, Automatica, vol 13, pp.235-242, (1977).

[17] Lakoff G., Hedges: a study in meaning criteria and the logic of fuzzy concepts, Journal of Philosophical Logic , vol 2, pp. 458-508, (1973).

[18] Loo S. G., Measures of fuzziness, Cybernetica, vol 20, No. 3, pp. 201-210, (1977).

[19] Mizumoto M., Tanaka K., Algebraic properties of fuzzy numbers, IEEE 1976 International Conference on Cybernetics and Society, Washington, D.C., (1976).

[20] Pappis C.P., Mamdani E.H., A fuzzy logic controller for a traffic junction, IEEE Transactions on Systems, Man, and Cybernetics, vol SMC-7, No.10, pp. 707-717, (1977).

[21] Procyk T.J., Linguistic representation of fuzzy variables, Fuzzy Logic Working Group, Queen Mary College, London, England, (1976).

[22] Procyk T.J., A self-organizing controller for single-input single-output systems, Fuzzy Logic Working Group, Research Report No. 6, Queen Mary College, London, England, (1977).

[23] Rescher N., Many-Valued Logic, McGraw-Hill, (1969).

[24] Saaty T.L., Measuring the fuzziness of sets, Journal of Cybernetics, vol. 4, No. 4, pp. 53-61, (1974).

[25] Saaty T.L., Exploring the interface between hierarchies, multiple objectives and fuzzy sets, Fuzzy Sets and systems, vol. 1, pp. 57-68, (1979).

[26] Tong R.M., Bonissone P.P., Linguistic decision analysis using fuzzy sets, Memorandum No. UCB/ERL M79/72, University of California, Berkeley, California, (1979).

[27] Tong R.M., Bonissone P.P., A linguistic approach to decisionmaking with fuzzy sets, IEEE Transactions on Systems, Man, and Cybernetics, vol SMC-10, pp. 716-723, (1980).

[28] Tsukamoto Y., Fuzzy logic based on Lukasiewicz and its applications to diagnosis and control, Ph. D. Thesis, Tokyo Institute of Technology, Tokyo, Japan, (1979).

[29] Wenstop F., Application of linguistic variables in the analysis of organizations, PH.D. Dissertation, School of Business Administration, University of California, Berkeley, (1975).

[30] Woods W. A., Transition network grammars for natural language analysis, Communications of the ACM, vol. 13, No. 10, pp. 591-606, (1970).

[31] Zadeh L.A., Fuzzy sets, Information and Control, vol 8, pp. 338-353, (1965).

[32] Zadeh L.A., Outline of a new approach to the analysis of complex systems and decision processes, IEEE Transactions on Systems, Man, and Cybernetics, vol SMC-3, No. 1, pp. 28-44, (1973).

[33] Zadeh L.A., The linguistic approach and its application to decision analysis, Proceedings of the Conference on Directions in Decentralized Control, Many-person Optimization and Large Scale Systems, U.C. Ho and S.M. Kitter eds., Plenum Press, (1975).

[34] Zadeh L.A., The concept of a linguistic variable and its application to approximate reasoning, (Part I) Information Sciences, vol 8, pp. 199-249, (Part II) Information Sciences, vol 8, pp. 301-357, (Part III) Information Sciences, vol 9, pp.43-80, (1975).

[35] Zadeh L.A., Fuzzy logic and approximate reasoning (In memory of Grigore Moisil), Synthese, vol 30, pp. 407-428, (1975).

[36] Zadeh L.A., Linguistic characterization of preference relations as a basis for choice in social systems, Memorandum No. UCB/ERL M77/24, University of California, Berkeley, (1977).

[37] Zadeh L.A., Fuzzy sets as a basis for a theory of possibility, Fuzzy Sets and Systems, vol 1, No. 1, pp. 3-28, (1978).

Approximate Reasoning in Decision Analysis
M.M. Gupta and E. Sanchez (eds.)

RECOGNITION OF LINGUISTICALLY INSTRUCTED PATH TO DESTINATION

Haruki Imaoka+, Toshiro Terano++ and Michio Sugeno+++

Man can arrive at his destination even if the instruction given to him is ambiguous. That is, man can deal with ambiguous concepts. In this paper, we analize this process and make a thinking model by using fuzzy set theory. There are two important factors in this process: fuzzy instruction given by the instructor and fuzzy information perceived on the street. Both fuzzy instruction and information are expressed by fuzzy sets. One of the main problems of this paper is how to compare these two fuzzy sets each other. For this purpose, the concept of truth qualification in fuzzy logic is applied. Using this method, we define the degree fo matching which represents the certainty that the path is right.

+ Research Institute for Polymers and Textiles, Tsukuba, Japan
++ Faculty of Engineering, Hosei University, Tokyo, Japan
+++ Department of Systems Science, Tokyo Institute of Technology, Yokohama Japan

KEY WORDS : thinking model, artificial intelligence, robot, path finding, truth qualification, linguistic instruction

1. INTRODUCTION

When we instruct somebody a route to a destination orally, he must interpret and complete it through some reasoning or imagination, because natural language is ambiguous in both expression and logic. That is, he must translate fuzzy instructions into nonfuzzy ones by using the information obtained on the street.

Generally speaking, computer is good at dealing with nonfuzzy concept and man is excellent in fuzzy concept. The latter is very flexible and adaptive. For instance, "almost true" means usually "true" in the human's resoning. But he modifies it to fit the new situation when his judgment turns to be false. This kind of flexibility is quite necessary for intelligent robot which can understand the oral instruction of human. For the analysis and the simulation of this problem, fuzzy set theory, especially its truth qualification rule, is effective. This kind of problem was first discussed by M. Uragami, M. Mizuno and K. Tanaka[1].

In this paper, we develope the thinking process of man who seeks his way to the destination instructed linguistically.

2. STRUCTURE OF THE WHOLE MODEL

The whole structure of simulation model consists of three major parts.

(1) town model which consists of the present state and the data base (map),
(2) instruction model of the path to the destination,
(3) thinking model of a man who goes to the destinaiton.

This structure is shown in Fig. 1.

In the town model, there are all ways, intersections and many other objects such as school, post office, etc. When any action is taken by a man, his state in the town is changed and new visual scene appears accordingly. Linguistic instructions about the path are given to him at the starting point and they are committed to his memory.

In the thinking model, his visual scene is compared with the memorized instructions, and the location, where he stands at present, is identified. Then he chooses the most suitable action, which causes a new scene. This circulation of information continues until he arrives at the destination. Thinking model is, the of course, most important in this system. It has the ability of reasoning and imagination which complete and make sure of the abmiguous information.

3. TOWN MODEL

The town model stores the map of the town as a database of which input is man's action and output is visual scene on the street. Action means here the change of man's position or the change of his direction. When the man is on the street, his actions are limited only to "GO ONE STEP" or "TURN TO THE OPPOSITE DIRECTION". And when he is at the intersection, the possible action is "TURN TO ONE OF THE WAYS".

The visual scene is also restricted within a very narrow range as shown in Fig. 2 where the dot expresses man's present position and the arrow means his direction. Man can see only four objects on the street but cognize eitht directions at the intersection. Moreover, he can perceive any object if it is between two ways at the intersection. As an example, when the man is at the position a, b and c in Fig. 3, visual scenes are as shown in Fig. 4 respectively.

4. FORM OF INSTRUCTION

Total instruction is defined as an ordered sequence of rules. Each rule consists of condition C and Action A. Further, condition is divided into two sentences: FIND sentence and LOCATION sentence. Therefore, a rule "i" is expressed as

$$C_i \to A_i, \quad C_i = (F_i, L_i)$$

, where F_i is the object to be found and L_i is its location.

Action means an order expressed by ACTION sentence and it instructs the action he should take at the subgoal. FIND sentence appoints the name of object and its attributes. This object can be considered as a subgoal on his way to the destination. LOCATION sentence expresses the distance between the previous subgoal and the next one. In actual computer simulation, we use dialogical way to obtain the rules from the linguistical instruction as shown in Fig. 5.

5. THINKING MODEL

We assume that both the instruction given by instructor and the information perceived on the street include some ambiguity which is represented by fuzzy sets. The problem is how to compare these two fuzzy sets. For example, if a fuzzy instruction such as "big building" is given, man wonders whether a tall building, he is looking at now, is big or not.

Now let A be a fuzzy set associated with a membership function μ_A which implies a fuzzy image in man's brain produced by instruction. And let B be also a fuzzy set with μ_B expressing fuzzy perception in the town. To compare these two fuzzy sets, we use "trueth qualification" suggested by L. A. Zadeh[2]. That is a way to obtain τ from A and B which satisfy the equation

$$(X \text{ is } A) \text{ is } \tau = X \text{ is } B \qquad (1)$$

, where $\tau : [0, 1] \to [o, 1]$ is a linguistic truth value.

Our problem is to obtain τ from A and B, which is called the converse problem of truth qualification and discussed by E. Sanchez[3], M. Sugeno and H. Imaoka[4], M. Gupta, Y. Tsukamoto and P. Nikiforuk[5]. In this paper, the last method is applied, because linguistic truth value is easily represented with a scalar value t which we call numerical truth value. It is very important in our study to introduce an order among alternatives.

The formulation of this method is as follows.

$$(X \text{ is } A) \text{ is } t = X \text{ is } B \qquad (2)$$

$$t = N(A/B) \qquad (3)$$

$$N(A/B) = 1/2 \{ \mathrm{Sup}(A \cap B) + \mathrm{Inf}(A \cap B') \} \qquad (4)$$

, where B' is the complement of B.

We define the degree of matching of two fuzzy sets with the value of t in Eq. (3).

The types of membership fucntion are limited within few kinds. As to the instruction, the following three types of membership function μ_A are adopted.

Type 1 $\mu_A = (-1/W_a(u-a) \wedge 1) \vee 0$ (5)

Type 2 $\mu_A = (-1/W_a|u-a| + 1) \vee 0$ (6)

Type 3 $\mu_A = (-1/W_a(a-u) \wedge 1) \vee 0$ & $\lim_{u\to\infty} \mu_A = 0$ (7)

These ar shown in Fig. 6.
As to the information perceived on the street, the types of membership function μ_B are as follows.

Type α $\mu_B = (-1/W_b|u-b| + 1) \vee 0$ (8)

Type β $\mu_B = (-1/W_b(b-u) \wedge 1) \vee 0$ (9)

These are the same to Type 2 and Type 3 respectively.

The degrees of matching of any combination of μ_A and μ_B can be calculated from Eq. (4) and the results are shown in Table 1.

We remark here the correspondence between the numerial truth value t and the linguistic truth value τ in Table 2.

By using this "degree of Matching", the thinking model can select the candidate paths out of all the possible ways on the street and rank them as follows.

The selection of the candidates is done by calculating the degree of matching of all the alternatives and the eliminating those whose value of t are under a given threshold.

The action should correspond to the alternative whose value of t is the biggest. But we must aware that the value of t will be changed according with the increase of the knowledge about the town.
The process of this thinking model is explained by some examples.

[Example 1] Interpretation of ACTION sentence

We suppose that the instruction is "TURN TO

THE RIGHT", and the man has just come to the position which is shown in Fig. 7. If this position is new for him, all the possible ways are examind. There are four ways he can go, W1, W2, W3 and W4, and the direction he perceives are represented by four membership functions which are shown with dotted lines in Fig. 8. The fuzzy instruction is shown in the same figure with a solid line. The degrees of matching of informations and the instruction are calculated as follows.

N(RIGHT, W1) = 0.07
N(RIGHT, W2) = 0.93
N(RIGHT, W3) = 0.50
N(RIGHT, W4) = 0.07

If we assume the threshold as 0.25, W2 and W3 are remained as the candidates. The final decision is, of course, W2.

[Example 2] Interpretation of FIND and LOCATION Sentence

We suppose the instruction is "FIND POST OFFICE", "LOCATION ABOUT 15 STEPS". Three cases are considered that the positions of man are S1, S2 and S3 in Fig. 9.

Case 1

When man is at S1, there are two alternatives. The first is to take an action here. That is, he believes that S1 is the true intersection instructed. The second choice is to go ahead, because he doubts that S1 is too near comparing with the instruction which indicates 15 steps, and he expects the true subgoal will be found ahead. In this case, fuzzy perception about the distance is expressed with the membership function of dotted lines in Fig. 10, where the solid line represents the fuzziness of the instruction. Since we have no knowledge about the distance of next post office, the membership function of the expected post office (EP) is as the chain line in Fig. 10.

The numerical truth values about these alternatives are as follows.

N(ABOUT 15/S1) = 0.42
N(ABOUT 15/EP) = 0.5

Though the degrees of matching are not so high, they can be candidates because they are higher than 0.25. And the final decision is to go ahead for seeking another post office.

Case 2

When man is at S2, there are three alternatives he can choose. These are to go back to S1, to turn right here and to go ahead. The fuzzy perception of each positions are shown in Fig. 11. The degrees of matching are as follows.

N(ABOUT 15/S1) = 0.42
N(ABOUT 15/S2) = 0.71
N(ABOUT 15/EP) = 0.5

Now he decides that S2 is the true subgoal and take an action here. In Case 3, he has four alternatives, but can make decision by the same way.

6. BACKTRACKING

The interpretation of fuzzy instruction is not always correct. Therefore, backtracking action is very important to recover the misunderstanding. This action consists of following five steps.
(1) Recognition that the present state is wrong,
(2) Decrease of the degree of matching which causes misunderstanding,
(3) Search of the former position where other possible alternatives are remaind,
(4) Returning to the previous position of which alternative has the highest degree of matching,
(5) Reinterpretation of the instruction.

The recognition of mistake is done in the first step, when all the alternatives have the lower truth value than the threshold. The second step is natural in order to select the other possibility, but it does not mean that this choice is completely eliminated. If there are no possible alternatives after cheking all of them, this may revive. In the third step, the more previous selections may be the cause of wrong decision if there remains no possible alternative in the former position. So this search should be continued until the cause is found. The fourth step means that man should return directly to the position where the wrong decision is done. In the fifth step, new interpretation is done with new list of selections.

The method of returning to the previous position in the fourth step is now discussed. The following notations are used here.

A, B, ...Z : position
#n : number of steps (distance)
N(= 2 ~ 8) : direciton of ways as shown in Fig. 2
-1 : opposite direction

The path which he has taken is expressed as a sequence of the above symbols, and the inverse sequence is created as follows.

$$(a,b,\ldots,\ell,m)^{-1} = (-1,m^{-1},\ell^{-1},\ldots b^{-1},a^{-1}) \qquad (10)$$

, where

a, b, ... stand for A, B, ..., #n, N, or -1.

and

$$\begin{aligned} A^{-1} &= A \\ (\#n)^{-1} &= \#n \\ N^{-1} &= 10 - N \\ (-1)^{-1} &= -1 \end{aligned} \qquad (11)$$

Next reduction rules are applied to find the shortest return rout.

$$\begin{aligned} &\#n,\ \#n' = \#(n+n') \\ &\#n,\ -1,\ \#n' = -1 \quad \text{if } n = n' \\ &\qquad\qquad \#(n-n'),\ -1 \quad \text{if } n > n' \\ &\qquad\qquad 01,\ \#(n'-n) \quad \text{if } n < n' \quad (12) \\ &N,\ -1,\ N' = N + N' - 1 \quad \text{if } N + N' < 10 \\ &\qquad\qquad N + N' - 9 \quad \text{if } N + N' > 10 \\ &A,\ A, = \wedge \\ &-1, -1 = \wedge \end{aligned}$$

where ^ means "delete".

An example is shown in Fig. 12. The memorized path is (A, #5, B, 5, #4, D, 3, #6, E, -1, #6, 7, -1, D, -1, #4, 5, -1, B, 3, #3, C, -1, #3, 3, #4, D, 5, #7, F).

The process of the reduction is as follows.
First
(A, #5, 3, #3, C, -1, #3, 3, #4, D, 5, #7, F)
Then
(A, #5, 5, #4, 5, #7, F)

At last we get the inverse sequence of the original path.
(F, -1, #7, 5, #4, 5, #5, -1, A)

7. RESULT OF SIMULATION

As an example, we consider a town of which map is as shown in Fig. 13. The meaning of the symbols used here are described in Table 3. We like to instruct a man, who is at the South-West corner of the town, the path to a mail-box marked with an asterisk.

The linguistic instruction is as follows. "Go straight to North from the park and turn right as the intersection which is about 15 STEP far from the park. If you walk about 20 STEP, there is a restaurant. Turn left there and stop at a mail-box which is on the left side a little way off the restaurant".
The form of this instruction is

START FROM PARK
HEAD NORTH
FIND THE INTERSECTION WHICH IS ABOUT 15 STEPS AHEAD
TURN TO THE RIGHT
FIND THE RESTAURANT WHICH IS ABOUT 20 STEPS AHEAD
TURN TO THE LEFT
FIND THE MAIL-BOX WHICH IS A FEW STEPS AHEAD AND ON THE LEFT HAND
STOP

The performance of the man simulated in a computer with this thinking model is shown as the solid line on the map. The thinking processes are interpreted as follows. He goes ahead to the North after confirmed the location of the park. At the first interseciton, he checks if this intersection is true one instructed. He judges this is true and intends to turn right, but there are two alternatives. He chooses the way to the East and goes about 20 steps, but there is no restaurant. He realizes this way wrong and goes back to the former intersection. Next he takes the way to the North-East. He finds a restaurant and takes a way to the North. After 7 steps walk, he finds a mail-box but this is too far. Then he comes back to the restaurant, and takes another way to the West. Since there is no mail-box along the street, he returns to the restaurant again. This time, there is no other alternative, then he awares this restaurant is not what is instructed. He takes the way to the East, because this can be considered almost straight. Another restaurant is found and he turns to left at this point. There is a mail-box, and he stops there.

We can see that his quess at the first intersection is already wrong. It is wonderful that he can come to the true destination, even though he makes many mistakes. This is because the thinking model has the ability of macroscopic judgement and the ability of learning.

The behavior of this thinking model is quite similar to that of human. This result is examined by many other simulations.

8. CONCLUSION

The ability of reasoning and imagination is indispensable to intelligent machines for performing the human instruction. In this paper, we suggest a thinking model which has this ability to some extent by using fuzzy reasoning. This model does not always attain the exact solution, but can aware the mistakes by itself and correct them under the ambiguous condition. The results obtained by this model are almost right. Those are similar to human thinking.

The next aim of our study is to give the model an ability of correcting the careless mistakes in the instruction. For this purpose, computer must have more common sense about the subject.

REFERENCES

1 M. Uragami, M. Mizuno and K. Tanaka: Fuzzy Robot Controls, J. of Cybernetics, 6:39-64, 1976
2 L. A. Zadeh: Fuzzy Logic and Approximate Reasoning, Synthese, 30, 407-428, 1975
3 E. Sanchez: On Truth-Qualification in

Natural Languages, ICCS, 1233-1236, Tokyo, 1978

4 H. Imaoka and M. Sugeno: A Model of Dialog Based on Fuzzy Set Concept, IJCAI, 419-421, Tokyo, 1979

5 M. M. Gupta, Y. Tsukamoto and P.N. Nikiforuk: Truth Qualifications and Numerical Truth Values, JACCA, 1980

Table 1 The Value of N(A | B)

μ_A	μ_B	N(A | B)		
Type 2	Type α	0,	$\lvert\varepsilon\rvert \geqq W_a + W_b$	$\varepsilon \triangleq (b - a)$
		$\dfrac{W_a + W_b - \lvert\varepsilon\rvert}{2(W + W_b)}$,	$W_a + W_b > \lvert\varepsilon\rvert > W_a$	
		$\dfrac{2W_a + W_b - 2\lvert\varepsilon\rvert}{2(W_a + W_b)}$,	$W_a \geqq \lvert\varepsilon\rvert$	
Type 3	Type α	0,	$- W_b \geqq \varepsilon$	$\varepsilon \triangleq (b - a)$
		$\dfrac{W_b + \varepsilon}{2(W_a + W_b)}$,	$0 > \varepsilon > - W_b$	
		$\dfrac{W_b + 2\varepsilon}{2(W_a + W_b)}$,	$W_a \geqq \varepsilon \geqq 0$	
		$\dfrac{W_a + W_b + \varepsilon}{2(W_a + W_b)}$,	$W_a + W_b > \varepsilon > W_a$	
		1,	$\varepsilon \geqq W_a + W_b$	
Type 1	Type α	ditto		$\varepsilon \triangleq (a - b)$
Type 1	Type β	0,	$0 \geqq \varepsilon$	$\varepsilon \triangleq (a - b)$
		$\dfrac{\varepsilon}{2(W_a + W_b)}$,	$W_a + W_b > \varepsilon > 0$	
		0.5	$\varepsilon \geqq W_a + W_b$	
Type 2	Type β	0,	$- W_a \geqq \varepsilon$	$\varepsilon \triangleq (a - b)$
		$\dfrac{W_a + \varepsilon}{2(W_a + W_b)}$,	$W_b > \varepsilon > - W_a$	
		0.5,	$\varepsilon \geqq W_b$	
Type 3	Type β	0.5		

Table 2 Correspondence of t and τ

t	τ
0	completely false
0.19	very false
0.25	false
0.31	more or less false
0.5	unkown
0.69	more or less true
0.75	true
0.81	true
1	completely true

Table 3 Symbol of Object

Symbol	Name
PA	Park
RE	Restaurant
BU	Building
PO	Mail box
PB	Police box
CS	Cigar store
ST	Station
SC	School
BA	Bank
BS	Book store

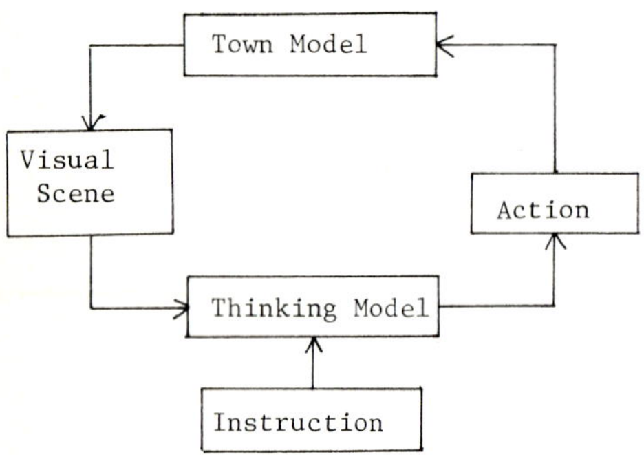

Fig. 1 Structure of the Whole Model

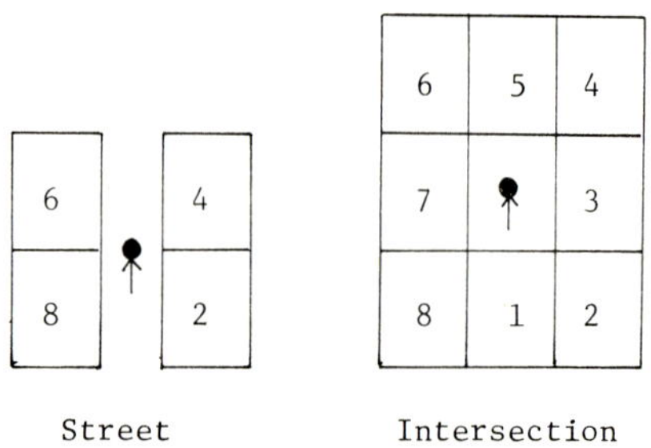

Fig. 2 Visual Scene

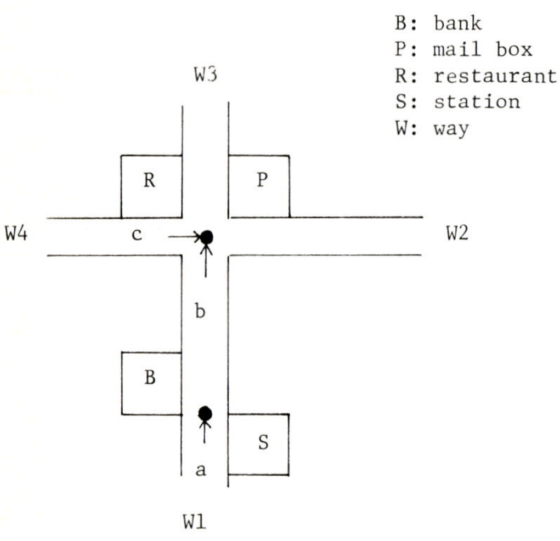

Fig. 3 Example of Town

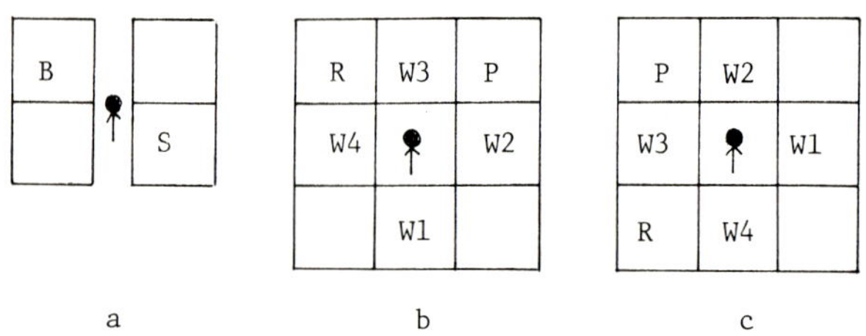

Fig. 4 Example of Visual Scene

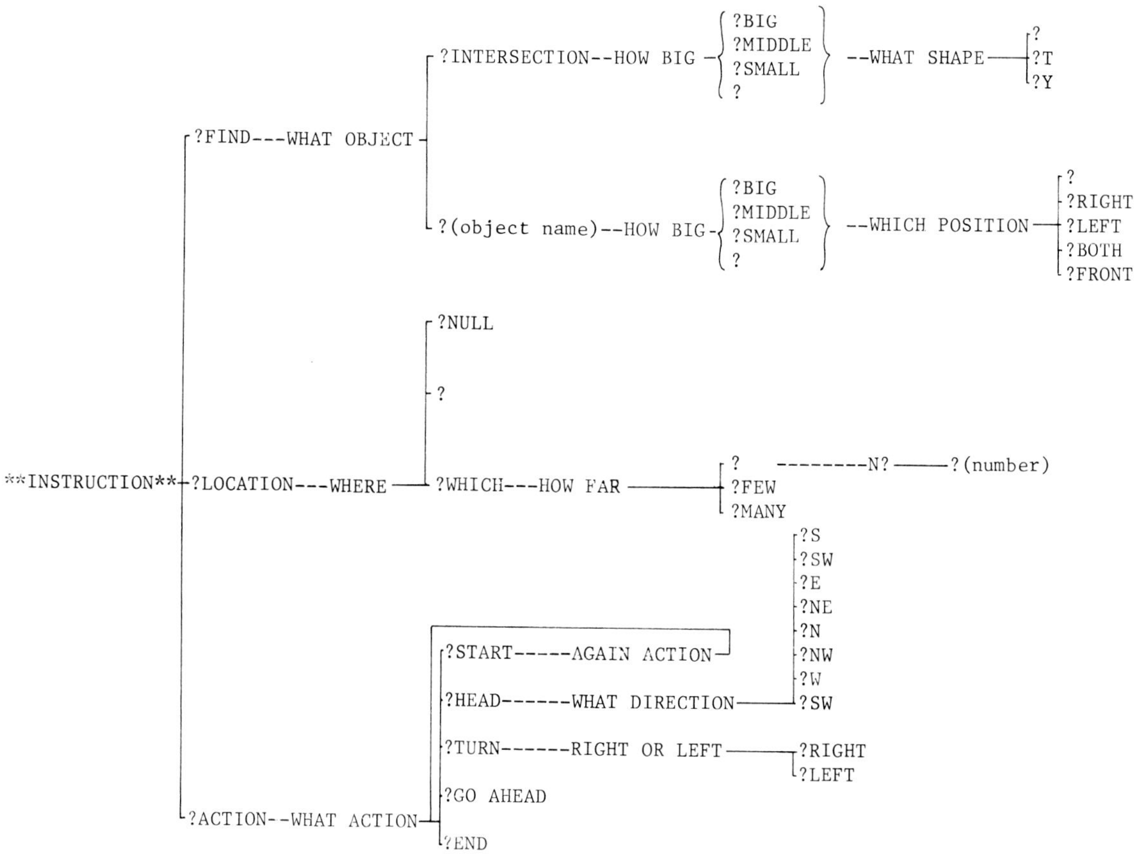

Fig. 5 Dialogical Composition of Instruction Rule

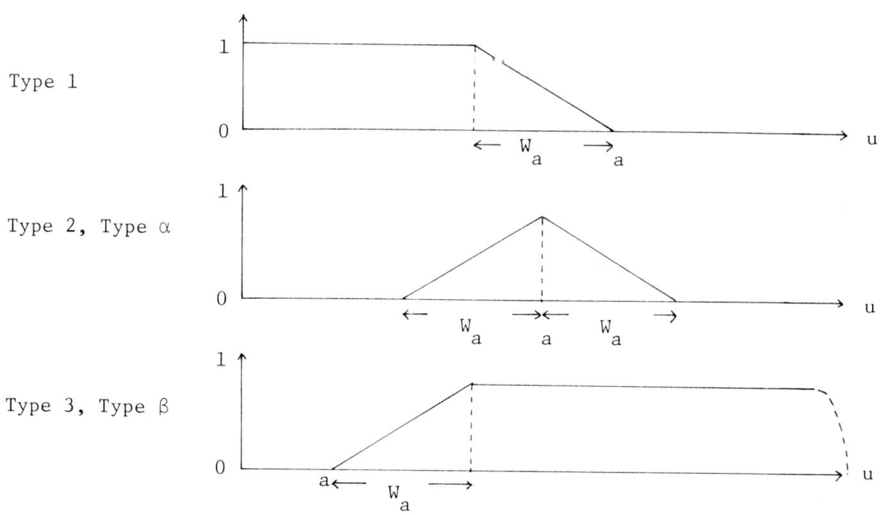

Fig. 6 Types of Membership Function

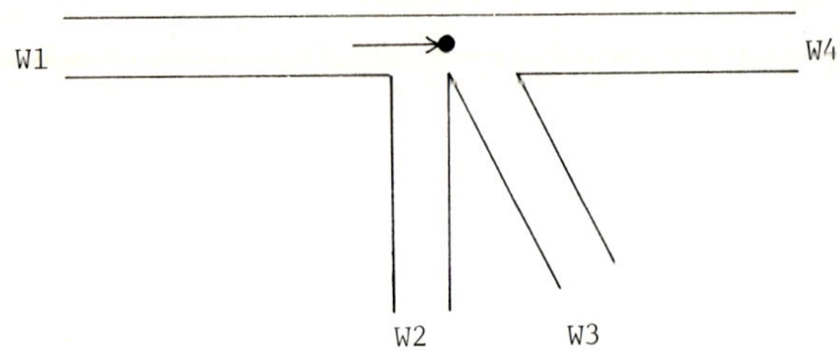

Fig. 7 Example of "TURN TO THE RIGHT"

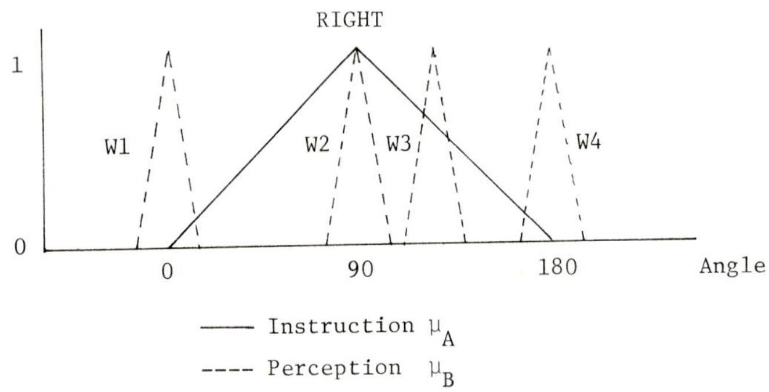

Fig. 8 Membership Function of Fig. 7

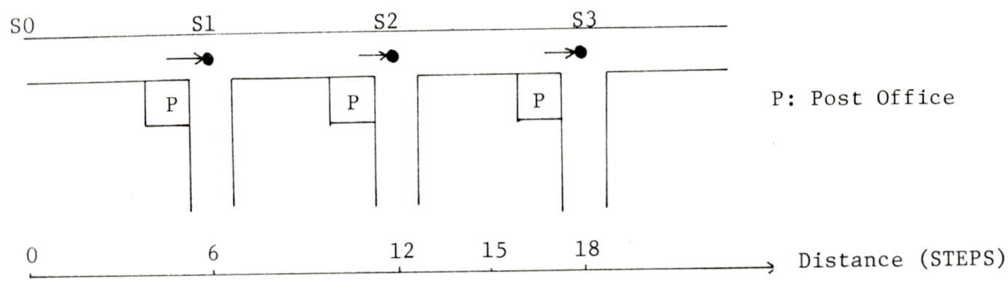

Fig. 9 Example of "ABOUT 15 STEPS"

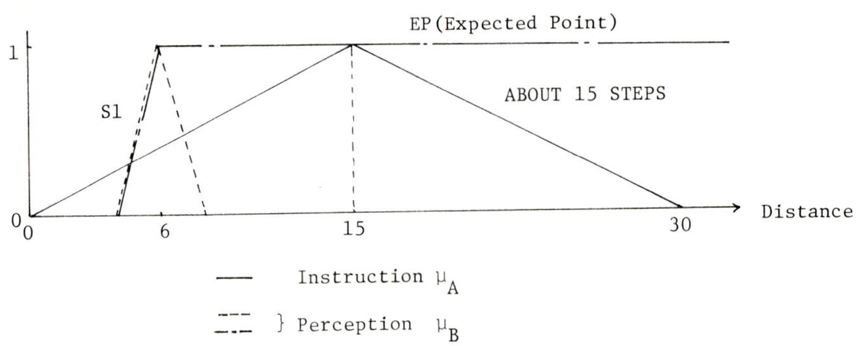

Fig. 10 Membership Function at S1 in Fig. 9

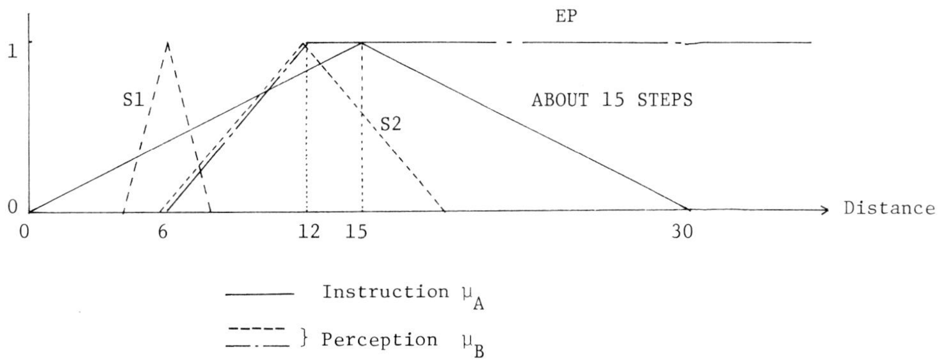

Fig. 11 Membership Function at S2 in Fig. 9

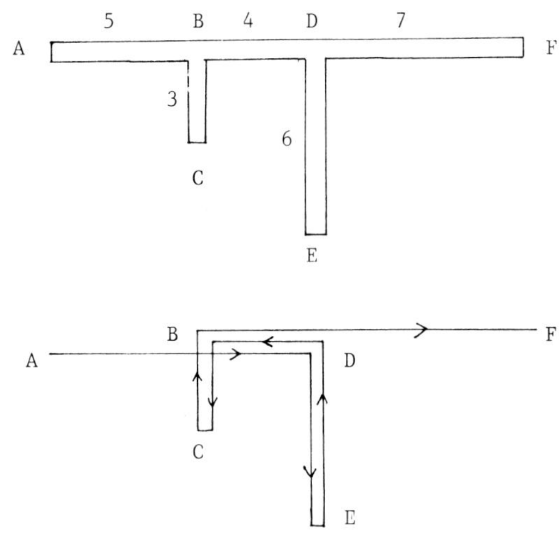

Fig. 12 Example of Backtracking

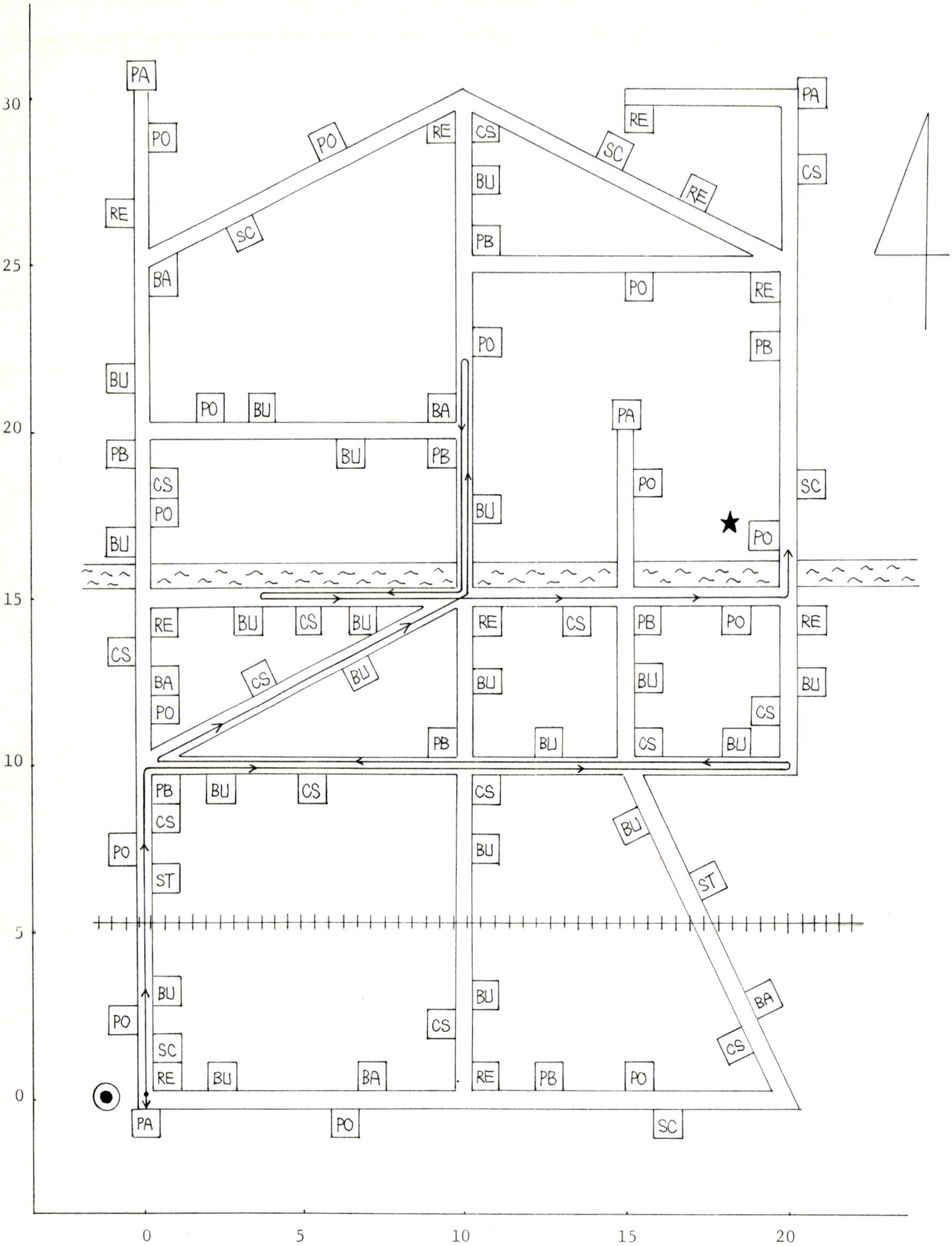

Fig. 13 Simulation Study

Approximate Reasoning in Decision Analysis
M.M. Gupta and E. Sanchez (eds.)

FUZZY SETS IN FEW CLASSICAL OPERATIONAL RESEARCH PROBLEMS

Stefan Chanas

Institute of Management
Technical University of Wrocław
Wrocław, Poland

The fuzzy set theory offers fresh opportunities for operational research, too. The theory makes possible considerations on some new problems so it extends possibilities of the well known classical models and methods. The latter is shown in the paper by presenting some results in network flows, network planning and assignment problems.

KEY WORDS: Operational research, Flow, Project, Assignment, Fuzzy set.

1. INTRODUCTION

A characteristic feature of operational research (OR) is its ability to adopt mathematical methods. This makes OR a scientific method, but simultaneously limits its application. The latter results from inflexibility of the classic mathematical apparatus which requires many difficult or impossible to prove concise assumptions. The "hard" mathematical apparatus often imposes a single-track approach to a decision problem being analyzed by OR methods.

Publication of Zadeh's work on fuzzy sets [16] in 1965 was the beginning of a rapid development of the so - called "soft mathematics". It seems that the new apparatus offers fresh opportunities for OR, too. We consider here the chances of adjusting mathematical methods used in OR to the nature of solved problems. The chance has been noticed by specialists and reflected in numerous publications on applications of fuzzy sets in OR and in decision making theory. The development has been accelerated since the publication of the interesting and stimulating work [1] by Bellman and Zadeh appeared in 1970. The work became a methodological "starting point" for other authors. The novelity of this approach is a identical treatment of constraints and goals in decision problems, their uniform modelling in the form of fuzzy subsets on the space of alternatives. This form allows for treating both quantitative and qualitative aspect of a decision problem because of different interpretations of the notion of a fuzzy set. The fuzzy set apparatus allows for the construction of some new models and methods used in OR and also provides some possibilities of generalization of known classic models and methods. Actually, we shall try to verify the last statement by presenting in this paper some generalizations of three known problems discussed in almost every typical OR handbook. These are: the problem of determining the maximal flow and the minimal out in a network as formulated and developped by Ford and Fulkerson [10]; the problem of project analysis, here we mean- above all- the classic and most popular CPM and PERT methods [12]; the assignment problem and the so - called bottleneck assignment problem [10].

2. FLOWS IN NETWORKS WITH FUZZY CAPACITY CONSTRAINTS

Now we shall present some generalization of the problem of determining the maximal flow and the minimal cut in a network with upper constraints on the arc capacities [5]. The difference versus the classical statement of the problem is in the vague formulation and in non-strictly fixed constraints and requirements which are allowed to be violated on a certain margin.

2.1. Formulation of the problem

Let us formulate the classic problem of maximal flow determination in a network, $S = \langle N,A \rangle$, with a fixed source, $s \in N$, and a destination, $t \in N$. N denotes a set of vertices of the network, $A \subset N \times N$ denotes a set of arcs. The determination of the maximal flow x_v ($x_v = \{x_{ij} / (i,j) \in A\}$) in network S from source s in destination t can be formulated in the form of a linear problem:

(i) $\max v$,

(ii) $$\sum_{i \in \Gamma_j^-} x_{ij} - \sum_{k \in \Gamma_j} x_{jk} = \begin{cases} -v & \text{for } j = s, \\ 0 & \text{for } j \neq s,t, \\ v & \text{for } j = t \end{cases}$$

(iii) $0 \leqslant x_{ij} \leqslant c_{ij}$.

v denotes the flow value, x_{ij} is the flow value in arc $(i,j) \in A$, Γ_j^- and Γ_j are sets of vertices preceding and following the vertex $j \in N$, respectively. Next, c_{ij} is the upper constraint (arc capacity) on the flow value x_{ij} in arc (i,j).

Now we shall generalize the problem (i) - (iii). Let us assume that the decision maker is interested in the flow value at least v_o, but he admits smaller values with a decreasing satisfaction degree to the limit of $v_1 \leqslant v_o$ beyond which the values do not satisfy him at all. Similarily, let the decision maker admits the capacity excesses in arc (i,j) to the limit of $\bar{c}_{ij} \geqslant c_{ij}$. The problem is to find such a flow which has a "possibly large" value and simultaneously in the "possibly best way" satisfies the capacity constraints. We see that the formulation is vague and the problem can be treated as a fuzzy decision problem, in which the goal as well as the constraints are fuzzy. Using the apparatus of fuzzy sets theory and taking into account the methodology proposed by Bellman and Zadeh [1] in the treatment of a decision problem in "the fuzzy environment" we now construct a formal model of the above problem.

Criterion (i) may be associated with a fuzzy set, G, in the space of alternatives (satisfying balance requirements (ii)) with the membership function:

$$\mu_G(x_v) = \begin{cases} 1 & \text{if } v > v_o \\ L(v_o,v_1;v) & \text{if } v_1 \leqslant v \leqslant v_o \\ 0 & \text{if } v < v_1 \end{cases} \qquad (2.1)$$

where $L(v_o,v_1;v)$ is a non - increasing (linear for instance) function in interval $[v_1,v_o]$ assuming the value of 0 for $v=v_1$ and 1 for $v = v_o$. Value $\mu_G(x_v)$ determines a decision maker's degree of satisfaction with respect to the satisfying of goal G by the flow x_v. Because that value depends on the value of v only, we shall use symbols $\mu_G(x_v)$ and $\mu_G(v)$ interchangeably. Similarly with each of the constraint in (iii) ($0 \leqslant x_{ij} \leqslant c_{ij}$) one can relate a fuzzy set, C_{ij}, with the membership function

$$\mu_{ij}(x_v) = \begin{cases} 1 & \text{if } x_{ij} < c_{ij}, \\ \bar{L}(c_{ij},\bar{c}_{ij};x_{ij}) & \text{if } c_{ij} \leqslant x_{ij} \leqslant \bar{c}_{ij}, \\ 0 & \text{if } x_{ij} > \bar{c}_{ij}, \end{cases} \qquad (2.2)$$

where $\bar{L}(c_{ij},\bar{c}_{ij};x_{ij})$ is a non-decreasing function (for example linear) assuming the value of 1 for $x_{ij} = c_{ij}$ and 0 for $x_{ij} = \bar{c}_{ij}$. $\mu_{ij}(x_{ij})$ - the feasibility degree of x_v with respect to the capacity constraint on arc (i,j) can also be understood as a measure of truth of the fuzzy statement "x_v satisfies $x_{ij} \leqslant c_{ij}$ as well as possible". Because $\mu_{ij}(x_v)$ depends only on the value of x_{ij}

we shall use symbol $\mu_{ij}(x_{ij})$ interchangeably, too. According to Bellman and Zadeh's criterion [1] the problem can be reduced now to finding a flow which maximizes the value of the membership function, $\mu_D(x_v)$, in fuzzy decision D:

$$D = \bigcap_{(i,j)\in A} C_{ij} \cap G,$$

$$\mu_D(x_v) = \mu_C(x_v) \wedge \mu_G(x_v) \to \max,$$

where $\mu_C(x_v) = \bigwedge_{(i,j)\in A} \mu_{ij}(x_{ij})$

$\mu_C(x_v)$ denotes a degree of a simultaneous realization of capacity constraints on all network arcs. The symbols $\cap$ and $\wedge$ stand for intersection and minimum operation, respectively. Let us deal now with properties of an optimal solution of the problem formulated above.

2.2 Properties of the optimal flow

Definition 2.1. A flow, x_v^*, is called the maximum flow if

$$\mu_D(x_v^*) = \max_{x_v} \mu_D(x_v).$$

Definition 2.2. A flow, x_v, with the greatest value of v among other maximum flows is called an optimal flow.

Definition 2.3. A cut in the network $S = \langle N,A \rangle$ separating the source s from the destination t is a set of arcs $(X,\bar{X}) \subset A$ connecting vertices $x \in X$ with vertices $y \in \bar{X}$ $(X,\bar{X} \subset N$, $X \cup \bar{X} = N$, $s \in X$, $t \in \bar{X})$.

For the sake of convenience we introduce the notations: $(\underrightarrow{X,\bar{X}})$ - the set of those arcs of the cut, $(X,\bar{X})$, which are directed from X to $\bar{X}$, $(\underleftarrow{X,\bar{X}})$ - the set of arcs directed from $\bar{X}$ to X. For real number flows the following theorem, which corresponds to Ford and Fulkerson theorem on the maximal flow and minimal cut, are valid. In the theorem some additional assumptions are needed. Namely we require that functions L and $\bar{L}$ in (2.1) and (2.2) are continuous.

Theorem 2.1. If x_v is an optimal flow there exists a cut, $(X,\bar{X})$, in the network satisfying the following conditions:

(i) $(i,j) \in (\underrightarrow{X,\bar{X}}) \Rightarrow \mu_{ij}(x_{ij}) = \mu_D(x_v)$

(ii) $(i,j) \in (\underleftarrow{X,\bar{X}}) \Rightarrow x_{ij} = 0.$

The above theorem is not true if only integer flows are assumed. In that case we have the following theorem.

Theorem 2.2. If x_v is an optimal flow then there exists in network S a cut, $(X,\bar{X})$, satisfying the following requirements:

$(i,j) \in (\underrightarrow{X,\bar{X}}) \Rightarrow \mu_{ij}(x_{ij} + 1) < \mu_D(x_v)$

$(i,j) \in (\underleftarrow{X,\bar{X}}) \Rightarrow x_{ij} = 0.$

The cut, $(X,\bar{X})$, appearing in Theorems 2.1 and 2.2 can be called the minimal cut because it forms a "bottle-neck" for the optimal flow. There exists an important difference between the idea of the minimal cut in the classic case and in the case discussed in the present paper. In the fuzzy case the minimal cut in the network cannot be determined without the knowledge of the optimal flow. Both the optimal flow and the respective minimal cut depend on the accepted form of the criterion G.

2.3 Algorithm for the determination of integer optimal flow

In the algorithm presented below subsequently constructed flows $\bar{x}_v$, $\bar{x}_{v+1}$, $\bar{x}_{v+2}$,..., are compared and each of them satisfies in "the best way" the capacity constraints in its class of flows with the same value i.e.

$$\mu_C(\bar{x}_k) = \max_{x_k} \mu_C(x_k) \quad \text{for } k = v, v+1, \ldots,$$

In that way an inspection of a finite number of flows is executed and the procedure allows for the identification of flows "near" to the optimal flow.

Algorithm

Step 1.

Find maximum flow $\bar{x}_v^1$ in the classical sense in network S assuming arc capacities equal to c_{ij}. Evidently $\mu_C(\bar{x}_v^1) = 1$. If $\mu_G(v) = 1$ then stop, $\bar{x}_v^1$ is optimal. If not go to step 2.

Step 2. Let $\bar{x}_v^1$ be an actual flow. Generate a flow, $\bar{x}_{v+1}^2$, satisfying in a maximum degree the capacity constraints. Go to step 3.

Step 3. Check if the following condition holds: $\mu_D(\bar{x}_v^1) > \mu_D(\bar{x}_{v+1}^2)$. If so, then stop and the optimal flow remains $\bar{x}_v^1$. If not, $\bar{x}_v^1 = \bar{x}_{v+1}^2$ and go to step 2.

The flow $\bar{x}_{v+1}^2$ in Step 2 of the algorithm is obtained by increasing the flow $\bar{x}_v^1$ by a unit on chain r linking source s with destination t and maximizing the value of the expression.

$$\mu^r(\bar{x}_v^1) = \bigwedge_{(i,j)\in\vec{r}} \mu_{ij}(\bar{x}_{ij}^1+1) \wedge \bigwedge_{(i,j)\in\overleftarrow{r}} \mu_{ij}(\bar{x}_{ij}^1-1) \to \max \qquad (2.3)$$

where $\vec{r}$ is the set of arcs of chain r accordingly directed, $\overleftarrow{r}$ - the set of arcs reversely directed; in addition we assume that if $\bar{x}_{ij}^1 = 0$ then $\mu_{ij}(\bar{x}_{ij}^1 - 1) = -1$. One of well-known algorithms for looking for the shortest path in the network can be easly adopted to searching for the optimal chain according to criterion (2.3) [eg. 7].

Let us illustrate the discussed algorithm with the calculation results obtained for a simple network given in Fig. 1. Apart from the input data c_{ij} and $\bar{c}_{ij}$ the values of arc flows, x_{ij}, with respective function values $\mu_{ij}(x_{ij})$ for the optimal flow are given in Fig. 1. In the example function L in the definition of μ_G is linear and $v_o = 15$ and $v_1 = 5$. Table 1 presents information about function values μ_C, μ_G and μ_D

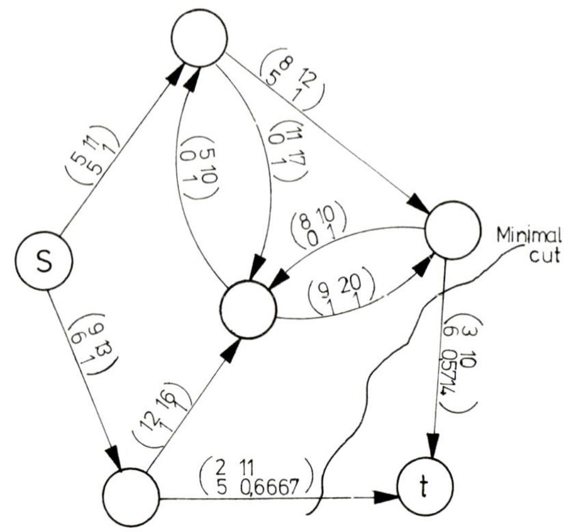

The numbers at arcs have the following meaning $\begin{pmatrix} c_{ij} & \bar{c}_{ij} \\ x_{ij} & \mu_{ij}(x_{ij}) \end{pmatrix}$

Figure 1: A sample network with input data and the optimal flow

for the optimal and few neighbouring flows.

The presented algorith can be adopted to some extension for the determination of optimal flow among real flows. It is sufficient to generate in the second step of algorithm the flow $\bar{x}_{v+\varepsilon}^2$ instead of $\bar{x}_{v+1}^2$, where $0<\varepsilon<1$. Evidently, one has to replace 1 by ε in formula (2.3). The proposed procedure does not give an exact solution. The exactness depends on the value of ε but the diminution of ε results in the increase of calculation time.

In [6] a more general problem then the one discussed here has been considered. The generalization takes into account additional lower constraints on arc capacities in the network. The authors solve the problem in a similar way as we do here but the proposed algorithm is more complex since the problem itself, is more complicated.

Table 1. Information about the optimal and neighbouring flows

v	$\mu_C(x_v)$	$\mu_G(x_v)$	$\mu_D(x_v)$
6	0.889	0.100	0.100
7	0.857	0.200	0.200
8	0.778	0.300	0.300
9	0.714	0.400	0.400
10	0.667	0.500	0.500
(11)	0.571	0.600	0.571
12	0.556	0.700	0.556
13	0.444	0.800	0.444
14	0.429	0.900	0.429
15	0.333	1.000	0.333
16	0.286	1.000	0.286

3. FUZZY APPROACH TO PROJECT ANALYSIS

Now, we present a generalization of CPM and PERT methods, classical methods of project analysis developped already in the fifties. The generalization admits a fuzzy determination of activity times in network models in the form of fuzzy sets on the time space.

3.1. Formulation of the problem

In the sequel we assume that the project can be represented as a directed, connected, acyclic graph $G = \langle Y,U \rangle$. $Y = \{1,2,\dots,N\}$ is the set of vertices, which represent project events. The set of arcs, $U \subset Y \times Y$, represents project activities. The events of the project are of "conjunction type" i.e. all activities "starting" from fixed vertex "i" are executed and their execution can be started at the time when all activities "entering" vertex "i" are completed. With no loss in the generality of consideration we assume that graph G has one initial vertex "1" ($\Gamma_1^- = \emptyset$) and one terminal vertex "N" ($\Gamma_N = \emptyset$).

In the classic CPM it is assumed that for every activity $(i,j) \in U$ a determined time, t_{ij}, for its execution is given. The problem consists in the determination of a series of characteristics of a great interest for planning and control of the project. These are: the minimum time for the completion of the project as the target time (the earliest time of the event "N" realization), the earliest and latest times of realization of the remaining events, the so-called critical activities and critical events being in a sense "a bottleneck" in the realization of the project - influencing the time of completing the project. The earliest moments, t_i^e, of occurring of events $(i=1,2,\dots,N)$ and consequently the target time, t_N^e, can be determined according to the following reccurence formula:

$$t_i^e = \begin{cases} 0 & \text{for } i = 1 \\ \max\limits_{k \in \Gamma_i^-} (t_k^e + t_{ki}) & \text{for } i \neq 1 \end{cases} \tag{3.1}$$

The latest moments, t_i^l, of occurance of events can be found by use of the following relation:

$$t_i^l = \begin{cases} t_N^e & \text{for } i = N \\ \min\limits_{k \in \Gamma_i} (t_k^l - t_{ik}) & \text{for } i \neq N \end{cases} \tag{3.2}$$

The times evaluated according to (3.1) and (3.2) are used in the calculation of the so - called slack times in events and activities. For instance the slack time in event "i" is the value, $L_i = t_i^l - t_i^e$, and the total slack time in activity (i,j) is given by $z(i,j) = t_j^l - t_i^e - t_{ij}$. The events for which $L_i = 0$ are called critical events and similarly critical activities are those with $z(i,j)=0$. The sequence with the starting point "1" and terminal point "N" composed of critical activities is called a critical path.

In PERT, which is actually a slight modification of CPM, random times of execution of activities are assumed. Practically, the analysis of the network is done by use of CPM introducing only the expectations and variances in activity times. The expectations and variations are evaluated according to formulae implied by the assumed distributions of activity times and the set of estimates delivered by some experts. For instance, in the first version of PERT [12], still the most popular beta distribution was assumed and the possibility to receive three estimates, a,b,m ($a\leq m\leq b$) by experts as the most optimistic, the most pessimistic and the most expected estimates, was assured. Under these assumptions the following approximate formulae for the activity time expectation, t_e, and variance σ^2 follow:

$$t_e = \frac{1}{3}\left[2m + \frac{1}{2}(a+b)\right] \qquad (3.3)$$

$$\sigma^2 = \frac{(b-a)^2}{36}$$

The method of PERT has often been criticized. Objections have been raised concerning assumptions about activity times as well as to formulae (3.3) and to the method of determining the project complection time. We shall not quote these objections and we shall not discuss their validity. Only one aspect of the matter must be noticed. Namely, real projects are usualy characterized by low repeatability. Thus, one cannot practically verify the assumptions concerning the probability distributions for a given project. Also, the expert estimates are not precise. It seems that the probability theory apparatus is too "strong" and inapplicable to the character of estimates at the disposal.

In papers [2,3,11] the idea of fuzzy approach to the project analysis was adopted. It is assumed that activity times are given in the network in the form of fuzzy sets, T_{ij}, on the space of time T. The fuzzy sets, T_{ij}, with the membership functions denoted by μ_{ij} ($\mu_{ij}: T \to [0,1]$) can be interpreted as the verbal statements of the estimates made by experts - as fuzzy variables, fuzzy numbers or possibility distributions in the sense of [17]. So the problem of determination of the project completion time arises. The time cannot be determined uniquely or precisely because of fuzzy activity times. Also, the problem of the notion of "critical path" in the new situation should be solved.

3.2 The completion time and criticality in the network with fuzzy activity times

We assume that fuzzy activity times, T_{ij}, are convex and normal fuzzy sets on time space T. It means that the following conditions hold

$$\forall_{\substack{\alpha\in[0,1]\\ t_1,t_2\in T}} \mu_{ij}(\alpha t_1 + (1-\alpha)t_2) \geq \mu_{ij}(t_1) \wedge \mu_{ij}(t_2) \qquad \text{(convexity)}$$

and

$$\sup_{t\in T} \mu_{ij}(t) = 1 \qquad \text{(normality)}$$

The extension principle of Zadeh allows for a natural generalization of arithmetic operations to the case of fuzzy data. Let A and B be fuzzy sets on T and let $*$ denote one of the arithmetic operations +, -, min, max.

Definition 3.1. $A * B = C$ iff

$$\mu_C(t) = \sup_{\substack{t_1,t_2\in T\\ t_1 * t_2 = t}} \min\{\mu_A(t_1), \mu_B(t_2)\}$$

Definition 3.2. The r-strong level, $r\in[0,1]$, of a fuzzy set A is the crisp set $A^r = \{t \mid \mu_A(t) > r\}$.

The following theorems are true:

Theorem 3.1. Let a fuzzy set A on T be convex. Then for all $r\in[0,1]$ A^r are intervals on T and of the form $A^r = \langle \underline{a}_r, \bar{a}^r\rangle$, where $\underline{a}_r = \inf A^r$ and $\bar{a}_r = \sup A^r$. With respect to the type of function μ_A these intervals may be one-sidely or two-sidely open or closed. For example if μ_A is continuous then we get open intervals $(\underline{a}_r, \bar{a}_r)$.

Theorem 3.2. If fuzzy sets A and B on T

are convex, then for all $r \in [0,1]$

(i) $(A+B)^r = \langle \underline{a}_r + \underline{b}_r, \bar{a}_r + \bar{b}_r \rangle$

(ii) $(A \vee B)^r = \langle \underline{a}_r \vee \underline{b}_r, \bar{a}_r \vee \bar{b}_r \rangle$

(iii) $(A - B)^r = \langle \underline{a}_r - \bar{b}_r, \bar{a}_r + \bar{b}_r \rangle$

(iv) $(A \wedge B)^r = \langle \underline{a}_r \wedge \underline{b}_r, \bar{a}_r \wedge \bar{b}_r \rangle$

Theorem 3.3. If fuzzy sets A and B on T are convex then $A * B$ are also convex ($*$ denotes one of the generalized operations in Definition 3.1).

Theorems 3.1 - 3.3 imply the following procedure for the determination of completion time. Let T_i be the earliest fuzzy time of occurence of event "i" with membership function $\mu_i (\mu_i : T \to [0,1])$. The times, T_i, can be found from reccurence formula which is a direct generalization of (3.1).

$$T_i = \bigvee_{k \in \Gamma_i^-} (T_k + T_{ki}) \quad i = 2,\dots,N. \qquad (3.4)$$

The starting time of a project, T_1, is given. If we assume for istance that the time is equal to zero then

$$\mu_1(t) = \begin{cases} 1 & \text{for } t = 0, \\ 0 & \text{otherwise.} \end{cases}$$

Evidently, the operations $\vee$ and $+$ in (3.4) are the generalization of fuzzy operations of maximum and addition as in Definition 3.1. In the case when the assumption of convexity for T_{ij} is valid the fuzzy times, T_i, can be determined by use of their r-strong levels. Then $T_{ij}^r = \langle \underline{t}_{ij}^r, \bar{t}_{ij}^r \rangle$ are intervals on T for all $r \in [0,1]$. T_i^r can be determined for every $r \in [0,1]$ by the formula following from Theorems 3.1 - 3.3:

$$T_i^r = \langle \underline{t}_i^r, \bar{t}_i^r \rangle = \langle \bigvee_{k \in \Gamma_i^-} (\underline{t}_k^r + \underline{t}_{ki}^r), \bigvee_{k \in \Gamma_i^-} (\bar{t}_k^r + \bar{t}_{ki}^r) \rangle \qquad (3.5)$$

Evidently, here $\vee$ and $+$ denotes ordinary, numerical operations of maximum and addition, respectively. Formula (3.5) allows for the determination of r-strong levels subsequently, according to the network structure, of times T_i and finally r-strong levels of the project completion time T_N. The time T_N itself and remaining times T_i (more precisely their membership functions μ_i) can be identified on the basis of r-strong levels by use of formula (3.6) in the following way:

Theorem 3.4 [14]. Let A be a fuzzy set on T and $\{A^r\}$, $r \in [0,1]$, be all r-strong levels of A, then

$$\mu_A(t) = \begin{cases} \sup \{ r \mid t \in A^r \} & \text{for } t \in A^0 \\ 0 & \text{otherwise} \end{cases} \qquad (3.6)$$

Evidently, because of numerical reasons the above procedure of calculation of T_N can be realized only in an approximate way by evaluation of T_i^r for a series of chosen r' s, for instance, $r = 0, 0.1, 0.2, \dots, 0.9$. In that case (3.6) allows for an approximate identification of membership function μ_i for T_i.

The results presented above may also be extended to the case of discrete time space T (T is the set of nonnegative integer numbers). In practice handling integer numbers to assess completion times of any activity or the whole project is convenient and sufficient for the question of accuracy. Of course the interval having integer ends $t_1, t_2 \in T$ would be understood as the set $\{t \mid t \in T, t_1 \leqslant t \leqslant t_2\}$, and the convexity of any set A as follows: A is convex if for any interval $[t_1, t_2]$ on space T the following inequality holds $\mu_A(t) \geqslant \mu_A(t_1) \wedge \mu_A(t_2)$ for all $t \in [t_1, t_2]$.

The direct generalization of formula (3.1) for the determination of the earliest times of events turns to be quite natural and reasonable. Nevertheless one cannot continue the generalization with formula (3.2) for the determination of the latest times of events. It is reasonable to generalize directly (3.2) only in the case when the calculation is initiated with an independently fixed determined or fuzzy target time, T_N, but not with time T_N determined by relation (3.4). In that case obtained results can be interpreted as the latest moments of events provided a fixed concrete completion time is assumed. In that situation the notion of criticality must be introduced otherwise than in the classic case. With fuzzy activity times it is not possible to define, in a unique way, the set of critical events or critical paths. Nevertheless one can say about the degree of criticality of an activity, an event or a path. Let $\bar{T}_i$, be "the earliest" time of the i-th event calculated by (3.4), while starting from the end of the network that is

$$\bar{T}_i = \bigvee_{k\in\Gamma_i} (\bar{T}_k + T_{ik}) \quad i = N-1,\dots,1 \qquad (3.7)$$

where $\bar{T}_N$ is given and

$$\bar{\mu}_N(t) = \begin{cases} 1 & \text{for } t = 0 \\ 0 & \text{for } t \neq 0 \end{cases}$$

In [11] the following definitions which seems quite natural and reasonable are given.

Definition 3.3. A fuzzy set, YC, on the set of vertices Y with the membership function

$$\mu_{YC}(i) = \text{Poss}\left\{T_i + \bar{T}_i \text{ is } T_N\right\}$$

is called a fuzzy set of critical events[1].

Definition 3.4. A fuzzy set, UC, on set U of activities with the membership function

$$\mu_{UC}(i,j) = \text{Poss}\left\{T_i + T_{ij} + \bar{T}_j \text{ is } T_N\right\}$$

is called a fuzzy set of critical activities.

The values of membership functions $\mu_{YC}(i)$ and $\mu_{UC}(i,j)$ can be interpreted as the degrees of criticality of event "i" or activity (i,j), respectively. Let us denote by P the set of all network paths going from vertex "1" to vertex "N". The realization time of path $p \in P$, denoted by T_p, is defined as the fuzzy sum of fuzzy activity times lying on this path

$$T_p = \sum_{(i,j)\in p} T_{ij}$$

The following definition of the critical path is natural.

Definition 3.5. A fuzzy set, PC, on set P of path with the membership function

$$\mu_{PC}(p) = \text{Poss}\left\{T_p \text{ is } T_N\right\}$$

is called a fuzzy set of critical paths in a project. The value, $\mu_{PC}(p)$, can be interpreted as the degree of criticality of path p.

In all three definitions 3.3, 3.4, 3.5 the problem of determination of the degree of criticality consists in the comparison of fuzzy values $T_i + \bar{T}_i$ with T_N in definition 3.3, $T_i + T_{ij} + \bar{T}_j$ with T_N in definition 3.4 and T_p with T_N in definition 3.5. Clearly the method presented here is not the only one possible. One could use an other preference on fuzzy outcomes [13].

We propose to realize all the operations in fuzzy multitudes using respective operations on r-strong levels. The concept of the so-called L-R - type fuzzy numbers developed by Dubois and Prade and simplified operations on them, as exact for + and - and approximate for $\vee$ and $\wedge$, is of a great interest [8,9]. The use of L-R numbers restricts - in an essential way - the range of possible mappings of the activity time but on the other hand provides some numerical advantages.

To end this section we present results of calculations executed for the network represented in Fig. 2. Table 2 gives fuzzy activity times on integer time space T. The times are given in the form of sets of pairs, the time value and corresponding membership function value. The completion time T_9 is equal to

$$T_9 = \{(19; 0.1), (20; 0.2), (21; 0.3), (22; 0.3), (23; 0.5), (24; 0.8), (25; 0.9), (26; 1), (27; 0.5), (28; 0.4), (29; 0.4), (30; 0.3)\}$$

The degree of criticality of activities and events are given in Fig. 2. The path (1,2, 5,9) is critical in degree 0.8, (1,2,4,7,8,9) in degree 1, (1,3,4,7,8,9) in degree 0.9

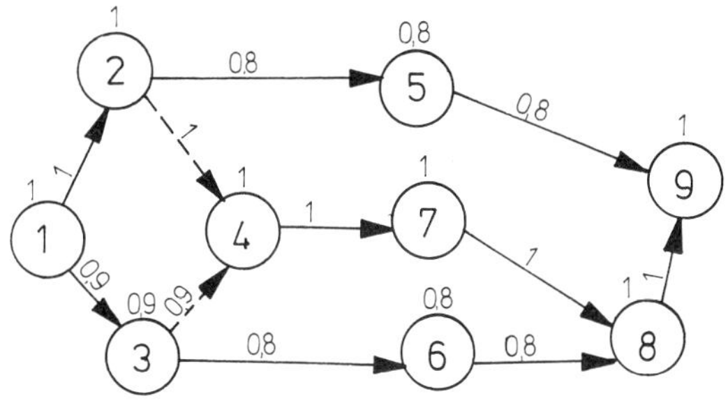

Fig. 2: Network for the example of calculations

and (1,3,6,8,9) in degree 0.8.

Table 2. Activity duration times

Activity denotation	Activity duration time
(1,2)	(2;0.2),(3;0.6),(4;1),(5;0.2)
(1,3)	(1;0.2),(2;0.4),(3;1),(4;0.7),(5;0.3)
(2,4)	(0;1)
(3,4)	(0;1)
(2,5)	(10;0.1),(11;0.5),(12;1),(13;0.6),(14;0.3)
(3,6)	(6;0.4),(7;1),(8;0.8),(9;0.2)
(4,7)	(7;0.3),(8;0.9),(9;1),(10;0.4)
(6,8)	(4;0.5),(5;1),(6;0.4)
(7,8)	(2;0.2),(3;0.8),(4;1),(5;0.4)
(5,9)	(7;0.4),(8;1),(9;0.8),(10;0.5)
(8,9)	(8;0.3),(9;1),(10;0.4)

4. FUZZY ASSIGNMENT PROBLEM

Both the models presented in the previous sections contain classic models as particular cases. Therefore they are some formal generalization of those models, too. In this section we present an assignment problem which is not, in this sense, a generalization of any classic model and operates "properly" only with fuzzy input data.

4.1. Classic assignment problems

Some real-world problems arise where decisions must be made concerning the assignment of each of a number of different machines to one of a number of different locations, each of a number of persons to one of a number of different positions, and so on. From a large number of known models related to the above stated problems we quote here two classic tasks. The first one is to find the assignment maximizing or minimizing a certain overall efficiency (total profit, overall costs). Formally, the problem can be stated as follows. Given n persons, n positions and efficiency estimates a_{ij} $(i,j = 1,2,\dots,n)$ where a_{ij} denotes the efficiency of assignment of the i-th person to the j-th position. The problem (I) consists in the determination of an assignment (n-element permutation $P = (p_1,p_2,\dots,p_n)$ which maximizes the overall efficiency

$$\max \sum_{i=1}^{n} a_{ip_i}$$

$P = (p_1,p_2,\dots,p_n)$ means that the person 1 is assigned to position p_1, person 2 to position p_2 and so on. The second problem (II) the so-called "bottleneck assignment problem" consists in the determination of an assignment which maximizes the minimal effectiveness

$$\max \min_i a_{ip_i}$$

Various methods of solution for both the above problems are known. Problem I can be solved using the so-called Hungarian Algorithm [10]. One of more advanced algorithms for the solution of II is given in [15].

4.2 Fuzzy effectiveness estimates

In many practical cases we have at our disposal neither objective criteria nor exact methods of estimating the effectiveness a_{ij}.

The estimates are often made by experts who have to take into account a series of criteria, also, of a qualitative character. In [4] there is a model described in which a fuzzy statement of estimates a_{ij} is allowed by use of fuzzy variables (fuzzy numbers). The model is not a direct generalization of any of the two classic tasks stated above though one could say that it links in some sense both the tasks. Now, let us formulate the problem and present its formal model. Let the effectiveness a_{ij} be given in a fuzzy way by use of fuzzy set A_{ij} on space U of estimates (the estimate scale). The sets, A_{ij}, can be interpreted as fuzzy variables, fuzzy numbers, possibility distributions. Let the membership functions of fuzzy sets A_{ij} be denoted by μ_{ij} ($\mu_{ij}: U \to [0,1]$). In the sequel, we assume that space U is discrete, $U = \{u_1, u_2, \dots, u_m\}$ because of numerical reasons. It seems reasonable to formulate the problem in the following way: find the assignment with possibly "high" estimates of the effectiveness and simultaneously with their "uniform" distribution. It means that one requires the individual effectiveness in the assignment to satisfy a certain condition (for instance to be "high") and at the same time to be close each to the others or in other words uniformly distributed. Here we give one possible formal approach to the stated problem

$$\max_P \max_{u \in U} w(P;\, u) \qquad (4.1)$$

where $w(P; u)$ is the membership function of the fuzzy set

$$A_{1p_1} \cap A_{2p_2} \cap \dots A_{np_n} \cap G \qquad (4.2)$$

provided the assignment, $P = (p_1, p_2, \dots, p_n)$, is fixed. The symbol $\cap$ denotes the intersection operation "$\cap$" for fuzzy sets or the operation "." of the algebraic product for fuzzy sets[2]. G is a fuzzy set on U and determines the meaning of non-sharp condition on the individual estimates in the assignment to be sought for instance one requires G to be "high" as in the above verbal formulation of the problem. In that case membership function μ_G of set G should be increasing from 0 to 1 in U, for instance a linear function. In other words the fuzzy set G, which is called in the sequel the estimate criterion, establishes the preference relation among individual number estimates on the estimate scale U. Generally G may have various forms and impose preferably, for instance, "medium" estimates or "low" estimates. Adopting G = "low" with the membership function decreasing from 1 to 0 in U would be equivalent to adopting a criterion of the specifically defined "minimization" of the assignment effectiveness.

Both the operations $\cap$ and $\cdot$ assumed in (4.2) have the same effect with the only difference in that that the algebraic product is more sensible to the change in the membership function values than the intersection operation.

4.3 Solution of the problem

Definition 4.1. The optimal assignment , P^*, in the sense of criterion G is defined by the following inequality

$$\forall_{P \neq P^*} \left[\max_{u \in U} w(P^*;u) \geq \max_{u \in U} w(P;u)\right].$$

In order to find permutation P^* one maximizes function $w(P;u)$ w. r.t all permutations $P \in \Pi$ (Π - the set of n-element permutations) as well as w. r.t all estimate values $u \in U$. Expression (4.1) can be transformed in the following way ($\wedge$ denotes the minimum operation if in (4.2) the intersection was assumed and the product if in (4.2) the algebraic product was assumed):

$$\max_{P\in\Pi} \max_{u\in U} w(P;u) =$$

$$= \max_{P\in\Pi} \max_{u\in U} \left[\left(\bigwedge_{1\leq i\leq n} \mu_{ip_i}(u) \right) \wedge \mu_G(u) \right] =$$

$$= \max_{u\in U} \max_{P\in\Pi} \left[\left(\bigwedge_{1\leq i\leq n} \mu_{ip_i}(u) \right) \wedge \mu_G(u) \right] = \qquad (4.3)$$

$$= \max_{u\in U} \left\{ \max_{P\in\Pi} \left[\left(\bigwedge_{1\leq i\leq n} \mu_{ip_i}(u) \right) \wedge \mu_G(u) \right] \right\}$$

Let us consider the first case when (4.2) contains the intersection. In that case the part of expression (4.3) closed in the braces for a fixed value of u has the following form:

$$z(u) = \max_{P\in\Pi} \min_{1\leq i\leq n} \mu_{ip_i}(u) \qquad (4.4)$$

The form is identical with the criterion for problem II as formulated in section 4.1 if one puts $a_{ij} = \mu_{ij}(u)$ $(i,j = 1,2,\dots,n)$. This fact allows for the formulation of the following algorithm for determination of the optimal assignment.

Algorithm I

(i) For every $k = 1,2,\dots,m$ solove problem II assuming $a_{ij} = \mu_{ij}(u_k)$. Denote by $z(u_k)$ and P_k^*, the value of function (4.4) and the corresponding solution for fixed k, respectively.

(ii) Among permutations P_k^* $(k = 1,2,\dots,m)$ choose permutation P_r^* satisfying the condition

$$\min \left[z(u_r), \mu_G(u_r) \right] = \max_{1\leq k\leq m} \min \left[z(u_k), \mu_G(u_k) \right]$$

This permutation, P_r^*, satisfies all the conditions required for the optimal permutation P^*.

In the case of the algebraic product in (4.2) the segment of expression (4.3) closed in the braces has the following form:

$$w(u) = \max_{P\in\Pi} \prod_{i=1}^{n} \mu_{ip_i}(u)$$

Since the monotonicity of function lg x is assured one can consider the equivalent criterion

$$\lg w(u) = \max_{P\in\Pi} \sum_{i=1}^{n} \lg \mu_{ip_i}(u) \qquad (4.5)$$

The criterion is identical with the criterion for problem I in section 4.1 provided $a_{ij} = \lg \mu_{ij}(u)$ $(i,j = 1,2,\dots,n)$. Thus optimal permutation P^* can be found in that case by use of the following algorithm:

Algorithm II

(i) For every $k = 1,2,\dots,m$ solve Problem I assuming $a_{ij} = \lg \mu_{ij}(u_k)$. Denote by $L(u_k)$ and P_k^*, the value of function (4.5) and the corresponding solution respectively.

(ii) Among permutation P_k^* $(k = 1,2,\dots,m)$ choose permutation P_r^* satisfying the condition

$$w(u_r)\, \mu_G(u_r) = \max_{1\leq k\leq m} \left[w(u_k)\, \mu_G(u_k) \right]$$

where $w(u_k) = \exp(L(u_k))$

This permutation, P_r^*, satisfies all the conditions valid for optimal permutation P^*.

Let us consider an example. We have four persons and four positions. The values of membership functions of effectiveness estimates A_{ij} in $U = \{0,1,2,\dots,10\}$ are given in Table 3. The last row in that table contains the information about adopted criterion G (the membership function of G). The solution is $P^* = (1,4,2,3)$ derived by both the above algorithms.

5. FINAL REMARKS

The application of the fuzzy set apparatus to modeling and analysis of decision problems seems to be very promising. The possibilities of classic methods can be

Table 3. Fuzzy effectiveness estimates A_{ij} and estimate criterion G

μ_{ij} \ u_k	0	1	2	3	4	5	6	7	8	9	10
11	0.1	0.3	0.5	0.6	0.7	0.8	0.9	1.0	0.7	0.5	0.3
12	0.4	0.6	0.8	1.0	0.9	0.8	0.6	0.5	0.3	0.3	0.2
13	0	0.1	0.1	0.2	0.3	0.4	0.6	0.7	0.8	1.0	0.8
14	0.2	0.2	0.2	0.3	0.5	0.6	0.7	0.8	1.0	0.9	0.7
21	0.5	0.6	0.7	0.8	1.0	0.8	0.6	0.5	0.4	0.2	0.2
22	1.0	0.9	0.8	0.7	0.7	0.7	0.6	0.5	0.4	0.3	0.3
23	0	0	0.1	0.1	0.2	0.4	0.6	0.8	0.9	1.0	0.9
24	0	0	0.1	0.2	0.4	0.6	0.8	1.0	0.9	0.8	0.6
31	0.8	0.9	1.0	0.9	0.8	0.7	0.6	0.4	0.2	0.1	0
32	0.1	0.1	0.1	0.3	0.5	0.6	0.7	0.9	1.0	0.9	0.8
33	0.2	0.3	0.5	0.7	0.9	1.0	0.9	0.8	0.7	0.6	0.5
34	0.1	0.1	0.2	0.3	0.4	0.5	0.6	0.7	0.9	1.0	0.8
41	0.7	0.8	0.9	1.0	0.9	0.7	0.5	0.3	0.3	0.2	0.2
42	0	0	0.1	0.2	0.2	0.3	0.4	0.5	0.6	0.8	1.0
43	0.3	0.3	0.3	0.5	0.6	0.7	0.8	1.0	0.9	0.8	0.7
44	0.5	0.6	0.7	0.8	0.9	1.0	0.9	0.8	0.7	0.6	0.5
G	0	0.1	0.2	0.3	0.4	0.5	0.6	0.7	0.8	0.9	1.0

extended and better adopted to real decision problems. For example the representation of experts' opinions in any project network model in the form of fuzzy variables more adequately characterizes the nature of these opinions and of project performance conditions than does the probabilistic approach. It seems that what the experts may say about the time of activity performance, in the situation of a unique project, is its possibility distribution rather than its probability distribution.

Also in the assignment problem, particularly in the situation when the role of assignees is played by people, taking into account inexact estimates of properties (influencing the assignment effectiveness) in the form of fuzzy sets seems more adequate than the deterministic approach and more natural than the probabilistic approach.

The generalization of the determination problem for maximal flow in a network presented in this paper is an example of respecting in a model some tolerances for the parameter values. The fuzzy sets apparatus in a natural way allows for introduction of that important element into the analysis of decision problems. The notion of tolerance is widely popular in engineering. It can also be used in the decision making problems, in particular if the tolerances become planning instruments.

The methods which employ the theory of fuzzy sets should be placed somewhere in the middle between deterministic and probabilistic methods. It seems that probabilistic methods should be used only in those cases when we have enough statistical data. In situations where uncertainty is not of statistical nature, where we are obliged to use unprecisely estimated data (often using experts' evaluations))the methods employing concepts of the fuzzy set theory are more appropriate. They are less labour - consuming and less sensitive to errors than the probabilistic ones.

FOOTNOTES:

[1]"Poss" denotes "possibility" as in [17]. Let us remind , following [17], that $\text{Poss}\{A \text{ is } B\} = \sup_t \min\{\mu_A(t), \mu_B(t)\}$.

[2]The definition of algebraic product of two fuzzy sets A and B is as follows: $A \cdot B = C \Longleftrightarrow \mu_C = \mu_A \cdot \mu_B$.

REFERENCES:

[1] Bellman, R. and Zadeh, L.A., Decision making in a fuzzy environment, Management Science 4 (1970) B141-B164.

[2] Chanas, S., Methods of design and analysis for project network model with non-sharply defined activity duration times, Ph.D. Thesis, Inst. of Management, Techn. Univ. of Wrocław, Report 220 (1977), in Polish.

[3] Chanas, S. and Kamburowski, J., The use of fuzzy variables in PERT, Fuzzy Sets and Systems 1 (1981) 11-19.

[4] Chanas, S. and Kakalanov, M., Assignment problem with fuzzy estimates of effectiveness, Zastosowania Matematyki (Applicationes Mathematicae) 1 (1980) 87-93.

[5] Chanas, S. and Kołodziejczyk, W., A maximum flow in a network with fuzzy arc capacities, Fuzzy Sets and Systems (to appear in 1982).

[6] Chanas, S. and Kołodziejczyk, W., Flows in networks with fuzzy capacity constraints, Inst. of Management, Techn. Univ. of Wrocław, Report 336 (1981).

[7] Dijkstra, E.W., A note on two problems in connection with graphs, Numerishe Mathematic 1 (1959) 269-271.

[8] Dubois, D. and Prade, H., Operations on fuzzy numbers, Int. J. of Systems Science 6 (1978) 613-626.

[9] Dubois, D. and Prade, M., Algorithmes de plus courts chemins pour traiter des donnees floues, RAIRO Serie R.O 2 (1978) 213-227.

[10] Ford, L.R. and Fulkerson, D.R., Flows in Networks (A RAND Corporation Research Study, Princenton Univ. Press, 1962).

[11] Kamburowski, J., Critical path analysis in a project with fuzzy estimates of activity duration times, Inst. of Management, Techn. Univ. of Wrocław, Report 39 (1979).

[12] Malcom, D.D., Roseboom, J.H., Clarc, C.I. and Fazar, W., Application of technique for research and development program evaluation, Operations Research 5 (1959) 646-669.

[13] Nakamura, U., Preference relations between fuzzy outcomes, Summary of papers on general fuzzy problems, The Working Group on Fuzzy Systems, Tokyo, Report 5 (1979).

[14] Negoita, C.V., Flondor, P. and Sularia, M., On fuzzy environment in optimization problems, Proc. Third International Congress of Cybernetics and Systems, Bucharest August 1975 (Abacus Press, London, 1976).

[15] Słomiński, L., An efficient approach to the bottleneck assignment problem, Bull. Acad. Polon. Sci. Ser. sci. tech. 25 (1977) 17-23.

[16] Zadeh, L.A., Fuzzy sets, Information and Control 8 (1965) 338-353.

[17] Zadeh, L.A., Fuzzy sets as a basis for theory of possibility, Fuzzy Sets and Systems, 1 (1978) 3-28.

Approximate Reasoning in Decision Analysis
M.M. Gupta and E. Sanchez (eds.)

THE THEORY OF FUZZY DECISIONS*

Kofi Kissi Dompere

Department of Economics
Howard University
Washington, D.C. 20059

In this essay, the theory of fuzzy decisions is presented as a natural development from the non-fuzzy decision theory. The environment is categorized as certain, uncertain, certain and fuzzy, and uncertain and fuzzy. The development of the theory is viewed in terms of interaction between the relevant spaces of criteria and constraints given the information set and the space of relevant variables. It is, thus, set-theoretic in its approach. The nature of algorithms that may lead to optimal fuzzy decision principles are analysed and discussed. A discussion on fuzzy rationality in both certain and uncertain environment concludes the essay.

KEYWORDS:

Fuzziness, certainty, uncertainty, measurability, Decision, Rationality.

0. DECISION MAKING.

History of ideas suggests that human behavior translates into decision, choice and action. From the viewpoint of epistemology, a clear and important distinction can be made between decision and choice [17] [18]. In this essay, however, such epistemological distinction will not be made. We shall assume as a point of entry a position that a decision is always translated into choice and hence they are interchangable. Our main concern is on the phenomenon of decision. The critical understanding of such a phenomenon of human behavior requires a favorable attitude of science. Thus we may speak of the science of decision which will be centered on the nature of human activity in choosing. We shall, thus, speak of decision agent and his behavior in a specified space.

Generally, the objective of decision scientist would be to ascertain the consistency that may be observed in any satisfactory decision process and thus deduce from the observed regularities certain rules that must be followed if the objective of the decision agent is to be realized. These deduced rules of successful decisions (as measured against objectives) are then used to provide a guideline for 'sensible' decision making.

The process of systematic explanation and/or abstraction of regularities and translation of these regularities into rules of 'good' decision will be called decision theory. Its scope of interest would, therefore, be a critical investigation into the meaning of selection rules and the development of consistent algorithms to realize these rules. The rules then are systematized as the calculus of discrimination on the basis of which a successful decision is arrived at. Any decision is said to be rational if it follows these rules. Since there are classes of decision problems, different systems of rational decision rules is invariably influenced by a number of factors that the analyst may consider as important. Given these factors, the structure of the rational decision principles that may be constructed depends on the assumptions and types of structural relationships imposed on these factors.

Most of the current theoretical structure of decision problems and the corresponding principles are formulated in such a way as to impose particular qualitative characteristics on human beings as decision agents. The most important of these characteristics is that of human ability to precisely specify ends and means in a decision process. In other words, the decision and algorithms are non-fuzzy. We shall refer to the selection rules developed under this condition as non-fuzzy decision principles and if certain conditions are met we shall qualify them as optimal. Since these selection rules and the corresponding algorithms are derived under conditions of classical mathematics we shall refer to them as classical non-fuzzy decision principles.

These non-fuzzy decision rules are useful, however, they are limited in their applicability to real world situations where nearly all real human decision problems are imprecise, ill-defined and vague in nature. The imprecision, ill-definedness and vagueness that tend to characterize various decision problems are predominantly subjective and linguistic in their essence and may be influenced by many factors that the decision agents may interact with.

The objective in this essay is to provide a uni-unified introduction to the analysis of decisions where imprecision, ill-definedness and vagueness, as characteristics of human decision may be endogenized. To do this we shall introduce a taxonomy of decision problems and consider a general formulation of such decision problems in canonical forms. We shall then state the logical framework of the classical non-fuzzy decision problems and principles. The non-classical fuzzy decision problems and principles are then formulated as natural extensions of the classical decision problems. We shall discuss some algorithms in realizing fuzzy decision principles. In the process, we shall bring into surface some basic differences and similarities in non-fuzzy and fuzzy logic in decision principles.

1. THE NATURE OF DECISION PROBLEMS.

The analytical structure of decision problems from both the view points of classical and non-classical persuations may start with some basic building blocks. We shall start with primitive notions of a decision agent and the space of his operations that we shall refer to as a decision space, Δ. The decision space is made up of spaces of variables, V, information (parameter), I, criteria, Λ constraints, Γ, and alternatives, Ω. The generic elements - of these spaces are respectively δ, v, i, λ, γ and ω except otherwise stated.

The space of variables may be divided into state and control spaces that may be represented respectively as X and U with generic elements x and u. Both the alternative and constraint spaces are defined over the space of variables given the information space. The space of alternatives indicates the possible goals while the constraint space specifies the feasible region of choice. The criterion space provides us with a set of ranking processes for the comparability of alternatives on the basis of which a decision is made. The decision, $\delta \in \Delta$ is made against the background of information about the variables, the constraints, alternatives, criteria and possible functional relationships. Thus the information space constitutes the environment in which a decision is made. The relevant information for a particular decision problem is summarized by parameter space, Θ, thus the parameter space may be viewed, as a subspace of the information space. The nature of parametric representation of the essential elements of the information would depend on the assumptions made about the environment. On the other hand, the structure of the decision, algorithms and decision principles that may be derived would depend on the information as viewed by the decision agent or the analyst. We shall provide few working definitions.

Definition 1.1.

A decision problem is said to be present in human action if more than one alternative can be demonstrated to exist for selection, i.e., $\#\Omega > 1$ (where $\#\Omega$ represents the cardinality of Ω).

Definition 1.2.

A decision problem is said to be trivial if Ω is a singleton set, i.e., $\#\Omega = 1$. It is called vacuous if Ω is a null set, i.e., $\Omega = \emptyset$ or $\#\Omega = 0$. A decision problem is said to be non-trivial if it is neither vacuous nor trivial.

Definition 1.3.

A decision problem is said to be objective (surjective) almost surely if the essential characteristics of the decision can completely be delineated in quantitative (qualitative) terms, otherwise it is said to be mixed.

With these definitions in mind we shall present the decision structure and its canonical representation.

2. DECISION STRUCTURE AND GENERAL CANONICAL REPRESENTATION.

The development of algorithms to realize selection rules may begin with the decision space, Δ, that represents the essential properties of a decision problem. This may be written as

$$\Delta = (\Lambda, \Omega, \Gamma, I, \Phi) \tag{2.1}$$

where Φ is the set of relevant personality characteristics of the decision agent. It includes, among other things, important properties of human beings as collectors and processors of information. The element Λ is defined over Ω while Ω and Γ are defined over a set composed of state and control variables of X and U respectively. The Λ may either be viewed as summarizing preferences over, or ranking elements in Ω.

Given that Θ is a set of parameters constructed from the information, I, in such a way that it summarizes the relevant information for the decision, we may write the general cannonical representation of the decision problem as

$$\underset{\omega \varepsilon A \cap B}{\text{Opt.}} \quad \lambda(\omega, \theta) \ \varepsilon \ \Lambda(\Omega, \Theta)$$

$$\text{S.T.} \quad \left.\begin{array}{l} A \cap B \neq \emptyset \\ B \subset \{\Gamma; \Theta\} \\ A \subset \{\Omega; \Theta\} \\ \Theta \subset \{I; \Phi\} \end{array}\right\} \qquad (2.2)$$

where A may be viewed as a set of goals or relevant alternatives and B the relevant constraint.

The decision problem represented by equation (2.2) simply requires the decision agent to collect information, process it and select a goal, from among all possible alternatives, that satisfies the physical limitations on choice, given the processed information, in such a way as to attain the best possible goal in accord with the personality characteristics and perference scale of the decision agent. The Θ and, generally, I may be viewed as the state of nature. The decision rule that may be realized from the family of algorithms will essentially depend on the alternative goals and information characteristics. Such a decision rule is general and may be written as

$$\delta = \delta(\omega, \theta), \ \delta \ \varepsilon \ \Delta \qquad (2.3)$$

with the understanding that $\omega \ \varepsilon \ (A \cap B) \subset \Omega$, $\theta \ \varepsilon \ \Theta \subset I$ given the personality characteristics Φ and a rank function, λ. The decision rule (2.3) is a complete decision rule in the sense that both ω and θ are under the action of the agent and it is said to be conditional on information set if θ is given.

Definition.

A decision rule δ is said to be completely optimal if the "best goal", ω^*, is attained with the "best information", θ^*, i.e.,

$$\delta^* = \delta(\omega^*, \theta^*).$$

It is said to be conditionally optimal if the optimality is conditional on the information set, i.e.,

$$\delta^* = \delta(\omega^*; \theta) = \max_{\omega} \delta(\omega; \theta).$$

It will be said to be informationally suboptimal if $\theta < \theta^*$ where $*$ is the optimal forcast from I.

The general cannonical representation of the decision problem and the corresponding decision rule allow us to speak of a family of optimal decision rules. The nature of such a family will depend on the information set (the environment) and the decision agent's interraction with it, where such interaction depends on the set of personality characteristics. So far we have not made any explicit assumptions about the information space, neither have we imposed any particular structure on the environment. Let us attend to this problem.

3. THE ENVIRONMENT AND DECISION PROBLEMS.

The decision problem and the solution function as described by equations (2.2) and (2.3) represent a family of families of decision problems. The specific family of the decision problem will depend on the type of environment assumed. Such environment would provide us with the information on the basis of which the structural parameters are obtained. Given the type of environment, each decision problem may be classified according to consistency and similarity conditions [19]. The specific algorithm designed to realize a decision rule would then depend on the family of the decision problems.

Let I be the environment space that may be partitioned into certain, C and uncertain C'. We also define over the same environment fuzzy, F and non-fuzzy, F'. We may represent these classification as

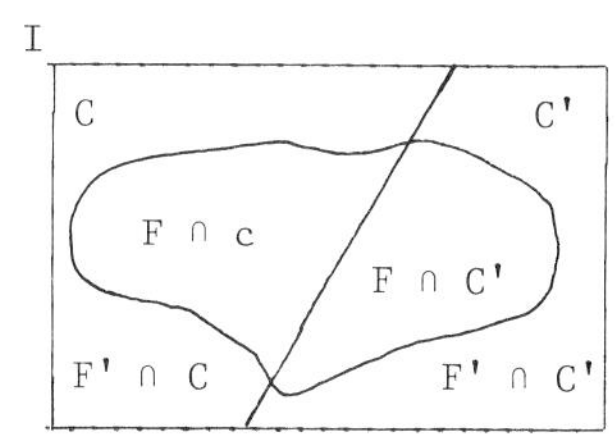

	C	C'
F'	Non-Fuzzy And Certain	Non-Fuzzy And Uncertain
F	Fuzzy And Certain	Fuzzy And Uncertain

Classification of Information Fig. 3.1

Brief definitions of fuzziness, uncertainty and their complements will be convenient.

Definition 3.1.

A decision environment is said to be uncertain in relevant regard if the information characteristics of the decision (in some measure) are not known almost surely otherwise it is said to be certain (in other words, questions regarding information about the decision problem have not been answered prior to the decision).

Definition 3.2.

A decision environment is said to be fuzzy if the relevant information characteristics about the structural properties of the decision are either known but vague or unknown and yet vague otherwise it is said to be nonfuzzy.

Definition 3.3.

A decision problem that combines vagueness and full information prior to the decision will be said to be fuzzy-certainty. If it combines vagueness and less than full information prior to the decision it will be said to be fuzzy uncertainty.

We shall note that fuzziness is said to occur in a decision process if there is the presence of either inexact measurement of some kind or vagueness of concepts. With this view, we shall adopt the following classificatory scheme for all decision problems (fig. 3.2). Since equation (2.2)

	C	C'
F'	α-class	σ-class
F	β-class	η-class

Fig. 3.2

Families of Decision

incorporates the essential elements of all these classes of decision problem we shall consider the specific characteristics of each family. We shall present the main structures of the α- and σ- classes in their canonical form since they have been extensively dealt with in the literature on decision. We shall consider the non-fuzzy decision problems and then the fuzzy ones.

The formal representation of such decision problems rests on proper specifications of ends and means. It may begin with building blocks of goals (objectives), information, alternatives and constraints, that together allows a proper representation of the <u>state</u> which may be viewed as the description of the environment, the <u>consequences</u> which may be viewed as the reward to the decision agent and the <u>act</u> which may also be viewed as a relation between the states and consequences.

The 'no-data-decision' problem requires the decision agent to choose a most preferred object from the set of acts where such objects of choice are preordered by preferences. The preordering among alternatives may be represented by a real-valued function referred to as objective function with desired properties. The events and their measurements are known not only certainly but also precisely. Thus the decision problem under certainty and non-fuzzy conditions may analytically be decomposed into: 1) define the set of acts; 2) define the set of objectives, 3) define the ranking relation; 4) define the limitations on acts and 5) find the act which yields the best objective according to the ranking. In set-theoretic terms, the decision problem may cannonically be represented as

$$\underset{\omega\varepsilon A\,\cap\,B}{\text{Opt.}}\quad \lambda(\omega;\,\theta)\ \varepsilon\ \Lambda(\Omega;\,\Theta)$$

$$\left.\begin{aligned} &A \cap B \neq \emptyset \\ &A \subset \{\Omega;\ \Theta \subset I\} \\ &B \subset \{\Gamma;\ \Theta \subset I\}, \end{aligned}\right\}\qquad (4.1)$$

where $A \cap B$ defines the <u>critical region of choice</u>. Equation (4.1) will include all classes of deterministic optimization problems such as linear and non-linear programming, etc. [2] [12] [20].

The algorithms of mathematical programming may be used to develop the optimal decision rules. The 'no-data-problem' optimal decision principle may be written as

$$\delta^* = \delta(\omega^*;\,\theta),\ \delta\ \varepsilon\ \Delta \qquad (4.2)$$

which is a family in the parameter space depending on θ. The sensitivity function of this optimal decision principle may then be written as

$$\frac{d\delta^*}{d\theta} = \sum_{\theta\varepsilon\Theta} \frac{\partial\delta(\omega^*;\,\theta)}{\partial\theta} = \psi(\theta) \qquad (4.3)$$

where δ^* is assumed to be information continuous. In other words, different information set defining the relevant parameters may alter the optimal decision rule. Examples of such a class is the consumption and production decision under full information [12] [20].

<u>THE σ-CLASS</u>

This class of decision problems is distinguished from the α-class by the presence of uncertain conditions. Even though the consequences are unknown, they are precise when they occur. In such a class of decision problems, not only do we have to deal with the problem of ranking of alternatives but also we have to deal with the measurement and ranking of the degree of uncertainty surrounding the outcome of each alternative since the degree of uncertainty may come to distort the ranking of alternatives under certain conditions. We thus face a problem of how to incorporate uncertainty into the formal representation of decision process.

In order to integrate into the decision process conditions of uncertainty, a measurement and ranking of relative uncertainty are required. A way to do this is through the construction of probability space. Suppose there is an uncertainty defined over the space of alternatives. Ω (such uncertainty may be extended to the space of constraints, Γ). We shall, therefore, consider $\omega\ \varepsilon\ \Omega$ ($\gamma\ \varepsilon\ \Gamma$) as a random variable. The degree of uncertainty surrounding the outcome of any alternative goal $\omega\ \varepsilon\ \Omega$ (or constraint, $\gamma\ \varepsilon\ \Gamma$)

is expressed in terms of how probable is the outcome. It is measured by probability that is expressed as a continuous sum in the sense of Lebesgue-Stieltjes as

$$P(\omega;\ \cdot) = \int_{\Omega} f(\omega;\ \cdot)d\omega = \int_{\Omega} dF(\omega;\ \cdot) \qquad (4.4)$$

where $f(\omega;\ \cdot)$ is a probability density function conditional on the set of available information. In a discrete case, we may write

$$P(\omega;\ \cdot) = \sum_{\omega\in\Omega} f(\omega;\ \cdot) \qquad (4.5)$$

The probability value satisfying certain properties is used as a measure of relative uncertainty surrounding the outcome of interest. The greater the value of $P(\omega;\ \cdot)$ the lower the uncertainty surrounding the decision goal. The probability measure over the alternatives may, therefore, be viewed as a unique representation of preordering of the degree of uncertainty that surrounds the outcomes of either decision goals or constraints [4]. It will be suggested later on that such a unique preordering of the degree of uncertainty is conditional on the absence of vagueness, and imprecision in both the concepts and measurement in decision.

Given that the degrees of uncertainty are uniquely preordered by probability, the expected consequences are then ordered by preferences. The preference ranking of the consequences is then induced by either expected utility or expected-valued function on the basis of which an optimal decision rule is to be abstracted. A difficulty arises, however, in the process of including the uncertainty ranking in the cannonical representation of the decision problem.

The difficulty may be overcome by assuming that we can meaningfully define a probability space over the decision space in such a way that it is more or less a subset. The probability space is a triplet, $\{\Omega, B_0, P\}$, where B_0 is a σ-field of Borel set on Ω and $\{\Omega, B_0, P\} \subset \Delta$. In some decision problems, it may be necessary to extend the probability space to the space of constraints and thus define another triplet of the form $\{\Gamma, B_1, P\}$ where B_1 is a σ-field of Borel set on Γ. Under such formalism, the decision problem under uncertainty may be canonically represented as

$$\left.\begin{array}{ll} \underset{\omega\in A\,\cap\, B}{\text{Opt}} & \lambda(\omega;\theta,P)\ \varepsilon\ \Lambda(\{\Omega, B_0, P\};\ \Theta) \\ \text{S.T.} & A \cap B \neq \emptyset \\ & A \subset (\{\Omega, B_0, P\};\ \ \Theta \subset I) \\ & B \subset (\{\Gamma, B_1, P\};\ \ \Theta \subset I) \end{array}\right\} \qquad (4.6)$$

The canonical representation of the decision problem under uncertainty (equation 4.6) requires three postulates of Savage [16]: 1) regular (complete and transitive) preordering among acts represented by expected utility (or a valued function) conditional on any nonempty event set of consequences; ii) a regular preordering among consequences measured by a utility or a valued function; and iii) a regular preordering among events, uniquely represented by probability, conditional on prior information. A typical class from the above cannonical form may be written as

$$\left.\begin{array}{ll} \underset{\omega\varepsilon A}{\max} & \int_{A\subset\Omega} \lambda(\omega)\ f(\omega)d\omega \\ \text{S.T.} & \int_{B\subset\Gamma} \gamma(\omega)\ \phi_0(\omega)d\omega \leq \bar{\pi} \end{array}\right\} \qquad (4.7)$$

where $\bar{\pi}$ is a predetermined value and $\phi_0(\omega)$ is a probability density function defined over the constrained space.

Under appropriate technical conditions, therefore, the above postulates lead to the "moral expectation theorem" where an optimal decision rule is obtained. From the view point of the theorem, the σ-class of decision problems may be decomposed into: 1) specifying the set of acts, ii) defining the performance (utility) ranking over the consequences (outcomes), iii) specifying probability ranking over the uncertainty surrounding the consequences and iv) constructing an algorithm to select an act that yields the most (in a specific sense) expected consequence. The corresponding optimal decision rule would be the best choice of $\omega = \omega^*$ conditional on a set of parameters and probability distributions over both the sets of alternatives and constraints. It may generally be written as

$$\delta^* = \delta(\omega^*;\ \theta,\ p) = \underset{\omega}{\text{Opt}}\ \delta(\omega;\ \theta,\ p) \qquad (4.8)$$

which is a family over the parameter and probability spaces. The sensitivity function to the above optimal decision rule may thus be written as

$$\psi = \psi(\theta,\ \ p) \qquad (4.9)$$

where the path of the optimal decision depends on the environment characterized by the relevant parameter space and the corresponding probability distribution.

From such a decision characterization, it may be suggested that the value theory should assist in defining and establishing preferences or some rank function over non-fuzzy consequences. Statistical inference of all forms, on the other hand, should bring the power of empirical observation to bear upon the assessment of probabilities of non-fuzzy consequences and evaluation of information about non-fuzzy parameters. Techniques of mathematical programming should lead us to develop algorithms (such as stochastic optimization) to realize optimal decision rules for non-fuzzy acts under uncertain conditions.

The σ-class of decision problems and the corresponding optimal decision principles are improvements over the α-class in that under properly specified uncertain conditions, the theory of decision that is constructed combines the techniques of statistical inference and mathematical programming in order to develop optimal decision principles. Under such theoretical conditions, the decision problem may be formulated in a general way where all the unknown parameters are treated probabilistically instead of some of them being treated as conditional point estimates.

5. FUZZY DECISION PROBLEMS.

The α- and σ- classes of decision problems require that both the concepts and measurable values over these concepts be of precise nature whether they are known in advance or not. Furthermore, the boundaries of all these alternatives are sharply defined. In other words, these classes of decision problem do not admit of vagueness of any form and hence the information on the basis of which alternatives are examined for ranking and choice is presented in a precise way.

While the understanding of these classes of decision problems is useful, it is limited in application in that in practice most decision problems are either vague in concepts or imprecise in measurement. Thus the theory of decision presented so far has little, if any, to say when the decision environment is vague, ill-defined and imprecise, in other words fuzzy. As such a different logical framework of calculus of decision is required. We shall present such a framework which will constitute the basic core of the concepts and algorithms that make up the essential logical processes of decision making in a fuzzy environment. The emphasis will be placed on the concept component of the fuzzy-decision logic rather than on the theory of algorithms. This stems from the observation that in almost all cases in the development of a particular theory the concepts and their meanings become powerful sources of confusion and hence causes of difficulties in the understanding of the logical framework and process in which the theory is being developed - in this case the calculus of fuzzy decision.

It is useful to divide fuzzy decision problems into fuzzy certainty and uncertainty which we have referred to respectively as β- and γ- classes. We shall treat the main concepts and basic algorithms of the β-class and present the essential directions of the development of the γ-class (it is useful to refer to [3] [5] [8] [14]).

5.1 THE β-CLASS.

The β-class of decision problems may be distinguished from other classes by the following characteristics: 1) All the relevant information regarding the decision is given to the decision agent; 2) The information on decision is, however, imprecise, the concepts and notions defined over the decision space may be vague or ill-defined while the measurements are inexact; 3) The information is summarized by fuzzy structural parameters. Such a decision problem may be referred to as "no-data-fuzzy-decision" problem. It is "no-data-problem" because all relevant information regarding the decision is known and it is fuzzy because the concepts, notions and measurements are vague, inexact and perhaps ill-defined.

The formal representation of this class of decision problems is similar to that of the α-class except that there is an added problem. The problem involves designing a method that will allow a proper inclusion of fuzzy ends and means in the decision-making process under conditions of certainty. The problem may be approached from many but interdependent vantage points [3] [5] [8]. We shall first discuss the concepts of fuzziness and fuzzy measure in the decision space and then present a canonical representation of decision problem under fuzzy certainty.

5.1A. CONCEPT AND MEASUREMENT OF FUZZINESS.

We now introduce the basic concepts and measure of fuzziness.

Definition 5.1.

A decision space is said to be fuzzy if some or all of the concepts and measurements defining the decision structure consisting of ends, means and limitations admit of shades of meaning and/or values.

Definition 5.2.

A number $0 \le \mu \le 1$ is said to be a fuzzy measure over a decision space if, for each element in the space, it specifies the essential differences among shades of meaning of concepts and shades of inexactness of measurements of the elements in such a way as to provide distinction and rank order of the elements. The function that assigns a fuzzy measure to each element in the space is referred to as a membership function [3]. If such a function exists, the space is said to be fuzzy measurable (see [11] for an attempt to deal with the degree of fuzziness in the space).

Definition 5.3a.

A fuzzy subset $\tilde{A}$ of Ω is a collection of a pair of points of the form

$$\tilde{A} = \{(\omega, \mu_{\tilde{A}}(\omega));\ \omega \in \Omega \text{ and } 0 \le \mu_{\tilde{A}}(\omega) \le 1\}$$

for any space or subspace of concern, the fuzzy measure can be normalized if some of the fuzzy values or all of them are greater than one by using the largest value plus one. The fuzzy values defined over the relevant space may thus be specified as $\mu(\omega) \varepsilon [0, 1]$ where ω belongs to a defined fuzzy set, $\tilde{A}$. If $\mu_{\tilde{A}}(\omega) = 0$ then ω is said not to belong to $\tilde{A}$ surely. It is said to belong to $\tilde{A}$ surely if $\mu_{\tilde{A}}(\omega) = 1$. The adverb "almost surely" will be used to modify belongs and does not belong depending on how close is $\mu_{\tilde{A}}(\omega)$ to one or zero.

Definition 5.3b.

A set

$$M = \{\mu_{\tilde{A}}(\omega);\ \omega \varepsilon \tilde{A} \text{ and } 0 \le \mu_{\tilde{A}}(\omega) \le \mu_{\Omega}(\omega) \le 1\}$$

is called a membership set where $\tilde{A}$ is fuzzy subset on Ω.

It is logically useful to assume that $\mu_{\tilde{A}}(\omega)$ is dense in the entire domain. For some examples of membership functions defined over a fuzzy measurable space see [3] [8] [14].

Definition 5.4.

The set of fuzzy goals, $\tilde{A}$ is a subset of the space of alternatives, Ω and is equipped with a membership function $\mu_{\tilde{A}}(\omega)$, written as

$$\tilde{A} = \{(\omega, \mu_{\tilde{A}}(\omega));\ \omega \varepsilon \Omega,\ \mu(\omega) \varepsilon M\} \qquad (5.1)$$

Example 5.1. A production enterprise has an objective of earning a yearly average profit that is <u>substantially greater</u> than a specified value- say a. The set of such fuzzy goals may be written and graphically represented as

$$\tilde{A} = \{(\omega, \mu_{\tilde{A}}(\omega));\ \omega \varepsilon \Omega,\ \mu_{\tilde{A}}(\omega) = [k|1 - \omega|e^{-(1-\omega)^2} + 1]^{-1},\ k > 0\}$$

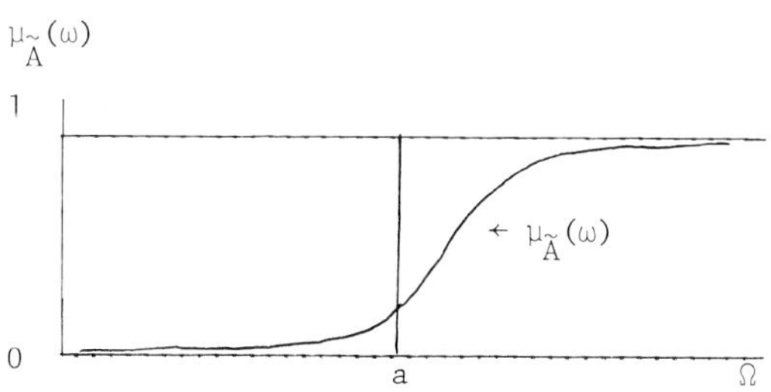

Fig. 5.1. A Fuzzy Production Goal.

Definition 5.5.

A fuzzy constraint $\tilde{B}$ is a subset of the general constraint space, Γ that is equipped with a membership function, $\mu_{\tilde{B}}(\gamma)$ and written as

$$\tilde{B} = \{(\gamma, \mu_{\tilde{B}}(\gamma));\ \gamma \varepsilon \Gamma \text{ and } \mu_{\tilde{B}}(\gamma) \varepsilon M\} \qquad (5.2)$$

Example 5.2. Continuing with example (5.1) the fuzzy constraint on the enterprise productive activity may be stated as 'the average cost must not be far greater than a specified value b. The set of such a fuzzy constraint may be written as

$$\tilde{B} = \left[(\gamma, \mu_{\tilde{B}}(\gamma));\ \gamma \varepsilon \Gamma,\ \mu_{\tilde{B}}(\gamma) = e^{-k||\gamma-b||^2},\ k = \begin{cases} 0, & \gamma \le b \\ \frac{b}{\gamma}, & \gamma > b \end{cases}\right]$$

where $||\cdot||$ denotes an euclidean norm. Graphically, we have

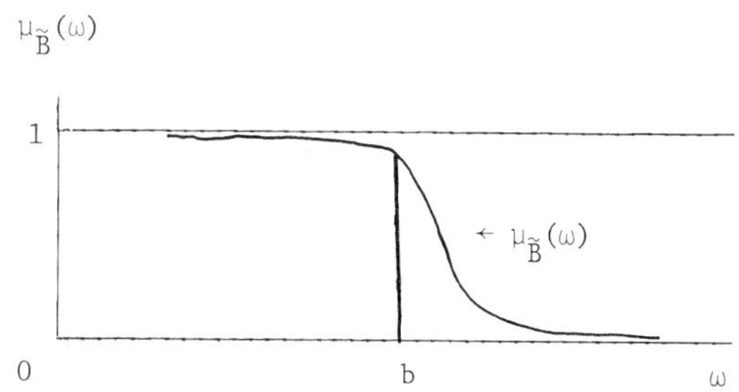

Fig. 5.2. A Fuzzy Production Constraint

Definition 5.6.

A fuzzy measurable decision space in a certainty environment consists of sets of ranking indices, alternatives, constraints, information, membership functions and personality characteristics that may be written as

$$\Delta = \{\Lambda, \Omega, \Gamma, I, \Phi, M\}. \qquad (5.3)$$

We note that a fuzzy decision space must always be accompanied by a set of membership functions. Each of the functions is a mapping defined over one or more of the set components of the decision space onto the closed interval [0, 1]. The sets of goals and constraints must always be equipped with an appropriate element in M. If the fuzzy decision space is not equipped with a membership set M then we shall write

$$\tilde{\Delta} = \{\tilde{\Lambda}, \tilde{\Omega}, \tilde{\Gamma}, \tilde{I}, \tilde{\Phi}\}$$

Each membership function may be conceptualized from many different but interdependent view points. One view point looks at the membership functions as ranking the degrees of shades of grades that an element may have in the relevant position of the fuzzy decision space. Alternatively, the membership functions may be viewed as ranking the relative positions of fuzziness occupied by each fuzzy element as measured against a precisely specified notion or value. The membership functions may even be viewed in some cases as acting as utility functions. The basic property of the membership functions is that they are more or less subjective and they depend on some or all of the personality characteristics of the decision agents. This subjective property is shared by the non-classical probability and ordinal valued functions.

5.1B. CANONICAL REPRESENTATION OF FUZZY-DECISION PROBLEM UNDER CERTAINTY.

Some difficulties may be encountered in the process of constructing membership functions in the decision space. These difficulties, however, will not be considered here. For any fuzzy notion and degree of closeness in the decision space, we shall assume that there is a well-behaved membership function (this may also be referred to as <u>fuzzy density function</u>, f.d.f.) with appropriate characteristics. We shall now depict a cannonical representation of the fuzzy decision problem.

Let $(\Omega, B_\omega, \mu_\omega)$ be a fuzzy measurable space of alternatives with a fuzzy measurable constraint space $(\Gamma, B_\gamma, \mu_\gamma)$ where $\omega \in \Omega$ and $\gamma \in \Gamma$. We can write the canonical representation of the "no-data fuzzy decision problem" in set-theoretic terms as

$$\underset{\omega\in\tilde{A}\cap\tilde{B}}{\text{Opt}} \quad \lambda(\omega; \tilde{\theta}, \mu_\omega) \in \Lambda(\{\Omega, B_\omega, \mu_\omega\}; \Theta)$$

$$\text{S.T.} \quad \left.\begin{array}{l} \tilde{A} \cap \tilde{B} \neq 0 \\ \tilde{A} \subset [(\Omega, B_\omega, \mu_\omega); \tilde{\Theta} \subset I] \\ \tilde{B} \subset [(\Gamma, B_\gamma, \mu_\gamma); \tilde{\Theta} \subset I] \\ \tilde{\Theta} \subset \{I \mid \Phi\} \end{array}\right\} \qquad (5.4)$$

Such a general representation of fuzzy decision problem under certainty conditions requires the following postulates: 1) regular (complete and transitive) preordering of fuzzy acts, ends and means according to either preferences or ordering index; 2) the preferences or scaling indexes are represented by membership characteristic functions and 3) the membership characteristic functions must be well behaved. In other words, the elements of all relevant fuzzy spaces are partially preordered by corresponding membership functions. The membership functions may be looked upon from the viewpoint of utility function (according to taste and preferences) in some sense where the utility function maps the elements in the decision space onto zero-one interval. Alternatively, they may be looked upon from pure scaling according to ε-closeness conditional on precisely specified value.

Under appropriate technical conditions these postulates and their implications lead to fuzzy rationality under conditions of certainty. From the viewpoint of fuzzy rationality, the β-class of decision problems may be decomposed into 1) specifying the set of preferred fuzzy ends, 2) specifying the set of preferred fuzzy means, 3) defining the set of fuzzy binding constraints, 4) defining the respective membership functions and appropriate fuzzy measurable functions over the preferred fuzzy goals, means and constraints and finally 5) constructing algorithms to select a fuzzy act which yields a feasible and most preferred fuzzy end. The decision rule resulting from such a procedure for solving the system represented by equation (5.4) will be referred to as <u>fuzzy optimal decision</u> principle. It may be written as

$$\tilde{\delta}^* = \underset{\omega}{\text{Opt}}\ \delta(\omega; \mu, \theta) = \delta(\omega^*; \mu, \theta) \qquad (5.5)$$

In other words, the path of fuzzy optimal decision depends on the fuzzy environment characterized by imprecise parameters and corresponding grade-characteristic values. If the path of the optimal fuzzy decision is assumed to be differentiable in the fuzzy parameter space then we can compute the fuzzy sensitivity function that may be written in the form

$$\frac{d\delta^*}{d\theta} = \sum_{\theta\in\Theta} \frac{\partial\tilde{\delta}^*}{\partial\boldsymbol{\theta}} + \sum_{\mu\in M} \frac{\partial\tilde{\delta}^*}{\partial\mu} = \tilde{\psi}(\theta, \mu) \qquad (5.6)$$

Let us now consider specific algorithms to equation (5.4) in order to realize an optimal fuzzy decision principle.

5.1C. THE BELLMAN-ZADEH APPROACH.

The important logical blocks of Bellman and Zadeh's pioneering approach [3] in constructing an operational fuzzy optimal decision rule from the canonical form of equation (5.4) consist of 1) a set of preferred imprecise objectives (called fuzzy goals), 2) a set of preferred vaguely binding constraints (called fuzzy constraints) as seen by the decision agent, iii) the use of membership functions defined over both sets and acting as ordinal ranking that indirectly take the place of utility functions. Viewed in this light, both the constraint and objective sets become fuzzy subsets of the general decision space. The intersection of these fuzzy subsets becomes the <u>critical region</u>, Δ_c of fuzzy decision.

Suppose that $\tilde{A}$ is a fuzzy subset of goals and $\tilde{B}$ a fuzzy subset of constraints equipped with their respective membership functions of $\mu_{\tilde{A}}(\omega)$ and $\mu_{\tilde{B}}(\gamma)$ where $\tilde{A} \subset \Omega$ and $\tilde{B} \subset \Gamma$. We may thus write

$$\Delta_c = \tilde{A} \cap \tilde{B} \qquad (5.7)$$

with a membership function that may be written as

$$\begin{aligned} \mu_{\Delta_c}(\delta) &= \min\,[\mu_{\tilde{A}}(\omega), \mu_{\tilde{B}}(\gamma)], \quad \delta \in \Delta_c \\ &= \mu_{\tilde{A}}(\omega) \wedge \mu_{\tilde{B}}(\gamma) \end{aligned} \qquad (5.8)$$

where ω and γ are equivalent in the same decision space. For one fuzzy goal and one fuzzy constraint the fuzzy optimal decision principle,

δ^* may be written as

$$\delta^* = \operatorname*{Sup}_{\omega} \mu_{\Delta_c}(\omega) = \operatorname*{Sup}_{\omega <=> \gamma} [\mu_{\tilde{A}}(\omega) \wedge \mu_{\tilde{B}}(\gamma)]$$

$$= \operatorname*{max\ min}_{\omega \rightleftarrows \gamma} [\mu_{\tilde{A}}(\omega), \mu_{\tilde{B}}(\gamma)] \quad (5.9)$$

In other words, the critical region, Δ_c of the general fuzzy decision space is what Bellman and Zadeh have viewed as goal-constraint confluence. The optimal fuzzy decision principle may thus be written as

$$\delta^* = \operatorname*{Sup}_{\omega} [\mu_{\Delta_c}(\omega);\ \omega \in \tilde{A} \cap \tilde{B}] \quad (5.10)$$

The optimal fuzzy decision rule requires us to choose an element that has the largest membership grade in the critical region. If the membership functions possess certain characteristics [3] then we may graphically represent the optimal decision rule of equations (5.9) and (5.10) as in Fig. 5.3. We shall follow a conversion that $\wedge$ implies min. and V implies a max.

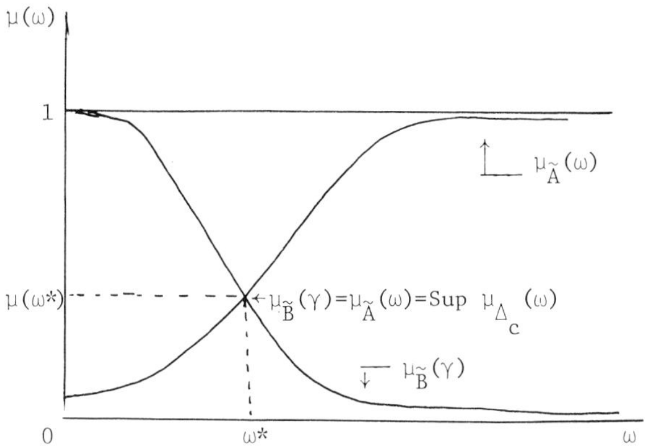

Fig. 5.3. A Fuzzy Optimal Decision

We may observe that the fuzzy optimal decision problem may be stated as a non linear programming problem that may be written as

$$\operatorname*{Opt.}_{\omega} \ \mu_{\Delta_c}(\omega)$$

$$\text{S.T.} \quad \omega \in \tilde{A} \cap \tilde{B}. \quad (5.11)$$

It is important to observe that the concept of critical region is crucial to all the classes of decision problems. This concept is emphasized by the set-theoretic representations of these problems. It is also important to notice that all these classes of decision problems may be reduced to programming problems in some essential way. In other words, the treatment of non-fuzzy decision is a natural extension of that of non-fuzzy decision.

Example 5.3. An enterprise seeks to determine a volume of output flow such that its average profit is significantly greater than a specified value, "a" and its average cost is not very much greater than a specified value, "b".

This is a microeconomic fuzzy production decision problem that is part of a general problem of fuzzy production planning which the author is currently working on. The problem may be extended in many directions. To solve this problem in its present form we shall assume that all relevant information, including input and output prices, regarding the fuzzy production decision is known or can be specified. Given this assumption the following logical steps may be taken.

1) Specification of the fuzzy set of profit goals: We shall assume that the production system is such that the fuzzy profit set may be specified as

$$\pi = \{(x, \mu_{\tilde{\pi}}(x));\ x \in [0, 1] \subset \Omega,\ \mu_{\tilde{\pi}}(x)$$

$$= [k|1 - x|e^{-(1-x)^2} + 1]^{-1}\}, k > 0$$

where Ω is the space of alternative goals with a generic element x. The value k may be chosen in such a way as to reflect the capital structure of the enterprise. Notice that

$$\lim_{x \to 1} \mu_{\tilde{\pi}}(x) = 1$$

$$\lim_{x \to 0} \mu_{\tilde{\pi}}(x) = 0, \text{ for } k >>> 0$$

2) Specification of the fuzzy set of cost constraints: The fuzzy cost constraint set may be specified as

$$\tilde{C} = [(x, \mu_{\tilde{C}}(x));\ x \in [0, 1] \subset \Gamma,\ \mu_{\tilde{C}}(x)$$

$$= e^{-h||x-b||^2},\ h \begin{cases} = 0, & x < b \\ = \frac{b}{x}, & x > b \end{cases}]$$

Note that

$$\lim_{x \to b} \mu_{\tilde{C}}(x) = 1 \text{ and } \lim_{x \to \infty} \mu_{\tilde{C}}(x) = 0$$

3) We may combine (1) and (2) and solve for the value of x by considering the membership functions as a simultaneous system of equations. We may thus write

$$[k|1 - x|e^{-(1-x)^2} + 1]^{-1}$$

$$= e^{-h||x-b||^2},\ h \begin{cases} = 0, & x < b \\ = \frac{b}{x}, & x > b. \end{cases}]$$

This is a complicated transendental equation in one variable that may be written as

$$e^{(1-x)^2}[e^{h||x-b||^2} - 1] + kx = k, \ 0 \le x \le 1$$

An approximate solution may be obtained by first approximation of Maclaurin expansion. Let this solution be x* as shown in the diagram below.

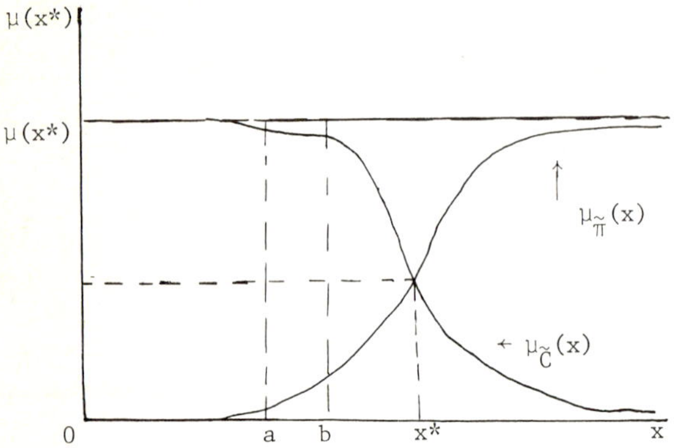

Fig. 5.4. Optimal Fuzzy Production Policy.

Now consider a simple production system where only labor, L, with price w is used. Furthermore, output, Q is produced at price p. For the optimal value of μ(x*) and x* we compute

$$(PQ - wL)/Q = x^*$$

and

$$Q^* = \frac{wL}{P - x^*}, \ \mu(Q^*) = \mu_{\tilde{\pi}}(x^*)$$

5.1D. SIMPLE EXTENSION.

Equations (5.9), (5.10) and (5.11) consider one fuzzy goal and one fuzzy constraint. Now suppose we have n goals and m constraints. The critical region, Δ_c of the fuzzy decision space may be specified as

$$\Delta_c = (\bigwedge_{i=1}^{n} \mu_{\tilde{A}_i}(\omega)) \wedge (\bigwedge_{j=1}^{m} \mu_{\tilde{B}_j}(\gamma)) \qquad (5.12)$$

where $(\cap_i A_i) \cap (\cap_j B_j) \neq 0$. The case where m = n = 1 gives equation (5.7). In general, the solution to the fuzzy optimal decision may not be unique; as such we may speak of a fuzzy set of maximal decision elements, $\tilde{M}$, that may be specified as

$$\tilde{M} = \{\omega^* \in \Delta_c; \ \mu_{\Delta_c}(\omega^*) = \sup_{\omega \in \Delta_c} \mu_{\Delta_c}(\omega)\} \qquad (5.13)$$

and thus $\delta^* = (\omega^*; \ \omega^* \in M)$ is an optimal decision.

Since $\tilde{M}$ may contain more than one fuzzy element, a question thus arises as to what choice must be made among the optimal elements in the set. Furthermore, in many practical cases a non-fuzzy choice is desired even though the decision problem is fuzzy. This problem may be dealt with in few alternative ways. One of such ways may be to further establish a preference over $\tilde{M}$. This perference may take the form of defining a membership function over $\tilde{M}$ and specifying the optimal decision as

$$\delta^{**} = \bigvee_{\omega^* \in M} \mu_{\tilde{M}}(\omega^*)$$

$$\text{S.T.} \quad \tilde{M} = \{\omega^* \in \Delta_c; \ \mu_{\Delta c}(\omega^*) = \bigvee_{\omega \in \Delta_c} \mu_{\Delta c}(\omega)\}$$

$$\Delta_c = (\bigwedge_{i=1}^{n} \mu_{\tilde{A}_i}(\omega)) \wedge (\bigwedge_{j=1}^{m} \mu_{\tilde{B}_j}(\gamma)) \qquad (5.14)$$

$$\delta^* = (\omega^*; \ \omega^* \in \tilde{M})$$

This is a membership optimization problem subject to both goals and constraints. Another approach is suggested by Kickert [8] through the center of gravity procedure where

$$\delta^{**} = (\omega^{**}; \ \omega^{**} = [\sum_{\omega^* \in \tilde{M}} \omega^* \mu_{\tilde{M}}(\omega^*)]/[\sum_{\omega^* \in \tilde{M}} \mu_{\tilde{M}}(\omega^*)]) \qquad (5.15)$$

for a discrete case. If the membership function is assumed to be continuous then

$$\delta^{**} = \{\omega^{**}; \ \omega^{**} = (\int_{\tilde{M}} \omega^* \mu_{\tilde{M}}(\omega^*) d\omega^*) / \int_{M} \mu_{\tilde{M}}(\omega^*) d\omega^*)\}. \qquad (5.16)$$

While it is necessary that the critical region of the decision space be fuzzy convex, it is not necessary that either the fuzzy constraint set or the fuzzy objective set be convex. A unique optimal decision is obtained if the critical region of the decision is strictly fuzzy convex.

So far the above development of algorithms to realize fuzzy rationality implicitly assumes equal importance for goals and constraints. It also assumes equal importance for differential goals and constraints in the case of multiple goals and constraints. In practice, this importance may vary depending on the nature of the problem. We shall now account for this problem through a process of weighting according to their relative importance and some process of goal-constraint aggregation.

Define a proportionality set A = [0, 1] and an index set J. The fuzzy decision problem may then be written as

$$\left.\begin{aligned} \max_{\omega} \mu_{\Delta_c}(\omega) &= \sum_{i \in J} \alpha_i(\omega) \mu_{\tilde{A}_i}(\omega) \\ &+ \sum_{j \in J} \alpha_j(\omega) \mu_{\tilde{B}_j}(\omega) \\ \text{S.T.} \ \sum_{i \in J} \alpha_i(\omega) + \sum_{j \in J} \alpha_j &= 1, \quad \alpha \in A \end{aligned}\right\} \qquad (5.17)$$

where α_i and α_j are chosen to reflect the

relative importance of goals and constraints. The differential importance may depend on other factors besides the personality characteristic. The problem defined by equation (5.17) is often referred to as convex-fuzzy-decision problem [3] [14].

By the definition of the intersection of fuzzy subsets, it is possible that the problem of absolute independence between the fuzzy goals and constraints may arise in the critical region of the decision space as specified by equation (5.12). The problem may be specified as

$$\Delta_c \begin{cases} \text{is said to be fuzzy independent of constraints if } \mu_{\tilde{A}}(\omega) \le \mu_{\tilde{B}}(\omega). \\ \text{is said to be fuzzy independent of goals if } \mu_{\tilde{B}}(\omega) \le \mu_{\tilde{A}}(\omega) \\ \text{is said to be completely fuzzy interdependent if } \mu_{\tilde{A}}(\omega) \gtreqless \mu_{\tilde{B}}(\omega) \text{ and} \\ \mu_{\tilde{A}}(\omega) \wedge \mu_{\tilde{B}}(\omega) \neq 0 \end{cases}$$

To avoid the problem of fuzzy independence of goals and constraints, the critical region of the decision space may be constructed as a product-fuzzy decision [14] that may be written as

$$\Delta_c = \{(\omega;\ \mu_{\Delta_c}(\omega));\ \mu_{\Delta_c}(\omega) = (\prod_{i\varepsilon J} \mu_{\tilde{A}_i}(\omega))(\prod_{j\varepsilon J} \mu_{\tilde{B}_j}(\omega))\}. \qquad (5.18)$$

The optimal fuzzy decision principle obtained from (5.18) is similar to (5.13 - 5.16).

5.2. A FUZZY-MATHEMATICAL PROGRAMMING ALGORITHM.

We have suggested above that the fuzzy decision problem may be constructed as a mathematical programming problem as in equations (5.11), (5.14) and (5.17). The algorithm that may be constructed to realize the optimal fuzzy decision rule is referred to as the fuzzy mathematical programming algorithm. Two approaches of the development of mathematical programming algorithm have been followed: i) through the - level set [21], ii) through the fuzzy utility function and fuzzy sets of nondominating alternatives [15]. Let us outline the basis approach of the fuzzy mathematical programming.

The α-Level Set.

In the search for optimal decision rule to the fuzzy decision problem, it is found that the optimization problem of the membership function defined over the critical region of the decision space may present some theoretical and applied difficulties if the function is not unimodel. The fuzzy optimal decision rule may be stated as

$$\bigvee_{\omega\varepsilon\bar{A}} \mu_{\Delta_c}(\omega) = \bigvee_{\omega\varepsilon\tilde{A}} [\mu_{\tilde{A}}(\omega) \wedge \mu_{\tilde{B}}(\omega)] \qquad (5.19)$$

This optimization problem may be transformed into a fuzzy mathematical programming problem through the use of appropriate set partitioning under a set of appropriate conditions.

Let us suppose that we have a set of alternative objectives, Ω on which an objective function, ϕ is defined such that $\phi\colon \Omega \to \mathbb{R}^+$. We may take $\Omega = \mathbb{R}^n$. Furthermore, let $\tilde{B} \subset \Gamma$ be a fuzzy constraint on Ω characterized by a membership function of the form $\mu_{\tilde{B}}\colon \Omega \to [0, 1]$. We shall assume that $\phi(\omega)$ is bounded from above in the form $\phi(\omega) \le u$. The fuzzy set of goals may then be defined as

$$\tilde{A} = \{(\omega,\ \mu_{\tilde{A}}(\omega));\ \omega \varepsilon \Omega \quad \text{and}$$
$$\mu_{\tilde{A}}(\omega) = \phi(\omega)/u\}. \qquad (5.20)$$

and the critical region of decision, Δ_c may be specified as

$$\Delta_c = \{(\omega,\ \mu_{\Delta_c}(\omega));\ \omega \varepsilon \tilde{A} \cap \tilde{B},$$
$$\mu_{\Delta_c}(\omega) = \mu_{\tilde{A}}(\omega) \wedge \mu_{\tilde{B}}(\omega)\}. \qquad (5.21)$$

The problem is to find the best decision element in Δ_c; in other words, to construct an algorithm that will solve

$$\bigvee_{\omega\varepsilon\Omega} \mu_{\Delta_c}(\omega) = \bigvee_{\omega\varepsilon\Omega} [\mu_{\tilde{A}}(\omega) \wedge \mu_{\tilde{B}}(\omega)] \qquad (5.22)$$

Under some appropriate set of conditions, this fuzzy optimization problem may be stated as a mathematical programming problem [14] [21].

Theorem 5.1.

$$\bigvee_{\omega\varepsilon\Omega} \mu_{\Delta_c}(\omega) = \begin{cases} \bigvee_{\omega\varepsilon R} \mu_{\tilde{A}}(\omega) \\ \text{St. } R = [\omega \varepsilon \Omega; \\ \quad (\mu_{\tilde{B}}(\omega) - \mu_{\tilde{A}}(\omega)) \ge 0] \end{cases}$$

To prove this theorem the following lemma is required (note V implies maximize).

Lemma 5.1.

$$\bigvee_{\omega\varepsilon\Omega} \mu_{\Delta_c}(\omega) = \bigvee_{\alpha\varepsilon[0,1]} [\alpha \wedge (\bigvee_{\omega\varepsilon B_\alpha} \mu_{\tilde{A}}(\omega))]$$

where $B_\alpha = \{\omega \varepsilon \Omega;\ \mu_{\tilde{B}}(\omega) \ge \alpha\}$ is the α-level set of $\mu_{\tilde{B}}(\omega)$ that induces a non-fuzzy set B_α in $\tilde{B}$.

The proofs of theorem 5.1 and lemma 5.1 may be found in [14] [21]. The essential steps may be outlined as

1. Given the proof of lemma (5.1) we define (a function) a point to set mapping of the form

$$\xi(\alpha) = \bigvee_{\omega\varepsilon B_\alpha} \mu_{\tilde{A}}(\omega)$$

where $\xi\colon [0, 1] \to [0, 1]$.

2. We define another function ψ such that ψ: $[0, 1] \to [0, 1]$ where

$$\psi(\alpha) = \{\alpha \wedge \xi(\alpha);\ \alpha \in [0, 1]\}.$$

We then observe that by lemma (5.1)

$$\bigvee_{\omega\in\Omega} \mu_{\Delta_c}(\omega) = \bigvee_{\alpha\in[0,1]} \psi(\alpha)$$

3. It is then shown that ξ has the following properties

a) $\xi(0) = \bigvee_{\omega\in\Omega} \mu_{\tilde{A}}(\omega)$

b) for $\alpha_1 \leq \alpha_2$, $\xi(\alpha_1) \geq \xi(\alpha_2)$

4. Assume that ξ is a continuous mapping on [0, 1], (in fact, it only needs to be upper semi-continuous) then by Kakutani's fixed-point theorem on unit simplex there is $\alpha_0 \in [0, 1]$ such that

$$\xi(\alpha_0) = \alpha_0 = \bigvee_{\omega\in B_{\alpha_0}} \mu_{\tilde{A}}(\omega).$$

Graphically, we have

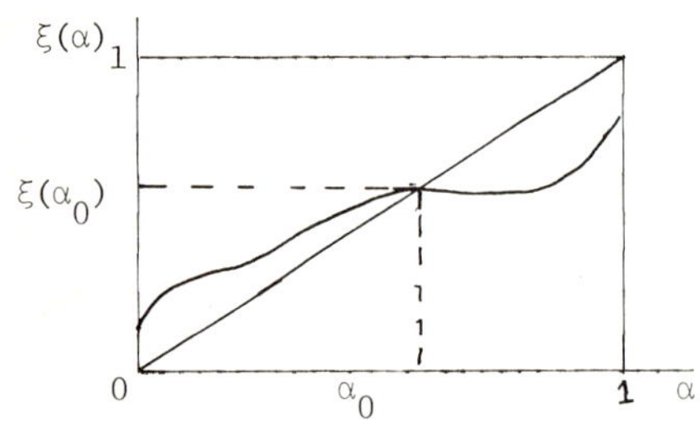

Fig 5.2.1: A Fixed-point Solution

5. By Calculus of fuzzy containment it is then demonstrated that $B_{\alpha_0} \subset R$ and hence

$$\bigvee_{\omega\in R} \mu_{\tilde{A}}(\omega) \geq \bigvee_{\omega\in B_{\alpha_0}} \mu_{\tilde{A}}(\omega) = \alpha_0$$

But $\bigvee_{\omega\in\Omega} \mu_{\Delta_c}(\omega) \geq \bigvee_{\omega\in R} \mu_{\tilde{A}}(\omega)$

These imply that

$$\bigvee_{\omega\in\Omega} \mu_{\Delta_c}(\omega) = \alpha_0 = \bigvee_{\omega\in R} \mu_{\tilde{A}}(\omega)$$

The proof is thus completed. In other words, α_0 is optimal if and only if

$$\alpha_0 = \bigvee_{\omega\in B_\alpha} \mu_{\tilde{A}}(\omega)$$

which gives us the optimal fuzzy decision rule. Observation: It is possible that there may exist more than one α_0 such that $\xi(\alpha_0) = \alpha_0$ and hence obtain a multiple solution. The α_0 is guaranteed to be unique if $\xi(\alpha)$ is not only upper semicontinuous but $\mu_{\tilde{B}}(\omega)$ is strictly fuzzy convex.

5.3. THE η-CLASS.

So far the theory of fuzzy decision has been developed under conditions of certainty; as such it has nothing to say when the environment is not only fuzzy but also uncertain. The class of decision problems that falls under fuzzy uncertainty is what we have referred to as the η-class. It has the basic characteristics of the β-class of decision problems and yet distinguished from it by the property that the essential information, summarized by relevant fuzzy parameters, is unknown in an uncertain world. This is the fuzzy-uncertainty decision problem where fuzzy data must be obtained in order to solve the fuzzy decision problem. It may be referred to as "fuzzy-data-decision" problem.

In an attempt to analyse this class of decision problems, a question arises as to what would be the proper representation of the simultaneous occurance of fuzziness and uncertainty in the relevant information that surround the decision problems. This is a nontrivial question in that the path of decision analysis that may be chosen will depend on the answer to the above question which will also affect the analytical representation of the problem, algorithm and decision rules that may be derived. It is important at this juncture to point out that the understanding of this η-class of decision problems is in primitive states of development (some attempts may be found in [8] [10] [23]).

Two logical approaches seem to present themselves in the simultaneous treatment of both fuzziness and uncertainty in decision problems. One approach may be an extension of the analysis of the σ-class into a fuzzy environment. This approach may lead to what may be called <u>fuzzy statistical decision theory</u>. Alternatively, the analysis of the β-class may be extended into uncertain environment. The resulting theory may be called <u>statistical fuzzy decision theory</u>. Let us outline the possible development of these two possible approaches.

5.3A. FUZZY STATISTICAL DECISION THEORY (FSDT)

The fuzzy statistical decision theory is an extension of statistical decision theory into fuzzy environment. The approach accepts an initial premise that probability measure is an appropriate representation of uncertain outcomes whether fuzzy or nonfuzzy. Given that probability is a suitable ranking of the degree of uncertainty, a question then arises as to how may fuzziness be incorporated into the decision making under uncertainty. The answer to this question may proceed from Zadeh's initial approach of defining probability measures over fuzzy events [7] [10] [23].

Consider a general set of alternative goals, Ω.

Let $\tilde{A}_i$ be a fuzzy event set for each $i \in J$, an index set and that $\tilde{A}_i \subset \Omega$. Let each fuzzy event set be equipped with a membership function $\mu_{\tilde{A}_i} : \Omega \to [0, 1]$. The collection of all these mappings is a membership set, M. We shall now define a fuzzy probability space.

Definition 5.1:

A fuzzy probability space is a triplet $(M,A,P;\Omega)$ where A is σ-algebra of Borel subsets of M, P a probability measure and Ω is a given set of alternatives.

The definition imposes Borel measurability on M and hence on $\mu_{\tilde{A}}$. We shall now define a probability measure on fuzzy event $\tilde{A}$ with a generic element $X_{\tilde{A}}$. Let ω be a value that $X_{\tilde{A}}$ may assume in Ω with $\mu_{\tilde{A}}(\omega) \in M$ then a probability measure on $\tilde{A}$ may be defined for continuous and discrete cases as

$$P(\tilde{A}; \omega) = P(X_{\tilde{A}} \leq \omega) =$$

$$\int_{-\infty}^{\omega} \mu_{\tilde{A}}(\omega)\ f(\omega)d\omega = E[\mu_{\tilde{A}}(\omega)] \tag{5.23a}$$

or

$$P(\tilde{A}, \omega) = \sum_{\omega\in\Omega} \mu_{\tilde{A}}(\omega)\ f(\omega)$$

$$= E[\mu_{\tilde{A}}(\omega)] \tag{5.23b}$$

and

$$P(X_{\tilde{A}} = \omega) = \mu_{\tilde{A}}(\omega)\ f(\omega) \tag{5.23c}$$

where $f(\omega)$ is the fuzzy probability density function defined over $\tilde{A}$. The expression $E[\mu_{\tilde{A}}(\omega)]$ is the expected value of the membership function of fuzzy subset $\tilde{A}$ provided that the sum converges absolutely on Ω.

The expected value of the membership function defined over the space of alternatives may be viewed as a representation of partial preordering of fuzzy uncertainty that surrounds the decision outcome. Given that the fuzzy uncertainty is partially preordered (the representation is not unique [10]), a question arises as to how can the fuzzy-uncertain consequences be preordered for choice. The preordering may be done with an expected-value function defined over the fuzzy-uncertain decision space. This decision space will be equipped with fuzzy probability space that will be a subspace of it (i.e., $[M,A,P;\Omega] \subset \Delta$). The fuzzy-uncertain decision problem is the optimization of the expected fuzzy value subject to an appropriate constraint set. In set-theoretic terms, it may canonically be represented as

$$\underset{\omega\in A\,\cap\,\tilde{B}}{\text{Opt}} \quad \lambda(\omega,\theta;\mu,p) \in \Lambda(\{M_\omega, A_\omega, P; \Omega\}; \Theta)$$

$$\text{S.T.} \quad \tilde{A} \cap \tilde{B} \neq 0$$

$$\tilde{A} \subset [(\omega; \{M_\omega, A_\omega, P\}); \tilde{\Theta} \subset I] \tag{5.24}$$

$$\tilde{B} \subset [(\Gamma; \{M_\gamma, A_\gamma, P\}); \tilde{\Theta} \subset I]$$

where M_γ is the membership set of the constraint set and A_γ its Borel set.

Let A be a subset of a typical production set with a corresponding fuzzy profit subset, $\tilde{\pi} \subset \Omega$ equipped with a membership function, $\mu_\pi(\omega)$ such that $F_0(A) = \tilde{\pi}$ is realized in an uncertain environment. Furthermore, let the realization of $\tilde{\pi}$ to be constrained by a fuzzy-uncertain cost set $\tilde{B}$. Under such conditions equation (5.24) may be explicitly written as

$$\max_{\omega} \int_{\omega\in\Omega} F_0(A)\ E[\mu_{\tilde{\pi}}(\omega)]d\omega \tag{5.25}$$

$$\text{S.T.} \quad \int_{\omega\in\Gamma} F_1(A)\ E[\mu_{\tilde{B}}(\omega)d\omega \leq k$$

where k is a constant and the constraint is fuzzy-uncertain. The production, profit and cost sets are immaterial to the decision representation of (5.25). The optimal decision rule $\delta^* \in \Delta$ to the above problem may be written as

$$\delta^* = \delta(\omega^*; \tilde{\theta}, e) = \sup_{\omega} \delta(\omega; \tilde{\theta}, e) \tag{5.26}$$

where e is the expectation of fuzzy event set contained in the space of alternatives and duly equipped with a membership function and a probability measure with a given information.

There are many unanswered questions that may be raised about the development of fuzzy statistical decision theory. Unfortunately we shall end here and discuss some main ideas about statistical fuzzy decision theory. However, we must say that the algorithms that may be developed to realize equation (5.25) may be similar to those of the σ-class.

5.3B. STATISTICAL FUZZY DECISION THEORY.

The statistical fuzzy decision theory, unlike the fuzzy statistical decision theory, is an extension of fuzzy decision theory into the world of uncertainty. Such a distinction may seem artificial and purely methodological. Nontheless, an important question may be raised as to whether the two approaches will yield the same optimal decision rule. This is a nontrivial question that perhaps can be answered after a substantial development of the theory of decision under fuzzy uncertainty. We shall outline the possible basic structure.

We first accept the premise that the membership function is an appropriate representation of the degree of fuzziness. The problem of decision under uncertainty is formulated along the line of the representation of the σ-class and the decision outcome is then fuzzified. The general canonical structure will be similar to equation (5.24) except that the way in which the essential parameters enter the system will be different. Without detailed explanation, we may write the corresponding form as

$$\underset{\omega \varepsilon A \cap B}{\text{Opt.}} \ \{\lambda(\omega;\theta,p),\ \mu_\lambda\} \ \varepsilon \ \Lambda(\{\Omega,\ B_0,\ p\},\ M_\lambda;\ \Theta)$$

$$\left.\begin{array}{ll} \text{S.T.} & A \cap B \neq \emptyset \\ & A \subset (\{\Omega,\ B_0,\ p\};\ \Theta \subset I) \\ & B \subset (\{\Gamma,\ B_1,\ p\};\ \Theta \subset I) \end{array}\right\} \quad (5.26)$$

Notice that the membership set is defined over the ends.

The problem of equation (5.26) may be solved in two stages. First we find the optimal decision rule to the non-fuzzy component in the form of equations (4.6) and (4.8). Let such optimal decision be of the form

$$\lambda^* = \lambda(\omega^*;\ \theta,\ p) \quad (5.27)$$

This optimal decision is then fuzzified relative to the value, λ^* leading to a problem that is equivalent to the β-class that will allow the use of fuzzy mathematical programming.

Secondly, a fuzzy set is defined for λ^* with corresponding membership function. Let such a set be $\tilde{\Lambda}$ with a membership function, $\mu_{\tilde{\Lambda}}(\lambda^*)$. The problem thus reduces to

$$\begin{array}{l} \underset{\lambda}{\text{Opt.}} \ \mu_{\tilde{\Lambda}}(\lambda^*) \\ \text{S.T.} \quad \lambda^* \ \varepsilon \ \tilde{\Lambda} \end{array} \quad (5.28)$$

The fuzzy mathematical programming technique may then be applied to obtain a fuzzy optimal decision rule that may be written as

$$\delta^* = \underset{\lambda^* \varepsilon \tilde{\Lambda}}{\text{Opt.}} \ \mu_{\tilde{\Lambda}}(\lambda^*) \quad (5.29)$$

where λ^* is optimal in non-fuzzy uncertain environment and δ^* is optimal decision in fuzzy-uncertain environment. Furthermore, it must be observed that λ^* is an expected value and hence $\mu_{\tilde{\Lambda}}(\lambda^*)$ is defined over expected value as a fuzzification process. This approach seems to be the one adopted by Van Eeden [8] [25].

6. CONCLUSIONAL REMARK.

The development of the theory of fuzzy decision has been presented as a natural extension of the theory of non-fuzzy decision through canonically set-theoretic representations. The general decision problem is partitioned into four classes of i) non-fuzzy certain, ii) non-fuzzy uncertain, iii) fuzzy certain and iv) fuzzy uncertain. Fuzzy and unfuzzy decision principles have been derived in set-theoretic terms with the specifications of optimal decision rules that correspond to the respective classes. It is pointed out that the theoretical development of decision problems under fuzzy uncertainty is at its elementary stages. Two approaches are fuzzy statistical decision theory and statistical fuzzy decision theory. A question arises as to whether these two approaches yield equivalent optimal decision principle. More research is needed not only on this question but on the whole question of relationship between fuzziness and uncertainty. This is a territory for both scientists and scientifically minded philosophers. The problem of philosophers of science, in this respect, would be to elucidate on the conceptual differences between fuzziness and uncertainty. On the other hand, the problem of fuzzy decision scientist is to construct appropriate structural representation of decision problems and algorithms under conditions of fuzzy uncertainty.

The problem that a decision practitioner may face is either choosing or constructing appropriate membership functions such that the degree of fuzziness is properly preordered in such a way that the ordering is complete. This problem is similar to the problem in utility theory.

REFERENCES:

[1] Asai, K. et al; "Decision-Making and Its Goal in a Fuzzy Environment" in [20].

[2] Beckman, M.J., Dynamic Programming of Economic Decisions, Springer-Verlag, New York, 1968.

[3] Bellman, R.E. et al, Decision-Making in a Fuzzy Environment", Management Science, Vol. 17 #4 1970.

[4] Berger, J.O., Statistical Decision Theory, Springer-Verlag, New York, 1980.

[5] Fung, L.W. et al., "An Axiomatic Approach to Rational Decision Making In a Fuzzy Environment" in [20].

[6] Gupta, M.M., et al, (Eds.), Fuzzy Automata and Decision Processes, North-Holland 1977.

[7] Kandel, A., et al, "Fuzzy Processes" Fuzzy Sets and Systems, Vol. 4, 1980.

[8] Kickert, W.J.M., Fuzzy Theories on Decision-making, Martinus Nijhoff, Boston, 1978.

[9] Kickert, W.J.M., Organization of Decision Making, North-Holland, 1980.

[10] Klement, E.P., et al., "Fuzzy Probability Measures", Fuzzy Sets and Systems, Vol. S, 1981.

[11] Knopfmacher, J., "On Measures of Fuzziness", Journal of Mathematical Analysis and Application, Vol. 49, 1975.

[12] Menges, G., Economic Decision Making, Longman Group, 1974.

[13] Mengés, G. et. al., Inference and Decision, Selecta Statistica Canadina, Vol. 1 Wiley, New York, 1971.

[14] Negoita, C.V. et al., Applications of Fuzzy Sets to Systems Analysis, Wiley, 1975.

[15] Orlovsky, S.A., "On Formalization of a General Fuzzy Mathematical Programming Problem", Fuzzy Sets and Systems, Vol. 3, 1980.

[16] Savage, L.J., The Foundations of Statistical Inference, Wiley, New York, 1959.

[17] Sayre, K.M., "Choice, Decision and Origin of Information" in [18].

[18] Sayre, K.M., et al., (Eds.), Philosophy and Cybernetics, Simon and Schuster, New York, 1967.

[19] Takahara, Y. et al., "A Unified Theory of Decision Principles", International Journal of System Science Vol. 11, #11, 1980.

[20] Takayama, A., Mathematical Economics, Dryden, 1974.

[21] Tanaka, H. et al., "On Fuzzy-Mathematical Programming, Journal of Cybernetics, Vol. 3-4, 1974.

[22] Zadeh, L.A. et al., (Eds.), Fuzzy Sets and Their Applications to Cognitive and Decision Processes, Academic Press, New York, 1974.

[23] Zadeh, L.A., "Probability of Fuzzy Event" Journal of Mathematical Analysis and Application, Vol. 23, 1968.

[24] Zimmermann, H-J, Fuzzy Programming and Linear Programming with Several Objective Functions", Fuzzy Sets and Systems, Vol. 1, 1978.

[25] Van Eeden, D., Fuzzy Random Variables in Decision Problems, Thesis, Department of Applied Mathematics, Technical University of Twente, Enschede, 1976.

[26] Adams, J.M., "Fuzzy Decision Trees, Fuzzy Sets and Systems, Vol. 4, #3 1980.

[27] Banon, G. "Distinction Between Several Subsets of Fuzzy Measures," Fuzzy Sets and Systems. Vol. 5, 1981.

[28] Hirota, K. "Concepts of Probalistic Sets", Fuzzy Sets and Systems, Vol. 5, 1981.

[29] Klement, E.P. et. al., "Correspondence Between Fuzzy Measures and Classical Measures", Fuzzy Sets and Systems, Vol. 7, 1982.

[30] Kling, R., "Fuzzy Planner: Reasoning with Inexact Concepts in Procedural Problem-Solving Language", Journal of Cybernetics, Vol. 3, 1974.

[31] Kuz'min, V.B. et. al., "Group Decisions I. In Arbitrary Spaces of Fuzzy Binary Relation" Fuzzy Sets and Systems, Vol. 4, 1980.

[32] __, "Design of Group Decision II. In Spaces of Partial Order Fuzzy Relations" Fuzzy Sets and Systems, Vol. 4, 1980.

[33] Lasker, G.E., Applied Systems and Cybernetics, Vol. 6,: Fuzzy Setts and Systems, Pergamon Press, New York, 1982.

[34] Lowen, R., "Convex Fuzzy Sets", Fuzzy Sets and Systems, Vol. 3, 1980.

[35] Negoita, C.V., "The Current Interest in Fuzzy Optimization", Fuzzy Sets and Systems, Vol. 6, 1981.

[36] Nojiri, H., "On the Fuzzy Team Decision in a Changing Environment", Fuzzy Sets and Systems, Vol. 3, 1981.

[37] Nurmi, H., "A Fuzzy Solution to a Majority Voting Game," Fuzzy Sets and Systems, Vol. 5, 1981.

[38] Nurmi, H., "Approaches to Collective Decision Making with Fuzzy Reference Relations", Fuzzy Sets and Systems, Vol. 6, 1981.

[39] Ponsard, C., "An Application of Fuzzy Subsets Theory to the Analysis of the Consumer's Spacial Preferences," Fuzzy Sets and Systems, Vol. 5, 1981.

[40] Stallings, W., "Fuzzy Set Theory Versus Bayesian Statistics", IEEE Transactions on Systems, Man and Cybernetics, Vol. 7, 1977.

[41] Takeda, E.,et. al., "Multiple Criteria Problems with Fuzzy Domination Structures", Fuzzy Sets and Systems, Vol. 3, 1980.

[42] Tanaka, H.T., et. al. "A Formulation of Fuzzy Decision Problems and its Application to an Investment Problem", Kybernetes, Vol. 5, 1976.

Approximate Reasoning in Decision Analysis
M.M. Gupta and E. Sanchez (eds.)

DYNAMIC CONFLICT RESOLUTION THROUGH A THEORY OF A DISPLACED FUZZY IDEAL*

Yee Leung

Department of Geography
The Chinese University of Hong Kong
Shatin, Hong Kong

A theory of a displaced fuzzy ideal is proposed for dynamic conflict resolution involving multiple criteria and multiple decision making units. The resolution process consists of two interactive and recursive stages. Based on the idea of a compromise solution, a concept of a fuzzy local ideal is constructed to resolve conflict within decision making units in the first stage. A notion of a fuzzy global ideal is formulated to resolve conflict among decision making units in the second stage. Throughout, displacement of a fuzzy local ideal or a fuzzy global ideal may occur with respect to new information gathered or changing perspectives of the conflict situation. Such a process of ideal displacement is imperative in determining the final compromise solution in the context of dynamic conflict resolution.

KEYWORDS: Dynamic conflict resolution, linguistic proposition, fuzzy local ideal, fuzzy global ideal, displacement of a fuzzy ideal.

1. INTRODUCTION

Conflict resolution processes involving multiple criteria and multiple decision-making units are in general dynamic in nature. The selection of an appropriate alternative under conflicting objectives and interest groups often requires an interactive and recursive procedure. Over the years, the idea of a compromise solution via a notion of an ideal solution (see for example [3, 4, 6]) has been a major analytical basis of conflict resolution. A concept of a fuzzy ideal [2] has also been proposed to resolve conflicts in a fuzzy environment in which information is inexact and our cognitive and decision making processes are fuzzy. Nevertheless, such a conceptualization of an ideal solution, exact or fuzzy, does not provide a dynamic resolution of conflicts characterized by a continuous process of information gathering and processing, constant feedback within and between decision making units, and changing cognitions and perspectives of the decision making environment.

To provide a dynamic analysis through the ideal solution framework, a theory of a displaced ideal emphasizing on an interactive and recursive decision process has been proposed [7]. To account for the prevailing fuzziness in the resolution process, value-based rules have also been incorporated in an extended model of a displaced ideal [1]. However, the displacement of a fuzzy ideal, possibly an important idea in conflict resolution, has not been analyzed. The objective of this paper is to present a theory of dynamic conflict resolution via the displacement of a fuzzy ideal.

In what follows, a general framework of conflict resolution involving multiple criteria and multiple decision making units is first described. Conflict resolution within a decision making unit is then discussed in section 3. Displacement of a fuzzy ideal is elaborated in section 4. Section 5 analyzes the resolution of conflict among decision making units. The paper then concludes by evaluating the applicability of the proposed theory in dynamic conflict resolution.

2. A GENERAL FRAMEWORK OF DYNAMIC CONFLICT RESOLUTION PROCESSES

Decision making in environmental management, socio-economic planning, international disarmament, selection of sites for public and private facilities, such as airport, highway, nuclear power plant, and obnoxious industrial plants, all involve multiple criteria and multiple decision making units (henceforth, refer to as DM units). Conflict occurs whenever a proposed alternative cannot simultaneously satisfy all the criteria designating conflicting goals or all DM units representing conflicting interests. Thus, the search of a compromise solution, based on the ideal solution method, becomes a natural approach to resolve conflicts under this situation. The framework of conflict resolution proposed in this paper is similar to the one discussed by Leung [1]. Displacement of a fuzzy ideal, however, is the key issue of analysis here.

* This paper was completed while the author was a Visiting Senior Fellow of the Center for Metropolitan Planning and Research and a Visiting Associate Professor of the Department of Geography and Environmental Engineering at The Johns Hopkins University in the spring semester, 1982.

In general, the conflict resolution process consists of two recursive stages. The first stage is conflict resolution within DM units. In this stage, each DM unit resolves its own conflict through a concept of a displaced fuzzy ideal. Fuzzy local ideal and the corresponding compromise solutions (to be discussed in section 3) are determined through an interactive and recursive procedure. Throughout the decision making process, displacement of the fuzzy local ideal occurs in accordance with the nature of the information gathered, internal and external feedbacks, abandonment or inclusion of alternatives, addition or deletion of criteria, and changes in the relative importance of criteria. Basically, the final local compromise solution can only be determined when further displacement of the fuzzy local ideal is not necessary.

The second stage deals with conflict resolution among DM units. Fuzzy local compromise solutions obtained in the first stage are turned in to the central coordinating committee, an independent entity or a group of representatives from the DM units, for evaluation. Then, the fuzzy global ideal is selected and the global compromise solution is determined (to be discussed in section 5). Similar to the internal conflict resolution within a DM unit, the final fuzzy global ideal and the associated global compromise solution may be ascertained only after several rounds of displacement of the initial ideal have taken place.

Though the whole conflict resolution process is divided into two stages, they are by no means to be independent. On the contrary, they are highly interdependent and recursive. For example, the determination of the fuzzy global ideal depends on all fuzzy local ideals and local compromise solutions. Any displacements of the fuzzy local ideals will lead to the displacement of the fuzzy global ideal. On the other hand, displacement of the fuzzy local ideal may be triggered by feedback information, such as the compatibility of the local compromise solutions and the commensurability of objectives or alternatives, from the second stage. Thus, the recursive conflict resolution process terminates only when a satisfactory global compromise solution is obtained and no further modifications are necessary.

The recursive two-stage conflict resolution process is depicted in Fig. 1. The formalization of the process is detailed in Sections 3, 4 and 5.

3. CONFLICT RESOLUTION WITHIN A DECISION MAKING UNIT

Let $Z = \{Z_1, \ldots, Z_k, \ldots, Z_l\}$ be a group of DM units which attempts to select a mutually satisfactory alternative in a joint venture.

In the first stage, for DM unit z_k, let $X = \{X_1, \ldots, X_i, \ldots, X_n\}$ be the set of initial feasible alternatives, and $Y = \{Y_1, \ldots, Y_j, \ldots, \ldots, Y_m\}$ be the set of initial criteria by which the performance of an alternative is evaluated. Based on the argument of a concept of a fuzzy ideal[2], let

$$\begin{bmatrix} p_1^1 & \cdots & p_j^1 & \cdots & p_m^1 \\ \vdots & & \vdots & & \vdots \\ p_1^i & \cdots & p_j^i & \cdots & p_m^i \\ \vdots & & \vdots & & \vdots \\ p_1^n & \cdots & p_j^n & \cdots & p_m^n \end{bmatrix} \quad (1)$$

be the performance matrix whose element p_j^i is a linguistic proposition of an alternative X_i, $i = 1, \ldots, n$, with respect to criterion Y_j, $j = 1, \ldots, m$.

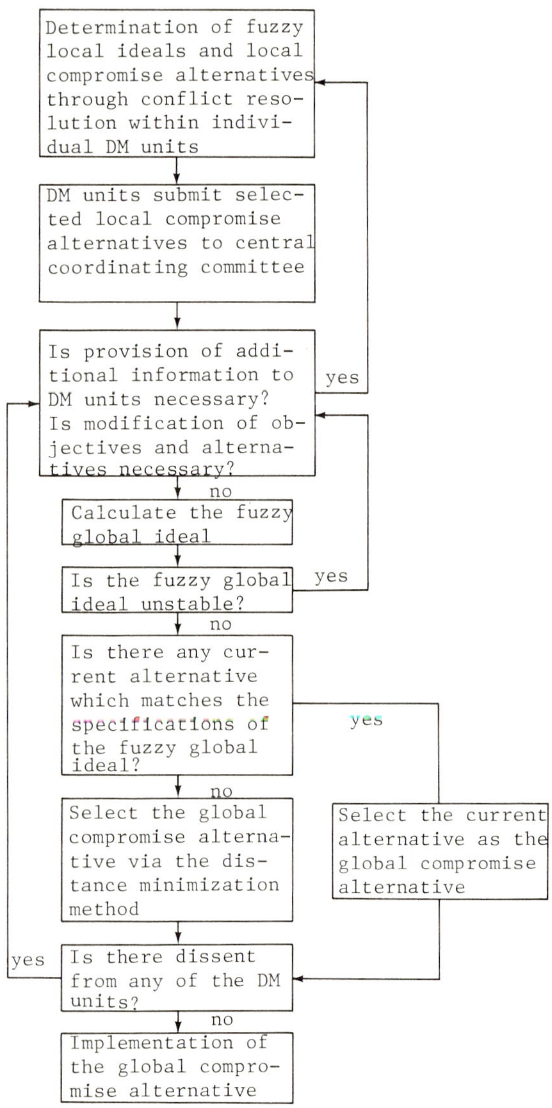

Fig. 1 An outline of a dynamic conflict resolution process involving multiple criteria and multiple decision-making units

The general format of the linguistic proposition p^i_j is

$$p^i_j : Y_j \text{ is } F^i_j, \quad (2)$$

which may be stated as

"with reference to alternative X_i, the criterion Y_j is F^i_j (a fuzzy subset)."

For example, "with reference to alternative X_i, net return (Y_j) is *approximately 10 million dollars* (F^i_j)."

By a theory of possibility [5], the linguistic proposition depicted by eq. (2) induces a possibility distribution, $\Pi^i_{Y_j}$, through the possibility assignment equation

$$Y_j \text{ is } F^i_j \rightarrow \Pi^i_{Y_j} = F^i_j, \quad (3)$$

such that

$$\text{Poss } (Y_j = y_j) = \pi^i_{Y_j}(y_j) = \mu_{F^i_j}(y_j). \quad (4)$$

Thus, the matrix of linguistic propositions in eq. (1) can be translated into a matrix of possibility distribution functions whose elements are $\pi^i_{Y_j}$'s. Since a possibility distribution function serves as a fuzzy restriction on the base variable, it in turn imposes a fuzzy interval,

$$[\underline{y}^i_j, \overline{y}^i_j] = \{y_j \mid \pi^i_{Y_j}(y_j) \leq \alpha\},$$

$$\alpha \in (0, 1], \quad (5)$$

where, $\underline{y}^i_j$ and $\overline{y}^i_j$ are, respectively, the minimum and maximum values of the interval, and α is a prescribed level of satisfaction, on the values of y_j under proposition P^i_j.

With respect to all alternatives, the ideal performance of an alternative under criterion Y_j may then be characterized by a composite linguistic proposition

$$P_j : Y_j \text{ is } F_j, \quad (6)$$

such that

$$\text{Poss } (Y_j = y_j) = \pi_{Y_j}(y_j) = \mu_{F_j}(y_j). \quad (7)$$

The term F_j is a fuzzy subset expressed as

$$F_j = F^1_j \text{ and } \ldots \text{ and } F^i_j \text{ and } \ldots \text{ and } F^n_j, \quad (8)$$

with a defining membership function

$$\mu_{F_j} = \mu_{F^1_j} \cap \ldots \cap F^i_j \cap \ldots \cap F^n_j. \quad (9)$$

Thus, the composite possibility distribution function

$$\pi_{Y_j}(y_j) = \mu_{F^1_j}(y_j) \wedge \ldots \wedge \mu_{F^i_j}(y_j) \wedge \ldots \wedge \mu_{F^n_j}(y_j) \quad (10)$$

is a composite characterization of criterion Y_j which restricts the spread of the values of y_j to a fuzzy interval.

$$[\underline{y}^*_j, \overline{y}^*_j] = \{y_j \mid \pi_{Y_j}(y_j) \geq \alpha\},$$

$$\alpha \in (0, 1]. \quad (11)$$

The values $\underline{y}^*_j$ and $\overline{y}^*_j$ represent, respectively, the minimum and maximum values of the interval. Since every element in this interval satisfies the specification of Y_j by each alternative, specifically $y_j \in [\underline{y}^*_j, \overline{y}^*_j] \Rightarrow y \in [\underline{y}^i_j, \overline{y}^i_j]$, then it can be considered as a fuzzy interval specifying a set of ideal values for Y_j.

With reference to all criteria, the fuzzy local ideal for DM unit Z_k is an ideal alternative which can be defined by a m-tuple of linguistic propositions

$$X^*_k = (Y_1 \text{ is } F_1, \ldots, Y_j \text{ is } F_j, \ldots, Y_m \text{ is } F_m), \quad (12)$$

or, by a fuzzy region taking the form of an m-cell

$$X^*_k = \{(y^*_1, \ldots, y^*_j, \ldots, y^*_m) \mid \underline{y}^*_j \leq y^*_j \leq \overline{y}^*_j, \ j = 1, \ldots, m\}. \quad (13)$$

It is an ideal because it satisfies all performance specifications, namely P_j's, of the individual criteria with reference to all alternatives. It is a local ideal because it may not satisfy other DM units' designations.

Since such an ideal alternative is ordinarily impossible to obtain, within Z_k conflict arises as to which alternative to select so that the chosen alternative has the minimum deviation from the fuzzy local ideal. A natural solution is that of a compromise solution with respect to the fuzzy ideal [2].

Due to the fuzziness of the local ideal, any of its element can be cognized as an ideal solution. Thus, for each element of the fuzzy local ideal, a set of local compromise solutions can be derived through a distance minimization procedure. Specifically, with respect to the maximum of the fuzzy local ideal, $(\overline{y}^*_1, \ldots, \overline{y}^*_j, \ldots, \overline{y}^*_m)$, for a prescribed value of the parameter p, $1 \leq p \leq \infty$, the local compromise solution, $\overline{X}_k = (\overline{y}^c_{k1}, \ldots, \overline{y}^c_{kj}, \ldots, \overline{y}^c_{km})$, is the alternative which minimizes the distance function

$$\left(\sum_{j=1}^{m} (1 - \mu_{\textit{close to } \overline{y}^*_j}(y^i_j))^p\right)^{1/p}$$

$$1 \leq p \leq \infty. \quad (14)$$

The local compromise solution set is then the collection of all these local compromise solutions for all p.

Similarly, if the minimum of the fuzzy local ideal, $(\underline{y}_1^*, \ldots, \underline{y}_j^*, \ldots, \underline{y}_m^*)$, is employed as an ideal solution, a set of local compromise solutions, with its element denoted as $\underline{X}_k^c = (\underline{y}_{k1}^c, \ldots, \underline{y}_{kj}^c, \ldots, \underline{y}_{km}^c)$, for all p can also be derived.

The above relationship between the fuzzy ideal and the local compromise solutions is depicted via a two-criteria example in Fig. 2.

In general, for each element of the fuzzy local ideal, a compromise solution set can be derived. That is, for a specific value of the parameter p, the local compromise solution, depending on which element of the fuzzy local ideal it is referring to, can take on different point-values.

The advantages and disadvantages of applying the concept of a fuzzy ideal to conflict resolutions will not be examined here (see [2] for discussions). Emphasis, however, is placed on the displacement of the fuzzy local ideal and the corresponding local compromise solutions. For clarity of presentation, displacement of a fuzzy ideal, local or global, is analyzed in a separate section. Nevertheless, it should be treated as an integral part of the conflict resolution process in the first and second stages.

4. DISPLACEMENT OF A FUZZY IDEAL

The continuous process of information gathering and the changing aspects of cognition of the conflic environment, as discussed in section 2, may displace the initial fuzzy local ideal. Thus, the initial local compromise solution may not be regarded as the final compromise alternative. It may also be displaced in accordance with the displacement of the fuzzy local ideal.

Basically, the displacement of a fuzzy ideal is induced by changing the linguistic propositions of the criteria. Such changes may be originated from varying the evaluations of alternatives with respect to the criteria, or from the deletion or addition of criteria or alternatives during the resolution process. In what follows, displacement of a fuzzy ideal in relation to changes in criteria evaluations is discussed first. Displacement resulting from the addition or deletion of alternatives is then examined.

4.1 Variations of Linguistic Propositions and Ideal Displacement

Generally, if the initial criteria and alternatives remain the same throughout the conflict resolution process, displacement of a fuzzy ideal then becomes a consequence of changes in the linguistic propositions of the criteria. Once the initial propositions are changed, the

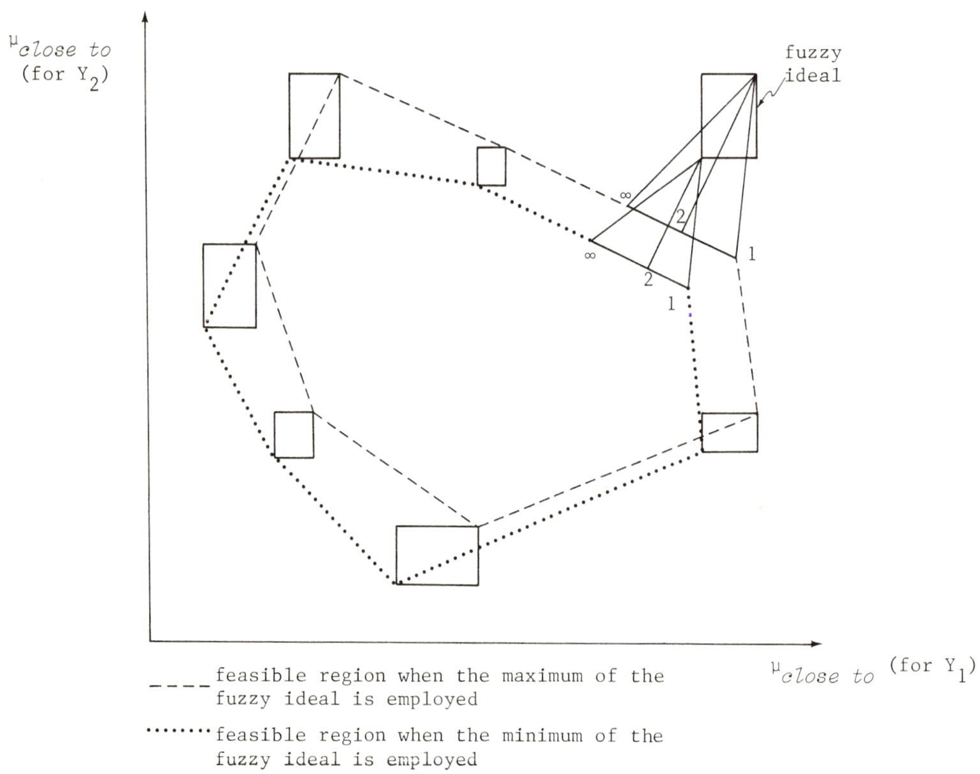

Fig. 2 Compromise solutions with respect to specific elements of a fuzzy ideal

new propositions in turn induce new possibility distribution functions which may impose new restrictions on the base variables of the criteria. Either the positions of the associated fuzzy intervals may be shifted or their sizes may be expanded or contracted. Since a fuzzy ideal is demarcated by a set of fuzzy intervals, changes in the fuzzy intervals may displace the initial fuzzy ideal. Such a process of displacement is summarized in Fig. 3.

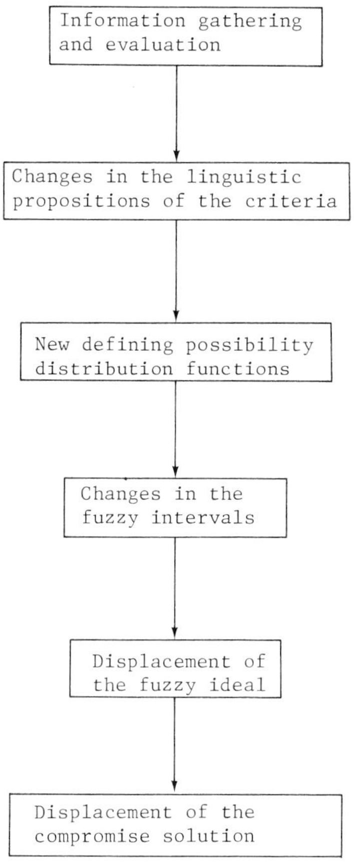

Fig. 3 A typical displacement process of a fuzzy ideal

In terms of the changing position and size of a fuzzy interval, three major types of displacement can be identified. For simplicity of presentation, the following discussions are restricted to a two-criteria case. The arguments, however, can be extended to the m-criteria situation.

4.1.1 Displacement of a fuzzy ideal due to dispositions of fuzzy intervals

This type of displacement only shifts the position of a fuzzy ideal, while its size remains constant. The displacement occurs when the reference point, a parameter, of a linguistic proposition is changed but its associated possibility distribution function remains the same. For example, the initial linguistic proposition of a criterion "net return is *close to* a_o" here, a_o is the reference point or a target) may be transformed into "net return is *close to* a_1." In this situation, except for the change of its parameter from a_o to a_1, the defining possibility distribution function, $\pi_{\text{net return}}$, takes on the identical form as that of the initial one, and the size of the fuzzy interval $[\underline{a}, \bar{a}]$ stays the same. Fig. 4 depicts such a displacement along the axis of criterion Y_1.

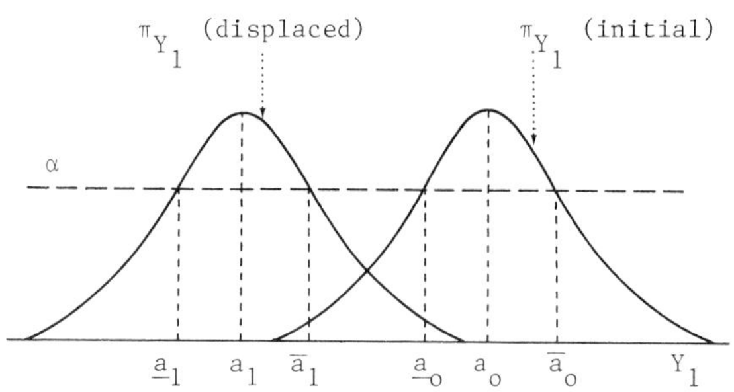

Fig. 4 Disposition of a fuzzy interval

In dynamic conflict resolution, this represents the situation in which decision makers are shifting the target an ideal alternative is expected to achieve. Further information or negotiation may have revealed that previously selected target may be impractical, suboptimal, or impossible to resolve existing conflicts. Shifting of the targets may enable a more efficient or satisfactory solution of the current problem.

Fig. 5 shows two typical displacements of a fuzzy ideal in a two-criteria case. Let the initial fuzzy ideal be characterized by a 2-cell, $\{(a, b) \mid \underline{a}_o \leq a \leq \bar{a}_o, \underline{b}_o \leq b \leq \bar{b}_o\}$, in accordance with the 2-tuple (Y_1 is *close to* a_o, Y_2 is *close to* b_o). Displacement of the initial fuzzy ideal in (A) indicates that the reference point of the initial linguistic proposition of criterion Y_1 has undergone changes depicted in Fig. 4. The new fuzzy ideal is now characterized by the 2-tuple, (Y_1 is *close to* a_1, Y_2 is *close to* b_o), or by the 2-cell $\{(a, b) \mid \underline{a}_1 \leq a \leq \bar{a}_1, \underline{b}_o \leq b \leq \bar{b}_o\}$. In (B), however, the displacement involves the dislocation of the reference points in the linguistic propositions of both criteria. The new fuzzy ideal is designated by the 2-tuple of linguistic propositions, (Y_1 *is close to* a_1, Y_2 is *close to* b_1), or by the 2-cell, $\{(a, b) \mid \underline{a}_1 \leq a \leq \bar{a}_1, \underline{b}_1 \leq b \leq \bar{b}_1\}$.

Theoretically, the initial fuzzy ideal can be displaced in any direction. Fig. 5 only depicts two possible directions of displacement. No matter which direction the fuzzy ideal is displaced, the basic mechanism which leads to the displacement is similar to what is discussed above.

4.1.2 Displacement of a fuzzy ideal due to changes in sizes of fuzzy intervals

Displacement under this category consists of changes in sizes of fuzzy intervals. Nevertheless, the reference points of the linguistic propositions remain constant throughout. Taking the initial linguistic proposition of a criterion "net return *is close to* a_o as an example, it may be transformed into "net return is *somewhat close to* a_o" or "net return is *very close to* a_o." Here, the reference point a_o remains the same. Its associated possibility distribution, however, changes in accordance with the modification of the initial linguistic proposition. For example, the possibility distribution function of "*somewhat close to* a_o" and "*very close to* a_o" may be defined as the dilation and concentration of "*close to* a_o" respectively. These new possibility distribution functions in turn place new restrictions on the spread, i.e. size of the fuzzy intervals, of the base variable (see Fig. 6).

This type of displacement reflects a policy of relaxing, constricting, or in general, regulating the performance requirement of an alternative with respect to a criterion during the interactive and recursive process of conflict resolution. Sometimes, conflict may not be resolved or a more efficient solution may not be obtained unless suitable changes of performance requirements are made.

Displacement of a fuzzy ideal in a two-criteria case is typified in Fig. 7a and b. Let the initial fuzzy ideal be characterized by the 2-tuple of linguistic propositions (Y_1 is *close to* a_o, Y_2 is *close to* b_o), which is translated into a 2-cell, $\{(a, b) \mid \underline{a}_o \leq a \leq \bar{a}_o, \underline{b}_o \leq b \leq \bar{b}_o\}$. Fig. 7a depicts the displacements of the initial fuzzy ideal along the Y_1 axis. In (A), the new fuzzy ideal can possibly be signified by the 2-tuple, (Y_1 is *very close to* a_o, Y_2 is *close to* b_o) or by the 2-cell $\{(a, b) \mid \underline{a}_1 \leq a \leq \bar{a}_1, \underline{b}_o \leq b \leq \bar{b}_o\}$. In (B), the initial characterizations are replaced by (Y_1 is *somewhat close to* a_o, Y_2 is *close to* b_o), or by $\{(a, b) \mid \underline{a}_2 \leq a \leq \bar{a}_2, \underline{b}_o \leq b \leq \bar{b}_o\}$.

When linguistic propositions of both criteria are transformed, displacement of the initial fuzzy ideal can take on various forms. As an illustration, Fig. 7b depicts two possible results. In (A), the new fuzzy ideal is most likely designated by (Y_1 is *very close to* a_o, Y_2 is *extremely close to* b_o) or by $\{(a, b) \mid \underline{a}_1 \leq a \leq \bar{a}_1, \underline{b}_1 \leq b \leq \bar{b}_1\}$, while in (B) it may be characterized by (Y_1 is *very very close to* a_o, Y_2 is *somewhat close to* b_o) or by $\{(a, b) \mid \underline{a}_2 \leq a \leq \bar{a}_2, \underline{b}_2 \leq b \leq \bar{b}_2\}$. Again, Fig. 7a and b only describe the basic mechanism of displacement related to the change in size of the fuzzy intervals. It is not intended to serve as an exhaustive account of all possible variations under this category.

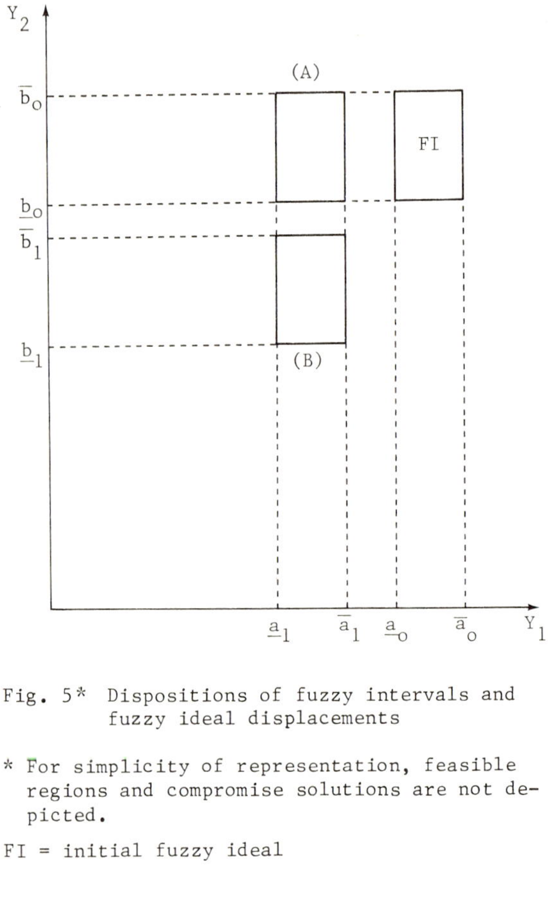

Fig. 5* Dispositions of fuzzy intervals and fuzzy ideal displacements

* For simplicity of representation, feasible regions and compromise solutions are not depicted.

FI = initial fuzzy ideal

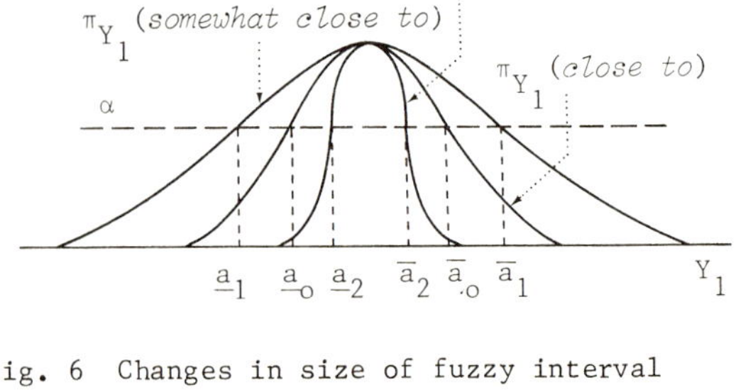

Fig. 6 Changes in size of fuzzy interval

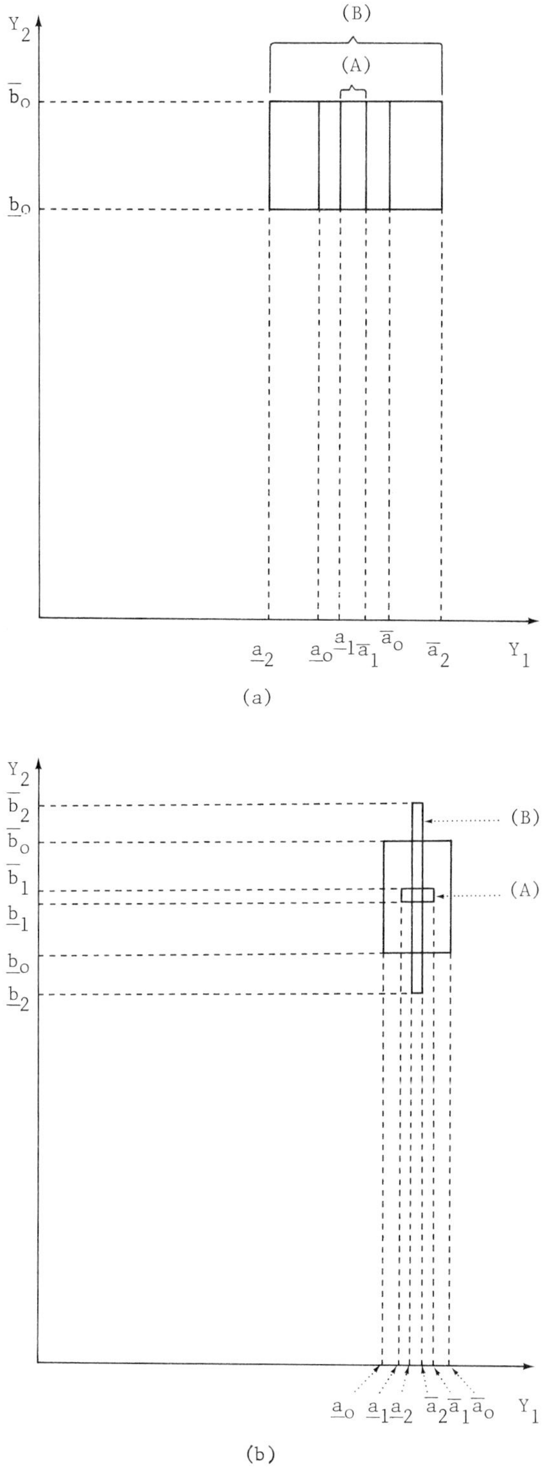

Fig. 7 Changes in sizes of fuzzy intervals and fuzzy ideal displacements

4.1.3 Displacement of a fuzzy ideal due to dispositions and changes in sizes of fuzzy intervals

This form of displacement is a combination of those described in 4.1.1 and 4.1.2 above. The fuzzy ideal is displaced because the reference points in the initial linguistic propositions are changed and the defining possibility distribution functions are different. For example, the initial linguistic proposition of a criterion "net return is *close to* a_o" may be changed into "net return is *very close to* a_1" which not only shifts the position of the initial fuzzy interval but also narrows its magnitude of spread. Fig. 8 depicts such a displacement along a single criterion.

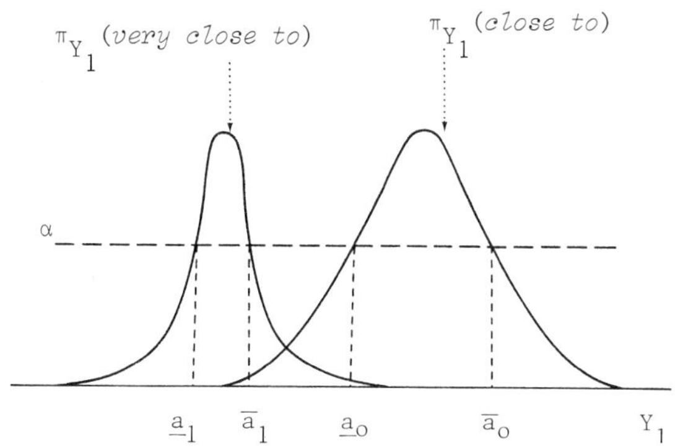

Fig. 8 Disposition and change in size of a fuzzy interval

During the process of conflict resolution, decision makers may find it necessary to shift the target of a criterion and adjust its performance requirement simultaneously in order to resolve conflict in a satisfactory way.

Fig. 9 demonstrates two typical displacements in a two-criteria case. Let the initial fuzzy ideal be designated by (Y_1 is *close to* a_o, Y_2 is *close to* b_o) or by $\{(a, b) \mid \underline{a}_o \leq a \leq \bar{a}_o, \underline{b}_o \leq b \leq \bar{b}_o\}$. Then, the displaced fuzzy ideal in (A) may be represented by the 2-tuple, (Y_1 is *very close to* a_1, Y_2 is *very close to* b_1), or by the 2-cell $\{(a, b) \mid \underline{a}_1 \leq a \leq \bar{a}_1, \underline{b}_1 \leq b \leq \bar{b}_1\}$. Similarly, the displaced fuzzy ideals in (B) may be characterized by (Y_1 is *somewhat close to* a_2, Y_2 is *extremely close to* b_2) or by $\{(a, b) \mid \underline{a}_2 \leq a \leq \bar{a}_2, \underline{b}_2 \leq b \leq \bar{b}_2\}$.

4.2 Variations of Alternatives and Ideal Displacement

In addition to various changes in criteria evaluations discussed above, the addition or deletion of criteria, without further elaborations here, can obviously lead to the displacement of a fuzzy ideal. Moreover, the deletion of inferior alternatives or the addition of viable alternatives is an attributing mechanism also. Sometimes, in the conflict resolution process, decision makers may realize that an alternative is inferior or undesirable, and the deletion of such an alternative may improve the final solution. On the other hand, a new alternative may be discovered during the process of recursive negotiation so that its inclusion may be beneficial to resolve conflicts. Thus, the deletion or inclusion of alternatives may be necessary in obtaining a more satisfactory compromise solution. When an existing alternative is deleted or a new alternative is added, ideal characteristizations of criteria may also be changed. That is, the linguistic propositions of the criteria may be transformed and new fuzzy intervals may be derived. Such a process leads to the change in the feasible region and the displacement of the fuzzy ideal. Fig. 10a, b and c typifies such a process. The initial fuzzy ideal and the associated feasible region are depicted in Fig. 10a. Transformation of the feasible region and displacement of the fuzzy ideal due to the deletion and addition of an alternative are shown in Fig. 10b and c, respectively.

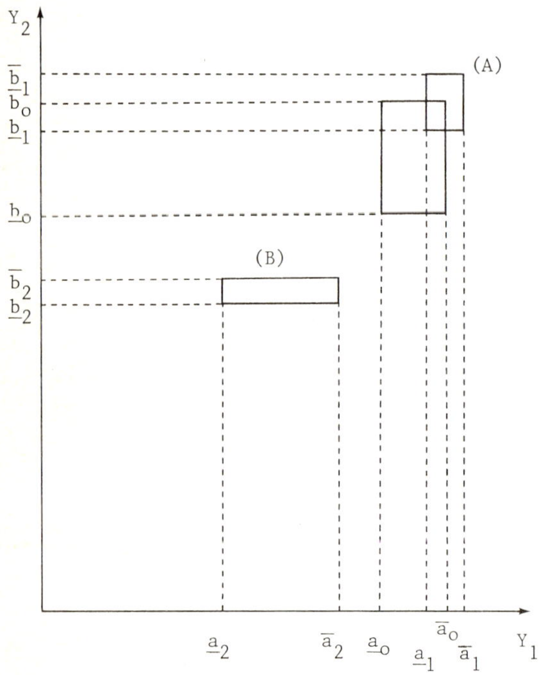

Fig. 9 Dispositions and changes in sizes of fuzzy intervals and fuzzy ideal displacements

The various forms of displacement discussed in subsections 4.1 and 4.2 appear to be versatile procedures through which a more efficient compromise solution can be obtained or the otherwise unresolved conflicts can be resolved. They may be employed by DM unit Z_k at any stage of the interactive and recursive process. Once the fuzzy local ideal is displaced, the associated sets of local compromise solutions are displaced accordingly. The recursive process continues until no further displacement of the fuzzy local ideal is necessary and a satisfactory local compromise solution is ascertained. DM unit Z_k will then employ the final fuzzy local compromise solution as a basis of negotiation with other DM units.

4.3 Remark

So far, a fuzzy ideal has been considered as a fuzzy region taking the form of an m-cell. Nevertheless, it may become a point-value ideal through the application of some zero-in procedures [2]. A zero-in procedure is essentially a defuzzification mechanism which enables decision makers to zero in on the most compatible element of the fuzzy ideal. The procedure is ordinarily performed on the possibility distribution functions. Therefore, displacements of the fuzzy ideal resulting from changes in the possibility distribution functions may displace the zero-in point-value ideal also. In general, if the displacement only involves changes in sizes, but not dispositions of reference points, of the fuzzy intervals demarcating the fuzzy ideal, eg. those in subsection 4.1.2, it will not displace the zero-in ideal. Displacement of the zero-in ideal will take place otherwise.

Since the zero-in procedures allow us to select the most compatible and the least compatible element of the fuzzy ideal as the ideal solution, then with respect to a specific value of the parameter p in the distance function we can derive the most compatible and the least compatible compromise solutions accordingly. By the same token, every point-value element in between can be derived accordingly. Thus, in place of a single point-value compromise solution as that obtained in conventional analysis, a set of compromise solutions ranging from the most compatible to the least compatible can be obtained.

In case only a single zero-in element of the fuzzy ideal is employed, and the associated compromise solution, $(y_1^c, \ldots, y_j^c, \ldots, y_m^c)$ is point value, let us assume that decision makers will transform y_j^c's into fuzzy numbers so that an m-cell

$$\{(y_1^c, \ldots, y_j^c, \ldots, y_m^c) \mid \underline{y}_j^c \leq y_j^c \leq \overline{y}_j^c, \; j = 1, \ldots, m\} \tag{15}$$

can be formulated. For example, if $y_j^c = 100$, it may then be interpreted as "*about* 100." The rationale of this approach is two-fold. First, if only a zero-in element of the fuzzy ideal is employed as the ideal solution, the corresponding point-value compromise solution most likely cannot cover the uncertainty which would have been there if the whole fuzzy ideal has been considered as the ideal solution. A remedy then is to treat y_j^c's as fuzzy numbers so that an approximation of the fuzzy compromise solution can be achieved. Secondly, by treating y_j^c's as fuzzy numbers, decision makers are incorporating performance flexibilities allowed for all criteria in the conflict resolution process.

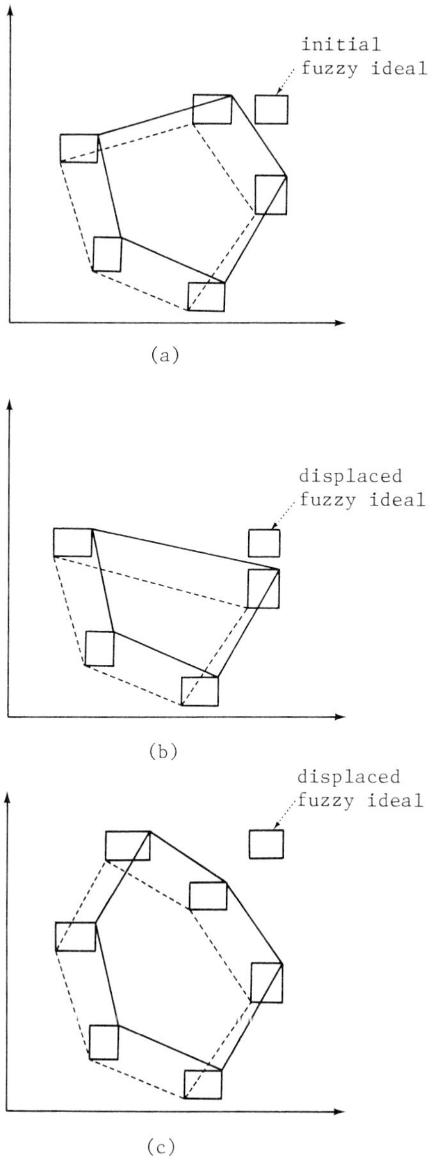

Fig. 10 Displacement of a fuzzy ideal due to the deletion (b) and addition (c) of an alternative

Thus, without loss of generality, let us assume that individual DM units equip themselves with local compromise solutions in the format of equation (15) to resolve intergroup conflicts in the second stage.

5. CONFLICT RESOLUTION AMONG DECISION MAKING UNITS

The conflict resolution procedure in this stage is similar to that in the first stage. Initially, all local compromise solutions are submitted to the central coordinating committee. A performance matrix consisting of all local compromise solutions is then constructed to serve as a basis of conflict resolution among DM units. The fuzzy global ideal is derived from the proposed local compromise solutions. The global compromise solution is in turn determined by a distance minimization procedure discussed.

Let

$$\begin{bmatrix} [\underline{y}^c_{11}, \overline{y}^c_{11}] \cdots & [\underline{y}^c_{1j}, \overline{y}^c_{1j}] \cdots & [\underline{y}^c_{1m}, \overline{y}^c_{1m}] \\ \vdots & \vdots & \vdots \\ [\underline{y}^c_{k1}, \overline{y}^c_{k1}] \cdots & [\underline{y}^c_{kj}, \overline{y}^c_{kj}] \cdots & [\underline{y}^c_{km}, \overline{y}^c_{km}] \\ \vdots & \vdots & \vdots \\ [\underline{y}^c_{l1}, \overline{y}^c_{l1}] \cdots & [\underline{y}^c_{lj}, \overline{y}^c_{lj}] \cdots & [\underline{y}^c_{lm}, \overline{y}^c_{lm}] \end{bmatrix} \quad (16)$$

be the performance matrix whose element

$$([\underline{y}^c_{k1}, \overline{y}^c_{k1}], \ldots, [\underline{y}^c_{kj}, \overline{y}^c_{kj}], \ldots, [\underline{y}^c_{km}, \overline{y}^c_{km}]) \quad (17)$$

represents DM unit Z_k's local compromise solution. The subscript k is employed to represent the k'th DM unit. Then, the fuzzy global ideal can be expressed as an m-cell

$$X^* = \{({}^*y^c_1, \ldots, {}^*y^c_j, \ldots, {}^*y^c_m) \mid {}^*\underline{y}^c_j \leq {}^*y^c_j \leq {}^*\overline{y}^c_j,\ y = 1, \ldots, m\}, \quad (18)$$

where,

$$\begin{aligned} {}^*\underline{y}^c_j &= \max_k \underline{y}^c_{kj}, \text{ and} \\ {}^*\overline{y}^c_j &= \max_k \overline{y}^c_{kj}, \text{ for all } j. \end{aligned} \quad (19)$$

It is defined as a global ideal because it satisfies the requirements specified by all DM units' local compromise solutions.

However, the fuzzy global ideal is usually impossible to obtain. Consequently, a compromise solution which has the least deviation from the fuzzy global ideal is desirable for conflict resolution.

With respect to the maximum $({}^*\overline{y}^c_1, \ldots, {}^*\overline{y}^c_j, \ldots, {}^*\overline{y}^c_m)$ of the fuzzy global ideal, for a specific value of the parameter p, $(\overline{y}^c_1\ \ldots, \overline{y}^c_j, \ldots, \overline{y}^c_m)$ is the corresponding global compromise solution which minimizes the distance function

$$\left(\sum_{j=1}^{m} (1 - \mu_{close\ to\ {}^*\underline{y}_j^c} (y_j^k))^p \right)^{1/p}, \tag{20}$$

$1 \leq p \leq \infty.$

Based on the minimum $({}^*\underline{y}_1^c, \ldots, {}^*\underline{y}_j^c, \ldots, {}^*\underline{y}_m^c)$ of the fuzzy global ideal, the global compromise solution $(\underline{y}_1^c, \ldots, \underline{y}_j^c, \ldots, \underline{y}_m^c)$ can likewise be determined. Thus, for each element of the fuzzy global ideal, a global compromise solution can be derived.

Again, displacement of the fuzzy global ideal may occur in this stage. It may be generated by the displacement of the fuzzy local ideals in the first stage, or it may be triggered by negotiations among DM units. Thus, the final global compromise solution may have to undergo several displacements should the fuzzy global ideal be recursively displaced.

After the final global compromise solution has been ascertained, the central coordinating committee will resubmit it to the DM units for approval. DM unit Z_k may request partial modifications of the alternative, depending on which criterion is not satisfactorily achieved. The dynamic conflict resolution process will continue until final consensus is achieved.

6. CONCLUSION

A theory of a displaced fuzzy ideal has been proposed for dynamic conflict resolution involving multiple criteria and multiple decision making units. Displacement of the fuzzy local and global ideals in an interactive and recursive two-stage process is demonstrated to be a crucial procedure to resolve intra- and inter-groups conflict. Though the applicability of the theory is subjected to future empirical verifications, its potential in resolving conflicts in a dynamic fuzzy environment is conceivable. Decision makers may find the current theoretical framework plausible or perhaps powerful to resolve real-life conflicts characterized by fuzzy cognitive and decision making processes in a dynamic information feedback system.

REFERENCES

[1] Leung, Y., A Value-based Approach to Conflict Resolution Involving Multiple Objectives and Multiple Decision-making Units. Paper presented at the International Symposium on Conflict Management, Kyoto, Japan (Aug., 1981)

[2] Leung, Y., A concept of a fuzzy ideal for multicriteria conflict resolution, in Wang, P.P. (ed.), Advances in Fuzzy Set Theory and Applications (Plenum, New York, 1982).

[3] Yu, P.L., A class of solutions for group decisions problems, Management Science 19 (1973) 936-946.

[4] Yu, P.L., Cone Convexity, cone extreme points, and nondominated solutions in decision problems with multiple objectives, Journal of Optimization Theory and Applications 14 (1974) 573-584.

[5] Zadeh, L.A., Fuzzy sets as a basis for a theory of possibility, Fuzzy Sets and Systems 1 (1978) 3-28.

[6] Zeleny, M., Compromise programming, in Cochrane, J.L. and Zeleny, M. (eds.), Multiple Criteria Decision Making (University of South Carolina Press, Columbia, 1973).

[7] Zeleny, M., The theory of the displaced fuzzy ideal, in M. Zeleny (ed.), Multiple Criteria Decision Making, Kyoto 1975 (Springer-Verlag, 1976).

Approximate Reasoning in Decision Analysis
M.M. Gupta and E. Sanchez (eds.)

CREATIVE DECISION-MAKING TROUGH FUZZY CATASTROPHES

Vladimir Dimitrov

Bulgarian Academy of Sciences*
Sofia, Bulgaria

Creative is a decision which leads to discovering new alternatives not preliminary known to the decision-maker. In the present paper the two-parametric cusp catastrophe is interpreted as a potential generator of creative decisions. The parameter u_1, estimating the grade of awareness or knowledge possessed by an individual h about the situation under which he(she) has to make a decision, and the parameter u_2, estimating the grade of emotional attachment of h to the goal which has to be achieved by making a certain decision, are essentially fuzzy parameters. A definition of a fuzzy catastrophe as one arising on the space of fuzzy parameters is given. Using the statement that each fuzzy catastrophe is unpredictable, it is grounded that each act of creating a new decision is principally unpredictable. A condition under which the fuzzy catastrophe manifold brings to generating creative decisions is proposed and analysed.

Keywords : Repetition Principle, Creative Decision, Thom-Arnold's Theorem, Fold Catastrope, Cusp Catastrophe, Generator of Creative Decisions.

1. INTRODUCTION

The modern decision-making is trivial in the sense that its main concepts are based on a principle saying: if a given problem situation s coinsides or is similar to another one, say s_o, then the decision d made on s coincides or is similar to the decision s_o made on s_o. The use of this principle, let call it Repetition Principle and denote RP, is justified by a natural tendency for minimizing the energy which a decision-maker h have to spend in order to find a decision with respect to given problem situation s - is it necessary to spend efforts for creating new decisions in the case of s, if it is already available a decision for s_o, and s is almost the same as s_o?

The utility function concept widely used in different decision-making models is based on RP; it is enough to remind the proof of Debreu's theorem of an utility function existence - a central assumption preceding his proof concerns the so-called "continiation property of preferences": $x_oRy_o \rightarrow xRy$, where x and y are alternatives closed to x_o and y_o, respect., and R is a binary weak preference relation.

The RP plays a fundamental role in the

* The present address is: International Institute of Manag. Sci., 129090 Moscow, Shepkina str., 8.

probabilistic decision-making - all models explaining the decision-making under risk and uncertainty use the repetition as a main informational source.

The transitivity property, used up to a high degree in the decision-making, extends the distance on which the "gravitational" force of RP acts - if there is a sequence of similar problem situations $s_1, s_2, \ldots, s_m$, the application of the transitivity property to the corresponding sequence of decisions $d_1, d_2, \ldots, d_m$, based on $s_1, s_2, \ldots, s_m$, leads to an implication of the following form: if
d_1 is preferred at least as much as d_2,
d_2 is preferred at least as much as d_3,
...
d_{m-1} is preferred at least as much as d_m, then d_1 has to be preferred at least as much as d_m.

A specific RP application to the collective decision-making is realized by the majority group choice rule - a rule mostly used for taking a droup decision: if a majority chooses one and the same decision, i.e. if one and the same point of view is repeated by a majority of group's members, then this point of view is automatically accepted as a common decision for all the group, no matter which and how worth are the decisions proposed by the individuals not included in the majority.

In spite of the fact, that for each of the cases of RP application considered above examples incompatible with the RP can be easily found in reality, the RP continues to penetrate deeply almost all models of the modern decision-making. Every such model is introduced by one and the same obligatory assumption: the decision-maker h ought to have on his(her) disposal all the alternatives relating to the goal he(she) pursues under given problem situation. Knowing the set of alternatives, all what h has to do, is to look for a way of some reasonable RP application in order to choose the most preferable alternative. But to choose an alternative among a beforehand given set of alternatives with respect to a beforehand stated goal, using a Principle which makes a cult of the Repetition, is nothing but making a trivial decision, no matter how great the involved computational efforts are.

Creative is a decision which leads to discovering new alternatives not given beforehand to the decision-maker. A creative decision is free from the "gravitational force" of the RP, since it is created out of the area of RP action.

2. NEGATIVE EFFECT OF REPETITION PRINCIPLE

Sooner or later the Repetition Principle (RP) destructs the functioning of any decision-making system operating on it, no matter it is a natural (man which makes decisions) or an artificial one (e.g. a computer programme which generates decisions). This fact is justified below.

Let s denote an arbitrary problem situation taking place on R^n - an n-dimensional euclidean space; the characteristics of s depend on n variables $x_1, \ldots, x_n$ uncontrolled by the decision-maker h. The only parameter, h can actually excercize any influence on, is the grade up to which h knows the situation s; let u denote this grade of awareness about s. The larger the values of u (defined on an one-dimensional space of real numbers R), the greater the amount of knowledge possessed by h about the regularities directing the rise of s and determining the way of its appearance before h. An increase of u with the time reflects the natural tendency of h to know deeper and better the situation s.

Let suppose that the decisions generated by h on s are in a full conformity with the Repetition Principle, that is, any gradual (smooth) change of s results in a corresponding gradual (smooth) change of the decision based on s.

Then the efficiency of an arbitrary decision generating process on s realized by h can be formally expressed by the following family of smooth functions

$$E: R^n \times R \rightarrow R \qquad (1)$$

Each exemplar of the family (1) relates to a decision generating process taking place under a fixed grade of knowledge about s. As far as the decision-making efficiency has to be held on the highest possible level, it makes sense to analyse how does the family (1) behave in the optimal case, i.e. when

$$\frac{\partial E}{\partial x_i} = 0 \ , \ i=1,\dots,n \qquad (2)$$

Evidently, different exemplars behave in a different way when passing through their optimal values - some of them stably keep these values under small changes of the uncontrolled variables $x_1,\dots,x_n$, others do not. But the family at a whole is stable and its optimal behaviour is determined by the following equation, defining the so-called "fold-catastrophe" manifold [1]:

$$x^2 + u = 0 \qquad (3)$$

The catastrophe is shown on fig.1:

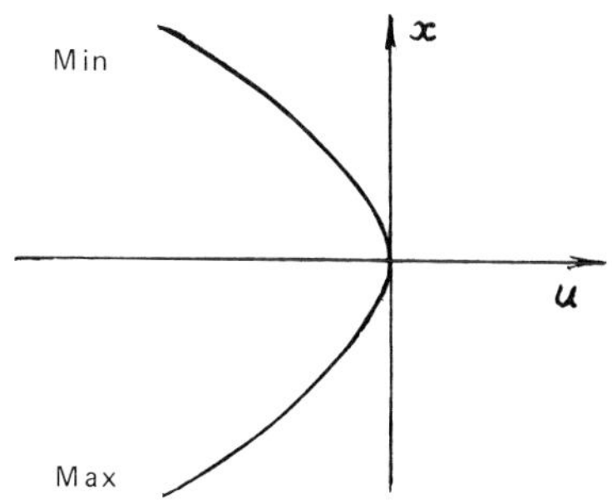

fig.1

It can be seen that some critical value of the controlled parameter u exists, for which the decision generating efficiency becomes zero and do not change with the further increase of u. (Note, that on fig.1 the origin of coordinates is chosen to coincide with the critical value of u.) By passing through this critical value the family (1) ceases to exist any more, and by the same token the functioning of the decision-making model whose efficiency is defined by (1) comes to an end.

As far as the values of the controlled parameter u can be estimated in a fuzzy way only (for more details about the fuzziness of u, see in Chapter 5 of the present paper) the critical value of u can not be precisely found; therefore the time of occurence of the fold catastrophe described above can not be predicted.

All said in this chapter can be briefly formulated as follows:

2.1 Statement

Any decision-making system (natural or artificial),

> operating on the Repetition Principle, sooner or later undergoes a catastrophe completely destroying its functioning.

It must be entirely different principle explaining the process of creating new decisions. This principle is implied by the Thom-Arnold's classification theorem - a central theorem of the catastrophe theory.

3. MODEL OF INDIVIDUAL DECISION-MAKING ABILITY

The decision-making ability of an individual is a function of many variables; some of them can be controlled by the individual, others can not. Let R^n denote a n-dimensional space of variables $x_1,\dots,x_n$, and R^r denote a r-dimensional space of controlled parameters $u_1,\dots,u_r$. For each collection of values taken by the parameters in R^r it is postulated the existence of a smooth real valued function $f\colon R^n \to R$ representing the potential ability of an individual, say h, to generate decisions - an ability realized permanently in the form of various decisions produced by h through his(her) all reasonable life. R is an one-dimensional space of real numbers on which some integral evaluation of the decision-making ability (d.m.a.) is possible. A highly estimated d.m.a. corresponds to an individual with a highly developed creative thinking; the decisions taken by such an individual are distinguished by originality and flexibility - they react immediately to any variation of the problem situation s.

3.1 Assumption

> The decision-making ability (d.m.a.) of an individual h can be formally represented by a structurally stable family of smooth functions
>
> $$F\colon R^n x R^r \to R \qquad (4)$$

In order to define what is meant under a structurally stable family of smooth functions it is necessary to explain the equivalence between two families.

3.2 Definition

> Two families $F,G\colon R^n x R^r \to R$ are equivalent in the vicinity of a given point $(x_o,u_o) \in R^n x R^r$, if in this vicinity they are determined two diffeomorphisms $e\colon R^r \to R^r$ and $y_u\colon R^n \to R^n$ for any $u \in R^r$ and a smooth mapping $z\colon R^r \to R$ such that

$$G(x,u) = F(y_u(x),e(u))+z(u) \qquad (5)$$

for all $(x,u) \in R^n x R^r$ belonging to the vicinity of (x_o,u_o).

Let remind that an arbitrary mapping $g\colon U \to R^m$ is called diffeomorphism if

$$\det\left[\frac{\partial g_j}{\partial x_i}\right] \neq 0, \text{ where } i=1,\dots n,$$

$j=1,\dots,m$, and U is an open set in R^m, $x \in U$.

3.3 Definition

> $F\colon R^n x R^r \to R$ is structurally stable, if it is equivalent to any family $F+P\colon R^n x R^r \to R$, where $P\colon R^n x R^r \to R$ is a sufficiently small family.

Each exemplar of the family (4) represents a function $f: R^n \to R$ related to some concrete point in the space of the controlled parameters R^r; by changing tha values of the controlled parameters, h can effect on his(her) decision-making ability.

Let consider an arbitrary exemplar $f: R^n \to R$ of (4).

3.4 Assumption

(i) An act of decision generating is possible with f only at some of its particular points, i.e. at a point $x \in R^n$ for which

$$\frac{\partial f}{\partial x_i} = 0, \ i=1,\dots,n.$$

(ii) An act of decision generating is possible with the family F only at some of its equilibrium points.

The following property of the family (4) is to be emphasized: F is structurally stable even if it contains non-stable exemplars.

Evidently, the larger the family F, the wider the spectrum of values admissible for the controlled parameters and the greater the number of encountered non-stable exemplars in F. The non-stable exemplars in F essentially influence the individual d.m.a. represented by F - they liberate it from the action of the Repetition Principle (RP). Indeed, according to 3.4 Assumption (i) any particular point of an arbitrary exemplar $f: R^n \to R$ of (4) stipulates a potential generation of a decision (let denote it d_o). However, if f is non-stable, then any small change of the variables in R^n will lead to a disappearance of d_o - it disappears together with the corresponding particular point. Consequently, the RP does not longer functionate - there is no decision at a situation (s) slightly differing from another one (s_o) characterized by a certain decision (d_o).

The mentioned above property of the family (4) can be shortly put into the following statement:

3.6 Statement

Every sufficiently large family (4) which is structurally stable represents an individual decision-making ability free from the action of the Repetition Principle.

4. CREATIVE DECISIONS TROUGH CATASTROPHES

In the present paper only two parameters u_1 and u_2 are considered; u_1 represents the so-called intellectual factor stipulating any act of decision generating and characterizing the grade of awareness or knowledge possessed by h about the problem situation under which h has to make some decision; u_2 represents the so-called emotional factor characterizing the emotional attachment of h to the goal which he(she) tends to attain through realizing an act of decision generating.

The higher the value of u_1 the more clear the problem situation for h; the higher the value of u_2, the more passionate the craving of h for the stated goal.

The spectrum of values taken by u_1 and

u_2 in practice is wide enough to garantee the existence of a sufficiently large number of exemplars in (4). But according to 3.6 Statement, beside the size of F it is necessary one more requirement to be satisfied in order to eliminate the action of the Repetition Principle (RP) on F - F must be structurally stable. This requirement is met through the validity of

4.1 Statement

The family F in (4) representing the decision-making ability of an individual, for any n and r=2 is structurally stable and equivalent to the cusp catastrophe of the form

$$F_{u_1,u_2}(x) = 1/4\ x^4+1/2x^2u_1+xu_2 \qquad (6)$$

where $x \in R^n$ and $u_1, u_2 \in R^2$.

The validity of the above statement follows immediately from the proof of the classification theorem of Thom-Arnold in the catastrophe theory[1].

On the base of the Statements 3.6 and 4.1 the following assertion is made:

4.2 Statement

The catastrophe (6) represents a potential generator of creative decisions free from the action of the Repetition Principle.

Ground of the Statement:

According to 3.4 Assumption (ii), the decisions are produced at the equilibrium points of the individual d.m.a., i.e. at those points $x \in R^n$ for which $\partial f/\partial x_i = 0$, i=1,...,n, where f is an arbitrary exemplar of (4). As soon as the equilibrium points can be either non-singular (indicating a stable equilibrium) or singular (indicating a non-stable equilibrium), all typical ways on which every two-parametric family of smooth functions can pass through its equilibrium points build an equilibrium surface called catastrophe manifold [1], shown on fig.2 and defined by the equation

$$\frac{dF_{u_1,u_2}}{dx} = x^3+xu_1+u_2 = 0 \qquad (7)$$

Fig.2 illustrates a process of formation of an abrupt change of the d.m.a.

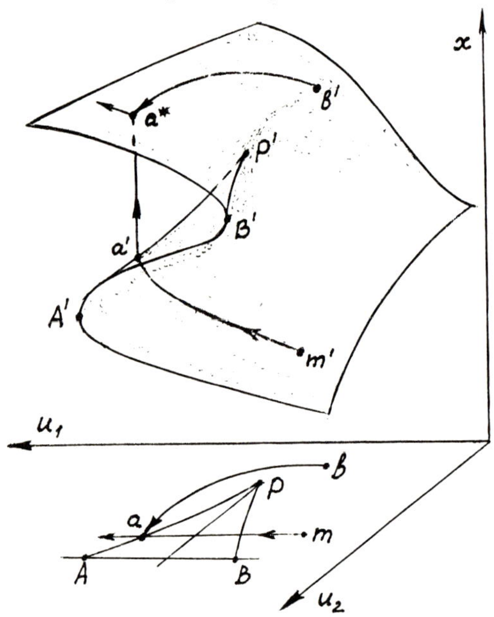

Fig.2

in result of gradual smooth changes of the parameters u_1 and u_2. On the right-hand side of the catastrophe manifold the non-singular points of the d.m.a. are located - their trajectories are smooth functions of u_1 and u_2; such "quiet" trajectories correspond to decisions generated in accordance with the RP - there is a continuous connection between the decisions. After the individual grade of emotional involvement in the decision-making process,

u_2, exceeds some level, the further increase of the "intelectual" parameter u_1 produces a sudden jump of the d.m.a.- this jump occures on A'P', i.e. for the values taken by u_1 and u_2 on the line AP (see fig.2). On the contrary, the decrease of u_1 can produce a fall of the d.m.a. - it occures on B'P', i.e. for the values taken by u_1 and u_2 on BP. If the "energy" accumulated by the d.m.a. in result of the upward jump is enough for overtaking the action of the RP, then an act of creating a new decision is accomplished. In this sense the cusp catastrophe (7) represents a potential generator of creative decisions free from the action of the Repetative Principle. Being free from it, the new decision (let denote it d^*) preserves its correspondence to the considered problem situation, since the parameters u_1 and u_2 continue to be related to this situation, and d^* serves for the same goal, to which the individual decision-making ability has been initially oriented.

5. FUZZINESS IN CREATIVE DECISION-MAKING

Let reveal now an essential characteristic of the parameters u_1 and u_2.

5.1 Statement

> The controlled parameters u_1 and u_2 determining the decision-making ability of an individual are essentially fuzzy (in the sense of Zadeh [2]), that is, they can be estimated in a fuzzy way only.

Ground of the Statement:

By definition u_1 estimates the grade of awareness or knowledge possessed by h about s - a problem situation under which the individual h has to make a decision. In order to estimate precisely u_1, h has to know all the truth about s; in such a case h would be able to determine exactly what part of this truth is available to him(her) before making a certain decision. But if h knew entirely s, then s should be no more "problem situation" for him(her) - so, there would be nothing to be solved about s. Unfortunately, every real-life situation which the decision-maker comes across can never become entirely known for him(her), excepting possibly a few trivial cases; that is why u_1 appears as an essentially fuzzy parameter to h.

The same assertion is valid for the parameter u_2 as well - how strongly tends an individual to the goals he (she) pursues by making a certain decision?, how much is he(she) attached to the consequences expected as a result of this decision? The answer of these questions can be given in a fuzzy way only, using words like "little, much, scarcely, strongly, moderately, not too much, passionately", etc.

5.2 Definition

> The Thom-Arnold's catastrophes are called fuzzy, if they arise on a space of essentially fuzzy parameters R^r.

5.3 Definition

> A catastrophe's occurence is principally unpredictable if no precise solution of the equation defining the catastrophe manifold is permissible.

5.4 Statement

> Every fuzzy catastrophe is

principally unpredictable.

Ground of the Statement:

As seen on fig.2 the catastrophic jump can happen if u_1 and u_2 take values on AP (if there are three real roots of (7) with two of them coinciding; the coincidence is with the minimal root) or BP (if (7) has three roots with two of them coinciding; the coincidence is with the maximal root) from the bifurcation set APB. According to 5.1 Statement, fuzzy estimates of u_1 and u_2 are only available for h. So, although an abrupt change in the d.m.a. is possible to occur (in accord with the Thom-Arnold's theorem) h is principally unable to find precisely the values of u_1 and u_2 under which the jump arises. In this sence the fuzzy cusp catastrophe is unpredictable. The same assertion is valid in the case when the number of the fuzzy parameters is more than two, i.e. for every fuzzy catastrophe.

From 5.1 and 5.4 Statements the following assertion can be extracted:

5.5 Statement

Every act of creating a new decision based on some cusp catastrophe is principally unpredictable.

Let G denote the "gravitational" force (strength of attraction) exercised by the past decisions taken on some problem situation s_0 due to the RP. G can be considered as a psychological factor determined by a specific property of the human brain to form stable patterns on its surface corresponding to the decisions taken in the case of s_0; these patterns are kept for a long time after the decisions have been made, and hinder the decision-maker to estimate truely the changes which appear in s_0. Some quantitative estimate of G could be available through a variaty of tests developed in the experimental psychology.

Let r be a "distance" on which G acts or a radius of the sphere of action of the RP for given h and s_0. The number of similar decisions taken by h before a necessity of a global transformation, that is, of creating new decision is recognized as unavoidable , can be used as an approximate estimate of r.

Let E be interpreted as an amount of "energy" expected to be released through some fuzzy cusp catastrophe defined on the d.m.a. of h. E is proportional to the height of the upward jump in the catastrophe manifold (7); as seen on fig.2 this height depends mainly upon the values taken by the fuzzy parameter u_2 - the stronger h craves for the stated goal, the heigher is the expected catastrophe jump on his(her) d.m.a. Of course the jump is impossible if there is not a sensitive increase of the other fuzzy parameter u_1 as well.

Then, the condition $E > r.G$ allows a proper functioning of the generator of new decisions.

Let a^* denote a point on the catastrophe manifold corresponding to some new decision d^* (see fig.2). After d^* is made, a connection between it and some of the decisions taken before the catastrophe jump can be easily established (line a^*b' on fig.2); the establishment of such a connection leads immediately to an extention of the area of the RP action, and by the same token d^* loses its property of being new one. Later on, at some next catastrophe jump of the d.m.a. another decision could be born anew, after it - another, etc. - so goes the process of generating new decisions until at least one human being, able to learn ($u_1 \neq 0$) and to feel ($u_2 \neq 0$) is on the earth.

6. CONCLUSION

According to the 5.5 Statement the fuzziness of the parameters stipulating the decision-making ability of an individual leads to unpredictability, that is, to unexpectedness of each act of generating a new decision. Does it exist a way of bringing nearer the time of realizing an upward jump in the individual decision-making ability? The answer of this question is easily read on fig.2:

- by increasing u_1, i.e. by a continuous deepening the knowledge about the problem situation on which the decision-maker comes across, and
- by keeping u_2 on a high enough level, i.e. by a strong adherence to the goals which the decision-maker has chosen to achieve.

Following these practical recommendations, the decision-maker would stop to be merely a simple repetative machine, generating finite number of decisions again and again through all the life, but would became a creator - a human being able to control entirely the energy accumulated by the "catastrophic" jumps which happen to occur on his(her) decision-making ability, and to direct this energy to a realization of the everlasting craving of the mankind for happiness and progress.

7. REFERENCES

[1] Poston, T. and Stewart, I., Catastrophe theory and its applications, (Pitman,London,1978).

[2] Zadeh, L., Fuzzy sets, Information and Control,8 (1965) 338-353.

Approximate Reasoning in Decision Analysis
M.M. Gupta and E. Sanchez (eds.)

A FUZZIFIED RELEVANCE TREE APPROACH FOR SOLVING THE COMPLEX PLANNING

Yasuyoshi Sekita* and Masaharu Mizumoto**

*Department of Hospital and Medical Care Administration,
School of Medicine, Tohoku University,
Sendai, Japan

**Department of Management Engineering, Faculty of Engineering,
Osaka Electro-Communication University,
Osaka, Japan

A new type of relevance tree approach, the fuzzified method, is developed by substituting reductionism concept for the fuzzy set one. Some properties of this method are clarified by comparing it with PATTERN method, one of the well known relevance tree approach. Regarding the results, several propositions and theorems are induced. This new method will be usable for solving complex problems or plannings.

Key words; Fuzzified relevance tree, PATTERN method, Fuzzy integral, Complex Planning, Random Digit Experimentation, Rank Correlation.

1. INTRODUCTION

The relevance tree method has been used as the most flexible principle available not only for normative forcasting, but also for decision making analysis. The PATTERN method (Planning Assistance through Technical Evaluation of Relevance Numbers), one of the well known relevance tree methods, has been applied to the NASA Air Space Project, development of medical care system, etc.[1] This method is based on the reductionism [3] and has many merits. However, difficulties occasionaly occur in dealing with complex problems. To eliminate the defects of the PATTERN method, we have developed a new type of relevance tree approach, "the Fuzzified Relevance Tree Method" by substituting reductionism concept for the fuzzy set one. This new method is clarified and evaluated by comparing it with the PATTERN method.

2. CHARACTERISTICS OF PATTERN METHOD

2.1 Relevance Tree

The PATTERN method, recognized as the technique to normative forcasting or decision making, is

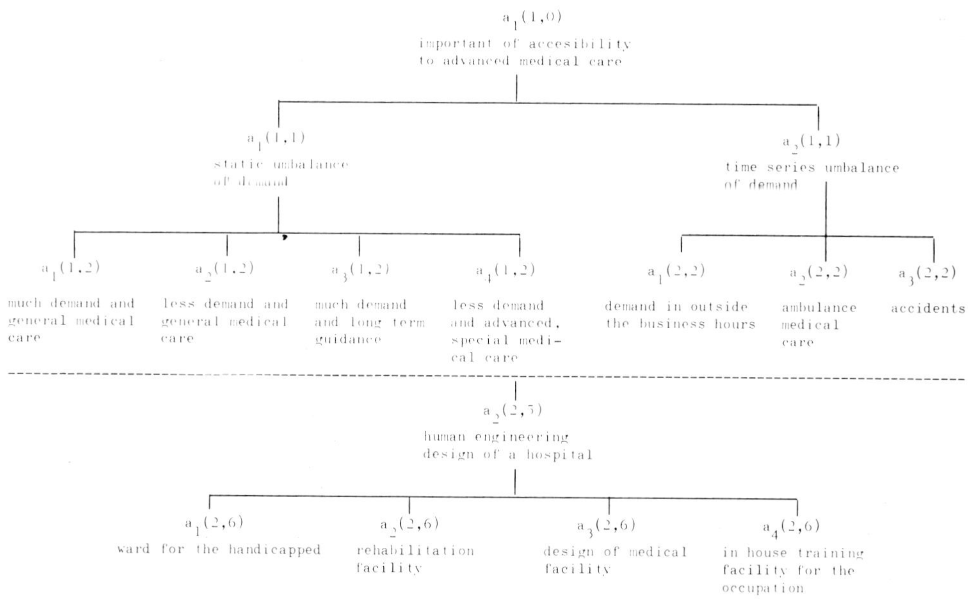

Fig. 2.1 An Example of the Relevance Tree [10]

constructed to reflect the objects in forcasting or decision making. The tree is expressed by a hierarchy including subobjects, strategies, policies, tasks, etc. The levels of the tree correspond to the levels in which the objects is reductioned. There are some issues on each level, and they are grouped on each level according to their relations with the issues on the upper level. We denote each issue in the i-th group on t-th level as $a_k(i,t)$. Figure 2.1 demonstates a representative case of the relevance tree [10]. Scenario writing is used in constructing the relevance tree.

2.2 Quantitative Evaluation on the Relevance Tree

Using the relevance tree, each issue $a_k(i,t)$ $(k=1,2,\cdot\cdot,m(t))$ is evaluated, usually by specialists, from several points of views. Criteria, c_p $(p=1,2,\cdot\cdot,q)$, are used for this purpose, and weights, $e_p \in [0,1]$ $(p=1,2,\cdot\cdot,q)$, of significance are subjectively attached to the criteria by the evaluators themselves. At each level in the PATTERN formulation, a matrix (Fig.2.2) is

CRITERIA: ITEM	WEUGHT	ISSUE IN (i,t): $a_1(i,t)\cdots a_k(i,t)\cdots a_n(i,t)$
c_1	e_1	$s_{11}\ \cdots\ s_{1k}\ \cdots\ s_{1n}$
.	.	. . .
.	.	. . .
c_p	e_p	$s_{1k}\ \cdots\ s_{pk}\ \cdots\ s_{pn}$
.	.	. . .
.	.	. . .
c_m	e_m	$s_{m1}\ \cdots\ s_{mk}\ \cdots\ s_{mn}$
RELEVANCE NUMBER $BR(a_k(i,t))$		$\sum_p s_{p1}\cdot e_p\ \cdots\ \sum_p s_{pk}\cdot e_p\ \cdots\ \sum_p s_{pn}\cdot e_p$

Fig. 2.2 Matrix of Significance Number

expressed for matching the issues against the criteria. Each entry in the matrix, called a "significance number", $s_{pk} \in [0,1]$, is calculated through the evaluation process based on the criteria c_p, and the weight e_p. The "relevance number" of an issue $a_k(i,t)$, $BR^*(a_k(i,t))$, is represented by $\sum_p s_{pk}\cdot e_p$ for an evaluator;

$$BR^*(a_k(i,t)) = \sum_p s_{pk}\, e_p\,. \tag{2.1}$$

It should be noted that the PATTERN formulation requires the criteria weights be normed to unity, that is $\sum_p e_p=1$. Total relevance figures, $TDR^*(a_k(i,n))$, for any particular issue $a_k(i,n)$ are defined by multiplying individual relevance numbers upwards to the top of the tree as follows,

Definition 2.1

$$TDR^*(a_k(i,n)) = \prod_{t=1}^{n} BR^*(a_{k(t)}(i(t),t)). \tag{2.2}$$

The priority of an issue at the lowest level can be determined by the value $TDR^*(a_k(i,t))$ of the issue.

Usually there are complex evaluators (f evaluators), and the relevance number, $BR(a_k(i,t))$ is obtained averaging $BR^*(a_k(i,t))$ through the evaluation process as follows,

$$BR(a_k(i,t)) = \sum_{j=1}^{f} BR_j^*(a_k(i,t))/f, \tag{2.3}$$

where j means the j-th evaluator. And the total relevance figures $TDR(a_k(i,n))$ is represented as follows,

Definition 2.2

$$TDR(a_k(i,n)) = \prod_{t=1}^{n} BR(a_{k(t)}(i(t),t)). \tag{2.4}$$

2.3 Merits and Demerits of PATTERN Method

Merits of the PATTERN method are as follows; a) The PATTERN method offers a consistent system through analysis of problems and evaluation. b) The three steps formed by scenario writing, reduction into issues and comparisons of issues, are similar to human thinking, and are familiar to us. c) In the process of scenario writing, details in the problem can be picked up. d) Policies as solving tools are explored logically by the relevance tree. e) Multi issues can be easily evaluated using the relevance tree. f) Evaluators themselves can clarify the evaluation of issues using the criteria and the significance number. g) Intuitive evaluation and the difference among them could be expressed quantitatively. h) The priority of policies can be ordered by TDR.

On the other hand, PATTERN method has the following defects. 1) Scenario writing procedures and construction methods of the relevance tree have not been completely clarified. 2) Methods of measuring the adequacy of the relevance tree have not been presented. 3) Too many issues are required to express details of subobjects (Jantsh [1] reported that there were more than 2300 issues related only to operational technical defects in the APOLLO planning in NASA). 4) Too much time is needed to construct and evaluate the relevance tree. Accordingly many specialists are required to apply this method for a long duration (it is said that six months was necessary for the technicians and OR specialists to construct the relevance tree related to space and military projects in Honeywell [1,2]). 5) An enormous cost is required to construct the relevance tree and to evaluate issues ($250,000 ~ 300,000 was spent in six months to construct the relevance tree in the Honeywell project). 6) There are no discussions about the mutual relation among criteria.

There is a belief that any complex problems (projects or systems) can be clarified by reductioning them in detail. Ironically, many of the above mentioned difficulties are attributable to reductionism on which the PATTERN method is based. This reductioning process is not identified uniquely in the PATTERN method. And too many level reduction of hierarchy makes it difficult to evaluate issues attentively. This complication becomes obvious by considering the following simple case of binary n level relevance tree. When the number of issues on the t-th level is 2^t, the total number of issues is $\sum_{t=1}^{n} 2^t$. If it takes three minutes to evaluate an issue (referring our experimentation with two criteria [9]), it necessitates about three hours in case of five hierarchy level and twelve full work days, for evaluation alone, in the case of ten level.

3. A FUZZIFIED RELEVANCE TREE APPROACH

To avoid the difficulty of expressing complex problem (system) in detail by reductionism, we have applied the fuzzy set concept to the relevance tree and call this as the "fuzzified relevance tree". The intuitive judgement used in the evaluating process of the PATTERN method is somewhat similar to the fuzzy set concept, and so it can be replaced by the fuzzy concept. Furthermore, the fuzzy concept reduces the number of issues.

Denote the k-th issue in i-th group on the t-th level of relevance tree as $a_k(i,t)$ ($k=1,2,\cdot\cdot$, $m(i,t)$; m depends on i and t) which is the identified symbol used for the explanation of the PATTERN method. Let denote $A(i,t)=\{a_k(i,t)\}_k$, $A_t=\{A(i,t)\}_i$. The object on the t-th level is expressed by the fuzzy set $\underset{\sim}{A}_t$ on the set A_t. The fuzzy set $\underset{\sim}{A}_t$ of a universe of discourse $A_t=\{a_k(i,t)\}_{i,k}$ is defined as a mapping $\mu_{\underset{\sim}{A}_t}(a_k(i,t))$; $A_t \rightarrow [0,1]$, and is expressed by the following ordered pairs,

$$\underset{\sim}{A}_t=\{(a_k(i,t),\ \mu_{\underset{\sim}{A}_t}(a_k(i,t))\},\ a_k(i,t)\in A_t,$$

where the value of membership function $\mu_{\underset{\sim}{A}_t}(a_k(i,t))$ is the grade that an issue $a_k(i,t)$ belongs to the fuzzy set $\underset{\sim}{A}_t$. Denote the conditional fuzzy relation proposed by an evaluator as $\mu_{\underset{\sim}{A}_t}(a_k(i,t)|a_{k'}(i',t-1))$, $(a_{k'}(i',t-1) \in A_{t-1}$, $a_k(i,t)\in A_t)$ when the fuzzy set $\underset{\sim}{A}_t$ is conditioned by an issue $a_{k'}(i',t-1)$. (Fig.3.1).

Define the evaluation value of an issue $a_k(i,t)$ on t-th level as $FR^*(a_k(i,t))$. If $\mu^p_{\underset{\sim}{A}_t}(a_k(i,t)|a_{k'}(i',t-1))$ denote the grade of conditional importance by an evaluator from the p-th evaluation criteria, the next equation is defined.

Definition 3.1

$$FR^*(a_k(i,t))=\bigvee_p \mu^p_{\underset{\sim}{A}_t}(a_k(i,t)|a_{k'}(i',t-1)). \tag{3.1}$$

The $FR^*(a_k(i,t))$ expresses the maximum fuzzy relation between t-1-th and t-th levels by considering the evaluation criteria, and corresponds to the $BR^*(a_k(i,t))$ in the PATTERN method.

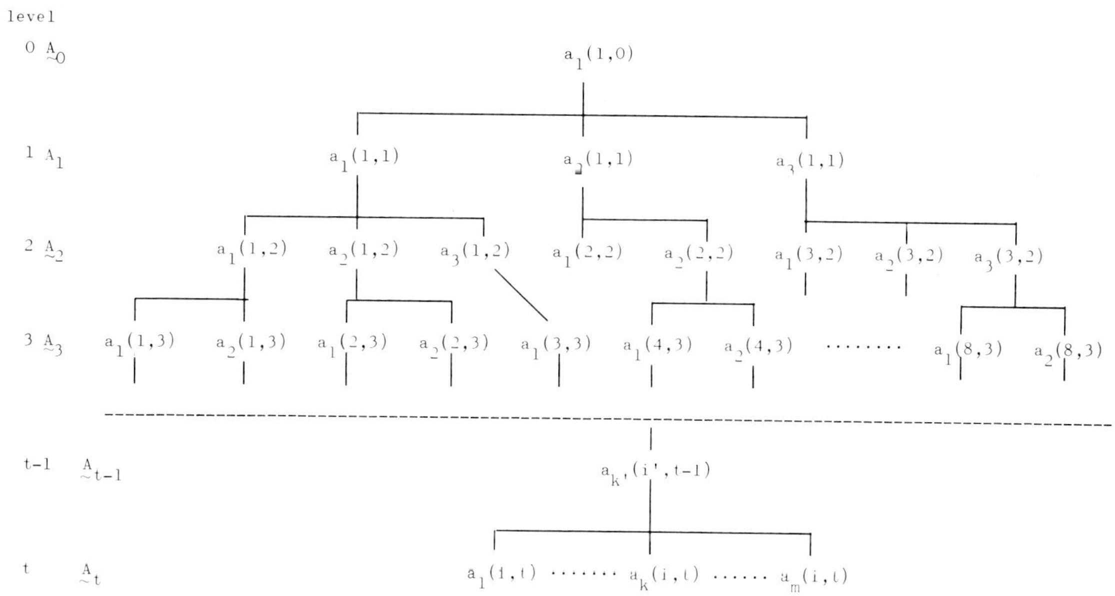

Fig. 3.1 Fuzzified Relevance Tree

Define the accumulated evaluation value $TFR^*(a_k(i,t))$ which corresponds to $TDR^*(a_k(i,t))$ in the PATTERN method as follows;

Definition 3.2

$$TFR^*(a_k(i,t))=FR^*(a_k(i,t))\wedge TFR^*(a_{k'}(i',t-1)). \quad (3.2)$$

Proposition 3.1

$$TFR^*(a_k(i,n))=\bigvee_{p(t),t}^{n}[\mu^{p(t-1)}_{\underset{\sim}{A}_{t-1}}(a_{k(t-1)}(i(t-1),t-1)\,|\,a_{k(t-2)}(i(t-2),t-2))\wedge \mu^{p(t)}_{\underset{\sim}{A}_t}(a_{k(t)}(i(t),t))\,|\,a_{k(t-1)}(i(t-1),t-1))] \quad (3.3)$$

where $\mu^{p(0)}_{\underset{\sim}{A}_0}(a_{k(0)}(i(0),0)\,|\,a_{k(-1)}(i(-1),-1)) = \mu^{p(0)}_{\underset{\sim}{A}_0}(a_1(1,0))$.

Proof: By the def.3.1 and def.3.2,

$$\begin{aligned}TFR^*(a_{k(n)}(i(n),n)) &= TFR^*(a_{k(n-1)}(i(n-1),n-1))\wedge FR^*(a_{k(n)}(i(n),n))\\ &= \bigwedge_t FR^*(a_{k(t)}(i(t),t))\\ &= \bigwedge_t(\bigvee_{p(t)}\mu^{p(t)}_{\underset{\sim}{A}_t}(a_{k(t)}(i(t),t)\,|\,a_{k(t-1)}(i(t-1),t-1)))\\ &= \bigvee_{p(t),t}[\mu^{p(t-1)}_{\underset{\sim}{A}_{t-1}}(a_{k(t-1)}(i(t-1),t-1)\,|\,a_{k(t-2)}(i(t-2),t-2))\wedge\mu^{p(t)}_{\underset{\sim}{A}_t}(a_{k(t)}(i(t),t)\,|\,a_{k(t-1)}(i(t-1),t-1))].\end{aligned}$$

Equation 3.3 demonstrates the necessity of accumulated evaluation based on the max-min criteria using the conditional membership grades through levels.

When dealing with group decision value of $FR^*(a_k(i,t))$, the following $FR(a_k(i,t))$ can be defined using the group fuzzy measure $\bar{g}(\cdot)$ and fuzzy integral [4,6].

Definition 3.3

$$FR(a_k(i,t)) = \bigvee_{s=1}^{f}[FR^*_s(a_k(i,t))\wedge\bar{g}(\cdot)] = \bigvee_{s=1}^{f}[\tfrac{s}{f}\wedge\sum_{j=1}^{s}FR^*_j(a_k(i,t))/j], \quad (3.4)$$

for $FR^*_{s-1}(a_k(i,t))\geq FR_s(a_k(i,t))$, $(s=2,3,\cdots,f)$, where s is the number of members in the group.

Definition 3.4

$$TFR(a_k(i,n))=TFR(a_{k'}(i',n-1)\wedge FR(a_k(i,n)). \quad (3.5)$$

Proposition 3.2

$$TFR(a_{k(n)}(i(n),n))=\bigwedge_{t=1}^{n}FR(a_{k(t)}(i(t),t)). \quad (3.6)$$

4. COMPARISON OF PROPERTY BETWEEN THE TWO METHODS

In order to compare $BR^*(a_k(i,t))$ and $FR^*(a_k(i,t))$, consider the case that $s_{pk}=\mu^p_{\underset{\sim}{A}_t}(a_k(i,t)\,|\,a_{k'}(i',t-1))$ for any p.

Proposition 4.1

$$FR^*(a_k(i,t))\geq BR^*(a_k(i,t)). \quad (4.1)$$

Proof: It can be induced that $\min_p(s_{pk})\leq\sum_p s_{pk}\cdot e_p\leq\max_p(s_{pk})$.

Then $FR^*(a_k(i,t))=\bigvee_p\mu^p_{\underset{\sim}{A}_t}(a_k(i,t)\,|\,a_{k'}(i',t-1))$

$=\max_p(s_{pk})\geq\sum_p s_{pk}\cdot e_p$

$=BR^*(a_k(i,t))$.

Theorem 4.1

$$FR(a_k(i,t))\geq BR(a_k(i,t)). \quad (4.2)$$

Proof: Using the def. 3.3 and def. 2.1, it is said that

$$\bigvee_{s=1}^{f}[\tfrac{s}{f}\wedge\sum_{j=1}^{s}FR^*_j(a_k(i,t))/j]\geq\sum_{s=1}^{m}FR^*_s(a_k(i,t))/f$$

Then $FR(a_k(i,t))\geq BR(a_k(i,t))$.

Lemma 4.1 $\sup_{\{x_t\}}(\min_t x_t-\prod_{t=1}^{n}x_t)=k_n^{1/n}-k_n$

subject to $\prod_{t=1}^{n}x_t=k_n$, $x_t\in[0,1]$ for every t.

Proof: In the case n=2, $0\leq\min(x_1,x_2)-k_2\leq k_2^{\frac{1}{2}}-k_2$. Then $\sup_{\{x_t\}}(\min_t x_t-\prod_{t=1}^{n}x_t)=k_2^{\frac{1}{2}}-k_2$ is induced under the condition $x_1=x_2$. Suppose $\sup_{\{x_t\}}(\min_t x_t - \prod_{t=1}^{n} x_t)=k_{n-1}^{1/(n-1)}-k_{n-1}$ when $x_t=x_{t+1}$ $(t=1,2,\cdots, n-2)$, then $\sup_{\{x_t\}}(\min_t x_t - \prod_{t=1}^{n} x_t)$ $=\sup_{\{x_t\}}(\min(\min_{t=1,2,\cdots,n-1}(x_t), \quad x_n)$.

This is obtained under the condition that $\min_{t=1,2,\cdots,n-1}(x_t) \quad =x_n$. Thus, $\sup_{\{x_t\}t=1,2,\cdots,h}(\min x_t - \prod_{t=1}^{n} x_t)$ $=\sup_{\{x_t\}t=1,2,\cdots,n-1}(\min(x_t) \quad -k_n) =k_n^{1/n}-k_n$, when $x_1=x_2=\cdots =x_n$.

Theorem 4.2

$$TDR(a_k(i,n)) \leq TFR(a_k(i,n)) \leq k^{1/n}-k,$$

where $\prod_{t=1}^{n} BR(a_{k(t)}(i(t),t)) = k$ (const).

Proof: By the proposition 3.2 and theorem 4.1, $TFR(a_k(i,n)) \geq \bigwedge_t BR(a_{k(t)}(i(t),t) \geq \prod_{t=1}^{n} BR(a_{k(t)}(i(t),t))$ because of $BR(a_{k(t)}(i(t),t))\epsilon[0,1]$. Using the lemma 4.1, $TFR(a_k(i,n))-TDR(a_k(i,n)) \leq k^{1/n}-k$.

Theorem 4.3

$$TFR(a_k(i,n))-TDR(a_k(i,n)) \leq n^{1/(1-n)}$$

$(1-1/n)$ for any $\prod_{t=1}^{n} BR(a_{k(t)}(i(t),t))$.

Proof: Denote $f(k)=k^{1/n}-k$. Then $f'(k)=1/n\cdot k^{1/n-1}-1$, $f''(k)=1/n\cdot(1/n-1)\cdot k^{1/n-2}<0$ for the nonnegative integer n. Thus the function f of k is unimodal concave, and $\sup_k(k^{1/n}-k)=n^{1/(1-n)}\cdot(1-1/n)$.

Theorem 4.4

It is difficult to use $TFR(a_k(i,n))$ for identifying the importance of the issues on the final level if $BR(a_k(i,t))$ has a property of approximately a random sample from the distribution on each level. The difficulty becomes magnified with the addition of more evaluators. On the other hand, $TFR(a_k(i,n))$ does not fall in this trap.

Proof: Denotes the p.d.f. of the distribution on t-th level as $f_t(x)$. It is induced that $BR(a_k(i,t))=\int_0^1 x\cdot f_t(x)dx=\mu_t$ for every $a_k(i,t)$. Then $TDR(a_k(i,n))=\prod_{t=1}^{n} BR(a_k(i,t))=\prod_{t=1}^{n}\mu_t$ for any k and i.

As the importance of issues on the final level affects the proposed purpose(zero level), the value of issues integrated on the lower level should reflect the evaluation on the upper level. We call the property which assures the connection of the lower level evaluation to the higher level one consistently as the "reversibility".

Theorem 4.5

The reversibility of evaluation between levels can be assured in our "Fuzzified Relevance Tree Method" under the condition that $TFR(a_{k'}(i',t-1)$ is smaller than the largest FR $(a_k(i,t))$ in $\{a_k(i,t)\}_k$, and the group can identify the fuzzy measures logically.

Proof: Let us consider the case that the issue $a_{k'}(i',t-1)$ is related to the issues $a_k(i,t)$ $(k=1,2\cdots, m(i,t))$ directly for each level. If the values $\{TFR(a_k(i,t))\}_k$ are integrated and the value becomes equal to TFR $(a_{k'}(i',t-1))$, we can say that the reversibility is assured between t-th level and t-1-th level. For this integration procedure, the fuzzy integral is applied. The fuzzy integral of $\{TFR(a_k(i,t))\}_k$ is written as $F(i,t)=\bigvee_k [TFR(a_k(i,t))\wedge g(A_t^k)]$, where g is a fuzzy measure, $TFR(a_k(i,t)) \leq TFR(a_{k+1}(i,t))$ $(k=1,2,\cdots, m-1)$, and $A_t^k= \{a_k(i,t), a_{k+1}(i,t),\cdots, a_m(i,t)\}$. From the property of fuzzy measure, it is said that $g(A_t^k) = g(a_k(i,t)) + g(A_t^{k+1}) + \lambda\cdot g(a_k(i,t))\cdot g(A_t^{k+1})$, where $\lambda >-1$. If we assume $g(a_k(i,t))$ can be identified as $TFR(a_k(i,t))$, then $g(A_t^k)=TFR(a_k(i,t)) + g(A_t^{k+1}) + \lambda\cdot TFR(a_k(i,t))\cdot g(A_t^{k+1})$. Thus $g(A_t^k)-TFR(a_k(i,t))=\{1+\lambda\cdot TFR(a_k(i,t))\}\cdot g(A_t^k)\geq 0$. From this result, $F(i,t) = \bigvee_k TFR(a_k(i,t)) = \bigvee_k [FR(a_k(i,t))\wedge TFR(a_{k'}(i',t-1))] = (\bigvee_k FR(a_k(i,t)))\wedge TFR(a_{k'}(i',t-1))$. If $\bigvee_k FR(a_k(i,t)) \geq TFR(a_{k'}(i',t-1))$, then $F(i,t) = TFR(a_{k'}(i',t-1))$. For this reason, reversibility is assured under the condition that $TFR(a_{k'}(i',t-1))$ is smaller than the largest $FR(a_k(i,t))$ in the feasible set $\{a_k(i,t)\}_k$.

The more issues there are in the group of relevance tree, the more reversibility will be assured. It is not important to note that we are not recommending the construction of a complexed relevance tree composed of many issues in a group, but a simple relevance tree which satisfies the reversibility. By introducing a simple evaluating procedure, alternatives of relevance trees can be selected to assure reversibility. Thus this theorem contribute to clarify not only the calculation definition and procedure, but also to the construction method for suitable relevance tree.

5. NUMERICAL EXAMPLE OF RANDOM DIGIT EXPERIMENTATION FOR TWO METHODS

It may be difficult to compare the two methods because of the following reasons; 1) The concept of s_{pk} is different from $\mu^p_{\underset{\sim}{A}_t}(a_k(i,t)|a_{k'}(i',t-1))$ intrinsically. 2) The value attached to an issue is determined freely in the interval [0,1] at every level of hierarchy depending on the evaluators. 3) No criteria has been established to evaluate the relevance tree in the PATTERN method.

In spite of these difficulties, we will attempt to elucidate the similarities of the important order of issues on the final level between two methods. In order to avoid the special evaluation formula, a random digit experimentation is introduced. The number of issues and levels of relevance tree should not be too large because of the property of our fuzzified relevance tree.

Let us assume the following conditions in our trial. 1) The binary relevance tree has three levels. 2) Only one evaluation criteria is used. 3) Random digit can be obtained from the two kinds of normal distribution. 4) Random digit experimentation is tried twenty five times in each case respectively. 5) There is only one evaluator, 6) The same value obtained through the examination is used for the calcuration of $TFR(a_k(i,3))$ and $TDR(a_k(i,3))$, that is, $s_{1k} = \mu^{1}_{\underset{\sim}{A}_t}(a_k(i,t)|a_{k'}(i',t-1))$. 7) The similarity of order of $TFR(a_k(i,3))$, $TDR(a_k(i,3))$ on final level is measured by the coefficient of rank correlation of Spearman, ρ, shown in the equation 5.1[2].

$$\rho = 1 - \frac{6\sum_i d_i^2}{N^3-N} \tag{5.1}$$

N; number of issues on the final level (number of paires)

d_i; difference of order between the i-th pair.

Using the normal distribution $\cdot$ $N(\mu,\sigma^2)$, two cases A and B are considered as follows;

case A; $\mu = 0.5$, $\sigma = 1$

case B; $\mu = 0.7$, $\sigma = 1$.

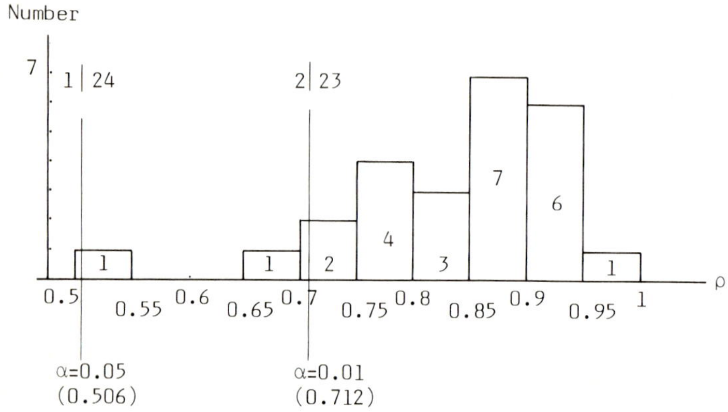

Fig. 5.1 Case A

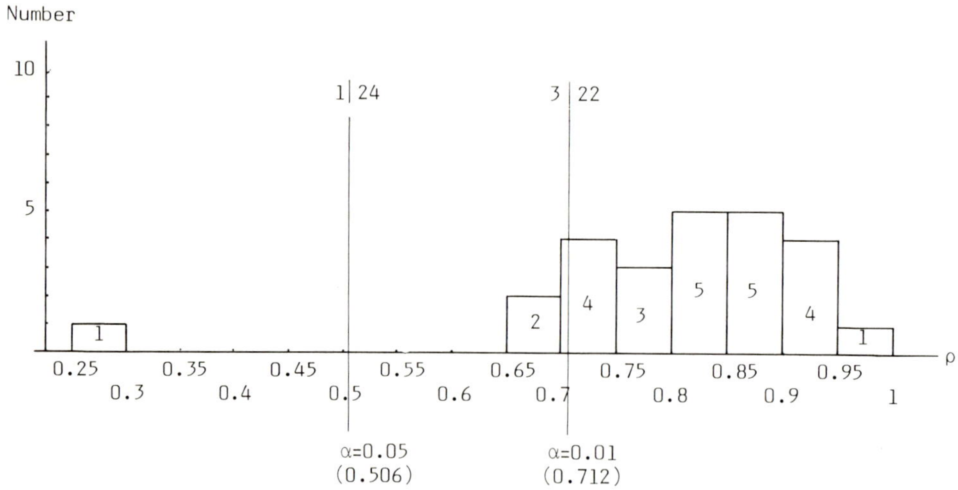

Fig. 5.2 Case B

Coefficient of rank correlation of Spearman

item value ··· normal random digits

case A ·· $\mu = 0.5$ $\sigma = 1.0$ $\sim N(0.5, 1)$

case B ·· $\mu = 0.7$ $\sigma = 1.0$ $\sim N(0.7\ 1)$

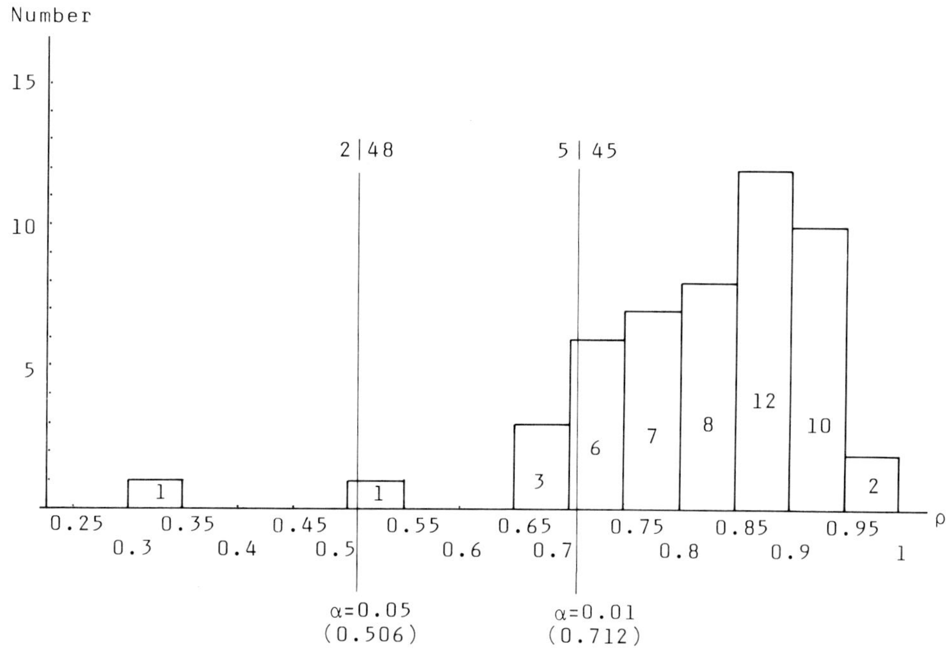

Fig. 5.3 case A∪B

Figure 5.1 ~Figure 5.3 show the histogram where the axis of spindle represents the number that the correlation values fall in the interval of horizontal axis in the cases of A, B, and A∪B, respectively. If we adopt the significant value $\alpha = 0.01$ or 0.05, then the outcome of the order on the final level in the fuzzified relevance tree is simillar to that of the PATTERN method from the statistical significance level.

6. CONCLUDING REMARKS

Although the relevance tree method can be useful for dealing with complex problems or plannings, difficulties sometimes arise in constructing a tree or evaluating issues, when there are too many issues and levels. In the strict application of reductionism, it may be difficult to reduce the issues and levels.

In our fuzzified relevance tree, the fuzzy concept substitutes for the reductionism, and suppresses the increase of issues and levels. To clarify the application of the fuzzy concept and to elucidate the property of fuzzified method, the well known PATTERN method was utilized as the object for the comparison. After developing several definitions for the fuzzified relevance tree method which relate to the PATTERN method, we are able to find some propositions and several theorems. That is, we could find the relation between $FR(a_k(i,t))$ and $BR(a_k(i,t))$, and $TFR(a_k(i,t))$ and $TDR(a_k(i,t))$, etc. The property of reversibility, assured in our method, will contribute not only to the foundation of our method, but also to give us criteria to construct an appropriate relevance tree. Random digit experimentation beyond the limitation of analytical approach was performed, and the order of issues on the final level between the two methods was compared using the coefficient of rank correlation of Spearman. Through the experimentation under several conditions, we could find the similarity of two methods from the statistical view point.

The most important thing remaining now is to apply our method in the practical field. The result will give us valuable materials and may contribute to modify our method.

FOOTNOTE

1) The PATTERN method has been applied to many field like follows; NASA Air Space Projects [1,2], Military Activities [2], Development of Medical Care System [10], Development of Medical Electronics [2], Development of Products [9], American Advertising [1,2], Decision Making in Governmental Organization [9].

2) If there are same orders, the following revised method is used here.

$$\Upsilon = 1 - \frac{6(S+U+V)}{N^3 - N}, \quad S = \sum_i d_i^2$$

$$U = \frac{1}{12}\Sigma(u^3 - u), \quad V = \frac{1}{12}\Sigma(v^3 - v),$$

where u, v is the number of same order on the level respectively.

REFERENCES

[1] Jantsh, E., Technological forcasting in perspective (OECD publications, Paris, 1967).
[2] Martin, W. and Sharp, J.M., Reverse factor analysis; A modification of relevance tree techniques, Technological Forcasting and Social Change 4 (1973) 353-373.
[3] Rosen, R., Some systems theoretical problems in biology, in Ervin Laszlo(ed.), The Relevance of General Systems Theory (George Braziller, 1972).
[4] Sekita, Y. and Tabata, Y., A health status index model using a fuzzy approach, European Journal of Operational Research, vol.3, no.1 (1979) 40-49.
[5] Sekita, Y., Some considerations of fuzzy hierarchical system, Osaka Economic Papers, vol.29, no.2 (1979) 59-68.
[6] Sugeno, M., Fuzzy measures and fuzzy integrals -A survey, in; M.M. Gupta, G.N. Saridis and B.R. Gaines(ed.), Fuzzy Automata (North-holland, 1977).
[7] Swager, W., Strategic planning III-Objectives and program options, Technological Forcasting and Social Change 4 (1977) 283-300.
[8] Zadeh, L.A., Outline of a new approach to the analysis of complex systems and decision process, IEEE Transaction on systems, Man and Cybernetics, SMC-3, no.1 (1973) 28-44.
[9] KIIS, The Report for the Application of PATTERN Method to the Process of Decision Making in Local Government Organization (in Japanese), KJ-74M08 (1975).
[10] MEDIS-DC, The Report for the Development of Medical Information System(in Japanese), III (1976).

PART EIGHT

FUZZY CLUSTERING ALGORITHMS

Approximate Reasoning in Decision Analysis
M.M. Gupta and E. Sanchez (eds.)

POSSIBILISTIC DATA STRUCTURES FOR THE REPRESENTATION OF UNCERTAINTY

Enrique H. Ruspini

HEWLETT PACKARD LABORATORIES

1501 Page Mill Road
Palo Alto, California 94304

Data abstractions for the representation of uncertainty in advanced information systems are proposed. Relevant constructs are described as relational aggregates of lower level constructs.

KEYWORDS: Information System, Data Base, Data Model, Uncertainty, Data Abstractions, Active Systems

1. INTRODUCTION.

Modern Information Systems are automated tools for the modeling of real world systems. Actual representation of the characteristics of the modeled systems is accomplished by use of symbolic entities which are called *data elements* or *data constructs* throughout the rest of this paper. In addition to their ability to represent the *existence* of real world entities, their attributes, properties, and relationships, Information Systems include capabilities for the definition, maintenance, and modification of these representations in a computing environment.

A represented set of real world entities is called a *data base*. It is also said that the database is a *data model* of the real world system. This definition is sometimes extended to indicate that a temporal sequence of data bases (obtained by successive modification) is a data model of a dynamically varying real world system.

Data bases can also be thought of as collections of representations of *facts* about the real world. In a data base two classes of facts are represented:

1) statements about the *existence* of real world entities, and

2) statements about *properties* of real world entities, expressed as *associations* or *relations* between pairs of real world entities.

More precisely, what is being represented is the *truth* of statements of either type about the state of affairs in the real world. This subtle but important semantic differentiation is not stressed in classical data bases, i.e. those primarily concerned with the representation of real world facts which are known or assumed to be true. In this case the representation of a proposition about the state of the real world is made equivalent to the representation of its known truth as only true facts are represented. Propositions known to be false can be represented by the truth of their negation.

Further, in the majority of existing applications the underlying data base is assumed to satisfy the close world assumption (CWA) (Reiter 1978). This assumption, which is customarily taken for granted but seldom explicitly stated in most data modeling applications, goes beyond equating representations of propositions with that of their truth. When the CWA holds true, facts not represented in the data base (or implied by them) are assumed to be false, therefore making the data base the representation of all true and relevant facts characterizing the state of a real world system. In contrast, in *open world* data bases, absence of explicit representations does not imply possible propositional falsehood but is generally an indication of the state of ignorance of the modeler about certain relevant aspects of the real world.

Modeling of real world systems as a collection of represented statements of the type:

Object X has Value V for Attribute A,

which are interpreted as representations of their truth, is adequate in many applications where the underlying physical system can be observed and measured to an acceptable degree of accuracy.

In many applications of interest, however, the physical system being modeled is known only in uncertain, imprecise or vague terms. In these cases, more sophisticated approaches to the representation of the truth of statements about the real world are required. *Possibility Theory (Zadeh 1978)* provides a convenient theoretical framework for the mathematical modeling of statements of the type:

The truth value of "Object X has value V for property P" is t.

As discussed by Zadeh, the mathematical constructs of Possibility Theory not only allow representation of vague and imprecise statements such as:

It is true that "the vehicle is a car" (Imprecision),

It is true that "the vehicle is large" (Vagueness),

but in addition allows representation of knowledge of the degree of belief and ignorance about the truth of statements:

It is very likely that "the temperature is 85 degrees" (Truth Uncertainty),

It is not known that "the weather is stormy" (Truth Ignorance),

This paper is devoted solely to the discussion of issues relevant to the representation of uncertainty as possibility distributions for probabilities. No effort will be made in this exposition to justify the use of possibility theory as a theoretical basis for uncertainty representation purposes as done by the author in an earlier paper (Ruspini 1982). Rather, the objective of this contribution is to present a number of data abstractions that provide a framework for the development of data models of real world systems observed under uncertainty conditions. Further, representations of these data abstractions as relational aggregates of lower level constructs are identified and discussed.

This paper is divided in six sections of which this is the first. Section 2 discusses the need for the development of special data abstractions for the representation of uncertainty. Section 3 discusses the role of lattices as the basic mathematical structure to represent the association between real world entities and the entity classes *(types)* to which they belong. As simple class membership is insufficient to provide unambiguous identification mechanisms for real world entities, special identifying structures developed for that purpose are discussed in Section 4. Section 5 is discussed to the discussion of relational approaches to the representation of propositions and the degrees of certainty, belief or likelihood placed by the data modeler on their validity as true statements about the state of the real world. Section 6 discusses certain additional constructs which are useful in the representation of knowledge about the real world.

2. THE NEED FOR UNCERTAINTY REPRESENTATION.

Ideally real world systems that are modeled using symbolic data constructs can be observed, characterized, or measured to an acceptable degree of accuracy by representation of propositions known to be true as valid descriptors of the state of the system being modeled. In all the early applications of Data Base technology, and in most of those existing today, the systems being represented can be adequately characterized by variables which can be observed or measured to acceptable levels of accuracy. In most financial systems, for example, such characterizations are not only possible but mandated by the modeling need to accurately assess financial states. However, even in areas such as financial and economical applications, it is possible to conceive schemes where representation and manipulation of imprecise, unknown or vague facts may result in the implementation of data based tools that aid in the understanding of the modeled system state and its dynamic behavior. For example, representations of the economy of a given country *(i.e., an economic model)* may include numerous examples of observations of economic variables which are known to contain error or are only partially believed due to the lack of credibility of the observational methods or sources. In spite of such uncertainty, the state of the system may be adequately characterized by combining the elements of information provided by the truth values of individual propositions.

Artificial intelligence applications have been concerned for some time with imprecision representation issues (Mylopoulos, 1980). Few developments have, however, considered issues of uncertainty representation. Notable exceptions to this statement are provided by some expert systems (Davis et al. 1977, Duda et al. 1977). In these cases the explicit methodologies developed have relied on the use of ad-hoc approaches, derived from probability theory and oriented towards treatment of the problem at hand. Manipulation issues have been stressed over those of representation while the underlying data structures are those provided by the application programming language rather than those developed to support the long term storage needs of structured data bases (e.g., relational structures).

The work presented herein, on the other hand, was strongly motivated by the need to develop structured approaches to the representation of uncertainty by Information Systems supported by modern data base management tools. The main objective of the research presented in this paper was to provide a migration path from theoretical approaches to the manipulation of multivalued logic truth values, such as those proposed by Zadeh (1979b) and Ruspini (1982), to specific data constructs that represent the major concepts and entities introduced by those approaches. To achieve this objective data abstractions were identified corresponding to the mathematical constructs used in the possibilistic treatment of probabilities. Further, these constructs are also expressed, whenever applicable, as relational aggregates of lower level data types. While there is no particular need or major advantage to the use of relational approaches (other than those that are intrinsic to any relational treatment), this representation is prototypical of the type of translation required to map the proposed constructs into structures that may be manipulated by existing data base management systems.

The research results being reported were obtained during the investigation of the concept of Active Information System. Active Information Systems are advanced information management capabilities developed to model large, complex real world systems which also have a complicated dynamic behavior. This behavior is itself characterized by a large number of frequent changes to the system state.

The main distinguishing characteristic of Active Systems is their ability to represent and manipulate the *information goals* of their users. Specifically, information goals are *computational goals*, that is statements indicating the need to produce certain values describing aspects of the present state and behavior of the system being modeled. These values are to be produced as the outputs of certain computational processes existing within the Active System *(Active Procedures)* which use as input data elements extracted from the data base. As the data base is continuously modified to maintain a timely description of facts about the real world (which may be expressed, however, by propositions that reflect uncertainty about the modeled system) it is possible that data base contents at a given instant in time *(a data base snapshot)* may or may not contain sufficient information to allow effective computation of the values specified as part of the goal statement. Active Systems perform continuous checks on the nature of the changing data base contents *(Data Base Introspection)* in order to assess the computability of information goals. The concept of Active System is discussed in detail in (Montgomery and Ruspini, 1981).

The data abstractions presented in this paper are those needed to support the representation needs of Active Systems describing physical systems which may be observed only under conditions of uncertainty. Rather than being a constraining limitation, this emphasis on Active System representation needs provides a more general class of constructs as active systems are a subclass of those advanced information management tools that must represent uncertainty about the state of the world. Further, special representation needs of active systems (e.g., representation of goals) are also characteristic of other types of systems which are concerned with uncertainty representation.

3. LATTICES.

The theoretical approach chosen for the representation of uncertainty is based on the translation of each truth-quantified proposition about the world into a possibilistic constraint on the value of a valuation (interpreted diversely as a degree of truth or a likelihood value) defined over a lattice.

Lattices are preferrable to families of conventional subsets (such as sigma algebras) due to their capability to support the representation of imprecise properties and attributes such as those that may be characterized by fuzzy sets defined over some domain. Since the fuzzy power set of a reference universal set is a complemented distributive lattice, but not a Boolean Algebra, lattices provide a better representation framework than other structures. In addition, lattices are adequate structures to represent propositional conjunction, disjunction and implication. In what follows it will be further assumed that the lattice structures utilized are those provided by *complete, complemented, distributive lattices* having a lattice supremum denoted by T (tautology) and an infimum denoted by F (inconsistency).

The role of lattices in the representation of uncertainty is that of defining useful *taxonomies*, i.e. classification schemes, of properties and attributes of objects. Lattice elements provide the basis for the formal translation of the predicate of the statement:

Object X has value V for property P.

In the above statement P is the name of a lattice and therefore, one lattice must be defined for each property of real world objects which may be observed or measured under uncertainty conditions. Correspondingly, V is a lattice element expressed commonly as a lattice-polynomial, i.e. an expression consisting of disjunctions and conjunctions of *atomic* lattice elements (Birkhoff 1940). For example, a propositional predicate which may be represented is:

"...has HAIR COLOR 'blonde' or 'light brown'",

where HAIR COLOR is a property (corresponding to a lattice domain) and where

'blonde' or 'light brown'

is a lattice polynomial formed by disjunction of two lattice elements.

For convenience in the representation of objects having more than one type (polymorphic entities), it will be assumed that lattice polynomials are in conjunctive normal form, i.e.

latt-polyn:=dclause AND dclause AND ...dclause

where

dclause:= atom OR atom OR ...atom.

Each of the above disjunctive clauses indicates that the object being represented belongs to a certain class while their conjunction indicates that the object belongs to (possibly) multiple types. Object-type relationships are defined by disjunctive clauses by associating each object with atomic elements larger than the element defined by the clause. In the above example, does not define (not being an atomic expression) a type association but the object is still defined as having the type 'fair' (assuming that 'fair' is an atom that dominates the disjunctive expression). In this sense, the proposed lattice representation extends the generalization approach of Smith and Smith (1977).

As discussed above, approaches to the representation of propositions are not, per se, sufficiently expressive for uncertainty modeling purposes. In addition to the ability to represent the components and roles of the propositions it is also required to model the truth-value of propositions. In the approach being presented in this paper, knowledge about the truth of a proposition is represented as a possibilistic *(or elastic)* constraint on the value that an isotone valuation takes over prescribed lattice-elements. The result of specifying an object's property value as a lattice element and the truth of the proposition

The 'object' has the 'property value',

is a data abstraction called a *Quantified Lattice Pointer,* or QLP for short. Quantified Lattice Pointers, which can be expressed in relational form as

qlp:= (latt-polyn, possib-constraint),

are *truth-quantified fields,* i.e. relational components having as values lattice-polynomials which are quantified to indicate the degree of the modeler's belief. The shorthand form *qlp-name#* is used throughout this paper to indicate specific fields being so qualified. As discussed in (Ruspini, 1982) possibilistic constraints are *fuzzy probabilities,* i.e. fuzzy subsets of the unit interval of the real line.

4. IDENTIFIERS.

Data abstractions which have been discussed so far have been introduced to represent levels of imprecision in the description of properties and attributes of objects and to model the degree of belief or likelihood placed by the modeler on the truth of a proposition asserting that a given object has a specified property. In order to identify unambiguously the objects being described it is necessary to consider a class of *identifier* data constructs. These constructs provide a mechanism for the internal identification of represented entities. They are specifically intended to represent *unique* real world entities, rather than *classes* of entities sharing a common property (as done by data abstractions based on lattices). This differentiation between *types* and *tokens* has been stressed in the Artificial Intelligence literature (Mylopolous 1980).

Uncertainty creates unique problems in the identification of real world entities. For example, a single real world entity may be represented (due to observational uncertainty) as several uniquely identified objects modeled in a data base. Special constructs (discussed in the next section) are required in these data models to represent potential identity of objects.

5. RELATIONS.

Relations model the known or assumed associations between objects and their properties. Specific constructs developed for the representation of these associations are based on relational data base models. Each relation is a set of *tuples,* each of which is an ordered collection of *field values* belonging to specified domains.

Some or all of these domains are identified as *key domains,* i.e. as parts of an unambiguous identifier of each tuple or relational instance. The unique requirements of uncertainty representation make necessary to revise the meaning of some of the basic concepts of the relational model as follows:

(a) As previously discussed certain field values are *Quantified Lattice Pointers,* i.e. tuples where the first component is a lattice polynomial (defined over some specified lattice) and where the second component is a possibilistic constraint on the values that a valuation may take on the lattice element identified by that polynomial. In the relational model all domains are *simple,* i.e., they correspond to ordinary sets.

(b) *Keys,* which are used to unambiguously identify relational tuples in the classical relational model do not longer serve that purpose in a data base representing imprecise and uncertain facts. For example, the relational tuples

HASHAIR (person 123, [fair, true]),

and

HASHAIR (person 123, [blonde, probable]),

are both instances of the relation

HASHAIR:= (person-id, haircolor=).

Under conditions of accuracy (i.e. a more precise lattice value cannot be specified) and precision (the truth value is either *true* or *false*), the QLP *haircolor* is functionally determined by the key field *person-id* but does not exhibit such functional dependence when uncertainty is introduced.

To maintain a conceptual correspondence with the relational model, a subset of domains will be said to be a *key* whenever values of fields belonging to those domains uniquely identify relational tuples under conditions of precision and certainty. Similarly, a relation will be said to be in *third normal form* if the restriction of its extension (i.e. set of component tuples) to existing tuples represented without uncertainty or imprecision is in third normal form as defined by the standard relational model definition.

Therefore, while certain domains are adequate to uniquely identify relational instances under conditions of accuracy and precision, they only identify sets of related tuples (i.e., different levels of similar property description for the same object) under uncertainty conditions.

(c) Under conditions of uncertainty it is possible that objects identified as unique real world entities in the data base may actually be different real entities and viceversa. Since partial belief or certainty may exist about the uniqueness of real world entities represented by different data base identifiers it is necessary to introduce special classes of data constructs such as

sameobject:= (object-id, object-id#).

Note that this type of constructs can be used to represent both identity as well as non-identity of objects (i.e. by assignment of complementary truth values).

(d) As individual relational tuples are representations of the truth-value (degree of belief, likelihood, etc.) of propositions of the type

Object X has value V for property P,

it is reasonable to require that each relational instance contain only one QLP field. While unambiguous interpretations of certain relations containing more than one QLP field can be made, it is always possible and preferrable to utilize relations exhibiting this property, called the *Simple Truth Quantification* property.

6. OTHER STRUCTURES.

In addition to the basic structures defined above to represent facts about the real world, other constructs are important to describe other types of knowledge about the real world. Of particular importance is *structural lattice knowledge,* which allows simplification of lattice polynomials. For example, the rule

IF E is a part-time employee OR E is a full-time employee THEN E is an employee,

can be used to simplify lattice-polynomial valued expressions defining the value of the field "EMPLOYEE-TYPE".

Predicates are functions defined over data base objects taking fuzzy probabilities as values. Of particular interest are *relational predicates,* i.e. predicates defined over tuples of a specified relation. In what follows, the term *predicate* will be used to denote relational predicates.

Knowledge rules, describing conditional implication statements of the type

If P is true then the the truth-value of Q is t,

are represented by the construct

rule:=(antecedent, consequent#),

where antecedent and consequent are both tuples of a specified relation.

Goals, previously discussed in the context of Active Information Systems, have the relational representation

goal:=(predicate, procedure, priority),

where *predicate* represents the need to compute certain relational tuples, *procedure* indicates the system process to be activated in the case of successful production of those tuples, and *priority* represents the relative importance of each goal.

ACKNOWLEDGMENTS:

Research reported in this paper was performed by the author while affiliated with the

Operating Systems Division of Logicon, Inc. Support for this research was provided by the Air Force Systems Command, Rome Air Development Center, Griffiss Air Force Base, Rome NY 13441.

REFERENCES:

Birkhoff, G., Lattice Theory, (American Mathematical Society, Providence, Rhode Island, 1940).

Duda, R.O. et al., Development of a Computer Based Consultant for Mineral Exploration, Annual Report SRI International, Nos. 5821 and 6415, 1977. Artificial Intelligence, 1977.

Hart, P.E., Progress on a Computer Based Consultant, Proceedings IJCAI 4, 1975.

Montgomery, C.A. and E.H. Ruspini, The Active Information System: A Data-Driven System for the Representation and Manipulation of Uncertainty, Proceedings VLDB 7, IEEE Press, 1981.

Mylopoulos, J., An Overview of Knowledge Representation, Procceedings of the Workshop on Data Abstraction, Data Bases and Conceptual Modeling, Pingree Park, Colorado, June 1980, ACM, New York.

Reiter, A. (1978), On Closed World Data Bases, Logic and Data Bases (H. Gallaire and J. Minker, eds.), (Plenum Press, New York, 1978).

Ruspini, E.H., Possibilistic Representation and Manipulation of Uncertainty by Information Systems, Computer, September 1982.

Smith, J.M. and D.C.P. Smith, Database Abstractions: Aggregation and Generalization, ACM TODS, 105-133, 1977.

Zadeh, L.A., Fuzzy Sets and Information Granularity, Memorandum No. UCB/ERL M79/45, University of California, Berkeley, June 1979(a).

Zadeh, L.A., Approximate Reasoning Based on Fuzzy Logic, Memorandum No. UCB/ERL M79/32, University of California, Berkeley, 1979(b).

Zadeh, L.A., Fuzzy Sets as a basis for a theory of possibility, Fuzzy Sets and Systems 1: 3-28, 1978.

Approximate Reasoning in Decision Analysis
M.M. Gupta and E. Sanchez (eds.)

NON METRIC FUZZY CLUSTERING ALGORITHMS AND THEIR CLUSTER VALIDITY

G. Libert and M. Roubens

Faculté Polytechnique
Rue de Houdain, 9
B 7000 Mons (Belgium)

Numerous methods were proposed to solve the problem of clustering. Among these, the fuzzy methods produce interesting results by allowing each data point to belong to different classes simultaneously instead of being assigned to one and only one cluster. They are briefly summarized and classified in metric or non metric procedures.
Then the choice of the number of classes which characterizes the best the structure that is present in the data is discussed. Some functionals which measure the cluster validity are reminded. A new one is defined and its statistical properties are emphasized.
A critical analysis and a comparison of these functionals are developed and the inferred conclusions are then illustrated by applications.

KEYWORDS : CLUSTER VALIDITY, FUZZY CLUSTERING, PRINCIPAL COMPONENTS ANALYSIS

1. METHODS

Suppose M points $\{x\} = E$ belong to a p-space. The problem of fuzzy clustering is partitioning the M points in K fuzzy subsets, K being fixed. For that, one searches for each point x a membership function to the fuzzy subset k, $\mu_k(x)$, with $0 \leqq \mu_k(x) \leqq 1$, $k=1,\dots,K$; $x \in E$.

Various metric and non metric methods were developed. A unified presentation of these and of those giving a hard partition ($\mu_k(x) \in \{0,1\}$) was proposed in [9].

In this paper, one only considers procedures producing fuzzy partitions.

1.1. Metric methods

A convenient distance measure d being chosen (Euclidean, diagonal, Mahalanobis, L_1, L_2 norms) in E, considered as p-space, R^p, an objective function is optimized. The most commonly used criterion was introduced by DUNN [7] and generalized by BEZDEK [4]. It generates the infinite family of fuzzy ISODATA clustering algorithms and is expressed as follows :

$$\min_{\mu_k} \sum_k \sum_x \mu_k^r(x)\, d(x, CG(k))$$

subject to constraints regarding μ_k

$0 \leqq \mu_k(x) \leqq 1$; $k=1,\dots,K$; $x \in E$

$\sum_k \mu_k(x)=1$; $x \in E$

r is given weighting exponent (r=2 corresponds to the method proposed by DUNN)

$$CG(k) = \frac{\sum_x \mu_k^r(x)x}{\sum_x \mu_k^r(x)}$$ is the fuzzy center of gravity of the fuzzy class k.

The criterion minimum is obtained with

$$\mu_k^{-1}(x) = \sum_m \left(\frac{d(x,CG(k))}{d(x,CG(m))}\right)^{1/r-1}$$

A metric fuzzy procedure similar to the "hill climbing" algorithm proposed in BALL and HALL [3] can be easily implemented and yields local solutions that depend on the initial partition, the starting point of the algorithm.

1.2. Non metric methods

Some problems are non metric in the sense that the data is defined as a dissimilarity measure between entities for each pair (x,y) belonging to E. The dissimilarity index d(x,y) satisfies

$d(x,y) \geqq 0$

$d(x,y) = d(y,x)$ for all $x,y \in E$

RUSPINI [11] has developed a well known algorithm which may be considered as a special case of the problem

$$\min_{\mu_k,\eta_k} \sum_k \sum_x \sum_y f[u(x), \mu_k(x)]\, g[u(y),\eta_k(y)]\, d(x,y)$$

$\eta_k(y)$ represents an auxiliary membership function ($0 \leqq \eta_k(y) \leqq 1$)

u(x) is the a priori weight assigned to each point $x \in E$ (eventually equal to 1/M), $\sum_{x \in E} u(x)=1$.

When $f[u(x),\mu_k(x)]=\mu_k^r/M$ and $g[u(y),\eta_k(y)]=\eta_k^s/M$

the criterion becomes

$$\min_{\mu_k,\eta_k} \sum_k \sum_x \sum_y \mu_k^r(x)\, \eta_k^s(y)\, d(x,y)$$

The following constraints are considered

$$0 \leq \mu_k(x) \leq 1 \ ; \ k=1,\dots,K; \ x\varepsilon E \qquad (1)$$

$$\sum_k \mu_k(x)=1 \ , \ x\varepsilon E \qquad (2)$$

$$\eta_k(y)\varepsilon\{0,1\} \ ; \ k=1,\dots,K \ ; \ y\varepsilon E \qquad (3)$$

$$\sum_k \eta_k(y)=1 \ ; \ y\varepsilon E \qquad (4)$$

The binary weight $\eta_k(y)=1$ means that y is assigned to the class k. The constraint (4) assumes that y is assigned to exactly one class and the conditions (1) and (2) introduce the degree of attractivity of each point x to the class k.

This hybrid procedure was proposed in [10]. It is hard by giving the opportunity to define a partition of E without using the classical rule of thumb : x belongs to the class k iff $\mu_k(x)>\mu_l(x)$ for all $l\neq k$. It is fuzzy in the sense that it can cope with "noisy" data points by considering the fuzzy membership function $\{\mu_k(x)\}$.

The program convergence is proved. A local solution can be obtained but generally the global optimum is reached with

$\eta_k(x)=1, \ \eta_l(x)=0, \ \eta_m(x)=0$ for all $m\neq k$

$\mu_k(x)=0, \ \mu_l(x)=1, \ \mu_m(x)=0$ for all $m\neq l$

It corresponds to the trivial solution : all the points belong to one class.
In order to remove this drawback, one ought to introduce a constraint on the number of classes.

By using the algorithm proposed in [9], this trivial solution is also given by the method MND2 based on the criterion

$$\underset{\mu_k}{\text{MIN}} \sum_k \sum_x \sum_y \mu_k^2(x) \ \mu_k^2(y) \ d(x,y)$$

$$0\leq\mu_k\leq 1 \ ; \ \sum_k \mu_k=1$$

Indeed, if one doesn't impose $\mu_k(x)=\mu_k(y)$ when y=x, one has

$\mu_k(x)=1 \ , \ \mu_l(x)=0, \ \mu_m(x)=0$ for all $m\neq k$

$\mu_k(y)=0 \ , \ \mu_l(y)=1, \ \mu_m(x)=0$ for all $m\neq l$; y=x

In order to have $\mu_k(x)=\mu_k(y)$ when y=x, the following algorithm must be implemented

1. Choice of an initial membership matrix $\{\mu_k(y)\}$

2. x=0

3. x=x+1
   Computation of $D(x,k) = \sum_y \mu_k^2(y) \ d(x,y)$ for k=1,...,K
   Optimisation of the quadratic program
   $\underset{\mu_k(x)}{\text{MIN}} \sum_k \mu_k^2(x) \ D(x,k)$ with $0\leq\mu_k(x)\leq 1$ and $\sum_k \mu_k(x)=1$

4. $\mu_k(y)=\mu_k(x)$ for k=1,...,K and y=x.

5. If x is smaller than M, go to 3.

6. Computation of the criterion. If a stopping test isn't checked, go to 2.

The algorithm converges to a local optimum which depends on the initial partition.

Remark : $\mu_k(x) = \frac{1}{K}$ for all k and for all x is a local solution and generally, this solution is reached when initial partition close to $\frac{1}{K}$ is chosen.
Numerical experience shows that quick convergence is achieved by using a hard partition in K classes as initial partition.

The optimum of the quadratic program defined in 3. can be readily obtained with the use of Lagrange multiplier.

$$\underset{\mu_k(x)}{\text{MIN}} \sum_k \mu_k^2(x) \ D(x,k) + \lambda[\sum_k \mu_k(x)-1]$$

leads to

$$\frac{\partial}{\partial \mu_k(x)} = 0 \ : \ 4\mu_k(x) \ D(x,k)+\lambda = 0$$

$$\frac{\partial}{\partial \lambda} = 0 \qquad : \ \sum_k \mu_k(x) = 1$$

$$\mu_k^{-1}(x) = D(x,k)\sum_m D^{-1}(x,m)$$

2. VALIDITY FUNCTIONALS

The most important problem of fuzzy clustering is neither the choice of the algorithm nor the distance to use but concerns the number of clusters to look for. Indeed, lacking in a priori knowledge of the data structure, there is no reason to choose a particular value of K and one must find a way to measure the effectiveness with which cluster structure has been properly identified by a fuzzy clustering algorithm. This is the so-called "cluster validity problem".

To solve this problem, one could try on finding K indicated by the criterion as optimum, i.e. the one for which the criterion falls below a decreasing trend in its value. Numerical experience with fuzzy criteria shows that this technique is often disapointing.

Many authors have proposed several measures of cluster validity associated with fuzzy K-partitions. The most known of these functionals are

$$F = \sum_k \sum_x \mu_k^2(x)/M \qquad [8]$$

$$NFI = (KF-1)/(K-1) \qquad [9]$$

$$F' = 1-NFI \qquad [2]$$

$$H = -\sum_k \sum_x \mu_k(x) \log_a \mu_k(x)/M, \quad 1<a<\infty \qquad [4]$$

$$H' = M\ H/M-K \qquad [5]$$

$$H'' = H/\log_a K\ , \quad 1<a<\infty \qquad [8]$$

$$P = -\log_2(\Pi_x(\sum_{i=1}^{I_x} (-1)^{i+1} \binom{K}{i} (1-i\ \mu_x)^{K-1})) \qquad [12]$$

I_x is equal to the greatest integer in

$1/\mu_x$, $\mu_x = \underset{k}{MAX}\ \mu_k(x)$.

BEZDEK, WINDHAM and EHRLICH [6] analysed the behaviour of these functionals. They computed their mean and variance when the membership function is thought of as the value of a random vector uniformly distributed in MF_K considered as the possible membership functions for a given K.

$$MF_K = \{\mu\varepsilon R^K : \mu_k \geq 0 \text{ for } k=1,\dots,K \text{ and } \sum_k \mu_k = 1\}$$

The resulting mean and the range of these validity measures are reported in table 1. The range is obtained with a quite fuzzy partition ($\mu_k(x) = \frac{1}{K}$) and a hard partition ($\mu_k(x)=0$ or 1).

Table 1

Index	Mean	Range	
F	2/K+1	1/K	1
NFI	1/K+1	0	1
F'	K/K+1	1	0
H(a=e)	$\sum_{k=2}^{K} \frac{1}{k}$	$\log_e K$	0
H'(a=e)	ME(H)/M-K	$\frac{M \log_e K}{M-K}$	0
H"(a=e)	$E(H)/\log_e K$	1	0
P	?	0	∞
NF"I	computable	0	1

NF"I is a new functional defined as

$$NF''I = (KF''-1)/(K-1)$$

$$F'' = ((\sum_x \mu_x/M) + \underset{x}{MIN}\ \mu_x)/2$$

At first, the justification of NF"I is intuitive. When one estimates the validity of a partition, one particularly considers the maxima of the membership functions. For this reason, one computes $\sum_x \mu_x/M$ which is a linear function of μ_x. Afterwards, the smallest maximum is added in order to emphasize the separation between clusters. If $\underset{x}{MIN}\ \mu_x$ is large, then F" is large. If $\underset{x}{MIN}\ \mu_x$ is small, F" is small and shows that the partition is not an adequate one due to overlapping clusters or "noisy" data points. By only using $\sum_x \mu_x/M$, this information doesn't necessarily appear because a small μ_x can be hidden by the mean of all the μ_x. F" is then divided by 2 in order that the variation range of NF"I is [0,1].NF"I is defined like NFI to take into consideration that a same F" value represents a better partition when K is larger.

The statistical properties of this functional can be established with the previous assumption. WINDHAM [12] proved the following theorem :

For K=2,3,... and $\frac{1}{K} \leq t \leq 1$ let

$$A_t = \{\mu\varepsilon MF_K : \underset{k}{MAX}\ \mu_k \geq t\},$$

then the proportion of membership functions in A_t is equal to

$$p(\mu\varepsilon A_t) = \sum_{i=1}^{I} (-1)^{i+1} \binom{K}{i} (1-it)^{K-1}$$

I is the greatest integer in 1/t

From this theorem, one deduces the distribution function of the maximum $F(t) = 1-p(\mu\varepsilon A_t)$

For K=2, one has

$I=1$

$F(t) = 1-2(1-t)$

$f(t)=2$ where $f(t)$ is the density function

$$E[\mu_x] = \int_{1/2}^{1} 2\ t\ dt = \frac{3}{4} = E[\sum_x \mu_x/M]$$

$$E[\underset{x}{MIN}\ \mu_x] = \frac{1}{2} \text{ and } E[NF''I] = \frac{1}{4}$$

For K=3, one has

. if $\frac{1}{2} \leq t \leq 1$, then I=1 and

$$F(t) = 1-3(1-t)^2 \quad , \quad f(t) = 6(1-t)$$

. if $\frac{1}{3} \leq t \leq \frac{1}{2}$, then I=2 and

$$F(t) = 1-3(1-t)^2+3(1-2t)^2,$$

$$f(t) = 6(1-t)-12(1-2t)$$

$$E[\mu_x] = \int_{1/2}^{1} 6t(1-t)dt + \int_{1/3}^{1/2} 6t((1-t)-2(1-2t))dt$$

$$= \frac{11}{18} = E[\sum_x \mu_x/M]$$

$$E[\underset{x}{MIN}\ \mu_x] = \frac{1}{3} \quad \text{and} \quad E[NF''I] = \frac{5}{24}$$

In the same way, the following results are obtained

K	E[μ]	E[NF"I]
2	3/4	1/4 =0.25
3	11/18	5/24 =0.208
4	25/48	13/72 =0.181
5	137/300	77/480=0.160
6	49/120	29/200=0.145

3. FUNCTIONALS ANALYSIS AND COMPARISON

In this section, main features of the validity measures are analysed and compared in function of K and μ_k. Conclusions concerning their practical utility are inferred. The next section confirms these conclusions by applications.

Consider K clusters and suppose that each point x has a membership function including one membership coefficient equal to μ and K-1 coefficients equal to $\frac{1-\mu}{K-1}$. μ is greater than $\frac{1-\mu}{K-1}$ and each set of membership coefficients to a cluster comprises at least one value equal to μ.

Table 2 gives values of F, H and F" for μ=1, 0.9, 0.8,...,1/K and for K=2,3,4,5. For a same μ value, F" is constant, F and H prefer the smaller K seeing that F must be maximum and H minimum. (F=1 and H=0 if $\mu_k(x)\varepsilon\{0,1\}$). Now, a μ value is more difficult to reach when K is larger, so

$$p(\mu\varepsilon A_{0.9})=0.2 \quad \text{for} \quad K=2$$
$$=0.03 \quad \text{for} \quad K=3$$

Consequently for a same μ, the better the classification is, the larger K is. F", F and H don't thus seem the best functionals. The same conclusion is valid for H' which leads still more quickly to a small K by the factor M/M-K.

TABLE 2: INDEXES VALUES IN FUNCTION OF K and μ

K	μ	F	H	F"
2	1.	1.	0.	1.
	0.9	0.82	0.325	0.9
	0.8	0.68	0.500	0.8
	0.7	0.58	0.611	0.7
	0.6	0.52	0.673	0.6
	0.5	0.5	0.693	0.5
3	1.	1.	0.	1.
	0.9	0.815	0.394	0.9
	0.8	0.66	0.639	0.8
	0.7	0.535	0.819	0.7
	0.6	0.44	0.950	0.6
	0.5	0.375	1.04	0.5
	0.4	0.34	1.09	0.4
	0.33	0.33	1.10	0.33
4	1.	1.	0.	1.
	0.9	0.813	0.435	0.9
	0.8	0.653	0.720	0.8
	0.7	0.52	0.940	0.7
	0.6	0.413	1.11	0.6
	0.5	0.333	1.24	0.5
	0.4	0.28	1.33	0.4
	0.3	0.253	1.38	0.3
	0.25	0.25	1.39	0.25
5	1.	1.	0.	1.
	0.9	0.8125	0.464	0.9
	0.8	0.65	0.778	0.8
	0.7	0.513	1.03	0.7
	0.6	0.4	1.23	0.6
	0.5	0.313	1.39	0.5
	0.4	0.25	1.51	0.4
	0.3	0.213	1.58	0.3
	0.2	0.2	1.61	0.2

Figure 1 shows the graphs of NFI, 1-H", P and NF"I in function of μ. NF"I is a linear functional. NFI and 1-H" are similar. The P values are very different for a same μ when K differs. This fact is illustrated in figure 2 where equivalence curves of these four functionals are drawn. The equivalence curve of a functional gives in function of K the values leading to a same functional value. (In figure 2, three families of equivalence curves are drawn). By example, one has for NF"I :

μ=0.9 (for K=2) equivalent to μ=0.867 (K=3), to μ=0.850 (K=4), to μ=0.840 (K=5).

μ changes quickly for P. However, in practice μ doesn't vary alike so that P will reach larger values and too large K will be selected.

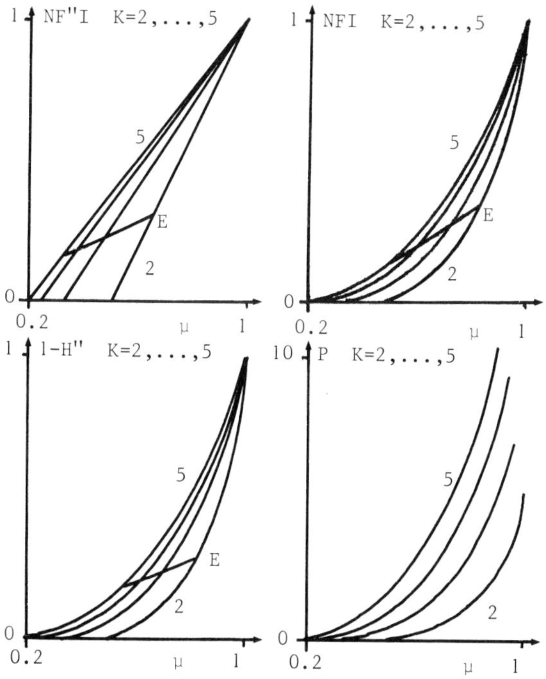

FIGURE 1 :
FUNCTIONALS GRAPHS IN FUNCTION OF K AND μ

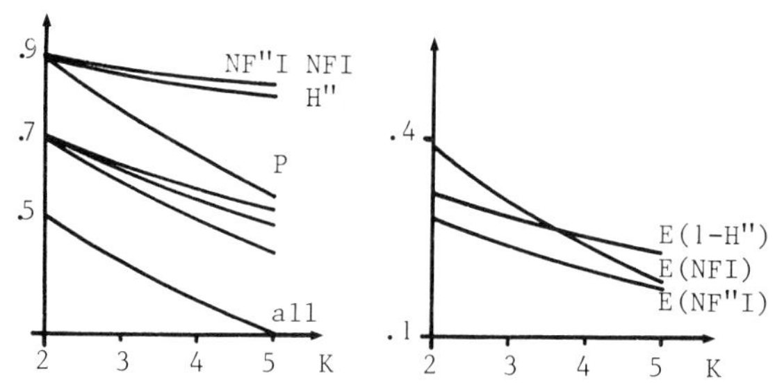

EQUIVALENCE CURVES FUNCTIONALS MEANS

FIGURE 2

The equivalence curves of 1-H" and NFI are similar. Identical graphs are obtained for NF"I and NFI but it's only true with the values of figure 1. With other $\mu_k(x)$, they aren't confounded but remain similar. This results from the dependence of NFI not only on μ but also on the other $\mu_k(x)$. By example, for K=3, NFI is equal to 0.16 if $\mu=0.6, \mu_2(x)=\mu_3(x)=\frac{1-\mu}{K-1}$ and if $\mu=0.467$, $\mu_2(x)=\mu$, $\mu_3(x)=1-2\mu$.
NF"I equals respectively 0.4 and 0.2

In order to take into account of NFI and 1-H" variations, the graphs of figure 3 are built. For K=2,3,4,5, all the possible values of NF"I, NFI, 1-H" and P are computed in function of μ. For K=2, the μ value leads to only one value of the other membership coefficient and the results of figure 2 are unchanged. On the other hand, if K is greater than 2, various values are possible for the other coefficients when μ is fixed. NF"I and P aren't modified because they depend only on μ but the range of NFI and 1-H" is greatly increased. By example, for K=3 and $\mu=0.5$, 1-H" can vary between

0.054 ($\mu=0.5, \mu_2(x)=\mu_3(x) = \frac{1-\mu}{K-1}$) and

0.369($\mu=0.5, \mu_2(x)=0.5-\varepsilon, \mu_3(x)=\varepsilon$; ε tends to 0).

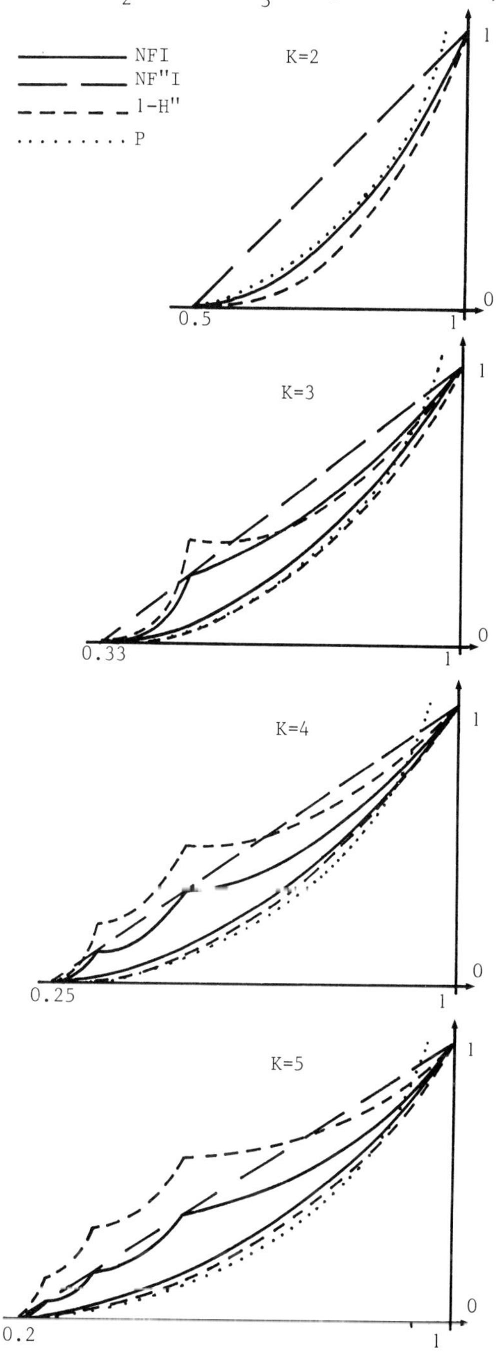

FIGURE 3 : GRAPHS IN FUNCTION OF K and μ

One remarks once more the similarity between 1-H" and NFI. However, these graphs show a little disadvantage of 1-H" by comparison with NFI. The possible values area of 1-H" completely includes the area of NFI and large values of 1-H" are more likely especially when K is large. Unfortunately, these values correspond to bad partitions. Thus, although 1-H" and NFI are very similar, 1-H" will select more quickly than NFI high values of K independently of the data structure.
It is illustrated in figure 2 by the graphs of the means of 1-H", NFI and NF"I computed under the assumption of membership function uniformity.
For $K \geq 4$, E(1-H") is effectively greater than E(NFI). The mean of 1-H" changes less than those of NFI. This fact apparently represents an important quality for 1-H". However as it was observed, this peculiarity is especially due to bad partitions. Consequently, the constancy of E(1-H") is not an advantage and, if one must choose between H" and NFI, it seems more advisable to use NFI.

Concerning P, figure 3 shows that still more than 1-H" and NFI, P is deviating from the linearity when K is increasing. Confusion results from that in particular for small values. Moreover, its expression is complicated and its use isn't easy. Indeed, the selection of K can be done only by drawing the plot of P in function of K in order to detect a discontinuance in the natural increasing trend of P.

The case is different with NF"I the maximum of which clearly indicates the best K. NF"I has also other advantages. It is a linear functional, its equivalence curve is similar to those of H" and NFI when a right partition is obtained and its mean doesn't too much vary in function of K. However, the last property isn't the most interesting one for the mean. Consider oncemore figure 1. In the graphs of NF"I, NFI and 1-H", a supplementary curve (E) has been drawn. It joins the values of the means for K=2,3,4,5. For these three functionals, the curves don't basically differ but one ascertains that the NF"I means curve is more on the left than the two others and that NF"I becomes comparable with E only for smaller μ values. So, for K=2, one has

NF"I(0.65)=E; NFI(0.79)=E; 1-H"(0.8)=E

In other words, NF"I is the less perceptible functional to the noise created by K. This property and the linearity are the most important qualities of this functional.

In conclusion, it seems that NF"I is the most advisable validity measure, that NFI and 1-H" are alike to each other and that P doesn't clearly and easily show the K values to select.

4. NUMERICAL EXPERIENCE

Numerical experience is based on the use of a metric procedure (ISODATA with r=2,...,6) and a non metric procedure (MND2). Normally, the considered examples must not be treated by MND2 since a distance (Euclidean) can be computed. However, the use of MND2 illustrates its performance and the effectiveness of the validity functionals.
For each of the data sets analysed below, the ISODATA algorithm is run for r=2,...,6 in order to see until which value of the weighting exponent the existing clusters can be distinguished. Indeed, when r is increasing, the membership coefficients become smaller and smaller and the borders between classes fuzzier and fuzzier.

Consider the RUSPINI data [11]. Graphs of functionals NFI, 1-H", NF"I and P for K=2,...,6 are drawn in figure 4. Obviously, all the functionals indicate K=4 for this standard example and few conclusions of the previous section are directly found again. NFI and 1-H" are very similar and 1-H" tends to exceed NFI when K is increasing. The trend discontinuance of P allows to easily detect K=4. NF"I is the validity measure which gives the most clearly the K value for all r. Indeed, even for r=6 and contrarily to the other functionals, the NF"I maximum distincly appears.

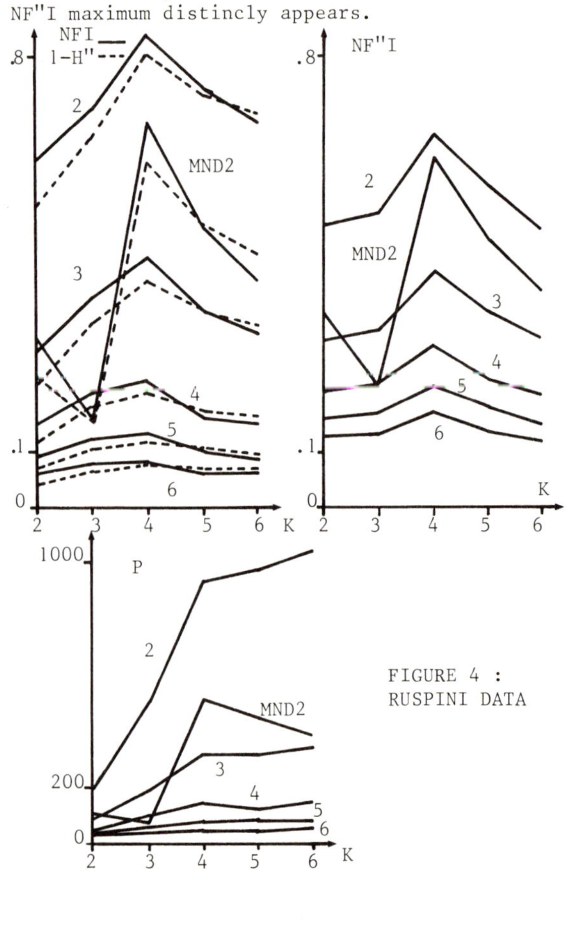

FIGURE 4 : RUSPINI DATA

Analyse now IRIS data [1] consisting of 150 four dimensional vectors. The components of a vector are the measurements of the petal length, petal width, sepal length and sepal width of a particular iris plant. There are 50 plants in each of three subspecies of iris represented in the data, so it is assumed that an effective validity functional will indicate the presence of three clusters. Values of the functionals are reported in figure 5. NFI and 1-H" always find K=2. For r=4,5,6,P chooses K=2 but for the other cases, which K value must be selected? K=2 or 3 ? NF"I detects K=3 for r=2,3 and for MND2.

It is thus the only one which can indicate the expected value. For r greater than 3, K=2 reappears but it's not surprising by taking into consideration the overlapping between two of the three clusters. This is illustrated in figure 6 which represents the projections of the 150 plants and of the 4 variables on the first principal plan resulting from a principal components analysis. This technique has been used in order to visualize the available information which cannot be seen in a 4 dimensional space. The underlined projections correspond to the plants misclassified by ISODATA (r=2) and the surrounded ones to the plants misclassified by MND2. Each algorithm leads to very satisfying results and it is easily understood that it is no more possible to build a boundary between the two overlapping clusters.

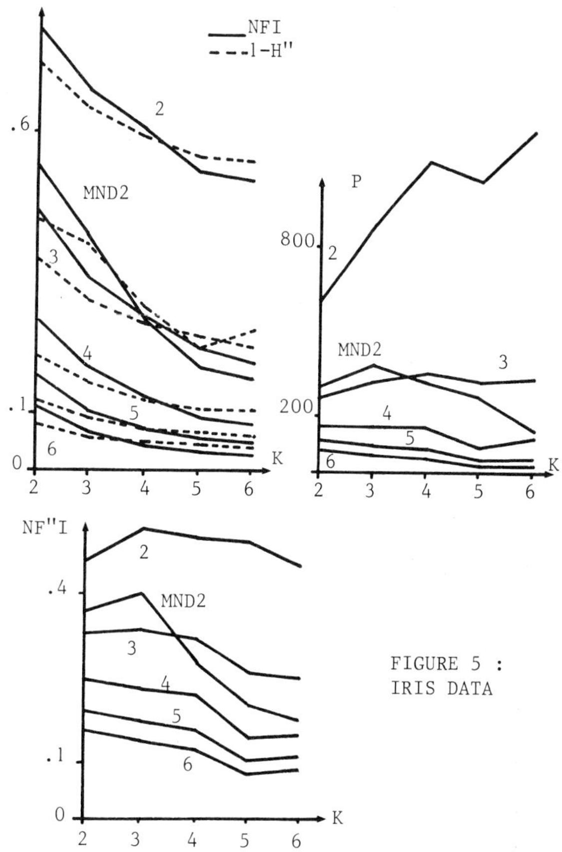

FIGURE 5 : IRIS DATA

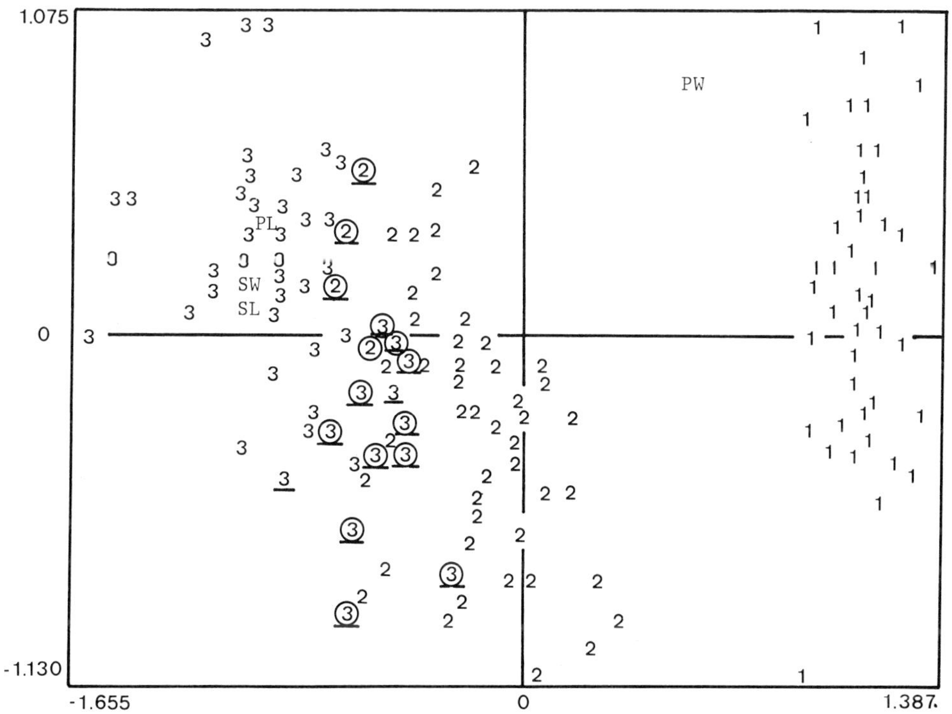

FIGURE 6 : PRINCIPAL COMPONENTS ANALYSIS OF IRIS DATA

Lastly consider the data of figure 7.

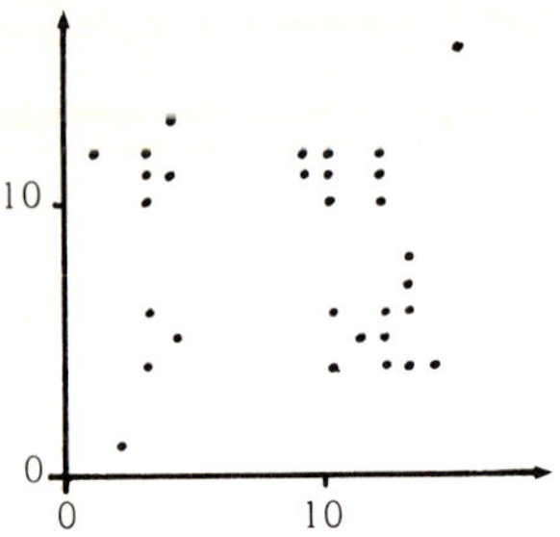

FIGURE 7

Functionals values are presented in figure 8. Although they are similar, NFI and 1-H" produce expected different results. For r greater than 2, 1-H" chooses a K value higher than the one of NFI. NFI, 1-H" and P find K=4 for only one case (r=2). On the other hand, NF"I always select K=4.

Remark : The partitions in 5 classes never correspond to the four important groups and the isolated point. Consequently, K=5 is never the best solution.

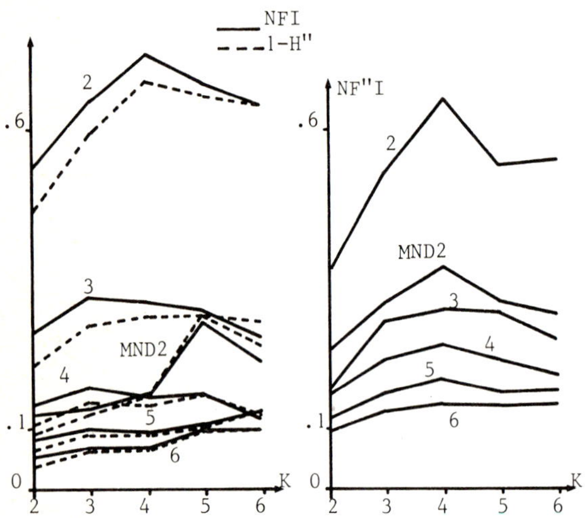

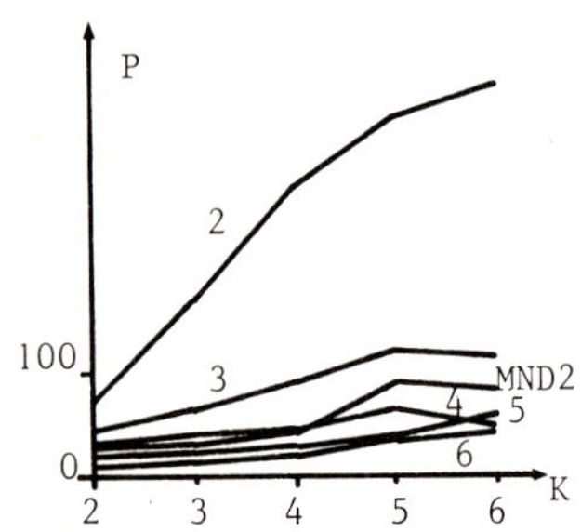

FIGURE 8 :
DATA OF FIGURE 7

CONCLUSION

MND2 algorithm, introduced for poorer data than those analysed in this paper, produces results comparable with those obtained by a metric method.

Functionals F, H, H' and F" aren't recommendable because their too high dependence on K complicates their use. This one needs a plot to show this effect and then, to detect K. The case is the same with P which rarely presents a maximum and the trend discountinuances of which don't always select the best K.

NFI (or 1-F') and 1-H" have the same behaviour but 1-H" chooses more often high K values. Both encounter difficulties to find K when clusters overlap. This is demonstrated by their weak resistance to the influence of increasing r.

NF"I seems to be the best validity functional to measure how well has a fuzzy clustering algorithm identified structure that is present in the data. NF"I is the less sensitive to r thanks to its linearity and it is the most independent on the number of clusters.

REFERENCES

[1] Anderson, E., The Iris of the Gaspe Peninsula, Bull. Amer. Iris Soc. 59 (1935) 2-5.

[2] Backer, E., Cluster analysis by optimal decomposition of induced fuzzy sets (Delft university press, Delft, 1978).

[3] Ball, G., and Hall, D., A clustering technique for summarizing multivariate data, Behavioral Sc. 12 (1967) 153-155.

[4] Bezdek, J.C., Cluster validity with fuzzy sets, J. Cybernetics 3(3) (1974) 58-72.

[5] Bezdek, J.C., Mathematical models for systematics and taxonomy, in Estabrook, G., (ed.), Proc. 8th Int. Conf. on Numerical Taxonomy (Freeman, San Francisco, 1975).

[6] Bezdek, J.C., Windham, M.P., Ehrlich, R., Statistical parameters of cluster validity functionals. To appear.

[7] Dunn, J.C., A fuzzy relative of the Isodata process and its use in detecting compact, well-separated clusters, J. Cybernetics 3 (3) (1974) 32-57.

[8] Dunn, J.C., Indices of partition fuzziness and the detection of clusters in large data sets, in Gupta, M., (ed.), Fuzzy automata and decision processes (American Elsevier, New-York, 1976).

[9] Roubens, M., Pattern classification problems and fuzzy sets, Fuzzy sets and systems, 1 (1978) 239-253.

[10] Roubens, M., Fuzzy algorithms and their cluster validity, EJOR. To appear.

[11] Ruspini, E., Numerical methods for fuzzy clustering, Information Sci. 1 (1970) 319-350.

[12] Windham, M.P., Cluster validity for fuzzy clustering algorithms, Fuzzy Sets and Systems. To appear.

Approximate Reasoning in Decision Analysis
M.M. Gupta and E. Sanchez (eds.)

TWO NEW METHODS IN FUZZY CLUSTER

Shih-pe Lou, Wha-cheng Cheng and Li-ming Chao

Research Section of Multivalued Logic & Fuzzy System,
Shanghai Railway Institute, Shanghai, China

In this paper two new methoes in Fuzzy Clustering were presented, namely, a new algorithm for finding the transitive closure of a Fuzzy matrix and a Fuzzy decision function were given. Applying the two new methods, the forecasting of the lasting raining in spring in Shanghai D.C. and the classification of conualent compounds and ionic compounds were solved. The results were satisfactory.

Keywords: Fuzzy clustering, weather forecasting, classification of compounds.

INTRODUCTION

Our purposes are to examine if the two new methods are valuable in application and compare them with other common methods in Fuzzy clustering. The fact is that they are simpler and better than Tammura algorithm and Prim algorithm which we ever used in solving the same problems.

Methods in Fuzzy Clustering

Sample Matrix

Supposing there are n samples X_1, X_2, ..., X_n, and each sample has m variables Z_1, Z_2, ..., Z_m, we get the sample matrix as follows:

$$M=\begin{pmatrix} x_{11}, x_{12}, \cdots\cdots, x_{1n} \\ x_{21}, x_{22}, \cdots\cdots, x_{2n} \\ \vdots \\ x_{m1}, x_{m2}, \cdots\cdots, x_{mn} \end{pmatrix}$$

Where

$X = (x_{1i}, x_{2i}, \ldots, x_{mi})$ =1, 2, ..., n

$Z = (x_{j1}, x_{j2}, \ldots, x_{jn})$ =1, 2, ..., m .

We can describe the sample matrix as

$$M=(x_{ij})_{mn}$$

Fuzzy Relation Matrix

$$\underset{\sim}{R}=(\mu_{ij})_{nn}$$

Where

$$\mu_{ij}=\frac{(X_i, X_j)}{\|X_i\| \, \|X_j\|}$$

Fuzzy Equivalent Relation

The Fuzzy relation R between the arbitrary elements x and y in set X is defined by the membership function

If $\mu_{\underset{\sim}{R}}(x, y)$ has the characters as follows:

1. Reflexive $\quad \mu_{\underset{\sim}{R}}(x, x)=\mu_{\underset{\sim}{R}}(x, x)$
2. Symmetric $\quad \mu_{\underset{\sim}{R}}(x, y)=\mu_{\underset{\sim}{R}}(y, x)$
3. Transitive

$$\mu_{\underset{\sim}{R}}(x,y)\geq\lambda,\ \mu_{\underset{\sim}{R}}(y,z)\geq\lambda \Longrightarrow \mu_{\underset{\sim}{R}}(x,z)\geq\lambda,$$

then we say R is a Fuzzy equivalent relation in X.

If R is reflexive and symmetric then we say R is a consistent relation in X.

In Fuzzy relation matrix R, we define the relation between X_i and X_j with μ_{ij}, namely

$$\mu_{ij}=\mu_{\underset{\sim}{R}}(X_i, X_j)$$

Obviously, $\underset{\sim}{R}$ is a Fuzzy consisten relation in X.

The key step in Fuzzy clustering is to transfer the Fuzzy consistent relation to Fuzzy equivalent relations. In the paper, we use a new algorithm for finding the transitive closure of a Fuzzy matrix to do so.

Transitive Closure of Fuzzy Matrix

Let $\quad \underset{\sim}{R}_k=(a_{ij}^{(k)}) \qquad k=0, 1, 2, \ldots, n$

Where

$$a_{ij}^{(k)}=\begin{cases}a_{ij} & k=0\\ a_{ij}^{(k-1)}\vee(a_{ik}^{(k-1)}\wedge a_{kj}^{(k-1)}) & 0\le k\le n\end{cases}$$

We assert

$$\underset{\sim}{R}_n=T(\underset{\sim}{R})$$

It is easy to prove that $T(\underset{\sim}{R})$ is a equivalent relation.

A Pratical Example in Meteorological Field.

Applying the new algorithm for finding the transitive closure of a Fuzzy matrix, the samples of the lasting raining in spring in Shanghai D.C. were classified, and the weather forecasting was made with the classification.

Selection of Weather Samples and Choosing the Meteorological Factors

We selected the weather samples of lasting raining in spring in Shanghai D.C. from 1950 to 1978 as the classified samples and choose ten factors in each sample. Some of these factors must be standardized with following formula:

$$\bar{x}_i=\frac{x_i-\min(x_i)}{\max(x_i)-\max(x_i)}$$

The Process of Classifying Samples

(1) Establishing Fuzzy consistent relations between samples with following formula:

$$\mu_{\underset{\sim}{R}}(X_i,X_j)\ \frac{(X_i,X_j)}{\|X_i\|\,\|X_j\|}$$

(2) Changing $\underset{\sim}{R}$ to a Fuzzy equivalent relation R with the new algorithm for finding the transitime closure of a Fuzzy matrix.

(3) Let $\lambda=0.94$, using level cut-set methods, the samples were classified to thirteen groups.

Forecasting Method

(1) Every group is a general subset of the sample set.

$$X^{(i)}=\{X_{i_1},\ X_{i_2},\ \ldots,\ X_{i_p}\}$$

X represents i- th group.

(2) Extending $X^{(i)}$ to construct Fuzzy subset X . The membership function of X is determined with following formula:

$$\mu_{\underset{\sim}{X}^{(i)}}(x)=\bigvee_{p=1}^{L}\frac{(x,\ X_{ip})}{\|x\|\,\|X_{ip}\|}$$

(3) Constructing pattern of lasting raining in spring in Shanghai D.C. as follows (it is a Fuzzy set, Complex pattern): $\underset{\sim}{X}=\bigvee_i \underset{\sim}{X}^{(i)}$

The membership function of X is $\mu_{\underset{\sim}{X}}(x)=\bigvee_i \mu_{\underset{\sim}{X}^{(i)}}(x)$

(4) Determing threshold value (in our example $\lambda_0=0.94$) the forecasting criterion is that

if $\mu_{\underset{\sim}{X}}(x)\geqslant\lambda_0$

then the lasting raining will occur in the day after tomorrow,

if $\mu_{\underset{\sim}{X}}(x)<\lambda_0$

then the lasting raining will not occur in the day after tomorrow.

The accuracy reached 82% in the forecasting in 1979.

Fuzzy Decision Function

There is a sample set $X=\{X_1,X_2,\cdots\cdots,X_n\}$ in m-dimension sample space, the samples in set X are from the subsets A and B, Where $A=\{X_{1A},X_{2A},\cdots\cdots,X_{aA}\}$, $B=\{X_{1B},X_{2B},\cdots\cdots,X_{bB}\}$, $a+b=n$.

Let W_A and W_B be the weights of A and B respectively.

then

$$W_A=\frac{1}{a}\sum_{k=1}^{a}X_{kA}=(\bar{X}_A^{(1)},\ \bar{X}_A^{(2)},\ \cdots\cdots,\ \bar{X}_A^{(m)})^T$$

Where

$$X_{kA}=(X_{kA}^{(1)},\ X_{kA}^{(2)},\ \cdots\cdots,\ X_{kA}^{(m)})^T$$

$$\bar{x}_A^{(i)}=\frac{1}{a}\sum_{k=1}^{a}x_{kA}^{(i)}$$

and

$$W_B=(\bar{X}_B^{(1)},\ \bar{X}_B^{(2)},\ \cdots\cdots,\ \bar{X}_B^{(m)})^T$$

$$X_{kB}=(X_{kB}^{(1)},\ X_{kB}^{(2)},\ \cdots\cdots,\ \bar{X}_{kB}^{(m)})^T\qquad \bar{x}_B^{(i)}=\frac{1}{b}\sum_{k=1}^{b}x_{kB}^{(i)}$$

Let

$$p^{(i)}=|\bar{x}_A^{(i)}-\bar{x}_B^{(i)}|,\quad Q=\sum_{i=1}^{m}p^{(i)},\quad w^{(i)}=p^{(i)}/Q,$$

$$W=(w^{(1)},\ w^{(2)},\ \cdots\cdots,\ w^{(m)})^T;$$

Obviously $\sum_{k=1}^{m}w^{(k)}=1$

Let

$$\mu_{ij}=\frac{(X_{iA},\ X_{jB})}{\|X_{iA}\|\,\|X_{jB}\|}\ ,\qquad \mu=\max_{i,j}(\mu_{ij})$$

Supposing X_{pA} and X_{qB} are the samples corresponding to μ,

$$X_{pA}=(x_{pA}^{(1)},\ x_{pA}^{(2)},\ \cdots\cdots,\ x_{pA}^{(m)})^T$$

$$X_{qB}=(x_{qB}^{(1)},\ x_{qB}^{(2)},\ \cdots\cdots,\ x_{qB}^{(m)})^T$$

Let

$$g(X_{pA},X_{qB})=\frac{\sum_{k=1}^{m}w^{(k)}x_{pA}^{(k)}x_{qB}^{(k)}}{\sqrt{\sum_{k=1}^{m}(x_{pA}^{(k)})^2\ \sum_{k=1}^{m}(x_{qB})^2}}$$

$X=(x^{(1)},\ x^{(2)},\ \ldots,\ x^{(m)})^T$ is an arbitrary sample in m-dimension sample space $\mathcal{X}$, the decision function is given as follows: $g(X)=g(X,W_A)-C$

where

$$g(X,W_A)=\frac{\sum_{k=1}^{m}w^{(k)}x^{(k)}\bar{x}_A^{(k)}}{\sqrt{\sum_{k=1}^{m}(x^{(k)})^2\ \sum_{k=1}^{m}(\bar{x}_A^{k})^2}}$$

If

$$g(X) > 0 \qquad X \in A$$

$$g(X) < 0 \qquad X \in B$$

The Classification of the Compounds.

There are twenty-five samples of compounds, in which ten are convalent compounds, ten are ionic compounds, and another five unknown samples, namely, we didn't know what classes they belonged to. We must analyse the twenty-five compounds, and find the relations among them, then deside which class the five compounds belong to.

There are six variables in each sample, they are

Z_1, Z_2, $(\frac{Z}{r})_1$, $(\frac{Z}{r})_2$, x_1 and x_2 . Z_1 is electronic number, r is the radios of electron, x shows connective degree of electrons.

The datum of the twenty-five samples are presented in table one

Table One

Sample	Z	Z	(Z/r)	(Z/r)	X	X
PCl_5	3	5	4.55	7.00	2.1	3.0
AlC_3	3	7	2.38	7.00	1.5	3.0
SbF_5	5	7	3.55	9.72	1.9	4.0
BF_3	3	7	3.57	9.72	2.0	4.0
AsF_3	3	7	2.46	9.72	2.0	4.0
B_2O_3	3	6	3.57	8.11	2.0	3.5
CO_2	4	6	5.19	8.11	2.5	3.5
N_2O_3	5	6	6.76	8.11	3.0	3.5
AsI_3	5	7	2.46	5.26	2.0	2.5
BCl_3	3	7	3.57	7.00	2.0	3.0
KCl	1	7	0.50	7.00	0.8	3.0
$SrCl_2$	2	7	1.05	1.00	1.0	3.0
$CaCl_2$	2	7	1.15	7.00	1.0	3.0
NaCl	1	7	0.63	7.00	0.9	3.0
AgF	1	7	0.70	9.72	1.9	4.2
NaBr	1	7	0.63	6.14	0.9	2.8
LiCl	1	7	0.76	7.00	1.0	3.0
$ScCl_3$	3	7	2.08	7.00	1.3	3.0
$CuCl_2$	1	7	0.80	7.00	1.9	3.0
PF_3	3	7	2.73	9.72	2.1	4.0
$GeCl_4$	4	7	3.28	7.00	1.8	3.0
$TiCl_4$	4	7	3.04	7.00	1.6	3.0
RbCl	1	7	0.47	7.00	0.8	3.0
KI	1	7	0.50	5.20	0.8	2.6
AgI	1	7	0.70	5.26	1.9	2.5

With Fuzzy decision function, we have

$W=(0.34,\ 0.07,\ 0.36,\ 0.12\ ,\ 0.1,\ 0.01)^T$

$X_{PA}=X_2=AlCl_3=(3,\ 7,\ 2.38,\ 7.00,\ 1.5,\ 3.0)$

$X_{gB}=X_{15}=ScCl_3=(3,\ 7,\ 2.08,\ 7.00\ 1.3,\ 3.0)$

$g(X_2,\ X_{15})=0.1167529$

$W_A=(3.7,\ 6.5,\ 3.816,\ 7.975,\ 2.1,\ 3.4)$

$g(PF_3)=0.0065443>0, \quad g(GeCl_4)=0.0219994>0$

$g(TiCl_4)=0.0205191>0;$

$g(RbCl)=-0.0210813<0, \quad g(KI)= -0.0246605<0.$

Therefore we forecast samples PF_3, $Gecl_4$, $Ticl_4$ to belong to class A-convalent compounds ; RbCl, KI to class B-ionic compounds.

The results of classification is concordant with the results of the experiment in chemistry.

REFERENCES

1. S.P.LOU & Z.X.Tong, An Algorithm for Finding the Transitive Closure of a Fuzzy Matrix, Journal of Shanghai Railway Institute, 1(1981), 37-42, (in Chinese).

2. E.M. Reingold, J.Neivergelt and N.Deo, "Combinatorial Algorithms: Theory and Practice" by Prentice-Hall, Inc, Englewood Cliffs. New Jersey 1977.

3. S. Tamura, S. Higuchi and K. Tanaka, "Pattern Classification Based on Fuzzy Relations" IEEE Trans. SMC-1, 1971, 61-66.

S.P.Lou graduated from Nanding University in 1962. He is the director of Multivalue Logic and Fuzzy Mathematics Research Section, Shanghai Railway Institute, Shanghai, China. Since 1981, he has been the Editor-in-chief of the journal of "Fuzzy Mathematics". His forty theses and three works on Fuzzy Mathematics, Multivalue Logic and Graph Theory have been published. He was given the Invention Achievement Award of the first grade by the Ministry of Railway of China in 1978.

W.C. Cheng graduated from Tangshan Institute

of Railway Technology in 1961. He is the editors of the journal of "Fuzzy Mathematics" published in China. He has been working on various topics in ptre and applied mathematics, such as fuzzy mathematics with its applications to weather forecasting, earthquake forecasting and pattern recognition and the evaluation of system reliability.

L.M. Chao graduated from Fu Dan University in Shanghai in 1968. His interests are in the area of fuzzy mathematics, discrete mathematics and computer science.

Approximate Reasoning in Decision Analysis
M.M. Gupta and E. Sanchez (eds.)

A FUZZY SET MODEL FOR THE EVALUATION OF BEST MANAGEMENT PRACTICES IN NONPOINT SOURCE WATER POLLUTION POLICY FORMULATION

Augustine O. Esogbue

School of Industrial and Systems Engineering
Georgia Institute of Technology
Atlanta, Georgia, U.S.A.

One of the dilemmas of State Planning Agencies in the U.S. relative to nonpoint source (NPS) water pollution control is the preponderance of factors which are essentially uncertain and fuzzy. The most prevalent technology for dealing with this problem is the so called best management practices. The effectiveness of these methods have not been hitherto scientifically determined or proved. This paper presents a methodology for evaluating their effectiveness. The approach is a hierarchical one employing the tools of fuzzy sets and fuzzy clustering techniques to collect, group, and analyze evaluative responses of planners and developers to essentially subjective questions. The output is two sets of quantitative values indicating to policy makers the effectiveness of BMP's recommended for controlling NPS water pollution.

KEYWORDS

Water Pollution Control, Best Management Practices, Fuzzy Hierarchical Model, Fuzzy Clustering Algorithm

INTRODUCTION

Water pollution control planning has now begun to focus on two major sources of water quality degredation--point source and nonpoint source. For quite some time, the attention of planners had been focused on point sources of pollution. There is however, mounting evidence that nonpoint sources of pollution are considerable contributers to the degredation of water resource quality.

For example, it is now known that a significant amount of the nutrients present in reservoirs and river basins is due to nonpoint sources.[5] Two major types of nonpoint sources have been singled out for intensive studies. These are agricultural and urban run off in nature. In each case, the technology for modeling and controlling the resultant problems lags behind that developed for point sources. This is due in part to the complexity of the problems which invariably are large and sociotechnical in nature.

THE PROBLEM

The accepted approach for the management of nonpoint sources of pollution is the concept of Best Management Practices (BMP's). A major objective of many of the 208 Areawide Planning Agencies in the United States today is the development and implementation of a set of BMP's suitable to the political, economic, social, and ecological uniqueness of their area.

Minton et al.[3] consider one of the more important questions to be asked concerning enforcements to be the relationship between Best Management Practices (BMP's) and receiving water standards. Those that are trying to implement a BMP program are finding themselves in violation of agency rules because receiving standards still have not been met. They must also concern themselves with the procedures a regulatory agency must use to determine the relative success of a BMP program.

Clearly then, the effectiveness of a set of BMP's must be determined to aid the implementation of such a policy. No satisfactory model for the determination of the effectiveness of BMP's exist today. This is due in part to the use of both structural and non-structural BMP measures. A structural measure would be a riprap sediment basin, etc., while a non-structural one would be street sweeping, litter control, etc. While experimental studies help to explicate the problem of the effectiveness of structural measures, they are inadequate for the equally important non-structural measures. The use of fuzzy sets based approaches to incorporate both of these measures is the subject of research reported in this effort. In particular, the effectiveness of the use of BMP's as a control alternative for nonpoint source pollution policy formulation is the central focus.

THE MODEL

Our model is an adaptation of a generic model developed earlier[1] and reported recently[2] with regards to the evaluation of public participation effectiveness measurement. It is essentially a multi-level hierarchical approach to the disaggregation of a problem into its constituent levels and sub levels.

As can be seen, the configuration of the model is cascade. A factor is evaluated by its directly descendant factors or subfactors. This configuration suggests that the only actual evaluation (data collection) that needs to be made is the evaluation of the resultant basic factors. Basic factors are defined as the factors which do not possess any descendant factors. Such factors are said to be dangling.

To measure the effectiveness of a set of proferred BMP's, we consider a number of constituent factors. Each factor is then broken down into subfactors which in turn are further subdivided into a number of descendant factors. We thus obtain a tree-like structure consisting of nodes and branches. A cascaded model of the system clearly results as shown in Figure 1 below.

Let $E(\cdot)$ = effectiveness of the set of BMP's depending on a set of constituent factors $\{x: x_1, x_2, \ldots, x_n\}$. We consider two measures $\{x^\alpha\}$ and $\{x^\beta\}$, the pessimistic and optimistic measures respectively. The pessimistic value, derived using the concept of pessimistic aggregation, assumes a worst case evaluation. It uses the operation of fuzzy intersection. The optimistic value, derived using the concept of optimistic aggregation assumes the best case evaluation and employs the operation of the union of fuzzy sets. Thus,

$$E(\cdot) = \{E(x^\alpha), E(x^\beta)\} \tag{1}$$

THE GENERIC MODEL

For nonbasic factors, i.e., those at higher levels in the hierarchy, we proceed as follows:

Let $f_{ij\ell}$ = descendant ℓ of subfactor f_{ij}, $\{\ell=1,2,\ldots,n_j\}$. Consider subfactor f_{ij} at level or stage 2 with descendant $f_{ij\ell}$. $j=1,2,\ldots,n_i$; $i=1,2,\ldots,s$. Thus

$$f_{ij} = \{f_{ij1}, f_{ij2}, \ldots, f_{ijn_j}\} \tag{2}$$

Let $x^\alpha_{ij\ell}(g)$ = pessimistic value of subfactor $f_{ij\ell}$ provided by evaluator g, $g=1,2,\ldots,G$, and $x^\beta_{ij\ell}(g)$ = optimistic value of subfactor $f_{ij\ell}$ provided by evaluator g. Then

$$x^\alpha_{ij}(g) = x^\alpha_{ij1}(g) \wedge x^\alpha_{ij2}(g) \wedge \ldots \wedge x^\alpha_{ijn_j}(g) = \bigcap_{\ell=1}^{n_j} x^\alpha_{ij\ell}(g) \tag{3}$$

Let $w^{(g)}_{ij\ell}$ = importance of subfactor $f_{ij\ell}$, $\forall\ \ell\varepsilon n_j$ provided by evaluator g. Then the weighted pessimistic evaluation,

$$_w x^\alpha_{ij}(g) = \bigcap_{\ell=1}^{n_j} (x^\alpha_{ij\ell}(g))^{w_{ij\ell}(g)} \tag{4}$$

Correspondingly, the optimistic value

$$_w x^\beta_{ij}(g) = \bigcup_{\ell=1}^{n_j} (x^\beta_{ij\ell}(g))^{w_{ij\ell}(g)} \tag{5}$$

Given $\{x^\alpha_{ij}(g),\ g=1,2,\ldots,G\}$, define a new set

$$\hat{x}^\alpha_{ij} \leftarrow \frac{\sum_{g=n_g}^{G'} x^\alpha_{ij}(g)}{G'} \tag{6}$$

where n_g = number of elements of G and G' is the number of clusters into which the set of G elements is divided.

Then at level 3, with descent f_{ij}, we have

$$f_i = \{f_{i1}, f_{i2}, \ldots, f_{in_i}\} \tag{7}$$

and

$$x^\alpha_i = \hat{x}^\alpha_{i1} \wedge \hat{x}^\alpha_{i2} \wedge \ldots \wedge \hat{x}^\alpha_{in_i} = \bigcap_{j=1}^{n_i} \hat{x}^\alpha_{ij} \tag{3}$$

or

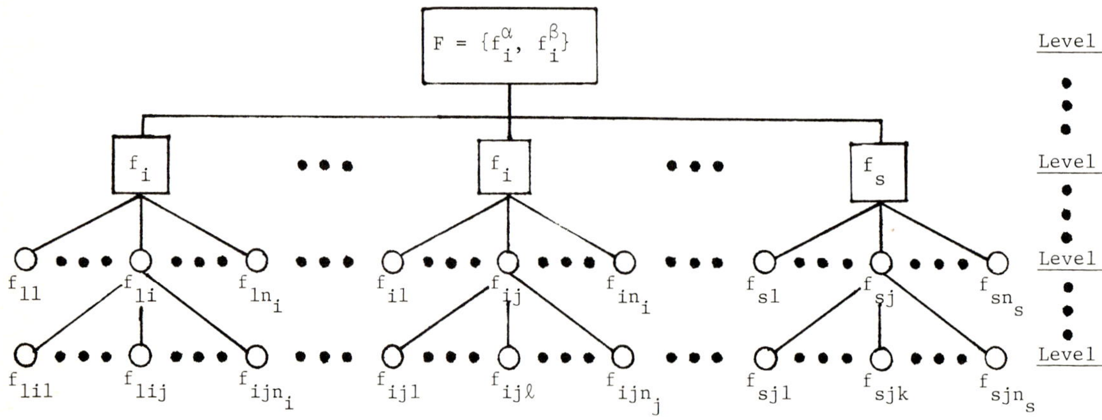

Figure 1. Measurement of BMP effectiveness as a 4 level cascade system.

$$_w x_i^{\alpha} = \bigcap_{j=1}^{n_j} (\hat{x}_{ij}^{\alpha})^{\hat{w}_i} \quad (9)$$

where

$$\hat{w}_i = \frac{\sum_{g=1}^{G} w_i(g)}{G} \quad (10)$$

and $w_i(g)$ = importance of factor i relative to all other factors descendant from level 3 as rated by evaluator g.

Correspondingly,

$$_w x_i^{\beta} = \bigcup_{j=i}^{n_i} (\hat{x}_{ij}^{\beta})^{\hat{w}_i} \quad (11)$$

Finally, define x^{α}, the pessimistic value of BMP effectiveness as x^{α}: $\{x_i^{\alpha}\}$ i=1,2,...,I

$$_w x^{\alpha} = \bigcap_{i=1}^{I} (x_i^{\alpha})^{\hat{w}_i} \quad (12)$$

where $_w x^{\alpha}$ is the weighted pessimistic value, and $_w x^{\beta}$, the weighted optimistic value =

$$\bigcup_{i=1}^{I} (x_i^{\beta})^{\hat{w}_i} \quad (13)$$

This approach has worked well in evaluating data which are imbued with a high degree of imprecision.

<u>For basic factors</u>, i.e., those at the lowest level of the hierarchy. These values together with the weightings of the component factors at each level are the only field data needed. They are derived by fuzzifying the linguistic variables. The primary terms of these fuzzy sets are first determined and then compatibility functions derived. The collected data are aggregated using fuzzy theory. Several clustering methods exist but the approach we use is heuristic.[2] From Figure 1 the data in question relates to the evaluation by each respondent of the various subfactors and their constituents in Level 1. Symbolically, these are: $\{f_{1i1},\ldots,f_{1ij},\ldots,f_{1jn_i}\}$, $\{f_{ij1},\ldots,f_{ijk},\ldots,f_{ijn_j}\}$ and $\{f_{sj1},\ldots,f_{sjk},\ldots,f_{sjn_s}\}$.

AN APPLICATION TO BMPs

The control of water quality from nonpoint source pollution is expected to respond to a set of planning criteria $\zeta = \{f_i\}$ which are essentially fuzzy with respect to implementation. We wish to quantify and evaluate these measures.

Let F = Effectiveness of a set of BMPs applied to meet the expectation of the set of planning criteria, ξ

$E(X^{\alpha}),(X^{\beta})$ = the pessimistic and optimistic evaluations respectively of system effectiveness, F

f_i = planning criterion i; for example, f_1

f_1 = the criterion of retaining sediment

f_{ij} = the consideration of planning criterion i on location j in the environment.

$f_{ij\ell}$ = the ℓ-th BMP used to meet criterion i on environmental location j

$X_{ij\ell}(g)$ = value of BMP $f_{ij\ell}$ provided by evaluator g familiar with the process. g=1,2,...,G.

Tables 1, 2, and 3 present sample factors and subfactors defined in the foregoing for the BMP effectiveness model. The fuzziness and imprecision characteristic of these variables is evident. The state of knowledge regarding their meaning and effectiveness is equally fuzzy and subjective. Thus it is important to derive some consensus of quantitative feeling as to their values. The experience of different users, developers and planners with these BMPs must be assessed in a systematic manner.

Table 1: Planning Criteria f_i, i=1,2,3,4

f_i	Description
f_1	Retain sediment
f_2	Retain or accomodate runoff
f_3	Minimize exposure to erosive elements and stabilize critical development areas
f_4	improve surface drainage

Table 2: An Example of f_{ij} - Location factors for f_1

f_{11} = Retain sediment on the general development area

f_{12} = Retain sediment along driveways on development site

Table 3: An Example of BMPs for Subfactor $f_{ij\ell} - f_{11\ell}$

(NOTE: See Table 5 for a definition of these BMPs)

f_{111} = Gabion

f_{112} = Riprap

f_{113} = Sediment barrier

f_{114} = Sediment basin

f_{115} = Sediment trap

f_{116} = Toe berm

In an actual application of this model to measure the effectiveness of BMPs, there were three levels in the model. The mathematical symbols and their meanings may be found in Table 4, the glossary of symbols. A questionnaire was designed to collect data for the study. Table 5 gives a sample of this questionnaire as it relates to planning criterion 1, the retention of sediment.

Table 4: Glossary of Symbols in Figure 1

Symbol	Meaning
Level 3:	
f_i	Planning criteria
f_1	Retain sediment
f_2	Retain or accomodate runoff
f_3	Minimization of exposure to erosive elements and stabilization of critical development areas
f_4	Improvement of surface drainage
Level 2:	
f_{ij}	Locations where BMPs are used
f_{11}	On the general development area
f_{12}	Along driveways on development site
f_{21}	On general development area
f_{31}	On general development area
f_{41}	On general development area

Table 4: (continued)

Symbol	Meaning
Level 1:	
f_{ijk}	BMPs used
f_{111}	Gabion
f_{112}	Riprap
f_{113}	Sediment barrier
f_{114}	Sediment basin
f_{115}	Sediment trap
f_{116}	Toe berm
f_{121}	Filter berms
f_{122}	Construction exits
f_{123}	Haulageways
f_{211}	Dikes
f_{212}	Downdrain structures
f_{213}	Subsurface drains
f_{214}	Level spreader
f_{215}	Storm drain outlet protection
f_{216}	Vertical drains
f_{311}	Buffer zones
f_{312}	Temporary seeding
f_{313}	Mulching
f_{314}	Topsoiling
f_{411}	Land smoothing

PRELIMINARY RESULTS AND ANALYSIS

Values of nonbasic factors, $f_{ij\ell}$ for this model were obtained through a mailed questionnaire administered to planners in the region. The relative weights $w_{ij\ell}$ were, for the purposes of model validation, randomly generated. The clustering of values provided by the evaluators into

Table 5: Sample Questionnaire for Planning Criteria 1

1. Retain Sediment

A. On the general development area.

BMP 1-A-1

Gabion - (large multicelled rectangular wire mesh boxes used in construction of revetments, dams, etc.)

Absolute system effectiveness		Cost Effectiveness	
0	1	0	1
Not effective at all	Very effective	Not cost effective at all	Very cost effective

Is this BMP operative in your area? Yes _____ No _____

BMP 1-A-2

Riprap - (revetment of loose rock or similar material on cut or fill face)

0	1	0	1
Not effective at all	Very effective	Not cost effective at all	Very cost effective

Is this BMP operative in your area? Yes _____ No _____

BMP 1-A-3

Sediment Barrier - (barrier or diversions of sandbags by bales of filtering materials)

0	1	0	1
Not effective at all	Very effective	Not cost effective at all	Very cost effective

Is this BMP operative in your area? Yes _____ No _____

BMP 1-A-4

Sediment Basin - (basin created by the construction of a barrier to retain runoff and trap sediment)

0	1	0	1
Not effective at all	Very effective	Not cost effective at all	Very cost effective

Is this BMP operative in your area? Yes _____ No _____

BMP 1-A-5

Sediment Trap - (impounding area formed by excavation of an area to trap sediment in storm water runoff)

0	1	0	1
Not effective at all	Very effective	Not cost effective at all	Very cost effective

Is this BMP operative in your area? Yes _____ No _____

Table 5: (continued)

BMP 1-A-6

Toe Berm - (compacted and vegetated ridge of soil to lower velocity of runoff water)

0	1	0	1
Not effective at all	Very effective	Not cost effective at all	Very cost effective

Is this BMP operative in your area? Yes ____ No ____

Importance

BMP	1	2	3	4	5	6
A-1						
A-2						
A-3						
A-4						
A-5						
A-6						

two groups was effected using the fuzzy clustering algorithm developed in 2. For comparative purposes, a fuzzy dynamic programming algorithm and a version of Bezdek's algorithm will also be used to analyze the data. The resultant effectiveness using our hierarchical model is $\left\{{}_wx^{\alpha}, {}_wx^{\beta}\right\} = \{0.272, 0.957\}$. The optimistic value appears high in this case. However, the actual weights will be generated through a delphi exercise using a panel of planners, developers, and citizens.

ACKNOWLEDGEMENTS

This research was supported in part by funds from the U.S. Department of the Interior, Office of Water Research and Technology under project B-147 GA at the Georgia Institute of Technology with the author as the principal investigator. The contributions of Dr. Daryl Chubin and Kok-Weay Looi are greatfully acknowledged.

REFERENCES

[1] Esogbue, A.O. and Ramesh, V., Dynamic programming and fuzzy allocation processes, Tech. Memo No. 202, Dept. of Operations Research, Case Western Reserve University (1970).

[2] Esogbue, A.O. and Ahipo, Z., A fuzzy sets model for measuring the effectiveness of public participation in water resources planning, Water Resources Bulletin, 18 (1982).

[3] Minton, G.R. et al., The relationship between best management practices and receiving water standards, Water Resources Bulletin, 14 (1978).

[4] Pheiffer, G.H. and Whittlessey, N.K., Controlling nonpoint externalities with input restrictions in an irrigated valley basin, Water Resources Bulletin, 14 (1978).

[5] Thackston, E.L. et al., Point source loads: not always cases in point, Water and Sewage Works (1978) 53-55.

PART NINE

BIOGRAPHICAL INFORMATION

Approximate Reasoning in Decision Analysis
M.M. Gupta and E. Sanchez (eds.)

BIOGRAPHICAL INFORMATION ABOUT THE EDITORS AND CONTRIBUTING AUTHORS

Klaus-Peter Adlassnig
Department of Medical Computer Sciences, University of Vienna, A-1090 Vienna, Garnisongasse 13, Austria.
Dr. Klaus-Peter Adlassnig is a Systems Analyst at the Computer Centre of the Vienna University Medical School. He received a diploma in Computer Sciences from the Technical University of Dresden in 1974. His research interests lie in the areas of medical computer sciences, especially medical diagnosis and therapy, evaluation of medical data and computer-aided instruction in medicine.

David I. Blockley
Department of Civil Engineering, University of Bristol, Bristol, England.
Dr. D.I. Blockley has been a Lecturer in Civil Engineering since 1969. He is a graduate of the University of Sheffield, obtaining the B.Eng. and Ph.D. degrees in Civil Engineering in 1964 and 1967 respectively. From 1967 to 1969 he was a Development Engineer for the British Constructional Steelwork Association. He is a Member of the Institution of Civil Engineers and in 1978 was awarded their highest prize, the Telford Medal, for his paper "Analysis of Structural Failures".
As Chairman of the Western Counties Branch of the Institution of Structural Engineers (1980-81), he was actively involved in both the theory and the practice of engineering. He is the author of many technical papers on structural design as well as acting as an engineering consultant.

Piero P. Bonissone
General Electric Company, Corporate Research and Development, 1 River Road, 37-567, Schenectady, NY 12345, USA.
Dr. P.P. Bonissone is a Systems Engineer in the Knowledge Based Systems Program at the General Electric Company, Corporate Research and Development in Schenectady, New York. He is also an Adjunct Assistant Professor of Electric Computer and Systems Engineering at the Rensselaer Polytechnic Institute, Troy, New York. He received a Ph.D. degree in Electric Engineering and Computer Sciences from the University of California, Berkeley, CA. His research interests include expert systems, fuzzy sets, natural language processing, decision analysis, pattern rcognition and interactive graphics.

Vladimir B. Cervin
RR 2, Harrow, Ontario, NOR 1G0, Canada.
Dr. V. Cervin has a Ph.D. in Social Psychology and a doctorate in the social sciences. He has just retired from the University of Windsor where he was Professor of Experimental and Applied Psychology and is now in private practice. He has published widely in the theory of learning and mathematical psychology and is currently interested in the application of fuzzy algorithms to description of the procedures of behaviour modification.

Stefan Chanas
Institute of Management, Technical University of Wroclaw, Poland.
Dr. S. Chanas is a Lecturer in Operations Research. He received a M.S. degree in Mathematics from the University of Warsaw in 1969 and the Ph.D. degree in Management Science from the Technical University of Warsaw in 1977. Currently, his research interests include operations research, decision making theory and the application of fuzzy set theory to these areas.

L.M. Chao
Research Section of Multivalued Logic and Fuzzy Systems, Shanghai Railway Institute, Shanghai, People's Republic of China.
Dr. L.M. Chao graduated from Fu Dan University in Shanghai in 1968. His interests are in the area of fuzzy mathematics, discrete mathematics and computer science.

Biswa Nath Chatterji
Department of Electronics & Electrical Communication Engineering, Indian Institute of Technology, Kharagpur, West Bengal, India 721302.
Dr. B.N. Chatterji is a Professor of Electronics and Electrical Communication Engineering. He received the B.Tech. (Hons.) and Ph.D. degree from Indian Institute of Technology, Kharagpur in 1965 and 1970 respectively. He worked as Assistant Development Engineer at Telerad Pvt. Ltd. Bombay and Senior Research Fellow at Central Electronics Engineering Research Institute, Pilani in the years 1965 and 1965-66 respectively. He joined the Indian Institute of Technology, Kharagpur in 1967 as a faculty member. His interests lie in the area of pattern recognition learning systems, system identification, signal processing, data reduction, picture processing, simulation techniques and microprocessor based systems. He has published extensively internationally and has written two books "Digital Computer Technology" and "System Identification Techniques". He leads the Control and Automation Engineering and Remote Sensing groups of Indian Institute of Technology, Kharagpur and is Fellow of the Institute of Electronics and Telecommunication Engineers (India) and India Society of Engineers.

B.B. Chaudhuri
Electronics and Communication Sciences Unit, Indian Statistical Institute, Calcutta, India.
Dr. B.B. Chaudhuri was born in 1950. He received the B.Sc. (Hons.) and B.Tech. degrees in 1969, 1972 and 1974 respectively and the Ph.D. degree from the Indian Institute of Technology, Kharagpur in 1980. His fields of interest include optical communication, image processing and pattern recognition. He has nearly 25 papers to his credit, He is a Computer Engineer in the Electronics and Communication Sciences Unit, Indian Statistical Institute, Calcutta. He is a Fellow of the Optical Society of India, Member of the Computer Society of India and Member of the IEEE. He is currently in the Department of Physics, Queen's University of Belfast where he is carrying out research as a Visiting Fellow.

Wuling Chen
Beijing Hospital of Traditional Chinese Medicine, People's Republic of China.
Dr. W. Cheu is a Physician. She is mainly interested in computerized medical diagnosis systems and medical data base.

Wei-min Cheng
Department of Automation, Tsinghua University, Beijing, People's Republic of China.
Dr. Wei-min Cheng was born in Shandon, China, 1923. He graduated in 1947 from the Department of Electrical Engineering of Tsinghua University. His research interests include optimal control, optimization, decision analysis and large scale systems. Professor Cheng is a member of The Board of Directors of The Chinese Association of Automation and The Board of Directors of The Chinese Association of Systems Engineering.

Wha-cheng Cheng
Research Section of Multivalued Logic and Fuzzy System, Shanghai Railway Institute, Shanghai, People's Republic of China.

Luo Cheng-zhong
Associate Director of Department of Mathematics, Beijing Normal University, People's Republic of China.
Professor L. Cheng-zhong is an Associate Professor at Beijing Normal University. His current research interest include fuzzy matrices, fuzzy groups and fuzzy algebras.

Vladimir Dimitrov
International Institute of Management Science, Shepkina Str. 8, 129090, Moscow, USSR.
Dr. V. Dimitrov was born in 1942 in Ezerche, Bulgaria. He received the Ph.D. degree in Engineering Cybernetics from the Politechnical Institute in Kiev, USSR. He has published over 50 papers on decision-making, fuzzy sets and the management of human systems. He worked until 1978 in the Mathematical Institute of the Bulgarian Academy of Sciences and is presently in the International Institute of Management Sciences in Moscow.

Kofi Kissi Dompere
Department of Economics, Howard University, Washington, D.C., 20059, USA.
Professor K. K. Dompere is an Assistant Professor of Economics. He graduated from Temple University in Mathematical and Economic Sciences. He is a Research Fellow of The African Institute of Applied Mathematical and Ideologial Sciences (AMIS) and a member of a number of international organizations of science. His research interests include fuzzy mathematics, optimal control theory, fuzzy decision theory and their applications to economics and statistics. In addition, he has special interest in the epistemoliogical problems of science.

Caroline M. Eastman
Department of Mathematics and Computer Science, Florida State University, Tallahassee, Florida 32306, USA.
Dr. C.M. Eastman is an Assistant Professor of Mathematics and Computer Science at the the Florida State University at Tallahasse. She received the B.A. degree in Applied Mathematics from Radcliffe College and the M.S. and Ph.D. degrees in Computer Science from the University of North Caroline at Chapel Hill. Her current research interests include data base management systems and information retrieval systems. She is the author of several papers in these fields.

Autustine O. Esogbue
School of Industrial and Systems Engineering, Georgia Institute of Technology, Atlanta, Georgia 30332 U.S.A..
Dr. A.O. Esogbue is a Professor of Industrial and Systems Engineering at the Georgia Institute of Technology, Atlanta, Georgia, an Adjunct Professor of Community Medicine at the School of Medicine, Morehouse College and an Adjunct Professor of Mathematics and Computer Science at Atlanta University. He earned his Ph.D. in Engineering from the University of Southern California, Los Angeles in 1968, his M.S. in Industrial and Management Engineering from Columbia University, New York in 1965 and his B.S. in Electrical Engineering from the University of California, Los Angeles in 1964. He was formerly a Development Engineer at the Water Resources Center, UCLA, Research Associate (engineering and medicine) at the University of Southern California, and an Assistant Professor of Operations Research at Case Western Reserve University, Cleveland, Ohio. His research interests include the application of mathematical programming and fuzzy sets to various decision processes particularly healthcare and water resources. He is co-author with Bellman and Nabeshima of "Mathematical Aspects of Scheduling and Applications" (Pergamon 1982).

V.V. Fedorov
Institute for Systems Studies, Moscow, USSR.
Dr.V.V. heads the Laboratory of Mathematical Statistics. He received a Ph.D. and D.S. in mathematics from the Moscow State University. His research interest is in the area of statistics and system studies. He is an author of Theorv of Optimal Experiments (Academic Press, 1972.)

Marius Fieschi
Laboratoire de Biomathematiques, tatistiques Medicales et Epidemiologiques, Informatique, Faculte de Medecine Marseilles, France.
Dr. M. Fieschi is currently Chef de Travaux de Faculte-Assistant des Hoptiaux in the Department of Medical Informatics of the Faculte de Medecine in Marseilles. He received his Ph.D. in Physics in 1972 from the Faculte des Science de Marseille and in Medecine de Marseille. He is mainly interested in applications in medical decision of artificial intelligence.

Dominique Fieschi
Laboratoire de Biomathematiques, Statistiques Medicales et Epidemiologiques, Informatique, Faculte de Medecine Marseilles, France.
Dr. D. Fieschi is currently an Attachee de Faculte-Assistante de Sciences Fondamentales in the Department of Medical Informatics Faculte de Medecine in Marseilles. She received a D.E.A. in Computer Science in 1973 from the Faculte des Sciences de Bordeaux. Her current research interests include applications in medical decision of artificial intelligence.

Joan M. Francioni
Department of Mathematics and Computer Science, Florida State University, Tallahassee, Florida 32306, USA.
Dr. J.M. Francioni received the B.S. degree in 1977 from the University of New Orleans, New Orleans, and the M.S. and Ph.D. degrees from Florida State University, Tallahassee in 1979 and 1981 respectively in Computer Science. Dr. Francioni is a member of Pi Mu Epsilon, Sigma Xi, and the Association for Computing Machinery.

Christian Freksa
Department of Biostatistics, Max Planck Institute for Psychiatry, Munich, West Germany.
Dr. C. Freksa is currently a Thyssen Foundation Research Fellow at the Max Planck Institute for Psyschiatry. He received a Ph.D. in Electrical Engineering and Computer Sciences with specialization in Artificial Intelligence from the University of California at Berkeley in 1981. His research interests include representation of imprecise knowlege, expert systems, and computer models of cognitive processes.

King-Sun Fu
School of Electrical Engineering, Purdue University, West Lafayette, IN., 47907, U.S.A..
Dr. King-sun Fu was born in 1930. He received the B.S. degree from National Taiwan University in 1953, M.A.Sc. degree from the University of Toronto in 1955, and Ph.D. degree from the University of Illinois in 1959, all in Electrical Engineering. From 1959 to 1960, he was a research engineer at Boeing Airplane Company. He joined Purdue University in 1960 as an Assistant Professor, was promoted to Associate Professor in 1963 and to Professor in 1966. In 1975 he was appointed Goss Distinguished Professor of Engineering at Purdue University. He is a Fellow of the Institute of Electrical and Electronic Engineers, a member of the National Academy of Engineering and Academia Sinica, and a Guggenheim Fellow. He received the Herbert N. McCoy Award for contributions to science in 1976, the Outstanding Paper Award of the IEEE Computer Society in 1977 and the 1981 ASEE Senior Research Award. He is the Vice President for Publications of the IEEE Computer Society, an Associate Editor of IEEE Transactions on Systems, Man and Cybernetics, Pattern Recognition, Computer Graphics and Image Processing, Journal of Cybernetics, and Information Sciences, and a member of the editorial board of the International Journal of Computer and Information Sciences. He is the first President of the International Association for Pattern Recognition (IAPR). He is author of the books, "Sequential Methods in Pattern Recognition" and "Syntactic Methods in Pattern Recognition", published by Academic Press in 1968 and 1974, "Statistical Pattern Classification Using Contextual Information", published by John Wiley & Sons in 1980, and "Syntactic Pattern Recognition and Applications" by Prentice-Hall in 1982, respectively.

Rongjian Guo
Institute of Automation, Academia Sinica, People's Republic of China.
Dr. R. Guo is a Research Associate in Control Engineering and Computer Science. His current interests include artificial intellegence, fuzzy mathematics and their application in medical field.

Madan M. Gupta (Editor)
Cybernetics Research Laboratory, College of Engineering, University of Saskatchewan, Saskatoon, Saskatchewan, S7N 0W0 Canada.
Dr. M.M. Gupta was born in Lansdowne India. He received the B. Eng. (Honors) degree in 1961, and the M.Sc. degree in 1962, both in Electronics-Communications Engineering, from BITS Pilani, India. In 1964, he was awarded a British Commonwealth Research Fellowship for studies in the United

Kingdom, first at the Queen's University of Belfast, and then at the University of Warwick. He was awarded a Ph.D. in Adaptive Control Systems in 1967 from the University of Warwick. From 1962 to 1964, he was a Lecturer in Electrical-Communication Engineering at the University of Roorkee, India. He joined the faculty of the College of Engineering at the University of Saskatchewan in 1967 as a Sessional Lecturer, receiving a full professorship in July 1978. He received a Senior Industrial Fellowship from the National Research Council of Canada in 1975-1976 to work with MacMillan Bloedel Research Ltd. Dr. Gupta has initiated research in the areas of optimization and adaptive control, fuzzy automata and decision processes, signal processing, and robotics. His present research interest also includes the detection and diagnosis of incipient cardiac abnormalities. He has published very widely and has edited two books entitled "Fuzzy Automata and Decision Processes (1977)" and "Advances in Fuzzy Set Theory and Applications (1979)", both published by North Holland. He is an Advisory Editor of the International Journal of Fuzzy Sets and Systems. He is very active in the IEEE and the IFAC, and has served on several international program committees. Dr. Gupta is a Senior Member of the IEEE and also a Member of the New York Academy of Sciences and many other professional societies.

Miklos Hajnal

Department of Process Control, Technical University of Budapest, Hungary.

Dr. M. Hajnal is a Senior Assistant Professor of Measurement and Control Engineering. He received the M.S. degree in Electrical Engineering in 1976 and the Ph.D. degree in data processing/pattern recognition in 1980 from the Technical University of Budapest. His interests in research and education include pattern recognition, picture processing, fuzzy systems and their application in materials testing, quality control and robotics.

Fumio Hara

Department of Mechanical Engineering, Tokyo University of Science, Kagurazaka, Shinjuku-ku, Tokyo 162, Japan.

Dr. F. Hara is an Associate Professor of Mechanical Engineering at the Tokyo University of Science and a Research Associate of the Institute of Industrial Science at the University of Tokyo. He received the Ph.D. degree in Mechanical Engineering from the University of Tokyo in 1970. His main research interests include fuzzy theory applications to evacuation problems, man-machine communications and safety in large-scale systems.

Haruki Imaoka

Research Institute for Polymers and Textiles, Tsukuba, Japan.

Mitsuru Ishizuka

Institute of Industrial Science, University of Tokyo, Roppongi, Minato-ku, Tokyo, 106, Japan.

Dr. M. Ishizuka is an Associate Professor of Electronics Engineering at the University of Tokyo. He received the B.S., M.S. and Ph.D. degrees in Electronics Engineering from the University of Tokyo. Previously, he was with Yokosuka Electrical Communication Laboratory, N.T.T. and Purdue University. His research interests include artificial intelligence, image processing and communications systems.

Ramesh Jain

Dr. R. Jain is an Associate Professor of Computer Science at Wayne State University, Detroit. His current research interests are in the areas of artificial intelligence, computer vision and computer graphics. He formerly worked at the Indian Institute of Technology, Kharagpur, India, the University of Hamburg, Germany and the University of Texas at Austin. He is a member of the IEEE, ACM, Pattern Recognition Society and AAAI. He received his Ph.D. in Electronics and Electical Communication Engineering from I.I.T., Kharagpur in 1975.

Michel Joubert

Laboratorie de Biomathematiques, Statistiques Medicales et Epidemiologiques, Informatique, Faculte

de Medecine Marseilles, France.
Dr. M. Joubert is an Assistant de Faculte-Assistant des Hopitaux in the Department of Medical Informatics of the Faculte de Medecine in Marseille. He received the Ph.D. degree in Applied Informatics from the Faculte des Sciences of Marseille in 1974 and the Ph.D. degree in Biologic Humaine in 1981 from the Faculte de Medecine in Marseilles working on applications of artificial intelligence to medicine. Mainly, his research interests focus on techniques for man-machine communication in the medical field.

Vadim Kh. Kaipov
Institute of Automatics, the Academy of Science, Kirghiz SSR, Frunze, USSR.
Dr. V.Kh. Kaipov is Head of the Laboratory, Institute of Automatics and is Senior Scientific Researcher in Information Theory and Cybernetics. He received a D.S. (Automatic Control) 1969. His research interests include applications of fuzzy sets theory to model synthesis, control of processes, theory of measurement and adaptive control.

Abraham Kandel
Department of Mathematics and Computer Science, Florida State University, Tallahasse, Florida 32306 USA.
Dr. A. Kandel is with the Department of Mathematics and Computer Science, Florida State University, Tallahasse . He is a Professor and Director of Computer Science. He received the B.Sc. from the Technion-Israel Institute of Technology and the M.S. from the Universiy of California, Santa Barbara, both in Electrical Engineering and Computer Science. From 1970 to 1978 he was with the Computer Science Department at the New Mexico Institute of Mining and Technology. During 1976-1977 he was with Ben Gurion University of the Negev and Tel-Aviv University, Israel. His current research interests include fuzzy systems, computer architecture, pattern recognition, and theoretical computer science. He is the author of more than 80 papers in these fields and is the co-author (with Dr. Samuel C. Lee) of the monograph "Fuzzy Switching and Automata: Theory and Applications" (Crane, Russak & Co., N.Y.,1979).

Etienne E. Kerre
Seminar for Mathematical Analysis, State University of Gent, Gent, Belgium.
Dr. E.E. Kerre is a member of the academic staff of the Seminar for Mathematical Analysis and Nuclear Power Technology at the State Universtiy of Gent. He received his doctoral degree in mathematics from the State University of Gent in 1970 for research concerning a theoretical approach to low energy electron diffraction. He is co-author of three books on basic mathematics at the undergraduate level. Since 1977 he has worked on fuzzy set theory and its applications. He has published several papers on fuzzy topological spaces. His main topics of research interest are fuzzy topological and algebraic structures, applications of fuzzy set theory to medical diagnosis, information retrieval and database management.

Laszlo T. Koczy
Department of Communication Electronics, Technical University of Budapest, Budapest, Hungary.
Dr. L.T. Koczy is a Senior Assistant Professor Digital Systems and Switching Exchanges. He received the M.S. degrees in Electrical Engineering and in Measurement and Control Engineering in 1975 and 1976 respectively, and his Ph.D. degree in Fuzzy Systems in 1977 from the Technical University of Budapest. His research interests include fuzzy systems, search algorithms and control of switching exchanges.

Gernot Kolarz
Ludwig Boltzmann Institut fur Rheumatologi und Fokalgeschehen, A-2500 Baden, Kaiser Franz Ring 8, Austria
Dr. G. Kolarz is Assistant Professor of Internal Medicine at the University of Vienna and Medical Director of a hospital for rheumatic diseases at Baden. His research interest are rheumatic diseases including computer-aided diagnosis in rheumatology.

V.B. Kuz'min
Institute for Systems Studies, Moscow, USSR.
Dr. V.B. Kuz'min is a senior researcher in the Laboratory of Methods for Generating and Choice of Preferable Systems Variants. He received his Ph.D. from the Institute of Systems Studies. He is an author of Geometry of Spaces of Crisp and Fuzzy Relations (Nauka, 1982). His interests include group decision making and fuzzy sets.

Piero Laface
Politecnico di Torino, Istituto di Elettrotecnica Generale Corso Duca degli Abruzzi 24, 10129 Torino, Italy.
Dr. P. Laface received his doctoral degree from the Politecnico di Torino, Torino, Italy. He has worked on signal processing and pattern recognition, especially in the field of automatic speech recognition. His main research interests are the application of pattern recognition and artificial intelligence techniques to real world data analysis.

Leonardo Lesmo
Instituto di Scienze dell'Informazione, Universita di Torino, Torino, Italy.
Dr. L. Lesmo, after receiving a degree in Computer Science in 1974 from the University of Turin, Italy, was a Research Assistant at the Istituto di Scienze dell Informazione of the University of Turin form 1974 to 1978. Since 1978 he has taught a course on databases. His current research includes expert systems and natural language processing.

Yee Leung
Department of Geography, Chinese University of Hong Kong, People's Republic of China.
Dr. Y. Leung is a lecturer of Geography at the Chinese University of Hong Kong. He received his B.Sc. degree in Geography from the Chinese University of Hong Kong, and the M.A. and Ph.D. degree in Geography and the M.S. degree in Systems Engineering from the University of Colorado. His research interests include humanistic systems research, urban and regional planning, and the application of fuzzy sets theory to spatial anaylsis and planning.

Gaetan Libert
Faculte Polytechnique, Rue de Houtain 9 B 700, Mons, Belgium.
Dr. G. Libert was born in Jemappes, Belgium, in 1953. He received the Ingenieur Civil degree from the Institute of Technology, Mons, Belgium in 1977, and completed a Ph.D. dissertation in Applied Statistics at that institution in 1981, where he was been a Research Scientist in the Department of Computer Science and Management since 1977. He has published several papers on time series analysis, cluster analysis and pattern recognition.

S.P. Lou
Research Section of Multivalued Logic and Fuzzy Systems, Shanghai Railway Institute, Shanghai, People's Republic of China.
Dr. S.P. Lou graduated from Nanking University in 1962. He is the Director of the Multivalue Logic and Fuzzy System Research Section, Shanghai Railway Institute, Shanghai, China. Since 1981, he has been the Editor-in-Chief of the journal Fuzzy Mathematics. He has published on fuzzy mathematics, multivalue logic and graph theory. He was given the Invention Achievement Award, first grade, by the Ministry of Railway of China in 1978.

Mou-chao Ma
Institute of Psychology Academia, Beijing, People's Republic of China.
Dr. Mou-chao Ma is a Research Associate in Psychology. He is an adviser to the Journal of China Advertising and a member of the Editorial Board of the Journal of Fuzzy Mathematics. He is currently interested in the empirical aspects of fuzzy set theory and fuzzy set methods, and their applications to psychological research.

Binrong Ma
Beijing Second Medical College, People's Republic of China
Dr. B. Ma is a Lecture of Mathematics. His research interests are biomedical mathematics and application of computer in medical information processing.

D.D. Majumder
Electronics and Communication Sciences Unit, Indian Statistical Institute, Calcutta, India.

Ramon Lopez de Mantaras
Facultat d'Informatica, Universitat Politechnica, Barcelona, Spain.
Dr. R. Lopez de Mantaras is an Adjunct Professor at the Department of Mathematical Methods in Computer Science of the Facultat d'Informatica in Barcelona. He received a Docteur de Specialite degree in Automatic Control in 1977 from the Universite Paul Sabatier in Toulouse, a M.S. degree in Engineering (Computer Science) in 1979 from the University of California at Berkeley and a doctorate in Computer Science in 1981 from the Facultat d'Informatica of the Universitat Politecnica in Barcelona. His research interests include learning systems, pattern recognition and expert systems.

Josep Aguilar Martin
Laboratoire d'Automatique et d'Analyse des Systemes (LAAS) du Centre National de la Recherche Scientifique (CNRS), Toulouse, France.
Dr. J.A. Martin is a Maitre de Recherche at the LAAS of the CNRS in Toulouse. He received the Docteur es Sciences degree in 1974 from the Universite Paul Sabatier in Toulouse. His interests include stochastic systems, learning systems, pattern classification and expert systems.

Masaharu Mizumoto
Department of Management Engineering, Osaka Electro-Communication University, Neyagawa, Osaka 572, Japan.
Dr. M. Mizumoto, a Professor of Information Science, received the B.Eng., M.Eng. and Dr. Eng. degrees in Electrical Engineering from Osaka University, Japan, in 1966, 1968 and 1971, respectively. In 1980-81 he was an Alexander von Humboldt Foundation Fellow at the Technical University of Aachen, West Germany. His research interests include fuzzy set theory and its applications to artificial intelligence, decision-making, data base systems and robot planning. He is an advisory editor of International Journal of Fuzzy Sets and Systems, an editor of Journal of the Institute of Electronics and Communication Engineers of Japan, a foreign correspondent of the Bulletin for Studies and Exchanges on Fuzziness and its Applications, and an honorary member of the editorial board of Journal of Fuzzy Mathematics.

Renato De Mori
Istituto di Scienze dell'Informazione, Universita di Torino Corso Massimo D'Azeglio 42, 10125 Torino, Italy.
Dr. R. De Mori received the doctoral degree in Electronic Engineering form Politecnico di Torino, Turin, Italy. In 1976 he became Professor and Head of the Institute of Computer Sciences at the University of Turin. He acted as Chairman of Sections devoted to Pattern Recognition and Artificial Intelligence at World IFIP and Pattern Recognition Conferences and is Associate Editor of the Journal Singla Processing. He is author of many papers devoted to computer systems, pattern recognition and artifiical intelligence. His interests are in syntactic pattern recognition, knowledge representation and organization of complex information systems.

Yajiro Morita
Tokyo Institute of Technology, 2-12-2 Oh-okayama, Meguro-ku, Tokyo 152 Japan.
Dr. Y. Morita is a Professor of Control Engineering. He received the B.E. degree (1955) in Mechanical Engineering from the University of Florida and the Ph.D. degree (1959) in Mechanical Engineering from the Pennsylvania State University. His research interests include temperature measurement and control technology and the fundamental theory of measurement.

Masao Mukaidono
Meiji University, Tama-ku, Kawasaki-shi, 214, Japan.
Dr. M. Mukaidono is a Professor of Electronics and Communication Engineering at Meiji University. He received a Ph.D. degree in Electrical Engineering (fail-safe logic system) from Meiji University in 1970. His research interests include multiple-valued logic, fault-tolerant computing systems and CAD.

Alan M. Norwich
Department of Industrial Engineering, Faculty of Applied Science and Engineering, University of Toronto, Toronto, M5S 1A4, Canada.
Mr. A.M. Norwich is a graduate student completing his Ph.D. in Industrial Engineering at the University of Toronto, where he earned the degrees of B.A.Sc. in Engineering Science and M.A.Sc. in Biomedical Engineering. He has presented and published papers on information theory and on fuzzy set theory.

Ario Ohsato
Yokohama National University, Tokiwadai, Hodogaya-ku, Yokohama 240, Japan.
Dr. A. Ohsato is currently an Assistant Professor at the Department of Computer Engineering, Faculty of Engineering. He received the B.E. Degree in Mechanical Engineering in 1976 from Yokohama National University. His current research interests include mathematical programming, system engineering, fuzzy set theory, especially theoretical aspects on composite fuzzy relations, and their application to medical information processing systems.

Yuzo Oka
Tokyo Institute of Technology, 2-12-1 Oh-okayama, Meguro-ku, Tokyo 152 Japan.
Dr. Y. Oka is a Research Associate in Control Engineering. He received the B.E. degree (1967) in Textile Engineering from the Tokyo University of Agriculture and Technology and the M.E. degree (1969) in Textile Engineering from the Tokyo Institute of Technology. His research interests include foundations of measurement and system evaluation.

A. F. Rocha
Department of Pysiology and Biophysics, Institute of Biology, UNICAMP 13,100 Campinos, Brazil.
Dr. A.F. Roach obtained his M.D. degree from the University of Sao Paulo in 1970 and his Ph.D. degree and title of Professor from the State University of Campinas in 1973 and 1981, respectively. He is interested in the application of mathematics to neurophsiology, begun while an undergraduate student, and on language neurophysiology, fuzzy reasoning and learning, started just after his Ph.D. thesis in the mathematical analysis of pressor responses to peripheral and central stimulations.

Marc Roubens
Faculte Polytechnique, Rue de Houtain 9 B 700, Mons, Belgium.
Dr. M. Roubens received the Licence in Mathematics degree in 1963 from the University of Brussels and the doctorate in mathematics degree in 1968. Since 1972, he is Professor of Statistics and Operations Research at the Institute of Technology, Mons, Belgium. He has published over 35 papers in Revue de Statistique Appliquee, Metrika, Fuzzy Sets and Systems, European Journal of Operational Research, Discrete Applied Mathematics and other Journals, volumes and proceedings. He is Editorial Associate of the European Journal of Operations Research.

Michel Roux
Laboratoire de Biomathematiques, Statistiques Medicales et Epidemiologiques, Informatique, Faculte de Medecine Marseilles, France. Service de Statistiques Informatique Medicales et Epidemiologiques. Hopital de la Timone Marseille, France.
Professor M. Roux is Chief of the University's Laboratory and of the hospital's department. He received the M.D. degree in 1969, finished Computer Sciences in 1971 became Junior Professor in

1972 and Senior Professor 1979. His main interests are propositional logic and inference systems, and their medical decision making applications.

Lorenza Saitta
Istituto di Scienza dell'Informazione, Universita di Torino Corso Massimo D'Azeglio 42, 10125 Torino, Italy.
Dr. L. Saitta has worked on problems of knowledge representation and fuzzy decision processes since receiving her doctoral degree in Nuclear Engineering from the Politecnico di Torino, Italy. Her main interests are in the fields of pattern recognition and artificial intelligence, particular speech recognition.

Elie Sanchez (Editor)
Service Universitaire de Biomatheematiques, Faculte de Medecine, 27 Bd Jean Moulin, 13385 Marseille, Cedex 5, France.
Dr. E. Sanchez is a visiting Research Associate at the University of California, Berkeley, currently on leave from the Faculte de Medecine of Marseille. He received a Ph.D. in mathematics in 1972 from the Faculte des Sciences of Marseille and a Ph.D. in Biologie Humaine in 1974 from the Faculte de Medecine of Marseille. His current research interests include approximate reasoning in medicine, possibility theory, fuzzy logic, fuzzy numbers equations and expert systems.

Takashi Sekiguchi
Yokohama National University, Tokiwadai, Hodogaya-ku, Yokohama 240, Japan.
Dr. T. Sekiguchi is a Professor of Control Engineering and Computer Engineering. He received the B.E. degree in Electrical Engineering in 1959 from Yokohama National University, and the D.E. degree in Electrical Engineering in 1975 from Osaka University, Osaka, Japan. He is mainly interested in modern control theory, sequence control theory, and computer-aided medical information processing systems.

Yasuyoshi Sekita
School of Medicine, Tohoku University, Seiriyo-chpo, Sendai 980, Japan.
Dr. Y. Sekita is an Associate Fellow of the Medical Care and Hospital Administration. He received the M.A. degree in Economics in 1973 from Osaka University and graduated with a Ph.D. in Economics in 1975. His research interests include the application of fuzzy set theory to complex planning, diagnosis, hospital administration and statistics.

Aleksey A. Seliugin
Frunze Polytechnical Institute, Frunze, USSR.
Dr. A.A. Seliugin is Reader at the Frunze Polytechnical Institute. He received a D.S. (Automatic Control) in 1976. His research interests include fuzzy sets and their application to model synthesis, control of processes, pattern recognition and computer systems.

Gerard Soula
Laboratoire de Biomathematiques, Statistiques Medicales et Epidemiologiques,Informatique, Faculte de Medecine Marseilles, France.
Dr. G. Soula is Chef de Travaux de Faculte-Assistant des Hopitaux at Marselle. He received his Ph.D. in Sciences (security of computers) from the Universite Paul Sabatier of Toulouse in 1976 and his Ph.D. in Biologie Humaine (fuzzy sets and medical diagnosis) from the Faculte de Medecine of Marseille in 1981. His present research interests are fuzzy logic, decision making and its applications in medical diagnosis and therapeutic.

Michio Sugeno
Department of Systems Science, Tokyo Institute of Technology, Yokohama, Japan.

Jiri Sustal
Department of Mathematics, Technical University of Brno, Hilleho 6, 60200 Brno, Czechoslovakia.
Mr. J. Sustal is a Lecturer in Engineering Mathematics. He has degrees in Mathematics and Electrical Engineering. His research interests include various cybernetical disciplines among them fuzzy sets and systems.

Toshiro Terano
Faculty of Engineering, Hosei University, Tokyo, Japan.

Z.X. Tong
Research Section of Multivalued Logic and Fuzzy Systems, Shanghai Railway Institute, Shanghai, People's Republic of China.
Dr. Z.X. Tong graduated from Nanking University in 1966. He is the Editor of the journal Fuzzy Mathematics published in China. He has been working on various topics in pure and applied mathematics, such as functions of complex variables, functional analysis, number theory, combinatorial mathematics, probability theory, fuzzy mathematics and combinatorial algorithms.

Pietro Torasso
Istituto di Scienze dell'Informazione, Universita di Torino, Torino, Italy.
Dr. P. Torasso received a degree in Computer Science from the University of Turin, Italy in 1974. From 1974 to 1978 he was a Research Assistant at the Instituto di Scienze dell'Informazione of the University of Turin. Since 1978 he has taught a course on artificial intelligence. His research interests include expert systems, natural language and learning methodologies.

Ismail B. Turksen
Department of Industrial Engineering, Faculty of Applied Science and Engineering, University of Toronto, Toronto, M5s 1A4, Canada.
Dr. I.B. Turksen is an Associate Professor of Industrial Engineering at the University of Toronto. He earned the degrees of B.S., M.S., and Ph.D. in Industrial Engineering and Operations Research, all from the University of Pittsburgh. He is a member of the Board of Advisors of the Encyclopedia of Computer Sciene and Technology and a senior member of the American Institute of Industrial Engineers. He was a member of the Board of Trustees of the American Institute of Industrial Engineers, Vice-President of Region XIV (Canada), and is the past President of Canadian Society for Industrial Engineering. He is a member of CORS/APEO. He has published and presented papers in the areas of operations research, information systems, scheduling, human error detection and control, and linguistic variable in fuzzy sets and systems.

A.I. Vereskov
Institute for Systems Studies, Moscow, USSR.
Mr. A.I. Vereskov is a researcher in the Laboratory of Mathematic Statistics. He received his M.S. degree from the Moscow State University. His interest includes statistics and system theory.

Chiu-feung Wu
Department of Automation, Tsinghua University, Beijing, People's Republic of China.
Dr. Chiu-feng Wu was born in Jiangsu, China, in 1936. He graduated in 1959 from the Department of Electrical Engineering of Tsinghua University, Beijing, China. He is a Lecturer at Automation at Tsinghua University. His current research interests are fuzzy decision, fuzzy control and distributed computer control.

Wen-li Xu
Department of Automation, Tsinghua University, Beijing, People's Republic of China.

Dr. Wen-li Xu was born in Jiangsu, China in 1947. He graduated in 1970 from the Department of Electrical Engineering of Tsinghua University, Beijing, China and received the M.Sc. degree in Control Engineering from Tsinghua University in 1981. His current research interests are optimal control, microcomputers and their applications.

James T.P. Yao
Purdue University, West Lafayette, Indiana, 47907 USA.
Dr. J.T.P. Yao is a Professor of Civil Engineering. He received the B.S.C.E. degree with honors, the M.S.C.E. and the Ph.D. degrees from the University of Illinois at Champaign-Urbana. His research interests include safety and reliability of structures, structural fatigue and structural control.

Cao Zhi-qiang
Institute of Automation, Academia Sinica, Beijing, People's Republic of China.
Dr. Cao Zhi-qiang graduated from the Department of Mathematics of the Chinese University of Science and Technology in 1969. He was an engineer at the Luoyang Tractor Factory, China from 1968-1978. In 1981 he graduated from the Graduate School of Academia Sinica. He has contributed book chapters on algebraic systems, on the application of fuzzy set theory to psychology, and numerous journal articles. His main research interests are in systems research, control theory, mathematical social sciences and psychology.

FUZZY INFORMATION AND DECISION PROCESSES

Edited By:

Madan M. Gupta
Cybernetics Research Laboratory
University of Saskatchewan
Saskatoon, Saskatchewan
Canada S7N 0W0

Elie Sanchez
Service Universitaire de Biomathematiques
Faculte de Medecine
Marseille Cedex 5
France

NORTH-HOLLAND
1982

CONTENTS TO "FUZZY INFORMATION AND DECISION PROCESSES"

FOREWORD vii

PREFACE viii

ACKNOWLEDGEMENTS ix

IN MEMORIAM: PROFESSOR JOSEPH KAMPE DE FERIET
HUNG T. NGUYEN xvii

PART ONE: FUZZY INFORMATION, AND ENTROPY

1. From Measures of Fuzziness To Booleanity Control
Teresa Riera and Enric Trillas 3

2. On Some Algebraic Aspects of the Measures of Fuzziness
Aldo De Luca and Settimo Termini 17

3. Ordering Via Fuzzy Entropy
Antonio Di Nola and Aldo G.S. Ventre 25

4. Ambiguity Based On the Concept of Subjective Entropy
Kaoru Hirota 29

5. Aspects for the Evaluation of Decision Situations
Ernest Czogała, Siegfried Gottwald and Witold Pedrycz 41

6. Complementation and Information on the Separating Power of a Fuzzy Set
Christiane Dujet 51

PART TWO: FUZZY PROBABILITY, FUZZY INTEGRALS, AND BELIEF FUNCTIONS

7. A Theory of Fuzzy Measures: A Survey
Erich Peter Klement 59

8. Some Problems In Fuzzy Probability
Cheng Zhaozhong and Liu Dsosu 67

9. The Structure of Fuzzy Lebesgue Measure
Zi-Xiao Wang 71

10. On Fuzzy Measure and Fuzzy Integral
S.T. Wierzchoń 79

11. Subjective Probability and Fuzzy Measures
Philippe Smets 87

12. Interpretation of Membership Functions of Fuzzy Sets in Terms of Plausibility and Belief
J. Kampé de Fériet 93

PART THREE: FUZZY MATHEMATICAL STRUCTURES

13. Modelling Vagueness
Heinz J. Skala 101

14. Approach to an Axiomatic Study on the Fuzzy Relations on Finite Sets
Jean-Pierre Olivier and Dany Serrato 111

15. A Generation of Fuzzy Category and Constructions of Invertible Elements in the Fuzzy Category
Ying-ming Liu 117

16. Graphs and Fuzzy Graphs
Umberto Cerruti 123

17. A f-Sets Universe $\tilde{V}$
Odile Botta and Marianne Delorme 133

18. Between Fuzzy Set Theory and Boolean Valued Set Theory
Zhang Jinwen 143

19. Cardinal and Ordinal Theories About Fuzzy Sets
Nicole Blanchard 149

PART FOUR: FORMALIZATION OF UNCERTAINTY

20. Some Foundational Problems in the Formalization of Vagueness
Guglielmo Tamburrini and Settimo Termini 161

21. On Several Representations of an Uncertain Body of Evidence
Didier Dubois and Henri Prade 167

22. Foundations for a Theory of Possibility
Robin Giles 183

23. Possibility Measures and Related Topics
Hung T. Nguyen 197

24. Characterizations of N-Ary Fuzzy Set Operations Which Induce Homomorphic Random Set Operations
I.R. Goodman 203

25. Treating a Fuzzy Subset as a Projectable Random Subset
Wang Pei-Zhuang and Elie Sanchez 213

26. Possibility Theory: As A Tool for Preliminary Analysis of Computer Security Systems
David C. Rine 221

PART FIVE: FUZZY OPTIMIZATION METHODS

27. Fuzzy Mathematical Programming
J.L. Verdegay 231

28. New Utilization of Fuzzy Optimization Method
Ghassan Kabbara 239

29. On Fuzzy Optimization
C.V. Negoita and A.C. Stefanescu 247

30. Multistage Decision Processes in a Fuzzy Environment: A Survey
Janusz Kacprzyk 251

PART SIX: AGGREGATION, MULTICRITERIA MODELLING, AND FUZZY ORDERING

31. The Performance of Fuzzy Algorithm Models for Aggregate Planning Under Differing Cost Structures
Dan B. Rinks 267

32. Fuzzy Set Methodologies in Multicriteria Modelling
Keith W. Hipel 279

33. A Method of Multicriteria Analysis
Emilio Freire and Anibal Ollero 289

34. Interactive Identification of Fuzzy Outranking Relations in a Multicriteria Decision Problem
Eiji Takeda 301

35. The Use of Fuzzy Numbers In Decision Analysis
Didier Dubois and Henri Prade 309

36. Choice Theory for Cardinal Scales
S.V. Ovchinnikov 323

PART SEVEN: FUZZY DATABASE AND QUESTION - ANSWERING

37. Freedom-0: A Fuzzy Database System
Motohide Umano 339

38. Some Problems in the Foundations of Fuzzy Set Theory
Maria Nowakowska 349

39. Fuzzy Databases and Their Applications
Billy P. Buckles and Frederick E. Petry 361

40. A Representation of Analogical Inference By Fuzzy Sets And Its Application to Information Retrieval System
Kiyohiko Nakamura and Sosuke Iwai 373

PART EIGHT: FUZZY SYSTEMS AND FUZZY LOGIC CONTROLLERS

41. Control of a Cement Kiln by Fuzzy Logic
Lauritz P. Holmblad and Jens-Jorgen Østergaard 389

42. A Mathematical Theory of Fuzzy Systems
Michel de Glas 401

43. An Expression for Fuzzy Controller
Wei-Min Cheng, Shou-Ju Ren, Chiu-Feng Wu, Tse-Hsing Tsuei 411

44. Heuristic Approach to Pump Operations Using Multi-Valued Logic
Masasumi Kokawa 415

45. Pansystems Methodology: A Transfield Investigation of Generalized System-Transformation-Symmetry
Wu Xuemou 423

PART NINE: BIOGRAPHICAL INFORMATION

46. Biographical Information about the Editors and Contributing Authors 437

TABLE OF CONTENTS OF "APPROXIMATE REASONING IN DECISION ANALYSIS", EDITED BY M.M. GUPTA AND E. SANCHEZ, NORTH-HOLLAND, 1982 449